A NATURAL HISTORY OF
AMERICAN
BIRDS

OF EASTERN AND CENTRAL
NORTH AMERICA
BY
EDWARD HOWE FORBUSH

Revised and abridged,
with the addition of over one hundred species by

JOHN BICHARD MAY

With ninety-six full color illustrations by LOUIS
AGASSIZ FUERTES, ALLAN BROOKS,
and ROGER TORY PETERSON.

This book, with *A Field Guide to the Birds*, forms the basic library of any ornithologist. A magnificent volume, illustrated with the best set of color plates in existence, it is the recognized classic in its field.

Bird identification, though an absorbing study, is but the first step to the more fascinating subject of birds' habits and habitats. *A Natural History of American Birds* contains the life history and a complete, accurate description of every bird to be found east of the Dakotas, Nebraska, and Kansas; it includes Florida to the south, eastern Canada to the north. For sheer readability these life histories have no equal. This is not only science; it is literature comparable to the best writing of the leading American naturalists.

The 96 full color illustrations are the work of America's top bird painters: Roger Tory Peterson, Louis Agassiz Fuertes and Allan Brooks. In accuracy of detail, fidelity of color and general beauty, this collection is unsurpassed. Fortunately the color plates for the book were made before the war, for to manufacture an identical set today would be prohibitively expensive.

A Natural History of American Birds is a book for both reading and reference, and its beauty will add luster to any library.

A NATURAL HISTORY OF

AMERICAN BIRDS

OF EASTERN AND CENTRAL

NORTH AMERICA

A NATURAL HISTORY OF

AMERICAN BIRDS

OF EASTERN AND CENTRAL

NORTH AMERICA

BY EDWARD HOWE FORBUSH

Revised and Abridged with the Addition
of More than One Hundred Species

BY JOHN BICHARD MAY

WITH NINETY-SIX FULL COLOR ILLUSTRATIONS

BY LOUIS AGASSIZ FUERTES

ALLAN BROOKS AND ROGER TORY PETERSON

BRAMHALL HOUSE · NEW YORK

THIS BOOK FIRST APPEARED AS
*Natural History of the Birds of Eastern
and Central North America*

This edition published by Bramhall House,
a division of Clarkson N. Potter, Inc.,
by arrangement with the Houghton Mifflin Company.
(A)

PREFACE

THE Commonwealth of Massachusetts issued in 1925, and in subsequent years, *Birds of Massachusetts and Other New England States*, by Edward Howe Forbush, consisting of three volumes. Some of these volumes are now unobtainable. *Portraits of New England Birds*, published by the Commonwealth of Massachusetts in 1932, is out of print. The Massachusetts Audubon Society promoted legislation making both these publications possible.

The Directors of the Massachusetts Audubon Society felt there was a public demand for a condensation of the great work of Mr. Forbush illustrated by Louis Agassiz Fuertes and Allan Brooks and that an edition should be available at a price considerably less than that of the original volumes. Consequently, in 1936, we presented legislation providing for an abridgment of the work in one volume to be published with the excellent plates of Fuertes and Brooks.

Through the good offices of the Secretary of the Commonwealth of Massachusetts and of our Committee on Legislation, arrangements for such publication were made with Houghton Mifflin Company, who had previously pleased bird lovers with their publication of the work of Bradford Torrey, John Burroughs, Florence Merriam Bailey, Ralph Hoffmann, and, more recently, Roger Tory Peterson.

Dr. John B. May, who assisted in the preparation of the original three-volume work, has included in the present book more than one hundred additional species, thus extending the range to cover North America east of the ninety-fifth meridian. There are four new color plates by Mr. Peterson.

From this publication the Massachusetts Audubon Society derives no remuneration. Its reward is the pleasure and profit of readers of the work.

ROBERT WALCOTT, *President*
Massachusetts Audubon Society

CONTENTS

ix

xvi

Birds occurring as 'stragglers' or 'accidentals' within the range of this volume, and western species whose normal distribution barely reaches the ninety-fifth meridian of west longitude.

LIST OF PLATES

INTRODUCTION

EDWARD HOWE FORBUSH was born in Quincy, Massachusetts, April 24, 1858. Even when a very young child he showed a keen interest in all outdoor life, in birds, insects, and plants. The common boyhood fad of 'collecting' natural history specimens soon became for him an engrossing and serious occupation. At the age of sixteen his knowledge of New England fauna and flora was recognized by his appointment as Curator of Birds in the Worcester Museum of Natural History, the first of a long series of honors awarded to him. While still in his teens he made his first extended collecting trip, to Florida, and this was followed in later years by others which led him as far afield as British Columbia and the Pacific coast and which, added to his thorough knowledge of the birds of his native New England, established his reputation as one of the foremost ornithologists of America.

In 1891 Mr. Forbush was appointed Supervisor of Gypsy Moth Suppression in Massachusetts and two years later he became the consulting ornithologist to the State Board of Agriculture. In 1908 he became the first official State Ornithologist of Massachusetts, and in 1920 he was appointed Director of Ornithology in the newly organized Department of Agriculture, a position which he held until, reaching the age of seventy years, he was retired under the compulsory retirement act.

In 1887 Mr. Forbush joined the American Ornithologists' Union and a few years later he was honored by election as a full Member of that organization. In 1912 his standing as an authority on economic ornithology and his work for conservation were recognized by his election as a Fellow of the Union, a distinction which is granted to but a few of the outstanding ornithologists of the United States and Canada. At the time of his death he was a member of the important Advisory Board of the Union, where his knowledge and judgment were of great value.

While still a young man he was president of the Worcester Natural History Society. Later he was one of the founders of the Massachusetts Audubon Society and for twelve years acted as its president. He was the first president of the New England (now the Northeastern) Bird Banding Association, and of the Federation of the Bird Clubs of New England. For more than twenty years he served as the New England representative of the National Association of Audubon Societies and was active in legislative matters affecting wild life, not only in New England but throughout all of North America. When the United States Department of Agriculture established an Advisory Board to assist in handling the regulations of the Migratory Bird Treaty with Great Britain, Mr. Forbush was one of the seven men who were asked to form the original board, and he served the government in this capacity until his death.

Mr. Forbush was a prolific writer and prepared a great many pamphlets and articles on popular and economic ornithology and on the conservation of our diminishing wild life. In addition to many newspaper and magazine articles, he wrote pamphlets under such varied titles as 'The Farmer's Interest in Game Protection,' 'The English Sparrow and the Means of Controlling It,' 'Food Plants to Attract Birds and Protect Fruit,' 'The Domestic Cat, Bird Killer, Mouser, and Destroyer of Wild Life,' 'The Utility of Birds,' and 'The Natural Enemies of Birds.' In 1907 the Commonwealth published his 'Useful Birds and their Protection,' which was immediately recognized as an extremely valuable and timely book, and which passed through several editions and is still in constant demand, being used as a textbook in many schools and consulted wherever economic ornithology is discussed. In 1912 he produced his 'History of the Game Birds, Wild-Fowl and Shore Birds of Massachusetts,' which placed before the public, for the first time, in clear and concise form, the actual facts regarding the decrease of many of our important birds which are hunted for food or for sport.

Had Edward Howe Forbush written nothing more than we have already mentioned, his place among scientific ornithologists and conservationists would have remained secure. But every step which he had taken was leading, consciously or unconsciously, toward his great and final work in the 'Birds of Massachusetts and Other New England States,' upon which the present volume is based. It represents the culmination of his many years of bird study and research, the outgrowth of his deep and abiding love for our feathered neighbors, the summit toward which all his earlier efforts had been leading him. It reflects in a multitude of ways the personality of their author, revealing many intimate though brief glimpses of the man himself. His never-ending joy in watching even the commonest birds, his thrill when as a boy he saw his first Ruffed Grouse and which was duplicated hundreds of times in later life, his discerning interest in the feeding habits of the little Red-eyed Vireo which first led him into a consideration of the economic value of our birds, his early awakened realization of the necessity of protecting and encouraging our bird population — all these are revealed in these pages, together with a thousand other little personal touches.

In the fall of 1923 it was my privilege to become one of Mr. Forbush's staff and to assist in the preparation of the 'Birds of Massachusetts.' On his retirement in 1928 I became his successor as Director of Ornithology in Massachusetts and upon the death of Mr. Forbush, in March, 1929, it devolved upon me to edit and complete his unfinished manuscript of the third volume.

The importance of this book as a source of ornithological information was immediately and widely recognized, but its price placed it beyond the reach of many bird lovers. In 1935 the Massachusetts Audubon Society petitioned the legislature for authority to prepare and issue a one-volume abridgment of the 'Birds of Massachusetts,' using any material needed from the original three volumes. This authority was granted and I was assigned the task of editing and abridgment because of my connection with the preparation of the original book and my editorial work on the third volume, and also because of my association with the Audubon Society as one of its directors. The scope of the work was broadened to include the birds of North America east of the ninety-fifth meridian of west longitude, necessitating the preparation of much new material and the addition of several new plates of birds. It also required a great many minor changes in addition to the abridgment from three volumes to one volume, such as the substitution of a word, a phrase, a sentence, or a paragraph, to adapt the descriptions written by Mr. Forbush to the wider field now covered by the work. The bird student interested in Mr. Forbush's complete text should refer to the original three volumes of the 'Birds of Massachusetts.'

The fourth edition of the 'Check-List of North American Birds' of the American Ornithologists' Union is the accepted authority in all matters of classification, scientific and vernacular names, and distribution. The only liberty I have taken with the nomenclature is the addition of the word 'American' before the common names of a few species where it has seemed to me to be desirable to distinguish our birds from similarly named European species, as, for example, the 'American' Golden Eagle, 'American' Osprey, and 'American' Avocet. In this I believe that I am merely being more consistent than the 'Check-List,' which has made similar changes in certain instances in revising its third edition, but has not done so in all cases.

The brief paragraphs under the headings 'Identification,' 'Voice,' and 'Breeding' I have abridged and amended from similar paragraphs by Mr. Forbush, many of my changes being adaptations from Roger Tory Peterson's admirable 'Field Guide to the Birds,' which every bird student should include in his equipment.

The 'Ranges' given in the present volume are based upon the fourth edition of the 'Check-List,' but in somewhat abridged form and with the omission of all references to 'casual' or 'accidental' occurrences. The birds treated comprise all species and subspecies which are commonly found, whether as breeding birds, winter visitors, or migrants, in a purely arbitrary geographical unit in eastern and central North America, including that part of the continent found east of the western boundaries of the Province of Ontario and the states of Minnesota, Iowa, Missouri, Arkansas, and Louisiana, and also including Newfoundland and the Bermuda Islands, but not including Greenland or the islands north of Ungava and Hudson Bay, the Bahamas, or the West Indies. Birds which are listed in the 'Check-List' as either 'casual' or 'accidental' in this area are not treated in detail, but are included in an Appendix at the end of the book.

With the many changes in the systematic sequences of the species in the revised 'Check-List,' it has seemed best to place all the illustrations together at the end of the book, retaining the numeration used in the original volumes. To the plates from the brushes of the late Louis Agassiz Fuertes and of Major Brooks have been added four new plates by Roger Tory Peterson, illustrating some twenty-seven species of birds which were not so treated in the original volumes.

I take this opportunity to express my deep appreciation of the work of Edward Howe Forbush, who was my friend and mentor throughout the years of our association together in the preparation of the 'Birds of Massachusetts.' In the difficult task of abridgment I have endeavored at all times to preserve the spirit of Mr. Forbush's writings and to retain, as nearly intact as is possible, the intimate descriptions of the haunts and habits of the birds, which he wrote with such sympathetic insight and which were the fruit of his long life of observation and study.

I also wish to express appreciation of the work of Mr. Forbush's other assistants, the late John A. Farley and the late James Mackaye, of Mr. Maurice Broun who contributed several of the bird biographies, and of Mrs. Alice B. Harrington, for many years secretary of the Division of Ornithology, as well as to the small army of bird observers and correspondents who contributed their parts in the preparation of the original volumes.

My own personal debt cannot be properly discharged without grateful recognition of certain ornithologists who have helped me with their friendship and advice, and upon whose authoritative writings I have drawn freely in my work. Foremost among these are Arthur Cleveland Bent, whose 'Life Histories of North American Birds' furnishes a tremendous storehouse of ornithological information; Dr. Frank M. Chapman and his 'Handbook of Birds of Eastern North America'; Arthur H. Howell and his 'Florida Bird Life'; Dr. Thomas S. Roberts and his 'Birds of Minnesota'; and the 'Field Guide to the Birds' by Roger T. Peterson.

JOHN BICHARD MAY

COHASSET, MASSACHUSETTS
October, Nineteen Thirty-nine

THE CLASSIFICATION OF BIRDS

CLASS AVES. BIRDS

BIRDS as a class have a close affinity to reptiles from which they are believed to have developed. Birds are distinguished from all other animals by their feathers.

The Class *Aves* has been divided into two subclasses, *Archaeornithes* and *Neornithes*, and the *Neornithes* into three Superorders, *Odontognathae*, *Palaeognathae* and *Neognathae*. All of the *Archaeornithes* and the *Odontognathae* have long been extinct and are known to us only by their fossilized remains. The *Palaeognathae* include such birds as the Ostriches, Apteryx, and Tinamous, none of which are native to North America. All North American birds belong to the Superorder *Neognathae*; this order is represented in the present volume by members of the following nineteen Orders: GAVIIFORMES, Loons; COLYMBIFORMES, Grebes; PROCELLARIIFORMES, Shearwaters, Petrels; PELECANIFORMES, Tropic-birds, Pelicans, Gannets, Boobies, Cormorants, Darters, Man-o'-war-birds; CICONIIFORMES, Herons, Storks, Ibises, Flamingos; ANSERIFORMES, Ducks, Geese, Swans; FALCONIFORMES, Vultures, Hawks, Eagles, Falcons, Caracaras; GALLIFORMES, Grouse, Quails, Pheasants, Turkeys; GRUIFORMES, Cranes, Limpkins, Rails; CHARADRIIFORMES, Oyster-catchers, Plover, Sandpipers, Avocets, Stilts, Phalaropes, Jaegers, Gulls, Terns, Skimmers, Auks, Murres; COLUMBIFORMES, Doves, Pigeons; PSITTACIFORMES, Parrots; CUCULIFORMES, Cuckoos; STRIGIFORMES, Owls; CAPRIMULGIFORMES, Goatsuckers; MICROPODIFORMES, Swifts, Hummingbirds; CORACIIFORMES, Kingfishers; PICIFORMES, Woodpeckers; PASSERIFORMES, Tyrant Flycatchers, Larks, Swallows, Crows, Jays, Titmice, Nuthatches, Creepers, Wrens, Mockingbirds, Thrashers, Thrushes, Gnatcatchers, Kinglets, Pipits, Waxwings, Shrikes, Starlings, Vireos, Wood Warblers, Weaver Finches, Blackbirds, Troupials, Tanagers, Grosbeaks, Sparrows, Finches.

PLATES

Page reference to the text description
is given under the name of each bird

PLATE 1

Horned Grebe
Page 8
Adult in breeding plumage   *Winter plumage*

Holboell's Grebe
Page 7
Adult in breeding plumage   *Winter plumage*

Pied-billed Grebe
Page 9
Adult in breeding plumage

All one-fourth natural size.

Louis Agassiz Fuertes.

PLATE 2

① ③ ④

② ④

Red-throated Loon
Page 5
① Winter
    plumage
② Adult in
    breeding plumage

Common Loon
Page 3
③ Adult in
    winter plumage
④ Adult in
    breeding plumage

All one-sixth natural size.

PLATE 3

Black Guillemot	Atlantic Puffin
Page 247	Page 249
Young in first winter plumage *Adult in breeding plumage*	*Adult in winter plumage* *Adult in breeding plumage*
Razor-billed Auk	
Page 242	
Adult in winter plumage	
Dovekie	Brünnich's Murre
Page 246	Page 245
Winter plumage	*Adult in winter plumage*

All one-fourth natural size.

PLATE 4

Parasitic Jaeger
Page 214
Light phase
Dark phase

Long-tailed Jaeger
Page 215
Adult

Skua
Page 215

Pomarine Jaeger
Page 212
Adult

All one-eighth natural size.

PLATE 5

Great Black-backed Gull
Page 218

Adult in breeding plumage   *Young in first winter plumage*

Atlantic Kittiwake
Page 225

Adult in breeding plumage   *Young in first winter plumage*

Kumlien's Gull
Page 218
Adult in winter plumage

Glaucous Gull
Page 216

Adult in breeding plumage

Immature in second-year plumage

Young in juvenal plumage

Iceland Gull
Page 217
Adult in breeding plumage

All one-eighth natural size.

PLATE 6

Herring Gull
Page 219
Adult in breeding plumage   *Young in first winter plumage*

Sabine's Gull
Page 226
Adult in breeding plumage

Bonaparte's Gull
Page 224
Adult in breeding plumage   *Young coming into first winter plumage*
Adult in winter plumage

Ring-billed Gull
Page 221
Young, juvenal coming into first winter plumage
Adult in breeding plumage

Laughing Gull
Page 222
Young in juvenal plumage   *Adult in breeding plumage*

All one-eighth natural size.

Black Skimmer
Page 240
Adult in breeding plumage

Eastern Sooty Tern
Page 234
Adult in breeding plumage

Caspian Tern
Page 238

Young in juvenal plumage   *Adult in nuptial plumage*

Royal Tern
Page 237

Adult in nuptial plumage   *Adult in winter plumage*

All one-sixth natural size.

PLATE 8

Arctic Tern
Page 231
Adult in breeding plumage

Forster's Tern
Page 228
Adult in breeding plumage
Young in first winter plumage

Roseate Tern
Page 233
Adult in breeding plumage

Common Tern
Page 229
Adult in breeding plumage   *Young in first winter plumage*

Least Tern
Page 235

Young in first winter plumage   Black Tern   *Adult in breeding plumage*   *Young in juvenal plumage*   *Adult in breeding plumage*
Page 239

All one-fourth natural size.

PLATE 9

Leach's Petrel
Page 14

Wilson's Petrel
Page 17

Sooty Shearwater
Page 11

Greater Shearwater
Page 12

Cory's Shearwater
Page 13

Atlantic Fulmar
Page 13
Dark phase

All one-fourth natural size.

PLATE 10

Double-crested Cormorant
Page 23
Young in first winter plumage

Adult in nuptial plumage

European Cormorant
Page 22
Young in first winter plumage

Adult in nuptial plumage

Gannet
Page 21
Young in first winter plumage

Adult

All one-sixth natural size.

PLATE 11

② ④ ⑤

① ③ ⑥

American Merganser
Page 91
Winter (nuptial)
  plumage
  ① *Adult male*
  ③ *Adult female*

Hooded Merganser
Page 89
Winter (nuptial)
  plumage
  ② *Adult female*
  ④ *Adult male*

Red-breasted
Merganser
Page 93
Winter (nuptial)
  plumage
  ⑤ *Adult female*
  ⑥ *Adult male*

All one-sixth natural size.

PLATE 12

① ② ③ ④ ⑤ ⑥

Mallard
Page 58
Winter (nuptial)
plumage

① *Adult male*
② *Adult female*

⑤ Common Black Duck
Page 60

③ Red-legged
Black Duck
Page 59

Gadwall
Page 62
Winter (nuptial)
plumage

④ *Adult male*
⑥ *Adult female*

All one-sixth natural size.

PLATE 13

① ② ③ ④ ⑤ ⑥ ⑦ ⑧ ⑨

Green-winged Teal
Page 66
Winter (nuptial)
  plumage
① Female
② Male

European Widgeon
Page 63
Winter (nuptial)
  plumage
③ Male
⑤ Female

European Teal
Page 66
Nuptial plumage
④ Male

Baldpate
Page 64
Winter (nuptial)
  plumage
⑦ Adult female
⑨ Adult male

Blue-winged Teal
Page 67
Nuptial plumage
⑥ Male
⑧ Female

All one-sixth natural size.

PLATE 14

① ② ③ ⑤
④ ⑥

Wood Duck
Page 70
*Winter (nuptial)
plumage*
① *Male*
② *Female*

American Pintail
Page 65
*Winter (nuptial)
plumage*
③ *Female*
⑤ *Male*

Shoveller
Page 68
*Winter (nuptial)
plumage*
④ *Male*
⑥ *Female*

All one-sixth natural size.

PLATE 15

Canvas-back (Page 73)

Adult male   *Winter (nuptial) plumage*   *Adult female*

Redhead (Page 71)

Winter (nuptial) plumage

Adult female

Lesser Scaup Duck (Page 76)

Adult female   *Winter (nuptial) plumage*   *Adult male*

Adult male

Greater Scaup Duck (Page 75)

Ring-necked Duck (Page 73)

Winter (nuptial) plumage

Aduli female   *Winter (nuptial) plumage*   *Adult male*   *Adult female*   *Adult male*

All one-sixth natural size.

PLATE 16

① ③ ④ ⑤ ⑥ ⑧ ⑦

Old-squaw
Page 80
① Adult female
 in winter plumage
② Adult male in
 winter plumage
③ Adult male in
 summer or breed-
 ing plumage

Buffle-head
Page 79
Nuptial plumage
④ Adult male
⑤ Adult female

American Golden-eye
Page 77
Nuptial plumage
⑥ Adult female
⑧ Adult male

Barrow's Golden-eye
Page 78
⑦ Adult male in
 winter (nuptial)
 plumage

All one-sixth natural size.

PLATE 17

① ② ④ ⑤ ⑦
③ ⑥

Eastern Harlequin Duck
Page 81
Winter (nuptial)
plumage
① Female
② Male

Northern Eider
Page 83
Nuptial plumage
④ Male

King Eider
Page 84
Nuptial plumage
⑤ Female
⑦ Male

American Eider
Page 83
Nuptial plumage
③ Female
⑥ Male

All one-sixth natural size.

PLATE 18

① ② ⑤ ⑥
③ ④ ⑦ ⑧ ⑨

American Scoter
Page 87
Winter (nuptial)
plumage
① Adult male
② Adult female

Surf Scoter
Page 86
Winter (nuptial)
plumage
③ Adult female
④ Adult male

White-winged Scoter
Page 85
Winter (nuptial)
plumage
⑤ Adult female
⑥ Adult male

Ruddy Duck
Page 88
⑦ Adult male in
nuptial plumage
⑧ Adult female
⑨ Adult male in
winter plumage

All one-sixth natural size.

Louis Agassiz Fuertes

PLATE 20

Common Canada Goose
   Page 49
   ① *Adult*

American Brant
   Page 51
   ② *Adult*

Black Brant
   Page 53
   ③ *Adult*

Whistling Swan
   Page 47
   ④ *Adult*

All one-eighth natural size.

PLATE 22

Great Blue Heron
Page 28

Adult in breeding plumage   *Young in juvenal plumage*

American Egret   Black-crowned Night Heron
Page 29   Page 35
Adult in breeding plumage   *Young in juvenal plumage*   *Adult in breeding plumage*

Snowy Egret   Little Blue Heron
Page 30   Page 33
Adult in breeding plumage   *White phase, or immature*   *Dark phase, or adult*

All one-eighth natural size.

PLATE 23

(2)
(1) (3) (4) (5) (6) (7) (8)

King Rail
Page 159
(2) *Adult in breeding plumage*

Northern Clapper Rail
Page 160
(1) *Adult in breeding plumage*

(3) **Yellow Rail**
Page 164

(4) **Black Rail**
Page 165

Virginia Rail
Page 162
(5) *Adult in breeding plumage*
(7) *Young in juvenal plumage*

Sora
Page 163
(6) *Adult in breeding plumage*
(8) *Young in autumn*

All one-third natural size.

PLATE 24

① ② ④ ⑤ ⑥ ⑧
③ ⑦ ⑨ ⑩

Red Phalarope
Page 210
① Adult male in
breeding plumage
② Adult female in
breeding plumage
④ Winter plumage

Wilson's Phalarope
Page 211
③ Adult female in
breeding plumage

Purple Gallinule
Page 165
⑤ Adult in breeding
plumage

Florida Gallinule
Page 166
⑥ Adult in breeding
plumage

American Coot
Page 168
⑧ Adult in breeding
plumage

Northern Phalarope
Page 211
⑦ Winter plumage
⑨ Adult male in
breeding plumage
⑩ Adult female in
breeding plumage

All one-fourth natural size.

PLATE 25

Wilson's Snipe
Page 181
Adult

American Woodcock
Page 178
Adult

Eastern Dowitcher
Page 200

Adult in winter plumage (autumn)

Adult in breeding plumage (spring)

All one-half natural size.

PLATE 26

① ③ ⑤
② ④ ⑥

American Knot
　Page 193
　① Young in juvenal
　　plumage (autumn)
　② Adult in breeding
　　plumage (spring)
Stilt Sandpiper
　Page 201
　③ Winter plumage
　　(autumn)
　④ Adult in breeding
　　plumage (spring)
Purple Sandpiper
　Page 194
　⑤ Adult in winter
　　plumage
⑥ Pectoral Sandpiper
　Page 195

All one-half natural size.

PLATE 27

⑤

① ③ ④

Baird's Sandpiper
Page 197
① *Adult in breeding*
   plumage (spring)

Red-backed Sandpiper
Page 198
③ *Adult in breeding*
   plumage (spring)
⑤ *Adult in winter*
   plumage (autumn)

White-rumped Sand-
piper
Page 196
② *Adult in winter*
   plumage (autumn)
④ *Adult in breeding*
   plumage (spring)

All one-half natural size.

PLATE 28

① ② ⑤ ⑦
③ ④ ⑥

Sanderling
Page 206
  ① Adult in breeding
     plumage (spring)
  ② Young in juvenal
     plumage (autumn)
  ③ Adult in winter
     plumage (autumn)

Semipalmated
Sandpiper
Page 202
  ⑤ Young in first
     winter plumage
     (autumn)
  ⑦ Adult in breeding
     plumage (spring)

Least Sandpiper
Page 198
  ④ Adult in breeding
     plumage (spring)
  ⑥ Young in first
     winter plumage
     (autumn)

All one-half natural size.

PLATE 29

All one-fourth natural size.

PLATE 30

③ ⑤
① ② ④

Greater Yellow-legs
Page 191
① Adult

Lesser Yellow-legs
Page 192
② Adult

Spotted Sandpiper
Page 186
③ Adult in breeding
plumage (spring)
⑤ Young coming into
winter plumage
(autumn)

Eastern Solitary Sand-
piper
Page 187
④ Adult

All one-half natural size.

PLATE 31

① Upland Plover
  Page 185

② Buff-breasted
  Sandpiper
  Page 204

Western Willet
  Page 190

③ *Adult winter*
  plumage (autumn)

Eastern Willet
  Page 189

④ *Adult breeding*
  plumage (spring)

All one-third natural size.

PLATE 32

② ⑥

① ③ ④ ⑤

American Oystercatcher
Page 169
② *Adult in breeding plumage*

Black-bellied Plover
Page 176
① *Adult in breeding plumage*
③ *Young in first winter plumage*

American Golden Plover
Page 174
④ *Young in first winter plumage*
⑤ *Adult in breeding plumage*

Killdeer
Page 173
⑥ *Adult in breeding plumage*

All one-third natural size.

PLATE 33

② ③ ④ ⑤

①

Ruddy Turnstone
Page 177

② Young in juvenal
plumage

③ Adult in breeding
plumage

Wilson's Plover
Page 173

① Adult in breeding
plumage

Piping Plover
Page 170

④ Adult in breeding
plumage

Semipalmated Plover
Page 172

⑤ Adult in breeding
plumage

All one-half natural size.

PLATE 34

Eastern Bob-white
Page 147

Adult male   *Adult female*

Canada Spruce Grouse
Page 133

Adult male   *Adult female*

European Partridge
Page 146
Adult

All about three-eighths scale.

PLATE 35

Heath Hen
Page 143
Adult male

Ring-necked Pheasant
Page 151

Adult male

Eastern Ruffed Grouse
Page 135
Adult male

Adult female

All about one-fourth scale.

PLATE 36
Passenger Pigeon
Page 253

Adult male   *Adult female*   *Young in juvenal plumage*

Eastern Mourning Dove
Page 252

Young in juvenal plumage   *Adult male*

All about one-half scale.

PLATE 37

Bald Eagle (Page 117)
Adult (About one-twenty-fourth scale)

Duck Hawk (Page 126)
Adult (About one-twelfth scale)

Cooper's Hawk (Page 104)
Adult (About one-twelfth scale)

American Osprey
Page 121
Adult
About one-twelfth scale.

Turkey Vulture
Page 94
About one-thirtieth scale.

Eastern Red-tailed Hawk
Page 105
Adult
About one-twelfth scale.

Marsh Hawk
Page 119
Adult female (About one-twelfth scale)
Adult male (About one-twelfth scale)

PLATE 39

Sharp-shinned Hawk
Page 101

Cooper's Hawk
Page 104

Adult female   *Young male in first winter plumage*   *Young female in first winter plumage*

Adult male

Eastern Goshawk
Page 100

Young male in first winter plumage   *Adult female*

All about one-fourth scale.

PLATE 40

Northern Red-shouldered Hawk
Page 108

Adult

Eastern Red-tailed Hawk
Page 105

Immature

Adult

Young in first winter plumage

Broad-winged Hawk
Page 110

Adult

Immature

All about one fourth scale

PLATE 41

Bald Eagle
Page 117

American Golden Eagle
Page 115

Adult

Immature
American Rough-legged Hawk
Page 113

Adult

Dark phase

Immature normal or light phase

All about one-sixth scale.

PLATE 42

White Gyrfalcon
Page 124
Adult

Immature

Adult, light phase

Black Gyrfalcon
Page 125
Adult, dark phase

All about one-fourth scale.

PLATE 43

Duck Hawk *

Page 126

Adult

* This plate is a gift to the Commonwealth of Massachusetts through the courtesy of Mr. and Mrs. Aaron C. Bagg.

PLATE 44

Eastern Pigeon Hawk
Page 129
Adult male

Duck Hawk
Page 126
Immature Male

Immature female

Eastern Sparrow Hawk
Page 131

Adult male

Adult female

All about one-third scale.

PLATE 45

American Barn Owl
Page 260
Adult

Long-eared Owl
Page 274
Adult

Short-eared Owl
Page 275
Adult

All about one-third scale.

PLATE 46

Great Gray Owl
Page 273
Adult

Great Horned Owl
Page 265
Adult

Northern Barred Owl
Page 272
Adult

Snowy Owl
Page 267
Adult female

All about one-sixth scale.

PLATE 47

Eastern Screech Owl
Page 261

Adult
Gray phase

Adult
Red phase

Saw-whet Owl
Page 278
Adult

American Hawk Owl
Page 270
Adult

Richardson's Owl
Page 277
Adult

All about one-third scale.

PLATE 48

Black-billed Cuckoo   Yellow-billed Cuckoo
Page 259   Page 257
Adult   *Adult*

Eastern Belted Kingfisher
Page 290

Adult male   *Adult female*

All about one-half scale.

PLATE 49

Eastern Hairy Woodpecker
Page 300
Adult female

Northern Downy Woodpecker
Page 302

Adult female

Adult male

Adult male

All about one-half scale.

PLATE 50

Arctic Three-toed Woodpecker
Page 305
Adult female
Adult male

American Three-toed Woodpecker
Page 306
Adult female

Adult male

All about one-half scale.

PLATE 51

Northern Pileated Woodpecker
Page 294

Adult male

Adult female

Yellow-bellied Sapsucker
Page 299

Adult male

Adult female

All about one-half scale.

PLATE 52

Red-bellied Woodpecker
Page 297

Adult male

Adult female

Red-headed Woodpecker
Page 298

Immature

Adult

Northern Flicker
Page 291

Adult female

Adult male

All about one-half scale.

PLATE 53

Chimney Swift
Page 284
Adult

Eastern Nighthawk
Page 282
Adult male

Eastern Whip-poor-will
Page 280
Adult male

All about one-half scale.

PLATE 54
Ruby-throated Hummingbird
Page 286

Adult female

Adult male

Flower — *Blue Vervain*

All about two-thirds scale.

PLATE 55

Northern Crested Flycatcher
Page 311
Adult

Olive-sided Flycatcher
Page 320
Adult

Eastern Kingbird
Page 308
Adult

Arkansas Kingbird
Page 310
Adult

All about one-half scale.

PLATE 56

Eastern Wood Pewee
Page 319
Adult

Least Flycatcher
Page 318
Adult

Yellow-bellied Flycatcher
Page 315
Adult

Acadian Flycatcher
Page 316
Adult

All about one-half scale.

Eastern Phoebe
Page 313
Adult

Alder Flycatcher
Page 317
Adult

PLATE 57

② ③ ④ ⑤

①

Prairie Horned Lark
Page 323
  ① Young in first
    winter plumage
  ② Adult female
  ③ Adult male

Northern Horned Lark
Page 321
  ④ Adult female
  ⑤ Adult male

All about one half scale.

PLATE 58

Northern Blue Jay
Page 337
Adults

Canada Jay
Page 335
Adult

All about one-half scale.

PLATE 59
Northern Raven
Page 342
Adult

Eastern Crow
Page 343
Adult

Fish Crow
Page 346
Adult

All about one-fourth scale.

PLATE 60

Eastern Red-wing
Page 465
Adult male in breeding plumage
Immature male
Adult female

Eastern Cowbird
Page 477
Adult male
Adult female

Bobolink
Page 459
Adult male in breeding plumage
Adult female

All about one-half scale.

PLATE 61

Orchard Oriole
Page 468
Adult male in breeding plumage
Young male in first winter plumage
Adult female

Baltimore Oriole
Page 469
Adult male in breeding plumage
Adult female

Eastern Meadowlark
Page 461
Adult male in breeding plumage

All about one-half scale.

PLATE 62

Rusty Blackbird
Page 471

Adult male in breeding plumage   Adult male in winter plumage   Young in first winter plumage

Starling
Page 399

Young in juvenal plumage   Young male in first winter plumage   Adult male in breeding plumage

Bronzed Grackle
Page 475

All about one-half scale.

Purple Grackle
Page 474

Male in breeding plumage   Male in breeding plumage but not quite typical

PLATE 63

Canadian Pine Grosbeak

Page 492

Adult male   *Immature male*   *Female*

Eastern Purple Finch

Page 491

Female or immature male   *Adult male*   Eastern Evening Grosbeak

Page 489

Female   *Adult male*

All about one-half scale.

PLATE 64

Red Crossbill
Page 500

Adult male   *Immature male*

Female

White-winged Crossbill
Page 501

Adult male   *Immature male*

Female

All about one-half scale.

PLATE 65

Holboell's Redpoll
Page 496
Adult male

Common Redpoll
Page 495
Adult male   *Female*

Hoary Redpoll
Page 495
Adult male

Greater Redpoll
Page 496
Adult male

All about one-half scale.

PLATE 66

Northern Pine Siskin
Page 497
Adult

American Goldfinch
Page 498

Male in winter

Male in summer

Female in summer

All about one-half scale.

Louis Agassiz Fuertes

PLATE 67

① ③
② ④

Lapland Longspur
  Page 536
  ① Female in winter
  ② Male in winter
Eastern Snow Bunting
  Page 537
  ③ Female in winter
  ④ Male in winter
All about one-half scale.

PLATE 68

Eastern Grasshopper Sparrow   Eastern Vesper Sparrow   Eastern Henslow's Sparrow
Page 508   Page 516   Page 510

                                 Eastern Savannah Sparrow   Ipswich Sparrow
                                 Page 507   Page 505

All about one-half scale.

PLATE 69

Eastern Seaside Sparrow
Page 513

Eastern Lark Sparrow
Page 518

Juvenal

Adult

Sharp-tailed Sparrow
Page 512

Acadian Sparrow
Page 511

Nelson's Sparrow
Page 513

All about one-half scale.

PLATE 70

② ③

① ④

White-throated
Sparrow
Page 528
① Immature
② Adult in spring

White-crowned
Sparrow
Page 527
③ Adult in spring
④ Immature

All about one-half scale.

PLATE 71

Eastern Field Sparrow
Page 525

Eastern Chipping Sparrow
Page 523

Eastern Tree Sparrow
Page 522

Slate-colored Junco
Page 520

Male

Female

All about one-half scale.

PLATE 72

Eastern Fox Sparrow
Page 529

Eastern Song Sparrow
Page 533

Lincoln's Sparrow
Page 530

Swamp Sparrow
Page 532

Immature   *Adult*

All about one-half scale.

PLATE 73
Rose-breasted Grosbeak
Page 484

Adult female   *Adult male in spring*

Eastern Cardinal
Page 483

Female in winter   *Adult male in spring*

Red-eyed Towhee
Page 502

Adult female   *Adult male*

All about one-half scale.

PLATE 75

Summer Tanager
Page 482

Male   *Female*

Western Tanager   Scarlet Tanager
Page 479   Page 480
Male   *Female*

Male in summer

Male in winter

All about one-half scale.

PLATE 76

Northern Cliff Swallow
Page 331
Adult male

Barn Swallow
Page 329

Adult male   *Juvenal*

Juvenal male

Juvenal female

Purple Martin
Page 334

Adult female   *Adult male*

All about one-half scale.

PLATE 77

Bank Swallow
Page 326

Male   *Female*

Rough-winged Swallow
Page 327

Male   *Female*

Tree Swallow
Page 324

Male   *Juvenal*   *Female*

All about one-half scale.

PLATE 78

Cedar Waxwing
Page 393
Adult male   *Juvenal*

Bohemian Waxwing
Page 392
Adult male

Migrant Shrike
Page 398
Adult male

Northern Shrike
Page 396
Immature   *Adult male*

All about one-half scale.

PLATE 79

Philadelphia Vireo   Eastern Warbling Vireo
Page 408   Page 408

Yellow-throated Vireo   Red-eyed Vireo
Page 403   Page 406

White-eyed Vireo   Blue-headed Vireo
Page 401   Page 404

All about one-half scale.

PLATE 81

Golden-winged Warbler
Page 413
Adult male

Lawrence's Warbler
Page 416
Adult male

Blue-winged Warbler
Page 415
Adult male

Nashville Warbler
Page 418
Male

Orange-crowned Warbler
Page 417
Juvenal male   *Adult male*

Brewster's Warbler
Page 416
Adult male

Tennessee Warbler
Page 417
Adult male

Juvenal male

All about one-half scale.

PLATE 82

Cape May Warbler
Page 423
Adult male
Young female

Eastern Yellow Warbler
Page 421
Adult male   *Young female*

Black-throated Blue Warbler
Page 424
Adult male
Female in autumn

Myrtle Warbler
Page 426
Female in spring   *Adult male in spring*

Audubon's Warbler
Page 428
Adult male in spring

All about one-half scale.

PLATE 83

Magnolia Warbler		Bay-breasted Warbler		Chestnut-sided Warbler	
Page 422		Page 435		Page 433	
Adult male	*Immature*	*Immature male*	*Male*	*Adult male*	*Immature male*

Cerulean Warbler
Page 430
Male   *Female*

All about one-half scale.

PLATE 84

Black-poll Warbler
Page 436

Black-throated Gray Warbler
Page 428

Adult male   *Female*   *Male in first winter plumage*   *Male*

Blackburnian Warbler
Page 431

Black-throated Green Warbler
Page 429

Female   *Male*   *Female*   *Male*

Yellow-throated Warbler
Page 432

Male   All about one-half scale.

PLATE 85

Northern Prairie Warbler
Page 439
Male

Northern Pine Warbler
Page 437

Adult female   *Adult male*

Northern Water-Thrush
Page 444
Adult

Yellow Palm Warbler
Page 441
Adult male

Western Palm Warbler
Page 440
Adult

Louisiana Water-Thrush
Page 445
Adult

Oven-bird
Page 442
Adult

All about one-half scale.

Kentucky Warbler
Page 446

Connecticut Warbler
Page 447

Immature male   *Adult male*   *Immature female*   *Adult male*

Mourning Warbler
Page 448

Yellow-breasted Chat
Page 451

Adult male   *Adult male*

Maryland Yellow-throat
Page 449

Immature male   *Adult male*   *Adult female*

All about one-half scale.

PLATE 87

American Redstart
Page 455

Adult male   *Female*   *Immature male*

Wilson's Warbler   Hooded Warbler
Page 454   Page 453

Female   *Male*   *Female*   *Male*

Canada Warbler
Page 454

All about one-half scale.   *Male*   *Female*

PLATE 88

Eastern Mockingbird
Page 367
Male

Catbird
Page 369
Male

Brown Thrasher
Page 371
Male

American Pipit
Page 390

Male in autumn   *Male in spring*

All about one-half scale.

PLATE 89

House Wren
Page 357
Short-billed Marsh Wren
Page 366

Carolina Wren
Page 362

Long-billed Marsh Wren
Page 363

Eastern Winter Wren
Page 359

All about one-half scale.

PLATE 90

Red-breasted Nuthatch
Page 354
Male

Female

Black-capped Chickadee
Page 347
Male

Tufted Titmouse
Page 351
Adult

Acadian Chickadee
Page 350
Male

White-breasted Nuthatch
Page 352
Female   *Male*

American Brown Creeper
Page 356
Male

All about one-half scale.

PLATE 91

Eastern Golden-crowned Kinglet
Page 388

Eastern Ruby-crowned Kinglet
Page 389

Female   *Male*   *Male*   *Female*

Blue-gray Gnatcatcher
Page 387

Male   *Female*

All about one-half scale.

PLATE 92

Bicknell's Thrush
Page 382

Gray-cheeked Thrush
Page 381

Olive-backed Thrush
Page 380

Eastern Hermit Thrush
Page 378

Veery
Page 383

Wood Thrush
Page 377

All about one-half scale.

PLATE 93
Eastern Bluebird
Page 385

Adult female   Juvenal male   Adult male

Eastern Robin
Page 373

Adult male   Juvenal

All about one-half scale.

PLATE 94

Painted Bunting
Page 487

Female   *Male*

Swainson's Warbler
Page 412

Brown-headed Nuthatch
Page 355

Pinewoods Sparrow
Page 519

Bachman's Warbler
Page 416
Male

Female

Kirtland's Warbler
Page 438

Slightly over one-half natural size.

PLATE 95

Ivory-billed Woodpecker
Page 307

Red-cockaded Woodpecker
Page 304

Eastern Ground Dove
Page 255

Florida Jay
Page 340

Burrowing Owl
Page 271

Chuck-will's-widow
Page 279

Nearly one-third natural size.

PLATE 96

Yellow-crowned Night Heron
Page 37

White Ibis
Page 44

Louisiana Heron
Page 32

Reddish Egret
Page 31

Roseate Spoonbill
Page 45

Great White Heron
Page 27

Florida Crane
Page 157

Limpkin
Page 157

All about one-eighth natural size.

PLATE 97

Audubon's Caracara
Page 123

Man-o'-war-bird
Page 26

Wood Ibis
Page 41

Water-Turkey
Page 25

Swallow-tailed Kite
Page 97

White Pelican
Page 19

Eastern Brown Pelican
Page 20

All about one-fifteenth natural size.

A NATURAL HISTORY OF

AMERICAN BIRDS

OF EASTERN AND CENTRAL

NORTH AMERICA

COMMON LOON

Gavia immer immer (BRÜNNICH).   PLATE 2.

Other names: Great Northern Diver; Big Loon.

IDENTIFICATION. — Length 28 to 36 inches: spread 52 to 58 inches. Size of small goose; black and white adult unmistakable in summer; in winter resembles Red-throated Loon, but larger and feathers of back *margined* with grayish where 'Red-throat' is *spotted* with gray or whitish; bill stout and usually straighter than that of Red-throat which often seems a little upturned.

VOICE. — Loud resonant calls like crazy laughter.

BREEDING. — *Nest:* A mere hollow in the ground or a mass of vegetation. *Eggs:* 2, olive-green to dark olive-brown, heavily marked.

RANGE. — Breeds from Labrador, Newfoundland, Nova Scotia, and Maine south to northern Indiana, northern New York, New Hampshire, and in Iceland; winters from the Great Lakes, Maine, and Nova Scotia (casually) to Florida and the Gulf coast and from the British Isles to the Azores, Madeira, and the Mediterranean and Black seas.

The Common Loon is a wonderful, powerful, living mechanism fashioned for riding the stormy seas. See him as he mounts high above the waves, neck and legs fully extended 'fore and aft,' and bill a trifle raised which gives to his whole form a slight upward bend, his wings beating powerfully and moving as steadily as the walking-beam of a side-wheel steamship. He is driving straight ahead into the teeth of the gale and making greater headway than the laboring steamer that steers a parallel course. Now he slants downward, and, striking just beyond the top of a towering wave, shoots down its inclined surface and rises again on the coming crest. Here, midway of the wide bay where the seas are running high and wildly tossing their white tops, with a wintry gale whipping the spray from them in smoky gusts, the Loon rests at ease, head to the wind and sea like a ship at anchor. The tossing and the tumult disturb him not, as he rides, light as a birch canoe. turning his white breast now and then on one side as he reaches unconcernedly backward to preen his feathers. His neck narrows at the water-line into a beautifully modeled cutwater. His broad paddles push his white breast to the tops of the great waves, where it parts the foam as he surmounts the crests and glides easily down into the gulfs beyond. The freezing spray that loads the fishing fleet with tons of ice seems never to cling to his tough and glossy plumage; or, if it does, he washes it off among the fleeing fishes away down in the warmer currents near the bottom of the bay.

Often toward nightfall I have heard his wild storm-call far out to windward against the black pall of an approaching tempest like the howl of a lone wolf coming down the wind; and have seen his white breast rise on a wave against the black sky to vanish again like the arm of a swimmer lost in the stormy sea. Sailors, hearing the call, say that the Loons are trying to blow up an 'easterly.' At times his cries seem wailing and sad as if he were bemoaning his exile from his forest lake. Such is the Common Loon in his winter home off the North Atlantic coast; for there he lives and braves the inclemency of the season. Of all the wild creatures

3

that persist in this region, the Loon seems best to typify the stark wildness of primeval nature.

In the breeding season Loons love the solitude of northern lakes where shores are shaded by fir and spruce and where the still pure water seldom mirrors a human face. Islands in quiet lakes are the favorite breeding-grounds of this species. The nest is on the ground close to the water's edge. Only two dark greenish, heavily marked eggs form a set. The young take to the water soon after they leave the eggs. They swim readily, using their feet alternately or both together, and soon learn to dive well and to remain for some time under water.

During his courtship the male frequently rushes about on the water, actually running almost erect upon the surface, with open bill and closed wings. He sometimes assumes a similar position and makes the same rushes when the young are threatened by his greatest enemy, Man.

Although the Loon is graceful and swift on the water, it is at a disadvantage on land. It has been asserted that it cannot under any circumstances rise in the air from land nor from the water unless aided by a head wind, and that it must have more room than can be furnished by a small pool, and even then it seems obliged to flutter and run spatteringly along the surface for some distance to get impetus enough to rise in the air. When the young are well grown, the family, often joined by some neighboring adults, frolic for a brief time on the water and then fall into line side by side, and, lifting their wings simultaneously, run an apparent footrace over the surface for some distance, and turning race back to the starting point. They repeat this over and over again. During these races the wings are held out and about half opened. At the end of the performance the male, female, and neighbors leave for other fishing grounds and the young scatter to find food. This play evidently tends to train the muscles of the young birds and to fit them for flight.

When the ice on the New England lakes starts to break up in the spring, the migration of the Common Loon begins. The Loons follow close to melting ice, and late in April the first birds appear on their nesting grounds in the Maine lakes and in southern Canada. All through this month small flights of Loons pass from time to time up the Atlantic coast from their southerly wintering quarters off the Florida and Carolina seaboard and in Chesapeake Bay; but the great migration to the Arctic regions comes about the 15th to the 30th of May. The great days of the loon-flight are usually warm with southwesterly winds. Then the birds fly low and fast. Morning and night they come. Passing the long sand beaches of New Jersey and Long Island, they go to the southward of Narragansett Bay and come up Buzzards Bay, crossing Cape Cod near the canal and so on into Cape Cod Bay, where they lay a course for the Bay of Fundy. Another flight keeps well out to sea and goes north outside Cape Cod, passing eastward of Truro and Provincetown, bound apparently for Nova Scotia, Newfoundland, and Baffin Bay. Their low flight on a southwest wind is very noticeable. When the wind comes from another quarter, they are likely to fly very high and so attract less notice.

A strong, swift, submarine diver, the Common Loon glides or flies at will far down the depths where it pursues its prey. Often little fish are swallowed under water. The Loon brings the larger and stronger fish to the surface, and mauls them there. If such a fish escapes, the bird dives in pursuit and soon overtakes its prey.

I have watched Loons to see how they reduce large fish so as to swallow them. In Nantucket Harbor I saw a Loon swallow two flounders within half an hour. One of them appeared to be

4

rather more than four inches in diameter. The Loon worked a long time with the flounder in its bill, apparently crushing it, possibly to contract it; finally the fish was swallowed with apparent ease. Fishermen say that the Loon 'rolls the fish up.'

The Common Loon is believed to feed chiefly on fish, but it feeds to some extent on crabs and mollusks, and also on frogs, leeches, aquatic insects, and water plants.

PACIFIC LOON
Gavia arctica pacifica (LAWRENCE).

IDENTIFICATION. — Length about 24 inches; spread 40 inches or less. In breeding plumage light gray or whitish top of head and hind neck distinguish it from Common Loon and black throat from Red-throated Loon with its grayish upper parts; difficult to distinguish in winter but much smaller than Common Loon while slender bill suggests that of Red-throated Loon.

BREEDING. — Similar to that of Common Loon.

RANGE. — Breeds on Arctic coasts and islands from Alaska to Baffin Island and south to York Factory, Great Slave and Athabaska lakes, and the Alaska Peninsula; winters mainly on the Pacific coast; accidental on the Atlantic coast.

Probably the Pacific Loon is the only race of the Black-throated Loon that has been taken in eastern North America. We have very few authentic records of its occurrence on the Atlantic coast which can be substantiated by specimens, though it is occasionally reported by experienced field observers. The bird is known to breed, casually at least, near James Bay. Its habits in general seem to be similar to those of the Common Loon. It breeds mostly about freshwater lakes and goes to salt water largely in winter.

RED–THROATED LOON
Gavia stellata (PONTOPPIDAN).   PLATE 2.

Other names: Red-throated Diver; Cape Drake; Cape Race; Cape Racer; Scapegrace; Little Loon; Sprat Loon; Pegging Awl Loon; Pepper-shinned Loon; Tutchmunk.

IDENTIFICATION. — Length 24 to 27 inches; spread about 44 inches. Smaller than Common Loon; in breeding plumage red throat patch makes it unmistakable; in winter distinguished by white spots on upper plumage where Common Loon has only light edgings; surest distinction is rather slender bill often appearing slightly upturned (or concave at nostrils), however bill varies in size and shape and often the two species are indistinguishable at a distance.

BREEDING. — Similar to that of Common Loon.

RANGE. — Breeds from northern Alaska and the Arctic islands of Canada and Greenland south to the Commander Islands, western Aleutian Islands, the Queen Charlotte and other northern British Columbia islands, northern Manitoba, southeastern Quebec, and Newfoundland, also throughout Arctic Europe and Asia; winters from the Aleutian Islands and the coast of British Columbia to Lower California, and from the Gulf of St. Lawrence and the Great Lakes to Florida, in Europe south to the Mediterranean, and in Asia to southern China.

The Red-throated Loon commonly appears in considerable numbers on the eastern coast in late September or October, but is rarely recorded in ponds or streams of the interior. Some

5

individuals of this species winter along the New England coast. In spring the larger number go north through the interior or else pass far out to sea, as the species is much less common in spring than in autumn. Like the Common Loon it begins moving northward along the coast in March and some are still passing in May.

In habits and appearance the bird is much like the Common Loon while with us, but it differs in one respect; it can rise readily and fly from even a small pool, springing into the air with little difficulty, even without the aid of a breeze; although like the Common Loon if frozen out of a pond in winter, it seems unable to rise from the ice and thus is captured or starved.

Because of its ability to rise from the surface of a small body of water, the Red-throated Loon often nests on the shores of tiny pools in the far northern Barren Grounds. The nest, with its two large, dark, and heavily marked eggs, is usually so located that the sitting bird, if startled, can quickly reach deep enough water to submerge and so disappear promptly from view.

Like the Common Loon, the Red-throated Loon uses its wings under water when necessary to increase its speed. Dr. George Suckley noted carefully the subsurface motions of one of this species which was attempting to escape out of a lagoon to the open water of the Straits of Fuca by swimming through a narrow outlet. Although slightly wounded it moved so fast that he was obliged to run as rapidly as possible to keep up with it. As the water was clear and shallow he was able to watch its motions. The neck was fully extended, and the bird used the wings as in flying in addition to the ordinary motions of the feet. 'Indeed,' he wrote, 'the bird was flying through the water instead of air.'

Mr. A. C. Bent, in his 'Life Histories of North American Diving Birds,' gives the following interesting account of the Red-throated Loon in the autumnal migration: 'The migration along the New England coast is mainly in October accompanying the main flight of the scoters. After leaving the fresh-water lakes of their summer homes they resort to the seacoast for migration and seem to prefer the fall and winter on salt water. When traveling they fly at a great height and in a direct course along the shore, a mile or two out from land; they usually fly singly, although often several are in sight at one time, widely scattered. There is, however, some sociability among them, most noticeable on foggy days, when they manage to keep in touch with each other by frequent interchange of call notes, as if helping each other to maintain the same general line of flight. They are even somewhat gregarious at times, gathering in small parties on the water to rest and calling to their passing companions; these gatherings are sometimes quite noisy, and are well known to gunners as "loon caucuses."'

This species while with us seems to feed mainly upon fish, and its food so far as known is similar to that of the Common Loon, but Mr. Bent says that it takes fish-spawn also.

HOLBOELL'S GREBE

Colymbus grisegena holboelli (REINHARDT).

PLATE I.

Other name: Red-necked Grebe.

IDENTIFICATION. — Length 18 to 21 inches; spread 30 to 32 inches. Size less than Black Duck, larger than other eastern grebes; in winter gray above, white below, and resembles Red-throated Loon but smaller and no white spots on back; neck more slender than any loon; white wing-patch shows in flight, but is concealed when at rest; resembles Horned Grebe in winter, but cheeks not so shining white, also adults have whitish upright spot toward back of head nearly surrounded by gray; bill longer than that of Horned Grebe; in summer white throat and cheeks in contrast to reddish lower neck distinguish it from Horned Grebe with black head and upper throat and yellowish-brown line through eye.

BREEDING. — *Nest:* Of grass, reeds, etc., usually among plants in shallow water of marshy lake, sometimes on muskrat house, often floating but attached to vegetation.

RANGE. — Breeds from northeastern Siberia, northwestern Alaska, and northern Canada south to northern Washington, North Dakota, and southwestern Minnesota; winters mainly on the Atlantic and Pacific coasts from Maine to North Carolina and from the Pribilof and Aleutian islands and British Columbia to southern California, also from southern Colorado, southern Wisconsin, southern Ontario, and the Ohio Valley casually to Tennessee, Georgia, and Florida, and in Asia south to Japan.

A bright clear day in January, a gentle breeze, a river mouth where the rippling flood flows into the sparkling sea, a lazy swell washing gently on the bar where a herd of mottled seals is basking in the sun, Oldsquaws and Golden-eyes in small parties — such a scene is a fit setting for the great grebe that winters on our coasts. Here we find the bird, nearly always shy and wary, resting low in the water, its head held horizontally, much like that of a loon, alert, diving 'like a flash,' and ready for any eventuality. Sometimes, loon-like, it floats with its head held under water while spying below for its prey. First we see it, then it has vanished! For nearly a minute we search the face of the waters in vain, when suddenly it reappears, but at a greater distance. Now as we hold the glass on it, it disappears again so quickly that we can hardly tell how it went. Like all grebes, Holboell's often dives with a sudden forward spring, but it can let itself down into the water backward either slowly or swiftly. Sometimes when alarmed it exposes only enough of its head to enable it to see, while keeping its body below the surface. It can do this for long periods, swimming so slowly and gently as to escape observation.

In New England Holboell's Grebe is usually the least common of the grebes, and stays mostly in wide waters where it can keep more than a gunshot from shore, but where no shooting is allowed, it becomes tame and unsuspicious. It may be seen off either rocky cliffs or sandy shores, and often is most common off isolated isles like Block Island or headlands like Nahant, where it sometimes gathers in great numbers. Occasionally it is seen far out at sea. Sometimes in spring or autumn one or two individuals, or even a small flock, may be met with in some of the larger fresh-water ponds, lakes, or rivers of New England; but otherwise the species is rather seldom seen in the interior of southern New England, except when severe cold waves freeze up large lakes to the westward in which, in ordinary seasons, many of the birds pass the winter.

In migration Holboell's Grebe assembles in flocks, and now and then numbers appear where food is plentiful along our shores, but usually the species is rather solitary. In migratory flights

7

along the coast it flies commonly not far above the water with head and neck extended and feet stretched out behind.

When feeding in salt water this fast swimmer overtakes the swiftest small fish. Occasionally it catches a fish too large to hold readily and swallow quickly, which wriggles away from the beak-hold. Then the eager bird dives 'like a flash' and seizes its prey again. Sometimes it carries such a fish into shallow water where it strikes, pounds and slaps it about until the victim succumbs. Then the active bird throws its own head up and backward until it seems to strike the back and so works the fish down its widely distended throat. The food of this bird on salt water seems to consist largely of fish and crustaceans. Mr. Bent says that in Manitoba it lives largely on crayfish, amblystomae and aquatic insects, and that it takes tadpoles, aquatic worms, small crustaceans, mollusks, and vegetable substances. It also takes earthworms and beetles.

HORNED GREBE

Colymbus auritus (LINNAEUS).

PLATE I.

Other names: Dipper; Hell-diver; Devil Diver.

IDENTIFICATION. — Length 12½ to 15 inches; spread about 24 inches. Size of Green-winged Teal but head and bill smaller; in breeding plumage easily recognized, with its black slightly crested head, brownish throat, and yellowish-brown line through eye; in winter its *pure white fore neck, cheeks and under parts* (white extending up from throat to nape), *absence of brown* in its plumage, its *straighter, slenderer* bill, and its large conspicuous *white wing-patch* (which always shows when wing is spread), distinguish it from Pied-billed Grebe; *smaller* size and short bill distinguish it from Holboell's Grebe.

BREEDING. — Similar to that of Holboell's Grebe.

RANGE. — Breeds from near the Arctic coast to Maine, Quebec, Ontario, Minnesota, northern Nebraska, and southern British Columbia, also in Iceland, northern Europe and Siberia; winters from Maine and New York to Florida and Louisiana, and from southern Alaska to southern California, in the region of the Great Lakes, and in central and southern Europe, northern Africa, the Azores, and the coasts of China and Japan.

In its full nuptial plumage the Horned Grebe is a handsome bird. In the sunshine its ruffed and crested head and rich, deeply colored neck and flanks glow resplendent. Even in the modest dark and white plumage of winter in which it is usually seen in the East, with its pure, satiny white breast, it is delicately handsome, and it seems as if aware of its distinction. Its head is carried proudly and when at ease it rides the water lightly and gracefully. Even in its finest plumage, however, it seems like a freak, with its fluffy tufted head and handsome fore parts, its rather ordinary-looking, plain back and its lack of any appreciable tail to balance its frontal beauties. Like all grebes the bird seems somehow to have been left unfinished; yet it is admirably adapted to its mode of life.

The Horned Grebe may be found almost anywhere along the Atlantic coast in winter, and is more common than the Holboell's Grebe; sometimes in migration it is locally abundant, not only on the coast but inland. Occasionally severe easterly storms drive large flocks into the ponds of the interior.

The flight of the Horned Grebe is strong and often direct and long-continued. In rising from the water it splashes along the surface for a long distance before it can gain sufficient impetus to launch itself into the air. In flight it appears much like a loon except for its small

8

size, the greater rapidity of its wing strokes, and its conspicuous white wing-patches. On the surface it swims with alternate strokes of its lobed paddles and dives quickly and gracefully with closed wings. I have never seen one open or use its wings under water, but Mr. C. A. Clark told me that he with a friend watched two Horned Grebes diving on Walden Pond in the Lynn woods. There were in the pond many small fishes, which the grebes pursued. The wings were held partly open and now and then a quick stroke was given with them. In catching the elusive fish the birds frequently darted their heads to the right or left as their prey dodged and doubled in flight.

No bird is more at home on the water than the Horned Grebe. It often sleeps there with its head on its back and the bill turned and buried under its scapulars. Like the Common Loon it turns on its side or back to preen the feathers of its breast.

On the Atlantic coast it passes in numbers during its migrations; and in October and November and again in March and April its greatest flights occur, usually a mile or two offshore. When migrating in the interior it often follows the course of a river, swimming with the current very early in the morning or just before dark. At times it flies at a considerable height.

The food of the Horned Grebe is known to consist largely of small fish, crustaceans, tadpoles, lizards, leeches, beetles, grasshoppers, locusts, many aquatic insects, a few snails and spiders, and some vegetal food.

PIED–BILLED GREBE

Podilymbus podiceps podiceps (LINNAEUS).   PLATE I.

Other names: Dabchick; Water-witch; Dipper; Didapper; Hell-diver; Little Diver.

IDENTIFICATION. — Length 12 to 15 inches; spread about 22 to 24½ inches. Smaller than a teal; in nuptial plumage black throat and spot on bill distinguish it; in late autumn or winter may be known by thick hen-like bill with curved upper mandible, general brownish tinge of fore neck and breast; no conspicuous white wing-patches.

VOICE. — Common calls loud and sonorous; suggest notes of a cuckoo; others, a loon.

BREEDING. — Similar to that of Holboell's Grebe.

RANGE. — Breeds locally from central British Columbia, Great Slave Lake, central Manitoba, southern Ontario, Quebec, New Brunswick, and Nova Scotia south to Florida, Texas, and parts of Mexico; winters from New York, and the Potomac Valley, Vancouver Island, British Columbia, Arizona and Texas southward, and in Cuba.

When autumn comes, when the leaves have turned to crimson and gold, when white frost lies on the meadows at sunrise, when noisy jays and busy squirrels are gathering their winter stores, then, on the winding reaches of some sluggish river where the pickerel-weed and arrow-plant grow and where wild rice and cattail flags wave in the breeze, we may find the 'Water-witches.' If undisturbed and at ease, they ride almost as lightly and buoyantly upon the water as an Indian canoe or an autumn leaf wafted along the surface. When apprehensive they sink slowly down, swimming with only the head or head and neck above water; but when really alarmed they go under so quickly that one can hardly see how they vanish. Often after such a disappearance the hunter searches in vain, for the scared bird swims under water until it reaches the water-plants on the margin, and there rests with only its bill and perhaps also its eyes above the surface, so deftly concealed that its hiding-place is rarely discovered. Its ap-

9

parent descent to the lower regions so quickly as often to escape a charge of shot, and its occasional complete disappearance, have given it the euphonious appellation of 'Hell-diver.'

In the breeding season the Pied-billed Grebe is shy and secretive, keeping generally well out of sight, but its presence may be detected by the sonorous notes which it often utters during the mating season. At this season it frequents cattail swamps, large marshes and stagnant, reed-bordered ponds where the nest is built. When the water is deep enough the nest floats, attached to stems of reeds, flags or bushes. Usually it is built high enough to keep the eggs above water, but they are rarely dry.

When the mother bird leaves her eggs, if time allows, she covers them with some of the 'muck and truck' from the nest. When the eggs have been thus concealed, the nest appears a mere heap of trash such as may be found anywhere in a marsh. The young can take to the water immediately after they are hatched and do so if disturbed. They swim and dive readily as soon as they strike the water but cannot stay very long beneath the surface.

This species like other grebes often carries the tiny young upon its back. In the face of danger the young are covered by the mother's wings while she swims away buoyantly. If she dives, she usually carries the young under water with her and emerges with them still concealed as it were in her pockets. Often the little ones ride about on the back of the mother entirely hidden beneath the scapulars or wing coverts, or with only their little heads peeping out. At such times, if the mother dives, the young often remain floating on the water and even when held under the wings, if the parent bird becomes frightened, the chicks sometimes come to the surface, perhaps because the mother uses her wings in swimming under water to hasten her flight.

The Pied-billed Grebe though swift and graceful in the water is quite awkward on land. It can walk or run slowly while standing on its feet with the body inclined forward at an angle, but if much hurried it throws itself forward on its belly and scrambles along with both wings and feet as if it were swimming.

The southward migration of this species begins during September in the northern United States. As the Pied-billed Grebe is mainly a fresh-water bird and frequents chiefly still or sluggish waters, it commonly moves southward when such waters freeze and remains in the South until the ice breaks up on the lakes and rivers of southern New England. In April its cuckoo-like notes may be heard again in the ponds and marshes where it breeds.

The food of the Pied-billed Grebe consists of small fish and other small forms of animal life, together with seeds and other parts of water-plants. Like all grebes they swallow feathers, balls of which are usually found in their stomachs, but the nutritive value of these to the grebe is unknown.

SOOTY SHEARWATER

Puffinus griseus (GMELIN). PLATE 9.

Other names: Black Hagdon; Black Hag or Haglet.
IDENTIFICATION. — Length 16 to 18 inches; spread 40 to 42 inches. Uniform dusky brown except paler under wings; appears black at a distance.
BREEDING. — On sea islands. *Nest:* A burrow in the ground. *Egg:* 1, white.
RANGE. — Breeds in Southern Hemisphere only; in summer north to Labrador, Greenland, Faroe and Orkney islands on the Atlantic coasts and the Aleutian and Kurile islands on the Pacific.

The Sooty Shearwater much resembles the Greater Shearwater in habits, but is not so numerous off the Atlantic coast. Wherever many of the latter species are seen, however, some Sooty Shearwaters usually will be found.

These shearwaters are excessively greedy birds, and are very bold and combative in securing food from other birds. They often follow fishing dories when the fishermen are baiting trawls, and as the gear sinks in the water at the stern of the dory, the birds dive after the sinking bait and frequently succeed in tearing it from the hook. Some are so greedy that they swallow it hook and all. In former times the fishermen retaliated by catching them by means of a floating bait in which a light hook was concealed. Thousands of shearwaters were caught in this way, and their bodies were used by fishermen for bait or for food. Among the thousands thus caught were proportionate numbers of Sooty Shearwaters.

Mr. Bent says that this species dives occasionally in pursuit of food 'using the wings freely under water,' and off the coast of Alaska I have seen them, when frightened at the approach of our steamer, dive awkwardly and swim or rather, fly, under water for a short distance before coming to the surface again and taking wing.

AUDUBON'S SHEARWATER

Puffinus lherminieri lherminieri LESSON.

IDENTIFICATION. — Length 11 to 12 inches; spread about 20 inches. Our smallest shearwater; resembles Greater Shearwater in markings but lacks white at base of tail.
BREEDING. — Similar to that of Sooty Shearwater.
RANGE. — Breeds on Bermuda, the Bahamas, and the Lesser Antilles; ranges over warmer parts of the western North Atlantic Ocean, occasionally reaching the coast from Florida to New Jersey.

Breeding on Bermuda and the Bahamas and ranging the open seas between, Audubon's Shearwaters may sometimes be observed from ships passing between our Atlantic ports and Europe, South America, or the Panama Canal, but they very rarely reach our coasts unless driven in by a severe storm. They are active little birds, using their wings more rapidly than their larger relatives. One hundred years ago Audubon described their feeding habits as he ob-

II

served them in the Gulf of Mexico. Their flight low over the water is an alternation of short periods of flapping and sailing; now and then they coast down to the surface and seem to run along on the water a short distance; they swim freely and dive easily for small fishes. The wings are used in underwater propulsion; probably all shearwaters use the wings in this manner. — (J.B.M.)

GREATER SHEARWATER

Puffinus gravis (O'REILLY).

PLATE 9.

Other names: Wandering Shearwater; Haglet; Hagdon; Hag; Gray Hag or Haglet; Common Atlantic Shearwater.

IDENTIFICATION. — Length 18 to 20 inches; spread 42 to 45 inches. Unmistakable two-colored effect on side of head; dark cap appears black by contrast with white of throat, with distinct line of demarcation; bill blackish.

BREEDING. — Similar to that of Sooty Shearwater.

RANGE. — Over entire Atlantic Ocean from Greenland to southern South America and South Africa, but breeds only on Tristran da Cunha Islands.

Shearwaters live most of their lives upon the sea. On the vast expanse of the Atlantic, where the mariner can see no land, where the sea heaves restlessly even in a calm or tosses and roars in wild commotion in the storm, there in the loneliness and desolation of the waters the shearwaters are at home. I have never seen one very near land, although sometimes they follow the fish near shore or even into some outlying harbor; but in summer, on the banks of Newfoundland and New England, wherever fishing schooners anchor, there the 'hags' are almost always to be found.

The Greater Shearwater breeds in the Southern Hemisphere, and visits the North Atlantic when winter reigns in southern oceans. Anyone cruising in summer a few miles off isolated points, such as Cape Ann, Cape Cod, Nantucket, or Montauk, may see a large, rather gull-like bird flapping and sailing near the surface of the water. Its dark brown upper plumage and sharply contrasting white under plumage and its manner of flight at once identify it as the Greater Shearwater. To see the birds in numbers, one should go to the fishing-grounds where great 'bottom fish' are hauled from the depths. Wherever the fish bite well, there these birds may be found; and a few fish livers cut in pieces and thrown overboard are likely to bring this and other species about the boat, together with gulls and petrels that are usually on the watch for such opportunities on the fishing-grounds.

Shearwaters are graceful birds on the wing, and in a high wind they scale about close to the water, with their long pointed wings slightly decurved. They circle and glide with the greatest ease. The Greater Shearwater often alights on the surface of the water to pick up floating food, swimming toward it with head erect and wings partially raised but not fully spread. In alighting it frequently strikes upon its breast with some force, but does not commonly plunge directly under water head first like a tern or a gannet. It can dive from the surface and swim well under water, and probably uses its wings beneath the surface in pursuit of sinking food or fleeing fish. All manner of fish is food for the shearwaters. They are particularly fond of the 'gurry' or waste thrown overboard by fishermen. On this food they grow fat, and they consume quantities of fish oil. Dr. C. W. Townsend says that they are very fond of squids, and a shearwater that he shot contained in its stomach the horny beaks of twenty-four of these animals. 'The hags feed on the squid, the gulls on the herring, and the gannets on the mackerel,' according to the Cape Sable Island, Nova Scotia, fishermen.

CORY'S SHEARWATER

Puffinus diomedea borealis CORY.   PLATE 9.

IDENTIFICATION. — Length 20 to 22 inches; spread 40 to 49 inches. Larger than Greater Shearwater; lack of sharp contrast between white throat and gray head differentiates from Greater Shearwater: bill yellowish.

BREEDING. — Similar to that of Sooty Shearwater.

RANGE. — Breeds on the Azores, Madeira, Salvage and Canary islands; wanders to Newfoundland and Brazil.

Cory's Shearwater is the largest of the shearwaters which visit the Atlantic coast. It does not differ from the Greater Shearwater in habits. It flies similarly, is the same greedy bird, and enjoys the same kind of food. Ordinarily it is seen only at some distance from land; more rarely it appears alongshore.

ATLANTIC FULMAR

Fulmarus glacialis glacialis (LINNAEUS).   PLATE 9.

Other names: Noddy; Oil-bird; Marbleheader; White Hagdon.

IDENTIFICATION. — Length 18 to 20 inches; spread about 42 to 45 inches. In flight unmistakable; straight, stiffly held, outstretched wings and long glides as the bird scuds along distinguish it from a gull.

BREEDING. — *Nest:* A slight depression on grassy shelves of sea-cliffs, sometimes grass-lined. *Egg:* 1, white.

RANGE. — Breeds from Franz Josef Land to northern Greenland; winters to New England coast; ranges north to lat. 85°, west to Melville Island, and south to Scotland and Ireland.

The gull-like Atlantic Fulmar — beautiful, with its intelligent dark eye set in its pure white head, its yellow bill, clear gray mantle and snowy underparts — is one of the best known of North Atlantic sea-birds. It is littoral in the breeding season only, when it is extraordinarily abundant, literally in myriads, at some of its favorite nesting-places which are mostly in high latitudes. After nesting is over, the Fulmars scatter far and wide over the gray wastes of the North Atlantic Ocean. Like other petrels, the home of the bird, except in the breeding season, is the open sea. With great powers of flight, it is a magnificent sea-bird, breasting the gale on sturdy wing or resting composedly on the water, no matter how high a sea is running. Fulmars are seen most often by whalers and fishermen upon whose ships the hungry birds are constant attendants. In Arctic and subarctic waters the offal from whalers and sealers attracts them. They crowd about and under the ship's stern, coming in greedy hundreds or even thousands from all quarters, when a whale is being cut up. Ravenous and audacious, they swarm in the oily wake, and come within a few feet of the sailors. Heedless of all else but the

13

refuse, they may be knocked over often with a boathook, while they regard the discharge of a gun so little that their dead fellows float unheeded within a few feet. The Atlantic Fulmar seems to like above all other food the blubber of the whale. For this it has a prodigious appetite, and sometimes it so gorges itself that it cannot rise from the water. Says Captain Collins: 'In former years many hundreds, if not thousands, of them were caught by the Grand Banks fishermen and used for bait. The voracity of these birds renders their capture by hook and line a comparatively easy task.'

Fulmars often associate with shearwaters and with them 'track' tirelessly the transatlantic steamships, both in midocean and nearer shore, following in their wakes, day by day, and picking up every bit of floating refuse cast overboard from the galley. The Fulmar usually feeds settled, albatross-like, on the water, though it sometimes 'dives wholly beneath the surface to grasp food,' a habit unusual among petrels.

Atlantic Fulmars have been much observed on their ancient breeding-ground, St. Kilda, one of the Outer Hebrides, to which island they resort in vast numbers. Their young are fed with oil by regurgitation.

The food of the bird largely consists of mollusks, cuttle-fish material and any animal garbage or other animal food that it can pick up. — (J.A.F.)

LEACH'S PETREL

Oceanodroma leucorhoa leucorhoa (VIEILLOT).   PLATE 9.

Other names: Leach's Fork-tailed Petrel; Fork-tailed Stormy Petrel; Fork-Tailed Petrel; Carey Chicken ('Kerry Chicken').

IDENTIFICATION. — Length 7½ to 9 inches; spread 17 to 18½ inches. General color dark dusky brown; shoulders lighter; rump white; a little larger and browner than Wilson's Petrel from which it is distinguished by its forked tail and short legs which in flight do not show beyond end of tail.

VOICE: *Notes:* Soft twitterings and squeakings near nest burrows.

BREEDING. — *Nest:* In burrow in ground or under a rock. *Egg:* 1, white, finely dotted at large end.

RANGE. — Breeds from southern Greenland and Iceland to Maine and Ireland, and from the Aleutian Islands to the Commander and Kurile islands; ranges south over the North Atlantic to the Equator and over the North Pacific to Japan and Midway Island.

In July, 1914, it was my good fortune to join Mr. William P. Wharton on the yacht Avocet for a cruise among the sea-bird colonies of the Maine coast. On the evening of the 13th, having found a considerable number of Leach's Petrels nesting on a small island, we concealed ourselves by lying on the lowest branches of some of the scattering spruce trees that grew near the shore. A higher layer of spruce limbs served us as cover, while the lower ones kept us off the ground. Herring Gulls which bred on the island were then coming in for the night, and many hundreds were seen winging their way toward us from distant shores. They alighted on the heaving sea in great flocks, and sat in massed array along the dark ledges, their white heads, necks, and breasts gleaming immaculate against the background of dun ledge and darkening waters. As we lay concealed, their complaining cries died away in the air overhead, until dark brought comparative quiet, except that a few wakeful gulls kept up intermittent cries; but the Night Herons were awake, and they broke the silence with raucous croakings.

14

Softly the warm, balmy summer night settled down. Eight o'clock, and still no sign of the petrels. Time dragged on, and we had almost decided that it was useless to wait, when at nearly nine a dark, indistinct shape flitted silently in from the sea, fluttered bat-like back and forth, and then dropped in the shrubbery. Soon another and another came, until the incoming was continual, while others seemed to be going out to sea, but may have been merely flying back and forth. Now queer sounds arose, in the air, on the ground about us, and even in the earth beneath, for these strange birds had burrows in the earth under the tree in which we reclined, and they crept into their holes seemingly beneath our very bodies where we lay across the mouths of their passageways. Tender chucklings, crowings, stammerings, and formless sounds that seemed like billing and cooing filled the air. Meanwhile there were flittings and flutterings, goings and comings, all about us. This went on for a good part of an hour, when apparently the first excitement had passed, and we arose and departed, vastly entertained by the experience.

Petrels are peculiar, eerie birds, and their habits are so strange that from time immemorial sailors have had a superstition that these small fowls are the precursors of storms and wrecks. There is some reason for such superstitions, as at the approach of a storm petrels often gather in great excitement about vessels. Our observations during the cruise of the Avocet seemed to prove that birds several times the size of the petrels have a strange, unaccountable fear of them. We took a petrel from its warm burrow in daylight and released it. It flew at once to the ocean, going toward a great flock of clamorous Herring Gulls sitting on a ledge near the island. Immediately every gull ceased its cries, took wing, and fled silently out to sea. Later we released petrels on other islands on which gulls or terns were breeding, and however numerous or clamorous were the birds immediately about us, the appearance of a petrel on the wing silenced their cries and caused a local exodus. No one has been able to account for this, so far as I know, and it may not be a universal experience; but it was ours. Let a hawk or an owl appear in one of these gull or tern colonies and the war cry is sounded, while the birds swarm from all directions to mob and harry the intruder until it is driven away; let a cat appear in a colony of Herring Gulls in the daytime, and its appearance is the signal for a general attack; but the small and apparently inoffensive petrel is avoided as if it were ghost or banshee.

One of the most interesting facts in the life history of this ranger of the wide and stormy seas is that you may find its nest in a burrow under a commonplace barberry bush in an island sheep-pasture. It digs fast. How it disposes of the earth is a question unanswerable to one who has seen only the long-occupied burrows unless, as the boy said of the chipmunk, it begins at the other end! But some loose soil is often seen at the mouth of a new excavation. When the bird is disturbed in its unfinished burrow, it can dig itself in very rapidly, apparently using both bill and feet, and as the soil is light, it possibly packs it down with its feet, as it digs onward. During the burrowing and nest-building both male and female may be found in the nest through the day, but after the single egg is laid only one bird, usually the male, remains there in daylight. Like other petrels, when disturbed in its burrow it has a habit of ejecting from the mouth an oily liquid with an offensive odor. This odor often indicates the breeding-places of the birds.

From late in May until September we never see a petrel about the breeding-grounds during the day, for while one bird of each nest remains in the burrow, the other probably roams far away over the sea, and the young are fed mainly if not wholly at night. Owing to their nesting habits, petrels must needs nest on islands where there are no small burrowing animals, such as minks, rats, or weasels, any of which would soon destroy a colony of these little birds. Any of man's destructive satellites, cats, dogs, or hogs, if at liberty, would soon extirpate them.

As a sea rover this species resembles the Wilson's Petrel, but it is now apparently rare in summer off the New England coast, though still found in numbers on the Grand Banks. Its habits at sea are somewhat like those of the other species, but Dr. R. C. Murphy says: 'Unlike Wilson's Petrel the Leach's Petrels settled frequently into the water, holding the tips of their wings high while they swam.' I have never seen this bird plunge or dive under water. On land it seems to alight only at the mouth of its hole, into which it creeps or waddles on its tarsi, and in leaving the burrow it makes use of its wings at once.

I find little data on the migrations of the petrels along the Atlantic coast. They pass at night or far from land, and their flittings are noted only by those 'who go down to the sea in ships.' Captain Collins says that petrels generally leave the Banks late in October or early in November, and return in April or May.

The food of Leach's Petrel seems to consist largely of oily matter which it gleans from the surface of the sea, together with small fish, mollusks, crustaceans, and other small oceanic creatures found on or near the surface.

STORM PETREL
Hydrobates pelagicus (LINNAEUS).

Other name: Mother Carey's Chicken.

IDENTIFICATION. — Length 5¾ inches; spread about 12 inches. Smallest of our petrels; blackish-brown with white rump, and some white showing under wing when in flight; round or unforked tail; webs of feet black.

BREEDING. — Similar to that of Leach's Petrel.

RANGE. — Breeds mainly on islands of the eastern North Atlantic and in the Mediterranean; ranges to coasts of Europe and Africa, and to Labrador, Newfoundland, Nova Scotia, and Maine.

The little Storm Petrel is probably the original 'Mother Carey's Chicken,' for it is the commonest petrel of the eastern Atlantic, where the name was first applied to these supposed harbingers of stormy weather. They are very irregular in their breeding, eggs having been found in their burrows from May to October, but after nesting duties are over they range the ocean widely, and are often seen on the fishing banks off Newfoundland, most frequently in August. They sometimes follow the wake of trans-Atlantic vessels for some time, in search of scraps of food dropped overboard. — (J.B.M.)

WILSON'S PETREL

Oceanites oceanicus (KUHL).

PLATE 9.

Other names: Long-legged Stormy Petrel; Wilson's Stormy Petrel; Sea Martin; Mother Carey's Chicken; Long-legged Mother Carey's Chicken; Stormy Petrel.

IDENTIFICATION. — Length 7 to 7½ inches; spread about 16 inches. May be distinguished from Leach's Petrel by almost square-ended tail; yellow-webbed feet project beyond end of tail in flight; wing-beats are more quick and fluttering, and it is given to short periods of sailing; a little darker and smaller than Leach's Petrel.

BREEDING. — Similar to that of Leach's Petrel.

RANGE. — Breeds on islands of the Southern Hemisphere; ranges all oceans except Pacific north of the Equator; ranges Atlantic north to Labrador and Great Britain.

Wilson's Petrel was long a bird of mystery. In summer it appeared in the North Atlantic, but it was never known to breed or even to go ashore unless driven there by high winds. Time solved the mystery. This petrel is one of the smallest of sea-birds. Its length is less than that of the Purple Martin. It is too small and delicate to withstand severe winter storms, and so times its migrations, therefore, as to live in perpetual summer. But like most of the shearwaters it reverses the ordinary migratory movement of the Northern Hemisphere. It breeds during the Antarctic summer in the Southern Hemisphere; then wings its way far northward toward the top of the world making a journey of about seven thousand miles; and passes the period of extreme Antarctic winter in the North Atlantic Ocean. It keeps to the wide seas and is rarely seen ashore in our latitudes unless driven in by very severe, prolonged gales.

Apparently Wilson's Petrel leaves its far southern breeding-grounds in March, and early in May its hordes appear in the North Atlantic. During summer the majority of the species seems to be distributed along the coast of North America and west of the Gulf Stream; but individuals may appear almost anywhere in the North Atlantic. In September and October they all move southward toward their breeding-grounds and the Antarctic summer.

Wilson's Petrel appears in numbers near the coast in June, July and August. The bird even penetrates into harbors; but commonly it is seen miles from any shore flapping and skipping along on the waves and often using both wings and feet at once, and thus both running (or skipping) and flying on the surface; hence, according to Dampier (1703), the name petrel (little Peter) after the Apostle Peter who also essayed to walk upon the waves. It seems credible, however, that the petrels were thus named in imitation of the notes of some species which resemble the word 'petterel.'

Wilson's Petrel may be seen during the summer from the deck of any vessel more than ten miles from shore. It is the common 'Stormy Petrel' or 'Mother Carey's Chicken' that follows steamships from American ports far out on the Atlantic, but unless viewed close at hand it is difficult to distinguish from Leach's Petrel except with a powerful glass. On a calm sea this species flies along close to the surface, flexing the wings like bats or fluttering almost like butterflies. In windy weather they sail more with set wings, using both feet at once and striking them down hard to leeward. They sometimes hop or bound from the surface of the wave, and appear to be tireless examples of perpetual motion as they often fly by night as well as by day; but Dr. R. C. Murphy, who watched them on a whaling voyage, says that at evening the birds dropped behind and he saw some settle on the sea. At about eight o'clock in the morning they appeared in the vessel's wake again. This indicates that the Wilson's Petrel rests at night on the sea.

Sometimes in daylight this species may be seen resting in flocks on the water. While they sometimes alight on its surface to pick up food, they usually gather this while flying and skipping along or while fluttering and stationary. They dance upon the sea, searching along the 'slicks' and picking up any bits of oily matter that may float, and sometimes plunge or dive beneath the surface. This Petrel when ashore is not only incapable of perching but even of standing upright unless by the aid of its fluttering wings. It walks on its tarsi; but by a powerful exertion of its wings it is enabled to run on its toes as it does on the surface of the sea.

Wilson's Petrel feeds largely on fish oil and on small oily morsels, both of which it gleans from the surface of the waves. Petrels gather about fishing-boats to feed on offal or bait or about whaling vessels for oil and scraps of blubber, and like other sea-birds may be attracted by throwing out pieces of fish liver, for which they will come close to the boat.

Order Pelecaniformes. Totipalmate Swimmers.

YELLOW–BILLED TROPIC–BIRD

Phaëthon lepturus catesbyi BRANDT.

Other names: Boatswain Bird; Longtail.

IDENTIFICATION. — Length 30 to 32 inches, of which tail may be 18 to 20 inches; spread about 34 to 38 inches. A white bird except for black lesser wing coverts and tertials, partly black primaries, and a black mark before and through eye; two central tail feathers very much prolonged; quick pigeon-like flight.

BREEDING. — *Nest:* On open ledges or in recesses and caves on sea-cliffs. *Egg:* 1, whitish, profusely speckled, clouded or blotched with browns and purplish.

RANGE. — Breeds in Bermuda and various islands of the West Indies and Bahamas; ranges north in summer to 40° N. lat. in the western Atlantic Ocean; winters from the Bahamas and West Indies south at least to Brazil and Ascension Island.

The homing instinct of birds is one of the unexplained mysteries. How do the Yellow-billed Tropic-birds find their way unerringly, in fair weather or in foul, across at least six hundred miles of open sea, to their ancestral homes in the water-worn or wind-weathered limestone cliffs of the tiny Bermuda Islands? Find their way they certainly do, for after a winter absence of several months, in late February or March the birds return to the islands and even to the same identical nesting holes which they have occupied in previous years, as banding records show quite conclusively.

This beautiful white bird with its long streaming tail feathers and its quick pigeon-like flight is one of the familiar sights for visitors to Bermuda. It makes long journeys out across the blue waters of the warm Gulf Stream for its favorite food of small surface fishes. Dr. A. O. Gross reports finding a species of flying fish in two stomachs which he examined, and wonders whether they were caught in the air or in the water.

The Yellow-billed Tropic-bird is only a rare straggler to the coast of North America, where we have occasional records scattered from Florida to Nova Scotia. After the erratic hurricane which devastated so much of New England on September 21, 1938, several Tropic-birds were found in Vermont, the first inland record for this maritime species, after they had been carried helplessly across several states and no one knows how many miles of seething waters by the great storm. — (J.B.M.)

WHITE PELICAN

Pelecanus erythrorhynchos GMELIN.   PLATE 97.

IDENTIFICATION. — Length 54 to 70 inches, spread from 8 to almost 10 feet. A great white bird with black wing-tips and long yellow bill and yellow pouch; short legs.

BREEDING. — In colonies on islands in inland lakes. *Nest:* On ground; of reeds, grass and sticks, or a mere depression in sand or pebbles. *Eggs:* 2 to 4, chalky white.

RANGE. — Breeds from central British Columbia and Great Slave Lake south to central Manitoba, southern Texas, and southern California; winters from northern California, the Gulf States, and Florida, and along both coasts of Mexico, and in the interior, as far as Panama.

The White Pelican is a majestic bird. Awkward and grotesque though it be in captivity, it is, nevertheless, a master of the air and its aerial evolutions at great heights exhibit a power and dignity which can be equaled only by the eagle.

In the spring of 1878, in Florida, I saw great flocks of these gigantic birds. When seen in the distance and magnified by the mirage, they presented the appearance of fleets of stately ships under sail on the calm lagoons. I never saw these birds, like the Brown Pelican, plunge from a height or dive for their food. On the coast they sat on the sands at low water, and as the tide flowed in, they sailed calmly and majestically out over the shallows, formed long lines at a distance from the shore and parallel to it, and then beating the water with their great wings, closed in toward the beach, driving before them the little fish, which they scooped up in their capacious pouches. Then after sitting sluggishly for a time the great white birds, with heads drawn backward on their shoulders, rose into the air in flocks and sailed grandly, sweeping in wide circles up into the blue dome, rising to enormous heights and floating there for long periods apparently to enjoy the cooling breezes of those high altitudes.

In 1878 White Pelicans might be seen almost anywhere along the east coast of Florida. Now some birds perhaps may still be found about the Mosquito Lagoon near the Government Reservation, but the species is slowly disappearing. Some of its great feeding-grounds in the northwestern States have been drained; from others it has been driven away; and there seems little hope that the species can be saved to North America unless a number of its principal breeding-places can be made bird reservations and guarded for all time. The best opportunity for protection now is in the Canadian Northwest, where White Pelicans breed on some of the islands in large lakes.

EASTERN BROWN PELICAN

Pelecanus occidentalis occidentalis LINNAEUS.   PLATE 97.

Other names: Common Pelican; American Brown Pelican; Blue Pelican.

IDENTIFICATION. — Length 45 to 54 inches; spread 75 to 84 inches. Size of large goose; long bill carried down front of neck; distinguished from White Pelican by dark color and smaller size; plunges from a height into water after fish.

BREEDING. — In colonies, usually on island, often in mangrove growth. *Nest:* In bushes or on ground; of sticks and grass. *Eggs:* 2 or 3, chalky white.

RANGE. — Breeds on South Atlantic and Gulf coasts of the United States and the Atlantic coast of Central and South America from South Carolina to Texas and south to Brazil, in the Bahamas and West Indies, on the Pacific coast of Colombia and Ecuador, and in the Galapagos Islands; winters from Florida and the Gulf coast southward.

In appearance pelicans are strange, weird creatures. Such peculiar birds have a great educational value. They seem like relics of a hoary past, alone in a modern world. They remind us of the flying reptiles of early ages, and should be preserved to perpetuate their curious forms and habits for the benefit of future generations of mankind. But it is only by dint of the strictest protection that they can exist side by side with modern civilization.

In Florida the Brown Pelicans fish largely in the sea and in lagoons near the coast. Often a long line of the great birds, each with a wing-expansion of more than six feet, may be seen flapping along over the waves of the incoming tide, flying parallel with the shore as they pass on their way to their fishing-grounds. With stiffened wings the leader sails low over the heaving sea, flaps a few strokes to get better speed, and then sails again. One bird after another in regular succession follows his example, sailing with wings widespread and head drawn proudly back, the line falling and rising over the waves and just clearing their summits.

Usually in fishing the pelicans scatter and fly from twenty to thirty feet above the surface. When a pelican sees a fish to its liking, it falls into the water with a splash like a barrel tossed from a ship's deck. The pneumatic cushion on its breast no doubt deadens the shock, but it also adds to the buoyancy of the bird which thus requires a great momentum to carry it well below the surface.

The motions of the bird seem clumsy in the extreme, but slow-motion pictures reveal careful and skillful timing in these dives from a height. At the start of the downward plunge, the wings are partly closed and the neck is curved so that the head is close to the shoulders. Just before the water is reached, the wings are extended behind with a quick short stroke, and the body turns so that the bird is upside-down as it strikes the water at an angle of perhaps seventy or eighty degrees. At the same moment the neck is straightened and the bill enters the water with the pouch upside-down in such a way that the force of the dive opens the pouch to its fullest capacity. The bird comes up to a sitting position on the water with the bill closed and pointed down so that the water drains out from the pouch, and in a moment the bird raises its bill above its head, and the swallowing movements can be plainly seen. Sometimes Laughing Gulls follow the fishing pelicans, and as the big birds come to the sitting position on the water, the little gulls flutter down and alight on the pelicans' backs or sometimes even on their heads, in their anxiety to get crumbs from the pelicans' feast.

The Eastern Brown Pelican is a mere straggler in the Northeast. In the hot summer months following the breeding season some pelicans wander northward. They are not now known to breed north of South Carolina, but many appear in summer in North Carolina and occasionally some are seen farther north.

GANNET

Moris bassana (LINNAEUS).   PLATE 10.

Other names: White Gannet; Solan or Soland Goose.

IDENTIFICATION. — Length 33 to 40 inches; spread about 72 inches. White adult with black wing-tips is unmistakable; in flight the long narrow pointed wings are very straight, and the head and tail are both 'pointed'; young are gray and when swimming look much like Common Loon in winter plumage; Gannets dive for fish from a considerable height and go deep under water.

BREEDING. — On sea-cliffs or near them, on islands. *Nest:* Chiefly of seaweed. *Egg:* 1, bluish-white and chalky.

RANGE. — Breeds on Bird Rock, Bonaventure and Anticosti islands in the Gulf of St. Lawrence, and on islets off southeastern Newfoundland, and off the British Isles and Iceland; winters from the coast of Virginia south to the Gulf of Mexico, Vera Cruz, and Cuba, and the coast of North Africa, the Canaries and the Azores.

In fall and spring, rarely in summer, and sometimes in winter, great white birds with long, black-tipped wings may be seen fishing off our coasts. They sail high over the sea, and at the right moment nearly close their pinions and shoot down like barbed arrow-heads into the waves with a resounding splash that sometimes tosses up spray eight or ten feet like a fountain. These birds are Gannets from the Gulf of St. Lawrence. Captain Collins says that the height of their flight above the surface when they are fishing varies according to the depth at which the fish are swimming. By noting the elevation from which the Gannets plunge, expert fishermen can tell how deep to set their nets. These birds often dive from a height of about one hundred feet, but a plunge of about sixty feet is more common. The bird plunges from a height to get sufficient impetus to carry it to a considerable depth below the surface. When the fish are near the surface, it sails close to the water and glides down diagonally upon them. But when small fish are at the surface, it sometimes rests on the water and pursues its prey on the waves, snatching them up with the bill.

The Gannet, it is said, cannot fish in a perfectly calm sea. Probably it is difficult, if not impossible, for so heavy a bird to rise from the water without help from the wind. Gannets have been washed ashore in numbers during a dead calm with a heavy swell running. The young leave the nest long before they are able to rise on the wing. They flutter or sail down from the cliff to the surface of the sea and there they remain until able to shift for themselves. Probably there is great mortality among them before the survivors gain full power of flight. They must keep at sea until they reach maturity, as comparatively few appear on the breeding-grounds in the speckled immature plumage.

From the deck of a coasting steamer in winter I have watched numbers of these great birds fishing far over the sea. The feet are not used for steering in flight, as in the short-tailed sea-birds like loons, grebes, and auks, but are carried under the tail. Gannets are active before a coming storm, and their snow-white forms contrasted against a murky sky as they sweep over the sea, now plunging, now rising again, always enliven the scene.

When the migratory fish begin their southward movement, the Gannets move with them. Wherever fish on which the Gannets feed are abundant, there the birds may be found. They move southward slowly, following the fish. In January or February, in mild winters, a few may be seen off Cape Cod and Block Island, but most of them go farther south, some even reaching the Gulf of Mexico. From the latter part of March to early May, according to the season, they again become common on our northern coasts as they move slowly toward their homes in the Gulf of St. Lawrence.

EUROPEAN CORMORANT

Phalacrocorax carbo carbo (LINNAEUS). PLATE 10.

Other names: Shag; Common Cormorant.

IDENTIFICATION. — Length 34 to 40 inches; spread about 5 feet. Size of a small goose; adult blackish; in spring with white throat-patch and white patch on flanks; young brownish with white belly; cormorants usually swim with bill pointed up above the horizontal; white throat patch of adult usually conspicuous, and in spring white patch on flank is diagnostic; young bird has whiter belly than *P. auritus*.

BREEDING. — In colonies, on cliffs or islands, sometimes in trees. *Nest:* Of sticks and seaweeds. *Eggs:* 4 to 6, bluish-white, chalky.

RANGE. — Breeds from the coasts of western Greenland and Cumberland Sound to the north shore of the Gulf of St. Lawrence and on the Magdalen Islands; winters from Greenland to New York (Long Island); also occurs in Europe.

If in the dead of winter one sees off our coast a large, dark bird flapping slowly along close to the water with outstretched neck and alighting on a spindle or a ledge where it stands nearly upright, probably that bird is the European Cormorant, or as it was formerly called, the Common Cormorant. Once it was a common bird along our northern coasts, but its breeding colonies on the Labrador coast and elsewhere were systematically raided by the fishermen and sealers and the inhabitants of those barren lands, and today it is rather a rare visitor to the New England shores in winter. The majority of the cormorants seen in spring and autumn migrating along the coast are the Double-crested Cormorant, but they do not ordinarily linger long in the North, where the wintering cormorants are usually the European species. Single birds or small flocks may be observed in late autumn, winter, and early spring on outlying ledges such as the Salvages off Rockport, the Cohasset and Scituate rocks near Minot's Light in Massachusetts, and the Cormorant Rocks near Newport, Rhode Island, where the birds often assemble to roost at night, or to rest and sun themselves by day. There are many such islets of sea-washed rocks off the Maine coast where these birds formerly gathered in considerable numbers, and where between October and May some may still be found.

A very characteristic posture of the cormorants of whatever species, is their 'spread eagle' attitude. Apparently the plumage of cormorants is not as water-repellant as that of ducks, and after swimming about for some time they become very bedraggled if not actually water-logged. Resting birds frequently spread their wings and hold them open for some time, seemingly to dry them in the sun or by wind action. — (J.B.M.)

DOUBLE–CRESTED CORMORANT

Phalacrocorax auritus auritus (LESSON).   PLATE 10.

Other names: Shag; Taunton Turkey; Nigger Goose.

IDENTIFICATION. — Length 29 to 35 inches; spread 50 to 53 inches. When perched, the cormorant's shape is unmistakable — upright figure, neck long and slightly curved, and tail used like a prop; when sitting in 'spread-eagle' style, with wings held out, it may be recognized instantly; in flight the dark cormorants resemble geese somewhat, but are silent, whereas geese are noisy; they often alternate brief flappings with briefer sailing; when swimming the body is low in the water and the bill usually pointed above the horizontal; adult Double-crested Cormorant never has white throat-patch or thigh-patch; young bird has light breast shading into darker on belly, while young European Cormorant has nearly white lower breast and belly.

BREEDING. — Similar to that of European Cormorant, but sometimes nests in swamps on inland lakes.

RANGE. — Breeds from central Alberta, northern Ontario, Gulf of St. Lawrence, and Newfoundland south to northern Nebraska, northeastern Arkansas, central Illinois, and Penobscot Bay, Maine; winters from Virginia south to Florida and on the Gulf coast.

In spring, late summer, or autumn long flocks of dark birds larger than Black Ducks may be seen almost anywhere along the North Atlantic coast, flying 'in single file' close to the water with slow-flapping wings and outstretched necks. When seen passing diagonally at a distance close to the waves, the long wings of each seem to overlap those of the next in line, all rising and falling very nearly together. Often in the shimmering summer haze, which operates to deceive the eye, this spectacle will almost delude the credulous into the belief that they have seen the folds of a sea serpent rolling along the waves.

Now and then one of these birds may be seen sitting erect on a spar-buoy; and the inexperienced young sometimes are tame enough to alight on a spile near some wharf or bridge unconcerned by passing vehicles or people. Usually when a cormorant flies off from such a perch above the water, it descends nearly or quite to the surface before it gathers headway. From this habit has arisen the southern superstition that the 'shag must wet its tail before it can fly.' When resting on the water this bird somewhat resembles a loon, but unlike the loon it has no pure white fore neck and breast. The cormorant's tail is longer than that of a loon and the bird has a hooked bill. This cormorant is a remarkably expert swimmer and diver, and often uses its wings as well as its broad paddles in the pursuit of swift fish in the depths. I have never seen the submarine activities of this species in its natural environment, but Dr. P. L. Hatch, who had abundant opportunity to watch the bird in its breeding-grounds in the clear lakes of Minnesota, says: 'Being principally fish eaters they spend most of the time in the water where their movements in pursuit of their prey are simply marvellous in velocity. With their totipalmated feet folded flatly into mere blades while carried forward and when struck out backwards opening to their utmost and the half-spread wings beating with inconceivable rapidity, they seem to fly through the waters at various depths in pursuit of their favorite food, the fish.'

It is thought that cormorants build (in part at least) their nests with seaweed that they obtain by diving. A statement by Dr. Charles W. Townsend in his 'In Audubon's Labrador' lends color to this belief. Referring to a trading-schooner which was sunk off the Labrador coast, he says 'This summer, when some fishermen visited a cormorant island near by, they found that the birds had decorated their nests with pocket-knives, pipes, hairpins, and ladies' combs — objects which they had obtained by diving to the wreck.'

When Double-crested Cormorants have a good breeding season in the North, they sweep south past the New England coast in great numbers in the autumnal flight. At times large flocks may be seen flying overland. This was the case in the autumns of 1905 and 1921. The flight of 1921 was the greatest that I have ever seen. The birds began to come in late August and by early September there were days when many flocks were flying. There were enormous numbers in September and October, and the flight continued until winter set in. In migration these birds fly high, sometimes in very long lines and often in the 'V' formation like Canada Geese. Sometimes such flocks are mistaken for geese, but their dark color, longer tails, smaller size, and silence in flight, while geese are vociferous, should differentiate them at once. In the return flight numbers usually appear coastwise between the middle of April and the middle of May.

FLORIDA CORMORANT

Phalacrocorax auritus floridanus (AUDUBON).

Other names: Nigger Goose; Water-turkey.
IDENTIFICATION. — Slightly smaller than Double-crested Cormorant but indistinguishable in the field.
BREEDING. — See Double-crested Cormorant.
RANGE. — Breeds in Louisiana, Florida, North Carolina, the Bahamas, and the Isle of Pines; winters north to Texas and throughout its breeding range (except the Carolinas).

This race and the Double-crested Cormorant are identical in appearance except for a slight difference in size, and their habits are very much alike. On the Gaspé coast of the Gulf of St. Lawrence the Double-crested Cormorant breeds in great rookeries of hundreds of nests, usually on cliffs or rocky islands, with practically no other species as neighbors, but the Florida Cormorant usually associates at this time with the Water-turkey and the various colony-nesting herons, egrets, and ibises, building in bushes or low trees often standing in water. In the West the Double-crested Cormorant sometimes builds its flat platform in the tules surrounding shallow ponds. — (J.B.M.)

MEXICAN CORMORANT

Phalacrocorax olivaceus mexicanus (BRANDT).

IDENTIFICATION. — Length about 25 inches; spread about 40 inches. Smaller than Double-crested Cormorant which it resembles; in breeding plumage face and gular pouch bordered with white.
BREEDING. — In colonies; in trees or bushes in shallow water. *Nest:* Of small sticks. *Eggs:* 4 or 5, bluish-white, chalky.
RANGE. — Resident from northwestern Mexico, southeastern Texas, southern Louisiana, Cuba, the Isle of Pines, and the Bahamas south to Nicaragua.

The habits of the Mexican Cormorant are not, in all probability, very different from those of our other American cormorants, but they have not been carefully studied and described. It is southern in distribution, but a few pairs nest on the Louisiana coast and it is occasionally found at interior points during its post-breeding-season wanderings. — (J.B.M.)

WATER–TURKEY

Anhinga anhinga (LINNAEUS).

PLATE 97.

Other names: Snake-bird; Darter; Anhinga.

IDENTIFICATION. — Length 34 to 36 inches; spread about 44 inches. Resembles a cormorant, but easily distinguished by longer, more slender neck, small head, slender, straight, sharply pointed bill, and long tail with brown tip often spread fan-like; adults chiefly black; *male* in spring with much white on scapulars; *female* with brownish head, neck and breast.

BREEDING. — In colonies with herons, etc. *Nest:* Of sticks. *Eggs:* 3 to 5, bluish-white, chalky.

RANGE. — Breeds from south-central Texas, east-central Arkansas, and southeastern North Carolina south to Brazil and Argentina; winters in nearly the same area north to southern California, Arizona, central Arkansas, and central Alabama.

Just across the Florida line from Thomasville, Georgia, and near Lake Miccosukee, is a small 'pond' which is, in miniature, typical of the great cypress swamps which from time immemorial, have sheltered hosts of breeding herons and egrets, ibises, and other birds, and it was at this pond that I first made the acquaintance of the Water-turkey, Snake-bird, or Darter, as it is variously called. Though spoken of as a pond, it looked from a distance more like a bit of primeval forest, with its huge cypress trees towering high above the surrounding cultivated region, but all the trees were growing in from one to four feet of amber-colored water, which, however, was almost completely covered with a floating mass of pondweeds and tiny duckweed or *lemna*. Great magnolias with glossy dark green leaves, their under surfaces brown in marked contrast, and smaller tupelos or sour-gums, filled the gaps between the cypresses, while the course of our little dugout canoe was obstructed by buttonball or titi bushes, rank growths of yellow or white pond lilies, the crowded 'knees' of the cypresses, and the interlaced trunks and branches of long-dead trees. Great turtles sunned themselves on fallen logs, and we watched carefully for the dangerous water-moccasins. Occasionally our guide pointed out to us what looked like a pair of knots on a submerged log, and only when they suddenly disappeared under water could we realize that they were the knobby eyes of alligators, waiting hungrily for luckless young egrets or herons to drop into the water nearby. Wood Ducks and Blue-winged Teal rose from the water at intervals, and from overhead came the croaks of marauding Fish Crows, the slow drumming of Southern Pileated Woodpeckers, and the calls of Florida Blue Jays and Red-bellied Woodpeckers, and we occasionally caught a glimpse of the vivid red of Florida Cardinals or the orange-yellow of the little Prothonotary Warbler.

Such is the haunt of the strange, prehistoric-looking Water-turkey or Snake-bird. We saw them perched singly or in small groups on the bare branches of blasted trees, with their characteristically erect posture, often with spread wings; soaring overhead in great circles, their fan-like tails, long necks and slender bills readily identifying them at the limit of vision; sitting on

25

their nests at various heights above the surface of the pond; climbing clumsily about in the trees or bushes; and swimming in the lemna-covered water, sometimes with the body low in the water like a cormorant and at other times with the body completely submerged and only the head and snake-like neck visible.

The adult male Water-turkey is a striking bird with a metallic sheen on its glossy black plumage which is only varied by the narrow whitish feathers of its shoulders, the white pencillings of its neck, and the brown tip of its turkey-like tail. The females are similar, but with grayish-buff head and neck and brownish breast, sharply defined from the black belly. Nestlings in their first plumage are covered with a dense mat of buffy down, very different from the blackish down of young Florida Cormorants, the sooty brown of White Ibises, or the pure white of nestling American Egrets, with which they are often associated in the great bird rookeries of Florida. — (J.B.M.)

MAN–O'–WAR–BIRD

Fregata magnificens MATHEWS.   PLATE 97.

Other names: Frigate Bird; Hurricane Bird; Frigate Pelican.

IDENTIFICATION. — Length 37½ to 41 inches; spread 7 to 8 feet. *Adult male* all black; *female* browner with breast and upper belly white; unmistakable with very long narrow wings and long deeply forked tail; only possible confusion might be with Swallow-tailed Kite, which is smaller and has small bill, white head, neck, rump, and under parts.

BREEDING. — In colonies. *Nest:* Of sticks on tops of bushes and small trees. *Egg:* 1, dead white in color.

RANGE. — Breeds in the Bahamas, West Indies, islands off the Caribbean coast of Venezuela, and the west coast of Mexico, and in the Galapagos Islands; winters north to Florida, Louisiana, and California.

Halfway down the west coast of Florida, at the entrance to Tampa Bay, is Pass-à-Grille, winter resort for many Northerners and a favorite spot from which to start fishing expeditions on the Gulf. It is a low island of dazzling white sand composed of disintegrated coral, limerock, and seashells, lying across Boca Ciega Bay from busy St. Petersburg. It is neighbored by many mangrove-covered islets so low that they are practically awash with every tide, but which afford shelter in winter to great numbers of pelicans, cormorants, and long-legged waders, while the shallow bay furnishes food for ducks of many species, and the beaches are daily patrolled by squads, battalions, and small armies of sandpipers and plovers. Overhead are wheeling many gulls — Herring, Ring-billed, and Laughing — frequent Black and Turkey Vultures, an occasional Osprey, or perhaps a Southern Bald Eagle from a nearby aerie. As we watch, a tiny speck against the sky develops the outlines of a Barn Swallow, with long narrow wings and long forked tail, but seeming to move with incredible slowness for our well-known mosquito catcher. And suddenly we realize that its size is dwarfed by its distance, and that we are watching the wonderful aerial evolutions of that master of aviation, the Man-o'-war-bird, with its eight-foot spread of narrow, sharp-elbowed wings, its long forked tail, and disproportionately small body. If it comes near enough, its powerful hooked beak is evident, and if it is a female, its light throat and upper breast distinguish it from the all-black male, while young birds have whitish heads as well as throat and breast.

26

The Man-o'-war-bird does not breed in the United States, but it is a common winter and less common summer visitor along the Florida coasts, and occasionally wanders to New England and Quebec, and far into the interior, especially after tropical storms which have driven the birds out of their usual range. It obtains much of its food by robbing other fish-catching birds of their booty, but it also picks up floating tidbits from the surface of the sea, swooping down from a height with almost incredible swiftness and suddenly checking its headlong career just above the water, seizing its prey with its long hooked beak, and lightly rising again apparently without wetting even the tips of its slim pointed wings. It has a marvelous capacity for sailing at great altitudes, and so calmly and easily does it ride the winds that it is even said to sleep on outspread wings above the storm, though this would be a hard thing to prove. — (J.B.M.)

Order Ciconiiformes. Herons, Ibises, and Allies.

GREAT WHITE HERON

Ardea occidentalis AUDUBON.   PLATE 96.

Other name: Great White Crane.

IDENTIFICATION. — Length 45 to 54 inches; spread about 6 to 7 feet. Averages slightly larger than the Great Blue Heron, which it resembles in proportions and in plumage arrangement, but entirely white, with yellowish bill and yellow-green legs; size, head plumes, and absence of 'aigrettes' distinguish it from smaller American Egret which is also an all-white heron but with black legs and yellow bill; the Wood Ibis is white with blackish naked head and black flight-feathers.

BREEDING. — On mangrove islands. *Nest:* Of sticks. *Eggs:* Usually 3, pale bluish-green.

RANGE. — Resident of southern Florida and the Florida Keys.

This beautiful bird, the largest of our American herons, occupies a very restricted range in 'tropical' Florida, the mangrove islands of the Bay of Florida between the Everglades and the Keys. While it has not met with the persecution given the so-called 'plume birds' by the millinery trade, its young have long been considered a great delicacy by the natives of this sparsely settled region, and its numbers were diminishing steadily, in spite of protective laws and an occasional arrest by alert bird wardens. Then came the great hurricane of September, 1935, which sent tremendous waves sweeping across the low islands, uprooting and carrying away the crowded mangrove trees, and completely destroying many of the islands themselves. Following this destruction, a very careful census was taken by agents of the National Association of Audubon Societies, and the existing population of Great White Herons was estimated at not over one hundred and fifty birds. Since then, under special protection, the numbers show an apparent healthy increase, a 1938 census showing about five hundred birds, but a species of such restricted range will always be in danger of extinction from some unexpected cataclysm.

The habits of the Great White Heron probably differ in no essential particulars from those of its congeners the Great Blue Heron or its southern race, the Ward's Heron, with which, indeed, it sometimes mates to produce the hybrid form known as Würdemann's Heron, a typical Ward's Heron with a pure white head and a yellowish bill. — (J.B.M.)

27

GREAT BLUE HERON

Ardea herodias herodias LINNAEUS.

PLATE 22.

Other names: Crane; Blue Crane.

IDENTIFICATION. — Length 42 to 50 inches; spread 65 to 74 inches. Distinguished by large size, very long neck and legs, and general bluish-gray color with largely white head and neck, and dark flight-feathers.

BREEDING. — In colonies in wooded swamps. *Nest:* Of sticks. *Eggs:* 3 to 6, pale greenish-blue.

RANGE. — Breeds from southeastern British Columbia, southern Manitoba, northern Ontario, central Quebec, and Nova Scotia south to Tennessee and South Carolina, west to Iowa and Nebraska, and in Bermuda; winters from New York and the Ohio Valley south to Florida, Texas and Panama.

The Great Blue Heron is by far the largest common wading bird of eastern North America. It is also one of the wariest. Its great height, telescopic sight and acute hearing give it an advantage over all other denizens of the marsh. It is quick to take the alarm and those that are shot are mainly inexperienced young of the year. In early spring after the ice has gone out of the rivers it may be seen wading in shallow waters, stepping slowly along, raising each foot high and slipping it noiselessly into the yielding element. While searching for its prey or standing motionless for many minutes at a time knee-deep in the flood, it patiently waits with indrawn neck until some luckless fish or frog has ventured near enough, when the sharp bill and long neck shoot forward and downward, the wiry body sways forward on the reed-like legs and the unfortunate prey, transfixed, or seized in the serrated beak, soon disappears down the capacious gullet. Then the statuesque pose is resumed and another period of waiting ensues. It flies heavily but with considerable speed and its powers of flight are great. The Great Blue Heron is regarded as a solitary bird and is often seen alone. During the breeding season, however, it lives in communities, and in migration it not only flies occasionally in companies and sometimes in large flocks, but in the autumnal migration I have seen from ten to twenty feeding not far apart about a salt pond or immersed to their bellies in a tidal river and scattered in a long line over the submerged flats. At such a time each bird holds its head high and remains quiescent or moves slowly forward until it sees its prey.

I have not seen the mating of this species, but in the nesting season I have climbed several tall trees to investigate the contents of the nests of heron communities. These nests are often used year after year and added to each season. When the parent comes with food, the well-grown young rise in the nest and as the adult usually alights at some distance from the nest and walks down a branch toward them the young reach, scramble, and climb toward the parent, each one eager to be first at the feast. The cackling of the young ones and the croaking of their parents make up a distracting combination of discordant sounds. The young are fed by regurgitation and from a distance the operation looks a little like an attempt at wilful murder as the parent stabs downward at the throats of the appealing young. As the wings of the young birds develop they strengthen them by climbing about among the branches, flapping their untried pinions to keep their balance and using wings, beak, and claws to keep from falling, though not always with success. Occasionally one falls to its death on the ground far below while the wings are still too weak to support its weight. Heronries are not always located in situations convenient for feeding, and the birds have been known to make daily round-trip journeys of scores of miles to procure food. When the young are fully fledged, they soon learn to fish for themselves and in late July or August they begin to scatter over the country.

From August until mid-November the birds are passing on their southward migration. The great November flight (which in New England occurs mainly alongshore) takes with it about all the remaining herons except occasional stragglers, a few of which may remain through the winter, though some such are starved and frozen before spring.

The Great Blue Heron is largely but by no means wholly a fish eater. The size of the fish eaten at times is surprising. Black bass weighing not less than one pound and a half each have been regurgitated by a young heron, and a piece of eel eleven inches long by another. This heron rarely frequents trout streams except where they flow through wide meadows. It takes minnows, crayfish, and various enemies of food fish. It eats many large insects and is fond of grasshoppers and locusts, field-mice, shrews and ground squirrels.

WARD'S HERON

Ardea herodias wardi RIDGWAY.

Other names: Florida Blue Heron; Blue Crane.
IDENTIFICATION. — Length about 52 inches, averaging slightly larger than *A. h. herodias*. Paler, with a much whiter head, darker neck, and olive-green instead of blackish legs.
BREEDING. — See Great Blue Heron.
RANGE. — Breeds from Kansas, southeastern Iowa, southeastern Illinois, southwestern Indiana, southern Alabama, southern Georgia, and southeastern South Carolina south to Oklahoma, southeastern Texas, the Gulf coast, and the Florida Keys; winters in Florida, southern Alabama, Texas, and southward to central Mexico.

AMERICAN EGRET

Casmerodius albus egretta (GMELIN).   PLATE 22.

Other names: Great White Egret; White Heron; White Crane; Long White; Big Plume Bird.
IDENTIFICATION. — Length 35 to 42 inches; spread 50 to 59 inches. Smaller than Great Blue Heron but plumage being entirely white, appears as large; distinguished from Snowy Egret and young Little Blue Heron by greater size, yellow bill, black legs and feet; in breeding season by long *decurved* plumes or 'aigrettes.'
BREEDING. — In colonies in marshes or wooded swamps. *Nest:* A flat platform of sticks. *Eggs:* 3 to 5 dull pale blue.
RANGE. — Breeds in Oregon and California, and from Arkansas, Tennessee, North Carolina, Florida, the Gulf coast and Mexico south to Patagonia; winters from Oregon, California, Texas, the Gulf of Mexico and South Carolina southward; in late summer ranges northward regularly to New Jersey and southern New England.

When as a boy in the wilds of Florida I first saw American Egrets I was amazed at their apparently large size and snowy whiteness. Their imposing figures stood out in the full sunlight in the chaste purity of their dazzling whiteness against the dark background formed by the shadows and black water of a deep cypress swamp. Their great flocks in those days were indeed a wonderful spectacle. Their large size and graceful plumes lend them a certain dignity that smaller herons do not possess. As they alighted on the ground the plumes springing from their backs seemed to float or rise in the air.

The migration of herons and some other southern birds to the northward after the breeding season is a well-known occurrence, and probably when the first settlers came to America, Egrets, which once bred in millions in southern swamps, extended their regular summer migration over practically the whole United States and into Canada; but since then, through man's greed and woman's vanity, the Egrets have been killed in the breeding season for their plumes and have been so nearly exterminated that they are now seen only in greatly reduced numbers. When I visited Florida in the winter of 1876–77, thousands of American Egrets were flocking in the Indian River region; ten years later they had become rare and hard to find. They have been saved from extinction chiefly through the efforts of the National Association of Audubon Societies which, under the leadership of William Dutcher and T. Gilbert Pearson, has stationed wardens in many heronries to protect the birds from the plume hunter.

These great white Egrets are very conspicuous and usually they seem to be aware of this and are very shy. In the land of their nativity they serve as sentinels to warn the wildfowl of danger. I remember once as a boy on Indian River creeping through the grass to get a shot at a flock of Pintails. Success seemed certain as I had advanced nearly within gunshot range when an old Egret that had been wading in the shallows stretched up his neck, saw something suspicious, and rising on broad white wings cried to heaven with rattling screams the news that the enemy was at hand. Those ducks immediately disappeared from that landscape.

The food of the American Egret is mainly, if not wholly, animal. It feeds largely upon fish, crawfish, frogs, lizards and insects.

SNOWY EGRET

Egretta thula thula (MOLINA).

PLATE 22.

Other names: Snowy Heron; Little White Egret; Little Plume Bird.

IDENTIFICATION. — Length 20 to 25 inches; spread 34 to 44 inches. Nearly size of Night Heron but slimmer; *pure white;* legs and bill mainly black, toes yellow; white young of Little Blue Heron has greenish legs, and white is less pure and often mottled with bluish; in breeding season Egret has long *recurved* 'aigrettes' on back.

BREEDING. — Similar to that of American Egret.

RANGE. — Breeds along coast from North Carolina to Louisiana and Texas; winters from Florida and Mexico southward; ranges northward after breeding season to Kansas and Maryland or farther.

It was my good fortune in the spring of 1877, by concealing myself behind some mangroves in a Florida swamp, to approach within about thirty feet of a dozen birds of this species while they were engaged in their courtship evolutions. They were standing on black mud from which the water had receded, and against this dark background and that of the mangrove roots their immaculate forms stood out in such bold relief that every detail of movement, shape and plumage was plainly visible. They strutted about, raised, spread and lowered their lace-like plumes, pursued one another back and forth, bowed and turned about, apparently bringing into action all their muscles and displaying their airs and graces. It seemed impossible that with all this impulsive and constant activity, with the birds apparently heedless of consequences, they should not besmear their plumage with mud to some extent at least, but marvelous to relate I could not detect a single spot upon their snowy forms. They did not feed, as it was playtime, and they were so engrossed in their antics that they never noticed me until one incautious movement on my part put them all to flight. Had I realized at the time that within ten years the species then so abundant in that region would be so greatly reduced in numbers, doubtless I should have made full notes describing the occurrence.

REDDISH EGRET

Dichromanassa rufescens rufescens (GMELIN). PLATE 96.

IDENTIFICATION. — Length 27 to 32 inches; spread 45 to 50 inches. Somewhat larger than Little Blue Heron, with heavier bill which is flesh-colored at base with black tip, rufous-chestnut head and neck and neutral-gray body; also a white phase but with bill as above.

BREEDING. — Similar to that of American Egret.

RANGE. — Breeds from the Gulf coast of the United States to Haiti, Jamaica and Guatemala; winters from southern Florida southward.

The Reddish Egret was formerly a common bird in suitable breeding localities on the coast of Florida, but the depredations of the plume hunters resulted in its almost complete extirpation in that region. In late years, however, it seems to be returning slowly to Florida, and there are a few small colonies in Louisiana. There are some large rookeries on the islands of the Texas coast, though the recent development of oil wells in the coastal areas threatens them seriously, both by the intrusion of noisy machinery near their nesting places, and by the spread of waste oil over their feeding-grounds.

The Reddish Egret is seldom found far from salt water, where it finds its favorite articles of food — small fish, varied with occasional crabs, frogs and tadpoles. Its nest is usually situated on low bushes or on the ground and is rather well built for a heron, being made of sticks and twigs and lined with smaller twigs, rootlets, straw and grasses. Even the downy young show two color-phases, and it is probable that this distinction remains unchanged throughout life. The earlier ornithologists considered the white bird a separate species, Peale's Egret, or else that the white bird was the immature, as in the case of the abundant Little Blue Heron.

The plumage of the Reddish Egret is noticeably loose and gives it the appearance of a larger, heavier bird than it really is. The feathers of the head, neck and back are long and narrow, especially in the breeding season, when it also bears long bluish-gray 'aigrette' plumes extending from the shoulders beyond the end of the tail. During its courtship displays and when threatening an enemy, these narrow feathers are erected and stand out like a porcupine's quills, giving the bird a very striking appearance. — (J.B.M.)

LOUISIANA HERON

Hydranassa tricolor ruficollis (GOSSE).

PLATE 96.

Other names: Lady of the Waters; Demoiselle of the Marshes; Silver-gray Heron.

IDENTIFICATION. — Length 24 to 28 inches; spread about 36 inches. A medium-sized heron with very long slender neck and equally long legs; dark slaty-blue head, neck, back, wings and tail; white belly in marked contrast is an excellent field mark; elongated brownish and white feathers on head and neck; back in breeding season has brownish-gray 'aigrette' plumes reaching to tail.

BREEDING. — Similar to that of American Egret.

RANGE. — Breeds from North Carolina and the Gulf States to the West Indies and Central America, and on the Pacific coast of Mexico; winters from Lower California and South Carolina southward; ranges northward in late summer to California, Indiana, New Jersey and Long Island.

The Louisiana Heron is the most slender of all our herons and when, in alarm, it stretches its neck upward to its limit, it certainly gives the impression of extreme attenuation. In compliment to its slender and graceful beauty, it has been called 'the demoiselle of the marshes.'

I have never seen the Louisiana Heron in the state for which it was named, but in Florida it is perhaps the most common of all the heron tribe. It is extremely abundant throughout the state, both in the great swamps of the interior and on the tidal shallows all along the coastline. There are many rookeries containing hundreds and even thousands of nests of this species, usually also sheltering several other varieties of long-legged waders.

This heron seems to be more versatile in its feeding habits than most of our herons, which depend largely upon patient waiting to bring their prey within reach of a lightning-like thrust of the needle-sharp bill. I have watched Louisiana Herons standing in this typical heron fashion, but I have also seen them running back and forth in the shallow water, sometimes in quiet pools and at other times where waves were breaking continuously on the shore; and I have seen them pursuing darting fish by running a few steps and then jumping into the air with flapping wings in a series of quick forward leaps, until their prey either was secured or else escaped. On one occasion, at Clearwater, Florida, I was watching a mixed flock of about a dozen Snowy Egrets, three or four Louisiana Herons, and a Little Blue Heron running about chasing minnows in the shoals over a tidal mud-flat, when a small flock of American Mergansers appeared and drove a school of fish into the shallow water near the herons. What a commotion followed! The water was barely deep enough for the mergansers to be completely submerged as they darted about, kicking up almost as much wake as a small boat would make, and wherever the ducks went the herons followed, running and jumping wildly in their eagerness to capture what fish escaped the mergansers. Crests were erected in the excitement, white wings and gray ones were in constant motion, and spray was flying during the few moments before the school of minnows, considerably depleted in numbers, reached the deep water of the channel once more. It was a lively and interesting interlude. — (J.B.M.)

LITTLE BLUE HERON

Florida caerulea caerulea (LINNAEUS).

PLATE 22.

Other names: White Heron; Little White Heron.

IDENTIFICATION. — Length 20 to 25 inches; spread 36 to 42 inches. Size of Night Heron but slimmer; adults in blue plumage can be confounded only with the Reddish Egret, which is larger and is practically unknown north of the Gulf States, or with the smaller Green Heron, which, seen at a distance, may appear bluish above, but the Little Blue is larger, slimmer, with legs and neck longer: the white young are distinguished from the Snowy Egret by greenish legs, light bill with dark tip and slaty-bluish spots on primaries; their white has a slightly bluish cast compared with the dazzling whiteness of the Snowy.

BREEDING. — Similar to that of American Egret.

RANGE. — Breeds from Delaware southward to Florida and the Gulf coast and in Arkansas, central Texas, Mexico and Central America; winters from North Carolina and Texas southward; ranges northward in late summer to Pennsylvania, southern New York, southern New England and casually farther.

The Little Blue Heron is one of the commonest herons in the Gulf States. I have seen literally hundreds of them feeding on the flats at low tide near Clearwater, Florida, and the proponents of any theory of protective coloration must have a hard time in explaining the difference in the coloring of the adult and immature birds of this species. The adults often blend beautifully with the background of blue water and the brownish sea-plants with which the flats are pretty well covered, but the white immatures stand out very conspicuously and can be seen at a long distance. One would think that the young birds, not yet old enough to know all the dangers that beset them, would need protective colors more than the wiser adults.

The birds are even more abundant in the fresh-water swamps than on the coastal lagoons, and their nesting rookeries are almost invariably on fresh water. They often nest with other herons in mixed rookeries, at which times their nests are usually located in crowded areas of willows or titi bushes at the edge of the heronry. Several pairs will often build their nests in the same small tree or bush.

The Little Blue Heron was formerly considered a casual or accidental visitor in the North, but in recent years it has appeared in considerable numbers in July and August. Like the American Egret they usually appear in hot weather and are most commonly seen on salt marshes or about fresh-water pools near such marshes. They often alight in trees near water, when not feeding. Most of those seen in the North are nearly pure white young of the year with very little blue on the primaries, though occasionally an adult in blue plumage is noted. This species usually hunts its prey of fish, frogs, tadpoles, lizards, crabs and insects by wading about in a slow and stately manner, or standing motionless waiting for its victims to approach within striking distance. — (J.B.M.)

EASTERN GREEN HERON

Butorides virescens virescens (LINNAEUS).

PLATE 21.

Other names: Little Green Heron; Green Bittern; Poke; Fly-up-the-creek; Crab-catcher; Indian Pullet.

IDENTIFICATION. — Length 15½ to 22½ inches; spread 23 to 26 inches. Smaller than American Bittern or Night Heron; always appears dark; back of adult looks bluish at a distance; flies with downward bend to wings even more pronounced than that of Black-crowned Night Heron; alights commonly on trees, stumps and dead limbs and jets tail when alarmed, often raising crest; rather short yellow legs.

BREEDING. — In woods near water, usually not in colonies. *Nest:* In bush or tree, a frail platform of twigs. *Eggs:* 3 to 6, pale greenish or greenish-blue.

RANGE. — Breeds from North Dakota, central Minnesota, northern Wisconsin, southern Ontario, southern Quebec and Nova Scotia south to the Dry Tortugas, the Gulf coast, Texas, Mexico and Central America, and west to central Colorado and New Mexico; winters from Florida and southeastern Texas to Central America and Colombia.

Hardly a shallow pond or wide stream may be found in eastern North America south of the St. Lawrence that is not visited either occasionally or frequently in spring and summer by one or more Eastern Green Herons. This, the smallest of our true herons, is commonly startled from its retreats by rowers, fishermen or idlers who frequent our lakes and waterways. Its usual manner of fishing is to steal carefully upon its prey with head drawn in and to strike like a flash when the proper moment arrives, but sometimes it varies this performance. Mr. Samuel H. Barker saw one, that had been standing on the edge of a plank projecting out of the water, plunge in after a fish that had come to the surface three or four feet away. The bird missed the fish, turned about, rose readily from the water and flew to the plank. This perch, he says, 'was surrounded on all sides by water from three to six feet deep.' Professor Lynds Jones tells of an Eastern Green Heron 'stretched out flat on a slanting log at a point where it projected from the water.' Beneath this log minnows found shelter. The bird rested motionless with its bill at the water's edge, when suddenly it darted its head under water and brought up a wriggling minnow in its bill, and, having swallowed it, remained motionless and ready as before. The bird came daily to this feeding-station and sometimes had to wait fifteen minutes before it could strike a fish.

Where Green Herons are abundant they nest in small colonies. Groups have been known to settle in apple orchards, but commonly each pair nests by itself in some remote and quiet place near water. Green Herons usually nest from fifteen to twenty feet from the ground in almost any dense tree. The white pine is a favorite. The stick nest is so frail that the eggs show through it, but after the young are hatched (or before) it is frequently built much larger and higher with grass and other warm material. In time the young learn to climb out of the nest and move around in the branches rather freely.

BLACK–CROWNED NIGHT HERON

Nycticorax nycticorax hoactli (GMELIN).   PLATE 22.

Other names: Quawk; Buttermunk; Bittrun; Bull Bittrun; 'Plunket'; Wagin; Grosbec.

IDENTIFICATION. — Length 23 to 28 inches; spread 43 to 48 inches. Size of American Bittern; adult with black bill, crown, and back, light bluish-gray wings and tail, and whitish under plumage; in flight, flaps rather slowly, at times sailing with wings slightly curved downward; young often mistaken for American Bittern but spotted with whitish and not so reddish-brown, and lacking black streaks on side of neck.

BREEDING. — In colonies, in marsh or wooded swamp. *Nest:* In tree or bush, sometimes on ground among reeds; of sticks, rushes, etc. *Eggs:* 1 to 8, light bluish-green.

RANGE. — Breeds from Oregon, Wyoming, southern Manitoba, and southern Quebec south to Paraguay; winters from northern California, Oregon and New York southward, occasionally farther north.

The Black-crowned Night Heron, as its name implies, is a night-bird. Its harsh cry is one of the well-known 'voices of the night' that may be heard in the dusk of summer evenings almost anywhere along the eastern coast and in the swamps of the interior. Its great red eyes seem to have some of the powers of night-sight that are bestowed upon the owl, as otherwise it could hardly see to fish at night. Nevertheless, it is not by any means altogether a night-bird, as, like all coast fishermen, it regulates the time of its fishing in coastal waters more or less by the tides, and like the owls it is often quite active in cloudy weather during the day.

Following is a description, from my manuscript, of a heronry among the sand dunes of Sandy Neck, Barnstable, Massachusetts, which I visited in July, 1908:

'As I neared the spot a few herons flapped stiffly away, with hoarse "quoks." Some croakings and many machine-like "chippings" were heard; and when at last my load dropped from my weary shoulders in the welcome shade of an oak grove, the heronry was so near at hand that the audible cries of both young and old had increased to a steady chorus.

'Evidently some enemies of the birds had been before me, for they had left their signatures on the visitor's book — a stretch of sand along the edge of the marsh. Tracks of foxes, old and young, and those of cats, crows and skunks, led into a little hollow, where a mat of dry creek grass had been thrown by the highest tides; and here well-worn paths led direct to the heronry, showing where nocturnal marauders had passed in to feast on young birds, eggs, dead fish, squids or other food dropped by the birds. Deeply indented hoof-marks in the sand showed where a big buck had passed along the edge of the wood, browsing as he went. The heronry was in a hollow among wooded hills, where there had been a pool in the spring, which was now dried up. The borders of the place were hedged about with thorny smilax and poison ivy, but inside the heronry the ground was comparatively clear. Here, well up on the trees, the large straggling nests were placed, from three to six nests on each tree. Young herons are inured to hardships from the first. Resting on the hard sticks which compose their crude unlined nests, exposed to every wind that blows over and through the ramshackle structure, they must become hardened or perish. The windless air was stagnant and fetid; swarms of stinging midges, deer-flies and mosquitoes attacked at will; and vicious wood-ticks, hanging from the vegetation, reached for me with their clinging claws, and crawled upon my limbs, seeking an opening to bury their heads in my flesh.

'Croaks and calls, flat cries and choking gasps filled the air, as the great flocks of the heronry

35

took flight, flapping and wheeling overhead. Here was a beautiful and stirring sight! Hundreds of waving plumes, pale, delicately tinted breasts, great red eyes, and wide-spreading pinions sailing over me just above the trees. The young birds, homely, awkward, speckled things with staring yellow eyes, were now out of the nests and had climbed to the tree tops high above that pestilential hole to a place where they could escape the mosquitoes, feel the breeze, and get a breath of the free air of heaven. They become adepts at climbing even before they finally leave the nest. On the approach of an intruder some will climb out and into the tree tops, to return again after the alarm has passed. In climbing they use feet, wings and bill and even the head. Rarely one will hook its head into a crotch from which it is unable to withdraw. I have seen them thus hanging dead. If one misses its footing and falls to the ground, it may become the prey of fox, cat, snapping turtle or other lurking enemy.

'While still in the nest they will strike at an intruder, opening the mouth widely, and making as formidable an appearance as possible, at the same time uttering a loud "*kak*" and perhaps also discharging the contents of the gullet at the enemy. Even now some of them, when approached, threw up gobs of half-digested fish that struck the ground with a thump. It is only courteous to proffer a visitor a meal, but these birds actually rob themselves to present one with a meal that they have already eaten!

'The day had been murky, hot and still, with hardly a breath of wind. On the ground under these trees the odor of ancient fish and that of the ammoniacal fumes accompanying decay were so nauseating that, having taken a few hurried snap-shots, I was ready to seek the open air to alleviate certain disagreeable symptoms. What a contrast in emerging from such a place to breathe the delicate fragrance of azaleas, and to hear mingled with the racket of the heronry the melodious voices of the Catbird and the Yellow-throat.

'I had intended, in my ignorance, to encamp for the night in that heronry; but this was plainly out of the question, and I determined to lie just outside, and so get the full benefit of the night wind over the water. So, at a bend in the shore line nearest the heronry, where the creek grass or thatch lay dry and deep, I shook down a bed, arranged my blankets and head net, and crept in to escape the flies, midges and mosquitoes that swarmed in one grand chorus as the light began to fail. Thus protected, molested only by a few hungry wood-ticks which penetrated my defenses, I lay awake far into the night, listening to the sounds of heronry, marsh and shore.

'Slowly the dull murk cleared away, then the rosy light melted out of the western sky, and the stars came out, but they were soon obscured by dark, drifting clouds. One star still burned clearly miles to the eastward, but that was the beacon of a lighthouse; and another light was shining from some window across the bay, where someone kept a late vigil, or some poor mortal tossed on a bed of pain. The sweet west wind blew in little gusts out of the dark silences over wide marshes and lapping waters. Shapeless and indistinct, seen darkly through my cheesecloth netting, some creature, perhaps a fox, stole swiftly across the strip of white beach sand; but, for the most part, all was still save in the heronry close by. There pandemonium had broken loose — evidently the birds were making a night of it. I had long wished to spend twenty-four hours at a night heronry, out of curiosity to know whether these birds really turn night into day, as their name implies. My experience here inclines me to the belief that, if they sleep at all, they must slumber in relays or take cat naps. In the twenty-four hours that I remained within hearing, there was not a minute when the sound of their voices was stilled, and there were always birds flying away to sea, shore or marsh, and others returning. They were quietest just after noon, and noisiest about all night, I believe; for, though I slept a little, sound or continuous slumber was impossible. I never before passed such a night except in some of the crowded swamps of Florida. No moon was shining, but nevertheless the babel of sounds increased as the night grew darker, until a nervous person might have imagined that the souls of the condemned had been thrown into purgatory, and were bemoaning their fate. One bird in particular in the edge of the wood near me set up a succession of most dismal groans, as if it were suffering slow torture. It kept up the performance intermittently throughout the night. The frog chorus of the young birds was varied. It sounded in some cases more like a hen calling for her chicks; now and then heavier notes were heard, reminding me of an old rooster clucking to his harem; cat-calls, infant screams, shrieks, yells and croaks swelled the chorus, all intermingled with the beating of heavy wings and the harsh "*quoks*" of individual birds that swept low over my camping place.'

When the young birds are well able to fly, they scatter in all directions from their breeding-place in search of food. Many of them go to the northward, sometimes hundreds of miles, others go west or south. In late September or October the adult birds gather in flocks and move southward. They assemble toward night and move in the dusk of evening; some flocks assume a V formation; while at other times immense irregular flights gather and flap away into the night.

Black-crowned Night Herons feed mainly along the shores of tidal rivers and estuaries, about the shores of fresh-water rivers and lakes or in fresh or salt marshes. Their food is taken either by silent watching or by walking or wading about and hunting over flats and marshes. At need some individuals do not hesitate to alight in deep water or to swim out into it.

YELLOW–CROWNED NIGHT HERON

Nyctanassa violacea violacea (LINNAEUS).   PLATE 96.

Other names: Grosbec; Quawk.

IDENTIFICATION. — Length 22 to 28 inches; spread 34 to 44 inches. Adult may be distinguished from Black-crowned Night Heron by darker plumage below, streaked back, black head with white stripe on cheek and yellowish or white crown; young are almost indistinguishable in the field but this species has heavier bill.

BREEDING. — Similar to that of Black-crowned Night Heron.

RANGE. — Breeds from southern Texas, Kansas, southern Illinois, southern Indiana, New Jersey and in the Bahamas and West Indies south to Brazil and Peru; winters from southern Florida southward.

The Yellow-crowned Night Heron in full breeding plumage is a striking and conspicuous bird. Though regarded as an accidental visitor in the Northeast, it probably occurs more often in summer than the records indicate. The tendency of young herons in America to migrate northward in summer is well known, and the young of this species so closely resemble those of the Black-crowned Night Heron that they may escape notice. The former resembles the latter in its habits, and haunts similar retreats. The Yellow-crowned bird, although it migrates at night and moves about much on clear nights, is often abroad during the day. Audubon asserts that if when flying over a line of gunners this bird is shot at and missed, it will

37

dive toward the ground and will continue to do this time after time whenever fired at. In this it differs from its black-crowned congener, which under such circumstances usually stops for no dive but turns away from the gunner and devotes its best attention to getting out of gunshot range.

The food of this heron is somewhat similar to that of the Black-crowned Night Heron, but it seems especially fond of crabs and crawfish. Audubon says that it eats small quadrupeds, young birds that have fallen from their nests, leeches and snails.

AMERICAN BITTERN

Botaurus lentiginosus (MONTAGU).

PLATE 21.

Other names: Stake-driver; Indian Hen; Meadow Hen; Bog Hen; Thunder-pump; Plum Pudd'n; Dunk-a-doo; Marsh Hen; Barrel-maker; Sun-gazer.

IDENTIFICATION. — Length 23 to 34 inches; spread 32 to 50 inches. About size of Black-crowned Night Heron; a large brownish slow-flying bird, with wide black streak on side of neck, broad brown black-tipped wings and long yellowish-green bill; flies with neck drawn in and long legs extended behind; alights on ground, seldom on trees or bushes.

BREEDING. — Amid marsh vegetation, occasionally in bushes. *Nest:* Of grasses, reeds, etc. *Eggs:* 4 to 7, olive-brown to pale olive-buff.

RANGE. — Breeds from central British Columbia, northern Manitoba, southern Ungava Peninsula and Newfoundland south to southern California, Kansas, the Ohio Valley and southern New Jersey; winters from British Columbia, southern Texas, Illinois, Indiana and Virginia south to Cuba, Guatemala and Panama.

The American Bittern is a hermit, dwelling in swamp and fen. Like all hermits, he is a peculiar character, and as the unusual piques our curiosity and even, among the ignorant, excites suspicion and superstition, the Bittern has been thought to have a sinister influence. Thoreau regarded him as the 'genius of the bog.' The Bittern seems to delight in the impassable morass where the 'floating island' tempts the unwary and where the first false step may plunge the incautious adventurer into foul and slimy depths. By preference our peculiar fowl seeks quaking margins of so-called bottomless ponds, cedar swamps, cattail beds, river marshes and meadows, the muddy thatch-bordered shores of tidal streams, where it follows the receding tide, or stagnant pools in the salt marsh and froggy slough. In such surroundings the Bittern's inconspicuous colors furnish sufficient concealment the moment it crouches low or retires among the reeds and even when wading in open water it has only to point its bill upward and draw its feathers close to its narrow body to be passed unnoticed, so close is its resemblance then to a dead limb, crooked stake or stump-root projecting from the water. The Bittern has such confidence in its invisibility that it often loses its life by starting up only when in danger of being trodden upon by the hunter. It flies so slowly and presents so broad and tempting a mark that many are shot and left where they fall. Therefore the Bittern is becoming rare in many places where formerly it was common. It is so inconspicuous and ordinarily keeps so much in hiding by day and its loud 'love notes' so much resemble the rural sounds of pumping and stake-driving that it is rarely noticed except by people who are much afield in its haunts or by those who are looking especially for it. Thoreau wrote 'the Bittern pumps in the fen.' What a story those few words tell! Again he remarks that the bird's notes sound 'as if he had taken the job of extending all the fences up the river to keep the cows from straying.'

The Bittern's so-called song and the accompanying contortions, together make up one of the most remarkable performances indulged in by any American bird. We cannot determine whether the sounds produced are all vocal or partly instrumental, nor can we say by what principle of acoustics this production, which never varies very appreciably, appears to imitate at one time pumping and at another stake-driving. Apparently the character of the sound which reaches the ear depends on the direction of the listener from the bird and possibly also on the point of the compass toward which the bird faces.

In 1922 I noticed that at my cottage at Wareham, Massachusetts, which was east of a meadow, we heard only stake-driving, but when I went to the marsh due south of the bird only pumping could be heard. The bird was perfectly concealed in the tall grasses and reeds so that one could not see which way he faced, but I passed carefully around him time after time and always heard on one side stake-driving only and on the other only pumping. There was a point, however, midway between the two where both could be heard together. The same experience was repeated day after day. When another observer accompanied me he could hear only the stake-driving from the east while I heard only the pumping from the south or west; while a third observer properly placed could hear both at the same time. Distance from the bird made little difference. The sound was the same and seemed nearly as loud at three hundred yards as at thirty. One could account for this only on the supposition that the bird during its performance always faced in the same direction, which actually was the case with a Bittern which I was able to see plainly in the Concord meadows. Probably should the Bittern face in different directions while pumping the 'tune' would seem to change, but we have no proof of this. Mr. William Brewster asserts that 'all three syllables may be heard usually up to a distance of about 400 yards, beyond which the middle one is lost' and the remaining two sound like 'plum pudd'n,' while at distances of more than half a mile the terminal syllable alone can be heard, resembling then the sound produced by driving an axe on a wooden stake. I had always supposed distance to be essential to produce the stake-driving effect, but this was not the case at Wareham. At the moment of emitting his dolorous love-song the violent contortions of the Bittern simulate those of a nauseated person in the very act of retching; yet the bird is not regurgitating food but apparently inflating its gullet with air.

The sound produced ('the song'), which it is agreed resembles the loud sucking of an old wooden pump, has been variously imitated in print by many writers, and to show what part imagination plays in such renditions, a few are herewith presented, all of which are supposedly descriptive of the same sounds: *Punc-a-pog; ugh plum pud'n'; plum pud'n'; pump-er-lunk; glump-te-glough; gung-gī-um; dunk-a-doo; pump-ah-gah; ponk-a-gong; chunk-a-lunk; kunk a whulnk; pomp aŭ gōr; pump ăŭ gah; umph-ta-googh; plunk a lunk; slug-toot; pung-chuck; chunk-a-lunk-chunk; quank-chunk-a-lunk-chunk; kung-ka-unk; puck-la-grŏŏk; waller-ker-toot.* A slight discrepancy in the consonants is noticeable. I doubt if the bird uses any. During the height of the mating season the Bittern has his 'spasms' often. In late April or early May he may emit his call from five to eleven times in succession, but in June and July the notes become much less frequent. While the booming of the Bittern is commonly a spring sound, it is sometimes heard in autumn. The bird is likely to be most noisy between twilight and midnight.

The 'stake-driver' note has been rendered thus: *Whack-a-whack, whack-a-whack*. At a distance only the reiterated *whack* reaches the ear.

There is a display of light-colored or white feathers which sometimes accompanies the above performance, especially when two males meet in the breeding season. This display consists of about nine or ten light-colored, fluffy feathers which appear on the male during the mating season. They are attached near the point of the shoulder or about where the humerus or arm bone springs from the body, and ordinarily are concealed under the wing. In display these seem to be usually erected and spread, one on each side of the back, like ruffs or 'little wings' nearly meeting behind the neck. Although usually more or less buffy or yellowish, they appear pure white in the sunlight. Another form of display is noted by Mr. Verdi Burtch, who says, 'as if by magic two beautiful, fluffy plumes arose from their concealment in the feathers of each shoulder and spread, fan-shaped, down around the neck to the breast.'

The migrations of the American Bittern are made mostly at night. The greater part of the spring migrants pass through the Northern States during the latter half of April and in early May. In autumn most of them move southward before October ends. An occasional famished straggler has been seen or taken in December and January.

The food of the Bittern consists mainly of frogs, snakes, small fish, crayfish and other small water animals, mice, moles and shrews, especially field mice, and a variety of insects. It is fond of grasshoppers and locusts and frequently may be seen in meadows or pastures near its usual haunts hunting grasshoppers.

EASTERN LEAST BITTERN

Ixobrychus exilis exilis (GMELIN). PLATE 21.

IDENTIFICATION. — Length 11 to 14 inches; spread 17 to 18 inches. A small secretive bittern hiding in reed beds and difficult to flush; unlike any other American bird; black top of head and black back, with buffy wing-patches, identify it.

CALL. — A soft *coo-coo-coo*.

BREEDING. — In fresh-water swamps, among vegetation. *Nest:* Of reeds or twigs. *Eggs:* 3 to 6, bluish- or greenish-white.

RANGE. — Breeds from North Dakota, central Minnesota, Wisconsin, Ontario, southern Quebec, southern Vermont, and southern Maine south to the West Indies and southern Mexico; winters from Georgia and southern Texas south to the West Indies and eastern Guatemala.

The Eastern Least Bittern is a queer little bird. Its slim head and neck and narrow, deep body fit it for passing between close-growing stems of reeds, flags and other water-plants, and it seems to be specially trained in climbing. I have seen it only when, like a rail, it was flying low and rather slowly over the tops of the reeds or climbing among their stems. When wading among tall reeds, one may rarely start this bird. It flies briefly in a rather bewildered way and drops down into the reeds a little farther on. It seems to keep more or less above the surface of the water, climbing about or running along from stem to stem, clasping them with its long flexible toes. When closely approached it is likely to straighten up, facing toward the intruder, with bill pointing skyward, and in this position among the shadows of stalks and blades it seems a part of its environment and is exceedingly difficult to distinguish. To show how readily this bird can pass between the crowded stems of reeds and flags, Audubon made an experiment with an individual alive. This bird was able to contract its body so as to pass between two books set an inch apart without moving them. When the bird was dead its body measured 2¼ inches in diameter. Occasionally it may be seen low down on some small tree or it may alight on a haycock or a fence rail. I have never heard of a real colony of this species, but sometimes a few pairs breed not far apart. Probably the Least Bittern is not so rare in the marshy regions of the Eastern States as the published lists would seem to indicate. The bird is perhaps even more secretive than the rails and is rarely seen except by those who spend much time in the marshes. I have heard its strange cooing notes in many places where I have never seen it. We know very little about its real distribution in the breeding season.

It migrates at night, often flying rather low, and thus, like the Woodcock, is sometimes killed or injured in migration by striking telegraph wires. Its principal spring migration probably occurs during the latter half of May, though stragglers arrive much earlier. In late August and September its principal southward passage occurs, though stragglers appear later.

NOTE. — The so-called Cory's Least Bittern, which is illustrated on Plate 21, is now considered merely a color phase of the Eastern Least Bittern.

WOOD IBIS

Mycteria americana LINNAEUS.   PLATE 97.

Other names: Gourd-head; Gannet; Iron-head; Flinthead; Preacher; Spanish Buzzard.

IDENTIFICATION. — Length 35 to 48 inches; spread 62 to 66 inches. Size near Canada Goose but with long legs; dark naked head, white body plumage, black flight-feathers and heavy down-curved bill; young are gray or partly white; in flight neck is fully extended and head not drawn in close to body as in herons.

BREEDING. — In colonies, in trees in swamps. *Nest:* A platform of sticks. *Eggs:* 2 to 3, chalky white.

RANGE. — Resident along the Gulf coast from Texas to Florida and north to South Carolina, also in West Indies, Mexico, Central America, and South America to Peru and Argentina; ranges widely after the breeding season.

The Wood Ibis is really a stork with a down-curved bill, and it is unfortunate that the name 'Ibis' has become attached to it. It is a large, heavy, powerful bird, and in its full plumage is not likely to be mistaken for any other bird. I have seen it only in Florida, where it usually frequents swamps and marshes. It seems to be extremely gluttonous, but when well fed it often exercises its wonderful powers of flight by mounting to great heights and wheeling and sailing there somewhat after the manner of the White Pelican. Wood Ibises sometimes gather in enormous numbers in southern swamps. Dr. T. Gilbert Pearson says in 'The Nature Lovers' Library':

'Of all the various species of Storks known to inhabit the earth, only two are found in North America. One of these, the Jabiru (*Jabiru mycteria*) of tropical America, occasionally wanders north to Texas, but the other species, the Wood Ibis, is with us in goodly numbers. They breed in the southern United States, chiefly in Florida. They are gregarious at all times, although now and then small bands wander away from the main flock. I once saw at least five thousand of these birds in a drove, feeding on a grassy prairie in central Florida. When disturbed by the report of a gun they arose, a vast white and black mass, and the roar of their wings coming across the lake resembled nothing so much as the rumbling of distant thunder.

'They breed in colonies numbering hundreds or thousands of pairs, and they always select the tallest trees for nesting sites. For several years the Audubon Society has been guarding a colony in "Big Cypress" swamp of south Florida. In the rookery nearly every tree has its nest and some of the cypresses with wide-spreading limbs hold six or eight of them. This colony occupies an area of from two hundred to five hundred yards wide and about five miles in length.

'I had the opportunity to witness the rather odd manner in which these birds sometimes get their prey. The water was low at this season and in the pine flats various ponds, which ordinarily cover many acres, were partially or entirely dried up. One of these, now reduced to a length of about one hundred feet and with a width perhaps half as great, contained many small fish crowded together. Thirty-seven Wood Ibises had taken possession of this pool and seemed to be scratching the bottom, evidently for the purpose of making the already thick water so muddy that the fish would be forced to the surface. The numerous downward strokes of the bare, bony heads fully demonstrated the effectiveness of their enterprise. "Gourd Head," "Iron Head," and "Gannet" are the appellations given to these birds by many swamp-dwellers to whom the name Wood Ibis is unknown.

'After the breeding season these Storks wander north as far as Pennsylvania and Michigan. Often one may find them on the wide marshes, either salt or fresh water, standing perfectly still for an hour or more at a time, the long heavy bill pointed downward and resting on the skin of the thick, naked neck. On such occasions they seem to represent the personification of dejection.'

EASTERN GLOSSY IBIS

Plegadis falcinellus falcinellus (LINNAEUS).   PLATE 21.

Other name: Black Curlew.

IDENTIFICATION. — Length 22 to 25 inches; spread about 36 inches. Heron-like build but heavy down-curved bill; rich chestnut color, with green or purple reflections on back, wings, tail coverts, and front of head; appears almost black at a distance; in flight neck is extended like a crane and unlike a heron.

BREEDING. — In colonies, in reeds or bushes, in swamps. *Nest:* Of twigs. *Eggs:* 3 or 4, glossless white, smooth or finely pitted.

RANGE. — Breeds in Florida, probably in Louisiana and Mexico, and in Haiti and Cuba; winters throughout range; recorded northward casually in late summer, to the northern states, Ontario, and Quebec.

I have seen the Eastern Glossy Ibis but once, for even in Florida it is today a rare bird. We were driving along the coast of the Gulf of Mexico near Sarasota late one December afternoon, when we noticed a scattered group of long-legged waders in the shallow water some distance out from shore. They seemed very dark for Louisiana Herons or Little Blues, and our glasses quickly revealed the heavy curved bill of the Ibis. They were moving about rather rapidly, probing in the mud apparently for food. When they flew, recognition was easier, for their glossy bronze plumage looks almost black, the head and neck are extended straight in front and the long legs straight behind; the curved bill points somewhat downwards as if too heavy to be held in horizontal position. Their dark color and curved bill have given them the popular name of 'Black Curlew.'

The Eastern Glossy Ibis usually nests in small groups associated with the White Ibis, the two egrets, and various other herons. A few pairs were nesting in the great White Ibis rookery at Lake Washington when I visited it in 1936 and were being very carefully protected by two wardens of the National Association of Audubon Societies. So it was with great surprise as well as pleasure that we learned of the discovery, in the spring of 1938, of a great rookery of Glossies, estimated at *twenty-five hundred* birds, not far from Lake Okeechobee in southern Florida. How such a congregation of these striking birds could have been overlooked before is hard to understand, but certainly there were many hundred birds nesting together there that year. May their tribe increase! — (J.B.M.)

WHITE–FACED GLOSSY IBIS

Plegadis guarauna (LINNAEUS).

IDENTIFICATION. — Size and general appearance almost identical with Eastern Glossy Ibis, but feathers about the base of the bill are white; this white extends back of the eye and under the chin.

BREEDING. — Similar to that of Eastern Glossy Ibis.

RANGE. — Breeds from southern Oregon and Utah to southern Texas and southern Mexico and locally in Louisiana, also in South America; winters from Louisiana, Texas, Arizona, and southern California to Mexico, and in South America.

This western species breeds in small numbers in Louisiana, and there is a single record of its breeding in Florida. In habits it is much like the Eastern Glossy Ibis.

Salt Lake City lies at the foot of the Wasatch Mountains, but it was only an aggravation to look up at the snow patches still lingering on their upper slopes, that blazing hot July day when I first met the White-faced Glossy Ibis. In spite of cold mountain water running down the gutters, the thermometers in the business section of the city registered one hundred and five degrees in the shade when we took the rural trolley-car towards Great Salt Lake. A few miles outside the city we crossed the edge of a shallow, tule-bordered fresh-water lake which was literally alive with water-birds and waders.

As the trolley shrieked to a stop and I alighted, a little group of seven birds rose from the shallows some distance away and flew off in single file. Almost black at first sight, when the sun caught the right angle they reflected bronzy-green and purple lights. They made a very characteristic silhouette against the sky, the extended neck and legs forming a straight line which slanted downwards a little from the raised head, while the curved bill also pointed downward in front. They flew with alternations of quick flappings and brief intervals of sailing, circled around the pond a couple of times, and lit again in the distance. Later I found others feeding in the shallows, probing in the soft mud as they restlessly moved about, now and then raising their heads for a brief inspection of the neighborhood. With the clear blue sky, the deeper blue of the water, the green of the waving tules, and the many other active birds, it made a picture long to linger in my memory. — (J.B.M.)

WHITE IBIS
Guara alba (LINNAEUS).   PLATE 96.

Other names: Spanish Curlew; White Curlew; Stone Curlew.

IDENTIFICATION. — Length 22 to 27 inches; spread 37 to 40 inches. A medium-sized heron-like bird with long legs, *long down-curved bill;* adult all white except black wing-tips, reddish bill and legs; young mottled brown and grayish, or brown above and grayish below.

BREEDING. — Similar to that of American Egret.

RANGE. — Breeds from Lower California, Texas, Louisiana, Florida, and South Carolina south to the West Indies, Venezuela, and Peru; winters from central Mexico and the coasts of Louisiana and Florida southward.

Crossing the Tamiami Trail in Florida, the attention of the passing tourist is often attracted by the sight of white birds standing in the short sawgrass of a burned area, wading about in the shallow water, or perched in groups in the trees or the dense bushes of a hammock a little distance from the road. If frightened, they rise almost as one bird and after circling about for a few moments, may alight again and resume their former occupations. In flight they show small black areas at the tips of the wings, the bill is long and pointed slightly downward, and in a good light is seen to be red with a darker end, the neck is extended straight ahead and the pinkish legs straight behind, while the line of the bird's body from head to tail is tilted downwards a little. Often the measured flappings are interrupted for a brief period of sailing. When traveling to and from their nesting or feeding-places they often form long wavering lines, while at other times they may ascend in a great spiral to a considerable altitude and perform interesting aerial evolutions. These birds are White Ibis, much smaller than the heavy-looking Wood Ibis with its black-bordered wings, or the pure white American Egret, and a little larger than the slender Snowy Egret with which they are often associated both when feeding and in their nesting rookeries.

Because it lacked the nuptial plumes which nearly sealed the fate of the egrets, the White Ibis is still a very abundant bird in parts of Florida, the nesting place at Lake Washington near Melbourne being estimated to contain upwards of twenty-five thousand pairs, with smaller numbers of other herons sharing the rookery. — (J.B.M.)

ROSEATE SPOONBILL

Ajaia ajaja (LINNAEUS).

PLATE 96.

Other name: Pink Curlew.

IDENTIFICATION. — Length 28 to 31 inches; spread 48 to 53 inches. Neck, back and breast white; rest of body and wings rose-pink with shoulders and tail coverts splashed with carmine; head bare, greenish-yellow; bill unique, 6 to 7 inches long, flattened like a spatula, two inches or more wide near tip.

BREEDING. — In colonies, on mangroves or in inland swamps. *Nest:* Of sticks, twigs and dry leaves. *Eggs:* 1 to 4, dull white, granulated.

RANGE. — Breeds locally from southern Texas coastal islands, Louisiana, Georgia (Okefinokee Swamp) central and southern Florida, the Bahamas, Cuba, and central Mexico south to Argentina and Chile.

Directly west of Miami but on the Gulf coast of Florida is the little village of Everglade, a few miles south of the Tamiami Trail and so off the beaten path of the northern tourists. Sportsmen know it as a favorable starting point for fishing expeditions, especially those in quest of that great trophy the 'Silver King' or tarpon. One morning in late December, 1934, I started out from Everglade with some friends for a cruise among the low mangrove-covered mud-lumps known as the Ten Thousand Islands of the west Florida coast, a favorite winter feeding region for many thousands of herons, egrets, ibises, and other birds.

Our motorboat threaded passage after passage among the crowded mangroves and across a chain of landlocked lagoons, until at last the way became too narrow, and three of us changed to a little outboard skiff to continue our exploration. Wherever we went herons rose before us, Little Blues, Louisianas, Ward's Herons, Snowy Egrets, and a few Americans, with Water-turkeys, Florida Cormorants, and many Black Vultures which were feeding on dead fish killed by a recent unusually cold spell of weather. White Ibises were abundant and now and then great, awkward-looking Wood Ibis passed over. At one point two Man-o'-war-birds circled quite low over our heads, their long wings and narrow tails identifying them at first sight. A few Great White Herons were seen, but the Swallow-tailed Kites, and Roseate Spoonbills, for which we were particularly searching, evaded our eager eyes. Finally we forced our little skiff through a screen of green branches into an opening perhaps a mile across, near the middle of which was what looked, at first glance, like a low white island, but which on our approach dissolved into a resting flock of White Pelicans, possibly six hundred in number, which rose in a great white cloud and circled around overhead until they were joined by two other flocks coming in from the south, and there were close to a thousand of the huge birds milling around overhead in a never-to-be-forgotten sight. After a brief period of wheeling evolutions, part of the flock drifted away to the north and the remainder came to rest again at the farther side of the pond.

As we started the outboard again, and headed around the shores of the lagoon, a little group of about a dozen pink and white, heron-like birds flew up from some mangroves, circled once or twice, and lit in the trees not far away. Slowly we approached them, our glasses glued to the spot, until we could get every detail of the beautiful birds, their white necks and breasts, their delicately pink wings with the carmine patch at the shoulders, and even their ugly greenish bare heads with the absurd spoon-like bill, that adds a touch of comedy to what otherwise would be an ideal of beauty. Even when at last they flew off into the distance, we almost held our breaths lest the spell be broken.

The Roseate Spoonbill was probably never a really abundant bird in Florida, and it was one of the earlier victims of the plume hunters, for its wings were valued for fans before the millinery trade popularized the use of aigrettes on hats. Today the Audubon Societies are waging a desperate fight to save the small remnant from any of the several menaces which in a single season might wipe out the few breeding Spoonbills of Florida and add this species to the list of vanished or extirpated birds. The few small rookeries are carefully watched and every effort made to protect the birds from disturbance. The Roseate Spoonbill is an unpredictable bird and its breeding habits are not any too well understood, so its protection is a difficult and uphill undertaking, but it is one which deserves the support of everyone interested in the preservation of our wild life. — (J.B.M.)

AMERICAN FLAMINGO
Phoenicopterus ruber LINNAEUS.

IDENTIFICATION. — Length 42 to 48 inches; spread 64 to 66 inches. Larger than Roseate Spoonbill, our only bird even suggesting a Flamingo in color; vermilion-scarlet in color with black flight-feathers, while Spoonbill is rose-pink and white with carmine shoulders.

BREEDING. — In colonies on low sand-bars or in shallow water. *Nest:* A pile of mud, 6 to 12 inches high. *Egg:* 1, rarely 2 or 3; dull white.

RANGE. — Breeds locally in the Bahamas, Cuba, Haiti, Yucatan, Guiana, and Peru; winters in the same range; formerly a regular visitor to southern Florida Peninsula, now only of casual occurrence there.

The story of the American Flamingo in Florida is mainly an historical one. Audubon reported the species as numerous near Key West about 1832. Würdemann described a flock of about five hundred near Indian Key in 1857. W. E. D. Scott observed about a thousand near Cape Sable in 1890 and R. H. Howe, Jr., about the same number there in 1902. Since then there have been no large numbers reported, and the reports have become few and far between.

On their few remaining breeding places in the Bahamas the birds have been relentlessly persecuted, the negroes using the young birds for food, while the whites have killed them for their plumage, but under more rigid protective measures there is some hope for their increase. Neither Mr. Forbush nor the present writer ever saw the American Flamingo in its native state, so I quote from W. E. D. Scott in the 'Auk' for 1890, writing of the Cape Sable region in extreme southwestern Florida:

'There, still a mile or more away, was presented a truly wonderful sight. Stretched out for fully three quarters of a mile, and about three hundred yards from the mainland shore, was a band of rosy, fire-like color. This band was unbroken, and seemed to be very even, though curving with the contour of the shore. Now and again a flame or series of flames seemed to shoot up above the level of the line. This proved when examined with the glass to be caused by one or more birds raising their heads to look about or to rest themselves, for when first noticed all were feeding, with their heads most of the time buried in the shallow water, searching the mud for the small shellfish which appear to be the favorite food at this point.

46

'Presently some of the birds saw the boats, and the alarm was given. Slowly the line began to contract toward the center, and the birds were soon in a compact body, appearing now like a large field of red upon the water, and the resemblance to flames was much increased by the constant movements of the heads and necks of the different individuals. In a few moments they began to rise and soon they were all in full flight, passing out of the bay and over the point of land to the east in long lines and in V-shaped parties, recalling to mind the flight of Wild Geese. If the color on the water was novel, that of the flock while in the air was truly surprising, a cloud of flame-colored pink, like the hues of a brilliant sunset. As far as we could descry the birds, the color was the great conspicuous feature.... As nearly as could be estimated there were at least one thousand birds in this flock, and of these all but about fifty appeared to be adults.' — (J.B.M.)

Order Anseriformes. Swans, Geese, and Ducks.

MUTE SWAN
Sthenelides olor (GMELIN).

IDENTIFICATION. — Length about 60 inches. Larger than Whistling Swan; distinguished by size, shape and color of bill, and habits; adult plumage pure white; bill reddish-orange with black swelling at base; young grayish.

RANGE. — A Eurasian species now feral in New York and New Jersey and probably elsewhere.

As the fourth edition of the 'Check-List' of the American Ornithologists' Union now includes several recently naturalized species of exotic birds, the Mute Swan is included here. It is the common 'Swan' of our parks and country estates, and escaped birds now occasionally breed in suburban regions. They may be seen frequently on the Hudson River near Westchester County. — (J.B.M.)

WHISTLING SWAN
Cygnus columbianus (ORD).   PLATE 20.

Other names: Wild Swan; American Whistling Swan.

IDENTIFICATION. — Length 48 to 55 inches; spread 72 to 88 inches. Pure white plumage of adult (young are grayish), very long neck and large size distinguish swans from geese; Mute Swan has orange bill with a black swelling at base, Whistling Swan has yellow spot on bill in front of eye, and the very rare Trumpeter Swan has a plain black bill.

BREEDING. — On Arctic islands or ponds. *Nest:* A heap of grass, moss, dead leaves, etc. *Eggs:* 2 to 7, usually 4 or 5, creamy or dull white.

RANGE. — Breeds mainly north of the Arctic Circle from northern Alaska to Baffin Island, south to the barren grounds of Canada, the Alaska peninsula, northeastern Siberia, and St. Lawrence Island; winters on Chesapeake Bay and its estuaries, on Currituck Sound and vicinity in North Carolina, and less numerously on the Atlantic coast from Massachusetts to Florida, on the Pacific coast from southern Alaska to Lower California, and formerly at least on the Gulf coast of Louisiana and Texas, and on the Pacific coast.

To an ornithologist there is no more thrilling sound than the high double or triple note of the leader of a flock of Whistling Swans and no more thrilling sight than that of the flock far up in the azure heights, their long necks stretched toward the Pole, their glistening white plumage catching the rosy rays of the rising sun as they sweep grandly onward in V-shaped flock formation toward their home in the Arctic wilds. Once they were abundant in migration along our coasts and many a lake, swamp or point of land received its name from them. Swan Lake, 'Swanholt,' Swan Neck, Swan Point, names not rare in New England, indicate the former presence of these noble birds. Now the few that pass over or through the northeastern states fly so high that they rarely are noticed, or they keep well out on wide water during daylight. Rarely their call is heard as they pass in the night to or from their inland feeding grounds in the lakes or rivers.

Swans feed mainly by floating upon shallow water, thrusting down their heads to the bottom and digging up roots or breaking off other parts of aquatic plants. They rarely dive for their food. They have been known to dive and swim under water, however, when wounded and pursued, when mating, or when in summer while molting and unable to fly they seek by diving to escape from eagles. Swans are powerful birds, extremely rapid swimmers and strong, swift fliers. They are so heavy that they must flap and paddle along the surface for some distance before they can clear the water, but when once in the air they probably can exceed the speed of any of our ducks or geese. In alighting they sail down to the water and glide along the surface like a boat, but hold the wings partly spread until their impetus is spent.

Their food consists of a great variety of vegetation, both aquatic and terrestrial, and various forms of animal life which they glean mainly from the bottom in shallow water.

TRUMPETER SWAN
Cygnus buccinator RICHARDSON.

IDENTIFICATION. — Length 58 to 72 inches; spread 8 to nearly 10 feet. Much larger than Whistling Swan; black bill lacks yellow spot before eye.

BREEDING. — *Nest:* A mass of grass, leaves and feathers. *Eggs:* 2 to 10, usually 4 to 6, creamy or dull white.

RANGE. — Formerly widely distributed, now nearly extinct; breeds in a few scattered localities in British Columbia, Alberta and the Yellowstone Park region in Montana, Wyoming and Idaho.

The Trumpeter Swan, a splendid white bird, the largest of all American wild-fowl, formerly nested on islands in many lakes or marshes in the latitude of New England and still farther south. It may have bred as far east as Ohio or western New York, but there are no definite records and so far as we know the bird always bred only in the Western States and in Canada. Formerly it frequented ponds of no great size, as well as large lakes, but was mainly a freshwater fowl, rarely seen off the coast. Its habits are similar to those of other swans. It seldom dives except to escape an enemy, but it can swim long distances under water. It gradually disappeared before settlement and the advance of civilization. Its eggs were taken and used as food. Its young were caught or shot for food before they were able to fly, and adult birds were killed at all seasons and at every opportunity. In Canada the same methods were used to bring about its extermination, and the trade in swan's-down offered further incentive for the destruction of the species. Today there are a few birds breeding in some of the wilder parts of Montana and Wyoming, otherwise they have retired to remote wildernesses in Canadian wilds seeking safe nesting-places.

At the approach of the frost king the Trumpeter leaves its breeding-grounds in the northwest and moves southward in triangular flock formation. The flocks move on like those of the Canada Goose, led by some old male, who, when tired of breasting the full force of the air currents, calls for relief, and falls back into the ranks, giving way to another. In migration they fly at such immense heights that often the human eye fails to find them, but even then their resonant, discordant trumpetings can be plainly heard. When seen with a glass at that giddy height in the heavens, crossing the sky in their exalted and unswerving flight, sweeping along at a speed exceeding that of the fastest express train, traversing a continent on the wings of the wind, their long lines glistening like silver in the bright sunlight, they present the grandest and most impressive spectacle in bird life to be found on this continent. When at last they find their haven of rest they swing in wide majestic circuits, spying out their landfall, until, their spiral reconnaissance ended and their apprehensions quite allayed, they sink gently down to the grateful waters to rest, drink, bathe and feed at ease.

COMMON CANADA GOOSE

Branta canadensis canadensis (LINNAEUS).   PLATE 20.

Other names: Wild Goose; Honker; Long-necked Goose.

IDENTIFICATION. — Length 34 to 43 inches; spread 59 to 66 inches. Largest of our wild geese; black head and neck, white cheeks, brown back, grayish under parts, black bill and feet.

CALL. — A loud *onk* or *onkle*, sometimes low and hoarse, and again pitched high.

BREEDING. — *Nest:* Usually on ground near water, of twigs, grasses, reeds, etc., lined with down. *Eggs:* 5 to 9, dull greenish, yellowish, or buffy-white.

RANGE. — Breeds from Mackenzie and northern Quebec to Labrador, south to the Gulf of St. Lawrence, James Bay, South Dakota, Colorado, and northern California, west to central British Columbia; winters from southern British Columbia, South Dakota, southern Wisconsin, southern Ontario, southern New England, and Nova Scotia south to Florida, the Gulf coast of Louisiana, Texas, Mexico, and southern California, and west to the Pacific coast.

Wild geese are the forerunners of winter and the harbingers of spring. While ice still covers our lakes, before even the wood frogs begin to croak, when the spring floods first begin to break up the frozen rivers, the geese are on their way; and when that 'flying wedge' sweeps fast across the sky, it brings to all who see or hear the promise of another spring. The farmer stops his team to gaze; the blacksmith leaves his forge to listen as that far-carrying clamor falls upon the ear; children leave their play and eagerly point to the sky where the feathered denizens of the northern wilderness press steadily on toward the pole, babbling of the coming spring, carrying their message over mountain and plain to village, city and farm as far as open water can be found. Coming after the long, cold winter, not even the first call of the Bluebird so stirs the blood of the listener. Again in autumn when the last great flight passes southward, flock after flock winging steadily on, we know that frost has closed the northern waters and that winter is at hand.

The Canada Goose is a distinctly American bird. It is the most widely distributed and well-known water-fowl on this continent. It migrates over nearly all of it and formerly bred over half the United States. Its habits are so well known that no extended description of them is necessary. The goose is a model of domestic faithfulness. Ordinarily a pair is mated for life. The young birds usually mate and breed in the third year. While the female incubates, the male keeps guard over her, and he is so strong and fierce in her defense that he will drive a fox, deer or even an elk away from the nest. When the downy young are hatched he still guards his little family. In July while the adult birds are molting, they lose all the flight feathers of their wings and for a time are unable to fly. At such times they skulk amid water-plants or readily dive to escape observation or the attacks of eagles. If surprised on land, they lie flat on the ground with outstretched neck, and if the surroundings lend themselves to the deception the back of the prone bird may be mistaken for a rock. Wounded geese often lie flat along the surface of the water with outstretched neck and so swim away. If waves are running high, they are then difficult to see at a distance. If closely pursued, they can dive and sometimes escape. Their flight is deceptive. The wing-beats are rather slow, but the great birds pass with such speed that the novice firing at the leader of a small flock is likely, if he scores at all, to hit one of the last birds in the flock.

When the geese have a good breeding season in the north, flocks begin to appear in the northern United States in September and all through October flock after flock passes southward, usually increasing in frequency toward the last of the month. All through November the flight continues but usually is at its height during the last ten days. If November is mild, however, this flight may continue into December and small flocks sometimes pass as late as the first week in January. A large part of the fall flight in the East comes down the coast from the Gulf of St. Lawrence. Others coming south from the interior join it, turning southwest when they reach the coast. When strong westerly winds blow, the flight may be drifted out over the sea and so many pass over Cape Cod; strong easterly winds on the contrary may send them inland. Many geese remain about the ponds of Martha's Vineyard, on the coast of Connecticut and sometimes about Muskeget all winter, except in very severe seasons. Sometimes during a January thaw some of these geese will make excursions into the interior, and then we hear of geese flying north; but there is rarely any real northward movement inland until late February or early March when geese begin to move eastward along the coast, and if the weather is mild, penetrate into the interior. In the interior they must wait until the ice breaks up and probably they cannot reach their most northern breeding-grounds until well into the month of May.

In spring and summer the Common Canada Goose feeds largely on insects, grasshoppers being a favorite food; and doubtless along the sea-coast in migration they get a few small clams and other shell-fish. Earthworms are not disdained, but the principal food seems to be vegetal in great variety. The roots of rushes and other parts of water-plants, tender grasses and shoots of grain, many seeds and grains including wild rice, berries, eel-grass and algae, all are taken.

HUTCHINS'S GOOSE

Branta canadensis hutchinsi (RICHARDSON).

Other names: Short-necked Goose; Little Goose; Mud Goose.

IDENTIFICATION. — Length 25 to 34 inches; spread 45 to 54 inches. A small Canada Goose, with light breast and under-body.

BREEDING. — See Common Canada Goose.

RANGE. — Breeds on Melville Peninsula, Southampton and Baffin islands, and probably in other parts of eastern Arctic America; winters on the Gulf coast of Mexico; migrates through Hudson Bay, and the Mississippi Valley.

This small race of the Canada Goose is occasionally reported from the eastern United States and Canada, but only careful measurement can determine its actual identity. Its normal migration route is from the region around and north of the entrance of Hudson Bay, south across the Bay, and down the Mississippi Valley to, eventually, the Gulf coast of Mexico. Stragglers apparently occasionally join migrating flocks of the larger Common Canada Goose, and have been collected in Ontario, Quebec, Maryland, and North Carolina, at least, and probably in other Atlantic coast states. The *Branta canadensis* group has recently been subject of considerable study and not all authorities are agreed as to the characteristics which define Hutchins's Goose, so that some early records of this race are now in doubt. But any very small goose with the markings of a Canada Goose, found east of the Mississippi River, is probably Hutchins's Goose. — (J.B.M.)

AMERICAN BRANT

Branta bernicla hrota (MÜLLER).   PLATE 20.

Other names: White-bellied Brant; Sea Brant.

IDENTIFICATION. — Length 23 to 30 inches; spread 42 to 52 inches. Smallest wild goose in the East; suggests a miniature Canada Goose but has partial white ring on neck instead of white cheeks, head, neck and breast black, and much white above tail and on under parts visible when swimming; wing-beats quicker and less labored than Canada Goose.

CALL. — A throaty *cr-r-r-ruk.*

BREEDING. — *Nest:* A depression on marshy ground, lined with down. *Eggs:* 4 to 8, whitish.

RANGE. — Breeds in the Arctic regions of eastern North America, on the coast of Greenland, and, apparently, the Spitzbergen Archipelago; winters on the Atlantic coast from Massachusetts to Florida, and less frequently on the Pacific coast, and the British Isles.

The American Brant is among the wariest of wild-fowl. Formerly its great flocks were seen both fall and spring in every land-locked bay and harbor where eel-grass grew upon the tide-washed flats, but as settlement increased and civilization extended all along the coast, the Brant, unprotected, constantly persecuted in migration and decreasing in numbers, withdrew, until at last it frequented only a few isolated points and islands such as Monomoy and Muske-get in Massachusetts, and the southeastern points of Long Island in New York. Since spring shooting has been prohibited, it has begun to come back into such favorable waters as Waquoit Bay on Cape Cod, from which long ago it was practically banished, but probably it will never return in its former numbers.

In ordinary flight over the water Brant fly low, but when they go overland they fly high, out of gunshot range. In migration the flocks are more likely to form in wide ranks or curved lines with the birds flying side by side than they are to assume a V-shape or any other definite formation. Often the flocks are 'bunchy.' As they come on, the black heads and necks are conspicuous, and as they pass, the white hinder parts are prominent in contrast with the black fore parts.

The Brant is an excellent swimmer, but seldom dives even when wounded and closely pursued, preferring usually to swim rapidly away with its head and neck stretched flat on the water, apparently in the hope of escaping observation. On land it is very nimble and light of foot. It runs at need almost with the agility of a sandpiper. Brants eat much sand as an aid to digestion, and just before beginning a migratory journey they are said to fill up with 'sand ballast.' The route by which the Brant comes down in autumn from its breeding places in far polar regions has never been fully worked out. It is known, however, that the birds that breed on the northwest coast of Greenland and those of the great lands lying to the westward of it begin to move southward late in August and early in September, as soon as the young are grown. They pass southward over desolate lands and freezing seas down the Boothia Peninsula and the west coast of Hudson Bay, into and down James Bay, and then turning to a point south of east they must cross the base of the Labrador Peninsula to the St. Lawrence River and the Gulf of St. Lawrence. There are rivers and lakes in the Labrador wilderness where they can rest in safety if rest becomes imperative. The birds which come across the Province of Quebec and cross the St. Lawrence River and the Gaspé Peninsula here save many miles over the route down the river; others apparently reach the Gulf farther east and go between Anticosti Island and the mainland; all turning south pass across Prince Edward Island and the neck of the Nova Scotia Peninsula and so on down to Cape Cod, Nantucket, Block Island and Long Island, while many pass on to Virginia and North Carolina. Considerable numbers now winter along the islands south of Cape Cod and on the coast of Long Island except when very severe winter weather, covering the flats with ice, drives them southward.

They begin to move north from the southern parts of their range in February, and in March their numbers considerably increase in their winter haunts in Massachusetts. In April large numbers have reached the Gulf of St. Lawrence by retracing the route followed in the fall, passing over Prince Edward Island. From June 10 to 15 large flocks leave the Island for their northward journey. Many flocks are said to turn up the St. Lawrence River in a general southwest direction, but apparently they all cross the base of the Labrador Peninsula somewhere and make for James Bay. Brant always go north in the spring along the east coast of James Bay and as they are not seen at that season on the west coast of Hudson Bay, they probably follow up the east coast directly north and so on by the shores of Baffin Island to their final destination, which they first reach about mid-June. On the way many cross Baffin Bay to west Greenland, while others may go more directly north to Ellesmere Island where numbers breed. It is probable that, as in the case of the White-winged Scoter, another flight goes north by the inland route, from Long Island Sound by way of the Hudson Valley and Lake Ontario.

The principal food of the American Brant in our waters is the common eel-grass (*Zostera marina*) of the tide flats. This they pull up when the water is low enough for them to reach (for they very seldom if ever dive for their food) and leave much of it floating on the water where they can feed on it again at high tide. In its northern homes it eats a variety of mosses and lichens and the stalks and leaves of Arctic plants, and in captivity it readily and eagerly feeds on corn and other grains.

NOTE. — Since the above was written the eel-grass has almost entirely disappeared on the Atlantic coast and the Brant have been obliged to change their feeding habits or succumb to starvation. Wintering Brant were found to be emaciated and weakened so that, while able to migrate northward in spring, very few young were raised, and the following fall only adults were seen. There has been some slight increase in the last few seasons, however, showing at least partial adjustment to the changed feeding conditions. — (J.B.M.)

BLACK BRANT

Branta nigricans (LAWRENCE).   PLATE 20.

IDENTIFICATION. — Similar to American Brant but breast dark and no abrupt change from black throat to whitish belly; in American Brant black extends down onto breast and then there is an abrupt change.
BREEDING. — See American Brant.
RANGE. — Breeds on Arctic coasts and islands from Siberia to about long. 100° W.; winters mainly on the Pacific coast from Vancouver to Lower California, and on the Asiatic coast to northern China and Japan.

There are a few eastern records of this western species, but it is only accidental on the Atlantic coast. It is enough like the American Brant in appearance to be easily overlooked, however, and it may be more frequent than the records indicate, and should be watched for wherever Brant congregate.

WHITE–FRONTED GOOSE

Anser albifrons albifrons (SCOPOLI).   PLATE 19.

Other names: Speckle-belly; Gray Brant; Laughing Goose; Yellow-legged Goose.
IDENTIFICATION. — Length 27 to 30 inches; spread 54 to 62 inches. Smaller than Common Canada Goose; a gray goose with pink or orange-yellow bill and narrow white fore-face; no black on head or neck; adult has 'speckled' belly; yellow feet.
BREEDING. — On tundra near fresh water. *Nest:* Of grass and feathers, lined with down. *Eggs:* 6 to 8, greenish-yellow or yellowish-white.
RANGE. — Breeds from the Yukon Valley east to Mackenzie, and on the west coast of Greenland, Iceland, Lapland, and the Arctic coast of Siberia to Bering Strait; winters in western United States east to the Mississippi Valley, from southern British Columbia and southern Illinois south to the coast of Louisiana and Texas and to central western Mexico, also to Japan, China, and northern Africa.

The White-fronted Goose was formerly a fairly common bird in the East but it is now a mere straggler in that region. It is still a common migrant in the Mississippi Valley where some birds winter, and is an abundant wintering bird in California. It is largely vegetarian

53

in its feeding habits, and in the wheat-growing states it has been accused of causing considerable loss to the farmers from its fondness for cultivated grain. Dr. H. C. Bryant writes of this species in Dawson's 'Birds of California' as follows:

'Easily picked out among feeding flocks of geese are the gray ones with orange-colored legs and feet, and breasts blotched with black. A closer view discloses the white forehead, giving rise to the name white-fronted goose. The loud harsh calls are stated by hunters to be of a peculiar quality, and to resemble the syllable "*wah*," and the Indians are said to imitate this call by patting the mouth. The species is sometimes called "laughing goose," in part, perhaps, on account of its grinning expression, but also no doubt because these "*wah-wah-wah*" notes are thought to resemble human laughter. The speckle-bellies call much less often than white geese and they are sometimes recognized by their silence. In flight, calls seem to be restricted to a few "*peer wekes*" by the leader....

'During the middle of the day white-fronted geese usually loaf on some body of water, or stretch of marsh, feeding early in the morning, in the evening, or during the night. The flights from the loafing grounds are oftentimes very regular, the time of arrival and departure not varying more than fifteen minutes. During periods of stormy weather, these geese often fly over in large flocks, apparently with no definite object in view other than change of feeding ground.' — (J.B.M.)

LESSER SNOW GOOSE

Chen hyperborea hyperborea (PALLAS).

Other names: White Goose; White Brant; Wavey.
IDENTIFICATION. — Length 26½ to 30½ inches; spread 55 to 61 inches. A white goose with black wing-tips; long neck and short bill distinguish Snow Geese from Gannet or White Ibis; young are grayish.
BREEDING. — On barren grounds near water. *Nest:* A hollow built up with grass, moss and other vegetation, lined with down. *Eggs:* 5 to 8, white with a yellowish tinge.
RANGE. — Breeds on Arctic coast from Alaska to Southampton Island and southern Baffin Island, and the islands to the north, also in Siberia; winters over the western United States, especially in California, east to the Mississippi Valley and from southern British Columbia, southern Colorado, and southern Illinois south to the Gulf coast from Florida to Texas and central Mexico.

The Lesser Snow Goose breeds on the Arctic tundras beyond tree-limit, and migrates southward along the Pacific coasts of Asia and North America, and through the Mississippi Valley region, so that it is always a rare migrant or straggler on the Atlantic coast. It was formerly an extremely abundant bird in winter in certain localities in California, Texas, and Louisiana, but its numbers are now greatly reduced.

In migration Lesser Snow Geese are usually seen very high, flying in a wide diagonal or curved line, in an irregular flock, or in an angular V-shaped formation like Canada Geese. They are not always as noisy in migration as Canada Geese and frequently pass without a sound; yet often they are quite vociferous. Against the blue sky they are striking in appearance, all white except the black primaries, their anserine silhouette readily distinguishing them from any other white birds with black on the wings like gulls, White Ibis, or Gannets. When seen close at hand the young are easily recognized from their gray or soiled appearance.

54

GREATER SNOW GOOSE

Chen hyperborea atlantica KENNARD. PLATE 19.

Other names: White Goose; White Brant; Wavey.

IDENTIFICATION. — Length 29½ to 32½ inches; spread 53 to 63 inches. Averages slightly larger than Lesser Snow Goose but indistinguishable in the field.

BREEDING. — See Lesser Snow Goose.

RANGE. — Breeds on Greenland and on Baffin and Ellesmere islands; winters on the Atlantic coast of Mary land, Virginia and North Carolina from Chesapeake Bay to Core Sound.

On the north shore of the St. Lawrence River and about thirty miles below the city of Quebec is Cap Tourmente, a rocky headland which rises an abrupt eighteen hundred feet above the tidal marshes that border the wide river, and here, for about six weeks each spring and fall, gather practically all the Greater Snow Geese of North America, to break their long migration flights between their little-known breeding-grounds in the Arctic and their winter feeding. resorts on our middle Atlantic coast.

One sunny afternoon in late April my son and I drove out the Saguenay road from Quebec, past Ste. Anne de Beaupré with its shrines and pilgrims, past St. Joachim, where the hard road swings inland on its way to Murray Bay, and then along a narrow farm road, muddy and slippery from recently melted snow, until, at the foot of towering Cap Tourmente, the way was blocked by the tidal marshes that crept to the very foot of the steep black cliffs. Here we left the car, and in hip boots, khaki breeches, and old sweaters, loaded down with cameras and field-glasses, we waded, bent almost double, down one of the narrow ditches that drain the flat marshlands, now bare of vegetation. Great cakes of ice were stranded here and there about us, and one bridged our ditch where it met the river-shore at high-tide mark, and kept us concealed during our cautious approach. Reaching this ice bridge at last, we slowly straightened up and looked beyond at a sight which I shall long remember.

Immediately in front of us was a huge white flock of Greater Snow Geese, the nearest birds less than a hundred feet away, the flock extending perhaps a half-mile upstream and nearer a mile downstream from where we crouched, and estimated to contain between ten and twelve thousand birds. It was a beautiful and inspiring sight, as the late afternoon sun, behind us, cast its low rays on the multitude of white birds, grouped together in a wide ribbon-like band where the blue waters of the St. Lawrence met the brown and gray of the salt marsh, not yet brightened by the green of returning spring.

Scattered among the Greater Snow Geese were some flocks of the larger Canada Goose, and we also identified a few of the much rarer Blue Goose, dark birds the size of the Snow Goose, the adults with a white head and neck, which often associate with the Snow Geese throughout the year. Offshore was a large raft of Black Ducks, a flock of scoters, and a few Common Loons, while gulls were circling lazily in the distance.

After we had watched the birds for some time, as they rested or preened themselves in deliberate manner, we stepped out from behind our icy screen and the great flock rose into the air with whistling wings, first those nearest us, then those farther and farther away, until the air was filled with the swirling flocks, a wonderful sight against the dark background of

55

Cap Tourmente towering nearly two thousand feet above the marshes at its foot. Circling past us at a distance, they soon settled again at the edge of the marshes, where we reluctantly left them.

Greater Snow Geese are rarely seen in the New England States, as they apparently pass over in their migrations without stopping between the St. Lawrence and Chesapeake Bay, flying silently and very high, perhaps at night, and only occasionally do flocks come down, usually in stormy or foggy weather, on our lakes or seashore. William Wood, however, writing of New England about 1630, speaks of a white goose almost as big as an 'English tame goose' that was seen in great flocks of two or three thousand, staying in the fall for five or six weeks and appearing again in March. But as W. L. Dawson remarked, 'snow banks of geese' have rapidly melted away before the 'incessant flashings of the white man's gun,' and such numbers will probably never again be seen by man. — (J.B.M.)

BLUE GOOSE

Chen caerulescens (LINNAEUS).

PLATE 19.

Other names: Blue Snow Goose; Blue-winged Goose; Blue Wavey; White-head.

IDENTIFICATION. — Length 25 to 30 inches; spread 53 to 56 inches. Between American Brant and Common Canada Goose in size; adult dark with white head and upper neck; young dark below and with dark head and neck.

BREEDING. — Similar to Greater Snow Goose.

RANGE. — Breeds in southwestern Baffin Island and Southampton Island; winters on the coast of Louisiana and Texas; migrates through the Mississippi Valley.

In 1925 Mr. Forbush wrote: 'Breeding of the Blue Goose in great swamps in the interior of northern Ungava is reported by Indians, and Eskimos report these birds in southern Baffin Land, where Capt. Donald MacMillan says he found many of them in the breeding season. As great flocks go up and down the east side of Hudson Bay in migration and as very few are seen on the west side, both Eskimos and Indians may be right.'

It was not until the summer of 1929 that the mystery of the breeding place of the Blue Goose was solved. Mr. J. Dewey Soper of the Canadian Department of the Interior had been searching for several summers for the nests of this species, and after spending a winter with two Eskimo companions on Bowman Bay on the shore of Foxe Peninsula on Baffin Island, on June 26, 1929, the first eggs were found. By July 20 the young were hatched, and a difficult trip by canoe was then made, to bring the first specimens of the eggs and downy young back to Cape Dorset, where close connections were made with the only steamer which visits the region annually.

On the same date — August 17, 1929 — that Soper reached Cape Dorset with his trophies, Dr. George M. Sutton landed on Southampton Island in northwestern Hudson Bay for a year's ornithological study, one of his main objectives being the nesting of the Blue Goose. Two weeks later Sutton visited a breeding-ground of this species where the Eskimos reported many birds nesting every year, but of course it was too late in the season to find eggs. The following summer, however, Sutton examined several occupied nests, and his observations have added much to our knowledge of this interesting bird and of its relations with the Lesser Snow Goose, with which he found the Blue Goose hybridizing freely.

In their winter home in southern Louisiana the Blue Geese, on account of their great numbers in a limited area, do much harm to marshy pastures. To get at their favorite food, the roots of certain species of grass, the geese dig holes which immediately fill with water; and after a continuance of this method of feeding shallow ponds result, and hundreds of acres of pasture land have had to be abandoned from this cause.

Blue Geese migrate southward in October across the region of the Great Lakes, occasionally stopping to rest and feed in the grain-fields of the Mississippi Valley. In June they reappear on the east coast of Hudson Bay northbound. On the Atlantic coast they appear very rarely as stragglers from their regular lines of migration. — (J.B.M.)

FULVOUS TREE–DUCK

Dendrocygna bicolor helva WETMORE AND PETERS.

IDENTIFICATION. — Length 20 to 21 inches; spread 31 inches. A peculiar-looking long-legged goose-like duck; general color yellowish-brown, darker above; wings, rump and tail chiefly black; tail coverts light buff showing both in flight and when swimming; at a distance looks blackish above, cinnamon below; legs extend beyond tail in flight.

BREEDING. — See below.

RANGE. — Breeds in central California, central Nevada, southern Arizona, southern Texas, and Louisiana south into Mexico.

The odd-looking Fulvous Tree-duck, half duck and half goose, with its long legs and rather long neck, is not likely to be confused with any other member of the duck tribe. While it breeds in the coastal regions of Louisiana, it is not a common bird there, and little is known about its habits. W. L. Dawson describes its habits in California, where it has apparently recently expanded its range. It is either polygamous or very lax about its household affairs, for he tells of a nest where three eggs were laid on each of three successive days, and there are reports of 'egg caches' containing from thirty to a hundred eggs! In California the nest is usually in the heavy grass of damp meadows, in the sedge which borders the marshes, or among the cattail thickets. Down from the bird's breast is not used to cover the white or buffy-white eggs, as is common with so many other ducks. — (J.B.M.)

COMMON MALLARD

Anas platyrhynchos platyrhynchos LINNAEUS.

PLATE 12.

Other names: Gray Mallard; Greenhead; Gray Duck (Female); Wild Duck; Domestic Duck; English Duck.

IDENTIFICATION. — Length 19 to 28 inches; spread 32 to 40 inches. Adult male has green head, narrow white ring around neck, ruddy breast, and upturned feathers on tail; speculum violet bordered front and back with white; female resembles Black Duck but lighter colored; speculum as in male.

NOTE. — Of female a loud harsh *quack;* of male a softer *kwek-kwek-kwek-kwek.*

BREEDING. — *Nest:* Usually on ground near water, of grasses, reeds, leaves, etc., lined with down. *Eggs:* 5 to 14, of various shades of greenish or yellowish.

RANGE. — Breeds from the Aleutian and Pribilof islands, Alaska, northern Manitoba, west coast of Hudson Bay, New Brunswick, and Nova Scotia south to Lower California, southern New Mexico, southern Texas, southern Kansas, southern Missouri, southeastern Illinois, southwestern Indiana, southern Ohio, and northern Virginia, also in Iceland, Europe, Asia, and North Africa; winters from the Aleutians, western Montana, Nebraska, Minnesota, southern Wisconsin, northern Indiana, Ohio, Maryland, and Nova Scotia (casually) south to southern Mexico, the Lesser Antilles, and Panama, and to South Africa, southern Asia, and Borneo.

The Common Mallard will breed almost anywhere if unmolested. Its adaptability has made it the chief wild duck of the world. It readily adapts itself to civilization. It does not require a secluded island in an isolated lake in some vast northern wilderness; it will nest on a little islet in a small pond in a city park, on a marshy spot near a noisy boiler factory, under sagebrush near a small waterhole in a desert with no other water for miles around or under a bush in a hillside pasture. It feeds readily on land and requires very little water. Although like all ducks it welcomes an ample supply, it can be happy in a puddle.

Like all wild-fowl, however, it prefers an aquatic courtship and mating. The male in his wooing antics displays his beauties upon the surface of the water, rearing up proudly, bowing to his mate, pursuing her here and there until she responds by nodding in her turn which seems to signify her acceptance of his suit. The nest usually is well concealed. When incubation begins, the male, like those of most other ducks, when thus left to their own devices, deserts the female and seeks only his own comfort and pleasure, leaving the mother to care for the young. The ducklings leave the nest probably within twenty-four hours after they are hatched, and go to water, where they readily dive, and in case of danger hide either beneath the surface or amidst the water-plants, with only the bill above water. If food conditions are not satisfactory where they are hatched, the mother leads them overland to other waters. By the latter part of August those that have survived are fully fledged, and in September the migration begins. The Mallard often mingles with other species of ducks, especially Pintails.

The Mallard is very adaptable in the matter of food. It eats many kinds of succulent water-plants, seeds, acorns, insects, particularly grasshoppers, many small aquatic animals and probably all the grains grown within its range. It is very fond of corn, wheat and wild rice and in the season of ripening grain is one of the best water-fowls for the table.

Mallards are very destructive to the larvae of mosquitoes and appear to be much more effective than fish in clearing stagnant pools where mosquitoes breed. It is a well-known fact that these larvae, hatched in stagnant water, live and develop there into the full-grown insects. Ducks feeding about such pools eat thousands of the larvae and by stirring up the water drown thousands more.

RED–LEGGED BLACK DUCK

Anas rubripes rubripes BREWSTER. PLATE 12.

Other names: Red-leg; Winter Black Duck; Clam Duck.

IDENTIFICATION. — Length 21 to 24 inches; spread 33 to 39 inches. Slightly larger than *A. r. tristis*, and with coral-red legs and yellow bill.

BREEDING. — Similar to that of Mallard.

RANGE. — Breeds in northern Quebec (Ungava), northern Ontario, and northern Manitoba; winters south to southern Texas, Arkansas, Louisiana, and Alabama, and from the Great Lakes and New England down the Atlantic coast to northern Florida.

The Red-legged Black Duck apparently is a virile bird, increasing its numbers and extending its range. If not already the principal wintering black duck of the Atlantic coast it soon will be at its present rate of increase. Its habits and food are similar to those of the Common Black Duck, but it migrates later in autumn. While the Common Black Duck begins to move during the latter half of September, the 'Red-legs' are rare then in Massachusetts. They come in larger numbers in late October and November and remain abundant all winter in suitable sheltered places such as the neighborhood of Plum Island off Newburyport and Ipswich, under the lee of Nahant beach, in Plymouth Harbor or Duxbury Bay. Some may be seen in open fresh-water ponds, especially where no shooting is allowed, but to see large numbers of these birds one must go to the salt water. This is a hardy race, many individuals of which remain in the North during the most severe winters. When the flats are frozen and they can get no food, they go to open springs to drink, and spend their days and nights mainly in sitting on the ice and slowly starving. In such winters many perish for want of food; or weakened by starvation they are killed and eaten by ravenous crows, gulls, eagles and foxes. Their habits and food are much the same as those of the Common Black Duck, but they are more addicted to salt water and tidal flats, are even more shy and do not come readily to live decoys. Black Ducks of both races get many small mussels and some very small clams after severe frosts come in the fall and early winter. Red-legged Black Ducks are very fond of such food. Clams found in their stomachs are often broken, but small shellfish, with shells thick and strong, mussels, quahogs and snails, are swallowed unbroken. No doubt these birds use their feet in working ('puddling') small clams out of the sand, but it is impossible to see the operation clearly as they are very shy, and usually work in the dusk of evening or at night by moonlight. They feed in very shallow water on the sand-flats or work in under the edge of the marsh, among the roots of the grass, and get only tiny clams which are not far below the surface.

COMMON BLACK DUCK

Anas rubripes tristis BREWSTER.

PLATE 12.

Other names: Dusky Duck; Dusky Mallard; Black Mallard; Summer Black Duck.

IDENTIFICATION. — Length 21 to 23½ inches; spread 32 to 36 inches. Size of female Mallard but darker; practically no dark borders to purplish-blue speculum; bill darker and legs lighter red than Red-legged Black Duck; both races very dark with silvery wing-linings.

NOTE. — Of female a loud *quack* similar to Mallard; of male a lower and shorter *quack*.

BREEDING. — Similar to that of Mallard.

RANGE. — Breeds in the Atlantic coast region from Maine to Delaware and west to northern Indiana, Wisconsin, and southern Ontario; winters from New England to North Carolina, Georgia, and Louisiana.

The Black Duck is the 'Wild Duck' of New England. Here it fills the place occupied in the Western States by the Mallard. It furnishes most of the duck shooting for gunners of the interior when the season opens in September and before the more hardy ducks have come down from the North. When the birds first come from inland waters and while they are feeding on wild rice and other vegetal food, their flesh is excellent, for it lacks the rank flavor acquired later in the season when the ponds are locked in ice and the birds, perforce, must feed on the tide-flats. Early in the season before the young ducks have become acquainted with the gunner and his wiles, it is not very difficult to take them, but all that then escape the gunner soon acquire sufficient 'education' to keep well out of gunshot as they pass by. The Common Black Duck is the wildest of them all, excepting only the 'Red-leg,' and he who would stalk these sagacious birds successfully must be as wily as a serpent.

The Black Duck is very much alive in every sense, and extremely active. It has many game qualities. It does not, like many ducks, drag itself slowly from the water into the air with laboring wings and splattering feet, but springs up at a bound. When it fears concealed danger from more than one quarter it often flies skyward; then, if not quickly shot down, it soon 'towers' beyond the reach of the shotgun. It is so swift in flight that most 'blunderers with a gun' will shoot far behind its tail. Although it does not ordinarily dive much for its food, when wounded it knows so well how to dive and hide under water that it often escapes to cover on shore where it hides away unnoticed. When mortally wounded it will sometimes push under vegetation on the bottom, die there and remain entangled in the clinging water-weeds or grass. Black Ducks are more or less nocturnal and when too much disturbed on their feeding-grounds in daylight, they fly out to sea or to the larger lakes to rest during the day and come into the smaller ponds and streams to feed at night, thus evading the gunner, but where not molested they feed during the day. Like all ducks they are active on bright moonlit nights.

Dr. C. W. Townsend gives an excellent description of the courtship of these birds. They begin by chasing one another about on the surface of the water. Those chased dive with splashing wings. The male often rises from the water in short flights and flies with body drooping a little and neck extended a trifle downward with bill open while he displays all his plumage, especially the white wing-linings. These flights are short and are ended by splashing down into the water near a female. There is more or less bobbing of the head in the surface antics and often there is an extended pursuit of the female by the male. They fly back

6c

and forth swiftly and close together, plunge into the water and race about on its surface for half an hour or more.

When the little ducklings are hatched they soon seek the water with their mother, and feed in shallow reaches of ponds among or near water-plants, where they can readily hide in case of danger. There, however, they are exposed to attack from large frogs and snapping turtles which sometimes seize and devour them, and if they get into deep water they may be swallowed by large trout or pickerel. In one way or another their enemies thin them out as the season advances. When the mother is suddenly surprised with her young she feigns to be wounded or helpless and so leads the intruder away. On one such occasion on the island of No Man's Land, a dog scented or saw the mother with her brood among the water grass at the edge of a small pond. As the brute ran into the water after them, the mother fluttered along just in front of his nose and while he followed the apparently disabled bird the young ones dived, swam along under water, came to the surface and dived again, keeping cunningly concealed amid the aquatic plants until the dog had been led far away by their devoted mother. Then they swam ashore, leaving the pond and creeping close to the ground through the short grass until they reached another small pond where they disappeared from our sight in the water-herbage. The tiny things could not have been more than a day or two old.

During the summer until the young can fly they learn to keep well concealed whenever an intruder approaches. By August they are on the wing and gather in small flocks in their favorite resorts. In September they are ready for migration. The Common Black Duck begins to migrate or work toward the salt water early in September. Nearly all the flight-birds seen near the coast in September are of this race. Sometimes in migration they fly very high. The flight is more or less intermittent but continues all through the autumn, and quite a number of this race winter in New England waters. In February, if the weather is mild, the northward flight begins, and in March as the ice breaks up the Black Ducks seek more and more the waters of the interior. While the ponds are still locked in ice, the birds seek open streams or 'spring-holes' or even small rain-water pools in pasture hollows until their favorite grassy ponds and watery swamps are released from their fetters of ice. The Black Duck feeds in fresh ponds and salt marshes, but if in the latter it must go once or twice daily to fresh water to slake its thirst.

The food of the Black Duck has been carefully worked out. Substantially three-fourths of the food is vegetal and one-fourth animal. Fully one-half of the vegetal food is derived from pondweeds, eel-grass, and wild celery. Grasses and their seeds form an important part, among them the grains, wild rice, also locally corn and wheat supplied to the ducks by gunners as 'bait.' Sedges are eaten and many seeds of weeds. Considerable numbers of reed seeds are eaten. About half the animal food consists of shell-fish, most of which are of no economic value, such as mussels, tiny clams, and snails. Crustaceans, including barnacles, sand-fleas, shrimps, and crawfish are eaten in appreciable numbers together with many insects. There is a very small proportion of fishes and their eggs.

FLORIDA DUCK

Anas fulvigula fulvigula RIDGWAY.

IDENTIFICATION. — Length 20 to 22 inches; spread about 30 to 32 inches. Slightly smaller than the very similar Common Black Duck (see Plate 12); paler, due to more extensive buffy edgings of feathers; throat light buff, *unstreaked;* speculum dull blue, lacking white border.

BREEDING. — *Nest:* On dry ground near fresh-water ponds; of grasses and leaves and rimmed with down. *Eggs:* 6 to 11, pale dull buff.

RANGE. — Southern and central Florida north to Alachua County, and along northwestern coast; resident throughout the year.

MOTTLED DUCK

Anas fulvigula maculosa SENNETT.

IDENTIFICATION. — Differs from *A. f. fulvigula* in having sides of head and neck more coarsely streaked with fuscous and more streaking on lower neck; the unstreaked buffy area of the throat much reduced.

BREEDING. — See Florida Duck.

RANGE. — Coasts of Louisiana and Texas, less commonly inland, along the Mississippi in Louisiana, and to central Texas; resident throughout the year.

These two races of *Anas fulvigula* are so similar to each other and to the two races of *Anas rubripes* in habits that no separate descriptions are necessary. A. H. Howell says that the Florida Duck is more strictly confined to fresh-water marshes than *A. rubripes*, however, but this does not seem to be the case with *A. f. maculosa*, which is an inhabitant of the coastal marshes of the western Gulf States. — (J.B.M.)

GADWALL

Chaulelasmus streperus (LINNAEUS). PLATE 12.

Other names: Gadwell; Gray Duck; Speckle-belly; Creek Duck.

IDENTIFICATION. — Length 18 to 22 inches; spread 34 to 35 inches. Smaller than Common Black Duck; slender, gray, with *white speculum* and white belly; male has black tail coverts; middle wing coverts chestnut.

BREEDING. — *Nest:* A hollow lined with grasses and down. *Eggs:* 7 to 12, creamy-white.

RANGE. — Breeds from Little Slave Lake and Hudson Bay to central British Columbia, California, southern Colorado, southwestern Kansas, northern Iowa, central Minnesota, southern Wisconsin, and Ohio (formerly), also in British Isles, Europe, and Asia; winters from Chesapeake Bay, southern Illinois, northern Arkansas, and southern British Columbia to southern Florida, Jamaica, and south-central Mexico, also in Europe and Asia.

The Gadwall breeds mainly in western Canada and winters largely in Louisiana and Texas. It keeps mainly to fresh water, and in autumn when it has been feeding on wild rice and succulent roots it is an excellent fowl for the table. Although it is one of the surface-feeding ducks and some ornithologists assert that it never dives for its food, it is in reality a skillful diver. Audubon says that it dives well on occasion, especially when wounded, and Dr. Hatch remarks that the Gadwall is an exceptionally good diver and rapid swimmer. The idea that any water-fowl never dives should be discarded. Individuals of all species of water-fowl dive. No one can be sure that all individuals of every species acquire the habit, but probably all dive more or less when very young, when courting, when wounded or when the wing-quills have been shed and the birds are unable to fly, and therefore must dive to escape their enemies. This applies not only to ducks and other small water-fowl, but also to geese, brant and swans, for individuals of all such species have been seen to dive.

The Gadwall rests high and buoyantly upon the water and when in air flies rapidly in small, compact flocks. When alarmed it springs at once into the air, climbing upward as readily as a Black Duck.

Early in September a few Gadwalls start south from their breeding-grounds, but the main flight begins in October. The spring flight may start in February, and a few of these birds may be seen rarely in March and April in New England.

EUROPEAN WIDGEON

Mareca penelope (LINNAEUS).   PLATE 13.

Other names: Widgeon or Wigeon; Red-headed Widgeon.

IDENTIFICATION. — Length 17½ to 20 inches; spread 29½ to 35 inches. Resembles Baldpate, but forehead and crown of male creamy and sides of head chestnut; females practically indistinguishable in the field, but sides of head show some reddish.

BREEDING. — Similar to Gadwall.

RANGE. — Breeds in Greenland, Iceland, northern British Isles, northern Europe and Asia; winters in the British Isles, southern Europe and Asia, and northern Africa, also regularly in British Columbia, California, the upper Mississippi Valley, and on the Atlantic coast from the Gulf of St. Lawrence to Florida.

The European Widgeon is very likely to visit ponds where wild celery and some of its favorite pondweeds grow. Any pond frequented by Scaups, Redheads and Baldpates is a good place to look for the Widgeon, which probably has visited most such ponds within its migration range in this country. In the British Isles, however, this species frequents salt-water bays and estuaries where it feeds largely on eel-grass or seaweed (*Zostera marina*). Like its American congener, the Baldpate, it can dive, but whenever diving for food becomes necessary it prefers to profit by the labor of others, and so it often accompanies the Brant for the purpose of stealing favorite food which that longer-necked bird brings to the surface. So far as I know, no one has yet reported a similar habit of the European Widgeon in this country, but it has been seen here in company with the Brant in salt water. Sportsmen can readily recognize it when in hand by its rich brown or reddish head and its gray axillars, for both sexes, old and young, have these distinctive marks, while the Baldpate has a grayish head and white axillars. If sportsmen would examine carefully all specimens of Widgeons taken by them and save any with gray axillars for the museums, we might get a better idea of the distribution of this species in this country than we have today. The habits of the Widgeon are much like those of the Baldpate. Its note, however, is quite different. Having watched the male and listened to his call at close range, my own impression of it differs from those of other authors. The note is given by the swimming bird, which raises its head high, but holds it horizontally, and appears to inhale a full breath and then expel it. The first note seems to come with the indrawn breath, the second with the exhalation. To me it sounds like *er-whew!* — the first note soft and low, the second high and shrill. In New England the European Widgeon appears late in October or in November, and may winter rarely in Massachusetts or Rhode Island, by going to the salt water after the ponds freeze. There are few New England spring records, and most individuals of this species seem to pass up the Mississippi Valley in spring, where they are more rarely seen in fall.

BALDPATE

Mareca americana (GMELIN). PLATE 13.

Other names: American Widgeon; Green-headed Widgeon; Southern Widgeon; California Widgeon; White-belly; Bald-head; White-face.

IDENTIFICATION. — Length 18 to 22 inches; spread 30 to 35 inches. Conspicuous white patch on fore-wing; male chiefly brownish with gray head, staring white crown and forehead, and white belly, large green patch on side of head; female and young usually lighter than European Widgeon and more grayish.

CALL. — Of male, a whistled *whee whee whew;* of female a loud *kaow, kaow.*

BREEDING. — Similar to Gadwall.

RANGE. — Breeds from northwestern Alaska to Oregon and east to Hudson Bay and Manitoba, south to northern Indiana, northern Nebraska, and northeastern California; winters from Chesapeake Bay, the Ohio Valley, Colorado, Vancouver Island, and southeastern Alaska to Panama and the Pacific coast of Central America.

In southern waters where Canvas-backs, Redheads, and Greater and Lesser Scaups, all excellent divers, are numerous and are diving continually on the feeding-grounds, bringing up succulent roots, bulbs, and other parts of submerged water-plants, the active Baldpate waxes fat by stealing tidbits from the hard-working diving ducks. The moment a bird comes to the surface, one or more Baldpates dash in, and sometimes one may succeed in snatching a morsel from the bill of the industrious diver. Probably in some localities they subsist to a considerable extent on the foliage of plants rooted up by the diving ducks, which may content themselves with eating the roots or bulbs, discarding the leaves. In examinations of the stomach contents of Baldpates the foliage of wild celery was the principal part of the plant found.

Apparently the Baldpate is not a skilful nor a very deep diver, but it can and does dive for food when necessity requires. It probably dives deep enough to dislodge the leaves or parts of eel-grass and wild celery, but possibly cannot dig up either plant from the bottom.

As Baldpates breed mainly in the western half of the continent, they must migrate east or northeast to reach the northern Atlantic States, and they are not so abundant there in spring, fall or winter as in the South Atlantic or Gulf States. Wherever their favorite foods may be had, they remain, if unmolested, so long as the foods last or until ice closes the waters. During many winters some numbers have remained until spring as far north as Martha's

Vineyard. Late in February their northward movement begins and early in May the vanguard of the species has reached the mouth of the Yukon River in Alaska.

AMERICAN PINTAIL

Dafila acuta tzitzihoa (VIEILLOT).   PLATE 14.

Other names: Sprig Tail; Pheasant Duck; Gray Duck; Picket-tail; Sea Widgeon.

IDENTIFICATION. — Length of male 26 to 30 inches, of female 20 to 24 inches; spread 33 to 36 inches. Long slim necks and long pointed tails distinguish Pintails from all other surface-feeding ducks; male has white breast and belly, white line running up neck into brown of head, generally gray back and sides, black tail coverts, very long tail; female grayish-brown but noticeably slender and with long slender tail; light edging of rear of wing is noticeable in flight.

CALL. — Of male a mellow whistle; of female a loud *quack*.

BREEDING. — Similar to Mallard.

RANGE. — Breeds from northwestern Alaska, northern Mackenzie, and James Bay south to central Iowa, central Nebraska, northern Utah, and southern California; winters from southern British Columbia down the Pacific coast to Central America and from northeastern Colorado, central Missouri, southern Illinois, southern Ohio, and Chesapeake Bay to the Bahamas, West Indies and Panama, also in the Hawaiian Islands.

The Pintail is one of the finest and most widely distributed water-fowl of the world. Elegant in form, beautiful in plumage, fleet, intelligent, cautious, and excellent upon the table, it has all the desirable qualities of a game bird. It is so suspicious and swift, and when alarmed gets away so quickly, that it taxes the skill of the sportsman to the uttermost. Any unusual object or the slightest motion of the hunter is enough to cause it to disappear instantly on the wings of the wind. It is normally a fresh-water bird frequenting rivers, lakes, and ponds, but it often feeds on flooded salt marshes. Along the coast when much pursued it will go to sea to rest during daylight, but returns to its favorite inland feeding-grounds when night has fallen. The American Pintail is one of the earliest of the water-fowl to appear in spring. Even in late February, while the rivers are still locked in ice, it may be seen sometimes in rain-water pools and unfrozen spring-holes, and usually it is here in March while floating ice still blocks the streams.

In safe retreats it seems to delight in leaving the water during the warm hours of the day and resting and dressing its plumage on some bar or open strand. When on the water it rides buoyantly and gracefully, its long tail held high, and when alarmed it springs into the air as readily as a Black Duck. There is no dragging or pattering along the surface with the active, clipper-built Pintail. Although a surface-feeding duck it can dive and swim readily under water, and like several other species it has been known when wounded to cling fast to some object on the bottom.

The Pintail also is one of the earliest of the ducks to return southward in autumn and sometimes comes along with the Blue-winged Teal, the first of the early ducks.

This bird is fond of pondweeds and the seeds of sedges and grasses, including the cultivated grains, especially rice, but it seems to get little but waste grain. It takes the seeds of common weeds, especially many of those growing near the water, and eats various succulent parts of many water-plants. It also destroys small mollusks and crustaceans and many insects such as beetles, flies, grasshoppers, dragon-flies, mosquitoes, water-bugs, etc.

65

EUROPEAN TEAL

Nettion crecca (LINNAEUS).   PLATE 13.

Other names: Teal; European Green-winged Teal.

IDENTIFICATION. — Length 12½ to 15 inches; spread 22 to 24 inches. Similar to Green-winged Teal; male with white streak on scapulars above fore-wing, no white vertical bar before wing, and creamy edge to green patch on side of head (not prominent); female and young indistinguishable in the field.

BREEDING. — On ground in marsh, field or woods. *Nest:* Of grass, sedges, weeds and feathers, lined with down. *Eggs:* 7 to 16, yellowish-white, greenish or buffy.

RANGE. — Breeds in Iceland, the British Isles, Europe, and Asia east through the Kurile and Aleutian islands, to Unalaska; winters south to the Canary Islands, Ethiopia, India, Japan, and the Philippines; accidental or casual in Nova Scotia and the Atlantic States south to North Carolina.

The European Teal has been considered for many years as a mere casual or accidental visitor to this country. When, however, Mr. A. C. Bent visited the Aleutian Islands in 1911 and found this species breeding commonly on the western and central islands, it was necessary to revise the breeding range of the species. It is not improbable that the species may breed elsewhere in Alaska.

The European Teal resembles the Green-winged Teal closely not only in form and plumage but also in habits. It frequents the same shallow fresh waters, and estuaries and marshes near the sea. Wherever the Green-wing is found the European Teal may be looked for along either coast of North America. In time it may be found to be only a very rare visitor in some American regions where it is now regarded as accidental.

The European Teal is chiefly vegetarian. It feeds more on the seeds of many plants than on their leaves or stalks. In spring it eats old waste grain; but snails, worms, slugs and insect larvae form a considerable part of its food.

GREEN-WINGED TEAL

Nettion carolinense (GMELIN).   PLATE 13.

Other names: Green-wing; Mud Teal.

IDENTIFICATION. — Length 12½ to 16 inches; spread 22 to 24 inches. Smallest of river ducks; adult male has chestnut head with green patch on side, generally gray plumage, breast light brownish, *white bar in front of wing;* yellow triangle under tail; female and young have head dusky brownish; both sexes and ages have greenish-brown speculum.

BREEDING. — See European Teal.

RANGE. — Breeds from northern Alaska, northern Manitoba, James Bay, and southern Ungava south to central California, northern New Mexico, northern Nebraska, southern Minnesota, northern Michigan, southern Ontario, western New York, and Quebec; winters from southern British Columbia, northern Nebraska, northern Missouri, southern Illinois, Kentucky, and Chesapeake Bay to the Bahamas, West Indies, Honduras and southern Mexico.

The lovely little Green-winged Teal is one of the swiftest fliers among game birds. Its speed has been estimated at 160 miles an hour, but to reach this rate it would have to be borne on the wings of a hurricane. It often flies in compact flocks, its line of flight either definite and direct or else vacillating, with quick turns in exact concert. In the water it is a buoyant swimmer and an excellent diver, but does not ordinarily dive except to escape some enemy. Much of the food of this teal is procured in very shallow water or on land. It is fond of wading and 'puddling' in a few inches of water in muddy places or on bare mud flats, in company with the sandpipers. It is particularly active on its feet, walks and runs well and often travels on foot for some distance on land either in search of food or in passing from pool to pool. When alarmed by the hunter, it springs direct from the water into the air and is soon out of danger; but if some members of a flock are shot down, the rest are likely to circle about and return and may even alight among their dead or dying comrades. The Green-wing is naturally tame and unsuspicious, and old people on Cape Cod have related often how the teal formerly fed with the barnyard ducks.

The natural tameness of this species has been its undoing. Excellent as a table bird it was in great demand in the market, and now in many places where formerly it was common and even abundant at times in migration, it has become uncommon or rare.

The Green-winged Teal begins to leave its northern breeding-grounds in October (although a few stragglers move southward in September), and until late in November it may be seen in its favorite waters in the Northern States. It frequents the fresh water by preference; but if the ponds and rivers freeze, it goes to salt-water estuaries until the fresh waters are freed from ice.

BLUE–WINGED TEAL

Querquedula discors (LINNAEUS).   PLATE 13.

Other names: Blue-wing; Summer Teal.

IDENTIFICATION. — Length 14½ to 16 inches; spread 24 to 31 inches. Adult male largely grayish with sky-blue fore-wing and white crescent in front of eye; blue of wing conspicuous in flight; female and young have less conspicuous blue on wing, distinguished from female Shoveller by smaller size and shorter, narrower bill.

BREEDING. — See European Teal.

RANGE. — Breeds from central British Columbia, central Manitoba, southern Ontario, New Brunswick, Maine, and Rhode Island south to western New York, Ohio, Indiana, Illinois, central Missouri, central Kansas, northern New Mexico, and northern Nevada; winters from South Carolina, Louisiana, Texas, Mexico, and southern California to the Bahamas, West Indies, and coasts of South America to Brazil and Chile.

Fleeing first of all wild ducks from the frost king and following the retiring sun toward the equator come the Blue-winged Teals. In the waning summer or with the full September moon they come; and swinging low out of the northern sky they sweep along the sedgy banks of some marshy river where wild rice and pickerel weed grow. Borne on swift whistling pinions, careering swiftly back and forth, they turn and return, and, as they swing and shift, show alternately light breasts and dark backs with flashing azure wings. Back and forth they rush, reconnoitering the landfall until, suspicions allayed, and satisfied at last, they check their speed with wings, feet and tail and alight all together on some still, marsh-bordered pool, the haunt of rails, muskrats, tortoises and frogs, where blackbirds tunefully emit their throaty notes and swallows flit on still summer evenings until the bats come out.

The Blue-winged Teal is fond of still waters and slow currents. It frequents small ponds and pools where it dabbles among the lily pads or the marshy borders of slow-running streams. Its flight, like that of the Green-winged Teal, is remarkably swift. It comes readily to decoys, particularly if live birds are used, and is normally tame and unsuspicious. In wet seasons it often alights in pools of rain-water. Formerly its flights were immense. As it flew and swam in close flocks, it offered an excellent target for the 'scatter gun.' Audubon tells of a gunner who reported that he had killed 120 at one discharge. Audubon himself records that he saw 94 killed by the simultaneous discharge of both barrels of a double gun.

In the first half of the nineteenth century the Blue-winged Teal was abundant in migration in the Northeast, but its numbers gradually decreased until it became rare. Now under protective laws it seems to be slowly increasing. It is one of the most prolific of all ducks and is said sometimes to hatch fifteen to seventeen young. If given reasonable protection its increase may continue.

Though this teal migrates southward very early and does not linger long in New England, a few may sometimes be seen in October and November, and rarely a bird or two may be recorded in winter. It is more often seen in spring in the wilder parts of northern New England than in the more southerly parts, and a few pairs have been known to breed there recently, though the majority of the species breed farther north or west.

SHOVELLER

Spatula clypeata LINNAEUS.   PLATE 14.

Other names: Spoonbill; Broadbill.

IDENTIFICATION. — Length 17 to 21 inches; spread 29½ to 35 inches. Male unmistakable; seen from below at a distance greenish head and neck seem black; from neck to front of wing, bird is white; chestnut lower body coming next seems dark and is spearated from black under tail coverts by narrow belt of white; thus five alternating areas, dark-white-dark-white-dark. Female and young brownish above, buffy below; might be mistaken for Blue-winged Teal except for length and shape of bill — this so long that in flight wings seem to be set too far back; Shoveller also usually flies less swiftly and in a more hesitating desultory manner than Teal.

BREEDING. — Similar to Mallard.

RANGE. — Breeds from the Bering Sea coast of Alaska to Great Slave Lake and the Saskatchewan Valley south to western Iowa, western Nebraska, Kansas, central Arizona, and southern California and from the Arctic Circle to southern Europe and central Asia; winters from southern British Columbia, California, eastern Texas, the lower Mississippi Valley, and the Atlantic coast from South Carolina south to the West Indies, the Pacific coast of Mexico, Central America and Colombia, and in the Hawaiian Islands, and in the Old World.

The Shoveller stands alone. No other duck in North America carries about such a long, broad, extremely specialized spatulate bill, and no other exhibits in the full plumage of the handsome male so peculiar an arrangement of striking colors. It bears no close resemblance to any other bird. It may be looked for occasionally anywhere in these states where muddy ponds and pools are found, especially near the sea-coast, where it is rarely seen in salt water. Its bill with its many comb-like processes is used to dabble in the mud from which the bird sifts out much of its food, and for this reason it frequents the small ponds or shallow mudholes which supply it with its favorite food.

The Shoveller is one of the first ducks to flee before the coming of winter, and the first severe frost will usually send it southward; but as its chief American breeding-grounds are in the western part of the continent, comparatively few ever reach New England. It comes singly, in pairs or in small companies and seeks the society of other ducks, such as Blue-winged Teal, Baldpate and Lesser Scaup. It should be looked for among other wild-fowl in September and early October. By December the vanguard has reached South America. They are a little later than most of the ducks on the return trip, for early April seems to be the average time of their arrival near the northern border of the United States.

The Shoveller is regarded as a rather 'slow' bird, comparatively unsuspicious and easily taken. It comes well to decoys and often seems slow and vacillating in flight, but in reality when aroused or frightened it is one of the most active and swift of water-fowl. When startled it springs quickly from the water with an audible flapping of its long wings and goes away with a rush. Its speed when alarmed and under full headway is difficult to estimate.

I have enjoyed watching the feeding habits of the Shoveller. At times there are no ducks more active on land or water. They dart about in pursuit of insects, splash in play and chase each other round and round. The great, peculiar bill is an excellent trap for both land and water insects, and, more than any other duck, the Shoveller uses the long comb-like pectinations of the spoon-shaped member to sift from water or ooze the food it most desires. I have watched many surface-feeding ducks swimming low in the water with head and neck extended and bill partially immersed. In this way they often drink, but perhaps still more often secure food which is retained by the sensitive tongue or the lamellated mandibles while the water and inedible residue passes out on either side; but no species that it has been my good fortune to observe practices this so often and so continuously as the Shoveller. Three or four Shovellers will form in line following one after the other, and then the leader will swing round in an ellipse, turning and following the hindmost, each one apparently straining through its bill the water stirred by the paddling feet of the one before it. Thus round and round they go with chattering bills, each one apparently enjoying the guttering exercise and getting some sustenance from the disturbed and turgid element. The male and female also circle about in this manner during courtship.

A bird so highly specialized as the Shoveller might be expected to subsist to some extent on minute objects not so readily separated from the ooze by ducks with ordinary bills un-provided with so fine a straining apparatus. An examination of the food of the Shoveller tends to confirm this theory.

WOOD DUCK

Aix sponsa (LINNAEUS).

Other names: Summer Duck; Wood Widgeon; Acorn Duck; Tree Duck.

IDENTIFICATION. — Length 17 to 20½ inches; spread about 28 to 29 inches. Smaller than Black Duck or Mallard; male has long crest on metallic green, blue and purple, white-lined head, and white throat; female largely brownish; in flight overhead Wood Ducks show a white or whitish belly where Black Ducks are dark; where markings can be seen at close range, the crested male with its unmistakable marks and the female with her white eye-ring and the white patch or line behind eye are recognizable.

BREEDING. — In a natural or artificial hollow in a tree in woods, swamps, or even orchards. *Nest:* Lined with down. *Eggs:* 8 to 15, pale buff to creamy-white.

RANGE. — Breeds locally throughout United States and southern Canada; winters from British Columbia to Illinois and Virginia and south to the West Indies and Mexico.

Loveliest of all water-fowl the Wood Duck stands supreme. Deep flooded swamps where ancient mossy trees overhang the dark still waters, secluded pools amid the scattered pines where water-lilies lift their snowy heads and turtles bask in the sun, purling brooks flowing through dense woodlands where light and shade fleck the splashing waters, slow flowing creeks and marshy ponds — these are the haunts of the Wood Duck. See that mating pair on the dark and shaded flood of a little woodland river; they seem to float as lightly as the drifting leaves. The male glides along proudly, his head ruffled and his crest distended, his scapular feathers raised and lowered at will, while his plumes flash with metallic luster wherever the sun's rays sifting through the foliage intercept his course. She coyly retires; he daintily follows, exhibiting all his graces, the darkling colors of his plumage relieved by the pure white markings of head and breast and the bright reds of feet and bill and large lustrous eye. What a picture they make, as, intent on one another, they glide along close together, she clothed in modest hues, he glowing and resplendent. He nods and calls in low sweet tender tones and thus, she leading, he pursuing, they disappear into the shadows where the stream turns upon another course. I have lain concealed beneath the foliage, and watched a flock of these exquisite creatures disporting themselves upon a woodland pool. Such a picture no pen can adequately describe. The changing colors of the water reflecting sun, sky and foliage, all are reproduced in the plumage of the active birds as they pass, turn and repass upon their favorite element.

The Wood Duck is part of Nature's heritage vouchsafed to the American people. It lives and migrates mainly within the United States. It breeds more generally throughout the land than any other duck. How have we kept that heritage? Once this beautiful bird was common to abundant throughout New England and in other favorable sections of the country, along all the watercourses, about the margins of lakes and ponds and all over our well-watered terrain. In heavily timbered regions they were even more abundant than the Black Duck or the Mallard. These ducks often built their nests in the hollow trees of the orchard or in the shade trees that overhung the farmhouse. Spring shooting which went on merrily even after the ducks had laid their eggs brought the species nearly to extinction in the early part of the twentieth century.

No doubt lumbering also had something to do with the decrease of this species, as it nests normally in the hollows of forest trees or in holes made by Pileated Woodpeckers. In their search for domiciles the females have been entrapped in chimneys and stovepipes; they have been known, where suitable trees were lacking, to nest upon the ground. The Wood Duck may become as abundant as in the past only by perpetual protection and by supplying it with artificial nesting-boxes simulating the hollow limbs of the forest.

Young Wood Ducks when hatched are well equipped for climbing, as they are provided with exceedingly sharp, pin-pointed, hooked claws and with hooked nails at the ends of their bills; so expert are they that in many cases when confined in a box or keg, they have been known to climb out, going up the perpendicular sides like flies walking on a wall. When the eggs begin hatching, the young remain quiescent in the nest for a day or two; but when the female alights on the ground or water and calls them, they quickly climb out of the nest. If the trunk of the tree leans, they may scramble down the bark backward or roll and tumble to the ground. If not, they fall fluttering lightly to the ground without suffering any serious injury, and the mother leads her brood proudly to the nearest water. As is the case with most ducks, the male leaves the female when the duties of incubation begin, but occasionally a male has been seen with his family before or after it has reached the water. The evident fitness of the ducklings for going to water as above described, and the fact that in zoological parks in Europe they get to the water in the same way, have inclined certain European ornithologists to the belief that the parent bird never carries them. There is incontestable evidence, however, that the young often are conveyed to the water by the parent not only when the nest is at a considerable distance from water but sometimes when the tree almost overhangs it.

In September the migration of the Wood Ducks begins. They move at first in small flocks or family groups and during late September or October quite large companies may be seen in favorite swamps and ponds or along the larger rivers. After October their numbers decrease and a winter Wood Duck in the latitude of southern New England is a rarity. In spring when the ice has left the ponds and streams and when the chorus of the wood frogs and hylas is heard in the land, the main northward flight of Wood Ducks appears, and they continue to pass through late March and early April.

REDHEAD

Nyroca americana (EYTON).

PLATE 15.

Other names: American Pochard; Red-headed Raft Duck.

IDENTIFICATION. — Length 17 to 23 inches; spread 30 to 33 inches. Male with *high forehead*, black lower neck and gray back should never be mistaken for male Canvas-back (although with similarly colored reddish head) with *low forehead*, brown neck and whitish back; nor for brown-headed female Golden-eye with whitish ring on neck just below head; in flight Redhead looks darker and shorter than Canvas-back. Female is more like female Canvas-back but low forehead and long bill of latter are as distinctive as in male; Redhead closely resembles the smaller female Ring-necked Duck.

BREEDING. — In sloughs and swamps near shallow lakes. *Nest:* Of reeds and flags, lined with down, often hidden under bent-over reeds, etc. *Eggs:* 10 to 15 or more, pale olive-buff to cream-buff.

RANGE. — Breeds from southern British Columbia and southern Manitoba south to southern California, central Nebraska, and Michigan; winters from British Columbia to Chesapeake Bay and south to Mexico and the West Indies.

There is no place in New England where Redheads can be seen during the fall, winter and early spring in such abundance as in some of the larger ponds on the south side of Martha's Vineyard where wild celery and pondweeds attract them. There in October and November hundreds may be seen in company with 'Blue-bills' riding the white-capped wavelets driven by the strong sea wind. Along the low, sandy lee shores of the pond rows of white froth gleam. The sun shines brightly on the sparkling waves; fleecy clouds race across the blue sky; gulls wheel and call over the beach ridge which divides the pond from the sea; and the long rafts of ducks lend added interest to the animated scene. Some are diving, some preening their feathers, others resting with heads on their backs. Occasionally one rises erect in the water with flapping wings.

Redheads in flight may not be known by any definite flock formation. Although they sometimes move in wide V-shaped flocks, they are quite as likely to fly bunched in dense flocks or in irregular formations. Like most ducks they like to swing about and reconnoiter before alighting; they then set their wings and sail down to the water, or sometimes fall rapidly from the sky in a zigzag course.

On Martha's Vineyard some of the market hunters of the old days were adepts in the art of 'wafeing.' The concealed hunter waved a red cloth in a way which attracted numbers of Redheads and Scaups within easy gunshot. Ordinarily these birds keep well away from the shore, but their curiosity is great and they come in readily to the sportsmen's decoys. They feed largely at night and rest much during the day, though they often fly about in flocks from pond to pond, especially early in the morning and late in the afternoon.

Redheads usually arrive in Massachusetts in October, are abundant in November and stay as long as the ponds are open. There are many winters during which they can remain on Martha's Vineyard with its relatively mild climate, but a severe cold wave that covers ponds and flats with solid ice will send them southward, and great flocks winter together on Chesapeake Bay and on the sounds and estuaries of the Carolinas and Georgia. In spring a few begin to move toward their summer homes before the ponds of the interior are clear of ice and often by the middle of March the movement becomes general.

As the Redhead is an excellent diver, its food is obtained largely beneath the surface and well away from shore, though it sometimes dabbles in very shallow water near the margin. Evidently it prefers to feed in fresh water where it dives to obtain the foliage, bulbs and roots of aquatic plants. Its vegetal food consists largely of wild celery, pondweeds and in fact the succulent shoots of almost any nutritious aquatic vegetation. It also includes some seeds and, according to Audubon, beech nuts and acorns. Its animal food is almost equal in variety but less in quantity. It eats fresh-water clams, snails, leeches, small fish, tadpoles, frogs, lizards and insects.

RING–NECKED DUCK

Nyroca collaris (DONOVAN). PLATE 15.

Other names: Ring-necked Scaup; ring-necked Blackhead; Ring-billed Blackhead; Ring-bill.

IDENTIFICATION. — Length 15½ to 18 inches; spread 25 to 30 inches. Resembles Lesser Scaup but head more puffy or crested and speculum bluish-gray; male with back blackish instead of grayish; white 'crescent' in front of wing continuous with white of under parts; at close range bill has white band near dark tip; female resembles larger female Redhead but has browner body, white eye-ring and light cheeks; chin and throat of female Ring-neck often continuously whitish.

BREEDING. — See Greater Scaup.

RANGE. — Breeds from central British Columbia, Manitoba, and western Ontario south to southern Wisconsin, northern Iowa, northern Nebraska, and central Arizona; winters from southern British Columbia down the Pacific coast to Mexico and from northern Arkansas, the Ohio Valley and Chesapeake Bay to the Bahamas, Mexico, and Guatemala.

The Ring-necked Duck is usually classed with the scaups, which it superficially resembles, but its affinity with the Tufted Duck of the Old World seems to be closer. Like the Lesser Scaup it appears to prefer fresh water to salt water, and is much more abundant in the interior of the country than on either the Atlantic or the Pacific coast. It commonly haunts rivers and shallow waters in preference to the open water of large lakes. In winter it is the most abundant duck in certain shallow lakes in Florida.

Its flight is extremely swift and like that of the Greater Scaup is accompanied by more or less whistling of the wings. The Ring-neck flies in small and rather scattered flocks or parties and does not mass in great companies on the water as do the scaups. Like *affinis*, when diving, the tail is always spread, and is deflexed as the head is dipped under the water. On its nesting ground it takes many aquatic insects, tadpoles, small frogs and snails and the seeds, roots and tender shoots of aquatic plants.

CANVAS–BACK

Nyroca valisineria (WILSON). PLATE 15.

Other names: Can; White-back.

IDENTIFICATION. — Length 20 to 24 inches; spread 34 to 36 inches. Low forehead and long wedge-shaped bill distinguish from somewhat similarly colored Redhead or female Golden-eye; adult male has reddish-brown head and neck and whitish 'canvas-colored' back; female duller colored; in flight its long slender neck and bill, all carried with a slight downward curve, give impression of wings being placed far back on body.

BREEDING. — Similar to Redhead, but eggs usually darker.

RANGE. — Breeds from Alaska and Great Slave Lake to central Manitoba, central western Nebraska, northern New Mexico, and western Nevada, occasionally east to southern Minnesota and southern Wisconsin; winters from southern British Columbia south along the Pacific coast to Mexico, and from northwestern Montana, northeastern Arkansas, southern Illinois, and Chesapeake Bay south to Florida, the Gulf coast of Louisiana, Texas, central Mexico, and rarely Guatemala.

On March 19, 1919, a southerly storm swept the south coast of Martha's Vineyard. Through all the preceding night the surf beat upon the sands with a sound like distant rolling thunder.

In the morning the wind shifted to the northward while the sound of the surf lowered to a sullen rushing roar which filled all the air, and the sea was obscured by drifting mist. Gulls wheeled along the shore, wild-fowl flew singly or in pairs across the misty sky, while the rain fell in great drops or drove in sheets and clouds like spray before sharp gusts from off the land. The sea had thrown upon the beach a windrow of sea-moss, kelp, rock-weed, sponges and all the flotsam of the tide. A flock of sheep attracted by the sea-wrack nuzzled along the beach. Toward night as the wind swung to the northwest, the sky began to clear and the westering sun threw his slant rays over the tumultuous waters. All along down toward Squibnocket the great rollers charged the shore, each like some great sea-monster boring in toward the beach, its high mane of white sea-foam towering at its forefront and its spray streaming backward like white smoke. The scene was magnificent as, lighted by the setting sun, Niagaras of foam were poured upon the beach.

On Watcha Pond hundreds of ducks, with heads to the wind, rode the waves in security. They were largely Scaups and Redheads, but here and there was a lordly male Canvas-back, his great white body standing out conspicuously among his darker and lesser companions.

Here if anywhere in New England we shall find the Canvas-backs. In the ponds of southeastern Massachusetts they appear more generally in fall than in spring; and in some winters may be seen in Waquoit Bay, rarely on Nantucket, and occasionally in Boston, Plymouth and other harbors, and in the ponds about Boston.

The principal breeding-grounds of the Canvas-back are in the wide prairie regions of western Canada, though it still breeds in some numbers in the states immediately south of this vast nursery of water-fowl. In its autumn migration the Canvas-back sometimes travels almost due east so that a few birds reach New England, but the great majority swing more to the southeast, and their favorite wintering grounds are on the shallow waters of Chesapeake Bay and Currituck Sound, though many also winter on the shores of the Gulf of Mexico and in California.

Until comparatively recent years the 'Cans,' as they were called, gathered in tremendous rafts, totaling thousands of birds, in favorable places on the shores of Maryland and tidewater Virginia, but their great popularity as a table delicacy nearly sealed their destruction, and today they are greatly reduced in numbers. They are prolific birds, and under modern conservation methods they should at least retain their present numbers, though we can probably not expect them to return to their former abundance.

The Canvas-back with its very large feet and large wide webs is a powerful swimmer and an excellent diver. It goes to the bottom and there grubs up roots and shoots of aquatic plants. It is the most celebrated of American ducks for the epicure and is supposed to acquire delectable flavor from feeding on the wild celery (*Vallisneria spiralis*). It is by no means a superior table bird except when feeding on its choicest vegetal aliments. The Redhead, Shoveller, and some other ducks are in some circumstances fully its equal on the table.

GREATER SCAUP DUCK

Nyroca marila (LINNAEUS).   PLATE 15.

Other names: Blue-bill; Blue-bill Widgeon; Broad-bill; Raft Duck; Big Black-head; Troop Fowl; Green-head.

IDENTIFICATION. — Length 17 to 21 inches; spread 29 to 35 inches. The two scaup drakes have dark heads, necks and breasts, blue bills, pure white speculum, light gray backs and white belly; abrupt transition from black breast to white belly is conspicuous in flight; head of Greater Scaup is metallic-green, that of Lesser shows purplish reflections; females have distinct white area around base of bill, head and upper parts brownish, and white speculum as in male.

BREEDING. — In sloughs or near marshy ponds. *Nest:* Of grass, flags, etc., lined with fine grass and down. *Eggs:* Usually 7 to 10 (or more); vary in color from greenish-gray to deep olive-buff.

RANGE. — Breeds from the Aleutian Islands and the Arctic coast of Alaska and Canada to the west coast of Hudson Bay, western Ungava and central Manitoba; winters on the Pacific coast from the Aleutian Islands to Lower California, and on the Atlantic coast from southern New England to North Carolina, and on Gulf coast of Florida, Louisiana, and Texas, occasionally on the Great Lakes and from Colorado to Arizona, also in the Eastern Hemisphere.

The Greater Scaup is known to most gunners as the Blue-bill or Broad-bill. It frequents salt-water ponds, bays, estuaries and large harbors as well as brackish or fresh-water ponds near the sea. Like the Redhead and the Canvas-back it is an excellent diver. The habits of the bird are much like those of the Redhead, with which species it may be often found in flocks. It feeds mainly by diving in deep or shallow water at some distance from the shore, though it sometimes dabbles along the margin. In diving it usually keeps the wings close to the body, though if wounded and pursued, it may at times use them to accelerate its speed beneath the surface.

In courtship the male lifts his head very high, and points the bill upward at an acute angle. When the female becomes responsive, she bows repeatedly. The Greater Scaup is normally an unsuspicious duck, possessed of great curiosity, and can be tolled close to the shore by one who is skilled in the process; but the birds learn by experience and soon become gun-shy. Scaups are gregarious birds. On the water they flock close together; and if only two are seen at one time, they will usually approach each other so that the concealed gunner who has patience can secure both with one shot. In rising they do not spring into the air like a Black Duck but must tread considerable water with many wing-flappings before they leave it. They fly usually in a compact flock, although if the flock is excessively large, it may string out to great lengths, bunching in places. There is no regular formation, though occasionally a small flock may assume the shape of a wedge. When set in their course, they fly direct and fast and occasionally turn from side to side.

The Greater Scaup feeds much at night, and at about sunset on winter evenings the flocks may be seen leaving their resting places in harbors and estuaries and passing out over the sea to their feeding-places on the mussel-beds where they eat small mollusks and crustaceans. In summer they take some insects. Among their food materials while with us are wild celery and eel-grass and its seeds.

LESSER SCAUP DUCK

Nyroca affinis (EYTON).

PLATE 15.

Other names: Little Black-head; Little Blue-bill; Raft Duck; Creek Broad-bill; River Blue-bill; Cove Blue-bill; Blue-bill Coot.

IDENTIFICATION. — Length 15 to 18 inches; spread under 30 inches. Slightly smaller than Greater Scaup, male with purplish head and less white on flight-feathers.

BREEDING. — See Greater Scaup.

RANGE. — Breeds from southern Alaska to Hudson Bay, and southeastern Ontario to southern British Columbia; winters from southern British Columbia south along the Pacific coast of Mexico and both coasts of Central America to Panama, and from northeastern Colorado, northeastern Arkansas, southern Illinois, New Jersey, and Chesapeake Bay to the Bahamas and Lesser Antilles.

The Lesser Scaup is so like the Greater Scaup that in the field it is difficult to distinguish one from the other. In some cases even their measurements overlap, and the usual difference in the shade of the gloss on the head of the male is not always evident. Possibly the two may interbreed. The Lesser Scaup, however, is an American bird, while the Greater Scaup has a much wider distribution. In winter the Greater Scaup frequents mainly the larger unfrozen lakes and the sea-coasts, while the Lesser Scaup is at all seasons more distinctly a fresh-water bird. Nevertheless at times both species may be seen together on salt, brackish or fresh water. The Lesser Scaup being more southerly in its winter range is the most numerous duck in winter on many of the lagoons and lakes of the Gulf States, where it is often called the 'Raft Duck,' because of its habit of collecting in enormous dense flocks or 'rafts' on such waters. In the winter of 1877–78 in Florida I saw one such 'raft' that extended a mile in length. When a boat approached such a gathering, only those nearest rose and flew over the 'raft' and settled on its farther side. The approach of any craft was followed by a continual thunderous roar of wings as the birds successively shifted their position to a place of greater safety. At night these great flocks were sometimes drifted by the wind to one shore or another which gave the crafty fox or the sneaking lynx an unusual opportunity. Gunners also after such a night crept to the shore in the early morning light to take advantage of such a chance for a raking shot.

The flight of the Lesser Scaup is swift and often very erratic. It is an excellent swimmer and diver, diving usually with closed wings. When wounded, it employs every artifice to conceal itself, keeping mostly under water and in some cases forcing itself under aquatic vegetation where it sometimes becomes entangled and drowns; or if all else fails, it may even seize some under-water plant with its bill, and as a last resort hold on until death ensues in its anxiety to escape its pursuer.

AMERICAN GOLDEN-EYE

Glaucionetta clangula americana (BONAPARTE).   PLATE 16.

Other names: Whistler; Brass-eye; Great-head; Garrot; Quandy (Female).

IDENTIFICATION. — Length 17 to 23 inches; spread 27 to 32 inches. A medium-sized, stocky duck with short neck and large head; male mainly black and white; at close range round white spot between bill and yellow eye distinguish it; much white on sides; female gray with round brown head, yellow eye, white speculum and light collar contrasting with brown head; male distinguished from Barrow's Golden-eye by shape of eye-spot and larger amount of white on sides and wings, and larger and less deep bill; in flight color pattern resembles mergansers but neck much shorter.

BREEDING. — In forested country near lakes or rivers. *Nest:* In hole in tree, lined with down. *Eggs:* 5 to 19, usually 12 to 15, various shades of greenish.

RANGE. — Breeds from Alaska, Hudson Bay and northern Labrador to Newfoundland, New Brunswick, central Maine, New Hampshire, northern Vermont, the Adirondacks, northern Ontario, northern Michigan, northern Minnesota, northwestern Montana, and interior British Columbia; winters on the Atlantic coast from Maine to South Carolina, on the Pacific from Alaska to Lower California, on the Great Lakes, and irregularly from Montana to Colorado and Arkansas, and elsewhere.

The American Golden-eye comes with the biting frost. No bird is more typical of winter on the New England coast. In days of brief winter sunshine when harbors are filled with floating ice, at daybreak keen and cold when hoar frost clusters on trees along our icy coast — then we may hear the clear, melodious whistle of the Golden-eye's fast-beating wings. At evening when the clouds reflect in evanescent tints the glory of a sun already sunk behind the western hills — then we may see his fleeting form speeding afar over the sea, tracing the pathway of the 'illimitable air.'

The species is well and widely known as 'Whistler' by gunners of the Atlantic coast, while the female is known to many as 'Quandy.' The bird is one of the hardiest of ducks, and may be seen in winter usually well outside the breakers, continually diving in pursuit of its favorite food. No other wild duck except the American Merganser shows so much white as the male Whistler. He rides the waves lightly, with the white feathers of sides and flanks thrown up in such a way as to cover most of the wing, and his white sides flash continually in the sunlight. The much darker, brown-headed females and young are often seen in company with the males, and do not appear to ride quite so high in the water. All dive usually with closed wings, and tails widely spread, but sometimes, perhaps when in haste, they open the wings and use them under water.

In late winter on our waters the hardy Golden-eye begins its courtship. The male swims about the female, often with head lowered and neck stretched along the water, but his most characteristic motion is that of raising his head upward and backward until with the bill pointing toward the zenith he utters his harsh note. Sometimes the head is thrown over until it almost touches the back. Often the bird dashes forward while the orange-colored feet strike backward and upward with such force as to throw strong jets of water into the air and at the same time display the brilliant coloring.

As the Golden-eye nests in hollow trees like the Wood Duck, its manner of getting the young to the water has attracted some attention. The young birds have been seen to tumble out of the nesting-tree and flutter down to the water. On the other hand other observers claim

77

to have seen them carried from the nest to the water on the back of the parent; while others still report that the young are conveyed in the bill of the mother, or in some way between her feet.

The American Golden-eye is largely a fresh-water bird and many remain all winter in the lakes and rivers of the interior, so long as the fresh waters are unfrozen; but when severe frosts close most inland waters, Golden-eyes flock to the coast. Like the scaups, Golden-eyes push northward early in spring. They move as fast as the ice breaks in the rivers, and in early May reach their most northerly breeding-grounds near the Arctic Circle.

BARROW'S GOLDEN–EYE

Glaucionetta islandica (GMELIN). PLATE 16.

Other names: Rocky Mountain Garrot.

IDENTIFICATION. — Length 20 to 23 inches; spread 30 inches or more. Male distinguished from American Golden-eye by greater amount of black on sides, outer surface of closed wing chiefly black; row of white spots on black scapulars, and angular white spot between bill and eye may be apparent; head purplish instead of greenish; females hard to distinguish but bill shorter and less acute angle.

BREEDING. — Similar to American Golden-eye. *Eggs:* 6 to 10.

RANGE. — Breeds in Greenland and Iceland and on the Labrador coast, and from Alaska south to the Sierra Nevada of California and east to Montana and Colorado; winters on the Atlantic coast from the Gulf of St. Lawrence to Massachusetts, on the Pacific coast from southern Alaska to central California, and irregularly in the interior from southern British Columbia to southern Colorado.

Probably this dark and handsome duck is not so rare on the North Atlantic coast as it has been regarded. When hunted it is one of the shyest of 'sea-fowl'; therefore very few are found in the hands of gunners. The females and young, which undoubtedly are more numerous than the males, so closely resemble the females and young of the American Golden-eye that the most expert ornithologist cannot always be sure of recognizing them in the field, and some have mistaken their identity even when in hand. The males are easily recognized, and often in winter I have seen from two to four males with five to twelve others which appeared to be females and young of the same species feeding on the mussel-beds off Red Rock at Lynn beach in Massachusetts. South of Cape Cod the bird seems rarer and it is a mere straggler on the Long Island shore.

In the Rocky Mountains from Colorado north this species is a common bird, nesting about many small lakes and ponds.

Courtship antics of these hardy vigorous birds may be seen on pleasant March days. There is more or less bowing or bobbing. The male swims rapidly about the female, erects the loose feathers of the head and now and then throws it backward until it nearly touches the back, when with the bill slightly opened and pointing to the sky the bird presumably utters its love note. Owing to distance and the sound of the breaking surf I have never heard a vocal sound from these birds. Barrow's Golden-eye is a strong swimmer, a powerful diver and swift in flight. With us it seems to feed chiefly on mussels, as it frequents mussel-beds, and, no doubt, like other diving ducks swallows these bivalves whole while under water, as it never seems to bring anything to the surface.

78

BUFFLE-HEAD

Charitonetta albeola (LINNAEUS). PLATE 16.

Other names: Butter-ball; Dipper Duck; Spirit Duck; Dipper; Dapper.

IDENTIFICATION. — Length 12 to 15 inches; spread 22 to 25 inches. Smaller than Blue-winged Teal, and 'chunkier'; male looks black and white with large head, black with purple gloss and large triangular white patch from below eye around back of head; black back; conspicuous white wing-patch; female a small dusky brownish duck with large head and whitish patch back of eye, which, with shape of bill, distinguish it from Ruddy Duck; male Hooded Merganser has white patch on side of head edged posteriorly with black, and slender bill; female brownish with single white patch back of eye.

BREEDING. — *Nest:* In hollow of tree. *Eggs:* 2 to 14, usually 6 to 8, buffy-drab to cream color.

RANGE. — Breeds from Alaska and British Columbia to Hudson Bay and south to northern Montana; winters from Alaska to central Mexico, and from Montana, the Great Lakes, and the coast of Maine south to northern Florida and the Gulf coast of Louisiana and Texas.

After a winter storm the handsome, hardy, vivacious little Buffle-head may be seen at its best. The sea still rages, and the white-topped surges pound and roar upon the seaworn ledges, tossing the spouting, snow-white spray high in the sunlit air. A piercing northwest wind cuts the spindrift from the rollers and carries it seaward in sheets. The western sun lights up the heaving sea and the acres of foaming white water that now at low tide rush upon the shallows of the beach. Most of the ducks have flown to the harbor or to the creeks in the salt marsh, but a few hardy White-winged Scoters and Old-squaws lie out on the open sea; close inshore, in shoal water and in the very boiling of the surf, groups of little Buffle-heads ride easily, swimming and diving as unconcernedly as if on some calm, untroubled pool. Now and then the surf seems to break directly over a bird; but at the instant when the towering crest seems to fall on its uplifted head, the head is no longer there. The little duck has dived either to the bottom for food or to reappear as before riding easily on the farther slope of the wave. The Buffle-heads play in the white-topped surf. They are perfectly at home and not in the least inconvenienced by foaming surge, raging wind or stinging cold. They seem cheerful, happy and contented, intent only on a supply of food that will enable them to withstand the cold and stress of winter on a wave-beaten coast.

On our shores Buffle-heads usually keep by themselves in small flocks on favorite feeding-grounds. They float lightly when undisturbed, with puffed-out heads drawn down between their shoulders, while the white feathers of the sides and flanks of the males are thrown up over the wings which seemingly are held close to the sides as the birds dive.

In migration Buffle-heads commonly appear late in October or in November in New England, and in March or early April return north in smaller numbers. In interior waters they are seen more frequently in autumn than in spring; they rarely occur in winter in the interior.

The food of the Buffle-head while on our coast consists largely of small marine forms of life. In the interior it takes small bivalves and minnows and on its breeding-grounds eats many insects and snails.

OLD–SQUAW

Clangula hyemalis (LINNAEUS).

PLATE 16.

Other names: Old Injun; Old Wife; Scolder; Scoldenore; South-southerly; Cockawee.

IDENTIFICATION. — Length 21 to 23½ inches; spread about 29 to 30 inches. Male unmistakable when long tail can be seen; in winter male has white dark-sided head, dark pointed wing without light speculum, blackish breast, and much white on body; female similar but with shorter tail; in summer male has brown head and neck with white patch on side of face; in flight Old-squaws have a spotted or pied appearance.

BREEDING. — On tundra. *Nest:* A depression on ground, in moss or grass, lined with down. *Eggs:* 6 to 10, greenish-gray.

RANGE. — Breeds on the Arctic coasts and barren lands of both hemispheres, south in North America to Labrador, Hudson Bay to Cape Jones and Churchill, southern Yukon Territory, down the Pacific coast to northwestern British Columbia; winters on the Atlantic coast south to Chesapeake Bay and North Carolina, on the Pacific coast to Washington and California, and in the interior on the Great Lakes and irregularly south to Texas, also in the Old World.

As the autumn sun retreats southward and leaves the Arctic sea in cold and darkness, the hardy Old-squaws follow the retiring orb and so reach the shores of New England. Clothed in a thick coat of down and feathers they easily withstand the winter's cold. After a February storm when a northwest gale clears the sky and lashes the surface of the sea into white-capped breaking waves, hundreds of these birds seek the lee of our headlands. While crossing on such a day from Woods Hole to Naushon Island, on the southern Massachusetts coast, we saw hosts of Old-squaws and many White-winged Scoters riding the waves. As our boat with close-reefed sail leaped and plunged over the choppy seas, the piercing wind continually dashed chilling showers of spray over us until deck, sail and rigging were encased with a heavy coating of ice. But the happy birds swarming into the air in flight before us or diving and playing on either hand showed not a trace of ice upon their plumage. The sea is their element and they seem to joy in riding crested surges. After such a winter storm on our coast while the bellowing surf still beats madly on the rocks, one may see the vigorous Old-squaws riding on the face of a towering wave and diving in time to avoid the white and toppling crest — perfectly at home on the wintry sea. This species is full of life and vigor. It is one of the swiftest ducks that flies. When alarmed its flight is often so erratic that it shows its back and then its breast as it turns and wheels. When shot at in flight, it will sometimes turn and plunge downward into the sea and swim away under water. In alighting it occasionally turns to check its impetus, but almost always plumps into the water with a great splash and often shoots straight ahead for some distance along the surface before its momentum is checked. It is a powerful diver, and as it goes under, always, so far as I have observed, spreads its wings somewhat. It is said to use them in under-water swimming.

The courtship of the Old-squaw is characterized by an act that I have never seen so prominently displayed by any other duck. As the male swims about the female, his tail is sometimes raised high and wagged horizontally, widely and rapidly like the tail of a dog; occasionally the wagging tail is only a trifle lifted. The male pursues the female both when she dives and when she flies. The male commonly throws the head over until it touches the back, and often both sexes stretch the neck out along the water.

Old-squaws are perhaps our most loquacious ducks. Their resounding cries have been likened to the music of a pack of hounds. The 'towering' of these birds is well described by Mr. George H. Mackay as follows: 'These ducks have a habit of towering both in the spring and in the autumn, usually in the afternoon, collecting in mild weather in large flocks if undisturbed, and going up in circles so high as to be scarcely discernible, often coming down with a rush and great velocity, a portion of the flock scattering and coming down in a zigzag course similar to the scoters when whistled down. The noise of their wings can be heard for a great distance under such conditions.'

EASTERN HARLEQUIN DUCK

Histrionicus histrionicus histrionicus (LINNAEUS). PLATE 17.

Other names: Rock Duck; Lord and Lady; Squealer; Sea Mouse.

IDENTIFICATION. — Length 15 to 18 inches; spread 24 to 27 inches. Male dark blue-gray with white patches; unmistakable at close range but at a distance white markings do not show and it looks all slaty-black except for chestnut on side; female resembles Buffle-head or Ruddy Duck, but small bill and two or three whitish patches on side of head identify her; young Old-squaw has whitish patch around eye.

BREEDING. — Usually near swift streams, on ground under rocks or logs, sometimes in hollow stumps. *Eggs:* 5 to 10, greenish-yellow or yellowish-buff.

RANGE. — Breeds in Iceland, Greenland, Baffin Island and northern Labrador, and probably in Newfoundland and the Gaspé Peninsula; winters south to the coast of Massachusetts and Long Island; resident in Iceland.

Harlequin! Rightly named, fantastically decorated, but nevertheless in beauty second only to the Wood Duck. The bird is so elegant that the people of the north coasts have well named its little companies the 'Lords and Ladies' of the sea. Unfortunately for most bird lovers, however, the beauty of these birds is reserved mainly for the far North, for mountain wildernesses or the wintry Atlantic where the waves dash on isolated, lonely offshore ledges.

It has never been my good fortune to see the eastern race of this rare and lovely duck, but in summer I have watched by the hour many flocks of Pacific Harlequins on the west coast near the Straits of Fuca. While suspicious of the slightest motion, this duck seems not to notice a motionless figure on the shore. While sitting once in a little cove I watched a flock of Harlequins at their play until they swam within a few feet of me. At my first motion, however, they churned the water into foam in their frantic flight. They are very playful birds and chase one another like children at a game of tag.

The Harlequin is equally at home on the quiet waters of some sheltered bay, on a rushing mountain torrent or amid the tumult of the crested seas that break in winter on our coast. The downy young soon reach their favorite element in some mountain stream where they dive and bob about in rushing waters and among the rocks, as much at home as are their parents on the restless sea.

The last of the Eastern Harlequins are leaving their breeding-grounds in Greenland when in early November the species first appears on the New England coast. Once they came in small flocks; now rarely more than a few individuals are observed together. They may be seen well offshore, along the rocky islands and ledges on the coast of Maine, off Cape Ann, or even about Martha's Vineyard or Nantucket, where a few sometimes spend part of the winter. Occasionally they reach Montauk Point on Long Island.

The food of the Eastern Harlequin in salt water consists largely of mussels and other mollusks and crustaceans (with some small fish) and is obtained mainly by diving.

LABRADOR DUCK
Camptorhynchus labradorius (GMELIN).

Other names: Pied Duck; Sand Shoal Duck; Skunk Duck.

Probably bred on the coast of the Ungava Peninsula and wintered on the Atlantic coast from Nova Scotia to New Jersey and possibly Chesapeake Bay, but now extinct.

The Labrador Duck or Pied Duck was first described by Gmelin. It is supposed to have bred in a limited area along the north coast of the Gulf of St. Lawrence, but may have gone much farther north. About all that we really *know* about its extinction is that the last recorded living specimen died by the hand of man near Long Island, New York, in 1875, and that according to Mr. William Dutcher, who made a painstaking investigation of the matter, there were in 1894 but forty-two specimens recorded in the museums of the world, of which thirty were then in North America. Since Mr. Dutcher made this report, a few additional specimens have been discovered in collections.

Statements that its breeding range was limited to the southern coast of the Labrador peninsula apparently are not substantiated by any direct evidence. We really know nothing about its nesting place or its nest and eggs. The opinion expressed by Professor Alfred Newton in his 'Dictionary of Birds,' that 'the shooting down of nesting birds witnessed by Audubon when he was among the islands on the Labrador coast could have produced no other result' than the extermination of the birds, is based on the supposition that this was their breeding range.

To the depredations of the natives may be added those of the eggers as described by Audubon, and those of the American feather hunters. As early as the middle of the eighteenth century vessels were fitted out on the New England coast for the express purpose of visiting Labrador and capturing birds that bred there, for their feathers. These excursions were made evidently in the breeding season, when the adult wild-fowl had lost the power of flight through the molting of their wing-quills, and before the young were able to fly. Amos Otis, a historian of Barnstable County, Massachusetts, asserts that large numbers of wild-fowl congregated to breed on barren islands off the Labrador coast where the crews of these feather vessels surrounded them, drove them together and killed them with clubs. He says that 'millions of wild-fowl' were thus destroyed, and a few years later (after 1760) their haunts were so broken up by this wholesale slaughter, and their numbers were so reduced, that feather voyages became unprofitable and were given up. If the Labrador Duck had been definitely known to breed in that region and only there we might with confidence attribute its extinction largely to the depredations upon sea-birds in the breeding season, which have continued almost to the present day. As it is, we can only conjecture that the Labrador Duck was exterminated by the hand of man.

Dr. D. G. Elliot said that between 1860 and 1870 he saw a considerable number of females and young males of the species in the New York market, but that the full-plumaged males were then exceedingly rare. Although we have no later record of the bird in that market, no one realized then that it was rapidly approaching extinction or that the last recorded specimen would be taken in 1875.

NORTHERN EIDER

Somateria mollissima borealis (BREHM).   PLATE 17.

Other name: Greenland Eider.
   IDENTIFICATION. — Ordinarily indistinguishable in the field from *S. m. dresseri;* the membranous processes extending from the bill toward the eye are narrow and pointed in *borealis*, broad and rounded in *dresseri;* there is less greenish color on the side of the head in *borealis*.
   BREEDING. — See American Eider.
   RANGE. — Breeds on the coastal islands of Greenland and eastern Arctic islands, south on the Atlantic coast to Labrador (Hamilton Inlet), and Quebec; winters from southern Greenland to the coast of Maine, rarely to Massachusetts and Connecticut.

AMERICAN EIDER

Somateria mollissima dresseri SHARPE.   PLATE 17.

Other names: Shoal Duck; Black and White Coot; Sea-duck; Wamp.
   IDENTIFICATION. — Length 20 to 26 inches; spread 39 to 42 inches. Large heavily built sea-ducks; male black under plumage, tail and top of head contrast strongly with white of breast and upper plumage; female warm ruddy brown above and below; sloping forehead and bill distinguish it from scoters.
   BREEDING. — Usually on rocky islands or shores. *Nest:* On ground, of moss, grass, weeds, etc., lined with down. *Eggs:* 3 to 10 or 12, pale greenish-olive.
   RANGE. — Breeds on coastal islands of southern Labrador, Newfoundland, eastern Quebec, Nova Scotia, and Maine, also on Hudson Bay and James Bay; winters on the sea-coast from Newfoundland and the Gulf of St. Lawrence to Massachusetts and rarely to Virginia.

The great, sturdy, handsome American Eider passes by the outer points along the New England coast, and thousands feed in winter on the shoals off Martha's Vineyard and Nantucket. This species is not often seen from the mainland, as it chiefly keeps to the sea. In migration its flocks may be seen on or near outlying rocks and ledges such as those off the Maine coast, off Cape Ann and Squibnocket, and those off Sakonnet Point, Rhode Island. Eiders are sometimes abundant in early April off Chatham, Massachusetts. They are rare farther south.

   Dr. C. W. Townsend says that the male American Eider in courtship frequently repeats his love-notes, which have so much volume that they 'can be heard at a considerable distance over water' and that the tones vary, much as do those of the human voice. Sometimes the head of the bird is drawn down with the bill on the breast and then raised until it is vertical; then the head is jerked stiffly backward and returned to its usual position. The eager bird frequently displays his black belly by rising almost upright on the water. At times he throws back his head and flaps his wings. The female may seem indifferent to this display or may show her appreciation by facing him and 'throwing up her head a little.'

At low tide Eiders may be seen in small companies sitting on wave-washed rocks that rise above the surface or floating on the water near them. Their favorite haunts lie about the sunken rocks where they chiefly find their food, and at night they leave the neighborhood of these rocks in flocks and fly out to sea.

In the autumnal migration Eiders appear off the New England coast early in November and less commonly in October. In spring all but a few stragglers have left by the latter part of April, at which time some may have appeared already in Canadian Labrador.

Their food is obtained mainly by diving from a point usually just outside the breaking wave. They detach mussels from the rocks and come up again outside the breaker. I have seen a male Eider lying on the surface of the sea in calm weather at low tide, and taking mussels off a rock, sometimes at the surface and sometimes by submerging head and neck, but this must be unusual. In our waters they feed largely on mollusks and crustaceans. On their breeding-grounds Eiders are said to eat many small fish. Little is known about the vegetal food of the American Eider.

KING EIDER

Somateria spectabilis (LINNAEUS). PLATE 17.

Other names: Wamp's Cousin; King Bird.

IDENTIFICATION. — Length 21 to 24 inches; spread about 28 inches. Smaller than American Eider; adult males have pearl-gray top of head, and black scapulars, and wing is black with a white patch; female usually more rusty or buffy-brown than sooty-brown female American Eider.

BREEDING. — Similar to American Eider but eggs smaller.

RANGE. — Breeds on coast of Greenland and the entire Arctic coast of North America south to northern Labrador, James Bay, St. Lawrence and St. Matthew islands, and Bering Sea, also from Spitzbergen to Siberia; winters from southern Greenland to the coast of New York, and the Great Lakes, and from Bering Sea to southern Alaskan islands, also in the Old World.

The King Eider is a bird of the cold northern seas, and seldom journeys much farther south than the Massachusetts coast in its migrations from its breeding-grounds on the Arctic islands and coasts. In its winter haunts it is quite local, and so is often absent from considerable areas where the commoner ducks like the Old-squaw, Golden-eye, or American Eider are found. In Massachusetts, for example, it is almost unknown on most of Cape Cod, on Nantucket, and on the south side of Martha's Vineyard, though small numbers can usually be found at the extreme western end of the Vineyard and near Dartmouth and Westport on the southern mainland of Massachusetts. At this latter place it is well known by the local duck hunters, who speak of the American Eider as 'Wamp' and the King Eider as 'Wamp's Cousin.' Probably this species crosses the head of Buzzards Bay in migration instead of circling Cape Cod, and makes this region a stopping place on the way to the east end of Long Island where some numbers also spend the winter. They are able to dive to the bottom in fairly deep water, and so usually keep pretty well offshore and are hard to identify except from a boat. Occasionally a few birds continue south to New Jersey or even to the Virginia coastal waters, but many more winter north of New England, on the Bay of Fundy and the unfrozen parts of the Gulf of St. Lawrence.

Mr. W. Sprague Brooks, who observed this species in Alaska, gives the following account of its courtship: 'On June 14 when approaching a small lagoon but still unable to see it owing to a slight elevation of the tundra before me, I heard a strange sound on the other side of the elevation. This peculiar noise came in series of three "Urrr-URRR-*URRR*," the last being the loudest, a sort of drumming call as when one expels air forcibly through the mouth with the tongue lightly pressed against the palate. I heard this noise once before during the winter made by an Eskimo and used with indifferent results for encouraging his dog team. I thought this call was an invention of his own at the time, but when in sight of the lagoon I found that the disturbance came from a small flock of King Eiders, three females and five males. They were on the beach and three males were squatted in a triangle about a female, each about a yard from her. They did much neck-stretching, as many male ducks do in the spring, and frequently bowed the head forward. The males constantly uttered the above drumming note. During this time the female was very indifferent to the attentions of her suitors, doing nothing more than occasionally extending her head towards one of them. After a brief period of these tactics, one or more of the males would enter the water and bathe vigorously with much bowing of heads and stretching of necks, to return to the beach in a few moments and repeat the foregoing performance.' — (J.B.M.)

WHITE–WINGED SCOTER

Melanitta deglandi (BONAPARTE).   PLATE 18.

Other names: Black White-wing; Bull White-wing; May White-wing; Eastern White-wing; Gray White-wing; Pied-winged Coot; Sea Brant; White-eyed Coot; Half-moon-eye.

IDENTIFICATION. — Length 19½ to 23 inches; spread 34 to 41 inches. Stocky, thick-necked, black or sooty sea-duck with large white wing-patches; male has small white eye-patch.

BREEDING. — *Nest:* On ground, of grass and twigs, lined with down. *Eggs:* 6 to 14, pale salmon-buff to cream.

RANGE. — Breeds from Alaska and central British Columbia to Hudson Bay, Ungava, the Gulf of St. Lawrence, central North Dakota, and northeastern Washington; winters from the Gulf of St. Lawrence to South Carolina on the Atlantic coast, from Alaska to Lower California on the Pacific coast, and irregularly in the interior, from British Columbia to Florida.

In the 'Auk' for 1891 Mr. George H. Mackay, in an excellent account of the scoters on the New England coast, expressed the opinion that the Surf Scoter was then the most numerous of the three species. Today the White-winged Scoter seems to be most abundant. For this change in relative numbers no single definite reason can be given. As our birds winter on the Atlantic coast and breed in the Far North or in the interior, making long journeys over land and sea, we cannot know all the circumstances and conditions which govern their increase and decrease. Shooting the birds in fall, winter, and spring, and the destruction of their nests and eggs by man have had their effect in reducing numbers, and these causes may have worked unevenly with the different species. On the New England coast it has been the custom of gunners to mark some of the most favorable points at which to intercept these birds on their migrations, and to anchor their boats in line, at suitable distances from one another, in such a way that the flight, keeping steadily on, must pass by or over some of the boats. In this way great numbers of birds were killed formerly, and many are thus taken still. In early years the species was one of the least shy and suspicious of the water-fowl. It seemed to be so stupid as to be attracted by almost any kind of a black wooden block or anything resembling a duck, and seemed to consider itself safe in the company of the most grotesque and clumsy and unnatural of wooden decoys. It flew low down, passing close by the gunner's boat, and about all the gunner had to do was to 'lead' the bird enough with the muzzle of the gun to be sure to put the charge into its head or neck, for the White-wing is swift on the wing. In recent years, however, the 'coots' have been 'hammered' so much along our coasts that they have learned a little caution. They fly higher over the boats, and judge better the distance called gun-shot range. This species, however, is as unsuspicious as any. A flock flying over a boat too high to be within range is sometimes brought down near the water by a shout or a gun-shot. The shaking of a gun-case or the throwing up of a hat may have a similar effect.

In autumnal migration the White-wings begin usually to pass Cape Ann a little later than the first of the American Scoters, but soon after the middle of September the flight is likely to be moving in force and reaches its height in October. Multitudes of this species spend the winter on the shoals and in the sounds off Nantucket, Muskeget and Martha's Vineyard. In April large flights pass northward and eastward, their movements, as always, being intermittent, and depending on conditions of wind and weather. Southwest winds seem to be favorable, but not absolutely necessary for these flights. In some years the birds dribble along steadily in small numbers; in other years great flights pass on a few favorable days. A part of the spring flight crosses Cape Cod and goes up the South Shore of Massachusetts; another part goes around outside of Cape Cod. Later in May there is a great flight to the west and northwest. The flight consists mainly if not entirely of mated adult birds ready for breeding, among which are a few of the other scoters. The flight is erratic, changing more or less in location and direction from time to time and from year to year, but all tend generally to keep the same approximate course. On the Connecticut coast it turns overland toward the Connecticut and Hudson valleys, crossing the land mainly at night and probably passing to the Great Lakes and from there to the inland breeding-grounds of the great Northwest, perhaps going on even to the shores of the Arctic.

SURF SCOTER

Melanitta perspicillata (LINNAEUS).   PLATE 18.

Other names: Skunk-head; Skunk-top; Skunk-bill; Bald-headed Coot; Butter-boat-bill; Gogglenose; Horsehead; King Coot; Mussel-bill; Patch-head; Surf Duck; Surf Coot; Surfer; Patch-polled Coot; Pishaug; Plaster-bill; Black Duck.

IDENTIFICATION. — Length 18 to 22 inches; spread 30 to 36 inches. Male black with white patches on forehead and nape, lacks white on wing; female dusky-brown with whitish patch on nape and two whitish patches on side of head.

BREEDING. — Similar to White-winged Scoter.

86

RANGE. — Breeds from Alaska and casually Greenland, south to the Gulf of St. Lawrence, Ungava, James Bay, northern Manitoba, and Alberta; winters on the Atlantic coast from the Bay of Fundy to Florida, on the Pacific from the Aleutian Islands to Lower California, on the Great Lakes, in the interior of southern British Columbia, and in Louisiana.

The name of the Surf Scoter is descriptive. It feeds much along the shore outside the breakers and often 'scoots' through a great wave as its crest breaks into foam, bobbing up like a cork on its farther side or, avoiding the breaking wave in another way, dives to the bottom to feed. It is not so common as the White-winged Scoter on the shoals at long distances from the shore and is usually rare in our interior waters, though sometimes driven to them by stress of weather, during migration. It has all the swimming and diving powers of the other scoters and uses both wings and feet for progression under water as occasion requires. Mr. Frank M. Woodruff has collected eiders and scoters on both Atlantic and Pacific coasts and in 'sailing down' the birds he has frequently stood by the mast where he could watch the progress of one of them under water. The wings were held about one-third spread and perfectly rigid. Used as planes or rudders they held the bird under water and on its course while the feet drove it onward. Both feet were used at once with powerful strokes. Mr. George H. Mackay asserts that in his experience wounded scoters when pursued and diving always use the wings as well as the feet.

Probably in the fall migration, which usually begins toward the middle of September and is at its height before the middle of October, continuing into November, most of the Surf Scoters pass outside Cape Cod, and great flights continue south of Long Island. The adults are the first to arrive; the young usually are much later. Late in March or early in April the return migration begins to pass our shores. This species and the American Scoter are likely to be on their way north before the White-wings begin to move, but after the middle of May there is a large movement of Surf Scoters.

AMERICAN SCOTER

Oidemia americana SWAINSON. PLATE 18.

Other names: Coot; Black Coot; Black Butterbill; Black Coot Butterbill; Butternose; Copperbill; Copper-nose; Yellow-nose; Yellow-bill; Punkin-blossom-coot; Whistling Coot; (for female and immature) Little Gray Coot; Smutty Coot; Smutty.

IDENTIFICATION. — Length 17 to 21 inches; spread 30 to 35 inches. Male all black plumage, yellow base of bill; female and young, identified by black cap, light sides of head, and absence of two whitish patches on side of head.

BREEDING. — Similar to White-winged Scoter. *Eggs:* Pale ivory-yellow.

RANGE. — Breeds from Siberia and the Bering Sea coast of Alaska to James Bay and Newfoundland; winters on the Atlantic coast from Maine to New Jersey and irregularly southward, on the Pacific from the Pribilof Islands to southern California, and to Japan and China, and in the interior to the Great Lakes, and irregularly farther.

Instead of being known as a coot, the American Scoter should be called the 'Black Duck,' for the male is the only American duck with entirely black plumage. Like all scoters it is tough, hardy, a quick and excellent diver, hard to kill and difficult to secure when wounded.

It can swim a long distance under water and uses both wings and feet at need for under-water progression.

As there are always some scoters in summer off the coasts of Maine and Nova Scotia, this species or either of the other two may be driven in on the New England coast at that season by a severe easterly gale; otherwise a very few non-breeding or crippled birds are seen there in summer, but the species is most abundant in fall and spring. Occasionally by the first of September a few small flocks pass along our coast, but usually no important movement occurs until the latter half of the month. At this season they are usually seen flying alongshore on days of light easterly winds. Such days appear to be favorable for their migrations. Strong westerly winds drive them offshore and strong easterly gales are likely to drive them into harbors and estuaries; on windy days they fly low in a long line, often headed by an old male. In calm weather they frequently fly quite high and not very far outside the beach. In October they continue to pass and are common, but in winter much less so, the majority of this species wintering off the Long Island and New Jersey coasts. The greater part of the spring flight northward along our coasts takes place in April and early May. By the latter part of May many scoters arrive on their breeding-grounds in the Far North.

All the scoters feed very largely on mussels which they can bring up from a depth of about forty feet in salt water. The principal food of the American Scoter seems to be mussels, but other bivalves, such as small sea-clams, short razor-shells, and small scallops, are taken in considerable quantity. In inland ponds or lakes which they sometimes frequent they take fresh-water clams.

RUDDY DUCK

Erismatura jamaicensis rubida (WILSON).   PLATE 18.

Other names: Butter-ball; Black-jack; Blue-bill; Broad-bill; Daub Duck; Dipper; Dapper; Dopper; Broad-bill Dipper; Creek Coot; Pond Coot; Dumb Bird; Goose Widgeon; Stiff-tailed Widgeon; Widgeon Coot; Hard-head; Tough-head; Steel-head; Sleepy-head; Hard-headed Broad-bill; Booby; Murre; Pintail; Spoon-bill; Gray Teal; Bumble-bee Coot; Salt-water Teal; Shot Pouch; Spike-tail.

IDENTIFICATION. — Length 13½ to 17 inches; spread 20 to 24 inches. Small size, stocky thick-necked form, and large upturned bill, distinguish the little Ruddy Duck; male in breeding plumage largely rusty red with white cheeks, black crown, and blue bill; in winter gray with white cheeks, blackish crown; female similar to male in winter but with dark line across whitish cheek; often 'cocks' its tail when swimming; short quick wing-stroke when flying.

BREEDING. — In marshes and sloughs. *Nest:* Near water, often floating among reeds, of dry stems of water-plants and lined with down. *Eggs:* 5 to 15, grayish-white to buffy-white, rough surface.

RANGE. — Breeds from central British Columbia to northern Manitoba and south to western Minnesota, northern Iowa, southeastern Wisconsin, southeastern Michigan, northern Illinois, central Texas, central Arizona, and Lower California; winters on the Atlantic coast from Chesapeake Bay (more rarely from Massachusetts), to Florida, the Bahamas, and West Indies, on the Pacific coast from southern British Columbia to Lower California, Guatemala, and Costa Rica, and in the interior from central Arizona, southern Illinois, and western Pennsylvania southward.

The following account is slightly altered from my own writing in the 'Nature Lovers' Library':

'The sprightly, comical little Ruddy Duck is a distinctly North America species and is distributed widely over the continent. It is perfectly at home on or under water and dislikes

88

to leave it, often preferring to attempt escape by diving rather than by flying. This makes it easy game for the gunner, as a flock will sometimes remain in a salt pond so small that any part of it may be reached from the shore with a shotgun, diving at every shot until those left alive essay to fly and most of them pay the penalty of their simplicity with their lives. They can dive so quickly that they often escape unharmed. Like the grebes they possess the power of sinking slowly down backward out of sight, but like them also they rise from the water with some labor and difficulty. They are extremely tough, hardy little birds and gunners know them by such names as Tough-head, Hard-head, Steel-head, etc. Other local names, such as Booby, Noddy, and Fool Duck, indicate a lack of respect for the birds' perspicacity.

'When the famous Canvas-back first showed signs of scarcity on the Atlantic coast, a price was put upon the head of the Ruddy Duck to meet the market demand. Unfortunately for its safety it feeds upon delicate grasses and other vegetable aliment in preference to sea-food. Therefore, its flesh is a passable substitute for that of the Canvas-back. So the market gunners have pursued it until its numbers are no longer legion and its chances for extinction are good.

'The male is a handsome bird in the breeding season, but presents rather a ridiculous appearance in mating time, as he swims pompously about with his head lifted proudly and drawn away back toward the spread tail, which is raised and thrown forward as if to meet it.

'This Duck nests in prairie sloughs, where the broods remain until after all the other breeding Ducks have departed. Old and young are regular gourmands and, according to Gurdon Trumbull, gunners near the mouth of the Maumee River told of finding them floundering helplessly fat on the water and in some seasons floating about dead or dying in numbers. But this was before the days of the market demand for their flesh. They do not have so much time to get fat now.'

In rising from the water the Ruddy Duck flutters and splatters along the surface. In flight it looks short and dumpy and usually flies low, but its fast-beating wings drive it along at only medium speed. Its diving for food is usually done in shallow water and it goes down not vertically but diagonally. It is an excellent diver, however, and its large feet and strong wings used together propel it to considerable depths.

This duck when swimming on the surface rides so low in the water as to seem partly submerged and it never has far to go to get below the surface. Being remarkably quick on land or water it 'gets under' like a flash when a gun is fired at it and it often escapes with its life.

HOODED MERGANSER

Lophodytes cucullatus (LINNAEUS).   PLATE 11.

Other names: Hooded Sheldrake; Wood Sheldrake; Pond Sheldrake; Pickaxe Sheldrake; Spike-bill; Hairy-crown; Hairy-head; Saw-bill Diver; Water Pheasant; Kokus Sheldrake.

IDENTIFICATION. — Length 16 to 19 inches; spread 24 to 26½ inches. Smallest merganser, smaller than Wood Duck; short, slender, *narrow* bill; male black and white with narrow or fan-shaped white-patched crested head, two black bars on front of wings, and brown sides; female with darker breast than other mergansers.

BREEDING. — In wooded swamps or forests near water. *Nest:* In hole in tree or stump, of grasses, weeds, and down. *Eggs:* 5 to 12, ivory-white.

RANGE. — Breeds locally throughout temperate North America from northern British Columbia, Manitoba, southern Ontario, and New Brunswick to New York, central Pennsylvania, eastern South Carolina, central Florida, southern Tennessee, northern Arkansas, northern New Mexico, and Oregon; winters mainly in Southern States north to Massachusetts, Pennsylvania, Lake Michigan, Nebraska, British Columbia, and southeastern Alaska, and south to Cuba and central eastern Mexico.

The cold and privations of winter have passed, and now in the solitude of small secluded pools, streams and ponds in swamp and forest the Hooded Mergansers disport themselves. Returning spring with its annual awakening kindles anew in their breasts the glowing fires of reproduction. The males, in all the splendor of their elegant spring plumage, seek and pay court to their prospective mates. Gallantly they dash back and forth, rippling the dark waters, expanding and contracting their flashing fan-shaped crests, now proudly rising erect on the water with bill pointed downward and head drawn back, now speeding in rapid rushes to and fro. The ardent males chase the females, pursuing them on the surface and even following them under water. I have lain prone amid grass and underbrush watching the kaleidoscopic changes of such a scene where several males, in splendid nuptial plumage, were coursing over the dark water in full display before an appreciative group of the other sex.

The Hooded Merganser is not ordinarily, like the American Merganser, a frequenter of swift waters, but seems to prefer slow streams and quiet, shaded pools. Nevertheless when wintering in the North, it goes by necessity to fast-running streams, river rapids or open spring-holes, and probably rarely seeks salt water, for I have never seen it in water more salt than brackish lagoons near the sea. It is not quite so wary as are the other mergansers and this lack of caution has led to its decimation. It is fond of decoy ducks which when employed by the gunner readily lead it to its doom. It is attracted readily to park ponds in which ducks are kept. It was formerly a common bird throughout a large part of the American continent. Now it is uncommon or rare over considerable areas. It is a swift and almost noise-less flier and easily threads its way among the branches of trees in its swampy woodlands. It lives in haunts similar to those of the Wood Duck, and as it also nests in hollow trees, it is known as the 'Wood Duck' to many people on the Pacific coast.

Its nesting cavities often are very high above the ground. In many cases the young climb out of the nest soon after they are hatched and jump, scramble, fall or flutter to the ground or water below. It is said that sometimes the mother takes them, one at a time, and flies with them to the nearest water.

In early September when the young are well grown and fledged, they gather in small companies, and soon their travels begin. Very few adult males appear, but often the females and young are common locally at this season. In winter an occasional bird or two may be seen in favorable seasons in small ponds near the coast or on open water in the rivers of the Northern States. In spring the main northward flight passes through in late March or April. During the seasons of migration they frequent the haunts of the Wood Duck and the Black Duck but do not often associate with them.

The Hooded Merganser is not at all dependent on fish, although, like its larger congeners, it eats them. It remains for considerable periods in ponds where there are no fish. It takes small frogs, tadpoles, insects, seeds and even the roots or bulbs of water-plants, and has been known to eat corn.

AMERICAN MERGANSER

Mergus merganser americanus CASSIN.　　　　　　　　　　　　　　　PLATE 11.

Other names: Buff-breasted Merganser; Fishduck; Sawbill; Sheldrake; Fresh-water Sheldrake; Pond Sheldrake; Swamp Sheldrake; Bracket Sheldrake; Goosander; Breakhorn.

IDENTIFICATION. — Length 21 to 27 inches; spread 34 to 39 inches. Largest American duck: male with black head, upper neck and back (no crest), white breast, sides and flanks; female with reddish head, gray back and sides, *white chin* and under parts; both sexes have conspicuous white speculum, and long narrow bill, in flight neck is much longer than in similarly colored Golden-eye.

BREEDING. — About lakes and rivers. *Nest:* In hole in tree, sometimes among rocks on ground; of grass, twigs, leaves, and down. *Eggs:* 6 to 17, pale creamy-buff.

RANGE. — Breeds from Alaska, Hudson Bay, Ungava Peninsula, and Newfoundland south to west-central Nova Scotia, southern Maine, central New Hampshire, central Vermont, central New York, southeastern Ontario, central Michigan, northeastern Wisconsin, northwestern Minnesota, northern New Mexico, and central California; winters from the Aleutian Islands, Great Lakes, St. Lawrence Valley, and Prince Edward Island to Florida, the Gulf States, and northern Mexico.

Few ducks are handsomer in life than an adult male American Merganser. After death the evanescent rich salmon tint of the breast fades and disappears. The Merganser is a fresh-water fowl. It is likely to appear in migration on any of the larger bodies of fresh water in the Northern States. The large black-and-white male is conspicuous, and therefore the species is better known to the country people than any other wild duck except the Black Duck. It seldom is seen on the surface of the open sea unless it has been driven out of fresh water near the coast, but it frequents estuaries and backwaters where the tide runs in and out. Wherever the species may be met with, individuals of both sexes usually are seen together, and the females and young are readily identified when in company with the unmistakable adult males. They frequent fresh-water ponds and lakes near the sea, and some, if not molested, often remain in such bodies of water all winter or as long as the surface remains unfrozen. They are seen commonly on the larger rivers and sometimes are the most numerous ducks on streams like the Connecticut and the Merrimac. They are vigorous, hardy, stout-hearted fowls. Ice, snow, and cold have no terrors for them. Sufficient food and open water are enough to insure their presence in the severest winters.

The American Merganser is an excellent swimmer and diver. Like the grebes it can dive almost with the flash of a gun. It either springs forward clear of the water, dips under with hardly a ripple or sinks quietly out of sight, employing the method that seems best suited to the occasion. Sometimes in under-water swimming its wings are not used, but in pursuit of swift fishes it uses both its strong, webbed feet and its powerful wings to force it through the water, much in the manner of the fast-swimming loon. Sometimes in shallow water it follows fish on the surface, using both wings and feet in the chase. At times it rises into the air, flies along over the water and flies down again into and under the water, possibly in continued pursuit of swift fish. Mergansers sometimes swim slowly on the surface with necks extended and heads partially submerged in the manner observed in surface-feeding ducks, but whether they take in food in this manner or merely drink thus is still unknown.

When rising from the water the Merganser has to use both wings and feet in running or pattering on the surface before it gets impetus enough to launch itself in the air.

Dr. C. W. Townsend, in the 'Auk' for 1916, thus graphically describes the courtship display of the male American Merganser:

'The courtship of the Merganser ... is fairly spectacular and differs widely from that of its red-breasted cousin, *M. serrator*....

'A group of five or six male Mergansers may be seen swimming energetically back and forth by three or four passive females. Sometimes the drakes swim in a compact mass or in a file for six or seven yards or even farther, and then each turns abruptly and swims back. Again they swim in and out among each other, and every now and then one with swelling breast and slightly raised wings spurts ahead at great speed by himself or in the pursuit of a rival.... They frequently strike at each other with their bills, and I have seen two splendid drakes rise up in the water breast to breast, and, amid a great splashing, during which it was impossible to see details, fight like game-cocks. The pursuit is varied by sudden, momentary dives and much splashing of water.

'The smooth iridescent green heads, the brilliant carmine bills tipped with black nails, the snowy white of flanks and wing-patches and the red feet, which flash out in the dive, make a wonderful color effect, contrasting well with the dark water and white ice. The smaller females with their shaggy brown heads, their neat white throat-bibs, their quaker blue-gray backs and modest wing-patches, which are generally hidden, are fitting foils to their mates.' The male frequently raises himself up almost on his tail and displays the beautiful salmon-yellow tint on the whole under surface of his body. 'Most of the time he keeps his tail cocked up and spread, so that it shows from behind a white center and blue border. Every now and then he points his head and closed bill up at an angle of forty-five degrees or to the zenith. Again he bows or bobs his head nervously and often at the same time tilts up the front of his breast from which flashes out the salmon tint. From time to time he emits a quickly repeated purring note, *dorr-dorr* or *krr-krr*.

'The most surprising part of the performance is the spurt of water fully three or four feet long which every now and then is sent backwards into the air by the powerful kick of the drake's foot....'

Although many American Mergansers still breed in northern New England, probably most individuals that are seen there in migration come from much farther north. The first October arrivals are early birds, as Mergansers are late migrants and pass south only when forced by ice and cold storms. They do not usually become common until late October and November. Even in December many may remain in the interior until ice closes most of the fresh waters and the ducks are driven south or to the sea. As soon as the ice begins to break up in March the Mergansers follow closely. In spring they migrate in numbers through New England in March and early April according to the season, resting for a time on the large ponds or streams as they go. In migration they usually fly very high in wedge-shaped formation, but in moving from place to place and especially upstream they commonly fly low over the water.

American Mergansers feed on fish, destroying many small minnows, but are not confined to an exclusive fish diet. They feed also on shell-fish, and nobody knows to what extent they may eat vegetal matter. Along the coast in winter they consume many mussels and other mollusks, swallowing shell and all; the shells are soon ground up in the stomach, and in the process of digestion are reduced to 'impalpable mud' at the end of the digestive tract.

RED–BREASTED MERGANSER

Mergus serrator LINNAEUS.   PLATE 11.

Other names: Shell-bird; Shelduck; Sheldrake; Salt-water Sheldrake; Saw-bill; Fish Duck; Sea Robin.

IDENTIFICATION. — Length 20 to 25 inches; spread 31 to 35 inches. Much like American Merganser of same sex and age; male has thin double crest and broad band of dark streaks across breast; female has throat gray, lacking sharply contrasted white chin of American Merganser.

BREEDING. — *Nest:* On ground, of grass, weeds, roots, etc., lined with down. *Eggs:* 6 to 16, dull creamy-buff, darker than those of American Merganser.

RANGE. — Breeds from the Arctic coast of Alaska, northern Ungava, and the coast of Greenland south to Newfoundland, Nova Scotia, New Brunswick, coast of Maine, northern New York, central Ontario, central Michigan, Wisconsin, central Minnesota, southern Manitoba, northern British Columbia, and the Aleutian Islands; winters on the Atlantic and Gulf coasts from Maine to Florida and Texas, and on the Pacific coast from southeastern Alaska to Lower California, and in the interior from the Great Lakes southward; also occurs in Europe, Asia and Africa.

The Red-breasted Merganser is one of the most abundant water-fowl that migrates along our coast, but it is almost unknown to inland people. On the Atlantic coast it breeds mainly about fresh-water ponds and streams near the sea, and as soon as the young are able to fly they seek salt water, on which they spend the greater part of the year. It may be found in the open sea, in sounds, bays and estuaries. It may seek shelter under the lee of islands or in ponds, but it seems to prefer sea-water. Like the loons it must be able to drink both salt and fresh water, for it breeds far in the interior in many northern lakes.

The Red-breasted Merganser is a skillful, rapid diver, at times using its half-spread wings as well as its feet for progression under water when pursuing swift fish, but seems not to be able to swim quite so fast or so far in this manner as the larger and more powerful American Merganser. Often on coming to the surface it rises erect and flaps its wings as if to shake off the water. It is wary and if wounded uses all manner of stratagems to escape from the gunner. It dives and conceals itself in submerged water-plants, swims away with only the bill above water and sometimes clings with its bill to some object on the bottom.

In mild days in March and early April the male Red-breasted Mergansers display their charms before the females. All seek some quiet bay and there in the sunlight under the lee of the shore, the bright males in their best feather gather with the females and pay them court. The male birds stretch up their heads showing their long, white necks, and then bob about with partially submerged breasts and widely opened beaks exhibiting their red bills and mouths to the best advantage. They rush back and forth, splashing the water with their flying feet and dashing sparkling jets three or four feet behind them. A male swims toward a female, throws his head out, forward and upward, with bill elevated, working his feet rapidly and sometimes flapping his wings, until under the urge of wings and splashing feet he rises upright in the water with head held proudly high and bill drawn in, turned down and resting upon his neck. The females often retreat and seem indifferent to their ardent lovers, but in time they grow more responsive and begin to bob and call in apparent excitement. This response often stirs up mad rivalry among the amorous males, which rush at each other with open bills in mimic war and sometimes seize their rivals, but I have never seen any resultant bloodshed.

93

The nest of the Red-breasted Merganser, like that of many other ducks, is built on the ground, usually well hidden by grass or sheltered by bushes, trees, rocks, or under the bank of a stream or pond. It is fairly well made, of grass, weeds, roots, or sometimes seaweed, and lined with gray down from the mother's breast. The American Merganser, and the smaller Hooded Merganser, on the other hand, nest in holes in trees or in the top of a broken stub, the other North American hole-nesting ducks being the Golden-eye and the beautiful little Wood Duck.

The female assumes the entire care of the young, while the male in his eclipse plumage either goes to sea or skulks amid rank water vegetation during the time when the flight-feathers of the wings are growing and he is unable to fly. The mother is very devoted to her young, and often in case of danger takes them on her back to insure their safety.

In late August or September, on their chosen breeding-grounds, the young Red-breasted Mergansers gather into large flocks led by some old female, and in October the main southward migration begins. The birds that appear in early fall seem to be all females and young, but probably some of them are adult males in their eclipse plumage, as usually they do not assume full adult winter plumage until November or later. By the second week in October this species usually is common locally on its chosen winter feeding-grounds either in shallow water near shore or over some outlying shoal. In October and November vast numbers pass along our shores. In December the numbers grow less but they are abundant locally all winter. Where they are much disturbed by gunners and power boats, they keep well offshore, where hundreds and sometimes thousands of them may be seen until midwinter, but usually they are found along the coast in small parties, often diving through the surf or feeding in secluded bays or estuaries.

Order Falconiformes. Diurnal Birds of Prey.

TURKEY VULTURE

Cathartes aura septentrionalis WIED.   PLATES 37 AND 38.

Other names: Turkey Buzzard; Buzzard; Red-necked Buzzard; Carrion Crow; John Crow.

IDENTIFICATION. — Length 26 to 32 inches; spread 68 to 72 inches. Size of small eagle: a large blackish bird with long and rather broad wings, medium rounded tail, and small naked red head (young have blackish heads); sails and soars much with wings held above the horizontal and separated primaries showing distinctly; tail usually closed, not spread fan-like; under surface of flight-feathers grayish in contrast to black under coverts.

BREEDING. — *Eggs:* Usually 2, creamy to dead white, blotched, splashed and spotted with browns, lavender, etc., laid on the ground among rocks or logs or in hollow log or a cave.

RANGE. — Breeds from southern British Columbia, southern Manitoba, northern Minnesota, Wisconsin, Michigan, southern Ontario, central New York, New Jersey, and Connecticut south to southern Lower California, the Gulf coast, and northern Mexico; winters throughout its regular range on the Atlantic slope but not north of the Ohio Valley, Nebraska, and California.

The Turkey Vulture, or 'Buzzard,' as it is commonly called in the South, leaves the ground with a bound and a few flaps, unless gorged with carrion, when it must disgorge much of its filthy cargo in order to enable it to get away; but when once in air and gaining height it moves with the ease of a master. No other American bird is so generally celebrated for its perfect

94

conquest of the aerial currents. It seems to sail and soar gracefully without effort and to gain altitude even in windless air with few motions of its widespread pinions, which carry it up as if by magic. It seems to materialize the flight of the dreamer who imagines that he floats through the air by the mere effort of his will.

There are, perhaps, not more than two or three Turkey Vultures to the square mile in their southern range, but on their aerial courses they patrol the land thoroughly, and probably there are few dead animals that escape their telescopic vision. Over hill and dale, lake and stream, farm, forest and village, the Buzzards wheel, adding life to the blue vault above, until one of the tireless birds sees some prospect of a feast. It may be that its keen eyes have spied a dead or dying animal, or a corpse rising to the surface of a stream, or even the village toper fallen by the wayside. Immediately the watchful fowl descends to the hoped-for feast, lowering its legs eagerly, long before it actually lights. Another, circling in the distant sky, sees that sudden 'stoop' and follows. Others in all directions mark the descending twain and wing their way to the common center. As they go they are seen from afar by others still, and soon every Vulture for miles around has assembled near the expected feast. Scores as they arrive alight on trees or fences, while a few of the boldest drop to the ground and with exceeding circumspection approach the object of their quest, for your Buzzard is a cowardly fowl and intends to take good care of his precious skin. They often gather thus, not only about dead animals, but also about the sick or disabled when death seems imminent. If the death of the victim seems assured they approach their prey. Over what follows let us draw the veil.

It is supposed that the Buzzards find their food entirely by sight; they frequently have failed to locate it when it has been covered by so frail a substance as paper; but their nostrils are large, and probably they have a sense of smell, as often they have hung about malodorous decaying bodies, apparently searching for them, but unable to discover them when hidden from sight.

BLACK VULTURE

Coragyps atratus atratus (MEYER). PLATE 38.

Other names: Carrion Crow; Black-headed Buzzard; Jim Crow; Black Buzzard.

IDENTIFICATION. — Length 24 to 27 inches; spread 54 to 59 inches. Smaller than Turkey Vulture, with shorter wings and short square tail; naked head blackish; conspicuous whitish area at base of primaries is excellent field mark; less graceful in flight than Turkey Vulture, sailing less and flapping frequently.

BREEDING. — Similar to Turkey Vulture. *Eggs:* 1 to 3, usually 2; grayish-green, creamy, or bluish-white, spotted and blotched with browns.

RANGE. — Resident from western Texas, Kansas, Missouri, southern Illinois, southern Indiana, Virginia, and southern Maryland south to Mexico and Central America.

In the South, especially near the coast, the Black Vulture is often a very common bird and with its larger relative, the Turkey Vulture, performs valiant service as a scavenger. Wherever animal waste, scraps, or garbage are thrown aside, these birds gather, and they are often to be seen along the highways feasting on the carcasses of animals which have been killed by speeding motor-cars. When stuffed to repletion on such foul matter they are very slow and sluggish in their movements, so that they often fall victim in their turn to the modern Juggernauts.

In some of the great rookeries of plume-birds in Florida the Black Vulture is a common neighbor of the herons and ibises, but the benefit is all to the Vultures, who are accused of eating both the eggs and the young birds whenever a chance offers. If a rookery is disturbed and the herons leave their nests even for a short time, the waiting Vultures begin their raiding without delay, and, with the Fish Crows, are among the worst enemies of the herons and other colony-nesting species. — (J.B.M.)

WHITE–TAILED KITE

Elanus leucurus majusculus BANGS AND PENARD.

Other names: Black-shouldered Kite; White Hawk; Black-winged Kite.

IDENTIFICATION. — Length 15 to 17 inches; spread about 40 inches. Pale bluish-gray above, lighter on head; white below; conspicuous black spot on upper wing coverts and smaller spot under wing; tail square, white except gray central feathers; narrow rather long wings.

BREEDING. — *Nest:* In trees, of twigs, lined with grasses, weeds, or moss. *Eggs:* 4 or 5, creamy-white, heavily blotched with browns.

RANGE. — Breeds locally in California, Texas, Oklahoma, and Florida south to Guatemala; winters throughout range.

The White-tailed Kite is an exceedingly attractive little bird, with its confiding and gentle disposition, its easy and graceful flight, and its low, plaintive whistle, but it is paying the penalty for being classed by many as a 'hawk,' and its numbers are very sadly diminished in this highly civilized land.

The flight of the White-tailed Kite is not particularly rapid and it does not show the spirit and dash of many of its relatives. When hunting its lowly prey it flies much in the open, beating back and forth across the fields and marshes with buoyant easy flight; or, with lightly fanning wings, wide-spread tail, and dangling legs, hovers briefly over its quarry, and then, elevating its wings over its body until they almost meet above its back, drops like a plummet to rise with a luckless grasshopper or field mouse clutched in its talons. At times it circles about at a moderate elevation, or sits quietly perched on a dead branch watching for its prey.

Mr. A. C. Bent gives it as his impression that 'this kite shows a decided preference for the vicinity of water, fresh-water marshes and streams; in such places it finds its food readily available all through the year, and it probably does not wander far away even in winter.' — (J.B.M.)

SWALLOW–TAILED KITE

Elanoides forficatus forficatus (LINNAEUS).   PLATES 38 AND 97

Other names: Forked-tailed Hawk; Snake Hawk; Forked-tailed Fish Hawk; Swallow-tail.

IDENTIFICATION. — Length 19½ to 25½ inches; spread 45 to 50 inches. Unmistakable (except possibly for Man-o'-war-bird); shape of gigantic Barn Swallow; white head and under plumage, glossy black above.

BREEDING. — In extensive woodlands and forested swamps. *Nest:* In top of tall tree, of twigs lined with moss. *Eggs:* 1 to 4, usually 2, whitish, heavily or sparsely spotted and blotched with browns and lavender.

RANGE. — Breeds locally from northern Minnesota, southern Wisconsin, southern Indiana, North Carolina, and South Carolina to Florida, Alabama, and eastern Mexico; winters south of the United States, occasionally in southern Florida.

The handsome, graceful Swallow-tailed Kite is pre-eminently a fowl of the air. In its chosen element it is supreme. It soars as gracefully as the Turkey Vulture, and in speed it is not often excelled. Its flight resembles in lightness the erratic flight of the Barn Swallow. It appears like a gigantic swallow as it catches insects in the air or flutters above the tree-tops; but anon it circles and soars straight up to heights beyond the scope of the human eye, remaining at times at such altitudes for from half an hour to an hour. Again, it swoops suddenly downward in the manner of the Nighthawk or turns over and over in the air. No pen can adequately describe the beauty, elegance and grace of its aerial evolutions. It is so much at home in the air that it devours its prey while on the wing, and it drinks by skimming rapidly like a swallow close to the surface of the water. I have seen it mostly flying over the wooded wildernesses of the South or perching on the tree-tops; but once seen it is not soon forgotten. Formerly it was a common bird as far north as the North-Central States, where it was seen in small flocks, but now it is only a straggler in that region, and is decreasing rapidly in the South. It is too tempting a target to exist long in thickly settled regions. In future it will be confined chiefly to the few remaining wildernesses of the South. It migrates southward early to the southern Americas but returns early in the spring to Florida.

The food of the Swallow-tailed Kite consists largely of snakes and other reptilian forms of life, frogs and insects, such as beetles, moths, caterpillars, crickets, grasshoppers, locusts, wasps and hornets. Large insects are taken chiefly by this bird while on the wing, either high in air or sweeping along the surface of the ground, but it sometimes alights and walks about in pursuit of grasshoppers. It is said also to be destructive to the cotton worm. It hovers over forest fires in pursuit of insects that escape the flames. Also it takes the eggs of reptiles, and there is one instance recorded by Dr. Rufus Hammond where an individual had swallowed some whole eggs of the catbird.

Apparently this bird does not pursue nor kill birds. It is a harmless, beautiful creature, and is considered beneficial because of the character of its insect food. It should be protected at all times by law, as it is now in danger of extirpation in North America.

MISSISSIPPI KITE

Ictinia misisippiensis (WILSON).

Other names: Louisiana Kite; Mosquito Hawk; Blue Kite.

IDENTIFICATION. — Length 14 to 15 inches; spread 36 inches. General bluish tone, almost white head, darker wings and black fan-shaped tail, small size and long pointed wings, distinguish this kite.

BREEDING. — In trees, 12 to 50 feet up. *Nest:* Of sticks lined with dead leaves or green leaves. *Eggs:* 1 to 3, whitish or bluish-white, normally unmarked.

RANGE. — Breeds from northeastern Kansas, southern Illinois, southern Indiana, and South Carolina south to Texas and Florida; winters in Florida and southern Texas and south to Central America.

The Mississippi Kite makes up in the grace of its flight what it lacks in color, for it is a very dull-appearing bird, with its generally bluish plumage, its dark wings and blackish tail, only lightened by its pale head and secondaries. Audubon said of this kite: 'Its flight is graceful, vigorous, protracted, and often extended to a great height, the Fork-tailed Hawk [Swallow-tailed Kite] being the only species that can compete with it. At times it floats in the air as if motionless, or sails in broad regular circles, when, suddenly closing its wings, it slides along to some distance, and renews its curves. Now it sweeps in deep and long undulations, with the swiftness of an arrow, passing almost within touching distance of a branch on which it has observed a small lizard, or an insect it longs for, but from which it ascends disappointed. Now it is seen to move in hurried zigzags, as if pursued by a dangerous enemy, sometimes seeming to turn over and over like a Tumbling Pigeon. Again it is observed flying around the trunk of a tree to secure large insects, sweeping with astonishing velocity. While traveling it moves in the desultory manner followed by Swallows; but at other times it is seen soaring at a great elevation among the large flocks of Carrion Crows and Turkey Buzzards, joined by the Fork-tailed Hawk, dashing at the former, and giving them chase, as if in play, until these cowardly scavengers sweep downwards, abandoning this to them disagreeable sport to the Hawks, who now continue to gambol undisturbed. When in pursuit of a large insect or a small reptile, it turns its body sidewise, throws out its legs, expands its talons, and generally seizes its prey in an instant. It feeds while on the wing, apparently with as much ease and comfort as when alighted on the branch of a tall tree.' — (J.B.M.)

EVERGLADE KITE

Rostrhamus sociabilis plumbeus RIDGWAY.

Other names: Snail Hawk; Hook-bill Hawk; Black Kite; Sociable Marsh Hawk.

IDENTIFICATION. — Length 16 to 18 inches; spread about 45 inches. Bill long and slender, strongly hooked. Wings much broader than in other kites, resembling those of Buteos; male dark slaty-blue except head and upper back which are lighter gray, and tail coverts, basal half of outer tail feathers and narrow tip of tail, which are white; female with upper parts rusty black, under parts streaked and mottled with brownish and buffy, some white on sides of head; young a more chestnut shade of brown much variegated.

BREEDING. — On bushes or rank vegetation in extensive fresh-water marshes. *Nest:* Of twigs and leafy sticks. *Eggs:* 2 to 4, dull white profusely marked with browns.

RANGE. — Breeds in peninsular Florida, Cuba, eastern Mexico, and Central America; winters from central Florida southward.

The highly specialized Everglade Kite feeds exclusively, as far as known, upon large snails of the genus *Ampullaria*, and it is therefore limited in its range in the United States to the vicinity of extensive fresh-water marshes in a restricted portion of the Florida peninsula. As drainage projects continue to dry up these marsh areas, the habitat of this interesting species becomes more and more restricted and there is real danger that this distinctive bird is due to disappear, before many years, as a breeding bird of the United States, unless active steps are taken to preserve it. Even as I write this, tremendously destructive forest fires have been sweeping over parts of the Everglades in Florida, the chosen habitat of this bird, not only destroying the surface cover but actually burning up the soil for a very considerable depth. These fires are the result of unintelligent drainage of the areas, which has lowered the water-level and allowed the rich vegetable loam to become dry and inflammable, loam which has probably taken thousands of years in its formation, and which cannot be renewed in less time. Not only are the birds and other wild life destroyed, but the rich agricultural land is ruined irreplaceably.

The feeding habits of the Everglade Kite are unique among members of the raptorial birds. The bird is an interesting example of special adaptations for a specialized food. Its bill is very long for that of a hawk or kite, and is very strongly curved or hooked. How the bird extracts the flesh of the big fresh-water snails upon which it feeds so exclusively, from their rather delicate shells, without destroying the latter, has been difficult to observe, but Herbert Lang, in the 'Nautilus' for 1924, described the operation as observed near Georgetown, British Guiana, and I quote my summary of his article from my own 'Hawks of North America':

'The snails remain in the water during the hotter part of the day, but in the early morning and late afternoon are found at the surface or creeping about on the marsh vegetation. The Kite quarters back and forth low over the water, suggesting a sea gull at a distance. Often it hovers over one spot for a considerable interval, then dives down to pick up a snail which it carries in its talons to some favorite perching place in a bush or low tree. Here it stands for several seconds motionless, on one leg, holding the snail in the long claws of the other foot. Soon the snail, which had withdrawn into its shell when picked up, closing tightly its operculum, begins slowly to extrude its slimy body. Suddenly, like a flash, the Kite grasps the body of the snail, between the operculum and the shell, in its blunt-edged but deeply hooked bill. The muscular contraction of the snail's body apparently detaches it from its attachment within the shell, and a moment later, with a shake of the Kite's head, the shell is tossed aside and the body swallowed, including the operculum. Favorite eating places are marked with considerable accumulations of empty snail shells.' — (J.B.M.)

EASTERN GOSHAWK

Astur atricapillus atricapillus (WILSON). PLATES 38 AND 39.

Other names: Blue Hawk; Partridge Hawk; Chicken Hawk; Big Blue Darter; Dove Hawk.

IDENTIFICATION. — Length of male 20 to 22 inches, spread 40 to 44 inches; length of female 22 to 26½ inches, spread 44 to 47 inches. A large long-tailed hawk with broad rounded wings; adult light gray below with barred tail and lighter above than any other Eastern hawk except male Marsh Hawk or White-tailed Kite, which are both much lighter; a black cap and white line over eye; young brownish above and striped below like large Cooper's Hawk.

BREEDING. — In forests. *Nest:* Very bulky, of sticks lined with finer material. *Eggs:* 2 to 5, bluish-white sometimes faintly spotted with browns.

RANGE. — Breeds from Alaska, northern Manitoba, southeastern Ontario, Ungava, and Newfoundland south to interior British Columbia, Michigan, northern New York, northern New England, and in the mountains to Pennsylvania and western Maryland; winters from Alaska and the southern Canadian provinces to southern California, northern Mexico, Texas, Missouri, Kentucky, West Virginia, and Virginia.

Among all the fierce raptores that inhabit the continent of North America, there is no hawk handsomer, braver, fiercer, or more powerful than the Goshawk. Its attack is swift, furious and deadly. In the death grapple it clings ferociously to its victim, careless of its own safety until the unfortunate creature succumbs to its steely grip. Its stroke is terrible. It is delivered with such force as sometimes to tear out most of one side of its victim, and its wing-power is so great that it can carry off rabbits and full-grown fowls. The Goshawk is a bird of the great northern coniferous forests, but in winter when pressed by hunger it hunts over all kinds of territory.

Every year in November or December some Eastern Goshawks enter the United States from the north, and about once in seven to ten years, coincidentally with a scarcity of the so-called snow-shoe rabbits (varying hares) and ptarmigans in the fur countries, Goshawks appear in large numbers. Apparently 'rabbits' so-called and ptarmigan are the principal food of Goshawks in their northern homes. When some sudden epidemic destroys most of the abundant rabbits the Goshawks must feed on ptarmigan until they have greatly depleted the supply, when they wander south, fierce and hungry. Sometimes these great flights consist chiefly of adult birds. Perhaps when food becomes suddenly scarce the hawks rear practically no young. During the summer they can subsist on birds, squirrels and mice, but when the birds go south and snow covers the runways of the mice, lacking rabbits and ptarmigan, the hawks and owls must eat each other or starve, unless they migrate. When they arrive in the United States they feed largely on grouse, and often attack poultry.

Many Goshawks are as shy as any other hawk. Some of them, however, coming from regions where they rarely see a human being, are quite unsuspicious, and many such are shot. Forced by hunger to migrate to this region, they become careless of their own safety when in pursuit of their prey. Their persistence at such times is well exemplified by the following experience related by the late Edward L. Parker. Mr. Parker had planted along a wire fence near his stable a tangle of shrubbery and vines to furnish food for birds and protection from their enemies. One morning the stable-man saw a large gray bird plunging at the thicket and beating against it. He soon perceived that a female pheasant had sought refuge under the dense shrubbery and that the hawk could not get at her. Presently the hawk succeeded in pushing under the thicket, but could not reach the pheasant, so it came out, flew back a short distance and, turning, hurled itself with great force against the yielding mass of small vines that covered the bushes. Meanwhile the pheasant had moved but little. The hawk then went over the thicket and dashed against the other side with such a shock that the frightened pheasant flew out and started for the woods. The hawk swiftly gained on her and had almost reached her when she rose to clear a high wire fence which enclosed the paddock. As the pheasant passed over the fence the hawk, which evidently did not see the wire until too late to avoid it, struck it with a bang, rebounding, evidently injured by the shock. However, it did not relinquish its pursuit of the pheasant but followed her with wobbling flight as she passed into the woods. Under the fence which the hawk struck there were a few feathers from its breast, one of which sent to me served to identify the bird.

Many instances could be related showing the audacity of the Goshawk. One day in the great British Columbian forest I had a good opportunity to collect a number of Longcrested Jays as a flock passed me high overhead among the tall trees. I had shot three or four when I noticed that not one had reached the ground. Shooting another I watched it fall, when a Western Goshawk swept out from among the trees into the very smoke from my gun and snatched it in the air.

In striking a bird on the wing the Goshawk does not dive from a height as a falcon often does, but overtakes its quarry by swift and powerful flight, coming, perhaps, down a slight incline from its post in some tree-top, and when near its prey sets its wings, throws its powerful feet forward almost beyond its head, and strikes its victim under the wing, driving in its powerful talons.

The Goshawk sometimes begins its feast by tearing off the head and legs and swallowing them. It decapitates a rabbit almost as if the head had been cut off with a knife. Birds are usually plucked. In some cases if the bird is large the breast is eaten first, sometimes the entrails are removed. The food of the Eastern Goshawk includes birds from the size of a Song Sparrow to that of a full-grown domestic cock, and birds form a considerable part of its sustenance. It feeds also on squirrels (red squirrels in particular), rabbits, mice, weasels and insects.

SHARP-SHINNED HAWK

Accipiter velox velox (WILSON).   PLATES 38 AND 39.

Other names: Pigeon Hawk; Chicken Hawk; Small Stub-winged Bullet-hawk; Little Blue Darter.

IDENTIFICATION. — Length of male 10 to 12 inches, spread 20 to 23 inches; length of female 12 to 14 inches, spread 24 to 27 inches. Rather longer and slimmer than either Sparrow Hawk or Pigeon Hawk, the two small falcons with which it is sometimes confounded; wings shorter and wider, more rounded; its flight an alternation of quick wing-beats and sailing, soaring at times, usually in small circles. Adults dark bluish-gray above; whitish, barred reddish-brown, below; under surface of wings and tail as seen in flight white, barred narrowly and darkly. Young browner above, body streaked brown below; female with reddish streaks, male with darker streaks.

BREEDING. — In tree in woods, 10 to 80 feet up. *Nest:* Of twigs, lined with strips of bark, etc. *Eggs:* 4 to 8, bluish-white or greenish-white, irregularly blotched and spotted with lilac and browns.

RANGE. — Breeds nearly throughout the United States and Canada from tree-limit in the north to the Gulf of Mexico; winters from southeastern Alaska, southern Minnesota, Michigan, Illinois, Indiana, Ohio, northern New England, and New Brunswick south to Central America.

The Sharp-shinned Hawk is remarkably swift, graceful and skillful in flight. It swings and circles through the forest aisles and even among thick branches with the greatest ease. Its usual cross-country flight consists of periods of steady flapping, with short intervals of sailing, but sometimes, especially during its migrations when hundreds may be seen passing at very considerable heights, much soaring is indulged in.

The courting activities and the building of the nest occur chiefly in April or early May. As is the case with other hawks the male often fights fiercely with any rival that makes advances toward his mate.

The birds having made choice of a nesting site are likely, if unmolested, to return to the same neighborhood year after year. Usually a new nest is built yearly. The nest is not hard to find, as often it is not over twenty or thirty feet high, and the hawks advertise it by scolding when any one appears in the immediate neighborhood. Often the little male will dart boldly at an intruder on the ground either before or after the nest-tree has been climbed. Frequently the female will stay on the nest until the tree is tapped, or even partly climbed. Sometimes her long tail may be seen sticking over the edge of the nest. She almost never flies because of someone merely walking beneath the tree. The eggs are laid usually on alternate days. Five little downy young 'Sharp-shins' in a nest are a beautiful sight. They fill the nest full to overflowing with their palpitating, snowy, fluffy mass, with five pairs of bright black eyes punctuating the fluff. The young remain in or near the nest for about four weeks, and during this time there is a constant and ever-increasing demand for food suitable for hawklets. As the young birds approach maturity probably each requires at least three or four small birds every day, or their equivalent, to supply sufficient aliment to insure rapid growth and development; and while the parents are bold and skillful hunters, they do not seem to be so uniformly successful in their forays as many ornithologists seem to believe them to be. If so, they would not find it necessary to brave so often the perils of the poultry yard in quest of little chicks. We are told that this hawk is 'feathered lightning' and that it can closely follow every turn of its victims, but the creatures on which it chiefly preys are so wary and agile as to be able often to escape the swift rush of the hawk, and by sudden dodging and twisting to gain a refuge in some dense and thorny thicket or pile of brush where the larger pursuer cannot enter; nevertheless the hawk sometimes follows one into a thicket, and not always in vain. In some cases where the hawk dashes into a flock it seems to be bewildered by the numbers of its potential victims, and fails to secure a bird. Sometimes the little raptore is so hard pressed for food that it is reduced to hunting mice, ground squirrels or insects, or even to stealing young birds from their nests.

One day on the Concord meadows a Red-winged Blackbird which had been accustomed to chase the rather slow-flying Marsh Hawk started after a Sharp-shinned Hawk that was crossing the meadow. Fatal error! The hawk immediately turned, but the blackbird evaded him and, realizing its mistake, attempted to gain the woods which, by turning and twisting, it finally reached ahead of its swifter but less agile pursuer. I was unable to see the end of that chase, but it was the longest and most persistent pursuit that I have known a hawk of this species to undertake. The hawk may have been angered by the attack of the blackbird, and that may have accounted for the determined chase. Its usual method is to flap and sail at a rather low altitude and to strike its prey by a quick drop or turn or a sudden dash at some incautious small bird, caught in the open and perhaps paralyzed by fear for an instant at the sudden approach of its redoubtable enemy.

Such hunting often is successful in thinly forested land where trees or shrubbery mask the approach, or even in open undulating land where the hawk flies low and where its coming is screened by a ridge or a patch of brush. In such a case on the coast of British Columbia, the hawk missed his victim. I was watching from my canoe a flock of small sandpipers, feeding on the strand, when suddenly the hawk shot like an arrow into their midst; he had thrust his feet forward to strike, when every little bird sprang away as with one accord; and so rapid were their concerted evolutions that the marauder never touched one, and soon gave up the pursuit.

Often the hawk will take a commanding position in a tree where it can overlook the haunts of its prospective victims and, partly concealed behind the leaves, wait and watch for its prey. Now and then a pack of Blue Jays will gather about one of these hawks, while he is perched, and revile him. At first their numbers and noise may confuse and baffle him, but if he is at all hungry let them beware, for then the hawk makes a sudden dash, bearing one of his assailants to the ground. The victim fights valiantly, but its cowardly companions retreat in disorder, leaving their comrade to its fate, which is soon settled by the impetuous little hawk.

The southward migration of this species probably begins in August, but we see few actually in migration before September. Then they pass in great numbers, and some are still passing in October or later. I shall never forget my first sight of this fall migration. We had been 'haying' in blue-joint grass on the river meadow, one hot day in early September and I was lying on top of a load of hay, which the horses were hauling to the barn, when, gazing upward into the blue, I became aware that in the far heights the sky was alive with birds. There were hundreds, sailing and drifting southward at different heights, and all that were near enough to be identified were Sharp-shinned Hawks. Several such flights have been observed since that day, and they always leave an impression of awe at the numbers and movements of the concourse.

In autumn great numbers of Sharp-shinned Hawks follow the flights of small birds across Lake Erie, starting from Point Pelee, Ontario, at the west end of the lake. Similar great flights of this hawk take place at Cape May, New Jersey, where the birds gather to await a favorable opportunity to cross Delaware Bay in their southward migration, and at Hawk Mountain in the Blue Ridge of Pennsylvania.

With fair winds these birds often fly very high in migration and drift onward, but with contrary winds they fly low, with much flapping and little sailing.

The individuals that winter in the latitude of New England are sorely pressed at times by want. Then they seem to have no fear of consequences, and strike their prey wherever it may be found. Frequently at this season they have dashed through windows in the attempt to reach caged birds, and they pursue their prey to the very doors of the houses; I have seen birds thus struck down beneath my very windows. They hunt in all weather, even in the face of a driving storm.

Having killed a small bird this hawk usually plucks off and discards about all the feathers, except a little down and some of the wing feathers, then tears off the head and feet and swallows them, after which it proceeds to devour the rest. It seems to be a common habit with many hawks and owls to swallow their prey whole if very small, but if not, to remove the head and legs or feet and eat them first, but this is not an invariable rule.

COOPER'S HAWK

Accipiter cooperi (BONAPARTE). PLATES 37, 38, AND 39.

Other names: Chicken Hawk; Quail Hawk; Big Blue Darter; Big Stub-winged Bullet-hawk; Privateer; Striker.

IDENTIFICATION. — Length of male 14 to 18 inches, spread 27 to 30 inches; length of female 16½ to 20 inches, spread 29 to 36 inches. Much like Sharp-shinned Hawk in coloration, form and habits; small male Cooper's may about equal size of large female Sharp-shin; end of tail rounded, that of Sharp-shin usually square.

BREEDING. — Similar to Goshawk.

RANGE. — Breeds from southern British Columbia, southern Ontario, southern Quebec, and Prince Edward Island to the southern border of the United States and Mexico; winters from southwestern British Columbia, Colorado, southern Illinois, southern Michigan (rarely), southern Ontario (rarely), southern New York, and southern Maine to Costa Rica.

Cooper's Hawk is a forest rover. It is cradled in the wind-swept woods, and fledged amid the creaking and groaning of great trees. Alert, swift and dauntless it roams the green wood with falcon-like freedom, carrying terror to the hearts of weaker creatures and leaving behind it a trail of destruction and death.

When the 'Cooper's' loud 'cucks' ring through the sunny, leafy woods of June, the hush of death pervades everything. All erstwhile cheerful thrushes and warblers become still and silent. There is indeed death in the air. This bird hunts more or less upon the wing, usually flying low near the ground or at a very moderate height above the trees, darting suddenly upon any victim taken by surprise. It gets up great speed almost immediately, and it alights on a perch with the quickness and readiness of a flycatcher. It will follow a bird into a thicket, often plunging through by sheer velocity, and so driving its victim out into the open and capturing it by its superior powers of flight, or by so terrorizing it that it becomes almost helpless from fright.

More commonly, however, this hawk secretes itself in a tree near some clearing, lake or stream, from which by sudden forays it surprises and captures its unsuspecting prey. Sometimes, with true cat-like grace, it will leap from limb to limb. Its long tail is loosely hung and it flirts easily and nervously. It will alight in a tree near a poultry-yard and watch its chance until, unobserved, it can glide rapidly along near the ground, or else drop straight down and bear away a chicken. Often the Cooper's will carry away a pullet almost as heavy as itself, scarcely clearing the grass. If scared by a shout (for the human voice is likely to terrify any wild creature) it may drop the pullet, which will run back to the farmhouse for safety, scarcely the worse for its experience save for the superficial bloody marks of the hawk's claws in its back. Again the Cooper's will kill a full-grown pullet or a hen too heavy to carry off. When opposed by the gallant cock, it has been known to grapple with him and leave him lying dead on the ground.

The Cooper's Hawk is so persecuted now that we may expect progressive decrease of the

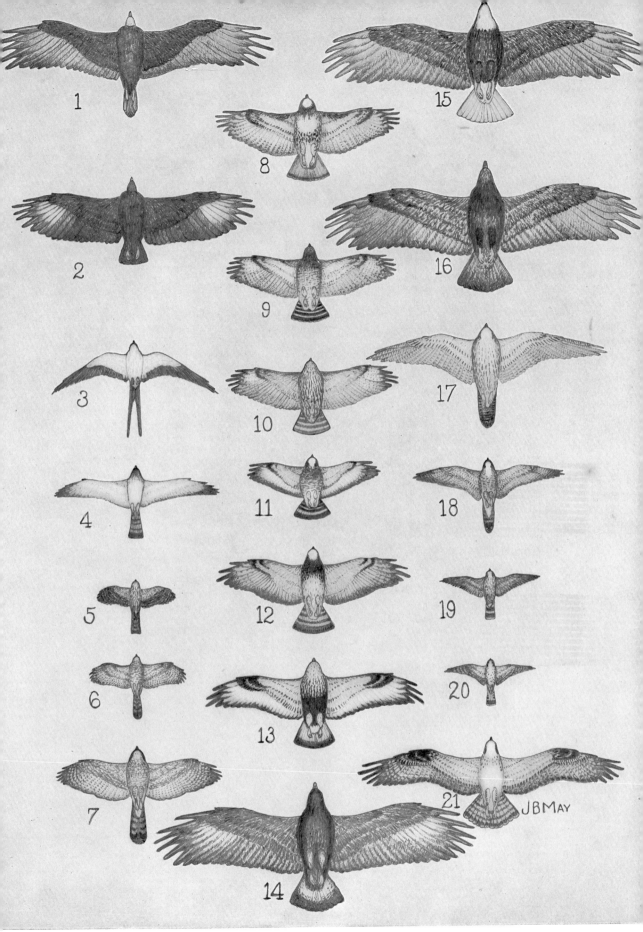

PLATE 38

1. Turkey Vulture. 2. Black Vulture. 3. Swallow-tailed Kite. 4. Marsh Hawk. *Adult male.* 5. Sharp-shinned Hawk. *Small immature male.*
6. Cooper's Hawk. *Small adult male.* 7. Goshawk. *Adult.* 8. Red-tailed Hawk. *Adult.* 9. Red-shouldered Hawk. *Adult.* 10. Red-shouldered Hawk. *Immature.* 11. Broad-winged Hawk. *Adult.* 12. Swainson's Hawk. *Adult.* 13. Rough-legged Hawk. *Immature. Light phase.*
14. Golden Eagle. *Immature.* 15. Bald Eagle. *Adult.* 16. Bald Eagle. *Immature.* 17. White Gyrfalcon. 18. Duck Hawk. *Adult.* 19. Pigeon Hawk. 20. Sparrow Hawk. *Male.* 21. Osprey.

species in the future. In the old days there were many nests of this bird in both coniferous and deciduous trees, some high up near the top of the pines or hemlocks, others out on the high limbs of tall oaks, hickories, or chestnuts, often necessitating high climbing for the adventurous youth who sought their eggs. Usually they build a new nest each year, somewhere in the neighborhood of last year's nest, for hawks like to return to the same nesting ground year after year; rarely the deserted nest of a Crow is occupied. As is the case with some other hawks, incubation may begin as soon as the first egg is deposited, or soon after, and there may be young of several sizes in the same nest. They remain there from twenty-one days to about twenty-five. During the last few days they exercise their wings in preparation for flight. When the nest is approached by a human intruder, the parent birds usually keep out of gun-shot and confine their protests to complaining 'cucks'; and although occasionally a bold bird will dart down toward the intruder, I have never known one to strike a man.

While the young are in the nest, considerable numbers of game birds, other birds and young poultry are slain for their subsistence. As soon as the young are strong on the wing, the family leaves the summer home and all roam at will, wherever food is plentiful, until the young birds have learned to hunt for themselves. In September and October, when the great southbound migration of small land birds is well under way, the Cooper's Hawks follow, often moving in company with other hawks in daylight migration, hunting more or less as they go.

The food of Cooper's Hawk consists more largely of game-birds and poultry than that of any other common hawk. The thievery of Cooper's Hawk is so adroit that often the bird is not seen or suspected, while the soaring hawks, such as the Red-shouldered or the Red-tailed Hawk, have to pay the penalty, because they are so conspicuous and may be seen occasionally soaring over the hen-yard. Cooper's Hawk is so powerful and active and so swift of flight that it can destroy animals of superior size and weight. It kills rabbits, grouse, ducks, squirrels and small birds, but when game is scarce it will content itself with snakes and other reptiles or even mice, grasshoppers and crickets.

EASTERN RED-TAILED HAWK

Buteo borealis borealis (GMELIN). PLATES 37, 38 AND 40.

Other names: Red-tail; Hen Hawk.

IDENTIFICATION. — Length of male 19 to 22 inches, spread 46 to 50 inches; length of female 21 to 25 inches, spread 48 to 56 inches. Largest common hawk except Osprey; in flight wings long and broad, with turned-up tips, and tail fairly long, broad, and usually spread fan-like; soars much like an eagle but wings relatively shorter; adult dark brownish above with a large whitish area on breast, wings chiefly whitish from below with a dark spot beyond bend, tips of flight-feathers dark; tail chestnut above, whitish below; young with tail not red but barred grayish and blackish.

CALL. — A long-drawn squealing whistle, *kee-aahrr-r-r-r.*

BREEDING. — In woodlands. *Nest:* Of sticks, often lined with grass, leaves, moss, etc. *Eggs:* 2 to 4, whitish, usually spotted and blotched irregularly, with browns, etc.

RANGE. — Breeds from Mackenzie, northern Manitoba, northern Ontario, southern Quebec, and Newfoundland south to central southern Texas, Arkansas, Alabama, northern Florida; winters from Kansas, northeastern Iowa, southern Illinois, Indiana, Ohio, central New York, and southern Maine to northeastern Mexico and the Gulf coast of the United States.

The Eastern Red-tailed Hawk is a fine, large, sturdy hawk and its soaring flight is almost as impressive as that of the Bald Eagle. It does not migrate very far in winter, merely moving out of the bleak and inhospitable parts of its northern range and shifting but a few hundred miles south of the southern border of its breeding range. Oftentimes a 'Red-tail' wintering in our climate will resort year after year to the same place, appearing with clock-like regularity in the late fall. In its spring migration it becomes most common in New England from about the second week in April until the last week in May. The migrating birds sail and soar at various heights, some of them at such lofty altitudes as to seem mere specks in the sky. Usually they are accompanied by Red-shouldered Hawks, and sometimes by Marsh Hawks and other species.

Some of the resident Red-tails begin making preparations to nest at a very early date, even as early as the last week in February in mild seasons, though eggs are rarely laid before the last days of March or early April. The nest when first built is not very large, but when it is used (probably by the same pair) from year to year and yearly additions are made, it may become in time almost as large as that of the Osprey. I have seen one or two such immense nests. A climber to the nest of one of these hawks is not in danger of attack by the owners. They usually content themselves with flying overhead, uttering cries of protest, though in some cases one or the other may swoop toward the intruder. Often only the female appears. The young grow slowly, and remain in or about the nest for a long time, but when once fledged they soon equal or exceed their parents in size.

I believe that this hawk rarely pounces upon its prey from on wing, though I have seen one, soaring, stoop toward the earth with a rush of wings, as if about to seize some animal from the ground. It prefers to sit quietly erect and motionless on an elevated perch such as a dead limb of some tall tree in a pasture or field, or at the edge of the woods, occasionally turning its head, but so slowly that the motion is almost imperceptible; here it scans its sur-roundings, ready to pounce on any mouse or other small mammal that presents itself.

This hawk is not so active as an Accipiter or as one of the falcons, but is more deliberate in action. Nevertheless, it is fast enough to pick a gray squirrel off a branch. If the squirrel proves an adept at dodging, the hawk may seek the assistance of its mate, and then, by alter-nately rising and swooping, one of the hawks gets its prey while the squirrel is dodging around the limb to evade the other.

In September and October, with favorable winds, the more northern members of the race may be seen wending their way southward over New England. Slowly they circle and drift at far heights, often up among the clouds. Now and then the keen far-seeing eye of one will detect the movement of some timorous field mouse far below. Nearly closing its wings it rushes head foremost through the air, falling like a hissing meteor from the clouds until it nears a convenient tree-top, when with spread wings and tail it checks its flight and alights gracefully on some dead projecting limb, only to fall presently on the trembling victim.

Not infrequently, during their migration, two hawks will do battle in the air. Grappling they fall, tumbling over and over, until at last, their safety endangered by the close proximity of Mother Earth, they separate, check their course and mount again towards the clouds. Sometimes they fly so high that they are only to be seen through rifts in the drifting vapors of the sky.

The food of the Red-tail consists very largely of mice. It kills rabbits, gophers and squirrels.

It takes comparatively few birds. When rattlesnakes or other snakes abound, a considerable number of these reptiles are among its victims. Though the farmers know it as the 'Hen Hawk,' it is not so destructive to poultry as are the Accipiters or the Goshawk. Nevertheless, when mice are scarce and hens are easily and safely obtained, now and then an individual Red-tail will get the chicken-killing habit and become destructive.

Dr. Fisher sums up the case for and against the Red-tail by stating that 'it has been demonstrated by careful stomach examinations that poultry and game birds do not constitute more than 10 per cent of the food of this hawk,' and that all the other useful animals eaten by it will not increase the proportion to 15 per cent. This leaves a balance of at least 85 per cent in favor of the hawk. It destroys so many noxious rodents and other destructive mammals that it should be allowed to live.

FLORIDA RED–TAILED HAWK

Buteo borealis umbrinus BANGS.

IDENTIFICATION. — Adult darker above than *B. b. borealis;* throat and middle of belly marked with broad conspicuous striping and banding of rich brown; tail feathers with dark markings near shafts; less diffused reddish below than *B. b. calurus,* the Western Red-tail.

RANGE. — Resident in southern Florida, Cuba, and the Isle of Pines.

KRIDER'S HAWK

Buteo borealis krideri HOOPES.

IDENTIFICATION. — Paler and with more white than *B. b. borealis;* viewed in the field it is noticeably whiter, with a lack of dark markings below and an almost white head.

RANGE. — Breeds from southern Alberta, southern Manitoba, and Minnesota south to Nebraska and Missouri; winters south to Wisconsin, Illinois, Mississippi, and Louisiana.

HARLAN'S HAWK

Buteo borealis harlani (AUDUBON).

IDENTIFICATION. — Much variation in individuals; most constant distinguishing point is the tail, which is usually closely and irregularly mottled with black, brownish, and white; upper parts may be grayer than *B. b. borealis* or a nearly uniform blackish; under parts vary from white more or less spotted with black or dusky to sooty brown or nearly black. Immature birds have the tail barred with grayish-brown and dusky.

RANGE. — Breeds from northwestern British Columbia, southwestern Yukon, and adjoining parts of Alaska south at least to southern Alberta; winters down the Mississippi Valley to the Gulf States.

There is still some difference of opinion among systematic ornithologists as to the correct classification of hawks of the Red-tailed group. J. L. Peters combines the Eastern and Western Red-tails in one race, and makes a separate species out of Harlan's Hawk. P. A. Taverner is inclined to regard both Krider's and Harlan's Hawks as merely extreme color-phases of the Western Red-tail. Judged by their habits, they are all one species. — (J.B.M.)

NORTHERN RED–SHOULDERED HAWK

Buteo lineatus lineatus (GMELIN).   PLATES 38 AND 40.

Other names: Hen Hawk; Chicken Hawk; Winter Hawk.

IDENTIFICATION. — Length of male 18 to 23 inches; spread 33 to 44 inches; length of female 19 to 24 inches, spread 39 to 50 inches. Nearly as large as Red-tailed Hawk; dark brownish above; ruddy under parts and lesser wing coverts; tail black with several *narrow* white bands (Broad-wing is smaller and has three broad black bands on tail alternating with conspicuous white bands); apparent translucent spot near tip of wing formed by narrow barring, is diagnostic, as are bright ruddy shoulders of adult; young have duller reddish shoulders and uniformly dark-streaked under parts, where young Red-tail has whitish breast and wide abdominal band of dark streaks.

CALL. — A prolonged piercing whistle, *kee-you, kee-you.*

BREEDING. — Similar to Red-tail but eggs usually more heavily marked.

RANGE. — Breeds from Ontario, southern Quebec, Nova Scotia, and Prince Edward Island south to southern Kansas, northeastern Tennessee, and North Carolina, and west to the edge of the Great Plains; winters from central Iowa, Illinois, Indiana, southern Ontario, central New York, southern Vermont and southern New Hampshire south to the Gulf coast and Texas.

There is no more pleasing spring sound than the lusty scream of the 'Red-shoulder' as it rings through the bare leafless woods as they stand up straight and brown against the pale blue sky of April. The Northern Red-shouldered Hawk probably is today the most generally common and conspicuous bird of its family in New England. When we speak of a hawk as common, we do not mean that it may be met with as often as a Robin or a Song Sparrow. The commonest hawk is rare compared with the Robin. The Red-shouldered Hawk is conspicuous because of its habit of circling up into the sky with widely extended wings, a habit which it shares with the less common Red-tail. In the last part of the nineteenth century when the latter commenced to decrease in numbers in southern New England, the present species began to increase, and soon largely took the place of its larger congener. In recent years its numbers seem to have fallen off somewhat in the same region. It seems, moreover, to prefer the more open and cultivated land, while the Red-tail is more at home within the borders of the forest and among heavily wooded hills. But since the larger and more stately bird has deserted many of its former woodland haunts, the smaller bird has regularly occupied them. The Red-shouldered Hawk will breed wherever it is allowed to settle in woodland or in small patches of large trees near open fields and meadows, where it finds its chief sustenance. Having once chosen an abiding place, it prefers to come back year after year to its old home, and often will use the same nest for years, rebuilding it somewhat and adding to it each year until its size and depth have increased considerably, and a good part of the structure is full of all sorts of old woods-dirt. Some of its nests would doubtless fill a bushel basket. Often in March it will begin to build a new domicile or repair an old one (chiefly with a broad encircling fringe of mossy twigs and branches and a freshened lining of the usual bark-strips, bits of oak leaves, lichens, etc.), both male and female working together, but rarely are eggs deposited in Massachusetts until well into April.

During the mating and until the eggs are laid the mated pairs are quite vociferous, and they betray their nesting place by their cries. After their eggs are laid the birds seem more quiet and secretive. Now and then a Red-shoulder will fly so quietly from the nest that she might be mistaken for an owl. Sometimes the female will scream at an interloper while she is still sitting on her nest, but as a rule, she flies from it while the invader is still fifty to seventy-five yards away. The females differ regarding shyness; some are very shy and leave the nest quietly before the intruder even catches sight of them. After the breeding season they seem to be as silent as any hawk. Usually shy, they sometimes become bold when an intruder visits the nest, although one rarely sits on the nest after climbing has begun. Sometimes the female will alight on a branch over the intruder's head, screaming long and loudly. I have even seen one dive furiously at my head with a rather terrifying roar of rushing wings when I merely walked within sight of her nest containing young. When the young are nearly fledged, with the down still clinging to their feathers, they leave the nest by day and climb about among the branches with flapping wings, thus exercising the muscles that control the pinions which are soon to bear them away from their home forever. It is well known that hawks, as well as many other species, will not tolerate the nesting of a pair of the same species near their home, though they may dwell in peace in the same grove with other rapacious birds.

This species, like the Red-tail, does not seem to be a very active hunter. It chases birds occasionally, but seems to be content mostly with sitting on some tree or pole where it can overlook a meadow, teeming with field mice, or the marshy border of some pond, where frogs and snakes abound.

When the leaves begin to turn and fall, many of these hawks leave the northern parts of their range and drift southward, at a considerable height, often in large scattered flocks and in company with other species. But some remain to eke out a precarious living along the larger streams or about the swamps, marshes, lakes or springs of southern New England.

The food of the Northern Red-shoulder consists very largely of small rodents, principally mice, batrachians and snakes. It catches few birds, but now and then an individual gets the poultry-killing habit. Evidently this is one of the most useful hawks. It should never be killed unless in the act of destroying poultry or game. As a rule it kills few small birds of any kind, and it destroys many snakes which are destructive to small birds and their eggs.

FLORIDA RED–SHOULDERED HAWK

Buteo lineatus alleni RIDGWAY.

IDENTIFICATION. — Slightly smaller than *B. l. lineatus;* adults lighter-colored and immatures darker; adults have grayish-white heads with no rufous feather edges, grayer tone to shoulder patch and much lighter faintly barred yellowish-buff under parts.

RANGE. — Breeds in Southern States from Oklahoma, Arkansas, Alabama, and South Carolina to Louisiana and southeastern Florida.

The Florida Red-shouldered Hawk is a common and easily recognized bird, with its breast so pale that it is readily distinguished in the field. It has not yet learned the caution which its more northerly relative has acquired by painful experience, and often allows quite close observation without taking alarm. Otherwise I know of no especial difference in its habits. — (J.B.M.)

INSULAR RED–SHOULDERED HAWK
Buteo lineatus extimus BANGS.

IDENTIFICATION. — Very similar to *B. l. alleni* but averages a little paler and slightly smaller.

RANGE. — The 'Check-List' gives its range as 'Florida Keys,' but Mr. A. C. Bent writes me, 'It breeds very sparingly, if at all, on the Florida Keys, but it is an abundant breeder all over the southern third of mainland Florida.'

BROAD–WINGED HAWK
Buteo platypterus platypterus (VIEILLOT).　　　　　　　PLATES 38 AND 40.

IDENTIFICATION. — Length 13 to 16½ inches, spread 32 to 38 inches; length of female 15 to 19 inches, spread 33½ to 39 inches. About size of slimmer Cooper's Hawk and much smaller than Red-tail or Red-shoulder; best field marks of adult are the showy black and white tail bars, visible from above or below (usually three black and two white) and 'clubbed' wings, with absence of red tail or ruddy shoulders of larger Buteos; wings long, broad, rounded at tips, and silvery-white below, with black tips to flight-feathers.

CALL. — A plaintive double note, *te-whee* or *pe-dee*, resembling note of Wood Pewee.

BREEDING. — Similar to Red-shoulder.

RANGE. — Breeds from central Alberta, southern Manitoba, Ontario, central Quebec, New Brunswick and Cape Breton Island south to the Gulf coast and Texas; winters from Florida and southern Mexico to Peru, occasionally north to Connecticut and Illinois.

The Broad-winged Hawk is generally uncommon or rare in the breeding season in those parts of New England from which the forests have been cleared. It is most common in hilly, forested regions and even there it is more or less local in distribution, though it is more common in the woods than the published records indicate. Mention of the 'Broad-wing' brings up a mental picture of the warm umbrageous woods of June, bright with the white of the flowering dogwood or ablaze with the pink azalea, with the little Buteo, with showy black and white tail, flying easily about and perching near, uttering the while its complaining *pe-dee*. It is a rather silent and sedentary woodland bird, except during the breeding season when intruders approach its nest, which it betrays by its 'scolding.' It is not often observed and identified save by those who, knowing it, go in search of it. As it rarely troubles poultry or pigeons about farmyards, its presence often is unsuspected in places where it breeds not uncommonly. Its powers of flight are so great that it is able to rise at will from summer heat to winter cold in the upper air. In warm summer weather it frequently soars to great heights with widely extended and almost motionless wings. The turned-up wing-tips and the general free and buoyant flight (almost soaring) of the Broad-wing are strongly reminiscent of the Red-tail. In flight, at least, the Broad-wing is a miniature Red-tail. Possibly no hawk ascends higher in the heavens than this rather small, inconspicuous species. Its broad, ample 'clubbed' wings, which name the bird so aptly when they are well seen, often make this hawk seem larger than it really is.

This species hunts either in the woods, flying above the tree-tops or coursing rather low over the open land. When it discovers its prey, it hovers sometimes until it sees a favorable opportunity to strike, when it swoops swiftly to the earth and rises with its prey in its talons. It will sit for long periods motionless on a perch watching for a movement of some small creature hidden in the leaves and grass and then pounce suddenly upon its prey, often leaping about among the leaves and other débris of the forest floor like a thing possessed, in its attempt to seize its victim. Having killed it, its captor either eats it on the ground or bears it away to the nest, or to some regular feeding-place by a stream or pool.

The Broad-wing normally nests rather near water in the unbroken forest, in a hollow among wooded hills, on a wooded hillside, near an old mill pond or beaver pond or along a running stream. Frequently in the Maine woods it chooses the black birch or the yellow birch, but it nests not infrequently in pines and hemlocks as well as in many species of deciduous trees. Near settlements the nest in some cases may be found where one would least expect it, in small patches of woods or near wood roads or the edges of open fields. Usually it is fairly high, from twenty-five to ninety feet, but nests have been found from three to ten feet from the ground. The parents complain when an intruder closely approaches the nest, but their cries may not be noticed, as on a windy day they may be mistaken for the creaking of the trees. As the nest is not usually occupied until May when the leaves have started to grow, it is not conspicuous, and so the birds avoid discovery. The young grow rapidly, but remain in or near the nest for at least four or five weeks while assuming juvenal plumage. Before they leave the nest for good, they frequently move about in or near it, flapping their wings and thus developing their flight muscles. Both parents feed the young, and green leaves or sprays of leaves are added daily to the nest; perhaps no other species of hawk is so much addicted to the use of green foliage. One or the other of the parents usually is at hand to guard and brood the young.

In autumn the Broad-winged Hawk migrates in large numbers along the Atlantic coastal region and also down the Mississipppi Valley. Possibly some of the birds which breed in northern New England come up the valley in spring, but probably most of those nesting here come by the coastal route. The species seems to be rare at all seasons along the seaboard of the Carolinas. Probably, therefore, the migration south of Virginia passes over the interior. The spring flight begins in March and April. Some continue to come in May, and in the Provinces they are seen moving even in June. The fall flight commences in late August or early September and continues into October. This flight, when both young and old come down, is the largest, and the great majority is composed of young birds. In fine weather, with favorable winds, they often fly very high, but strong northwest winds drift them towards the coast and necessitate low flight to escape the great force of the wind at high altitudes. Then they appear in large numbers with hawks of other species along the coastal regions of Connecticut, Long Island and New Jersey, and many are killed during these flights by gunners who lie in wait for them. Broad-wings fly sometimes in flocks, but more often are much scattered. During favorable winds they soar or sail much, and drift with the wind.

The Broad-winged Hawk feeds largely on small mammals, reptiles, batrachians and insects, and ordinarily destroys very few birds. Most of the birds found in the stomachs examined were fledglings taken from the nest or when learning to fly. Chickens are taken rarely. Young rabbits, red squirrels and chipmunks occasionally are killed, and many mice, particularly wood mice, also a few moles and shrews. Snakes and frogs are freely eaten. Lizards are taken in numbers and sometimes small fish where they are abundant. It eats many of the large larvae of night-flying moths and many other caterpillars, also many beetles, grasshoppers and crickets; among the crustaceans eaten are fiddler crabs and crawfish; if stomach examinations are made, at least one large green larva will almost always be found at the proper season for this creature.

SWAINSON'S HAWK

Buteo swainsoni BONAPARTE.   PLATE 38.

Other names: Prairie Hawk; Prairie Buzzard; Grasshopper Hawk; Gopher Hawk.

IDENTIFICATION. — Length of male 19 to 21 inches, spread 47 to 51 inches; length of female 19 to 22 inches, spread 47 to 57 inches. Two color-phases, with intermediates; adult in light phase resembles Red-tail but mainly white below with very wide dark band across upper breast separating white throat and nearly white belly, a white patch on either side of rump, tail with numerous inconspicuous bands, and wings rather narrow for a Buteo; dark phase may be entirely sooty brown, or upper plumage dark and lower as light as in light phase.

BREEDING. — In woods, groves, or isolated trees. *Nest:* On ground, bush or tree, of sticks, leaves and grass. *Eggs:* 2 to 4, dull whitish, varying from unspotted to heavily blotched.

RANGE. — Breeds from interior British Columbia, Fort Yukon, Great Slave Lake, and Manitoba south to northern Mexico; winters in southern South America, only occasionally north of the Equator; occasionally wanders east of normal range.

Swainson's Hawk is a 'buzzard' of the open country, although it usually nests in trees. Its home is always near wide, open lands, and it will even nest in low bushes or on the ground in its favorite regions. Its habits are somewhat similar to those of the Red-tailed or Red-shouldered Hawks, and young birds might be mistaken for either of these. It does not require extended notice here, as it is merely a straggler east of the Great Plains, though perhaps it occurs here more often than the records indicate.

In hunting it courses over the open prairies with slow, rather sluggish, circling flight until it sights its prey, when suddenly it is transformed into an alert and skillful hunter. Frequently it sits perched on a fence post or other low observation point for considerable periods of time, watching for the movements of rodents or insects, and at such times it may often be approached quite closely. At times it has been observed hopping about on the ground in a sprightly manner while pursuing grasshoppers or other insects. At other times it catches flying insects while on the wing. At Yellowstone Canyon I once watched a number of Swainson's Hawks catching newly hatched 'dobson-flies' or adult helgramites, which they grasped with their talons and then, while still in full flight, lowering the head, ate 'from the hand' without difficulty. — (J.B.M.)

SHORT–TAILED HAWK
Buteo brachyurus VIEILLOT.

Other name: Little Black Hawk.

IDENTIFICATION. — Length about 17 inches; spread about 35 inches. Two distinct color-phases, apparently without intermediates: adult in light phase, above dark slaty-gray or grayish-brown, under parts pure white except sides of breast which are rufous-brown, tail barred black and gray with white tip, under surface of wings shows primaries largely white with black tips and secondaries barred; adult in dark phase dark brownish-black all over except whitish forehead, occasional concealed spots or bars on under parts, grayish under surface of wings, and grayish tail barred with black.

BREEDING. — In extensive forested swamps. *Nest:* Of cypress twigs, and moss. *Eggs:* 1 to 3, pale bluish-white, unmarked or irregularly spotted or blotched.

RANGE. — Breeds in Florida, eastern Mexico, and Central America south to Peru, Bolivia, and Brazil.

The little Short-tailed Hawk is one of the rarest hawks in North America and is found within the United States only in a limited area on the Florida peninsula, where it has probably never been an abundant bird even for a raptor, and where today it is perhaps seriously threatened with early extirpation unless active measures are taken at once for its protection and preservation.

The Short-tailed Hawk is usually unsuspicious and gentle in disposition, and it is attractive in appearance and harmless in its feeding habits. It is an expert on the wing and often sails for a long time, in typical Buteo fashion, high above the swamps and woodlands, apparently without a movement of its extended wings and tail. It should be easily recognizable from its shape and size and its characteristic color patterns. It is one of the few species of North American birds which exhibits true dichromatism, that is, has two distinctly different color-phases which are irrespective of age or sex, and it is of especial interest for that reason. — (J.B.M.)

AMERICAN ROUGH–LEGGED HAWK
Buteo lagopus s. johannis (GMELIN).   PLATES 38 AND 41.

Other names: Black Hawk; Mouse Hawk; Ruff-leg.

IDENTIFICATION. — Length of male 19½ to 22 inches, spread 48 to 52 inches; length of female 21½ to 23½ inches, spread 52 to 56 inches. A large hawk with relatively broad wings rather pointed at tips (for Buteos) and rather long tail: two color-phases with intermediates; light phase is noticeable for conspicuous masses of dark and light areas and especially for *broad blackish abdominal band;* dark phase may be all black but usually shows a white base to tail.

BREEDING. — On ledge or cliff, sometimes in tree. *Nest:* Of sticks and roots, lined with grass and feathers. *Eggs:* 2 to 5, whitish to buffy, spotted and blotched more or less.

RANGE. — Breeds from Aleutian Islands, northwestern Alaska, Victoria Island, southwestern Baffin Island, northern Quebec (Ungava), and northeastern Labrador south to northern Alberta, north shore of Gulf of St. Lawrence, and Newfoundland; winters from southern British Columbia, Colorado, Minnesota, the northern boundary of the United States, and southern Ontario, south to southern California, southern New Mexico, Texas, Louisiana, and North Carolina.

When cold weather comes in the Hudsonian Zone with its accompaniment of deep snow and thick ice, an army of Rough-legged Hawks moves southward toward the United States. When starting on migration they soar to a great height and then set their course. Probably they travel at such high altitudes that they are seldom noticed in migration. They seem to be able to see well in the gathering dusk, as they hunt very early in the morning and after sunset when mice are active. As they fly low when hunting, and often over lowlands, such as meadows or marshes, it is not difficult to make out the location of the white patch on the upper part of the long tail.

From autumn until spring they may be seen in their chosen haunts, slowly flapping along not far above the ground or sitting erect on the tops of small trees or posts watching for their favorite prey. Occasionally one soars to considerable heights with motionless wings and tail fully spread. Dr. C. W. Townsend well describes the flight of his hawk as follows:

'The flight of the Rough-legged Hawk is graceful and indicative of skill and power. In soaring, the wings and tail are spread to their full extent; the first half-dozen primaries are spread out separately like fingers and curve upward at their tips. On motionless wings, if the wind be favorable, this bird may often be seen soaring high up over the land. In April and May, I have several times seen two of them, probably a pair, rising up higher and higher as they circled, and, arrived at a considerable elevation, striking out in flight for the northeast.

'When soaring they may be seen looking down, and I have several times seen them partially close their wings, lower their long feathered tarsi and drop like a plummet. On one occasion the bird secured a large mouse with which it flew to the marsh and perched on an ice cake. On another occasion a fine Rough-leg pounced successfully on a cotton-tail rabbit and bore it off.

'In searching the ground for game of this sort they often fly slowly, alternately flapping and sailing, from fifty to a hundred yards up in the air. Occasionally they hang over one place by hovering, and often drop their legs preparatory to pouncing on the prey and draw them up behind when they change their minds. If the wind be favorable, they hang suspended in the air as motionless as a kite. The wind needed for this is an up-current over the brow of a steep hill or cliff. In this case gravitation acts like the kitestring, and by skillful disposition of the plane of the wings to the up-current, the bird remains motionless if the wind is steady. When the wind is irregular and flawy, the bird swings about more or less, just as a kite acts under similar circumstances. When the wind drops for a moment the bird hovers.'

It is now a well-known fact that the food of the American Rough-legged Hawk in the United States consists chiefly of field mice, while on its breeding-ground its principal prey is the lemming.

Probably the Rough-legged Hawk, viewed from the standpoint of the farmer, is one of the most useful birds in the country. Nevertheless it has been slain in large numbers by both farmers and sportsmen, either because it is large and slow, making a good target, or because they believe it to be harmful.

AMERICAN GOLDEN EAGLE

Aquila chrysaëtos canadensis (LINNAEUS).   PLATES 38 AND 41.

Other names: Mountain Eagle; Ring-tailed Eagle; Royal Eagle.

IDENTIFICATION. — Length of male 30 to 35 inches, spread 75 to 84 inches; length of female 35 to 41 inches, spread 82 to 92 inches. Larger than any hawk but suggests very large dark Buteo with rather longer wings, upcurved and separated primaries when soaring; light spot at base of primaries; yellowish-brown ('golden') head and nape; young have upper tail white with dark terminal band.

BREEDING. — In mountainous country. *Nest:* A bulky mass of sticks, etc. *Eggs:* 1 to 4, whitish, usually marked with browns and claret.

RANGE. — Breeds in mountainous regions from northern Alaska, northwestern Mackenzie, and perhaps in the Canadian Provinces east of the Rocky Mountains south to northern Lower California, central Mexico, western Texas, Oklahoma, and formerly to North Carolina; in winter south casually to Louisiana, Alabama, and northern Florida.

Since man came up from barbarism the stately Golden Eagle has been considered the noblest of birds. He it is that typifies royalty among the feathered tribes, and has caused the eagle to be named the king of birds. In the olden days when falconry flourished in Europe the Golden Eagle was flown by kings. He was the pet of royalty, and was looked upon as a bird of great distinction. Comparing him with our national bird, the Bald Eagle, we find that he seems built of finer clay. His beak is not so large and coarse as that of the White-headed Eagle; his feet are smaller, though the talons are very long, keen and powerful; his form seems to be more compact. In the air he makes even a finer figure than the Bald Eagle; he soars grandly in wide circles, wheeling above the clouds, and his hunting is like that of the 'noble' falcons. He hunts chiefly mammals and birds which he captures by open approach, speed and skill. At obscure heights he hangs suspended until an opportunity comes, when he closes his wings and shoots down upon his victim like an arrow from the bow, coming so swiftly as to take his prey by surprise, and striking it dead in an instant, while the Bald Eagle lives largely on dead fish and carrion or by robbing the Osprey. The Golden Eagle builds her nest usually in the wild and savage wilderness and in its sublimest solitudes on giant mountain crags, while the Bald Eagle builds her nest chiefly in trees in low country along the coast or near the larger streams or bodies of water where she can find her chief food.

A study of ornithological literature and some attention to the traditions of the people furnish convincing evidence that the Golden Eagle formerly bred in the mountainous regions of the East, from which it has been extirpated by gun, trap, and poison; so that now it is seen there only casually, unless possibly a few may breed even now on some of the more remote mountains of Maine and in the southern Appalachians. However, it never was common there, as few Eastern mountains are vast and lofty enough to suit its temperament. Heavily feathered to the very toes, it can endure the extreme cold of high latitudes and great altitudes; but when food becomes scarce it wanders far in search of it, and so reaches the Eastern States mainly in winter during a dearth of food in the North. Its migrations are, therefore, mostly wide wanderings in search of food.

Although I have handled a large number of specimens I have seen but one that was fully adult, as all the others had more or less white at the base of the tail. Evidently the old birds have learned to take good care of themselves and so seldom reach the museums. As a species it is wild, and difficult to approach, although on a western ranch the bird will become so used to droves and the attendant riders that it will take little notice of a horseman. Although a fearless bird the Golden Eagle has learned to beware of mankind. Any person may disturb its nest, if he can reach it, without the slightest fear of an attack from the birds. On all such occasions they keep far away in the upper air and manifest little if any concern.

The food of the American Golden Eagle consists chiefly of birds and small mammals. It does not hesitate to attack animals much heavier than itself. Wild turkeys, geese and other water-fowl, herons, small fawns (rarely good-sized deer), grouse, rabbits, squirrels, raccoons, skunks, prairie dogs, marmots, young pigs, cats and foxes are destroyed by the powerful bird. When urged by hunger it has been known to kill young lambs, kids, calves, and poultry, but it feeds its young largely on wood rats, squirrels and mice. It is a cleanly bird, plucking or skinning its prey before eating, and keeps its plumage in excellent condition by bathing and preening, which, by the way, is customary with most birds of prey.

NORTHERN BALD EAGLE

Haliaeetus leucocephalus alascanus TOWNSEND.

IDENTIFICATION. — Length 34½ to 43 inches, spread 82 to 98½ inches. Indistinguishable in field from Southern Bald Eagle, which see.
BREEDING. — In forests near lakes or ocean. *Nest:* Usually in tall tree, a mass of sticks. *Eggs:* 1 to 4, white.
RANGE. — Breeds from northwestern Alaska to Ungava and south to British Columbia and the Great Lakes; winters south to Washington, Montana, and Connecticut.

As the Northern Bald Eagle is virtually identical with the Southern Bald Eagle, except for its larger size, and as it has been recognized only recently as a distinct race, we have no very definite information regarding its breeding or wintering range. Probably the larger eagles that winter near the Great Lakes and along the Maine coast are referable to this race. When the waters of the north are frozen and the wild-fowl have left for the south, doubtless many of these eagles go to the coast for food and thus work southward along the shores of New England. I have seen in winter a number of eagles in Frenchman's Bay, Maine, where both seals and eagles were seen on floating ice, as much at home as within the Arctic Circle. I have seen many Northern Bald Eagles also in British Columbia, where in the salmon season they commonly feed on dead or dying salmon that they find on the beaches or along the streams. The habits of this eagle apparently are the same as those of the Southern Bald Eagle, the other subspecies, with some allowance for differences in latitude and environment.

SOUTHERN BALD EAGLE

Haliaeetus leucocephalus leucocephalus (LINNAEUS).   PLATES 37, 38 AND 41.

Other names: Bald-headed Eagle; White-headed Eagle; Gray Eagle (Young).

IDENTIFICATION. — Length of male 30 to 34 inches, spread 72 to 85 inches; length of female 35 to 37 inches, spread 79 to 90 inches. A very large raptor with long broad wings; adult unmistakable with white head and tail and all dark body; immature very dark but with considerable mottling of whitish areas on tail (not 'banded' as young Golden Eagle); body plumage more or less mottled with white spots on dark feathers; tarsus yellow and unfeathered (feathered to toes in Golden Eagle).

RANGE. — Breeds in suitable locations throughout United States to central Mexico; winters throughout most of its range.

I well recall the day when, as an impressionable lad, I first saw the Bald Eagle wheeling majestically up the sky until it rose to a height almost beyond the utmost compass of my straining vision, and there — a mere speck in the blue — it sailed away until it vanished in the vast spaces of the upper air. The great bird had been fishing about Podunk Pond in West Brookfield, Massachusetts, and, startled at the sound of my gun, had passed away from that mundane scene apparently as lightly as a drifting cloud. Since then I have seen many Eagles on the shores of the Atlantic and Pacific oceans and witnessed many of their aerial evolutions, but never since have I experienced the feeling of awe with which I watched this living embodiment of the emblem of American freedom ascending grandly into the autumnal sky. My emotions on that occasion were somewhat similar to those experienced when I first viewed in the near distance the great dome of the capitol at Washington, for around both bird and building cluster many memories and traditions of a great country and a mighty people. Our Eagle may deserve some of the epithets that have been heaped upon him; he may be a robber, a skulker and a carrion feeder; nevertheless he is a powerful and noble bird and a master of the air.

The Bald Eagle ordinarily seems a heavy bird in flight and very deliberate as it flaps along with its rather long neck extended and its feet stretched out behind under its tail, but it is capable of great speed at need, and instances are known where it has overtaken and struck down swift-flying water-fowl. Sometimes its speed is extraordinary. It can overtake and master the Swan, the Canada Goose, and the Brant, and it has been seen to strike down a flying Pintail. In the North I have not seen the Bald Eagle attack any bird, but in the South it often chases ducks, which may elude it by diving, although a persistent Eagle may finally tire out and capture an unwounded duck. Wounded ducks and Coots are captured frequently, while unwounded Coots are taken with ease.

From Halfway Pond, the source of the Agawam River, to Popponesset on Cape Cod, the Eagles follow the alewives when they begin in April to run up the streams. An old resident of Wareham told me that in his early days he had seen as many as thirty Eagles in one day following up the Agawam River. At my farm at Wareham on the banks of the Agawam there was in 1900 a tall dead pine that we called the 'eagle tree,' on which Eagles often perched while scanning the river for alewives. A few years later the tree fell, and after that the great birds used another about half a mile up the river which has now gone the way of all trees. I have often approached quite near a young Eagle perched in one or the other of these trees.

The history of the Bald Eagle is that of all our larger birds. Formerly breeding commonly in the primeval forest, the species has been greatly reduced in numbers, and over wide areas the breeding birds have been extirpated. Possibly from fifty to one hundred pairs of Bald Eagles still nest and rear their young in the forests of Maine and along its coast. But in the Kennebec Valley the nests are much less numerous than they were years ago. A few pairs nest in New Hampshire from about the region of Lake Winnepesaukee northward, and a pair or more may still breed in the region about Lake Champlain.

The Bald Eagle is by nature a fish eater, and fish form his principal food. He takes them alive or dead, and when opportunity offers he seizes those already caught by the Osprey. When some mortality occurs among fish, causing them to die by thousands, eagles often assemble in numbers to the feast.

The keen eye of the Eagle is proverbial. Eaton tells us in his 'Birds of New York' how, as he watched an Eagle soaring at a great height over a lake, the bird started diagonally downward in a dive toward a floating fish, which it picked up three miles from the spot over which the bird had been soaring, and brought it ashore. The bird was so far away from the observer when it picked up the fish that he could not see it in the bird's talons with a six-power glass.

Afar in the sky or on a branch of some tall tree near the water the Eagle's eye follows the fishing Osprey and marks every plunge. When the Osprey rises with a fish the Eagle shows his speed and power. With flashing eye and quickening wing, he speeds toward the laboring Fish-hawk, which exerts itself to the utmost to escape, but usually in vain. A strong, swift Osprey with a small fish sometimes escapes, but a heavy fish is too great a handicap. Reaching the Osprey, the speeding Eagle passes under his victim; the Osprey, turning and twisting in the air, rises to escape, but the Eagle, having driven the lesser bird high enough for his purpose, threatens it with beak and claws. Striking at the Fish-hawk, and sometimes almost enveloping the poor bird with his great beating wings, he drives it here and there, trying to frighten it so that it will drop the fish. Usually intimidation accomplishes his object, but if not, the eagle strikes the Osprey with force enough to send it reeling through the air. At last it relaxes its hold on its prey. As the fish falls, the Eagle with a few swift strokes catches it with one foot, or if the Osprey has dropped it at a moment when the Eagle is not in a position to snatch it immediately, he poises an instant, then shooting downward with partly closed and hissing pinions, he overtakes his booty in its rapid descent and bears it away to a dead branch of some tall tree to eat it at his leisure. At least this is the picture drawn by those who claim to have seen the action.

I have never seen the Eagle actually seize the fish in its fall. In my experience the great bird is quite likely to allow the fish to drop. Twice I have seen one shoot down from a far height with breath-taking speed, only to check his flight near the surface with vibrating wings and wide-spread tail, while the fish just below him disappeared with a splash in the water. At any rate the Eagle does not depend on the Osprey, but watches for dead fish, and if he finds none, and no Osprey is at hand, he catches them himself or pursues some other quarry. His usual method is to flap or soar at no great height above the water, occasionally hovering; and at the proper moment he glides diagonally downward with set wings, grasps the fish without plunging under water and carries it to the shore; or he sits perched on some tall tree near the water and when a good opportunity presents itself, sails down on set wings and picks up his victim. Rarely he strikes a fish too large to raise from the surface, but he holds to it tena-

118

ciously as long as possible until eventually he either tows it ashore or is himself dragged under water and forced to relinquish his hold and come to the surface for air.

The Bald Eagle is a brave bird, but tales of its attacks on human beings must be received with caution. An adult Eagle usually has had enough sad experiences with mankind to teach it circumspection. Sometimes immature birds seem to be full of curiosity regarding man and his ways, but attempts on the part of an Eagle even to approach human habitations are likely to be promptly met with a charge of shot or a rifle ball, and the birds that escape with their lives soon become very shy.

The Bald Eagle is virtually harmless. It plays the part of scavenger about the shores of many bodies of water. Only once have I known it to disturb poultry, and never have I heard of an unwounded bird killed by it in this region. It should be rigorously protected at all times by law and public sentiment to save it, if possible, from extirpation.

MARSH HAWK

Circus hudsonius (LINNAEUS).   PLATES 37 AND 38.

Other names: Bog Hawk; Mouse Hawk; Frog Hawk; Snake Hawk.

IDENTIFICATION. — Length of male 17½ to 20 inches, spread 40 to 45 inches; length of female 19 to 24 inches, spread 43 to 54 inches. Larger than crow, with long wings and tail; upper tail coverts always white; beats about over open lands and marshes, flapping along low down with some sailing, and wings held slanting upward from shoulder. Adult male lightest in color of any hawk in northeast region; light gray above, nearly white below; black tips to flight-feathers. Female and young rich brown above, lighter brown below.

BREEDING. — In meadows or open lands among coarse vegetation. *Nest:* On ground, of grass and weeds. *Eggs:* 3 to 8, whitish usually unmarked.

RANGE. — Breeds from Alaska, northern Ontario and Newfoundland south to Lower California, Texas, southern Illinois, Ohio, Maryland, and southeastern Virginia; winters from southern British Columbia to southern New Hampshire and south to Florida, the West Indies, and Colombia.

The slender graceful Marsh Hawk is a bird of tireless flight. It is one of the 'ignoble' hawks — a lowly mouse hunter; a 'harrier' of the marsh, hunting mainly close to the ground. It seldom alights on a large tree, where I have seen it but once, although it rests occasionally on very small trees, shrubs, haycocks, or fence posts. It feeds usually upon the ground, nests there and probably often roosts there.

This hawk is not confined to the marsh in its peregrinations, as it may be seen hunting on the dryest kind of sandy lands or on upland pastures, and in some parts of the Western prairie country it nests on high ridges. It is seen rarely in the woods, except about woodland lakes or rivers or small ponds near the borders of the forest. Its flight and its appearance in the air about the shores of Lake Umbagog, in Northern New England, are graphically described by William Brewster as follows:

'Even when its shores are almost everywhere submerged in May, and early June, they are not infrequently included within the regular daily beats of adult male Marsh Hawks in full nuptial plumage, looking almost as white as gulls, and indeed not always to be distinguished from them, when seen at a distance skimming low over blue water, or against a dark background of evergreen foliage. Flying ever in the buoyant, unhurried manner so characteristic of their race, now renewing waning impetus by a few deliberate wing-strokes, next gliding for several rods on wings set with the tips held well upwards, much as those of a gliding Turkey Vulture are held, tilting their bodies more or less perceptibly from side to side and rarely pursuing a perfectly straight course for more than a few yards at a time, they may skirt the shore for miles, following all its windings closely, and keeping just outside the outer ranks of living trees, but taking no especial pains to thus avoid outstanding dead ones. For the most part such flight is apt to impress one as unheeding if not perfunctory, but all the while the bird is doubtless keenly scanning every stump and floating log within its range of vision, while every now and then it will hover low over rafts of driftwood collected in sheltered coves, to scrutinize them with obviously eager interest. . . . A Marsh Hawk engaged in low and for the most part straight-onward, gliding flights is not unlikely to remind one, as has been said, of a Turkey Buzzard similarly employed, because of the decided upward angle, nearly, if not quite, 45°, at which its wings are held, and of the lateral tilting of its body. But when, as often happens, it soars in circles, perhaps hundreds of feet above the earth, its wings are set almost level, like those of a soaring Buteo which it otherwise resembles in general carriage, but from which it may easily be distinguished, even at distances too great to make out its characteristic color and markings, by its slenderer body, and longer tail. At the Lake I have repeatedly seen Marsh Hawks mount in this manner, with rarely a wing-beat, until they were almost lost to sight overhead, and apparently above the crests of the higher mountains.'

With the warm days of April many Marsh Hawks, leaving their southern winter homes, appear in the North. Some already are mated when they arrive and they may mate for life, as pairs have been observed in winter hunting together.

The courtship of the Marsh Hawk is carried on largely in its favorite element. In warm spring days a pair may be seen soaring to a great height, when one will suddenly plunge far downward and turn a complete forward or sidelong somersault in the air. Sometimes one falling thus from a height will turn over and over again in the manner of a tumbler pigeon. As it bounds up and down in the air, it seems to move more like a rubber ball than a bird. This tireless behavior usually occurs over the marsh or meadow that they have chosen for a home. When two of these birds are mated or mating they keep together much of the time, either on the ground or in the air. When the female alights the male follows her and walks or flies around her. On the ground he bows to her and swells with amorous ardor. Sometimes the male flies alone across the marsh rising and falling alternately and with each fall turning a complete somersault. Again he 'carries on' in the same way while flying in her company. He is a good father, as he assists at times in nest building and also in incubation and in caring for the young, but his principal function after the young have hatched is that of providing food for the family. Hunting tirelessly along marshy borders of some lake or stream, he beats over the ground until he perceives the movement of some mouse, frog or other suitable prey in the grass, when, rising a little in the air and poising for an instant with rapidly vibrating wings, he falls upon his victim; or, if in his flight he catches sight of some fleeing timorous prey beneath him, he turns like a flash and snatches it up, or, having overrun it, he, in his eagerness to check his flight, may even turn a complete somersault in striking his victim; then rising high, he flies swiftly homeward. As he nears the neighborhood of his domicile he hails his mate with shrill cries, and she, replying, leaves her precious charge and rises to meet him. When directly over her, he drops his prey and she, turning partly over in the air, catches it with her claws as it falls, or if not near enough darts after it and dexterously snatches it ere it reaches the ground, then drops to her nest, while he either follows her or turns again to his hunting.

The Marsh Hawk nests on the ground among tall grasses, bushes, or other vegetation in a meadow or swamp not far from water. The eggs are apparently laid at intervals of several days, as the young birds in a nest vary considerably in size and development.

In late August or early September the autumnal migration of the Marsh Hawk begins, and some birds continue to move southward until late in November. The principal migration seems to move along the coastal plain.

The Marsh Hawk is a useful species over most of its range, but along the Atlantic coast it is more harmful than in many other regions. Even there, however, it probably is worthy of full protection as, were this hawk exterminated, the injury done by the mice, rats and squirrels that it now consumes and their progeny, would soon far exceed that attributable now to the hawk.

In the rice fields of the South it is extremely useful, as it frightens the 'rice birds' and keeps them moving and thus interrupts their depredations, while in the game preserves it destroys cotton rats, which rank among the greatest enemies of the Bob-white.

AMERICAN OSPREY

Pandion haliaëtus carolinensis (GMELIN). PLATES 37 AND 38.

Other name: Fish-hawk.

IDENTIFICATION. — Length 21 to 24½ inches; spread 54 to 72 inches. Nearly as large as a small eagle; unmistakable, very dark brown above, often with considerable white on upper head, but back of neck never white like that of Bald Eagle; mostly white below; with very long, bent, 'crooked' wings; often seen over water; flaps rather slowly and sometimes sails and soars; often hovers high over water and then plunges down and in; as it flies away, its flapping flight, with flexible wings, resembles very much similar flight of Great Blue Heron.

CALL. — A shrill, rapidly repeated whistle suggesting 'peeping' of young chickens.

BREEDING. — Usually near sea or large lake, sometimes in colony. *Nest:* Very bulky, of sticks, corn-stalks, etc. *Eggs:* 2 to 4, white or buffy-white, heavily marked with browns.

RANGE. — Breeds from Alaska, Hudson Bay, southern Labrador, and Newfoundland south to Lower California, the Gulf States, and the Florida Keys; winters from Florida and the Gulf States to the West Indies and Central America.

The American Osprey is one of the few large birds that is still a familiar sight to the inhabitants of New England, but it has decreased greatly in recent times. There is every reason to believe that it was once a common breeding bird along the whole coast of New England and locally in the interior. It breeds commonly now only where it is protected. In such cases it assembles in colonies, as on the border of Rhode Island and Bristol County, Massachusetts, where the farmers protect the species. It is said that while these birds are incubating their eggs and rearing their young, they will not allow other hawks in the vicinity of their nests, and, as the young chickens are allowed to run at large at that season, the Ospreys protect the chickens from the forays of other hawks. For this reason the farmer desires to have a pair of Fish-hawks nesting as near the farmyard as possible. Here and there someone has erected a tall pole in the dooryard with a cartwheel fixed horizontally across its top. This makes a convenient and safe location of which the Osprey is not slow to take advantage. When I first visited this colony in 1900, there were apparently about seventy-five nests; probably the colony has decreased since that time. The region lies along the shores of Narraganset Bay and its estuaries, which then were an ideal fishing-ground for the birds. The country near the coast, being quite open and cultivated, did not offer many suitable nesting-sites for the Fish-hawks. Most of the conveniently located, large, isolated trees were already occupied, and some of the birds were forced to use telegraph poles or even chimneys as supports for their domiciles.

A few Ospreys arrive in interior southern New England in March, but most of them return to their inland breeding-grounds there early in April, and some begin to repair their old nests, for the Osprey is accustomed to utilize the same nesting-site year after year. In building on to the old nest and repairing it a great mass of material is gotten together, in time, so that the nest becomes nearly as large as that of an eagle. Some of them are enormous, and when fixed in the top of some tall dead tree one may be seen for miles. I have observed similar great nests on the Maine coast on tall rocks jutting up from the water in a bay or estuary. On Gardiner's Island, New York, where the birds are protected, many of them build their nests on the level ground, while along the coast of some of the Southern States nests may be found resting upon the tops of sand-dunes on sea islands.

The Osprey's well-known method of fishing is to flap along over the water at a height of from thirty to one hundred feet, scanning the depths below. When it sees a desirable fish near the surface, it hovers for an instant and then closing its wings shoots downward, plunging into the water with great force and often disappearing from sight. The force of the bird's plunge is so great that it must strike the surface head first, as any deviation from its course on entering the water might result in injury. Rising to the surface it rests a mere instant, flaps into the air and starts for its nest or some tree where it intends to devour its victim. In flying away with the fish it always turns it head foremost.

The American Osprey appears to be an affectionate bird; while the young are in the nest one or the other parent usually is within call, always ready to defend its offspring. When the young are fledged and able to fly well, they begin to practice catching fish for themselves. They require no teaching, as individuals that have been brought up by hand and have never seen their parents catch fish, will begin fishing for themselves as soon as they have fully mastered the intricate problem of flight. At first they have very little success. I have seen a young bird plunge into a river seven times in succession without securing a fish, but the bird did not appear to be in the least discouraged, for it continued to follow the river and scan its waters in search of a victim. The adults also now and then fail, and a wetting is all they get. They frequently drop part way, only to check their fall with spread wings and tail when the fish has gone too deep.

When the frosts of autumn chill the coast waters and many fishes begin to move southward, the Ospreys follow, but before they go many of them repair their nests with strong, freshly broken sticks as if to prepare them to withstand the storms of winter.

The food of the Osprey consists principally of fish. Now and then perhaps a frog or some other small aquatic animal is taken, and more rarely a water-snake. The fish captured are principally surface fish of little value, such as carp, suckers, pike, alewives, menhaden and sunfish — fish which normally swim near the surface. Sometimes catfish are taken, including the hornpout of New England. All the evidence available points to the conclusion that the Osprey is harmless to poultry, birds and game, and that most of the fish that it takes are species of little value to mankind. Fishermen usually welcome it as a guide to good fishing. All things considered, this great, handsome, picturesque and interesting bird must be regarded as a subject for perpetual protection.

AUDUBON'S CARACARA

Polyborus cheriway auduboni CASSIN.   PLATE 97.

Other names: Mexican Eagle; Mexican Buzzard; King Buzzard.

IDENTIFICATION. — Length 20 to 25 inches; spread about 48 inches. A long-legged, large-headed hawk with heavy beak, and bare skin around eye; head slightly crested, crown black; back, wings, and belly rusty black; throat dingy white or buffy; breast barred; wings blackish but a light area near tip; tail narrowly barred and with broad black terminal band.

BREEDING. — In tree, often a palmetto. *Nest:* Of twigs and green sticks. *Eggs:* 2 to 4, white or creamy or darker, variously marked with browns.

RANGE. — Resident from northern Lower California, southwestern Arizona, Texas, and Florida south through Mexico and Central America.

Audubon's Caracara is a bird of the open country, preferring prairie regions and seldom seen in heavily wooded areas, and nesting usually in mesquite thickets or among palmettos and scattered small trees. It is principally a scavenger and carrion eater and is often found associated with Black and Turkey Vultures at their feasts. It occasionaly devours small animals, rodents and reptiles being its most common prey.

The appearance of Audubon's Caracara is striking and characteristic. On the ground, its longer legs and its habit of walking instead of hopping differentiate it from other hawks. Its straightaway flight is often sluggish-appearing, with alternate flappings and sailings, but at times it is strong, rapid, and direct. It frequently skims low over the ground, and at other times circles high overhead. When perched, it sits very erect 'with a strange grandfatherly appearance.' When emitting its raucous call, from which it gets its name, the head is thrown back until it seems to rest upon the bird's shoulders.

In flight, the Caracara's long straight wings with widely separated primaries, rather long tail, stiffly outstretched neck, and the conspicuous whitish areas on neck and breast, near tips of the wings, on upper and lower tail coverts, and base of tail, make an unmistakable and easily recognized picture. The great beak is yellow, and the broad cere (the fleshy base of the beak) and the bare area around the eye, are carmine. — (J.B.M.)

WHITE GYRFALCON

Falco rusticolus candicans GMELIN.   PLATES 38 AND 42.

IDENTIFICATION. — Length of male 21 to 22½ inches, spread 48 to 49 inches; length of female 23 to 24 inches, spread 49 to 51½ inches. A large white hawk with long pointed wings; flight, rapid wing-beats alternating with short periods of sailing.

BREEDING. — About rocky cliffs near the coast. *Eggs:* 2 to 4, creamy-white to reddish-brown, usually thickly marked, laid on bare ground.

RANGE. — Resident in eastern Arctic America, Greenland, Spitzbergen, and Franz Josef Land (probably); casual south in winter to southern Canadian provinces, Maine, Montana, and in Europe.

The White Gyrfalcon is, like the Snowy Owl, a bird of Arctic regions, chiefly, beyond the tree limit. This is the greatest and most powerful of all the northern falcons. In the days when falconry was in vogue, it furnished sport for kings. Commander Donald B. MacMillan, the Arctic explorer, says of it, 'This bird stands as the dominant king of northern bird-land, fearless, aggressive, and the swiftest of all. In lonely and inaccessible places it builds its nest, scorning the friendship of bird or man. Although the Gyrfalcon lived within two miles of our house, we rarely saw it. A rapid white dash and the bird was gone.' The voracity of this powerful falcon was shown, according to Commander MacMillan, by an enormous pile of bones of the Dovekie accumulated near its nesting-place. In preparing a Dovekie for its use the Gyrfalcon bites off head and wings, plucks out the feathers, and swallows the body whole. When digestion has disposed of the soft parts, the bones are disgorged. The only specimens that I have seen alive were three young birds, fully fledged, that were brought in 1925 from an aery in northern Greenland by Commander MacMillan. From his vessel he saw the aery of the falcon and three well grown young high up on a sea-cliff, and he sent an Eskimo to climb the cliff and secure the birds. The man finally reached them, got them down and, placing them in the bow of his skin boat, paddled back to the ship. In the meantime one had fallen overboard and been picked up. There was no room for them below decks on the crowded, heavily laden vessel, which was then homeward bound, so a cage was made for them on deck. The voyage home was very rough and the young birds were drenched time and again by the boarding seas, but while they complained and shivered in misery, they were so tough and hardy that they lived and prospered. On their arrival at Boston they were consigned to the Zoological Garden at Franklin Park, where they were kept in a large cage out of doors with concrete floor and a dead tree for a perch. As there are no trees in northern Greenland, they never seemed to regard the tree as a resting-place and did not use it, but sat constantly on the cold concrete or rocks.

The Gyrfalcon's flight is lofty and swift. It progresses by quick flappings, interspersed occasionally with a short sail. It takes its prey either by a swift stoop from a height or by a chase, overtaking its victim by dint of speed, lung power, and endurance. It can catch in this way many swift water-birds. It is said to strike down in flight such large birds as Eider Ducks and Snow Geese. Its food is quite varied but consists largely of lemmings, Arctic hares, guillemots, ducks, Dovekies, shore birds, Snow Buntings, and Kittiwakes.

BLACK GYRFALCON

Falco rusticolus obsoletus GMELIN.   PLATE 42.

IDENTIFICATION. — Length of male 20 to 23 inches, spread 44 to 50 inches; length of female 22 to 25 inches, spread 49 to 55 inches. Typical falcon outlines and large size will identify the species, but the subspecies cannot be distinguished in the field, the light phase of *F. r. obsoletus* being very similar to the dark phase of *F. r. candicans*.

BREEDING. — Similar to White Gyrfalcon.

RANGE. — Breeds from Point Barrow to Labrador; wanders south in winter to northern tier of states.

When Mr. Forbush wrote his 'Birds of Massachusetts and Other New England States' the third edition of the 'Check-List' of the American Ornithologists' Union was accepted in matters of classification and nomenclature. He therefore listed and illustrated two species of gyrfalcon, with three races of one species, namely *Falco islandus*, White Gyrfalcon; *F. rusticolus rusticolus*, Gray Gyrfalcon; *F. r. gyrfalco*, Gyrfalcon; and *F. r. obsoletus*, Black Gyrfalcon. The fourth edition of the 'Check-List,' appearing in 1931, lists only one species with three subspecies, from North America; *F. r. candicans*, formerly *F. islandus*, White Gyrfalcon; the Asiatic Gyrfalcon, *F. r. uralensis*, occasionally found in extreme northwest North America; and *F. r. obsoletus*, Black Gyrfalcon, to which all records from northeastern and north central North America, not *F. r. candicans*, are now referred.

The Black Gyrfalcon is apparently more southern in its distribution than its congener the White Gyrfalcon, breeding on rocky cliffs in Labrador and along the Arctic shores of North America, where it feeds largely upon sea-birds, though, unlike most falcons, it also feeds freely upon mammals, from hares to lemmings and field mice. Breeding in a treeless or nearly treeless region, it seldom alights in trees during its occasional southern wanderings, but prefers a resting-place on a ledge, boulder, or haycock, or even the ridgepole of a building at times.

One of the most interesting results of the recent observations made at Hawk Mountain in Pennsylvania, where thousands of hawks of many different species pass during the autumn migrations and where formerly they were slaughtered indiscriminately, has been the sight identification of several individual Gyrfalcons. This is considerably south of what we might consider the 'normal' range of this rare straggler, the 'Check-List' giving it as found 'casually' in New York and 'also probably' in Pennsylvania. A Gyrfalcon could be confused only with a large Duck Hawk, and only when light conditions prevented recognition of their very different colorations. — (J.B.M.)

DUCK HAWK

Falco peregrinus anatum BONAPARTE. PLATES 37, 38, 43 AND 44.

Other names: American Peregrine Falcon; Ledge Hawk; Great-footed Hawk; Rock Hawk; Bullet Hawk.

IDENTIFICATION. — Length of male 15 to 18 inches, spread 38½ to 43 inches; length of female 18 to 20 inches, spread 43 to 46 inches. Size about that of Cooper's Hawk; adult dark slate above, buffy with black spots below; young brownish above, streaked below; a dark bird of swift flight on rapidly beating sharp-pointed wings and rather long, rounded (almost pointed) tail; flight resembles that of a pigeon; distinguished from other hawks when near at hand by its conspicuous black cap and its black 'moustache' on a light background; does not soar very much in circles, but sails easily and plunges from a height on its prey or overtakes it by rapid flight.

BREEDING. — On ledge of cliff. *Eggs:* 2 to 6, deep, creamy color very heavily marked with rich browns.

RANGE. — Breeds locally from Alaska, Baffin Island, and Greenland south to Lower California, central Mexico, Missouri, Tennessee, and Connecticut; winters from Vancouver Island through California, and from Colorado, Illinois, and Massachusetts south to the West Indies and Panama.

The Duck Hawk is the American representative of the Peregrine Falcon, a noble bird, a 'falcon gentil,' that was used for hawking by the knights and ladies of the days of chivalry. Its American representative is, virtually, identical with the European bird in spirit, habits, form, size and coloration, with the exception of lighter and less marked lower fore parts. In size and color it approaches the European bird so closely that in some cases it is difficult or impossible to distinguish one from the other. Even in captivity this capable bird knows no fear; he retains his dignity, equipoise and boldness.

Every person who ranges the woods knows that jays are accustomed to assemble and hector certain hawks and owls. There is one hawk, however, that the jays let severely alone, and that is the Duck Hawk. This swift and powerful falcon is the jay's worst enemy. From its mountain heights this hawk surveys the shining waters and the valleys spread below. Its piercing eye selects its prey in full flight, and it falls on its victim like a thunderbolt from the sky. It is the master of the air within its wide domain.

The favorite retreats of this hawk are cliffs or crags overlooking some broad river valley with a stream meandering far below. It often watches from a dead tree on the steep mountain side, but more often patrols the valley at a considerable height or swings upward in wide circles until it reaches such an altitude that it is unseen or forgotten by its prospective victims. Its flight is one of the most wonderful exhibitions of speed and command of the air shown by any bird. At times when heading into the wind it will slide off sidewise, covering a mile thus in a matter of seconds. It can so regulate its flight at will as seemingly to bound upward for one hundred or two hundred feet like a flash and apparently with the greatest ease. It can overtake and capture any of our birds in flight except possibly the Chimney Swift, and the only hope its victims have to elude it is by dodging its rushes, until they can dive into some tangle of vines and shrubbery. Fierce and audacious in pursuit of its victims, it does not hesitate to rush with incredible rapidity into the very farmyards in pursuit of poultry or pigeons, and to strike down its terrified quarry in the near presence of its arch enemy, man.

In March and April many Duck Hawks come in from the south. Their line of migration follows chiefly the coast, but in New England some of them are on their breeding-grounds in March, and a few have been seen in winter about their nesting-places. Eggs are laid late in March or early in April. The mated pair often hang about its breeding-cliff to guard the nesting-place from interlopers or squatters of their own kind long before the eggs are laid. When choosing an aery the falcon usually finds a high shelf on some cliff for her future home. It must be high enough to command an extended view. It must be free from danger from falling rocks, and it must be inaccessible to quadrupeds and unwinged bipeds. Danger from rocks falling from the cliff is lessened either by choosing a shelf near the top or by occupying a recess or small cave under firm overhanging rock. Commonly the eggs are laid on a projecting cliff which gives a wide view, but this is not always the case. If the cliff is very high, the aery may be situated in some recess halfway up. Occasionally it is so near the summit as to be readily accessible from above, but probably this is exceptional. Often when the birds are watched, they will not go to it or will use great caution in approaching it. Usually the young are ready for flight before June 1. In the meantime one may fall over the edge of its rocky shelf to its death on the broken talus far below. While the young are developing, the parents continually bring them small birds that they kill while ranging far and wide over the valley below. In about four weeks the natal down is nearly all replaced by the brown of juvenal plumage. The whole family lingers near the aery till snow flies, but only one pair nests there the next spring. When the fledglings have become skillful in flight, both young and adults in practice or in play often strike at birds which apparently they have no intention of capturing.

When a Duck Hawk 'stoops' from a great height upon its prey, its plunge is so lightning-like that the bird seems to have been evolved out of a clear sky, and the sound of its rush is like that made by a rocket. The sudden arrowlike fall of this bird from far heights is one of the most impressive sights in bird life. However, it does not always strike thus, but frequently perches on some tall tree at the water's edge and launches out at water-fowl flying by. Mr. C. J. Maynard asserts that in such cases the eye can hardly follow its movements, and it overtakes and strikes swift-flying ducks in this manner with the greatest ease.

When I was hunting one day on the Banana River, in Florida, a flock of Blue-winged Teals came flying over the water. The rapid flight of these Teals is well known to sportsmen. Suddenly, from somewhere, a Duck Hawk shot through that flock like a meteor, struck down three birds, one after another, and passed swiftly on, leaving the little ducks lying dead on the water. For some reason diving ducks, when resting on the surface, seem to have no fear of this falcon — perhaps because it rarely strikes anything on or in the water, but prefers to take its prey on the wing in sportsmanlike fashion; nevertheless individuals have been known to dive into the water, osprey-like, or to strike wooden duck decoys riding on the surface.

The courage and intrepidity of this falcon are so great that it sometimes attacks very large birds. Commander Donald MacMillan says that he once saw one drop like a comet out of the blue sky and knock down a Blue Goose with such force as to partially disable it. He was positive that in this case the falcon threw her wings far back and struck the goose with her breast. Others have reported similar observations. This hawk usually does not trouble other birds of prey unless they approach its aery. Then let them beware!

Water-fowl of considerable size are the usual prey of the Duck Hawk, and while some of them are swift fliers, they cannot turn quickly enough to evade the falcon's rush. The smaller shore birds are more successful in eluding its pursuit, but it captures some of them. When its young are small it shows great aerial skill in catching small birds on the wing, some of which are adepts at dodging, as for example the Phoebe and the Barn Swallow. Swifts are believed

127

to be the swiftest of all birds, and it has been generally asserted that the Duck Hawk is unable to overtake them. I have never found the feathers of a swift near a Duck Hawk's aery, but a farmer in the Connecticut Valley states that he saw this falcon capture a Chimney Swift. Many swifts, he says, were coursing above the fields, when the falcon made several dashes at them, but missed. At last as one turned to evade the rush, the hawk swung over on its back, and reaching up one foot as it shot by, caught the swift in its powerful grasp.

On May 20, 1917, I climbed a mountain above an aery, and then worked down to it from the top of a precipice five hundred feet above the river. The single young one — the only one left from the clutch of three eggs — was more than half-grown and covered with white down. There was nothing that could be called a nest on this rock shelf, but the nesting-place was surrounded by small bushes growing from the scanty mold that had accumulated there. Here the young bird sat and viewed the world from the shadow of the overhanging rock. He was surrounded by feathers of many Blue Jays and some feathers of other small birds which had been brought by his parents. He called intermittently to his sharp-winged, powerful screaming mother, sailing high overhead. Soon the male joined her, and both swooped down at me with menacing cries. One of the birds suddenly shot straight down like a feathered arrow-head from a height of about one hundred feet directly over my head, and passed me with a startling rush of wings, bounding upward to its original height without any perceptible motion of its pinions, which were held less than half open. What tremendous power and spirit these birds evince! Later both of them hung in air against a gale that rushed furiously over that mountain top, and hardly a motion of a flight-feather could be detected. What held them, as if by sheer force of will, against such a wind far above that rocky summit?

On June 10 I visited the aery again. Lowering clouds in sheets of white mist drifted above the mountain top, now hiding the valley below, now unveiling the lovely landscape. The woods were wonderfully beautiful; the leaves were fully developed, and the miracle of spring and summer was consummated. The young falcon, a few weeks earlier a little downy white chick, was now a hawklet, nearly full-grown, with wings and tail ready for flight and only a few down-filaments of his chick plumage remaining. On June 11 he launched out over the gulf on strong and perfect pinions, riding in a moment the unstable, shifting element that man, after centuries of failures, has only just begun to conquer.

The Duck Hawk feeds for the most part on birds, including usually those from the size of a Snow Bunting to that of the largest ducks and grouse. Domestic fowls are occasional victims, and pigeons are a favorite prey in settled regions. In cities like Boston, New York, and Philadelphia, Duck Hawks occasionally resort in winter to some tall building where they can overlook the city and prey on the street pigeons which abound there. Very small birds such as the smaller sparrows and warblers seldom are troubled by this species, except perhaps when its young are small and are fed almost entirely on small birds. Among the feathers found about the nests of this species those of Pheasants and Ruffed Grouse appear occasionally, but I have observed very few remains of mammals.

EASTERN PIGEON HAWK

Falco columbarius columbarius LINNAEUS.   PLATES 38 AND 44.

Other names: Blue Bullet; American Merlin; Little Corporal.

IDENTIFICATION. — Length of male 10 to 10½ inches, spread 23½ to 26 inches; length of female 12 to 13½ inches, spread 24 to 26 inches. A heavy, stocky hawk with the long sharp-pointed wings of a falcon; resembles a pigeon in flight, with rapid wing-beats; sails more or less with extended wings; long, pointed wings and dark breast distinguish it from Sharp-shinned Hawk, with longer tail and shorter rounded wings. Adult male bluish above; whitish, darkly streaked, below. Female and young dusky brownish above, streaked below; distinguished from Sharp-shinned Hawk by stockier form and 'rowing' flight of the long, pointed wings; 'Sharp-shin' is slimmer and often larger.

BREEDING. — In coniferous forests. *Nest:* Near top of tall tree, of sticks lined with grasses, leaves, moss, etc. *Eggs:* 4 to 7, vary from white to purplish-brown, spotted and blotched.

RANGE. — Breeds from tree-limit in eastern Canada south to Newfoundland, Nova Scotia, northern Maine, Ontario, northern Michigan, and southern Manitoba; winters from the Gulf States through eastern Mexico to Ecuador, and in the West Indies.

The handsome, speedy little Eastern Pigeon Hawk is a small falcon resembling the Duck Hawk in power and speed, but, being much smaller and of less weight, it cannot attain such momentum as is exhibited in the swift dashes of the latter. It has received its name either because it was accustomed to prey on wild pigeons or because of its resemblance to a pigeon in form and flight. This hawk breeds in Canada almost entirely, and is seen in the eastern United States chiefly in the fall migrations, when from September to November it follows southward the flights of smaller birds. Oftentimes it appears quite tame. Although the Pigeon Hawk is naturally a forest bird and breeds in the woods, on its migrations it hunts mainly in open lands or about the shores of the larger streams or bodies of water and along the sea-coast. It likes to take a stand on post, pole or tree where, having an unobstructed view, it can survey at leisure the wild life of the locality, and from which it can launch forth in swift pursuit of some passing bird, or plunge into some nearby thicket after some timid warbler or sparrow. Its usual method is to chase the prospective victim, which in most cases it can overtake with apparent ease; but in my experience it is frequently baffled by the sudden doublings of the pursued, until it gives up the chase or the hunted bird escapes by suddenly diving into water or dense shrubbery. I have seen a Pigeon Hawk chase a small flock of Common Terns without even touching one, and once in Florida I watched one pursuing for a long time a flock of sandpipers, but it was unable to catch one as long as the chase was maintained within my field of vision. The hawk seemed to be able to overtake them and to follow their flash-like turns quite closely, but could not lay its claws on a single bird; snipes and sandpipers continually escape, and probably the hawk cannot often take a vigorous shore bird in full possession of its faculties, but a weak, sickly or wounded bird would stand little chance before it.

The following beautifully written description is from the pen of the late William Brewster: '1895. September 24. — About seven o'clock this morning a Pigeon Hawk drove a flock of ten or a dozen Blue Jays into the birch grove near our camp on Pine Point and during the next ten minutes circled or hovered low over or near them. As long as they remained perched he made no attempt to attack them, although the foliage was everywhere too thin to afford them much shelter. Nor did they stay in it long at a time, being too restless and venturesome.

Whenever one rose on wing above the trees and tried to steal away, as happened every half-minute or less, the Hawk instantly gave chase, vibrating his pinions ceaselessly, rapidly, and tremulously, as those of the Duck Hawk are moved on similar occasions, and flying with such exceeding velocity that my eyes could scarce follow him. His lavish expenditure of speed and energy in pursuit of the slow-winged Jays seemed almost as absurdly needless as that of a race horse might be were he employed to run down a cow or a goat. Of course I expected to see the Hawk capture his prey at the end of every swoop, especially when, with evident eager hope of such result, he checked his impetus more abruptly than birds of his kind are often able to do and thrust forward his widespread talons; but the Jay always dodged them at the last available moment by dropping suddenly into a tree-top. After keeping straight on for a short distance the little Falcon would then circle and rise to make ready for renewed assault. He never hovered directly over the Jays when they were in the trees, but invariably kept well off to one or another side of the flock, as if to offer them what might seem a tempting chance to escape, although it may have been done for the purpose of enabling him to avoid steep descent when making his dashing swoops. These were ordinarily from twenty to forty yards in length, and trending so slightly downward that the total drop was no more than six or eight feet for the entire distance, which was often covered by the Hawk before the Jay had flown one quarter as far. Altogether his admirably swift and graceful forays furnished one of the most beautiful and interesting spectacles of the kind that I have ever witnessed, despite their unvarying ill-success. Although appearing to make them in dead earnest he may, perhaps, have been merely amusing himself. Such, apparently, was the impression of the Jays; at least they did not take him seriously enough to seem very much afraid of him.'

There is one bird, however, that this hawk rarely misses. It will follow every twist and turn of the English Sparrow and soon overtakes its victim. Then its talons flash out and the chase is ended. Blackbirds, Meadowlarks and sparrows in flight over the water or over the salt marsh are easy victims, and occasionally a swallow is caught. Sometimes the hawk in pursuit of a bird will rise abruptly in the air above it and then plunge diagonally downward upon it with the speed of an arrow. Such tactics must be successful in some cases, but when the fleeing quarry eludes the rush, the impetus of the hawk's plunge carries him by, and thus the victim gains ground.

The food of the Eastern Pigeon Hawk consists chiefly of small birds, small mammals and insects. In autumn it hangs about flocks of slow-flying birds, such as blackbirds, and has been seen to dive through a flock of them and come out with 'one in each fist.' It picks up many sickly or crippled birds, and captures birds from the size of a warbler to that of a flicker or a small dove. Apparently this hawk does little harm to game or poultry but is destructive to small birds. The mice and insects and English Sparrows that it takes should be set down to its credit.

EASTERN SPARROW HAWK

Falco sparverius sparverius LINNAEUS. PLATES 38 AND 44.

Other names: American Kestrel; Killy-hawk; Windhover; Grasshopper Hawk; Mouse Hawk.

IDENTIFICATION. — Length of male 9 to 10½ inches, spread 20 to 22 inches; length of female 9 to 12 inches, spread 23 to 24½ inches. Small size, narrow pointed wings and rather long tail distinguish from all but Pigeon Hawk; reddish-brown back, three upright black marks on side of head; male has wings ashy blue, tail chestnut with black subterminal band and white tip; female has back, wings, and tail cinnamon narrowly barred with black.

BREEDING. — In natural or artificial cavity in tree, or about a building. *Eggs:* 4 to 7, vary from white to cinnamon, usually heavily marked but very variable.

RANGE. — Breeds from the Upper Yukon, northern Ontario, and Newfoundland south to California, eastern Texas, and the eastern Gulf States except Florida; winters from southern British Columbia, Kansas, central Illinois, southern Ontario, Ohio, and southern Vermont south through eastern Mexico to Panama.

The pretty little Eastern Sparrow Hawk seems to have become more common of late than it formerly was. It adapts itself to civilization, and has learned to utilize for nesting purposes bird-houses and nesting-boxes and nooks and crannies in churches, factories and other buildings, instead of the old woodpeckers' holes and hollow branches which it formerly used.

In New England Sparrow Hawks usually begin mating some time in April. It is quite possible that they mate for life as some other hawks are supposed to do. The female seems to take the initiative in mating, when they play about in the air in a peculiar way which is well described by William Brewster as seen by him in May at Lake Umbagog on the border of Maine and New Hampshire. His description of this mating play is succeeded by another note on play of another kind: '1880, May 17. — A pair of Sparrow Hawks are haunting the shores of the flooded river-meadows near the Lake House with the evident intention of breeding somewhere there. Today I saw them sitting not far apart on the tops of neighboring dead balsams. Every now and then one, always the male, I thought, would mount high in air to fly very rapidly, in a wide circle over and around where the other was perched, bending the tips of his wings downward and quivering them incessantly, at the same time uttering a shrill clamorous *kee-kee* cry, oft repeated. Sometimes both would start off together, to chase one another far and near, describing all manner of beautiful curves and occasionally sweeping down almost to the surface of the water. On realighting they invariably chose the very topmost twigs, often very slender ones, and settled on these with no less abruptness than precision, yet with admirable grace, scarce checking their speed until the perch was well-nigh reached and just then deftly folding their shapely wings.' '1888, September 12. — In a broad expanse of hilly burnt ground bordering on the Dead Cambridge above the Sluice we saw a Sparrow Hawk amusing himself at the expense of two Flickers. Calling *clac-lac-clac-lac-clac-lac* he would first hover over them for a few seconds, and then dart down close past them, to rise and hover again. Whenever they took flight he accompanied them, describing graceful curves and circles above and around them. That all this was done without malice on his part seemed obvious, and the Flickers evidently so interpreted it, for they showed no fear of him and more than once flew into a tree where he had just settled, alighting within a few feet of him.'

Such behavior is common among Sparrow Hawks, as they are playful and frolicsome creatures. Oftentimes birds pay no alarmed attention to the hawk and equally the hawks do not seem to regard the birds, but if pressed by hunger they do not hesitate to attack birds fully as large as themselves, and then a Flicker or a Blue Jay may be the first victim, and very rarely it has been seen to strike a 'Quail.' It is a common habit of this hawk, while hunting, to hang suspended in the air by its hovering wings while watching for an opportunity to pounce on some insect or mouse in the grass. Mr. Aretas A. Saunders says that while he watched one hovering close by, it squealed several times like a mouse, and he wonders if it was trying to entice a mouse from its concealment. Both parents join in the care of the eggs and young, and they are liberal providers and fierce defenders. They have been known to attack the Crow and both Red-shouldered and Red-tailed Hawks in defense of their young. Occasionally, however, one 'catches a tartar.' This was the case with one observed by Mr. S. G. Emilio in an attack on a Pigeon Hawk. After several swoops by the Sparrow Hawk, which its enemy deftly avoided, the latter turned on its assailant and pursued it for its life, but the Sparrow Hawk, by an unexpected exhibition of speed, escaped.

The principal part of the food taken to the young consists of mice and insects, but if for any reason such food is hard to obtain, small birds are substituted. The young remain in the nest about three weeks, but are fed by the parents for some time after they are able to fly. When the young are strong on the wing and have become expert in feeding themselves, in late August or early September, the great majority of our Sparrow Hawks begin to move southward; probably most of the birds of this species seen here in winter are migrants from farther north. In migration as well as in their summer home Sparrow Hawks roam over all kinds of country; they pass over unbroken forests, over the summits of our highest mountains and cross large lakes and arms of the sea, but they seem to hunt more in open country than in the woods. Grasshoppers form their chief food, when obtainable. Where grasshoppers are abundant, Sparrow Hawks appear to feed almost wholly on these insects, and rarely trouble birds.

LITTLE SPARROW HAWK

Falco sparverius paulus (HOWE AND KING).

IDENTIFICATION. — Smaller and darker than *F. s. sparverius;* tail and wings shorter in proportion; bill large and heavy; 'rufous of upper parts very dark.'

RANGE. — Resident in Florida peninsula and the southern portion of the Gulf States north to central Alabama.

Sparrow Hawks are very abundant birds in Florida. In summer the resident race is supposed to be the Little Sparrow Hawk, but in winter the Eastern Sparrow Hawk visits the same region, which complicates field observations badly. Their habits there are identical so far as I know, except that the northern bird is migratory and the southern race a permanent resident. — (J.B.M.)

HUDSONIAN SPRUCE GROUSE

Canachites canadensis canadensis (LINNAEUS).

IDENTIFICATION. — Similar to *C. c. canace*, but a grayer bird, more white and purer gray in the male, but even more marked in the female, which is much more purely black and gray with much less buffy or ochraceous. Males are probably indistinguishable in the field but females are less rusty than *C. c. canace*.

BREEDING. — In swampy coniferous woods. *Nest:* On ground, of twigs, leaves, and grasses. *Eggs:* 8 to 16, usually deep buff spotted with browns.

RANGE. — Boreal forest region from the Labrador Peninsula west to the eastern base of the Rocky Mountains west of Edmonton, Alberta.

Dr. Charles W. Townsend wrote of this bird in Mr. Bent's 'Life Histories of North American Gallinaceous Birds': 'The Hudsonian Spruce Grouse thrives best in regions where man is absent. In fact it remains so woefully ignorant of the destructive nature of the human animal that, unlike its cousin, the Ruffed Grouse, it rarely learns to run or fly away, but allows itself to be shot, clubbed, or noosed, and, in consequence, has earned for itself the proud title of "fool hen." As a result, wherever man appears, the Spruce Grouse rapidly diminishes in numbers, and, in the vicinity of villages or outlying posts, is not to be found. It is a bird of the northern wilderness, of thick and tangled swamps, and of spruce forests, where the ground is deep in moss and where the delicate vines of the snowberry and twinflower clamber over moss-covered stubs and fallen, long-decayed tree-trunks.

'The plumage of Spruce Grouse often makes them difficult to distinguish from their surroundings, and if their tameness depends on this protective coloration, they are overconfident, for, in a setting of reindeer lichen or snow, or an open branch of a spruce, they are very conspicuous. When flushed they generally fly only a few yards or even feet, and alighting in trees, they continually thrust the head and neck now this way, now that, and appear to be blindly trying to discover what has disturbed them. As a rule the flight is noiseless, or a slight sound only is heard, but at times they rise with a loud whir of wing-beats.' — (J.B.M.)

CANADA SPRUCE GROUSE

Canachites canadensis canace. (LINNAEUS).   PLATE 34.

Other names: Spruce Grouse; Spruce Partridge; Swamp Partridge; Heath Hen; Fool Hen.

IDENTIFICATION. — Length 15 to 17 inches; spread about 23 inches. Slightly smaller than Ruffed Grouse; male recognized by barred black and gray upper plumage and black and white under parts; female and young brownish, barred black and brown above where Ruffed Grouse is spotted and mottled.

BREEDING. — See Hudsonian Spruce Grouse.

RANGE. — Breeds in southern Manitoba, southern Ontario, southern Quebec, New Brunswick, and Nova Scotia south to northern Minnesota, northern Wisconsin, northern Michigan, northern New York, and northern New England.

In the dense spruce, fir, cedar and tamarack swamps of the great Maine woods the Spruce Grouse dwells. Where giant, moss-grown logs and stumps of the virgin forest of long ago cumber the ground, where tall, blasted stubs of others still project far above the tree-tops of today, where the thick carpet of green sphagnum moss deadens every footfall, where tiny-leaved vinelets radiate over their mossy beds, there we may find this wild bird as tame as a barnyard fowl. In the uplands round about, there still remain some tall primeval woods of birch and beech and rock maple where the moose and bear have set their marks upon the trees. In winter the deer gather in the swamps, and there their many trails wind hither and yon. Gnarled, stunted trees of arbor vitae, some dead or dying, defy the blasts of winter, while the long, bearded usnea droops streaming from their branches. Black-capped Chickadees, Acadian Chickadees, and Red-breasted Nuthatches curiously gather about the intruder.

One day in early September while following a trail through such a swamp which borders Sandy Stream, and hurrying to reach camp before dark night closed down, we almost stumbled over a male Spruce Grouse standing in the trail. The bird was somewhat startled and flew heavily up into a near-by spruce, alighting near the tip of a little limb about twenty feet from the ground. As the limb drooped under his weight, he walked up it to the trunk, hopped up a branch or two higher, and immediately began to feed on the foliage. After a few minutes of this he moved a little into another tree and continued feeding. Pounding on the trunk with an axe did not alarm him, and it was only after several sticks had been thrown and one had hit the very limb on which he sat that he was induced to fly.

The Canada Spruce Grouse is disappearing from the inhabited regions of northern New York and New England, although it holds its own fairly well in some of the wilder tracts. It is a forest recluse, much more arboreal than the Ruffed Grouse, confined rather closely to spruce, larch and cedar swamps and thickets in densely wooded regions, though found also among firs, hemlocks and other trees and on higher, drier lands, but rarely in open meadows or clearings.

The male in courtship struts about with the red comb-like patches above the eyes distended, breast-feathers ruffled, wings lowered and tail upraised and spread; he drums also, making a sound somewhat like the more rapid part of the drumming of the Ruffed Grouse, but less loud and resonant. This sound is produced by the wings, which beat upon the air with quick nervous strokes, while the bird is fluttering up ten or fifteen feet into a tree, or flying down from a branch. He has been seen to drum also while climbing the leaning trunk of a tree, while hovering in the air, and while merely flying up or down to or from the top of a stump. The usual flight of an unhurried Spruce Grouse is rapid and comparatively noiseless. The bird has been seen to start up silently from the ground and to drum during the latter part of the flight, and occasionally he drums when leaving the ground, but stops before the flight is completed. When this grouse is flushed suddenly from the ground, the sound of the wing-beats resembles that made by the wings of the Ruffed Grouse under similar circumstances, but is not quite so loud.

The food of the Canada Spruce Grouse consists largely of wild berries in late summer and autumn and of shoots, foliage and buds of spruce, larch and fir in winter. It is fond of insects and eats many, including grasshoppers, in spring and summer, and also parts of low-growing plants. The young are said to subsist mainly on insects and spiders.

EASTERN RUFFED GROUSE

Bonasa umbellus umbellus (LINNAEUS).   PLATE 35.

Other names: Partridge; 'Patridge'; Pheasant.

IDENTIFICATION. — Length 15½ to 19 inches; spread 22 to 25 inches. A large red-brown or gray-brown bird of the woodlands resembling a small domestic fowl in shape; blackish 'ruff' on neck, and fan-shaped tail with black or brownish band near end; when flushed rises with rapid noisy whirring flight.

BREEDING. — In wooded regions. *Nest:* On ground, a depression lined with dead leaves. *Eggs:* 7 to 17, whitish to pale brown, faintly marked with brownish.

RANGE. — Breeds from southern portions of Minnesota, Wisconsin, Michigan, Ontario, and New York, and from Massachusetts, south to eastern Kansas, northern Arkansas, Missouri, Tennessee, and Virginia, and in the mountains to northern Georgia and northern Alabama.

How quickly memory leaps athwart the years to the day long ago when as a child I flushed my first 'Partridge.' I can see now those dim and windless woods at break of day. The woodland songsters were awake and tuneful, and the woods rang with the staccato notes of the Oven-bird, when I started little bunny from the undergrowth. As I sprang forward hoping to catch the furry thing, a large bird, whose thundering pinions seemed to fill the air with their sudden breath-taking roar, rose almost beneath my feet and sped away through flying leaves and bending twigs into the shadowy recesses of the forest. My heart seemed to stop beating as I stood amazed, while little Molly Cottontail made good her escape.

An old cock Grouse treading his native forest floor is a sight to gladden the eye. Can you not see him? There, near the foot of that great white birch! He stands erect, his raised ruffs with their dark metallic sheen glistening in a ray of sunlight that sifts in through the tree-tops. With crested head erect and carried high, with bright and banded tail held clear and widely spread, he turns, pauses, listens, now turns again, throws forward his proud head, and steps lightly along, raising his feet well up, moving over the inequalities of the ground with a gently undulating motion, his broad tail raised or lowered at will, his dark wild eye flashing on all around; his frame instinct with electric life and vigor drawn from rugged New England hills. A perfect full-winged bird he stands, decked in his nuptial plumage, ready for love or war. Now his keen senses have detected the presence of his chief enemy, man. With a quick flirt of wings he has slipped over a low stone wall and is gone — hidden in friendly, sheltering thickets. This grouse is the king of American game birds, and doubtless has no superior among the grouse of the world.

In my early days the grouse often lay close and rose almost under foot, but now many of them have learned caution by sad experience and rise farther and farther away. When the country was first settled, this bird was one of the most tame and unsuspicious of the fowls of the air. It was known as the 'Fool Hen.' It was so tame that many were killed with stones or knocked over with sticks. They were then fair game for the small boy. Forty-five years ago in the wilderness I saw birds of this species that walked boldly up to within a few feet of the hunter, or even sat on a limb just over his head. An occasional unsophisticated bird may be seen that will seek human companionship, and even allow itself to be picked up and handled, but such birds are rare and usually are short-lived. Where they are hunted, the survivors have become 'educated,' and they resort to all kinds of tricks to escape the hunter and his dog.

135

When frightened and in full flight this grouse seems reckless. It does not, like the Wood Duck, so control its movements as to avoid the twigs and branches of trees, but dashes through them. I have seen one in such a case strike bodily against a limb and fall to the ground. This bird had been fired at in a neighboring wood, and had crossed the open with tremendous speed to another wood where it struck the limb. Aside from the shock the bird was unhurt. Often in autumn (the so-called 'crazy' season) the swift-flying birds dash against houses or through windows, and some have been known to go through the glass of moving motor-cars or trolley-cars and even into locomotive headlights. So careless are they of obstructions that a high wire fence around a covert is likely to kill all the Ruffed Grouse within its confines. From September to November, whether hunted by man or not, some of them rush wildly about from place to place by day or by night. At this time they may be found in the most unlikely places, and some individuals kill themselves by striking against buildings far from the woods.

The Eastern Ruffed Grouse is a woodland bird. It may at times go far afield, but almost always it keeps within easy reach of cover. The rocky wooded hills of southern New England are its favorite summer home. In winter it seeks shelter in valleys and swamps under the protection of thickets or coniferous trees.

In early spring the drumming of the 'Partridge' is one of the everyday sounds of the forest or thicket, although it is said to have been heard in every month of the year and in every hour of the day and night. It is less common in autumn than in spring, and in winter is very rarely heard. The deep-toned *thump, thump, thump*, like the muffled beating of a great heart, followed by a quickly accelerated, drumming roll, like far-distant thunder, is produced by the wings, and probably by the concussion of swift blows upon the air, although the wings seem to strike against the feathers of the breast. The bird stands erect on log, stump, fence, mound or rock, with ruffs more or less raised and spread and tail trailing behind. The wings are raised quickly until they almost come together over the back and then are struck forward until they nearly touch the breast. The drumming is not produced by striking the wings together over the back, as such a contact would make a sharp crack like that heard when the wings of a domestic pigeon come together in this way. The sound seems pervasive and ventriloquial. Sometimes it appears to be more plainly audible at a distance of half a mile than when heard near-by. Often it is exceedingly difficult to locate the drummer, but if the observer can find the drumming log, he may be able to approach the bird while it drums. However, he must be very quiet between times, as the bird is very watchful while on the drumming log, except during the act of drumming. This drumming has to do with the mating season; it denotes virility and combativeness. Then, it is at once a call to the female and a defiance to rival males, and often results in a meeting of the sexes or a fight between two cock birds. At other seasons the action is mainly an expression of the extreme vitality and vigor of the male, though the bird has been known to copulate in autumn.

In the mating season the male often struts like a turkey-cock with wings lowered, head and neck drawn back, and tail, crest and ruffs raised high. The ruffs and tail are then fully spread — the tail a perfect fan, the two ruffs almost encircling the neck and merging into one. The female also, under excitement, sometimes struts in the same way, although her ruffs are smaller and less conspicuous. After mating, the female steals away and makes her nest, apparently hiding it from the male, whose behavior if he finds it is said to resemble that of the traditional 'bull in a china shop.' On stormy days the female sits closely; but during continuous severe weather she must leave at times to get food. Ordinarily she is absent from the nest for hours at a time, but this does not seem to affect the vitality of the eggs, except during cold storms.

Like the eggs and young of all ground-nesting birds those of this grouse are subject to the attacks of any prowler of the woods. Occasionally a wandering cat finds the nest, steals on the mother bird at night and makes a meal of her. Once I saw a skunk eating the eggs in a nest while the bird fussed about in an ineffectual attempt to drive him away. The fox also is an unwelcome visitor. It seems probable that the bird on her nest gives out no scent, and that when a dog or a fox finds it, the brute merely stumbles upon it as humans often do. Quite often a nest situated near the den of a fox is unmolested, though foxes kill and eat grouse whenever they can catch them, as the feathers around their burrows and the traces left on the snow in winter plainly testify.

When the eggs are hatching as well as when the young are very small and unable to fly, the mother on the approach of danger simulates a crippled condition, and attempts to lead the enemy away in futile pursuit of herself, while the little ones, if out of the shell, scatter and hide beneath the undergrowth or the dead leaves on the ground.

When all goes well, the young remain for a short time in the nest, then at the call of their parent they leave it, never to return. They roam through the woods, scattering about, picking up insects from ground and foliage and drinking dewdrops from the leaves. The mother accompanies or follows them with head held high, alert for any enemy that may be creeping upon their trail. Thus they travel wild and free, but never go very far from the place of their nativity. When they become wet or chilled, the mother gathers them under her wings, and broods them quietly on the forest floor under the sighing trees. At evening she settles down, wherever night overtakes her, and calls them to her to sleep. If during the day she hears some faint suspicious sound near-by, she coos very gently to the young as if to attract their attention. They seem to disregard the cooing; but if she discovers an approaching enemy, she utters a quick warning cry, and in an instant the young are hidden; they dart into near-by cover or creep under the dead leaves on the ground. Sometimes, if not greatly alarmed, the mother will strut before the intruder with fan-like tail raised high, and ruffs and crest erect, crying and clucking to attract the attention of the enemy to herself; she may act like a wounded bird to tempt the intruder to pursue her, or she may merely run away squealing loudly. Her behavior at such times is very variable. Very rarely, when the young are in danger, the male bird appears and takes his turn at running toward and strutting near the intruder, and he has been known to care for a brood after the death of the mother bird. When all danger is passed, the mother calls and assembles her brood and leads them quickly away. The young usually seem to keep silent, but sometimes utter a piping cry. The little wings grow rapidly, and after the first week the chicks can flutter short distances. In ten days the wings are quite well developed, and soon, under favorable conditions, the chicks will fly fifty to one hundred yards.

In warm days the grouse hollows out saucer-shaped depressions by the roadside or in some dry, dusty place in the wooded upland, and resorts to these places for dust-baths to rid itself of vermin. As the summer wanes and wild fruits and seeds develop, the young birds change their diet from insects and succulent green vegetation to fruits and seeds. Late in August, if not before, the old male may join the flock, which now consists of four to twelve birds. As autumn comes on, they frequent the vicinity of oak and chestnut trees, hazel bushes, wild apple trees and wild grapevines to feed on the fruit. Then comes the hunting season, when the birds are driven and scattered far and wide among the hills. They are now putting on their snowshoes — growing the pectinations on both sides of each toe which so broaden the sustaining surface of the feet that the snows of winter will better bear their weight.

During summer and autumn they have learned to roost high in the trees, but with the coming of snow and cold they stay on the ground at night under shelter of low branches, and in storm and darkness allow the snow to cover them. Later, as the snow grows deeper, some fly and dive directly into and under it at nightfall, thus leaving no trail. In this snug shelter they pass the night. Even here, however, the prowling nocturnal fox sometimes finds them and catches them unawares by a swift pounce and a plunge into the drift, where his tracks and the feathers of the victim tell the tale. Sometimes a hard crust forms over the snow at night and imprisons the birds beneath the surface, but their strength and endurance usually enable them to break out; again, a crust may form in the daytime and thus shut the birds out from their sleeping quarters. Then they sleep on the surface, beneath the low and sheltering limbs of spruce, hemlock, pine or juniper, often in a hole hollowed in light snow, fallen on the crust. Here again the crafty fox sometimes surprises the sleeping bird. Some of these birds drop into the soft snow and pass the night in snug depressions made by their bodies, from which by raising the head they can see an approaching enemy.

The Ruffed Grouse is a hardy bird. It can withstand extreme cold and privation, and can subsist if need be on twigs and dead leaves. The stomach seems to digest the bark off the twigs, leaving them white and bare. In very severe winters with heavy snow crusts when the trees for long periods are covered with ice, some of the weaker birds may succumb, but ordinary winters have no terrors for them. Their pectinated toes serve as snowshoes to bear their weight on the lightest crust or on packed drifts.

The food of the Eastern Ruffed Grouse in spring and summer consists very largely of insects and young growing plants. Tender grass is eaten freely. Perhaps the plant most sought after in the New England coastal region is the cow-wheat, a low-growing plant with small white blossoms which thrives almost everywhere that this bird is found. Ruffed Grouse in confinement are so fond of it that they eagerly eat quantities of it, consuming the entire plant, root and branch. Edible mushrooms are taken eagerly. Fern leaves which remain green in swamps under the snow of winter are eaten then as well as at other seasons. The grouse is extremely fond of grasshoppers, locusts and crickets, and often seeks them in their season in fields and meadows near the woods. Ants, beetles, cutworms and other caterpillars, also bugs, including leaf hoppers and tree hoppers, are eaten.

CANADA RUFFED GROUSE

Bonasa umbellus togata (LINNAEUS).

Other names: Northern Ruffed Grouse; Partridge; Birch Partridge.

IDENTIFICATION. — Averages a little larger than *B. u. umbellus*, distinctly darker and usually grayer above, with more black in upper plumage and less reddish; brown markings below heavier and more distinct, very conspicuous.

BREEDING. — Sea Eastern Ruffed Grouse.

RANGE. — Northern Ontario and northern Quebec to eastern North Dakota, northern Minnesota, northern Michigan, central New York, northern Massachusetts, and Maine.

Deep in the Maine woods a long ridge slopes steeply down to a gentle stream where trout break the still surface and where the beaver builds its house. The rotting wrecks of forest trees are strewn along the ledges, their great gnarled roots flung high where the storm winds have thrown them. Beside these symbols of decay there springs the perennial life of the earth. From the forest floor rises a new wood of little spruces and firs, interspersed with dainty wood plants; seedlings spring up even from the tops of moss-grown stumps and logs. Thus from the primitive richness of the earth the forest ever renews itself. Great trees of birch, beech and rock maple stand guard over all. They have secured a firm foothold by clasping their clinging roots around great rocks and thrusting them down deep into the crevices of the ledge.

Here in the forest shades a Canada Ruffed Grouse, 'quitting' softly, runs up the face of the ridge, pauses to look back, and then disappears in the deeper shadows.

Near the summit of Mt. Greylock, Massachusetts, picturesque wrecks of old spruce trees burned by fire, seared and scarred by lightning and broken by ice storms still stand defying the winter gales that sweep the mountain, their tops high above the thickets. The undergrowth is composed largely of northern shrubs and dwarfed trees such as the moosewood and mountain maple. There in the shelter of the thickest shrubbery we shall find this grouse. In these shades nearly three thousand feet above sea-level, it finds a safe retreat. In summer we find this bird often on the higher elevations. In winter it may retire into the lowlands, but it makes no extended migrations. The Canada Ruffed Grouse is really the typical forest grouse of New England, as it occupies the greater part of the territory, and haunts regions similar to those occupied by the Eastern Ruffed Grouse, but it is more typical of the Canadian faunal region, and is found commonly in most of the forested region from northern New England to Michigan and Minnesota, and northward into Canada.

Its habits and food are similar to those of the Eastern Ruffed Grouse, but it feeds to a greater extent on the foliage, seeds and fruit of northern plants and on northern insects.

NOVA SCOTIA RUFFED GROUSE

Bonasa umbellus thayeri BANGS.

IDENTIFICATION. — 'Similar to *B. u. togata* but general color of upper parts darker, more dusky or sooty, less grayish; the whole under parts, except throat, heavily and regularly banded with dusky, the dark bands much blacker and much more boldly contrasted against the ground color — less blended.'

RANGE. — Nova Scotia and probably eastern New Brunswick.

This bird is probably identical in haunts and habits with other northern Ruffed Grouse, where their environment is similar.

WILLOW PTARMIGAN

Lagopus lagopus albus (GMELIN).

Other names: Willow Grouse; Willow Partridge.

IDENTIFICATION. — Length 14 to 17 inches; spread about 23 inches. Near size of Ruffed Grouse; feet feathered to toes; in winter white with blackish tail; in summer rich brown in effect, but feathers barred and streaked, and white wings; in spring mottled brown and white, scarlet comb over eye; autumn mottled brown and white.

BREEDING. — *Nest:* A hollow in ground or moss, lined with feathers, grass or leaves. *Eggs:* 6 to 20, deep reddish-cream with confluent blotches of dark browns.

RANGE. — Breeds from Banks Island, west coast of central Greenland, and the eastern Aleutian Islands south to northern Quebec (Ungava), and central Mackenzie, and in the mountains to central Alberta and northern British Columbia; winters south to southern Quebec, central Ontario, southern Saskatchewan, and southern Alberta.

Ptarmigans are dwellers in Arctic wastes or high mountain ranges where Alpine conditions prevail. The Willow Ptarmigan is a bird of the snow — white as the snow itself in winter. When it desires to rest during the day, it scratches a hole in the snow as a refuge from the cold wind. At night, to get shelter from the storm, it flies down into the snow and sleeps there. It is a bird of great vitality, of strong and swift flight. It has been known to distance a pursuing Goshawk. In autumn many birds of this species leave their breeding-grounds and fly south for hundreds of miles. No one knows how far they can fly without resting, but many of them cross Great Bear Lake and Great Slave Lake, though some are unable to make the passage and are drowned on the way. In these winter migrations a straggler here and there reaches the northern United States, but these are mere accidental wanderers, venturing far south of the main body of their kind. These Ptarmigans, like the northern hare, change color with the season, becoming white in winter and brown in summer. In the transition stages when the snow occurs more or less in patches on the ground, their plumage looks like patchwork.

In the northern summer they feed on berries, foliage, and insects. In winter they subsist largely on the twigs of willows, alders and other shrubs and in the spring they eat the buds of willows, birches, alders, poplars, mountain ash and other trees or shrubs, also grass, insects and spiders.

UNGAVA PTARMIGAN

Lagopus lagopus ungavus RILEY.

IDENTIFICATION. — 'Like *L. l. albus*, but with a heavier bill.'
RANGE. — Northern Quebec (Ungava) probably to the northeastern shore of Hudson Bay.

ALLEN'S PTARMIGAN

Lagopus lagopus alleni STEJNEGER.

IDENTIFICATION. — Distinguished from *L. l. albus* by having 'the shafts of both primaries and secondaries black, and by having the wing-feathers, even some of the coverts, marked and mottled with blackish.'
RANGE. — Resident in Newfoundland.

These two races of Willow Ptarmigan differ in only minor ways from the widely distributed and decidedly variable *L. l. albus*, so that expert ornithologists have considerable difficulty in assigning museum specimens to their proper classification, and of course it is impossible to distinguish them in the field. — (J.B.M.)

ROCK PTARMIGAN

Lagopus rupestris rupestris (GMELIN).

Other name: Barren-ground Bird.
IDENTIFICATION. — Length about 13 inches; smaller than Willow Ptarmigan. Feet feathered to toes; bill more slender than in *L. l. albus;* in winter all white except black tail and *black bar from bill through eye;* in spring mottled and with scarlet comb over eye; in summer decidedly barred with dark and ochre with little white intermixed; in autumn lighter in general, with vermiculations giving a 'fine pepper-and-salt' effect.
BREEDING. — Similar to Willow Ptarmigan but eggs more heavily marked.
RANGE. — Northern British Columbia, southern Yukon, central Mackenzie, Keewatin, southern Baffin Island, and the Ungava Peninsula.

The haunts of the Rock Ptarmigan are the Barren Grounds of the Far North and the desolate mountains at or near the limit of trees. There it is resident throughout the year, though there is some slight migratory change of location, governed apparently more by the food supply than by any need of seeking a warmer climate. The Ptarmigan is beautifully adapted to life in this region of great seasonal changes, for its summer and winter plumages are entirely different, to meet the changes in its habitat. In winter the Rock Ptarmigan is all white except for its blackish, white-tipped tail and a short black line from the bill to the eye. In summer it is mainly a rich rusty brown narrowly barred with black and with white tips to the feathers, with white flight-feathers and white belly, and with the tail largely black. In changing plumage the birds are variously mottled with remnants of the old plumages and bits of the new just coming in.

My experience with Ptarmigan has been very brief, but it was in typical ptarmigan habitat, in the extreme northwestern corner of British Columbia, between Skagway in Alaska and Carcross in Yukon Territory. It was on a barren plateau surrounded by higher mountains whose snowfields supply the many small streams which unite to form the mighty Yukon River. The surface of the land was more rock than soil, varying from wide flat exposures of ice-planed ledges to low cliffs and tumbled piles of talus, and back of this the sheer precipices and towering peaks of the mountains. In the hollows between the rock exposures were hundreds of small pools the haunts of Red-throated Loons and ducks of several species. Along the brooks connecting the pools were thickets of willow and alder, upon which the Ptarmigan feed in winter and spring, while creeping out over the ledges were grasses and alpine flowers and low bushes of blueberries and other heaths, which form a large part of the birds' food in summer and fall.

L. M. Turner says of the Rock Ptarmigan: 'They prefer more open ground and rarely straggle even into the skirts of the wooded tracts. The hilltops and "barrens" (hence often called barren-ground bird) are their favorite resorts. As these tracts are more extensive in the northern portions of Labrador and Ungava, these birds are there very abundant.... In the month of May the nuptial season arrives and is continued until about June, when nesting and laying begin. The birds are by this time scattered, each pair now taking possession of a large tract of stunted vegetation, among which they make their nest and rear their young.' — (J.B.M.)

WELCH'S PTARMIGAN

Lagopus rupestris welchi BREWSTER.

While the circumpolar Willow Ptarmigan has been assigned five subspecies from North America in the fourth edition of the A.O.U. 'Check-List,' our American races of the Rock Ptarmigan number eleven, mostly restricted to small areas in Alaska. Welch's Ptarmigan is the race which is accredited to Newfoundland, but such keen ornithologists as P. A. Taverner and A. C. Bent question the validity of the supposed subspecific characters, as Ptarmigans are extremely variable birds. — (J.B.M.)

HEATH HEN

Tympanuchus cupido cupido (LINNAEUS).   PLATE 35.

Other names: Hethen; Eastern Pinnated Grouse.

Former range included southern New Hampshire, Massachusetts, New York, Pennsylvania, New Jersey, and probably the shores of Chesapeake Bay in Delaware and Maryland; now extinct.

The story of the Heath Hen can be stated very briefly. Once it was extremely abundant throughout its limited breeding range. It was excellent eating and easily killed. It rapidly decreased in numbers with the coming of the white man to America, until it was confined to a small area on the island of Martha's Vineyard in Massachusetts. Here desperate attempts were made to preserve the bird, but in 1916 a disastrous fire swept over the low thickets of shrub oak, pitch pines, and berry bushes where the birds were nesting, destroying the eggs and many of the devoted mothers. From that date the birds rapidly decreased until one lone survivor was known to remain. This bird disappeared in the fall of 1931, a few months after I had last seen it at close range from a blind erected by Dr. A. O. Gross for photographing the bird, and the race is now undoubtedly extinct. — (J.B.M.)

GREATER PRAIRIE CHICKEN

Tympanuchus cupido americanus (REICHENBACH).

Other names: Pinnated Grouse; Prairie Hen.

IDENTIFICATION. — Length about 18 inches; spread about 28 inches. Similar to Heath Hen (see Plate 35), but tufts of elongated feathers on side of neck wider and with round, not sharp, ends; grayer and not so strongly marked below.

BREEDING. — Among vegetation in open places. *Nest:* On ground, a slight depression lined with grasses. *Eggs:* 7 to 17, dark olive-buff to grayish-olive, with fine and large sepia spots.

RANGE. — Ranges from west-central Alberta, southeastern Saskatchewan, and southern Manitoba to eastern Colorado, Arkansas, Missouri, southern Illinois, western Indiana, and northwestern Ohio; formerly to Ontario, Pennsylvania, and Kentucky.

The Prairie Chicken was well named. Its eastern relative, the Heath Hen, was an inhabitant of brushy lowlands of the coastal plain, which, at least in its last stronghold, Martha's Vineyard, were covered over much of their extent with almost impassable thickets of shrub oak, blueberry, bayberry, wild cherry, beach plum, and pitch pine, with an under-carpet of checkerberry and creeping bearberry, and tied together in places by catbrier and poison ivy. With this difference in habitat went a corresponding change in food habits, the Heath Hen subsisting in great part upon acorns, berries, and seeds of these plants, while the Prairie Chicken inhabited much more open country, and, with the coming of cultivation, has followed the grain-fields beyond its original habitat into Canada. When attempts were made to introduce the Prairie Chicken to New England in the hope that it would breed with the Heath Hen, the new importations apparently did not find suitable feeding or nesting conditions, and soon disappeared.

The Greater Prairie Chicken is a true bird of the open that thrives near settlements, provided man does not follow his usual custom and kill them off too rapidly. Usually its nesting-site is among grasses and weeds or low bushes in very open situations, and is either in a natural hollow of the ground or in a slight excavation made by the bird herself, and often with very little nesting material added, though the nest is skillfully hidden by the surrounding vegetation.

The mother is usually a close sitter, leaving the duties of incubation only long enough to get a little food, and carefully protecting the eggs from storms and especially from too much heat. When the young are hatched they leave the nest almost as soon as dry, and immediately begin to search for food, for, as with most gallinaceous birds, the mother protects and guides her young but probably never feeds them.

While the Greater Prairie Chicken is able to survive pretty severe weather in winter, when it roosts at night in hollows it has made in snowbanks, there is evidence that it is migratory to some extent in the northern part of its range. It not only makes shifts of habitat based on a search for better feeding conditions but also makes extended north and south seasonal flights, or true migration journeys.

The Greater Prairie Chicken has already disappeared from considerable of its original range, and while this is somewhat balanced by its recent extension of range toward the northwest, there is no doubt that its total numbers are diminishing and that unless its conservation is wisely handled it will follow the Heath Hen to extinction, another of man's victims. — (J.B.M.)

ATTWATER'S PRAIRIE CHICKEN

Tympanuchus cupido attwateri BENDIRE.

IDENTIFICATION. — Smaller than *T. c. americanus*, and darker in color, more tawny above, usually with more pronounced chestnut on the neck.

BREEDING. — See Greater Prairie Chicken.

RANGE. — Inhabits the coast region of Texas and southwestern Louisiana.

George F. Simmons says of this southern race that in the Austin region of Texas, where it is now extirpated, it inhabited the open prairies and grain-fields inland, and grassy knolls along the coast, and that its habits were much the same as those of the Greater Prairie Chicken. Referring to its history he says, 'They disappeared rapidly as the country was settled up and as cultivated fields took the place of the extensive, wild, unfenced prairies; and hunters quickly killed the few remaining birds.' Its range is now quite limited and its numbers much reduced. — (J.B.M.)

NORTHERN SHARP–TAILED GROUSE

Pedioecetes phasianellus phasianellus (LINNAEUS).

IDENTIFICATION. — Length about 17 to 18 inches; spread about 27 inches. A pale grouse of the northern prairie region, with a short, pointed tail, which distinguishes it from Greater Prairie Chicken in similar haunts but with short, rounded tail, from Ruffed Grouse with wide, fan-shaped tail, and female Ring-necked Pheasant with long, pointed tail.

BREEDING. — *Nest:* On ground, a hollow lined with leaves, grass, and a few feathers. *Eggs:* 10 to 15, dark olive-buff with small dark brown spots.

RANGE. — Inhabits central Alaska, northern Manitoba, and northern Quebec (Ungava) to Lake Superior, and casually to Parry Sound, Ontario, and the Saguenay River, Quebec.

The Sharp-tailed Grouse, with its three races, or subspecies, is widely distributed across Canada and in parts of the western United States. It is not as much a bird of the open grassy prairies as the true Prairie Chicken, but is fond of willow thickets, low rolling hills more or less bush-covered, and open glades in woodlands. Its habitat is reflected in its food, which in some localities is largely composed of seeds and grains, in others and at certain seasons, of buds and sprouts of willows, birches, aspens, and various shrubs. It also eats berries and rose-hips, and the Prairie Sharp-tail, at least, is very fond of grasshoppers.

Like many other members of the grouse family, the Sharp-tail is subject to periodical fluctuations in numbers. Norman Criddle made an interesting study of this phenomenon in Manitoba and has shown with graphs the coincidence of grouse abundance with grasshopper outbreaks. In 1932 the Northern Sharp-tailed Grouse apparently reached one of these periodic peaks of abundance and the birds overflowed in considerable numbers southward into parts of Quebec and Ontario where they were practically unknown previously. — (J.B.M.)

PRAIRIE SHARP–TAILED GROUSE

Pedioecetes phasianellus campestris RIDGWAY.

Other names: Pintail Grouse; Spike-tail; Sharp-tail; Speckle-belly; White-belly; Brush Grouse; White-breasted Grouse.

IDENTIFICATION. — Length about 17½ inches, spread about 27 inches. Paler, more 'creamy-colored' than *P. p. phasianellus*, not so gray as *P. p. columbianus*.

BREEDING. — See Northern Sharp-tail.

RANGE. — Southern Alberta and southern Manitoba to Wyoming, eastern Colorado, central Nebraska, eastern South Dakota, Minnesota, and western Wisconsin.

This southern race of the Sharp-tailed Grouse was known as the 'Prairie Chicken' to the early settlers of Minnesota and the northern prairie states, where it was later replaced by the true Prairie Chicken or Pinnated Grouse, *Tympanuchus*, as the Sharp-tail retreated with the advance of agriculture, and the Pinnated Grouse followed the grain-fields to the north and west.

Seton writes of the habits of the Prairie Sharp-tailed Grouse: 'During the summer months the habits of the chicken are eminently terrestrial; they live, feed, and sleep almost exclusively on the ground, but the first snow makes a radical change. They now act more like a properly adapted perching bird, for they spend a large part of their time in the highest trees, flying from one to another and perching, browsing, or walking about among the branches with perfect ease, and evidently at this time preferring an arboreal to a terrestrial life.'

The Sharp-tail indulges in a spring dance resembling that of the Prairie Chicken. E. S. Cameron reports it as follows: 'At this date (April 18) the ball is opened by a single cock making a run across the open space as fast as he can use his legs, the tail being inclined stiffly over the back, while the wings are dragged, so that a large white area is exposed behind. The vivid yellow superciliary fringe is erected, and, all the feathers of the neck standing on end, a pink inflated sac is disclosed. At the same time the head is carried so low as almost to touch the ground, so that the bird is transformed in appearance and, as observed through binoculars at some distance, looks to be running backwards. He then returns at full speed, when another cock comes forward toward him, both advancing slowly, with vibrating tails, to meet finally and stand drumming their quills in a trance with tightly closed eyes. After perhaps a minute one bird peeps at the other, and seeing him still enraptured, resumes an upright graceful carriage, anon stealing gently away. His companion is thus left foolishly posing at nothing, but presently he too awakes, and departs from the arena in a normal manner. Meanwhile the remaining cocks, one after another, take up the running till all have participated, but the end of each figure seems to be the same. Two birds squat flat on the ground with their beaks almost touching for about twenty minutes, and when they do this they are out of the dance for that day. The dance appears to terminate by some bird, either a late starter or one more vigorous than the rest, being unable to find a partner to respond to his run. Having assured himself of this, he utters a disgusted clucking, and all the grouse fly away at intervals as they complete their term of squatting.' — (J.B.M.)

EUROPEAN PARTRIDGE

Perdix perdix perdix (LINNAEUS).   PLATE 34.

Other names: Hungarian Partridge; Bohemian Partridge; English Partridge; Gray Partridge.

IDENTIFICATION. — Length 12 to 14 inches; spread 18 to 22 inches. Size between Ruffed Grouse and Bobwhite. Short gray neck, brownish-gray body, chestnut tail; dark horseshoe mark on breast.

BREEDING. — In fields and waste lands. *Nest:* On ground, of grasses and leaves. *Eggs:* 9 to 20, olive.

RANGE. — Introduced from Europe; now naturalized in Wisconsin and several western states and provinces; introduced in East but not well established as yet.

The European Partridge frequents open and cultivated fields, grain-fields, meadows and waste lands, all of which it prefers to the woods, though it will often seek cover in thickets. In spring after most of the weed seeds are gone it haunts clover fields. As a game bird in the East it has not proved a great success, as it has not had sufficient protection, and it often nests in grass fields and meadows where its nest and eggs are destroyed by early mowing. It seems to thrive best in light soils in a farming community where grain-growing is the principal industry, and it has become well established in some of the Western States and provinces. In Bohemia it is said to live largely in the hop and beet fields. Like the Bob-white this Partridge sleeps on the ground, the individuals of a covey forming a circle with heads outward to guard against night prowlers, and like the Bob-white also it is not usually polygamous. When the mating season arrives, the birds may be seen pursuing each other in the fields. The males fight fiercely for the possession of their chosen females. The female is said to cover her eggs with leaves when she leaves the nest until all are laid. During the time of incubation the bird seems to give out no scent, and dogs rarely find the nests. When the young are hatched the male takes his turn in brooding them. The parents are very solicitous in their care, and endeavor to lure an enemy away by their cries and antics. The male often defends his mate and young against birds larger than himself. After the breeding season the partridge when alarmed crouches close to the ground, where, like the Bob-white, it is very difficult to detect, even on bare ground. It may lie thus until nearly trodden upon, so secure does it seem to feel in its invisibility, but it is said not to lie so well to dogs.

EASTERN BOB–WHITE

Colinus virginianus virginianus (LINNAEUS).   PLATE 34.

Other names: Quail; Bob-white Quail; Partridge (in the South).

IDENTIFICATION. — Length 9½ to 10¾ inches; spread 14 to 16 inches. Much smaller than Ruffed Grouse; black and white markings on head of male are conspicuous, buff markings of female less so; a plump little *walker*; when flushed wings whir loudly and it flies at no great height with high speed and fast-beating wings, then scales with wings sharply curved downward; named from common note.

CALLS. — A clear whistled *Bob-white* or *Poor-Bob-white*, and other low whistles.

BREEDING. — In field or near edge of woods. *Nest:* On ground, of grass and leaves. *Eggs:* 7 to 17 (or more), pure white.

RANGE. — Breeds from South Dakota, southern Minnesota, southern Ontario, and southwestern Maine south to southeastern and northern Texas, the Gulf coast, and northern Florida, west to eastern Colorado; introduced in Bermuda.

During my boyhood the cheery, heartening call of the Quail was one of the most common and welcome sounds of spring and summer. The plowman resting his team gave ear to the gladdening sound and it mingled with the ring of the whetstone on the scythe. Since those days many hundreds of the birds have been introduced from the South; others have been artificially reared and liberated, but by 1915 the note had become a rare one near the city of Worcester, where much of my boyhood was passed. Bob-whites were very abundant in southern New England when the country was settled. Thomas Morton (1632), who located in what is now a part of Quincy, Massachusetts, records that he saw sixty of these birds in one tree. They continued abundant up to about the middle of the nineteenth century.

Many sportsmen naturally attribute the decrease of the birds in the North to 'hard winters.' Occasionally a severe winter destroys the greater part of the Bob-whites in New England, left over from the shooting season. Within easy motoring distance of the large cities, however, too many gunners roam the fields, and Bob-white has a small chance to survive unless protected at all times by law, as now in Ohio.

147

A hard winter will not destroy all the New England Bob-whites, though it may kill off all the most northern outposts and ninety per cent of the others, but if these prolific birds could have sufficient protection after such a winter, they would soon recover their former numbers. It is well to record here that 106 of my correspondents, chiefly gunners, attribute the decrease of these birds mainly to the gun. They are right. Overshooting, if allowed, will exterminate the birds.

There is an old saying among the gunners that if the coveys are not shot into and thus broken up, the birds will not pair and breed. This old saw came to us from England. The birds would breed faster if no gun was ever fired at them. During the Civil War when practically every Southern able-bodied hunter was in the army, and when the negroes had no guns, Bob-whites increased enormously. Their numbers in South Carolina were much greater at that time than they have ever been since.

It is a well-known fact that the greatest danger faced by Eastern Bob-whites in winter is a hard crust on the surface after a heavy fall of snow. When heavy snow comes, the bevy gathers in its usual circle on the ground near some thicket or under some sheltering branch, and soon is covered deep by fast-falling snow. If then rain comes, followed by freezing cold, a crust which they cannot break forms above the birds. Imprisoned thus under the snow they may be able to move about a little, and get some food from the ground, but if the crust does not thaw, they must eventually starve, and during severe winters large numbers sometimes perish in this way.

In many of the Southern States Bob-white is still an abundant bird. This is partly due to the milder winters, but it is also largely because of the smaller human population in some regions, and in others because of the modern 'conservation' practices carried on by the owners of large estates. Bob-white is an extremely prolific bird, and under reasonable conditions will hold his own against his enemies. In many parts of the South shooting is very carefully restricted so that there is always ample breeding stock carried over each year, and in addition shelter and food are supplied in adequate amount. As a result of this intelligent treatment, quail hunting continues to furnish sport for a veritable army of gunners, without apparent diminution in the supply of feathered targets. In much of the North, with its more crowded population and with the land held in many small parcels instead of in great private preserves, a very different condition prevails, and it is only by the distribution of great numbers of quail reared in game farms that the supply is kept from exhaustion.

The home life of the Bob-white has much of human interest. Bob-white appears to be a cheerful, good-natured little fowl, but does not hesitate to do battle with his rivals for the favors of his chosen mate. He is a good husband and father, as he has been seen to engage in nest building, and although the female alone probably usually attends to the duties of incuba-tion, the male has been known to incubate the eggs long and faithfully after the death of his mate and to care for and raise a brood bereaved of its maternal parent.

Sometimes a female will lay a remarkable number of eggs. In confinement one female has been known to lay 102 eggs in a season, another 106, and another 124, nearly all of which proved fertile. Sometimes a very large number will be found in one nest. The eggs are packed in solidly with the small ends down, and if the number is very large, they are arranged in two layers. It is said that if the eggs are handled or disturbed, the bird will desert them. The incubating bird normally leaves her eggs every afternoon in pleasant weather for rest and recreation, often not returning to her duties for several hours. Usually the vitality of the eggs is not injured by this seeming neglect, but if the eggs become addled, the female continues to incubate for a long time. In one case she was known to sit for 56 days. In leaving the nest the bird ordinarily flies directly from it and comes back to it in the same way.

When hatching time comes, each chick breaks a hole through the shell, using for the purpose the little horn or spur near the end of the upper mandible (which drops off about three days after the chick is hatched). Next it breaks the shell in a line all around the egg so that the shell separates as if it had been cut in two with a knife, and the struggling little chick pops out into the world. All the birds of a brood hatch at nearly the same time, and they are active and able in case of necessity to run away almost at once. The young, like their parents, are adepts at hiding. They usually seek shelter, then squat and become indistinguishable, and such is their apparent confidence in their invisibility that they will actually remain until trodden upon. The driver of my slow-moving, heavy farm team on seeing a female Bob-white fluttering before him in the road stopped the team, and found several tiny young ones in the ruts. Two had already been crushed by the wheels. Often when the young are in danger, one or both parents simulate lameness or helplessness so artfully as to draw off a dog or a cat and lead it away from the little ones.

The young ones grow rather slowly, and their little wings do not develop quite so fast as in the Ruffed Grouse or the Spruce Grouse, but they begin to use them at an early age. Wings are needed indeed, as the little ones must run the gauntlet of many enemies. Storms are fatal to many, as they soon get chilled in the wet grass, and chills are deadly to young birds. As soon as they are large and strong enough to dispense with the maternal brooding, they learn to squat in a close circle on the ground at night, usually near some cover, and there, tails together, heads out, alert for trouble in any direction, they pass the night, with the parents usually in the circle or near by. The circular formation gives them the advantage of mutual contact and warmth, and in case of an alarm with one simultaneous spring forward and upward every bird in the flock gets wing room.

There is some evidence that where Bob-whites are abundant, some of them, possibly young birds, migrate short distances in autumn, going generally not far and southward, but I have seen no statement anywhere to indicate that they return in spring. Ordinarily Bob-white probably passes its life in or near one neighborhood, although at times some may be driven away from their home by persecution or lack of food. In such a case marked birds have been taken in a near-by town.

He who wishes to increase the number of the species should provide them with food and shelter in winter. For this purpose high brush piles should be built, and weeds should be cut as soon as the seeds ripen. A sheltered place should be selected on the south side of a little grove or thicket, where a pile of weeds should be laid down to a depth of about a foot; a layer of strong brush should be added, then another layer of weeds, another of brush, and a cap over the whole composed of a deep layer of weeds or boughs from a coniferous tree. There should be a rock or two on the heap or a few slanting stakes to hold it against strong winds. The brush allows the sun and wind to enter the pile and makes a refuge into which the birds can creep. The brush must be strong so that no layer of heavy snow can crush it down. It may be necessary toward spring to add to the food supply barn sweepings, millet seed, or small grains. Probably no better feeding-place and shelter than this can be devised.

The greatest possible attraction for this bird in summer is a fruiting mulberry tree and in autumn a field of buckwheat, and next to this a weedy potato patch or a field of small grain.

Bob-white has many natural enemies. As it feeds mainly on the ground and passes the night there, no bird is more constantly menaced by prowling foes. Hawks, owls, crows, foxes, skunks, weasels, squirrels, rats, mice and snakes all destroy the birds or their eggs. Roaming dogs snap up the young or eat the eggs. The domestic cat is one of their most destructive enemies, often cleaning up a whole brood.

Bob-white is so exceedingly prolific, however, that its many enemies make little impression on its numbers, and it readily may be increased by protection, winter feeding and control of its enemies. The Pennsylvania plan of catching a few bevies and keeping them in confinement through the coldest part of the winter has manifest advantages.

The food of the Eastern Bob-white is largely vegetal, consisting of seeds of trees such as the maple, pine, oak and beech, numerous smaller seeds, many wild fruits, grasses and leaves; also many insects. The bird eats enormous quantities of the seeds of the common kinds of weeds, such as ragweed, chickweed, and sorrel. Among the wild fruits that it takes are bayberries, mulberries, the fruit of Solomon's seal, greenbrier and sassafras, thimbleberries, blackberries, strawberries, apples, wild and ground cherries, fruit of the sumacs, holly, black alder, climbing bittersweet, frost grape, flowering dogwood, sour gum, blueberries, huckleberries, nightshade, black haw, honeysuckle, wintergreen, elder and partridge berries, sarsaparilla and woodbine berries. The bird is very fond of mulberries and will go into the trees for them, but eats comparatively little cultivated fruit. It eats more or less green food such as grass, clover, sorrel, plantain and the leaves of weeds. It is, however, a glutton for insects in spring and summer, and eats them in every month of the year whenever and wherever it can get them. The young seem to feed principally on insects. Among the insects taken are quantities of several of the most destructive insect pests such as cutworms, army worms, cabbage worms, Colorado potato beetles, chinch bugs and many other bugs, two species of cucumber beetles, May beetles, weevils, grasshoppers, locusts, flies and plant lice. In winter the bird eats whatever it can find, dried wild fruits, dried grasses and leaves of weeds, also weed seeds and insects living or dead, grass seeds and small grains wherever they can be found. Along the coast dried eel-grass is eaten. Bob-whites require gravel, and when snow covers this they suffer or even die. At that season flocks often learn to eat with poultry.

FLORIDA BOB-WHITE

Colinus virginianus floridanus (COUES).

IDENTIFICATION. — Slightly smaller than *C. v. virginianus* and colors darker, with much more black, especially on under parts.

RANGE. — Florida, except the extreme northern part and the Keys.

The Florida Bob-white has adapted itself to the varied terrain of the peninsula to the extent of being found in the palmetto scrub of the so-called prairies, the sandy open 'piney' woods, about the borders of the brushy hammocks, and wherever cultivated land is found. — (J.B.M.)

RING–NECKED PHEASANT

Phasianus colchicus torquatus GMELIN.

PLATE 35.

Other names: Chinese pheasant; Chinese Ring-neck; Oregon Pheasant.

IDENTIFICATION. — Length of male 33 to 36 inches, length of female about 20 inches. A large game-bird with a long, tapering tail; head of male appears black, breast bronze, sides yellow with black spots; female brown, smaller than male, tail pointed but much shorter than male; Sharp-tailed Grouse has *short* pointed tail and is paler.

BREEDING. — In open country. *Nest:* on ground, of leaves and grass. *Eggs:* 6 to 16, olive-brown to pale bluish-green.

RANGE. — Introduced species of probably mixed blood, now acclimated in various parts of United States and Canada.

The first successful introduction of pheasants into the eastern United States was in 1887. After several unsuccessful attempts the birds became established. The English Pheasant has been bred under artificial conditions so long that it does not do well in the wild, and the probability is that the blood of the Ring-neck predominated in the strain that finally became established there. So far as can be determined, *P. colchicus torquatus*, the chief progenitor of our pheasants, is the only race of pheasants the descendants of which have been able to establish themselves in a wild state in eastern North America. With special care and protection they seem to hold their own in the more open lands where the Ruffed Grouse cannot long survive, and where the Pheasant has become a valuable acquisition to our supply of feathered game.

The Ring-necked Pheasant is a proud, stately, handsome bird, active, daring and aggressive; well adapted to sustain itself in a mild climate even under adverse circumstances, but not quite hardy enough to endure the severe winters of the higher and more northern parts of New England. In its native land it is a dweller chiefly in river valleys, grain-fields, flats, meadows, marshes and low rolling scrubby or forested hills, and it thrives best here in such situations. It enters woodlands and commonly finds shelter in tracts of low bushes and briers. It frequents open woods with a thick undergrowth of shrubbery, briers and grasses, with open glades and streams. It is rather rarely seen in trees as it roosts more or less on the ground in summer, but in autumn and winter it roosts much in trees, and in winter when food on the ground is covered with snow, it has been seen in trees feeding on buds or wild berries.

The bird is not so well adapted to the climate of the Northern States as is the Ruffed Grouse, for it feeds chiefly on the ground and needs a continuous supply of grain or weed seeds to carry it through the winter. After sleet storms Pheasants have been found attached to the ice by their long tails which have 'frozen in.' This seems to indicate that possibly some of them roost more or less on the ground even in winter. A severe winter with deep snows makes life hard for the Pheasants, as most of their accustomed food is then covered with snow. When the snow becomes crusted, they can find little food, and, unless they have learned to subsist on buds, they may require to be fed at such times with grain. When deep snows come, they search diligently for food, often approaching farmhouses, and even coming into the outskirts of villages to hunt for garbage or anything edible that may be thrown out by the inhabitants.

In the Southern States Nature is kinder to the alien Pheasant, and its principal enemies,

151

besides man, are cats and rats, which destroy many of the young birds as well as the eggs, and occasionally even full-grown birds.

The Ring-necked Pheasant is polygamous, and a single cock is likely to sport a harem of several hens. The cocks are vigorous, powerful birds, and, like the males of other polygamous species, they fight viciously for the possession of their chosen females. In autumn as the young birds begin to develop and to imitate the crowing of their elders, they commence fighting, and in early spring, beginning even in February in some places, fighting and mating go on apace. While in winter the sexes keep largely apart, in spring they begin to intermingle, and during the strutting and crowing of the mating season the males become quite noisy and conspicuous. The bare skin about their heads becomes a deeper red, they carry their wings lower and their tails higher, and appear more proud and stately. Like the domestic cock whenever they find some choice store of food, they gallantly call up the females to the feast.

When the young Pheasants are hatched, they soon leave the nest, never to return. Like the Ruffed Grouse the mother broods them here and there and takes them under her wings at night wherever darkness overtakes them. She leads her brood about as does the domestic hen, finds food for them and calls them to it. At first they get their water from their food, the rain and the dewdrops, but later they seek water at some pool, lake or stream. When the mother is surprised by an enemy, she flies up with a sudden uproar of wings, making herself conspicuous and inviting pursuit, while the young run and hide. They are adepts at the game of sneaking away to safety, and some usually manage to escape the attacks of their many enemies, of which the domestic cat, the weasel, and the Great Horned Owl are particularly destructive. In winter the Goshawk is perhaps the greatest enemy of the full-grown birds. This pheasant is remarkably intelligent and makes good use of all its keen faculties to preserve its life. It may become accustomed to the presence of the farmer in the fields and seem quite un-suspicious, but let the sportsman appear with gun and dog, and its behavior is soon altered. It is a swift flier and knows a few tricks by which it often makes out to elude the hunter and his dog.

The animal food of the Ring-necked Pheasant includes many insects, worms, and other small forms of animal life; its vegetal food is comprised very largely of parts of wild plants, including great quantities of the seeds of pernicious weeds and a considerable amount of grain. Most of the grain, however, is either waste grain picked up in the stubble or in corn-fields, or grain fed to them by people interested in their preservation.

EASTERN TURKEY

Meleagris gallopavo silvestris VIEILLOT.

Other names: Wild Turkey; Gobbler; Great American Hen.

IDENTIFICATION. — Length of male about 48 inches, spread about 60 inches; length of female about 36 inches. Similar to domestic Turkey but upper tail coverts and tips of tail feathers chestnut, with no white or pale buffy.

CALL. — Gobbling similar to that of domestic Turkey.

BREEDING. — In a thicket. *Nest:* A hollow in the ground lined with a few leaves. *Eggs:* 8 to 20, buffy-white to yellowish-buff, with small dots of clay-color, etc.

RANGE. — Resident in western Oklahoma, eastern Texas, the Gulf Coast, and northern Florida to southeast ern Missouri, eastern Kentucky, and central Pennsylvania; formerly to Nebraska, Kansas, South Dakota, southwestern Ontario, and southern Maine; now somewhat mixed with domestic and western stock in eastern portion of its range.

Much of the story of the Eastern or Wild Turkey is hinted in the word 'formerly' in the description of distribution of this species, as given above. While the species is completely extirpated throughout much of its former range, it may still be found in some numbers in parts of the South, where it is very carefully protected by northern sportsmen on their shooting preserves, and also in some of the wilder parts of the Gulf States, where it has survived because of the scarcity of human neighbors. Attempts at restoration have been made with considerable success in a few Northern States, notably Pennsylvania, where possibly a little of the native stock still existed, and has been augmented by much southern stock from game farms.

In his early book, 'A History of the Game Birds, Wild-Fowl and Shore Birds,' Mr. Forbush treated the history of this bird in considerable detail, and the following is a condensation of that account. Although it refers principally to New England, the bird's history is much the same in other regions. — (J.B.M.)

'The discoverers and early explorers of North America found this bird ranging almost the entire length of the Atlantic coast line, from Florida to Nova Scotia, where it roved in great flocks, and often migrated in multitudes in search of food. It seems to have been particularly numerous in Massachusetts and New England. The first settlers found it a vital asset of the land and a substantial source of food supply.

'Champlain (1604) says that the Indians of the Massachusetts coast described a large bird that came to eat their corn. From their description he judged it to be a Turkey. He landed on Cape Cod, and as the Cape was then well wooded, it doubtless was inhabited by this bird.

'William Wood (1629–34, Massachusetts) writes: "The Turky is a very large Bird, of a blacke colour, yet white in flesh; much bigger than our English Turky. He hath the use of his long legs so ready, that he can runne as fast as a Dogge, and flye as well as a Goose: of these sometimes there will be forty, three-score, and a hundred of a flocke, sometimes more and sometimes lesse; their feeding is Acornes, Hawes, and Berries, some of them get a haunt to frequent our English corne: In winter when the Snow covers the ground, they resort to the Sea shore to look for Shrimps, & such smal Fishes at low tides. Such as love Turkie hunting, must follow it in winter after a new falne Snow, when hee may follow them by their tracts; some have killed ten or a dozen in halfe a day; if they can be found towards an evening and watched where they peirch, if one come about ten or eleaven of the clocke he may shoote as often as he will, they will sit, unlesse they be slenderly wounded. These Turkies remaine all the yeare long, the price of a good Turkie cocke is foure shillings; and he is well worth it, for he may be in weight forty pound."

'Shooting and trapping the birds at all times soon had its inevitable effect, and the Turkey retired rapidly before the advance of settlement, and soon it could be found only in the wildest parts of the country. In Massachusetts Turkeys were most numerous in the oak and chestnut woods, for there they found most food. They were so plentiful in the hills bordering the Connecticut Valley that in 1711 they were sold in Hartford at one shilling four pence each, and in 1717 they were sold in Northampton, Mass., at the same price. In the last part of the eighteenth century most of the Wild Turkeys had been driven west of the Connecticut River, but there were still a good many in the Berkshire Hills and along the Connecticut Valley on both sides of the river.

'De Kay (1844) wrote that the Turkey had disappeared almost entirely from the Atlantic States, but that a few were still to be found about Mt. Holyoke in Massachusetts, and in Sussex County, New Jersey, as well as in some of the mountainous parts of New York. Wild Turkeys are believed to have existed on Mt. Tom and Mt. Holyoke longer than anywhere else in Massachusetts. There was a flock on Mt. Tom in 1842, a few in 1845, and a single Turkey in 1851. Some remained on Mt. Holyoke nearly as long. In the History of the Sesqui-Centennial Celebration of South Hadley, the statement is made that a few Turkeys were left on Mt. Holyoke later than 1851. It is said that a year or two before the outbreak of the Civil War a party of hunters from Springfield and Holyoke went to Rock Ferry, and there divided, a part ascending the north peak of Mt. Tom and the others crossing the river to Mt. Holyoke, north and east of the well-known roosting place of the birds. The latter party beat the woods and drove the few surviving Turkeys to the southerly end of the mountain, whence they took flight for Mt. Tom, but before the poor creatures could alight, the guns of the ambushed hunters had exterminated them.

'Since then the Wild Turkey has disappeared from Canada and from most of the Atlantic seaboard, although a few are still to be found in Virginia and other Southern States, and it is still common in some western localities.

'The habits of this Turkey have been well described by Audubon, and no extended notice of them is necessary. Although it is a bird of the woods, where it roosts high in the tall timber in the deep fastnesses of which it hides, it likes to come out in the open and search in the tall grass of field, meadow or prairie for insects of which it is fond. When discovered in such a situation it usually tries to steal away through the long grass; if followed it runs rapidly, and if closely pressed rises and flies, often a long distance, generally making for timber if possible, where it disappears like magic in the thickets. I well remember when I started my first old gobbler from the long prairie grass. The rising sun at my back was just throwing its level beams across the grassy sea as I emerged from the timber, between the bird and its retreat. At the sound of my gun the great bird rose resplendent from the grass, gorgeous with metallic reflections, its broad wings throwing off the sun rays like polished bronze and gold — a sight, as it sailed away, to be long remembered.

'In the mating season the males strut, gobble and fight in the manner of the domestic Turkey. The female steals away by herself to make her nest, and guards her secret carefully from her many enemies, of which the male is not the least, for he will destroy the eggs or the young birds if he finds them. The young are very weak when first hatched and will hardly survive a good wetting; Audubon says that when the young have become chilled and ill the female feeds them the buds of the spicebush (*Benzoin benzoin*); but, however she manages, she often succeeds in rearing the brood. The fox and lynx are among her most dangerous enemies at this time, but later, when the young birds have learned to fly and to roost in the trees, the Great Horned Owl takes its toll from their numbers.

'The Wild Turkey adapts itself to circumstances in regard to food, eating acorns, berries, buds, weed seeds, grass seeds and other vegetable food. It is also fond of grain, and this no doubt led to its extirpation in Massachusetts. The gunners watched in the corn-fields, or laid long lines of corn in ditches, where they could rake a whole flock, or baited the birds into

154

pens, in which whole broods were captured. But the birds, both young and old, often are useful to the farmer, for they are fond of insects, particularly grasshoppers.

'The varied food of this bird gives it the finest flavor of any fowl that I have ever tasted, and its great size and beauty contribute to make it, to my mind, the noblest game bird in the world. It is destined to vanish forever from the earth unless our people begin at once to protect it.'

FLORIDA TURKEY

Meleagris gallopavo osceola SCOTT.

IDENTIFICATION. — Similar to *M. g. silvestris* but darker in general tone; the color of the tail and upper tail coverts are the same in both races, distinguishing them from the domestic turkey with its white or whitish coloration.

RANGE. — Inhabits peninsular Florida, north at least to the region about Gainesville.

There are no notable differences in the habits of the races of Wild Turkey, except so far as changes in environment affect feeding, nesting, and so forth.

Order Gruiformes.   Cranes, Rails, and Allies.

WHOOPING CRANE

Grus americana (LINNAEUS).

Other name: Great White Crane.

IDENTIFICATION. — Length 49 to 56 inches; spread 76 to 92 inches. Largest of American wading birds; flies with slow heavy flappings or sails in high circles with neck always fully extended and legs trailing horizontally behind; adult white with black wing-tips and red (bare) face; (Wood Ibis has black head and neck and black secondaries as well as primaries); young more or less rusty or brownish mixed with white.

BREEDING. — On open marsh or prairie. *Nest:* A platform of rushes, etc., often in water. *Eggs:* 2, greenish-brown thickly spotted with browns and purplish.

RANGE. — Now very rare and mainly restricted to southern Mackenzie and northern Saskatchewan in summer, and Texas in winter; formerly bred from Mackenzie and Hudson Bay south to Nebraska and Iowa and in migration not uncommon east to Atlantic coast from New England to Georgia.

In size the great Whooping Crane stands alone, a relic of the past. It overtops all North American waders, even the Flamingo, which though nearly as tall is less in bulk. A search through the writings of the early explorers and settlers on the Atlantic coast leads to the belief that this great bird was once a transient there, and was at least an occasional visitor to some New England States. Emmons in his list of Massachusetts birds (1833) rates the Whooping Crane as a rare but regular visitant, 'breeding in this climate.' Dr. Thompson, in his 'Natural History of Vermont' (1842), says that it is seen in the state only in migration. DeKay (1844) includes it in his list of the birds of New York. Being an edible fowl, however, and of great size, it gradually disappeared before the rifle of the hunter and the settler, and is now confined mainly to the interior of the continent, where it is nearing extinction.

In moving about on its feeding-grounds this species flies low and heavily, but in migration it rises to tremendous heights, from which, however, its resonant cries may be clearly heard. Audubon asserts that he has heard its call at a distance of three miles. This bird, like the Trumpeter Swan, has a long convoluted windpipe which is sometimes nearly five feet in length and which is believed to add force and resonance to its voice. Nuttall, in describing the flight of cranes up the Mississippi Valley in 1811, said that the bustle of the great migrations and the passage of the mighty armies filled the mind with wonder.

Its chief inland haunts are savannas, marshes, prairies, and the low grassy shores of rivers, lakes, and lagoons, while formerly on the Atlantic coast it frequented river valleys and the lowlands of the coastal plains. It is extremely wary, feeding usually in open regions where its great stature enables it to keep watch in all directions. Its food consists largely of vegetal matter — grain, seeds, roots, etc. — and it also takes a large quota of animal food, consisting of mice, moles, snakes, lizards, frogs, insects, worms, and many small forms of aquatic animal life.

SANDHILL CRANE

Grus canadensis tabida (PETERS).

Other names: Brown Crane; Blue Crane; Turkey.

IDENTIFICATION. — Length 40 to 48 inches; spread about 80 inches. About size of Great Blue Heron but heavier; a gray bird that flies with neck stretched out at full length and legs trailing behind; bald red forehead; young similar but much browner above.

BREEDING. — In marshes and wet prairies. *Nest:* Of grasses, weeds, roots, mud, etc. *Eggs:* 2, similar to those of Whooping Crane.

RANGE. — Bred formerly from British Columbia, Saskatchewan, Manitoba, and southwestern Michigan south to California, Colorado, Nebraska, Illinois, and Ohio and in migration east to New England; now rare east of Mississippi and rare or extirpated as a breeding bird in southern half of its former range, but still breeds from northeastern California, Wisconsin, and Michigan northward; winters from California, Texas, and Louisiana south to Mexico.

The great Sandhill Crane once roamed the Atlantic coast in migration. Like the Wild Turkey it disappeared with the coming of settlement and civilization and is no longer found on the Atlantic coast north of Georgia, except as an extremely rare straggler. Probably it never came to New England in very great numbers, as this is largely a hilly forested country, and cranes prefer more level and open lands.

It is an extremely wary bird. It feeds usually in open meadows, marshes, savannas, or prairies, taking its food mainly from the ground or near it and raising its head frequently to watch and listen for danger. It is very difficult to approach within gunshot range, as it always shows great fear of mankind, but when wounded and brought to bay, it exhibits the utmost courage and fights desperately. Audubon tells of being driven into a river up to his neck in water to escape an enraged crane with a broken wing which waded into the water to its belly in pursuit. A wing-tipped crane is exceedingly agile and is capable of evading blows and darting its long bill through a man's eye to his brain. I can well believe Audubon's tale, as I once had a fencing match with a winged bird which attacked me so savagely that I felt obliged to end the contest with a charge of shot. This species can defend itself successfully against any dog, and doubtless has few dangerous enemies besides man.

This crane, like its relatives, takes much vegetal food. The roots of plants and tubers, including potatoes and sweet potatoes, corn and other grains and seeds make up a part of its food. It destroys the eggs and probably the young of rails. On the other hand, it feeds on mice and insect pests.

FLORIDA CRANE

Grus canadensis pratensis MEYER.   PLATE 96.

IDENTIFICATION. — Slightly smaller than *G. c. tabida*, and darker.
RANGE. — Peninsular Florida and southern Georgia (Okefinokee Swamp), casually to South Carolina and probably to southern Alabama and Louisiana.

The Florida Crane is not confined to the prairies and savannas, but may be seen at times in the open 'piney' woods, where its raucous cries arouse the echoes, though it is most commonly seen on wet prairies and its nest is almost always located in a shallow pond grown up to flags and other marsh vegetation. The nests are usually built of grass, sticks, and palmetto leaves and may be three to five feet across and a foot or more thick, with a slight depression in the center for the eggs, which are usually two in number.

Like most cranes, the Florida Crane has an interesting mating dance. The birds usually assemble in some numbers on a knoll on the nearly level prairie and dance about, skipping high in air and even flying up a little way from the ground occasionally, turning about, moving with high prancing steps and bowing repeatedly in all directions. Both males and females engage in the dance. At times a single pair may be seen so occupied and even a lone bird may take a few 'dance steps' from time to time.

The Florida Crane has a rather easily recognized flight. The neck is extended straight ahead and the feet straight behind, and the wings beat with a slow, steady rhythm, but with a peculiar jerky motion which is characteristic. Sometimes the birds ascend to quite an elevation and circle around for some time. — (J.B.M.)

LIMPKIN

Aramus pictus pictus (MEYER).   PLATE 96.

Other names: Courlan, Crying Bird; Nigger Boy; Indian Pullet.
IDENTIFICATION. — Length 25 to 27 inches; spread 40 to 42 inches. Near size of American Bittern but stands higher; flies with neck extended and legs extended or hanging down; body color dark brown, streaked and blotched with white; head and neck paler; bill long, slightly down-curved.
NOTE. — A loud mournful wail suggesting cry of a child.
BREEDING. — In saw-grass marshes. *Nest:* Of leaves and other vegetation among grass tufts. *Eggs:* 4 to 8, cream-buff to dark olive-buff, with longitudinal blotches of drab and browns at larger end.

RANGE. — Peninsular Florida west to Wakulla River, and north to Okefinokee Swamp in southern Georgia; also in Cuba.

About twenty miles south of Tallahassee, Florida, the road to the Gulf of Mexico crosses a fair-sized river of beautifully clear water, bordered with the typical rank growths of Florida streams, arrowhead and spider lilies, 'bonnets' and long streamers of pondweeds, while up river are tall cypresses draped in Spanish moss towering above the gum trees and other lowlier growths. Now and then an Osprey flaps across the water and hovers a moment before dropping to its surface for a fish; Water-turkeys soar high overhead, their distinctive outline, with long neck and small head, rather long wings, and long fan-shaped tail readily identifying them; Turkey Buzzards sail over and Black Vultures flap intermittently as they search for carrion; and beautiful pure-white Egrets pass at intervals, or a line of White Ibises with their black wing-tips, curved reddish bills, and long legs trailing behind.

This is the Wakulla River, which rises full-grown from the clear depths of Wakulla Springs a few miles above the highway bridge, and which is said to be the largest spring in the world, with water so transparent that its bottom may be seen at a depth of one hundred and eighty-five feet. On one side of the spring is a grove of tall deciduous trees, live-oaks and magnolias, tupelos and swamp maples, haunt of Pileated and Red-bellied Woodpeckers, Tufted Tits and noisy Crested Flycatchers, and tiny flitting warblers, but to the north and east stretches the jungle, with its dense shelter of water- and muck-loving flowers, vines, bushes and trees, impassable for man except by way of the winding channels of the slow-moving river. And here is a chosen home of that strange marsh bird, the Limpkin, Courlan, or Crying-bird, once an abundant inhabitant of all suitable places in Florida, but now rare and locally distributed. Their harsh cries may be heard all day long and through the night, and they may often be seen perched, statue-like, on a low branch of a cypress, wading about in the shallow water, or supported on the rank aquatic vegetation as they search for food, or perhaps balancing precariously on the blunt point of a cypress knee, bowing and teetering, before striding rapidly away into the dark recesses of the jungle. They are easily recognized, with their dark brown body plumage sprinkled with white spots and streakings, their grayish head and neck, long legs, and long slightly curved bill, but their voices render them unmistakable and unforgettable. William Brewster has described the habits and notes of the Limpkin as he studied them in Florida sixty years ago: 'We certainly were not ignored by the vigilant Courlans, for any sudden noise, like the splash of a paddle in the water or the rapping of its handle against the boat, was sure to be instantly followed by a piercing *kur-r-ee-ow, kurr-r-ee-ow, kurr-r-ee-ow, kr-ow, kr-ow*, from the nearest thicket; or perhaps several would cry out at once as rails will do on similar occasions. For the most part the birds kept closely hidden, but at length we discovered one feeding on the shore. His motions were precisely similar to those of a rail, as he skirted the oozy brink, lifting and putting down his feet with careful deliberation. Occasionally he detected and seized a snail, which was quickly swallowed, the motion being invariably accompanied by a comical side shake of the bill, apparently expressive of satisfaction, though it was perhaps designed to remove any particles of mud that may have adhered to his unique food. Finally he spied us and walked up the inclined trunk of a fallen tree to its shattered end, where he stood for a moment tilting his body and jerking up his tail. Then he uttered a hoarse rattling cry like the gasp of a person being strangled, at the same time shaking his head so violently that his neck seemed in imminent danger of dislocation. Just as we were nearly within gun-range he took wing, with a shriek that might have been heard for half a mile. His flight was nearly like a heron's, the wings being moved slowly and occasionally held motionless during intervals of sailing.'

In North America the Limpkin is found only in Florida, and there its haunts are restricted to regions where its favorite food, a large fresh-water snail, may be found. Drainage projects have reduced its breeding area very greatly and threaten it seriously. It has long been hunted for food and used as a target by thoughtless tourists, so that its numbers are greatly depleted and protection is necessary if it is to continue its status as an attraction for bird-lovers in Florida. Its reaction to protection is well demonstrated at Wakulla Springs, where since the building of the hotel all shooting has been stopped, and the birds are increasing in numbers and becoming extremely tame, in spite of the hundreds of visitors to the spring and the river jungles, and the coming of noisy outboard motorboats. — (J.B.M.)

KING RAIL

Rallus elegans elegans AUDUBON.   PLATE 23.

Other names: Meadow Hen; Fresh-water Marsh Hen; Mud Hen; Great Red-breasted Rail; Prairie Chicken.

IDENTIFICATION. — Length 17 to 19 inches; spread 21½ to 25 inches. Largest of North American Rails; brighter in color than Clapper Rail; coloration chiefly reddish; breast cinnamon rather than buffy or grayish as in Clapper; resembles Virginia Rail but much larger and lacks grayish cheeks of latter.

CALL. — A loud *bup, bup, bup, bup, bup, bup, bup,* increasing to a roll in the middle.

BREEDING. — In fresh-water marshes. *Nest:* Of weeds, grasses, etc., on or near ground or over water, among reeds, etc. *Eggs:* 6 to 16, buffy or creamy, blotched and speckled with brown and lilac.

RANGE. — Breeds from Nebraska, southern Minnesota, southwestern Ontario, New York, and Massachusetts south to Florida, Louisiana, and Texas, and west to Kansas; winters in southern part of its range north to New Jersey.

The great King Rail is the largest and handsomest representative of the family in North America. Tall grasses, reeds, sedges, arums and cattail flags commonly screen it from human eyes, except on those rare occasions when startled by a sudden intrusion it rises and flaps or flutters slowly along for a short distance above the tops of the marsh vegetation. It is more partial to uplands than most of our rails and sometimes wanders into grass or grain-fields. It frequents fresh-water marshes, though often found near the sea-coast or even occasionally within the confines of salt marshes. When not in fear of molestation it sometimes leaves its cover and comes out on mud-flats or into stubble-fields. In seasons of high spring floods it has been known to retreat from its flooded marshes and nest in fields and on hillsides. It seems to be an erratic wandering bird, which is more often heard than seen. It is considered as merely an occasional visitor in Massachusetts, but as large Rails are reported on Cape Cod in summer with young, this species must breed occasionally in that region.

Some King Rails seem to remain in the North or to wander northward in autumn or winter. There are winter records in Wisconsin, Michigan, Ontario, New York, Connecticut, Rhode Island, Massachusetts, New Hampshire and Maine.

N. S. Goss, in his 'Birds of Kansas,' says of the King Rail: 'Its flights, when not suddenly

159

started, are at dusk and during the night. It springs into the air with dangling legs and rapid strokes of its short wings; but if going any distance, its legs, like its neck, are soon stretched out to their full extent, flying rather slowly and near the ground.... Its call note, or "*Creek, creek, creek, creek,*" and of flight, "*Cark, cark, cark,*" can often be heard both night and day, and at times during the early breeding season they are almost as noisy as the guinea hens. If it were not for its voice its presence would seldom be known, as it skulks and hides from its pursuers, and when hard pressed runs into the deeper waters within the reeds and rushes, preferring to swim (and can also dive) to taking wing, knowing that it is safter within its watery, grassy cover, for which it is so well adapted.'

NORTHERN CLAPPER RAIL

Rallus longirostris crepitans GMELIN.   PLATE 23.

Other names: Mud-hen; Salt-marsh Hen.

IDENTIFICATION. — Length 13 to 16 inches; spread 19 to 21 inches. Smaller than King Rail, larger than Virginia; gray and buffy rather than brown and ruddy; much less distinctly marked than King Rail; rarely seen away from coastal region.

CALL. — A harsh clattering cackle, beginning loud and fast, ending lower and slower.

BREEDING. — In salt marshes and on coastal islands. *Nest:* On ground under drift or in grass. *Eggs:* 8 to 13, buff or clay color, speckled and blotched with browns, grays and lavender.

RANGE. — Breeds on salt marshes of the Atlantic coast from Connecticut to North Carolina; winters mainly south of New Jersey.

The large and rather neutral-colored Northern Clapper Rail is a denizen of the salt marshes and brackish coastal regions of the Middle Atlantic States, and it is still an abundant bird throughout much of its range. It is a noisy bird and is more often heard than seen, for it has the typical rail habit of slipping about in the dense growths of salt-marsh plants, invisible to the prying eye of the bird student, now and then giving utterance to its harsh cackling cry, *cac, cac, cac, cac, ca, caha, caha,* first from one direction and then from another, as if, as Dr. Chapman says, the rails were children in a game of blindman's buff. If there is a particularly high tide they are sometimes forced out of their shelter in the tall vegetation and they may be seen running over the floating 'thatch' or drifting around on bits of flotsam, waiting for the waters to subside. Easterly storms during the breeding season sometimes work great destruction to the nests of these birds, the eggs being floated away and destroyed, or the young scattered and drowned. Marauding Fish Crows also destroy many of the eggs and young where the Rails nest together in communities. — (J.B.M.)

WAYNE'S CLAPPER RAIL

Rallus longirostris waynei BREWSTER.

IDENTIFICATION. — Generally darker color than *R. l. crepitans*; more ashy under parts and fewer markings on under tail coverts.

RANGE. — Resident on salt marshes of southern Atlantic coast from southeastern North Carolina to New Smyrna, Florida.

The chain of low islands along the coasts of South Carolina and Georgia, and the broad tidal marshes which lie between them and the mainland, are the principal haunts of Wayne's Clapper Rail. It differs in no important essentials of its habits from the Northern Clapper, or its Southern relative, the Florida Clapper. It is a prolific bird, often raising two broods totaling two dozen offspring annually, but it has many enemies to contend with, the two worst being man, who hunts the birds tirelessly, and the occasional high tides which, driven by an easterly storm, may flood the breeding-grounds and destroy all the eggs or young over large areas of marshlands. — (J.B.M.)

FLORIDA CLAPPER RAIL

Rallus longirostris scotti SENNETT.

IDENTIFICATION. — This race is even darker in general coloration than *R. l. waynei*, and slightly smaller.

RANGE. — Limited to the Gulf coast of Florida and the Atlantic coast north to Jupiter Inlet.

MANGROVE CLAPPER RAIL

Rallus longirostris insularum BROOKS.

IDENTIFICATION. — Similar to *R. l. waynei* but feathers of upper parts more broadly edged with grayish; sides of head beneath and behind eye light neutral gray, sides of neck and breast washed with same.

RANGE. — Apparently found only in mangrove swamps of the Florida Keys.

Little is known about the habits of this race of extreme southern Florida. It probably differs somewhat from the other races of Clapper Rails in feeding habits on account of its quite different environment, the ecological factors in the mangrove swamps being very unlike those of the salt marshes of the Atlantic coast. — (J.B.M.)

LOUISIANA CLAPPER RAIL

Rallus longirostris saturatus RIDGWAY.

IDENTIFICATION AND RANGE. — A more richly colored race of Clapper Rail, resident on the salt marshes of the coasts of Texas, Louisiana, Mississippi, and Alabama.

Mr. A. C. Bent says of this race that its habits differ in no material way from those of the Atlantic coast races, except that it is a little more often found in brackish swamps some distance inland from the coast. — (J.B.M.)

VIRGINIA RAIL

Rallus limicola limicola VIEILLOT.   PLATE 23.

Other names: Small Mud-hen; Long-billed Rail; Little Red-breasted Rail.

IDENTIFICATION. — Length 8½ to 10½ inches; spread about 13 to 14½ inches. Not half size of King Rail which it resembles in coloration; near size of Sora but has long down-curved bill, red eye and reddish breast.

BREEDING. — Similar to that of King Rail.

RANGE. — Breeds from southern British Columbia, southern Ontario, southern Quebec, New Brunswick, and Nova Scotia, south to northern Lower California, Utah, Missouri, southern Illinois, Kentucky, New Jersey, and eastern North Carolina; winters from Utah and Colorado to Lower California, Guatemala, and the lower Mississippi Valley States, and from North Carolina to Florida.

The Virginia Rail frequents such localities as those inhabited by the King Rail, and has similar habits. Like the latter, it is, for the most part, a bird of fresh-water marshes, rarely breeding in salt marsh. In autumn it sometimes may be found in grain-fields or stubble-fields. It seems more secretive than the King Rail. Although secretive like all rails, it is not usually so shy as the Sora and, while keeping more or less hidden, will often come near an observer or permit a close approach. It is fond of marshy, oozy pools where button bushes grow, of jungles of cattails and of river meadows flanked by wild roses. Among reeds, bushes, briars, rushes, grasses and wild rice it follows the numerous hidden passages, which cross and recross one another, in which, unseen, it can race rapidly from place to place at the least alarm. It runs at great speed and passes readily between stems set so close that passage seems impossible. Its flight is feeble and it rarely flies where it can escape under cover. If forced to the brink of a swampy pond and in immediate danger of discovery, it may plunge in and swim away under water by using its partly spread wings, and may hide beneath some stump or bank or conceal itself among the water-plants with only the bill above water. If there is but a small ditch or slough to cross, it may run lightly over the surface on lily pads or other floating vegetation or, if the water is clear, it may swim quickly across, its head bobbing forward with each foot stroke, until it disappears on the farther side in the moving greenery of marsh vegetation. This bird is much more common in its favorite retreats than our infrequent views of it would indicate. Like all rails it is active in the twilight, and its common notes may be heard sometimes intermittently for hours along our river marshes. During the breeding season its rarer grunting notes also are uttered.

This bird is a rapid and excellent climber, scaling at times rushes, shrubs, vines and even small vine-embowered trees in its search for seeds and berries or in pursuit of insects, of which it destroys quantities. It seems to be especially eager in quest of locusts, grasshoppers and beetles. It is fond of wild rice, wild oats and the seeds of grasses and reeds. It takes small crustaceans and even small snakes and fishes and also feeds on earthworms, snails and other of the smaller aquatic animals of the marsh.

SORA

Porzana carolina (LINNAEUS). PLATE 23.

Other names: Sora Rail; Carolina Rail; Rail-bird; Chicken-bill; Meadow-chicken; Crake; Ortolan; Rail-bird.

IDENTIFICATION. — Length 7¾ to 9¾ inches; spread 12 to 14½ inches. Slightly smaller than Virginia Rail; distinguished by short yellow bill, grayish breast, and in adult, black fore-face and throat.

BREEDING. — Similar to that of Virginia Rail but eggs darker and with heavier markings.

RANGE. — Breeds from central British Columbia, Manitoba, the lower St. Lawrence River, New Brunswick, and Nova Scotia south to Lower California, Utah, northern Missouri, southern Illinois, southern Ohio, Pennsylvania, and Maryland; winters from California, Arizona, Texas and Florida through the West Indies and Central America to Venezuela and Peru.

The Sora is *the* 'Rail-bird' of New England. It is a more abundant migrant in our meadows and marshes than any other rail and probably outnumbers them all. Its favorite breeding-haunts are river meadows, cattail swamps and fresh-water marshes in general, together with brackish marshes near the sea; in migration it frequents also salt marshes and tidal streams. Lowlands along slow-flowing rivers are favorite spots for migrating Soras. The term 'thin as a rail' applies to this as well as to all rails. Any rail can compress its narrow body at will. At the least alarm the Sora slips easily and rapidly away amid the grass stems, or if pressed too hard by a fast dog, it rises above the grass tops, flutters away weakly like a wounded bird, with legs dangling loosely, and drops to earth again almost at once as if unable to fly far. But the short-winged fluttering Sora has landed on vessels hundreds of miles at sea. Numbers fly to Bermuda, about six hundred miles from the Continent. The bird goes north to Greenland and is supposed even to cross the Gulf of Mexico. Probably favoring winds assist it in its long migratory night flights.

Like all rails it takes readily to water, swimming on the surface, diving at need and using its wings for propulsion under water. Mr. C. J. Maynard asserts that he once saw one run nimbly along the bottom of a brook in water about one foot deep. It was able to do this, he says, by clinging to aquatic plants, and it went about fifteen feet while thus submerged.

When closely pursued, the Sora hides readily beneath the surface by clinging to grass or reeds with its feet and breathing through its upthrust bill, or sometimes it crosses narrow waters by fluttering and splashing along the surface like a Coot. While naturally secretive, it is also curious, and I have seen it come out from its hiding places to survey a slowly drifting canoe or a gunner hiding in the marsh. In September a loud shout, a gunshot or a paddle

struck upon the water will sometimes start the Soras to cackling and their *cuck cuck* may be heard all over a marsh where not one of the birds is visible. If one wishes to see them, he must sit down quietly in some open spot and wait. If his patience is greater than that of the birds, they may appear. Occasionally a dog may force one to fly and even overtake and catch it in the air, so low and slow is its flight. Where unmolested it becomes quite tame, and it is said that on the Western prairies it formerly came about the farmhouses and fed with the chickens.

This rail has a wonderful variety of notes which it gives forth at night as well as by day, and it is sometimes unusually vocal on moonlit nights. Apparently individuals have some ability as imitators. On three different occasions I have heard a very remarkable avian monologue, interspersed with apparent imitations of Whip-poor-will, Flicker, Screech Owl and Bob-white, which I could only attribute to the Sora, and during which several common notes of the Sora were given frequently. Once I had a very brief glimpse of the performer as it plunged into the water, but can only say positively that it was a rail of some kind.

YELLOW RAIL

Coturnicops noveboracensis (GMELIN).

PLATE 23.

Other names: Little Yellow Rail; Yellow-breasted Rail; Yellow Crake; Clicker.

IDENTIFICATION. — Length 6 to 7¾ inches; spread 10 to 13 inches. A small yellowish rail, darker above, and with a conspicuous white wing-patch showing in flight.

BREEDING. — *Nest:* On ground near marshes. *Eggs:* 4 to 15, buffy with brownish dots at larger end.

RANGE. — Breeds in North Dakota and California and probably in Minnesota, Wisconsin, northern Illinois, Ohio, Massachusetts, Maine, Nova Scotia, central Quebec (Ungava), northern Manitoba and southern Mackenzie; winters in the Gulf States and north to North Carolina, and in California.

The Yellow Rail is seen rather rarely in the Northeastern States. It is probably more common in migration than is believed generally, as it is very small and its habits are secretive. It might even be abundant at times and no one be aware of it except an occasional marsh-haunting gunner. It is difficult to flush one without a swift dog, and even then the dog is quite as likely to catch the bird alive as to start it from the grass. It is even more reluctant than the other rails to take flight, but when forced to take wing it flies in the same hesitating, fluttering manner as the other rails for a few yards and then drops, with uplifted wings and dangling legs, into the grass again. It can swim and dive well in case of necessity.

The Yellow Rail seems to prefer the higher margins of marshes, grassy meadows and savannas. It is sometimes found in grain-fields and among garden crops. It also frequents wet meadows and the higher parts of salt marshes at times.

BLACK RAIL

Creciscus jamaicensis stoddardi COALE.

PLATE 23.

Other name: Little Black Rail.

IDENTIFICATION. — Length 5 to 6 inches; spread 10½ to 11½ inches. Appears like a little black chicken: slaty or blackish with black bill but white cross-bars on upper plumage show at close range; black downy young of other species of rail sometimes mistaken for this species.

BREEDING. — On ground in marsh or meadow. *Nest:* Of grasses. *Eggs:* 6 to 9 or more, buffy or creamy-white, profusely speckled with browns and lilac.

RANGE. — Breeds from Massachusetts, Iowa, and Kansas south to New Jersey, Virginia, and Florida; winters mainly south of United States to Guatemala and casually in the Southern States.

The little Black Rail is probably not so rare within its range as it is supposed to be, but the region about Boston is near the northern limit of its normal distribution on the Atlantic coast. It should be looked for in marshes and damp meadows. It is not particularly shy but is very secretive and keeps well under cover, running with head low and neck extended so that it might readily be mistaken for a field mouse. Sometimes when frightened it squats close to the ground and hides, pushing its head under cover. In this position it is occasionally caught by man, dog or cat. It rarely flies until almost trodden upon. Its small size and skulking habits serve as its best protection, and as it frequents marshes overgrown with rank vegetation and nests there or in fields of rank grass and grain, it seldom emerges from cover and is an extremely difficult bird to find or observe. Like all rails, it is more or less nocturnal, flies and migrates chiefly at night, and is heard far more than seen. Its characteristic notes when heard will identify it, but a sagacious bird dog is usually required to take it or at least to assist in its capture.

PURPLE GALLINULE

Ionornis martinica (LINNAEUS).

PLATE 24.

Other name: Blue Pete.

IDENTIFICATION. — Length 12 to 14 inches; spread about 22 inches. Size near that of American Coot but slimmer; deep purplish-blue head and neck (appearing black at a distance) and bright, glossy green upper plumage distinguish this species from the Florida Gallinule; blue frontal shield, red bill tipped with yellow, and yellow legs.

BREEDING. — In swamps and marshes. *Nest:* A shallow platform of rushes, etc., in rank vegetation. *Eggs:* 6 to 10, whitish to buffy, sparsely spotted with browns and grays.

RANGE. — Breeds from Texas, Louisiana, southern Alabama, and South Carolina south through Mexico and the West Indies to Ecuador, Paraguay, and Argentina; winters from Texas, Louisiana, and Florida southward.

The elegant and tropically colored Purple Gallinule is second in grace and beauty among the water-birds only to the male Wood Duck. Its long-toed yellow feet enable it to run rapidly over lily pads and other water vegetation, but unless frightened or pursuing elusive prey it is rather deliberate in its movements. It is a great runner, however, and an active climber and does not hesitate to climb into shrubs, vines and trees where it often perches. It swims well, but usually keeps more to cover than to open water. It feeds on insects, worms, small snails and other small aquatic animals and wild-fruit seeds and other parts of plants.

Mr. A. C. Bent, in his 'Life Histories of North American Marsh Birds,' thus describes the Purple Gallinule in its southern home: 'The extensive marshes which border the upper waters of the St. Johns River in Florida gave us, among other thrills, our first glimpse of the Purple Gallinule in its chosen haunts. . . . The, so-called, open water through which we had to pole our skiff, wound in tortuous channels among the islands and through the saw-grass; it was completely filled with a rank and luxurious growth of yellow pond lilies, or spatterdocks, locally known as "bonnets," through which we were constantly pushing the skiff with two long poles, the pointed prow making a passageway between the thick, fleshy stalks and great broad leaves. . . . Common white pond lilies were quite numerous in the open places; and among the "bonnets" they were in full bloom. Water-turkeys, wood ibises, white ibises, and various herons were seen flying over or found nesting in the willows. Least bitterns, sora rails, and boat-tailed grackles were breeding in the saw-grass and the loud notes of the grackles and redwings were heard all over the marshes. And in the larger open spaces, where the "bonnets," "lettuce" and pond lilies grew we saw the purple gallinules, together with their more common relatives the Florida gallinules and coots. We were thrilled with the striking beauty of this handsome species, as we saw for the first time its brilliant colors in its native haunts. One cannot mistake it as it flies feebly along just over the tops of the "bonnets," with its long yellow legs dangling. And how gracefully and lightly it walks over the lily pads, supported by its long toes, nodding and bowing with a dovelike motion and flirting the white flag of its tail.'

FLORIDA GALLINULE

Gallinula chloropus cachinnans BANGS.   PLATE 24.

Other names: Gray Pond-hen; Meadow-hen; King Rail; Red-billed Mud-hen; Bonnet-walker; Pad-walker; Rice Hen.

IDENTIFICATION. — Length 12 to 14¾ inches; spread 20 to 23 inches. A gray duck-like bird but with a hen-like red bill and red frontal plate; lacks glossy green and purple of similarly shaped Purple Gallinule and has flank-feathers streaked with white unlike white-billed American Coot.

BREEDING. — In fresh-water marshes. *Nest:* A platform of reeds and grasses, on ground or floating. *Eggs:* 8 to 14, darker and spots bolder than those of Purple Gallinule.

RANGE. — Breeds from California, Nebraska, Minnesota, southern Ontario, New York, and Vermont south to the West Indies, Mexico, and Panama, also in Bermuda and the Galapagos Islands; winters from southern California, Texas, and South Carolina southward.

The Florida Gallinule is the 'Water-hen' of America. Its generic name *Gallinula* means 'little hen,' and it walks, talks and squawks like a veritable 'biddy' of the barnyard. It behaves, however, like a connecting link between the hens and the ducks, as it swims and dives like a duck. It prefers to keep under cover, but when forced into open water it often dives to escape observation, and when pursued can conceal itself under water as readily as on land. In habits it resembles the other gallinules and even the American Coot, except that it is less inclined to swimming and more to wading than is the latter. While the Coot keeps much in open water, the Florida Gallinule keeps more under cover. Like the Purple Gallinule, its large, long-toed feet serve like snowshoes to support it as it walks or runs over the surface of the water from one lily pad to another or over the tangled leaves and stems of other floating water-plants. Though not usually very shy it is secretive like the rails, and by keeping under cover eludes observation. Thus, where uncommon, it might escape notice, were it not for its loud calls in the breeding season which are so much like the common clucks and cackles of the barnyard that when coming from the henless watery waste of the marshlands they attract the attention of the ornithologist. When the bird is discovered it is usually walking about with quick upward jerks of the tail, the white of the under tail coverts flashing as the tail is alternately raised and lowered. If swimming, the bird rests lightly on the water like a duck, its head moving forward and backward with every stroke, like that of an American Coot. When feeding in shallow water it sometimes 'tips up' in the manner of surface-feeding ducks. Although it prefers the cover of the marsh rather than the open water, it is unlike the rails in that it is rather more readily flushed. In the breeding season the bright scarlet of the bill and frontal plate is conspicuous.

Brewster described the wooing of the bird as follows:

'Late one afternoon we suddenly heard a great outcry, and soon our pair of Gallinules appeared; the female, who was much the plainer-colored in every respect, swimming swiftly, her tail lowered and about in line with the back; the male flapping his wings on the water in his eagerness to overtake her. This he soon succeeded in doing, but just as he clutched at her with open bill, evidently with amorous designs, she eluded him by a sudden clever turn. He then swam around her in a narrow circle, carrying his tail widespread and erect, his neck arched, his scarlet front fairly blazing and apparently much enlarged and inflated. Seeing that she would not permit his approaches, he soon gave over the pursuit and returned to his favorite raft, while the female swam into the bushes. During the chase one of the birds, presumably the male, uttered repeatedly the following cry: *ticket — ticket — ticket — ticket* (six to eight repetitions each time). This was doubtless a wooing note, for we heard it on no other occasion.'

The eggs of this and the preceding species are found in different stages of incubation and some of the young hatch much earlier than others. The nestlings resemble little black chickens, and like the young of rails they run about soon after they are hatched.

Its food is both vegetal and animal; grass-seed and small grains (in the South particularly rice) are eaten, but it also destroys many aquatic insects, grasshoppers and locusts.

AMERICAN COOT

Fulica americana americana GMELIN.

PLATE 24.

Other names: Blue Peter; Blue Marsh-hen; Crow Duck; Crow-bill; Pelick; Puldoo; Sea-crow; Pond-hen; Pond-crow; Meadow-hen; Water-hen; Mud-hen; Mud-duck; White-bill.

IDENTIFICATION. — Length 13 to 16 inches; spread 23 to 28 inches. Size of small duck but small head and short white bill distinguish it; a slaty bird with black head and neck, white tips to secondaries, and white under tail coverts; yellowish-green legs.

BREEDING. — Similar to Florida Gallinule but eggs clay color to creamy-white, uniformly dotted with small black or brownish spots.

RANGE. — Breeds from central British Columbia, southern Mackenzie, Ontario, southern Quebec, and New Brunswick south to Lower California, Tamaulipas, Arkansas, Tennessee, New Jersey, and in Florida, West Indies and Nicaragua; winters from southeastern Alaska, Colorado, Illinois, Indiana, Massachusetts (casually), and Virginia south to the West Indies and Costa Rica.

The American Coot is a rather clumsy, simple bird with a gawky, silly expression of countenance, whence perhaps its name and the expression 'a silly coot,' as applied to human beings. It is chiefly a fresh-water bird, though sometimes seen in salt marshes or on the surface of bays or estuaries of the sea. It should not be confused with the scoters commonly called 'coot' alongshore, for these are actually ducks, not coots, and in New England are chiefly seen on salt water.

Formerly the Coot was much more abundant through most of its range than it is today. It is so unsuspicious that it is easily taken. Millions doubtless are killed annually by sportsmen, boys, settlers, farmers, and by all kinds of novices in the use of a gun. Probably for this reason Coots, being prolific breeders, go south in the fall in numbers much greater than those that return in spring.

Their only safety lies in betaking themselves to wide waters or to ponds and sloughs surrounded by impenetrable morasses. These are the situations they love, and in the South in winter they gather in such waters until their dark masses cover practically the entire surface. At a sudden alarm there arises an uproar of wings and splattering feet, for the Coot must run splashing and fluttering along the surface when it starts to fly. Almost immediately the pond is cleared, but the Coots, instead of departing for parts unknown at the first alarm, like a wild duck, have only retreated into the cover of the surrounding morass and soon appear again along the margin, spreading gradually over the water until the pool is again covered with their gabbling hundreds. While wading in such morasses in water and mud waist or armpit deep for want of a better method, I have observed their antics and studied their simple habits. Some individual birds will go down and bring up food in water twenty feet or more in depth, while others seem to find it almost impossible to get under the surface. Coots seem to dive more quickly and directly downward than ducks.

In rising from the water Coots flutter and flap along, splashing and paddling with both wings and feet until, clear of the water, they flutter feebly into the air with legs and feet hanging, but when well under way they make fairly good headway, with feet trailing behind. In habits they resemble both gallinules and ducks. They search for food by both wading and swimming as well as by 'tipping up' and diving. When in cover they are prone to hide like rails and are not so easily flushed as are the gallinules.

The little, black, downy young tumble out of the nest into the water soon after they are hatched, but often when these first reach the water there are others still unhatched and the eggs must be cared for. So the mother remains on the nest and continues incubating, while doubtless the father cares for the earliest chicks. For many nights the mother calls them all back to the nest where she broods them through the hours of darkness.

Coots feed very largely on vegetable matter. They eat tender grass in the manner of domestic fowls and are fond of various pondweeds (*Potomagetons*), but they do not disdain their share of animal life, particularly in the breeding season when insects and snails form a good part of their fare. Roots, bulbs, buds, blossoms and seeds of various tender water-plants are eaten.

Order Charadriiformes.   Shore Birds, Gulls, Auks, Etc.

AMERICAN OYSTER–CATCHER

Haematopus palliatus palliatus TEMMINCK.   PLATE 32.

Other names: Oyster Bird; Clam Bird; Red-bill Snipe.

IDENTIFICATION. — Length 17 to 21 inches; spread 30 to 36 inches. About size of Crow; a conspicuous unmistakable bird; long red bill; pied plumage which seems black and white and flashes strikingly when in flight.

BREEDING. — On sand-dunes or beaches. *Nest:* A hollow marked by a few bits of shells. *Eggs:* 2 to 4, creamy-buff spotted with dark brown and lined faintly with lavender.

RANGE. — Breeds locally on Atlantic and Gulf coasts from Virginia (casually to New Brunswick), to Texas and Brazil, the West Indies, and on the Pacific coast from Tehuantepec to Colombia; winters from Virginia southward.

If we can believe the statements of Audubon, the American Oyster-catcher once nested north as far as the coast of Canadian Labrador. As the Black Oyster-catcher ranges north to Alaska and the European Oyster-catcher to Greenland, our bird may well have bred on the Labrador coast in the old days. If so, it is not the only bird that has disappeared from that region since the settlement of the country. Unfortunately no one corroborates Audubon's statement. It formerly nested in New Jersey and possibly even on Long Island, but now the remnant of its race is disappearing from Virginia, and one must go to North Carolina to be sure of finding nesting birds.

Many years ago in Florida I watched these birds feeding on the oyster-bars, disabling the small 'coon' oysters with a clip of the powerful bill. These oysters are exposed at low tide, and the birds know how to open them as well as any professional oyster-opener. They feast on them until their flesh has the flavor of an oyster. These conspicuous great birds were common then, wading about on bars which were exposed at low tide and going to fresh-water ponds back of the beach to drink and bathe. Their color patterns in flight are so conspicuous that the dullest eye cannot fail to find them. Apparently, they know their danger and constantly keep far out of gunshot. I never saw one far from the coast or from some lagoon near the sea. They frequent wide open beaches and flats and avoid cover of any kind. They pay no attention to decoys and would have an excellent chance to survive were it not for the fact that they deposit usually but two or three eggs, deposited on open beaches or stretches of sand, which in the North have become too populous for their safety. Notwithstanding their comparatively short legs, they are swift runners. They are excellent swimmers, dive well at need and fly swiftly.

The food of the American Oyster-catcher consists largely of mussels, limpets, oysters, shrimps, small crabs, small clams, razor-clams, sea-worms and other forms of marine life, and many insects. It probes deeply in the sand for small shellfish and knocks others off the rocks.

PIPING PLOVER

Charadrius melodus ORD.   PLATE 33.

Other names: Beach-bird; Beach Plover; Butter-bird; Clam-bird; Mourning-bird; Pale Ring-neck; Ring-neck; Peep-lo; Tee-o; Feeble.

IDENTIFICATION. — Length 6 to 7¾ inches; spread 14 to 16 inches. A pale, plump sandpiper-like bird, the color of dry sand above; black band above white forehead and partial or entire black band around neck; in flight shows much white in wings.

NOTE. — A plaintive, piping whistle.

BREEDING. — On sandy beaches. *Eggs:* Usually 4, creamy or clay color finely dotted with browns, laid in hollow in sand marked by small pebbles and bits of shell.

RANGE. — Breeds locally from southern Alberta, southern Ontario, southern Quebec, Magdalen Islands, Prince Edward Island, and Nova Scotia south to central Nebraska, northeastern Illinois, northwestern Indiana, northern Ohio, northwestern Pennsylvania, and coasts of New Jersey, Virginia, and North Carolina; winters on the Atlantic and Gulf coasts from South Carolina to Texas and northern Mexico.

In the latter part of the nineteenth century the dove-like little Piping Plover came very near extirpation on most of the Atlantic coast. Destroyed by spring and summer shooting, it had become rare where once it was abundant and was rapidly disappearing, when the Massachusetts Legislature enacted a law giving it protection at all times. Now, protected similarly by Federal law, it is increasing in numbers and reoccupying its former breeding-grounds, wherever the summer population is not too numerous for its comparative safety. Its gentle notes are now heard throughout the summer on all the more lonely sand beaches from the Carolinas to the St. Lawrence. It is a bird of the sandy shore. Wide beaches, backed by dunes, are its favorite breeding-places, where it runs along the sand at such speed and so gracefully and smoothly that it seems to be gliding swiftly over the beach.

The following from one of my note books gives some idea of the means by which this bird and its young avoid their enemies:

'I was watching a pair of adults trying to lead me away from their young. They threw themselves on the ground breast downward and drooping the flight-feathers or primaries, raised and agitated the secondaries until the motion resembled the fluttering pinions of young birds; meantime pushing themselves along with their feet. As the wings were not spread, the primaries were not noticeable and so the imitation of the struggles of the helpless young was complete. Immediately we began a careful search for the nest, looking in all the usual hiding places in or under the tufts of beach-grass, but no nest could we find. As the old birds continued their plaintive cries and circled about we extended our search, expecting to find some half-grown young flattened out somewhere on the beach. Finally by searching over the sand we found a nest exactly like that of the Least Tern on the open beach. A few little pebbles had been grouped in a slight hollow, and there, partly beside the pebbles and partly on them lay three lovely little downy chicks and one egg. I attempted to photograph the parents but they would not come to the young, and as the little ones had already begun to run about we sunk an old barrel in the beach and put them and the egg in it, that we might know where to find them on the morrow. The day was foggy and cold, and during the night a thunderstorm drenched everything, but the next morning the egg had disappeared and four lively youngsters were running around in our barrel. They were now so strong and swift that if one were liberated it was rather difficult to catch it. If hidden it was almost impossible to find it.

'One of my early experiences will serve as an illustration of the difficulty of finding young beach-birds. One day I saw in the distance a downy young Piping Plover running on the beach. Watching it with a powerful glass until it squatted, I marked the spot carefully, walked over and picked it up. I then took it to an open flat part of the beach and released it. It ran a little way, and I have never seen it since. The most careful search failed to solve this puzzle.

'To go back to our little plovers in the barrel. We kept them there two days until we made sure that the parents never feed the young. They brooded them quite constantly, but brought no food whatever and we made certain that the young were able and willing to find their own food within twenty-four hours after they were out of the shell. It was seen that unless they were liberated from the tub they would soon starve to death. On the third day they had become so active and vigorous as to lead one quite a chase.'

Although some Piping Plovers may be seen on our beaches from late March to late October, the great majority of the breeding birds come here in April and early May and depart in August. The late birds probably are hardy migrants from the eastern Canadian Provinces.

CUBAN SNOWY PLOVER

Charadrius nivosus tenuirostris (LAWRENCE).

IDENTIFICATION. — Length about 6 inches; spread about 14 inches. Slightly smaller and even paler than Piping Plover, with longer, slender black bill (Piping Plover has bill orange-yellow at base); stripe above forehead and spot on either side of breast (remnants of ring) brownish-black; legs black.

BREEDING. — Similar to Piping Plover, but 2 or 3 eggs are olive-buff spotted and scrawled with black and gray.

RANGE. — Breeds on the Gulf coast from Florida to Texas and apparently in Haiti and Porto Rico, also on salt plains of Kansas and Oklahoma; south in winter to the Bahamas, Cuba, Haiti, Porto Rico, Yucatan, and Venezuela.

To the New England bird student, the sand-dunes and neighboring beaches of Plum Island, Wingaersheek, Duxbury Bay, and Sandy Neck are dazzling white in the summer sun, composed as they are of tiny light-reflecting grains of white quartz and other resistant portions of disintegrated granite from our 'stern and rock-bound coast.' But when, seeking warmth in winter, we visit the beaches of Florida, the whiteness of our northern sand is dull in comparison with the blinding white of the barrier beaches of broken shells and bits of coral.

And it is for protection on this glittering expanse of palest sands that the little Cuban Snowy Plover has developed its very light coloration that blends so perfectly with its background and which makes it almost invisible until a movement of the bird catches the eye and reveals its plump little form, its slender bill and black legs, distinguishing it from the very slightly grayer Piping Plover, with which it is often associated, or from the abundant Sanderlings with their more contrasting pattern in flight.

The Cuban Snowy Plover differs in no important traits from the more familiar Piping Plover, except that it is more southern in distribution. — (J.B.M.)

SEMIPALMATED PLOVER

Charadrius semipalmatus BONAPARTE.   PLATE 33.

Other names: Ring-neck; Little Ring-neck.

IDENTIFICATION. — Length 6 ½ to 8 inches; spread 14 to 16 inches. Resembles Piping Plover but much darker above (color of wet sand, while Piping Plover is color of dry sand); black line from bill to eye and outlining white forehead; smaller than Killdeer with short tail and only one black band across breast; slightly smaller than Wilson's Plover and with shorter bill with yellowish base.

BREEDING. — *Nest:* A depression in ground sometimes lined with grass. *Eggs:* 4, whitish, greenish-buff or yellowish, spotted with browns.

RANGE. — Breeds on Arctic coast from Bering Sea to Baffin Island and Greenland south to British Columbia, southern James Bay, north shore of Gulf of St. Lawrence, New Brunswick, and Nova Scotia; winters from central California, Louisiana, and South Carolina to Patagonia, Chile, and the Galapagos.

Dr. C. W. Townsend in the 'Birds of Essex County' gives an excellent account of the Semipalmated Plover as follows:

'The Semipalmated Plover, or Ring-neck as it is universally called, is one of the abundant birds of the beach in flocks of from two or three up to forty or fifty. They are found alone or associated with Peep or other shore birds. They also visit the sloughs of the salt marshes, and are occasionally seen still farther inland.

'The flocks on the wing, although sometimes compact, are apt to fly in loose order. On the sand, the birds at once spread out, not keeping together like Sandpipers, so that the pothunter spends many anxious moments waiting for a good combination, and often to his chagrin misses them all as the frightened birds take wing. Unlike the Sandpipers also, but in true plover fashion, instead of moving along close to the wave line with heads down, diligently probing the sand, they run rapidly about in different directions with heads up, often pausing and standing still as if in thought, occasionally jerking or bobbing their heads and necks nervously, and ever and anon dabbing quickly at some morsel of food.

'Like all shore birds, the Ring-neck often snatches moments of sleep in the day, especially during high tide when their best feeding-places are covered. At these times it is not uncommon to see whole flocks huddled together fast asleep on the upper part of the beach, their heads turned to one side and thrust into the feathers of the back. There are always a few birds awake and on the lookout, and by close watching one may see even those apparently asleep, open their eyes occasionally. Ring-necks also sleep with heads sunk down between the shoulders. Their sleepiness in the day is accounted for by the fact that they feed and migrate by night as well as by day....

'Like all shore birds also, the Ring-neck is often exceedingly fat in the autumn and I have known the fat of the breast to split open when the bird struck the ground after being shot when flying at a height. The fat is not only everywhere under the skin but it envelops all the viscera, and the liver is often pale from fatty infiltration. How birds under these circumstances are able to fly so vigorously on their long migrations, or even to fly at all is certainly a mystery.'

WILSON'S PLOVER

Pagolla wilsonia wilsonia (ORD).
PLATE 33.

Other names: Ring-neck; Stuttering Plover.
IDENTIFICATION. — Length 7 to 8¼ inches; spread 14 to 16 inches. Slightly larger than Semipalmated or Piping Plovers; long heavy black bill and black half-ring on upper breast, not completed on back of neck.
BREEDING. — Similar to Semipalmated Plover.
RANGE. — Breeds from Virginia to the northern Bahamas and Florida and along the Gulf coast to Texas; winters from Florida to Texas and south to the West Indies, Honduras, Guatemala, and the coast of Brazil.

Wilson's Plover shows a strong resemblance to the somewhat smaller and slightly darker Semipalmated Plover, but it is easily recognized by its proportionately larger and stouter, black bill. It is southern in distribution, nesting on the sandy beaches of the Middle and Southern Atlantic States, where it is often a fairly common bird in summer.

Its habits are very similar to the paler-colored little Piping Plover, though it sometimes abandons the sand beaches and the wash of the surf for the tidal flats, where its browner back makes it less conspicuous than its smaller relative would be when away from the sun-drenched sand. Its nest is a mere hollow in the sand, sometimes encircled by bits of broken shells, and the rather pointed eggs are very difficult to see against their background of sand and tiny pebbles. — (J.B.M.)

KILLDEER

Oxyechus vociferus vociferus (LINNAEUS).
PLATE 32.

Other names: Killdeer Plover; Kildee; Meadow Plover.
IDENTIFICATION. — Length 9 to 11¼ inches; spread 19 to 21 inches. A medium-sized plover with white collar and two black bands across lower neck and upper breast; lower back tawny to chestnut; much white in wings shows in flight; longer tail than most shore birds; bobs head frequently when on ground.
VOICE. — A noisy bird, often calling *kill-dee, kill-dee* shrilly.
BREEDING. — In marshes, fields and gardens. *Nest:* A hollow on ground usually lined with pebbles or grasses. *Eggs:* 4, drab to creamy-buff, thickly streaked and blotched with black, browns, and lavender.
RANGE. — Breeds from northern British Columbia, northern Ontario, and southern Quebec south to the Bahamas, Florida, central Mexico, and southern Lower California; winters from southern British Columbia, Colorado, Missouri, southern Illinois, western New York, and New Jersey south to Bermuda, the Greater Antilles, northern Venezuela, and northwestern Peru.

The Killdeer is a friend of mankind. Although it sometimes nests about the edges of the salt marsh, it seems generally to prefer to rear its young about cultivated land and gardens (but not in fields where grass or grain grows thickly), probably because it finds that the insects on which it feeds are abundant in such situations. When a nest is approached the female, usually watchful, sneaks away while the intruder is a long distance off, but if she is surprised on the nest or if the interloper closely approaches eggs or young, she uses every artifice to lead him away, floundering along the ground, shrieking and beating the earth with her wings as if in terrible agony. Thus she may induce the novice in Killdeer wiles to follow her. If so, when she has led him far enough astray, she miraculously recovers; her mate meantime wings his way near by with clamorous cries. As in the great shore-bird group in general the eggs are four in number, placed with their smaller ends together at the center of the nest. If this arrangement is disturbed the Killdeer will soon restore it.

The funny little downy young are recognizable as Killdeers as soon as their natal down has dried, for their markings resemble those of the parents. From the first they are able to pick up their own living, as they are hatched in a time of plenty. Killdeers are fond of newly plowed land. They follow the plow and the cultivator in search of grubs and worms. Corn, potato, turnip, clover, alfalfa and other fields and gardens furnish them an abundance of insect food. The Killdeer is an exceedingly swift and graceful bird on the ground or in the air. To 'run like a Killdeer' is a common saying in the South. On the wing it performs wonderful evolutions, particularly in the mating season, showing off the bright markings of its wings, rump and tail to excellent advantage. It flies and cries in the dusk of evening, on moonlit nights, and before daylight in the early morning.

AMERICAN GOLDEN PLOVER

Pluvialis dominica dominica (MÜLLER).   PLATE 32.

Other names: Black-breast; Field-bird; Golden-back; Green-back; Green Plover; Green-head; Pale-breast; Pasture-bird; Squealer; Toad-head; Trout-bird; Brass-back; Frost-bird; Muddy-breast; Pale-belly; Threetoes; Bullhead; Field Plover; Prairie Pigeon.

IDENTIFICATION. — Length 9¾ to 11 inches; spread 20½ to 23 inches. Slightly smaller and more slender than Black-bellied Plover with shorter bill and longer wings (relatively); *no black axillars;* in spring black below, golden-brown above; in autumn brown below; generally more yellowish above and below than Black-belly in autumn; shows no conspicuous white on wings or upper tail coverts.

NOTE. — A harsh whistle, *queedle* or *quee.*

BREEDING. — *Nest:* A hollow in earth lined with a few leaves. *Eggs:* 4 or 5, buffy-olive, heavily spotted with brown and black.

RANGE. — Breeds on Arctic coast from Point Barrow probably to Baffin Island and south to Manitoba; winters on pampas of central South America; migrates in autumn mainly over Atlantic Ocean from Nova Scotia and New England, in smaller numbers down the Mississippi Valley, and along the Pacific coast; migrates north chiefly up the Mississippi Valley.

As the American Golden Plover does not normally visit the Atlantic States in spring and as its usual route to South America in fall takes it out to sea from Nova Scotia to South America, it never was abundant in New England except in autumn, and then only when driven off its usual route by high adverse winds. At such times it appeared in enormous numbers not only along the coasts but on the hills of the interior. In spring it passed up the Mississippi Valley in countless hordes and this great migration continued annually until about the time that the hosts of the Passenger Pigeon began to disappear. Then the Golden Plover commenced to come into the chief game markets of the United States in barrels to take the place of the pigeons. After that the decrease of the species was rapid and it narrowly escaped extinction, pursued as it was by gunners, not only throughout its spring passage up the Mississippi Valley but also in its fall flights wherever it landed either on our coasts or the Bermudas, the Antilles or in South America. All along its route in the settled and civilized parts of both continents it was unremittingly slaughtered except when at sea, and there its ranks probably were decimated by storms.

An easterly gale with heavy rain during the fall migrations in the latter part of August or the first part of September is very likely now to bring a number of American Golden Plovers to outlying points of the New England coast such as Plum Island, Ipswich, Cape Cod, Nantucket and Martha's Vineyard. Some adults still retain most of the breeding plumage at that time.

I have never had a good opportunity to watch the habits of this bird and therefore quote an excellent account written by my friend, Mr. George H. Mackay of Nantucket:

'Various authorities state that along the Atlantic coast the food of the Golden Plover consists principally of grasshoppers, on which they become very fat. I can only say, in answer to this statement, that in my experience I have never seen them eat any, and I have watched them when on the ground quite near, as well as through a strong field glass. I have also examined the stomachs of a good many which I have shot on Nantucket, and have never found any grasshoppers in them, nor in fact anything but crickets (which seem their principal food there), grass seeds, a little vegetable matter, like seaweed, coarse sand, and small stones. I have also frequently shot them with the vent stained purple, probably from the berries of the *Empetrum nigrum*. I have rarely seen a poor or lean bird that landed while making the southern migration. While they are not all in the same condition they are, as a rule, quite fat. The eye is dark hazel, very lustrous, and appealing, and is their most beautiful feature to my mind. Those birds killed soon after landing have the bottoms of their feet quite black; after living on the Island awhile, they turn whitish. I have no reason to offer for this change.... When scattered over considerable ground, as is usual after they have been any length of time on their feeding-ground, every bird apparently on its own hook, if alarmed, a note is sounded; they then rise so as to meet as soon as possible at a common center, which gained, away they go in a compact body. When high up in the air, flying on their migration, I have often noticed the flocks assume shapes that reminded me of the flight of Geese; they also fly in the form of a cluster, with one or more single lines out behind; also broadside in long straight lines, with an apparent velocity of about one and a half miles a minute, measured by the eye as they pass along the headlands. When flying near the ground they course over it at a high rate of speed, in every variety of form, the shape of the flock constantly changing, and frequently following every undulation of the surface, stopping suddenly and alighting when a favorable spot is noticed. They are extremely gregarious, and I have had the same flock return to my decoys as many as four times, after some of their number had been shot each time. When approaching the decoys every bird seems to be whistling, or, as I have often expressed it, uttering a note like *coodle, coodle, coodle*. During the middle of the day they are fond of seeking the margins of ponds, where they sit

175

quietly for a long time, if undisturbed. When disturbed they are almost certain to return, in a short time, to the same spot from which they have been started, that is, if they have been resting or feeding there any length of time.'

In the fall migration on our coast the adults usually appear first. They have a habit when on the ground (particularly when first alighting) of raising the wings high over the back and slowly folding them down. W. H. Hudson tells us that sometimes when a few birds flying high over the pampas see others on the ground they drop rapidly and almost vertically, with fixed wings, to the earth, producing a loud sound resembling the blowing of a horn.

BLACK–BELLIED PLOVER

Squatarola squatarola (LINNAEUS). PLATE 32.

Other names: Black-breast; Black-heart; Bull-head; Beetle-head; Chuckle-head; Bottle-head; Gump; Gray Plover.

IDENTIFICATION. — Length 10½ to 13¾ inches; spread 22 to 25 inches. Largest of American plovers; in spring unmistakable; large head, high white forehead, stout bill, black fore parts, grayer back than Golden Plover; in flight all ages or sexes show *white in wing, and black axillars,* also white upper tail coverts and white black-barred tail.

FLIGHT NOTE. — A loud ringing *pee-oo-ee.*

BREEDING. — Similar to Golden Plover.

RANGE. — Nearly cosmopolitan, widely distributed in both hemispheres; in western hemisphere breeds on Arctic coasts and islands from Point Barrow to Southampton and Baffin islands; winters from southern British Columbia, California, Louisiana, and North Carolina south to Brazil, Peru, and Chile; in migration occurs throughout the United States and in Greenland and Bermuda.

The Black-bellied Plover is misnamed, as the black extends below only to the thighs. The Golden Plover is the real black-bellied bird.

With the ebbing tide thousands of acres of Cape Cod Bay marshes and flats are laid bare. In late May these flats are the haunts of myriads of shore birds and marsh birds. At high water the shore birds scatter over the higher parts of the marsh or the upper beaches, but when the tide is out their table is spread, and then they gather on the flats, scattering here and there, and following the receding brine to pick up what the retiring sea has left. Then their flocks spread over the flats for miles and miles. In the latter half of May the predominant birds are the Black-bellied Plovers, giants among the smaller shore birds. They may be found anywhere along the edges of the sand-flats or where the streams from the marshes pour their shallow floods far over the sands. At the first of the ebb they station themselves on the higher sand-bars near shore; as the tide recedes they follow, until some have reached the outermost spits a mile or more from the shore. For hours they patrol the sandy strand, and then there is a change. The army is on the retreat. The tide is coming in. Preceded by a line of foam or froth, the wavelets wash fast along the sands to reclaim their own. As the sea advances over the wide land-wash the shore birds are the first to go, but gulls and terns stay on until the whirling wavelets wash all round them and they seem to be sitting on the surface of the sea. The shore birds are forced back at last to the beach, and finally, driven from their last sandy feeding-ground, they wing their way far up into the marsh. The incoming waves bring fishes, crabs,

176

algae and various other forms of sea life to feed the birds again when later the tide has retreated. During the ebb and flow a person seated in a stranded boat with a telescope at hand may observe at his leisure the habits of the Black-bellied Plover. While the tide is out they run about with heads up, apparently without aim or purpose, but now and then one thrusts its open bill down into sand or water and pulls up a long marine worm. These seem to be a favorite food, and the birds apparently like to wash the sand from them if there is water near by. A plover sees a turnstone taking something from the sand, steps up quickly and strikes at the smaller bird to drive it away. Another wades into the incoming wash until its breast is partly submerged and then ducks and splashes, throwing water over itself like a timid girl bather. Two beautifully plumaged adult birds apparently run a race for several rods, trotting, and stepping high, with heads in the air. First, one is ahead, then the other; then they turn and run towards us side by side a yard apart. The race continues for about three minutes, during which there is no stop for eating, though twice one snatches up something. Then one flies away, with the other in full pursuit. This looks like courtship, and as one was a little brighter in plumage than the other, the birds probably were a pair, and one at least had 'intentions.' About one in five of the birds in the various groups is a full-plumaged male and perhaps one in a hundred seems to be still in full winter plumage, while between the two extremes are all sorts of 'speckle-bellies.' Two small birds in winter plumage appear to be fed by two larger ones in full plumage, but we can see no food pass, and probably the exercise is mere billing, a form of greeting like that of kissing among human kind. The Black-bellied Plover is a glorious bird and well worth watching. It is usually shy, however, and keeps well beyond ordinary gunshot range.

In the spring migration it is rare in April but usually appears on the New England coast in considerable numbers by the middle of May, and is often abundant until about June 1. Now and then stragglers are seen during June even as far south as Florida. By the first week in July a few adult birds, stragglers from the North, appear on Cape Cod, but the great southward flight comes in August, the young birds coming later than the adults. In flock formation the plovers fly in lines, V's or in massed flocks, like those of many ducks.

RUDDY TURNSTONE

Arenaria interpres morinella (LINNAEUS).   PLATE 33.

Other names: Chicken-bird; Chicken-plover; Chicken; Rock-bird; Rock-plover; Bishop-plover; Calico-back; Calico-bird; Chicaric; Creddock; Red-legged Plover; Streaked-back; Sparked-back; Brant-bird; Horse-foot Snipe; Sea-quail; Salt-water Partridge.

IDENTIFICATION. — Length 7¾ to 10 inches; spread 16 to 19½ inches. Size about that of Killdeer but more robust and tail shorter; pied black, white and chestnut plumage, adult with diagnostic head markings; short straight or slightly upturned bill and short orange legs; in flight shows black and white in wings and tail, and three white streaks down back, with black patch near base of tail.

BREEDING. — *Nest:* A hollow in ground lined with leaves. *Eggs:* 4, olive-brown, cream color or drab, spotted with light brown and lilac.

RANGE. — Breeds from western and northern Alaska to Southampton and Baffin islands; winters from central California, Texas, Louisiana, Mississippi, and North Carolina south to southern Brazil and central Chile; occurs in migration over North America in general.

177

The handsome, busy Ruddy Turnstone has increased under the protection of the Federal law until it is becoming quite a common bird in migration along much of the Atlantic coast. It is so striking and its habits are so peculiar that it well repays the watcher who is able to observe it at close range or with a glass. It likes to delve about the foot of a rocky cliff or on a stony beach where great rocks project above the sea and where rock-weed and kelp abound. In such surroundings its colors seem to blend with its environment and there it is perfectly at home. As its name implies, it digs and pushes with its beak under stones and overturns them. It roots over heaps of mosses and overthrows clods, but is not by any means always thus occupied, for often it runs along the sand like any sandpiper and follows the retreating waves. At half tide I have often found it far from its rocky shores on wide sand-flats, where it runs about in shallow pools, seeking its prey, and occasionally prying up and overturning a large shell of sea-clam or quahog in anticipation of finding some lurking prey beneath. It swims well at need and seems to enjoy wading and bathing. On May 24, 1923, a warm, sunny day, I watched Semipalmated Sandpipers, Semipalmated Plovers and Ruddy Turnstones bathing on the Yarmouth flats. Thirteen lovely Turnstones in elegant nuptial plumage were bathing where the waters of a little creek spreading out over the sand-flats met the incoming tide. The tide was advancing so fast that the birds did not need to wade in, but on the shallows where the wavelets flowed in swiftly but softly, they dipped and fluttered in an inch of water which rapidly grew deeper. Here they splashed about, throwing the sparkling drops over their bright and strikingly marked plumage, from which all water seemed to roll off as if from a duck's back. Some, however, must have soaked in, for as each pretty bather finished its ablutions, it fluttered up into the air a foot or two and flying along for three or four feet alighted on a little sand-bar that still showed above the tide, and so shaking its plumage threw off the remaining drops, meantime displaying all its beauties — its white, black-banded tail fully spread and its pied head, chestnut back and black and white wings glistening in the sunlight.

The Ruddy Turnstone feeds on crustaceans, small mussels and other marine objects and on the eggs of the great crab commonly called Horsefoot or Horse-shoe. In the autumn it often becomes very fat.

AMERICAN WOODCOCK

Philohela minor (GMELIN).   PLATE 25.

Other names: Little Whistler; Whistler; Bogsucker; Timber Doodle; Hill Partridge; Wood Snipe.

IDENTIFICATION. — Length 10 to 12 inches; spread 16 to 19½ inches. Largely nocturnal or crepuscular in habits; when flushed its stocky form, russet coloration, broad fluttering wings, long bill, and whistling sound of wings identify it; protective coloration renders it almost invisible when motionless on ground; Wilson's Snipe is slenderer, darker above, with longer, pointed wings.

CALL. — A nasal *peent.* SONG. — Given in flight, a warbling, twittering whistle.

BREEDING. — In damp woodlands and bushy meadows. *Nest:* A hollow in the ground lined with a few dead leaves. *Eggs:* 3 or 4, creamy-buff to buffy-brown, spotted with browns and grays.

RANGE. — Breeds from southern Manitoba, northeastern Minnesota, southern Ontario, northern Michigan, southern Quebec, New Brunswick, and Nova Scotia south to eastern Colorado, southern Louisiana, and northern Florida; winters from southern Missouri, the Ohio Valley, and southern New Jersey south to Texas and central Florida.

The American Woodcock is a most interesting bird. It has been studied by ornithologists for more than a century, and still its periodical mysterious appearances and disappearances and its lines of migration are not fully understood. We know that the Woodcock is an early bird. Occasional individuals appear in February as far north as Massachusetts. These may have wintered there or in Connecticut, but the main flight usually appears in March and the first part of April. We know that some of the early birds reach Nova Scotia and some of the later ones may go on even to Newfoundland; but we know little regarding the extent of their flight to the northeast.

Some of the American Woodcock's common habits are well known and have been described often. Its young are rather weak and dependent and, unlike the young of the Ruffed Grouse, easily taken; they quickly learn to fly, but in the meantime are frequently carried from place to place by the mother, who clasps them between her thighs, or between her legs and her body, or with her feet. It is said that rarely she carries them on her back.

In the mating season the male, seeking the female at evening, bows and calls repeatedly and often rises high in air, with erratic flight and a variety of peculiar notes; on returning to the ground he struts about with lowered wings and spread tail like a turkey-cock, and while strutting thus with his upraised tail almost touching the back of his retracted head, he is sometimes so absorbed that he actually trips over twigs or sticks in his path; he bows, *peents* and sometimes raises his bill vertically as high as possible, stretching the neck to the utmost, and then pulls down his head until his eyes appear to lie on his shoulders.

To those who have not witnessed the song-flight of this bird, the following graphic description sent to me by Mr. Harry Higbee will be interesting:

'As the bird mounted into the air, it did so each time on a long plane — exactly as an airship rises — and the rapid wing-strokes and vibrant whistling notes given at the same time served to heighten the effect of this similarity. When well into the air the bird turned and mounted higher and higher; still continuing its rapid whistling notes as it rose in diminishing circles. When at the apex of this flight — seemingly two hundred feet or more overhead — these whistling notes were changed to louder and more distinct call notes, which were followed by the outburst of melody given in a descending scale, similar to the "flight song" of the Oven-bird. This song was given while the bird circled overhead, gradually descending on fluttering wings, and finishing with rapid downward sweeps and long "volplanes" toward the earth, when it dropped suddenly down within a few yards of the place from which it had arisen. The entire performance in the air seemed to occupy about five minutes, and as soon as the bird alighted again in the grass it began the peculiar calls with which it had started. These calls seemed to be given at intervals of about five seconds, and in some instances at least the bird moved about before it again arose. Sometimes a low gurgling note, seeming to be given with a sudden expulsion of air, could be heard between these calls. Once or twice an answering call was heard from the long grass near by, and just before dark another Woodcock — presumably the female which had been the object of these outbursts — flew up from the ground near by and disappeared over the tree-tops, seeming to settle down again not far away. This bird, which arose while the other one was in the air, made no distinguishable whistling sound as did its mate when rising.'

The function of the long, grooved, sensitive bill is understood to be that of feeling its way to grubs and worms buried in soft earth or mud, and then opening at the flexible tip to seize and draw them out. Wherever it feeds, its 'borings' are found where its bill has probed deeply, and its 'chalkings' (white excrement) also indicate its presence, for the Woodcock is a mighty eater and blessed with enormous digestive powers.

We know that the American Woodcock probes the soil with its long bill in search of earthworms and grubs, but beyond this we know little of its habits, for the bird is active during the twilight and in the night, and in daylight it may be as sleepy and stupid as an owl. Wherefore it lies to a dog until forced to rise, and then flutters up and over the tops of small trees or undergrowth, to drop again almost immediately into another hiding place.

The primitive ground-nest of the American Woodcock with its spotted gray or buffy eggs, which sometimes is buried by a late snowstorm; the close sitting of the parent bird, which sometimes may be touched with the hand or even lifted from the nest; the stratagems by which the mother strives to entice the intruder away from her young; the bold front she sometimes assumes in the attempt to drive the enemy away — all these are but parts of an oft-told tale. The little chicks with their comparatively short bills and striped downy bodies are exceedingly interesting, readily tamed and might be artificially reared. If the breeding season be not too dry, young Woodcocks apparently prosper, but in a very dry season they seem to disappear, and then the fall flights are disappointing.

In July and August when molting, Woodcocks retire to briery thickets, and then and in September they are often found in the most unlikely places, such as pastures and fields of corn, strawberries, potatoes or asparagus. The movements of the birds in August cannot be fully accounted for. Some short migrating flights may begin before the month ends. During the September moon, however, many birds bred in the hill country move south or into the valleys, but the moonlight nights of October usually see the main flight. A very few Woodcocks winter irregularly in southern New England.

The numbers of the Woodcock are greatly reduced when, as sometimes happens in spring, they reach the North in March only to be overtaken by severe cold or overwhelmed by a blizzard. In the South they are sometimes driven by storms and cold from their wooded fastnesses in the hills and swamps to the coastal regions, where the starving birds die or are slaughtered. Sometimes also, in winter, high water in the swamps sends them out to meet death at the hands of the pot-hunter, but their greatest danger, the country over, lies in the multiplication of gunners. In the upper Mississippi Valley region the Woodcock is now very much reduced in numbers. Its greatest refuge and breeding-ground at present is the Atlantic coast territory, particularly New England and the southern part of the Maritime Provinces. If we do not adequately protect it here, its extirpation is only a question of time.

The food of the American Woodcock consists largely of earthworms. When the summer and autumn are unduly dry and worms go down into the subsoil, the birds lose weight rapidly, but they eat many beetles, grubs and other insects which they search for among the fallen leaves or dig from the ground.

WILSON'S SNIPE

Capella delicata (ORD).

PLATE 25.

Other names: Snipe; English Snipe; Jack Snipe; Alewife-bird; Squatting Snipe.

IDENTIFICATION. — Length 10¼ to 11¾ inches; spread 16¼ to 20 inches. Larger than Spotted Sandpiper; extremely long bill, dark striped plumage, white belly, and rather weak harsh cry as it flushes from the grass and goes off in zigzag or 'crazy' flight, identify it; usually found on low meadows or marshy land.

CALL. — A nasal, rasping *scaipe, scaipe.*

BREEDING. — In wet meadows and marshes. *Nest:* On ground lined with grass. *Eggs:* 3 to 4, very variable, heavily marked.

RANGE. — Breeds from western Alaska, northern Manitoba, the Ungava Peninsula, New Brunswick, and Newfoundland south to southern California, eastern South Dakota, northern Iowa, northern Illinois, northern Indiana, central Ontario, and northwestern Pennsylvania; winters from southeastern Alaska, southern Montana, central Colorado, and southern Virginia through Central America and the West Indies to Colombia and southern Brazil, casually north to Minnesota and Nova Scotia.

When the spring rains and mounting sun begin to tint the meadow grass, when the alewives run up the streams, when the blackbirds and the spring frogs sing their full chorus, then the Wilson's Snipe arrives at night on the south wind. Whoso wades in the marsh at this season will see the startled Snipe spring from the grass, rising up five or six feet perhaps against the wind, and with a harsh cry, '*escape escape,*' proceed to do so in the most erratic, crazy fashion.

The most remarkable performance of this bird is its song-flight. Thoreau says of it: 'Perhaps no one dreamed of a Snipe an hour ago, the air seemed empty of such as they; but as soon as the dusk begins, so that a bird's flight is concealed, you hear this peculiar spirit-suggesting sound, now heard through and above the evening din of the village.' Again he says: 'Persons walking up and down our village street on still evenings hear this *winnowing* sound in the sky over the meadows and know not what it is.' Thoreau hears his first Snipe of the season 'A-lulling the watery meadows, fanning the air like a spirit over some far meadow's bay.' How few people seem to hear or recognize this remarkable sound! Sometimes on cloudy days (rarely in fair weather) this performance may be seen in full daylight. It is called the booming, drumming or bleating of the Snipe, but these words entirely fail either to indicate or to describe the sound.

On April 30, 1911, a dark day with lowering clouds, I was standing near a bog in Westborough, Massachusetts, listening to a Brown Thrasher's rollicking song when I heard an intermittent *who-who who-who who-who who-who who-who* — a sound somewhat like the strong wing-beats of some powerful water-fowl in flight as its passing wings are heard in the dusk of the coming night. This occurred at intervals of a few seconds and shifted rapidly about in the sky. I looked in vain for the source of the sound, and as I moved on to the northward, it faded in the distance. Returning half an hour later I heard the winnowing sound again, and finally with my glass made out the bird against the sky. He was circling high — so high that when he passed over me I could barely see his long bill with the aid of my glasses! Each of his circuits must have covered a mile in its circumference and each encircled the Bittern's Bog, where possibly the female of his choice lay hidden. There was a strong breeze from the southwest. The Snipe seemed to rise diagonally through the air, with rapid wing-beats, and then to glide off sidewise and downward in a curious, wavering, sidelong manner, his wings apparently beating as before, but his body seeming to wobble a little, and his wings to pursue an erratic course. During the diagonal downward plunge the sound was produced, after which the bird continued on in its great circle, soon making another sidewise plunge from another point of the circumference of its line of flight. After I first saw the bird the performance lasted nearly half an hour. At times the bird was perhaps three hundred yards from the earth; at other times much lower, but always beyond gunshot. Finally at about 5.30 he circled directly over the bog, and with set wings pitched almost straight down into the grass.

The sounds produced in this flight are supposed to be made by the outer quills of the wings or tail. European ornithologists believe that the European Snipe produces its so-called 'bleating' by means of the two outer tail feathers, which stand out clearly from the others during the downward plunge.

The song-flight apparently is a part of the mating display of this bird, but in courtship the male struts about the female with wide-spread erected tail, proudly carried head and drooping wings, sometimes ascending spirally into the air high above her, and uttering his love notes as he comes down. When the Wilson's Snipe is on the ground, its striped plumage resembles so closely its environment that it has only to stand still or crouch in the open meadow to be perfectly concealed.

Wilson's Snipes on the average are far more abundant in spring than in fall in New England. Considering the large number killed on the southward migration, the numbers should be less in spring. This anomaly must be accounted for by the fact that the greater part of the birds go south by sea in the fall and come north by land in the spring. Sea-going Wilson's Snipes have reached Bermuda and many winter in the West Indies and eastern South America. Sometimes they are driven back by storms on Cape Cod, Nantucket, Martha's Vineyard, Block Island or Long Island and some of them have been known to pass the winter in such localities. Locally a few winter on the mainland, near flowing springs or in springy swamps.

Wilson's Snipe walks usually with bill directed a little downward, and in feeding plunges it vertically down into the soft earth or mud. Sometimes it pulls out earthworms and at other times secures large numbers of crane-fly larvae. Where it feeds, its borings are less prominent than those of the American Woodcock on its chosen feeding-grounds. It eats cutworms, grasshoppers, mosquitoes, wireworms, click-beetles, water-beetles, seeds of smartweed and other plants, and more or less other vegetal matter has been found in snipes' stomachs.

LONG–BILLED CURLEW

Numenius americanus americanus BECHSTEIN.   PLATE 29.

Other names: Sickle-bill; Old Hen Curlew; Big Curlew.

IDENTIFICATION. — Length 20 to 26 inches; spread 36 to 40 inches. Largest of our shore birds, with very long down-curved bill, but length of bill varies greatly and cannot always be relied on in distinguishing from Hudsonian Curlew; Longbill is more buffy and lacks *contrasting stripes* on head; when flying overhead *bright cinnamon* wing-linings are diagnostic.

BREEDING. — In wet meadows and dry prairies, on ground. *Eggs:* 3 or 4, ashy-yellow to greenish, blotched and spotted with browns, lilac, and black.

RANGE. — Breeds in Utah, southern Idaho, and eastern Nevada; winters from central California and southern Arizona south to Guatemala; now a straggler east of the Mississippi.

The Long-billed Curlew, largest of all American shore birds, must have been once irregularly common in New England. Old gunners have assured me that it was frequently seen on the coast of Massachusetts as late as the sixties of the nineteenth century. When I first went to Florida in 1877 there were many then on the wilder parts of the east coast, but the bird soon practically disappeared from the entire East. It is now rare or wanting in a large part of the West, where it once bred, and only the strictest protection can save it from early extinction. In the East it resorted chiefly to the sea-coast.

This bird is naturally shy, except in defense of its young or when one of its companions is wounded. When one or more have been shot down its companions often return and with piercing cries flutter over the wounded ones until in some cases nearly all fall victims.

The great Long-billed Curlew frequents mud-flats, beaches, creeks in the salt marsh on the sea-coast, and meadows and prairies in the interior.

It probes with its long bill into the holes of crabs and crawfish. In addition to the usual food of shore birds it eats many berries and a few seeds.

HUDSONIAN CURLEW

Phaeopus hudsonicus (LATHAM).   PLATE 29.

Other names: Jack Curlew; Jack; Foolish Curlew; Blue-legs; American Whimbrel.

IDENTIFICATION. — Length 15 to 18¾ inches; spread 31 to 33 inches. A curlew on the Atlantic coast is almost certainly a Hudsonian; distinguished from most shore birds by large size and down-curved bill; smaller, grayer, and usually with shorter bill than Long-billed Curlew; curved bill and extended legs are noticeable in flight.

CALL. — A series of clear, penetrating, staccato whistles.

BREEDING. — *Nest:* A depression in moss or sod on tundra. *Eggs:* 4, similar to Long-billed Curlew.

RANGE. — Breeds on coast of Alaska and east to northern Manitoba; winters from Lower California to Honduras, from Ecuador to Chile, and from British Guiana to the mouth of the Amazon; migrates mainly along Atlantic and Pacific coasts but regular migrant in spring in the interior.

The Hudsonian Curlew is now practically the only curlew to be seen on the Atlantic coast. It is considered rare in spring, when a few may be seen, but many small companies pass along the coast from the latter part of July until well into September. They alight mostly on outlying points where few people see them. They are more often seen flying along the sea-coast, from just outside the beach to ten or twelve miles offshore. In feeding they usually frequent tide-flats at low water, retiring sometimes to wide salt marshes to rest and feed at high tide, and they sometimes frequent beach-grass near sandy shores. In flight the flocks are often formed like those of geese or ducks.

Mr. George H. Mackay has written an excellent account of the habits of this bird in which he says that it feeds on fiddler crabs, grasshoppers and large, gray, sand spiders; also on beetles and 'huckleberries.' It probes the sand or mud deeply with its bill in search of crustaceans and other forms of aquatic life. Mr. J. H. Wheeler writes from Tabucintac, New Brunswick, that this species feeds on cloudberries and blueberries. Mr. L. L. Jewel, writing in the 'Auk' of Panama birds, says: 'One of the bird surprises of my life was to see a Hudsonian Curlew tiptoe and catch butterflies within twenty feet of my front door at Gatun. The clearings in and around town seemed very attractive to these birds and they were fairly tame. Marching or advancing by rushes, always with graceful dignity, sometimes singly but more often in groups of four or five, they foraged through the shorter grass, picking up or catching on the wing their insect food.'

ESKIMO CURLEW

Phaeopus borealis (FORSTER). PLATE 29.

Other names: Doe-bird, sometimes spelled Dough-bird; Prairie Pigeon.
IDENTIFICATION. — Length 12 to 15 inches; spread about 26 to 30 inches. Smaller than Hudsonian Curlew; primaries dark, not barred; wing-linings reddish-brown; lacks well-defined light strip through center of crown; bill shorter than adult Hudsonian.
RANGE. — Formerly bred on the Barren Grounds, migrating down the Atlantic coast from Labrador to New Jersey and thence over the ocean to South America where it wintered from Chile to Patagonia; now extinct or nearly so.

The Eskimo Curlew formerly was one of the extremely abundant birds of America. It was said to have visited Newfoundland in autumn in millions that darkened the sky. Audubon, Dr. Elliott Coues and Dr. A. S. Packard tell of immense flights. In the Prairie States the numbers so resembled the tremendous flights of Passenger Pigeons that they were called 'Prairie Pigeons.' A single flock on alighting in Nebraska was said to have covered forty or fifty acres of ground. Breeding in the Barren Grounds of Canada, they migrated in August southeast to Labrador and Newfoundland, fed there to repletion on curlew berries (*Empetrum nigrum*) and snails, and waxing fat started out across the sea for South America. An easterly storm, like the West Indian hurricanes that sometimes occur in August and September, occasionally drove them on the New England coast. A high westerly gale might send some of them even to European shores, where the species has been taken occasionally. Traveling south, they were driven at times by westerly winds to Bermuda. They often touched on the Lesser Antilles and then passed across the sea to the coast of Brazil and so on to Argentina and Patagonia. The spring route through South America is unknown, but this curlew probably crossed the Gulf of Mexico, arriving in March in southern Texas, and passed up the western Mississippi Valley region to South Dakota and thence on north to the breeding-grounds.

The destruction of the Eskimo Curlew followed that of the Passenger Pigeon, whose place it took in the markets of the country. In the spring migration in the West it was slaughtered at times by wagonloads. Market hunters made it their business to follow the birds from state to state during the migration. On the Atlantic coast in autumn the curlews met with a similar reception, while the South Americans hunted them in winter. From 1870 to 1880 they began to decrease. Between 1886 and 1892 they diminished very rapidly and after that were never seen in numbers on the Labrador coast. Since that time the records show comparatively few

184

birds killed in any part of their range. The last specimen known in New England was a lone bird shot September 5, 1913, at East Orleans, Massachusetts.

The Eskimo Curlew was considered a great table delicacy, and although a very useful bird in the prairie states where it fed on such destructive insect pests as the Rocky Mountain locust, it was rapidly and completely destroyed like the Passenger Pigeon for the price that it brought in the market.

UPLAND PLOVER

Bartramia longicauda (BECHSTEIN).   PLATE 31.

Other names: Bartramian Sandpiper; Highland Plover; Land Plover; Grass Plover; Uplander; Hill-bird; Prairie Plover; Pasture Plover; Field Plover; Prairie Pigeon; Prairie Snipe; Quailly.

IDENTIFICATION. — Length 11 to 12¾ inches; spread 21 to 23 inches. Larger than a Killdeer; no conspicuous field marks but general color buffy-brown; relatively short bill, small head, long neck and long tail distinguish it; habit of holding wings raised high on alighting is characteristic.

ALARM NOTE. — *Quip-ip-ip-ip.* SONG. — A prolonged mellow rolling whistle, *wh-e-e-e-e-e-e-e-e-e-e-o-o-o-o-o-o-o-o-o.*

BREEDING. — In wet meadows or dry fields, on ground. *Eggs:* 4, similar to those of Woodcock.

RANGE. — Breeds from northwestern Alaska, central Manitoba, central Wisconsin, southern Michigan, southern Ontario, southern Quebec, and southern Maine to southern Oregon, Colorado, southern Missouri, southern Illinois, southern Indiana, and northern Virginia; winters on the pampas from southern Brazil to Argentina and Chile.

The tale of the destruction of this lovely bird is a sad one. Harmless and eminently useful, it nevertheless is one of the most luscious morsels to delight the epicurean palate, and so the greed of man has almost swept it from the earth. The market demanded it and got it. It occupied open and cultivated fields and wide prairies. It was not a bird to hide in sheltering forests or thickets; it lived in the open for all to see and when the market hunters and netters had destroyed the Passenger Pigeon, when they turned to a new supply for the insatiable market demand, they found it in the birds of the open land, the Upland Plover, Eskimo Curlew, Golden Plover and Buff-breasted Sandpiper which then swarmed in spring in the Mississippi Valley. In comparatively few years thereafter these birds, destroyed by hundreds of thousands, were nearly extirpated from the land.

I well remember when in my boyhood the Upland Plover nested in the fields behind my father's house in Worcester, Massachusetts, when during the warm, clear nights of early May the notes of this gentle bird fell from out the sky in all directions as the flocks migrated to their summer homes. Then it bred in the fields all over New England, but from the fifteenth of July until the last plover went south they were pursued by gunners everywhere. They were followed in the same way north, south, east and west as their price in the city markets continued to rise.

A decrease is noted in every state where the bird was formerly abundant. The gunner is not to be blamed for all this. Civilization brings many adverse influences. Millions of unrestrained dogs and cats destroy young birds or catch the mother at night on her nest; mowing and reaping machines and late plowing take their toll. Now, although this bird is protected at all times by statute, the law cannot be fully enforced, and there is no protection for it on the pampas of South America where it passes the winter. Our children's children may never see an Upland Plover in the sky or hear its rich notes on the summer air. Its cries are among the most pleasing and remarkable sounds of rural life. They rank with the mating music of the American Woodcock and the Wilson's Snipe. That long-drawn, rolling, mellow whistle as the bird mounts high in air has the sad quality of the November wind. Except the wail of the wind there is nothing else like it in nature. It is an ethereal sound which might well pass for the utterance of the fabled 'wind spirit,' and its *quitty quit*, as it rises startled from the grass, is a distinctive, unique and pleasing call unlike that heard from any other bird. Its long legs seem made for wading in pond or marsh, yet I have never seen it in the water. It wades in the grass of field or prairie and approaches its nest from a distance by walking cautiously through the grass, head held low and squatting lower and lower, and leaves it with like caution.

SPOTTED SANDPIPER

Actitis macularia (LINNAEUS). PLATE 30.

Other names: Tip-up; Tip-tail; Land-bird; Teeter; Teeter-bob; Teeter-tail; Teeter-peep; Twitchet; Peet-weet; Perr-wipe; Pee-weet; Teeter Snipe.

IDENTIFICATION. — Length 6¾ to 8 inches; spread 13 to 14 inches. In spring the black-spotted white breast is distinctive; young birds and winter adults are white below with an ashy tint to upper breast; in any plumage a broad white bar across wing is noticeable in flight; extreme lifting and bobbing of head is characteristic.

CALL NOTE. — *Peet-weet* or *teeter-teet*, with many repetitions.

BREEDING. — *Nest:* On ground, of grasses, leaves, seaweed, etc. *Eggs:* 3 to 5, creamy or drab, spotted and blotched with dark browns, blackish, and grays. Typical 'pear-shaped' sandpiper eggs.

RANGE. — Breeds from tree limit in northwestern Alaska, northern Manitoba, northern Ungava, and Newfoundland south to southern California, southern Louisiana, central Alabama, and northern South Carolina; winters from southern British Columbia, Louisiana, and South Carolina to southern Brazil, Peru, Bolivia, and Argentina.

The cheery little Spotted Sandpiper is the best known and most widely and commonly distributed shore bird that inhabits North America. In these respects it rivals even the Killdeer, for although its breeding range does not extend so far south, it is much more common in the northern part of its range. Its characteristic attitudes and motions are thus graphically described by Dr. Elliott Coues in his 'Birds of the Northwest':

'This bobbing of the head and fore parts (of the Solitary Sandpiper) is the correspondent and counterpart of the still more curious actions of the Spotted Tattlers, or "Tip-ups" as they are aptly called, from this circumstance: a queer balancing of the body upon the legs, constituting an amusement of which these last-named birds are extremely fond. As often as the Tip-up, or "Teeter-tail," as it is also called, stops in its pursuit of insects, the fore part of the body is lowered a little, the head drawn in, the legs slightly bent, whilst the hinder parts and tail are alternately hoisted with a peculiar jerk, and drawn down again, with the regularity of clockwork. The movement is more conspicuous in the upward than in the downward part of the performance; as if the tail were springhinged, in constant danger of flying up, and need-

186

ing constant presence of mind to keep it down. It is amusing to see an old male in the breeding season busy with this operation. Upon some rock jutting out of the water he stands, swelling with amorous pride and self-sufficiency, puffing out his plumage till he looks twice as big as natural, facing about on his narrow pedestal, and bowing with his hinder parts to all points of the compass. A sensitive and fastidious person might see something derisive, if not actually insulting, in this, and feel as Crusoe may be presumed to have felt when the savages who attacked his ship in canoes showed the signs of contumaceous scorn that De Foe records. But it would not be worth while to feel offended, since this is only the entirely original and peculiar way the Tip-up has of conducting his courtships. Ornithologists are not agreed upon the useful purpose subserved in this way, and have as yet failed to account for the extraordinary performance.'

Soon after the middle of May the mated birds decide upon a nesting-place where they scratch and scuffle out a hollow, which, by the joint endeavor of both, is soon ready for the eggs. The female often begins to incubate as soon as the first egg is laid, and for this reason some eggs may hatch before the others, but usually the young emerge within the space of two days subsequent to the hatching of the first egg. As with various other birds the devoted male often feeds his sitting mate. The comical motions of the adults become even more ridiculous when indulged in by the tiny young, which are no sooner out of the parental nest than they discover the 'same uncontrollable ambition' in their posterior ends and 'say "how do you do" backward, with imperturbable gravity.' After they have been hatched, if undisturbed, they remain for a day or two in the nest, but if frightened, they can run and hide almost immediately.

The Spotted Sandpiper swims and dives readily. It can dive from the surface of the water or from full flight, at need. Under water it progresses by using its wings, which it spreads quite widely, and in shallow water it can go to the bottom and run a short distance with head held low and tail raised like a Water Ouzel or Dipper. When the adults are disturbed on the borders of lake or river, they usually start up with many *peet-weets* and fly out low over the water, often scaling with quivering down-bent wings, rocking from one side to the other, soon to swing in and return to shore farther on. Sometimes they alight in trees, and often they perch on fence posts, rails, stone walls and moored boats.

In the North they seldom flock at all, but in the South in winter they sometimes assemble in large companies.

EASTERN SOLITARY SANDPIPER

Tringa solitaria solitaria WILSON. PLATE 30.

Other names: Barnyard Plover; Black Snipe; Wood Tattler.

IDENTIFICATION. — Length 7½ to 9 inches; spread 15 to 17 inches. A little larger than Spotted Sandpiper; very dark above, olive legs and dark slender bill; wings dark above and below; tail largely white at sides with dark central feathers; teeters much like Spotted Sandpiper but does not *exaggerate* so much with its hinder part.

BREEDING. — Unique among shore birds. *Eggs:* 4 or 5, pear-shaped, greenish-white, heavily marked, laid in an abandoned nest of some bird (Robin, Grackle, etc.), in the woods.

RANGE. — Summers from central Alberta, northern Manitoba, northern Ungava, and Newfoundland south to Nebraska, northern Iowa, Illinois, Indiana, northern Ohio, and northern Pennsylvania, but breeding range is not clearly known; winters casually in Florida, and from southeastern Texas, the West Indies, and Costa Rica to Ecuador and possibly Argentina.

The Eastern Solitary Sandpiper is remarkably graceful and active on foot or on the wing. Its aerial evolutions will equal or exceed those of Wilson's Snipe. It gets insects on the wing as readily as do many of the smaller birds. I have described elsewhere its ingenious method of stirring the silt in the bottom of a ditch by moving one foot so rapidly and gently that though the water was not roiled its insect prey was started from the bottom and seized by its ready bill. I have never known any other bird to perform this feat so skillfully, and I know from experiment that I cannot in any way stir this ooze without clouding the water. Dr. Elliott Coues in his 'Birds of the Northwest' described the habits of this bird in his inimitable way:

'They cannot be said with entire propriety to be "solitary," though this name is well enough to indicate less social propensities than most of the waders possess. I generally found from two or three to half a dozen together; frequently only one at a time; occasionally, but not often, upwards of a score, that seemed, however, to be drawn together by their common tastes in the matter of feeding-grounds, rather than by any gregarious instinct. They are, moreover, pretty exclusive in their own set; rather declining than encouraging familiarity on the part of other waders; though the Peetweets and others sometimes intrude hoydenish society upon the more sedate and aristocratic members of the long-legged circle. They should rightly, however, rather embrace, than merely endure such company, for they are of easy-going contemplative natures, and their sharper-eyed associates often do them good service in sounding alarms.

'These Tattlers indulge on all occasions a propensity for nodding, like Lord Burleigh or the Chinese mandarins in front of tea shops; and when they see something they cannot quite make out, seem to reason with themselves, and finally come to a conclusion in this way; impressing themselves heavily with a sense of their own logic. They go through the bowing exercise with a gravity that may quite upset that of a disinterested spectator, and yet all through the performance, so ludicrous in itself, contrive to preserve something of the passive sedateness that marks all their movements. . . . The Solitary Tattlers . . . are fond of standing motionless in the water when they have satisfied their hunger, or of wading about, up to their bellies, with slow, measured steps. If startled at such times, they rise easily and lightly on wing, fly rather slowly a little distance with dangling legs and outstretched neck, to soon realight and look about with a dazed expression. Just as their feet touch the ground, the long, pointed wings are lifted till their tips nearly meet above, and are then deliberately folded. The Esquimaux Curlews and some other birds have the same habit. The Tattlers are unusually silent birds; but when suddenly alarmed, they utter a low and rather pleasing whistle as they fly off, or even without moving.'

This is the only sandpiper that habitually frequents wooded highlands. It may be found on some of the higher wooded mountains as well as in the lowlands, and is rather rarely seen on the seashore. It appears in migration in greatest numbers about the middle of May and again in the latter half of August and early September when from six to nine birds may sometimes be found about a small pond.

EASTERN WILLET

Catoptrophorus semipalmatus semipalmatus (GMELIN). PLATE 31.

Other names: Humility; Pied-wing Curlew; White-wing; White-winged Curlew, Bill-willie, Pill-willet.

IDENTIFICATION. — Length 14 to 16 inches; spread 24 to 29 inches. Larger than Greater Yellow-legs; long, wide, white patches contrasting with blackish on both surfaces of wings very noticeable both in flight and when wings are held raised in first alighting.

CALL NOTE. — *Pill-will-willet.*

BREEDING. — On beach or sand-dune. *Nest:* A few grasses in a hollow. *Eggs:* 4, very variable.

RANGE. — Breeds on the Atlantic coast in Nova Scotia, and from New Jersey to Florida, and on the Gulf coast to Texas, also in Bahamas and Greater Antilles; winters from North Carolina and the Bahamas to Brazil.

The Eastern Willet, a great, strikingly marked shore bird, has been gradually reduced in numbers until it has become one of the rarest of shore birds on the North Atlantic coast. Samuels (1870) said that it occasionally bred within the limits of New England, usually preferring a sandy island to the main shore; 'but,' he wrote, 'it sometimes selects a locality in a marsh for its nest, and has been known to breed in a rye field twenty miles from the seashore.' This is interesting historically, as the bird has been long since extirpated from New England as a breeder. Samuels asserts that the nest is built about the last week in May, which would extend the breeding season into June.

The Eastern Willet was not considered a very edible fowl, but its eggs were highly prized for the table. This consideration and its availability as a target for the shotgun were sufficient to insure its extirpation as a breeding bird throughout much of its range.

Like other large shore birds it is very solicitous for the safety of its young. The mother throws herself before the intruder and simulates lameness to entice him away or flutters overhead with wild shrill cries of distress, exposing herself recklessly to the aim of the gunner. Mr. Arthur T. Wayne tells how he watched an anxious pair of Willets with newly hatched young until he saw one of the parents carry the young, one at a time, across the marsh and over three creeks to an island a quarter of a mile away.

Often, like the Wilson's Snipe and other shore birds, in the breeding season the Eastern Willet alights on dead trees or even on living ones. It is an habitual wader, often wading in up to its belly, and it swims readily and well. Wherever it is common it is usually seen in flocks, but now on the northern Atlantic coast single birds are more often noted. Probably a few Eastern Willets which appear on the coast of New England early in July come here from Nova Scotia where they breed, but most of the birds taken later in the season are specimens of the Western Willet.

WESTERN WILLET

Catoptrophorus semipalmatus inornatus (BREWSTER).

PLATE 31.

Other names: Same as Eastern Willet (see page 189).

IDENTIFICATION. — Length 15 to 19 inches; spread 28 to 31 inches. Larger but indistinguishable in field from Eastern Willet; summer adult is paler above and not so conspicuously marked.

BREEDING. — See Eastern Willet.

RANGE. — Breeds from east central Oregon, southern Alberta, and southern Manitoba south to northeastern California, western Minnesota, and northern Iowa; winters from northern California on the Pacific coast and from the coasts of Texas, Louisiana, and Florida south to Ecuador, Peru, and the Galapagos Islands; in fall migration occurs in southern Ontario and on the Atlantic coast from New England south.

The habits of the Western Willet are similar to those of its eastern relative, and while on the Atlantic coast it haunts the same localities. Like the Eastern Willet, it has a characteristic habit of holding its wings straight upward when it alights, thus displaying their conspicuous black and white pattern. A very good description of the habits of this bird is given by Grinnell, Bryant and Storer in 'The Game Birds of California,' from which the following extract is taken:

'In its chosen haunts the Willet stalks about in search of the aquatic animals which constitute its food, sometimes wading breast deep in the water. Its half-webbed feet allow it to swim easily and this the bird often does when lifted beyond its depth by a wave, or when pursued.... These birds are often more suspicious than most other large shore birds. The Willets do not decoy so readily, and even when passing over decoys the least movement will frighten them, after which no amount of skillful whistling will induce them to return.

'A flock of six observed on the Alameda marsh, upon rising flew in the zigzag manner of sandpipers, but with longer straight flights preceding the changes in direction. When the birds alighted on a sand bar they stood very erect, and now and then spasmodically raised the head still higher for an instant in a haughty manner — a backward bow! During high tide the birds retired inland along the sloughs where they stood heel deep, preening, and at short intervals they seemingly rinsed their bills.

'The flight of the Willet when well under way is quite direct, with a flat wing-beat. The wings rarely rise above the level of the back, and consequently the upper surface of the body is almost continually in view. The bird sails with set wings only when descending from a higher to a lower level, or when about to alight. A change in the direction of flight is seemingly accomplished by a difference in the intensity of the two wing-beats and a rolling of the body. The feet, which extend considerably beyond the tail, probably assist somewhat in steering. During high tide, when the feeding-grounds of the Willet are covered with water, the birds choose some higher situation which will not be inundated, and there they rest, many of the flock tucking their heads under their wings as they sleep. There is, however, one or more constantly on watch, and on the approach of danger a shrill cry of alarm is sounded, the flock at once taking wing and rapidly making off to some safer place.'

The bird is already growing rare in some of the states west of the Mississippi, where it formerly bred commonly, and unless it can be stringently protected, it will in time disappear.

Many individuals migrate easterly or southeasterly in autumn and so reach the Atlantic coast, from New England at least to the Carolinas. In spring apparently they go west from Florida and then move northward west of the Mississippi.

GREATER YELLOW–LEGS

Totanus melanoleucus (GMELIN). PLATE 30.

Other names: Winter Yellow-leg; Winter Turkey-back; Cucu; Big Yellow-leg; Horse Yellow-leg; Greater Tattler or Tell-tale; Yelper; Tell-tale Snipe.

IDENTIFICATION. — Length 12¼ to 15 inches; spread 23 to 26 inches. Distinguished from all shore birds except Lesser Yellow-legs by large size, slender appearance, gray upper plumage and white under parts, conspicuous white tail coverts, and long yellow legs; from Lesser Yellow-legs by size and larger, stouter bill.

COMMON CALL. — A rather penetrating, insistent, mellow, whistled series all on one pitch, usually in threes or fours, *whew-whew-whew.*

BREEDING. — In forested regions. *Eggs:* 4, grayish-white boldly marked, in a depression in the ground.

RANGE. — Breeds from Alaska, central Alberta, southern Ungava, and Labrador to southern British Columbia, southern Manitoba, Anticosti and Mingan islands, and Newfoundland; winters from California, Texas, Louisiana, and South Carolina south to Patagonia.

Every marshland hunter knows the Greater Yellow-legs as a telltale. This shy, wild bird seems always on the lookout for danger and its cries of alarm are well understood by every wild denizen of marsh and shore. It frequents mainly the mud-flats, estuaries and pools in the marsh or along the shore, where it wades sometimes up to its body in the water. In August and early September, when interior waters are low, it may be seen in small numbers about their margins. At all seasons it is rather rare along the outer sea-beaches. The following by Dr. C. W. Townsend is excellently descriptive of the habits of the species:

'This beautiful and interesting bird is rarely to be found on the beach, preferring the sloughs of the marsh or the muddy creeks, where it can catch small fish in the water and probe the soft mud with its long bill. Persistently sought by the gunner, eagerly responding to the easily imitated call, and offering on its approach to the decoys an extremely easy shot, the Greater Yellow-legs still remains common, although its numbers have been greatly reduced in the last twenty years. Like all shore birds, its numbers on the coast vary greatly in different years, owing not so much to the actual number of birds as to the direction of the flight, whether along the coast or farther out to sea. This, in turn, depends largely on the weather conditions.

'In flying, the Greater Yellow-legs is a conspicuous object. Its long yellow legs are extended out behind, its long neck and bill in front, while its white rump flashes out as the bird turns or flies away. The wings, dark and pointed, are curved downward with vigorous strokes, as the bird flies and scales alternately. In alighting, it first sets its wings, sails gracefully downward, drops its long legs, and as soon as it is firmly on the ground it frequently spreads and lifts its wings straight up over its back, then folds them carefully, and after "tetering," in which process it moves its whole body up and down on its legs as a fulcrum, it proceeds to go about the business of the day in feeding.

'The courtship song of the Greater Yellow-legs comes up from the marshes of Essex County throughout the month of May, but is heard in greater volume during the two middle weeks. It has a sweet and pleading character and seems to say *wull yer? wull yer?* Although it differs from the Flicker-like call described in the original Memoir, which may be heard at the same time, it too has a decided Flicker-like flavor. It is heard throughout the day, but in the evening until it is nearly dark, the marshes often resound with the plaintive callings.

'In walking in the shallow water of a pond these long-legged birds kick out their legs behind as if to rid them of weeds or grass. They dab at the mud or water like a plover instead of deliberately probing it like a sandpiper with head down. They often pick off insects from the grass or the surface of the water, and I have found small fish in their stomachs.'

In its long spring migration from Patagonia or other South American regions to Canada and Alaska the Greater Yellow-legs appears on the northern Atlantic coast in greatest numbers in May, and on the return flight is most common in late August and September or early October.

The food of this species seems to consist more largely of small fish than that of other shore birds. A small party of these Yellow-legs may be commonly seen in shallow water running rapidly in different directions in pursuit of little fish. Each bird, darting its bill into the water from time to time, now and then succeeds in catching one of the tiny creatures, which is swallowed with little effort. Occasionally, however, a bird catches a fish so large and long that it can be swallowed only with great difficulty. In addition to its fish diet the species takes the usual toll of mollusks and crustaceans and in the interior a great many insects.

LESSER YELLOW-LEGS

Totanus flavipes (GMELIN). PLATE 30.

Other names: Summer Yellow-legs; Small Cucu; Yellow-leg Tattler.

IDENTIFICATION. — Length 9¼ to 11¼ inches; spread 19 to 21½ inches. Similar to Greater Yellow-legs but one third smaller and bill more slender.

BREEDING. — Similar to Greater Yellow-legs.

RANGE. — Breeds from Alaska, northern Manitoba, and Ungava to northern British Columbia, Alberta, and southern Manitoba; winters in Chile, Argentina, and Patagonia, and casually in Mexico, Louisiana, Florida, and the Bahamas; rare in spring on the Atlantic coast.

The Lesser Yellow-legs is one of the most generally common of our migrant shore birds along the Atlantic coast. Its double whistle may be heard in August or early September about all large bodies of water. The spring flight of this species goes largely up the Mississippi Valley. It seems to be uncommon to rare in spring north of South Carolina, from which state it migrates in a northwesterly direction. Dr. P. L. Hatch gives the following account of its appearance at this season in Minnesota:

'From the first to the tenth of April the Yellow-legs appear about the shallow pools and muddy ponds in small parties. In these they wade about constantly for hours at a time when unmolested, and when driven to wing, fly very swiftly away in an irregular, snipe-like manner, making a loud, whistling note, illy adapted to concert melody. Their flight is wonderfully compact, the flock moving as if by one impulse through all the gyrations incident to indecision where next to go, which, however, often results in their return to the same pool when the gunner has concealed himself effectually. From the repeated observation of this phenomenon in many species of bird life, I am convinced that in such cases only the individual leading the flock takes the least cognizance of their surroundings, all others maintaining an instinctive attention to the motions of the leader alone. If by an exceptionally sudden surprise the flock is momentarily deranged, in an instant the former compactness is resumed as if nothing had occurred, which would be impossible upon any other conceivable hypothesis. The noisy, whistling notes of the species soon become familiar to the gunner, which some of them learn to imitate so well that the deluded flock easily falls into the range of his deadly missile. Their meat is scarcely less palatable than the best of the snipe kind. By the first of May most of them have gone, probably much farther north, to multiply by reproduction and return here again about the first week in September.'

This description of the species in the interior in spring may well be supplemented by another by Mr. J. T. Nichols, describing its habits in autumn on the Atlantic coast:

'The Lesser Yellow-legs frequents the shallow pools in the salt marshes, and is seen now and then on the mud-flats or on stranded layers of eel-grass along the shores of coves and bays. It is also very partial to brackish meadows with standing water.

'It is a very gregarious bird, and pairs or small flocks are more frequently observed than solitary individuals. It often associates with other species, such as the Dowitcher, Robin Snipe, and Greater Yellow-legs. In comparison with the last-named species, it generally travels in larger bodies, and is much less suspicious, stooling more readily and alighting closer to the blind. Its flight is similar, though perhaps not quite so strong as that of the larger bird, which at times covers distance with surprising speed. In all its movements and attitudes — whether wading among the decoys in water up to its thighs, bathing, running about over a mud-bar, standing at rest with neck drawn in, scratching its bill with a foot, or curving its slender wings in easy flight — the Lesser Yellow-legs is an exceedingly graceful bird.'

We see so few of these birds in the Atlantic States in spring that their arrival is always a welcome sight, but in the fall migration Lesser Yellow-legs appear in some numbers in August and early September along the margins of lakes and rivers, wherever flats or bars are exposed by low water. They frequent sewer-beds, fresh and salt marshes, flats exposed at low tide, and sometimes may be seen even on the beach. They are more gregarious than the Greater Yellow-legs, and collect in larger flocks. They are not quite so shy as the larger species, and like that and the godwits, if one is wounded, the others, in their anxiety, are likely to return and flutter overhead, regardless of the gunner, until their ranks are sadly thinned.

AMERICAN KNOT

Calidris canutus rufus (WILSON). PLATE 26.

Other names: Red-breasted Sandpiper; Gray-back; Silver-back; Rosy Plover; Robin Snipe; Blue Plover; Buff-breast; Gray Red-breasted Plover; Wahquoit; Whiting.

IDENTIFICATION. — Length 10 to 11 inches; spread 20 to 21 inches. Large and stout compared with small sandpipers; larger than Ruddy Turnstone; rounded chunky form; short legs; colored a little like Dowitcher, but short bill and gray back distinguish it; light rump not conspicuous in flight, as in Dowitcher or Yellow-legs and only a faint white line shows in wing; in breeding plumage, reddish breast distinguishes it from all but Dowitcher and Red Phalarope; young birds are gray above and white below.

NOTE. — A soft *wah-quoit.*

RANGE. — Breeds on Arctic islands from Greenland west possibly to Alaska; migrates along both coasts of America and through Alberta; winters in South America south to Patagonia, and rarely on coasts of Florida and South Carolina; present in summer from Florida to Virginia on the coast.

In the days of our grandfathers the Gray-backs or Wahquoits, as they were called, swarmed along the coasts of Cape Cod by the thousand. Spring and autumn their hosts were marshaled on the flats of Barnstable County, and around Tuckernuck and Muskeget islands they collected in immense numbers and rose in 'clouds' before the sportsman's gun. As the nineteenth century closed they were becoming rare all along the coast, but now under protective laws their numbers are beginning to increase. They appear in spring usually during the latter half of May (about the 20th) and feed in company with Ruddy Turnstones or Black-bellied Plovers, sometimes with Red-backed Sandpipers and a few Sanderlings. They usually pass rapidly on to the North. While here they feed much on beaches and flats at low water, wading in shallow small pools or little streams, that flow over the flats to the sea, retiring to the high beach or the salt marsh to rest and feed at high tide. They leave New England about the first week in June and proceed to Arctic regions. There in the breeding season the male has a pleasing flight song. By mid-July the adults are seen on their return, some still retaining much of the breeding plumage. They continue to pass all through August. The young come later than the adults and are usually here in greatest numbers in the latter part of August and the first part of September. The Atlantic coast seems to be their chief route of migration between their Arctic homes and South America, though some pass through the Mississippi Valley and down through Mexico.

While the American Knot has one of the widest seasonal ranges of any North American bird, nesting on the Arctic coasts and wintering as far south as Tierra del Fuego, stragglers from the great migration flocks sometimes linger on the shores of our Southern States from South Carolina to Florida and the Gulf of Mexico, where they join in patrolling the beaches and the muddy shores of the shallow inlets, with the Ruddy Turnstones, Red-backed Sandpipers, Black-bellied Plovers, and the larger Willets.

PURPLE SANDPIPER

Arquatella maritima (BRÜNNICH).   PLATE 26.

Other names: Rock-bird; Winter Rock-bird; Rockweed Bird; Rock Plover; Rock Snipe; Winter Snipe; Winter Peep.

IDENTIFICATION. — Length 8 to 9½ inches; spread 14 to 16 inches. Size of Sanderling but more robust; only shore bird commonly seen in New England in winter; *dark color*, white belly, short yellow legs, yellow base of bill, and *squat* rounded figure distinguish it; considerable white on dark wing shows in flight; usually found on offshore ledges.

RANGE. — Summers from Melville Island, Ellesmere Island, and northern Greenland south to southern Baffin Island and southern Greenland (also in Eastern Hemisphere); winters from southern Greenland and New Brunswick to New York.

The Purple Sandpiper winters farther north than any other member of the shore-bird family. It nests in Greenland and from Melville Island to Baffin Island, and journeys only a few

194

hundred miles southward to its winter habitat, while many other sandpipers travel thousands of miles to South America at the same season.

Its favorite haunts are rocky islands offshore, and in New England at least it is very rarely found upon the mainland. Its food is found on these rocks below the high-water level, and during the period of high tide the plump little birds may be seen resting in scattered flocks, sometimes consisting of a hundred or two hundred birds, wherever the inequalities of the ledges afford some slight shelter from the wintry blasts which sweep across the open Atlantic and often send the salt spray completely over the smaller islets. As the tide begins to drop the birds move around restlessly, often flying from one small island to another, and as soon as the band of gray-white barnacles is exposed, feeding commences. A little later the festoons of rockweed will also be exposed with their wealth of tiny marine creatures upon which the Purple Sandpiper feeds. They seem to prefer the eastern or seaward side of the ledges except in the stormiest weather, probably because the recurring surges of the sea continually turn over the heavy fronds of the seaweed, exposing fresh surfaces to the eager little birds searching for snails and other mollusks, and for minute crustaceans. Though slush ice is forming in the shelter of the rocks and the spray freezes wherever it strikes, they wade about in the shallow rock pools or in the wash of the waves, merely fluttering up into the air a few inches when an especially high wavelet threatens to overcome the little waders. They seem actually to revel in the commotion of the waters, though in stormy weather they may seek the lee side of the islands for their feeding.

From Nova Scotia and New Brunswick along the rocky coast of Maine, to the ledges of Cape Ann and the Scituate and Cohasset rocks in Massachusetts, the Purple Sandpiper is a fairly common winter resident from November or December to March or April. South of that the birds are rarely seen, the sandy stretches of Cape Cod and Long Island offering little attraction to a bird of the specialized feeding-habits of the Purple Sandpiper. Late in May or in early June the birds have returned to their northern breeding-range for the short summer season. — (J.B.M.)

PECTORAL SANDPIPER

Pisobia melanotos (VIEILLOT).   PLATE 26.

Other names: Grass-bird; Jacksnipe; Brown-back; Brownie; Marsh-plover; Dowitch; Squat Snipe; Squatter; Creaker Pert; Creaker; Grass Snipe; Meadow Snipe.

IDENTIFICATION. — Length 8 to 9½ inches; spread 15 to 18 inches. Size of Sanderling or larger, smaller than Knot; stocky, short-necked, short-legged; legs yellowish or greenish; closely resembles Least Sandpiper in spring plumage but more than twice as large; has no white wing-bar, and white of lower breast and abdomen is more abruptly bounded by brownish or buffy, heavily streaked, dark breast; when on wing, the pale gray tail with dark middle feathers sometimes is noticeable; feeds chiefly on marshes and mud-flats.

FLIGHT NOTE. — A reedy *kriek, kriek*.

RANGE. — Breeds on Arctic coast from northeastern Siberia to northern Alaska, and to Southampton Island; winters in South America from Peru to Patagonia; rare migrant on Pacific coast; common migrant in fall in the Mississippi Valley and on the Atlantic coast, rare in spring, especially on Atlantic coast.

The Pectoral Sandpiper, known to many gunners as the 'Grass-bird,' is well named, for it is mainly a bird of grassy lands. It prefers such environment, and in its season may be found, on the Atlantic coast, chiefly in the upper parts of the salt marsh, where the 'black grass' grows, or even in fresh-water meadows or upland pastures. In the interior of the continent it has been found in the mountains as high as thirteen thousand feet, but in the Eastern States it prefers damp lowlands and sometimes may be found wading in mud-holes in the marsh, running over mud-flats or even occasionally following the retreating waves on the sea-shore. It usually comes in at night in small flocks, sometimes in considerable numbers or even great flights; in some seasons it is hardly seen at all. The flocks seem to prefer salt marshes, where the grass has been cut, and although they migrate in compact 'bunches,' when they alight they scatter about over the marsh to feed, singly or in pairs. When squatting or hiding in the short grass they seem to have confidence in their protective coloration and will often lie close, jumping suddenly and flying erratically away only when nearly stepped on by the gunner. In its Arctic home the male bird develops its gullet until, when filled with air, it appears nearly as large as the bird's body. With the aid of this sac the bird in its nuptial flights produces a peculiar booming note.

The Pectoral Sandpiper arrives in the North Atlantic States in greatest numbers during the latter part of August or in September, though now and then a bird or two will appear as early as the last week of June. In May it is a rather rare migrant when on its way from South America to its home within the Arctic Circle.

Its food consists largely of insects. It takes grasshoppers, weevils, cutworms, beetles, wireworms, mosquitoes, horse flies, small snails, and small shellfish, together with some vegetal matter.

WHITE–RUMPED SANDPIPER

Pisobia fuscicollis (VIEILLOT). PLATE 27.

Other names: Bonaparte's Sandpiper; Bull-peep; White-rumped Peep; White-tailed Stib.

IDENTIFICATION. — Length 6¾ to 8 inches; spread 14 to 16½ inches. In breeding plumage resembles both Pectoral and Baird's Sandpipers (smaller than former, slightly larger than latter); distinguished from both in *flight* by white of its upper tail coverts which extends *across* the rump; difficult to distinguish when on ground with wings covering white spot, but generally more black on back and scapulars than the other species, especially in midsummer; in winter plumage grayer than either; in transition plumage some black spots show in gray of upper plumage; larger than Semipalmated Sandpiper and in breeding dress breast is dark in front of wing where former is nearly white.

RANGE. — Breeds along the Arctic coast from northern Alaska to Southampton and southern Baffin islands, reported east to Greenland in summer; winters from Paraguay to Patagonia and the Falkland islands; in migration most abundant in the Mississippi Valley but uncommon in Alberta and on the Atlantic coast.

The White-rumped Sandpiper, though an abundant bird in migration in the Mississippi Valley, is not generally common on the northeastern Atlantic coast. Stragglers appear there from the North late in July, but most of them come late in September or in early October. Again in May they return, but usually in much smaller numbers. On the coast they come in small parties, by themselves, but often a single bird or a few are seen with Semipalmated Sandpipers and 'Ring-necks' on the beach. They are particularly fond of rocky beaches, where

196

they run over the weed-covered rocks or wade up to their bellies in salt-water pools between tide marks. They frequent the borders of creeks and pools in the salt marsh, and are seen also in springy places in the uplands. In the interior they may be found at times in meadows, sometimes in company with 'Grass Birds' (Pectoral Sandpipers) or along the shores of shallow ponds or pools. In flight when seen from the rear their white upper tail coverts are very conspicuous. In the late fall, in its habitat on the sandy shore, the plain gray of its winter plumage and the white of its rump suggest a diminutive Knot. It is usually rather unsuspicious, and allows a close approach wherever it has not been harassed by law-breaking gunners, but when molested soon becomes wild.

This species remains in Argentina until late April and in Brazil until May. Most of the spring records in the United States are in May, and there are June and July dates in Ontario and Saskatchewan, respectively. In early July the southward movement begins, and in early September the vanguard has reached Cape Horn, the southernmost part of the bird's range. Thus this wonderful flight covers the entire length of both western continents.

BAIRD'S SANDPIPER

Pisobia bairdi (COUES).   PLATE 27.

Other names: Bull-peep; Grass-bird.

IDENTIFICATION. — Length 7 to about 7½ inches; spread 15 to 16½ inches. Like a very large Least Sandpiper with breast tinted buffy; seen with Semipalmated Sandpipers is a little larger, more buffy and breast darker; with Least Sandpipers, plainly larger; with White-rumps can be identified surely in flight by its dark rump; with Pectoral Sandpipers is smaller, not so brown, rather less distinctly streaked above and below and bill shorter and more slender; as this bird can be closely approached its short, straight, slender bill will help to distinguish it from larger shore birds; this readily separates it from Red-backed Sandpiper, which has a longer, down-curved bill.

RANGE. — Breeds along the Arctic coast from western Alaska to Baffin Island and probably Greenland south to Mackenzie; winters in Chile, Argentina, and Patagonia; occurs regularly in migration from the Rocky Mountains to the Mississippi Valley, and irregularly in autumn on the Pacific coast from Alaska to Lower California, on the Atlantic coast from Nova Scotia to South Carolina, and on the Gulf coast of Florida.

On the south shore of Martha's Vineyard where shallow pools are formed from the overflow of ponds and marshes just inside the beach ridge — there Baird's Sandpiper loves to feed. In late August or early September when the grass has been cut, this bird comes in small parties of four to eight and hunts about the margins of partly dried-out pools, threading its way among the stubble or poking about upon the bare mud. It is very intent on its own business, assumes a crouching attitude as if near-sighted, and works slowly along, weaving in and out among the Least or Semipalmated Sandpipers with which it associates. Under such circumstances it may be readily recognized, as it will allow a quiet observer to approach within twenty feet. Its larger size and generally buffy-brownish appearance distinguish it at once from its smaller and more agile companions. Probably in autumn it is less rare than it is rated on our coast, and a few may remain here later than the records show, as the bird is commonly confused with other small sandpipers. Occasionally it feeds on the beaches, but seems rather to prefer inland ponds and even uplands. It is common in migration in the

Rockies, where it seeks grasshoppers and locusts on the high benches. It has been seen there near the summit of the highest mountains at an altitude of fourteen thousand feet and has been taken repeatedly in northern Chile at ten to twelve thousand feet. It often is found at considerable distances from water.

LEAST SANDPIPER

Pisobia minutilla (VIEILLOT). PLATE 28.

Other names: Peep; Mud-peep; Meadow Ox-eye; Green-legged Peep.

IDENTIFICATION. — Length 5 to 6¾ inches; spread 11 to 12¼ inches. Smallest of our sandpipers; sparrow size; known from Semipalmated Sandpiper by lighter greenish-yellow legs (never black or blackish like those of Semipalmated Sandpiper); neck and sides of breast usually more streaked in spring and darker in fall than those of latter; bill more slender.

RANGE. — Breeds from northwestern Alaska, northern British Columbia, and Labrador south to the Upper Yukon, Magdalen Islands, Newfoundland, and Nova Scotia; winters from southern California, Texas, and North Carolina through the West Indies and Central America to Brazil, the Galapagos Islands, and central Patagonia; in migration occurs throughout the United States and west to Siberia and north to Greenland.

The Least Sandpiper or 'Peep' is naturally an exceedingly unsuspicious bird. If an observer remains motionless, the little things will sometimes come almost to his feet in their busy search for food. They run about the feet of much larger shore birds, and even associate with ducks feeding alongshore. Apparently these larger birds seldom molest them. They are very gregarious, and frequent salt marshes and mud-flats on which they find their food, also inland meadows and the muddy margins of rivers and ponds, especially in August when the water is low. They are not uncommon, however, on the sea-beach, though not nearly so abundant there as are the slightly larger Semipalmated Sandpipers. The male has a twittering, tremolo flight-song in the nuptial season, which may be heard occasionally over the marsh in late May or early June. The habits of this species are well known, but anyone who has not observed them may easily do so, as they are always here during the month of May and during August and the first week of September.

In their migrations to South America they must fly long distances over the sea, as many arrive in the Bermudas during the autumnal migration. These islands lie in a direct line and about halfway between Nova Scotia and the Lesser Antilles.

RED–BACKED SANDPIPER

Pelidna alpina sakhalina (VIEILLOT). PLATE 27.

Other names: American Dunlin; Red-back; Lead-back; Fall Snipe; Brant-bird; California Peep; Crooked-bill; Simpleton; Stib; Winter Ox-eye; Little Black-breast; Winter Snipe.

IDENTIFICATION. — Length 7½ to 9¼ inches; spread 14½ to 15¾ inches. A little larger than Sanderling; size of Spotted Sandpiper but bill longer; unmistakable in spring plumage with red back, black belly and rather long, slightly curved bill; in autumn its dark plain brownish-gray or ashy-brown plumage and long bill, slightly curved downward toward tip, differentiate it from the light-colored straight-billed Sanderlings with which it associates; it shows a grayish band across breast and in flight white lines in wings.

RANGE. — Breeds in Arctic America from the mouth of the Yukon to Hudson Bay; migrates through the Great Lakes; winters on the Pacific coast from southern British Columbia to southern Lower California and on the Atlantic and Gulf coasts from New Jersey to Florida and southern Texas; also breeds in Siberia and winters south to the Malay Archipelago.

When most of the smaller sandpipers have departed, when sharp frosts have closed the inland marshes and waters of the Arctic regions, when the honk of the wild goose is heard in the land, then in late September or October the Red-backed Sandpipers appear. In some seasons a considerable flight passes in November. A few of them reach the latitude of New England early and in gay summer plumage, but by the time the majority arrive they are mostly in modest gray winter dress, though some adults still retain some red feathers on their backs. They feed mainly on sand-beaches and sand-flats in company with Sanderlings or other lingering shore birds, but they appear often along the muddy margins of creeks in the salt marsh. Usually they come in very small flocks or in companies of three or four. They are rather restless, run rapidly, and frequently fly from place to place. In spring their numbers are fewer, as they migrate northward largely through the interior and by way of the Great Lakes and Hudson Bay, but a few may be seen occasionally on wide sand-flats in May in full spring plumage. Now and then a few are reported on our coast in June, July and August. The Red-backed Sandpiper flies in compact flocks, the members of which scatter over the flats to feed. On mud-flats they move about rapidly, probing the mud with their bills, and sometimes even submerging the head in water in their eager search for food.

Mr. H. J. Massingham writes as follows regarding the Dunlin, the European form of this sandpiper, whose habits are apparently identical with those of the Red-backed Sandpiper:

'April and September are the signal months for the great migratory flights of the dunlin, chestnut-backed, with a black patch on the lower breast in spring, and ash-gray and white when the nuptial dress is cast, the most commonly distributed of all the Limicolae about our shores. The afternoon sun leans its rays into the repose of the marshes, when suddenly one of these tremendous floods of life surges over them, sweeping down in the distance like a cloud detached from the sky, an invasion of Valkyrie with all the wild discipline and exultation of speed and none of the menace or terror. The little birds approach over the water in a dense column of perfect order, in a humming volume of a sea-like monotone, accompanied by a soft purr from thousands of throats. Then, as though they swam into the spell of an influence breathed like a perfume from the brown flats beneath them, the determination of the course is stayed, and, swerving at right angles with a unanimous tilt of the body, flashing a single sheet of white from their breasts, they fall into a compact ballet of movement a few feet from the ground. Changing pattern, direction, color and formation with every turn, each individual yet keeps the same distance from his neighbor, the same momentum, and the same angle of the body, as though pulled hither and thither with lightning rapidity from the ends of an infinite number of invisible and equidistant threads, all radiating from a common point. Thus they cut one design after another out of the fabric of space — three thousand leaderless birds, executing intricate movements with the single cohesion of one body, supported upon one pair of wings, a thing more wonderful than a single thought issuing from the collaboration of a myriad brain-cells, since the myriad contained in one body have found subtle contact with those of thousands of other bodies as apart, and from that urge of harmonious energy blossoms one flower, dressed in thousands of petals, swaying to and fro in the varying breeze of its own delight and impulse. Thus the dunlin dance the air in chorus, until the marshland pulls them gently to its breast, and they sink into it, breaking up at once into a jargoning crowd of individuals, twinkling and dibbling helter-skelter over the saltings.'

EASTERN DOWITCHER

Limnodromus griseus griseus (GMELIN).

PLATE 25.

Other names: Red-breasted Snipe; Brown-back; Red-breast; Robin Snipe; Driver; Kelp Plover; Deutscher; Fool Plover; German Snipe.

IDENTIFICATION. — Length 10 to 12½ inches; spread 17½ to 20 inches. *Long bill;* size close to Wilson's Snipe; rump and tail appear silvery-gray at a distance; bird looks very dark at a distance, and so resembles Wilson's Snipe, but the Snipe does not habitually haunt sand-bars, beaches and mud-flats, as does the Dowitcher; in spring and summer reddish breast and long bill distinguish adult Dowitcher; in flight a narrow white patch shows on back, not so white as that of the Yellow-legs.

FLIGHT NOTE. — Suggests the bird's name, *dowitch* or *dowitcher.*

BREEDING. — *Nest:* Unknown until 1925; 'a hollow in a lump of moss, scantily lined.' *Eggs:* 4, olive-green, more or less spotted and blotched with browns, etc.

RANGE. — Breeds from central Alberta to the west side of Hudson Bay, Churchill, and northward; winters from Florida and the West Indies south to central Brazil and Peru; migrates regularly on the Atlantic coast of the United States and less abundantly in the interior and on the Pacific coast.

Along the low sandy shores of the outer arm of Cape Cod the Eastern Dowitcher stops to rest and feed on its way to its northern home. It is a bird of inner beaches and still waters. It prefers inner beaches in sandy harbors near where the sea continually moans on outlying bars. Wide sand-flats along the inner shores of Cape Cod Bay or small shallow ponds just inside the outer beaches are favorite resorts. At low tide it often feeds on sand- or mud-flats or along the estuaries in the salt marsh, and it is very rarely seen in fresh marshes where Wilson's Snipe sometimes abounds. In the spring migration it usually remains with us in small numbers during a brief period in the latter part of May or until early June, but in autumn its numbers are larger and, though usually not very common in its accustomed haunts, in some seasons a large flight of young birds passes south along our coast during the latter part of August. The species was once abundant on the Atlantic coast. It became rare during the latter part of the nineteenth century and now is increasing again, owing to wise laws prohibiting shooting and sale. Early in July a few Dowitchers appear all along the Atlantic coast from Massachusetts to North Carolina. They seem to come overland from Ungava. Apparently the Dowitcher habitually migrates down the Atlantic coast. A part of the flight seems to leave the Carolinas in autumn and go by sea to the Antilles. In returning the majority of the birds appear to leave the coast of the Carolinas and migrate north through the interior. Dowitchers may be seen in spring plumage in May and again in July, but most of the birds of the fall migration are in adult winter, first winter or changing plumage.

This species often feeds by thrusting its bill deep into mud and water, securing marine worms and other small animals buried there. If feeding on soft mud it seems to rest its weight partly on its bent tarsi, but on sand it runs about like any sandpiper. Often it wades in water up to its belly, probing the bottom. It swims readily, nodding its head and jerking its tail with each stroke. It does not habitually follow the receding waves, but feeds in sheltered places. When resting on the beach at high tide Dowitchers often squat behind tufts of grass which they seek as a protection from the wind. The Dowitcher often may be found in the company of the smaller sandpipers and also with the Lesser Yellow-legs, from which it may be readily distinguished by its long bill and shorter legs. In flight it is usually seen in small parties which move in concert, performing aerial evolutions, all moving together as one bird.

LONG–BILLED DOWITCHER

Limnodromus griseus scolopaceus (SAY).

Other names: White-tailed Dowitcher, and others applied to Eastern Dowitcher (page 200).

IDENTIFICATION. — Length 10¾ to 12½ inches; spread 18 to 20½ inches. Indistinguishable in the field from Eastern Dowitcher; averages slightly larger, and darker in plumage.

RANGE. — Breeds from Point Barrow to the mouth of the Yukon and east to northwestern Mackenzie; winters from central California, Louisiana, Florida, Cuba, Jamaica, and Mexico south to Panama and Ecuador; in migration on the Pacific coast and in western Mississippi Valley.

The haunts and habits of the Long-billed Dowitcher are the same as those of the Eastern Dowitcher when on our coast. The former is supposed to be much more western in distribution, but in the fall migration many wander eastward to the Atlantic coast. Probably this alleged race is not so rare in the East as the records would indicate, as it is impossible to distinguish the two forms in the field and an expert can tell them apart only with difficulty even when in the hand. The measurements of bills of the two forms often overlap in length so that the length of the bill cannot be relied upon as a field mark. In the migration southeastward the Long-bill is said to reach Florida in larger numbers than does the other race, the majority of which are supposed to put out to sea before they reach the land of flowers.

STILT SANDPIPER

Micropalama himantopus (BONAPARTE).   PLATE 26.

Other names: Bastard Yellow-legs; Stilted Sandpiper; Mongrel; Frost Snipe; Green-leg.

IDENTIFICATION. — Length 7½ to 9¼ inches; spread 15½ to 17 inches. A small bird, but its long legs and bill make it appear as large as a Dowitcher; in fall plumage it resembles young Yellow-legs, but its body is smaller and its legs are *greenish* and not bright yellow; the tail and tail coverts show whitish in flight, but it lacks the long gray rump and the white on the back shown in flight by the Dowitcher; in spring it may be recognized by its dark back, barred under plumage and long, *greenish*-yellow legs; among small sandpipers it is readily recognized, as its long legs raise its body above the others.

RANGE. — Breeds from near the mouth of the Mackenzie to Coronation Gulf and Hudson Bay (Churchill); winters in South America to Uruguay and Chile; in migration occurs in interior Canada, the western Mississippi Valley, the West Indies and Central America, less commonly on the Atlantic coast and coast of British Columbia.

The Stilt Sandpiper is an unusual bird that seems nowhere to be very common now, although there is evidence in the western Mississippi Valley as well as in New England that it was once common to abundant at times in migration. In spring it is a mere straggler in the East, as it passes north mainly west of the Mississippi, arriving in Saskatchewan and Mackenzie soon after the middle of May. Little is known about its breeding-range or breeding-habits. As soon as the breeding season is over a part of the birds move southeastward from Mackenzie or Keewatin toward the Atlantic coast. Some, going overland, apparently cross Ontario to New England, and either follow the coastline down or put out to sea on the way to South America. They are usually most common there during the month of August, though a few arrive in July.

This bird, like other sandpipers, when flying in flocks, wheels and turns, showing first the upper and then the under side. It is usually seen here singly or in very small numbers, sometimes with the Yellow-legs, along beaches, in salt marshes or on the flats where it wades deeply and plunges its bill (sometimes partly opened) into the mud.

It is said to feed occasionally like the Avocet or the Roseate Spoonbill by wading and swinging its partly opened bill through the water from side to side somewhat as a mower swings his scythe. In muddy pools it sometimes plunges its head beneath the surface in securing food from the bottom. Probably its food while here does not differ much from that of other sandpipers.

SEMIPALMATED SANDPIPER

Ereunetes pusillus (LINNAEUS).

PLATE 28.

Other names: Peep; Sand Peep; Beach-Peep; Bumble-Bee Peep; Hawk's Eye; Oxeye; Black-legged Peep.

IDENTIFICATION. — Length 5½ to 6¾ inches; spread 11¼ to 12¾ inches. A little larger than Least Sandpiper; similar but has a whiter, less streaked breast in fall and legs and feet very dark practically *black*, while those of Least Sandpiper are lighter and greenish or greenish-yellow.

RANGE. — Breeds from northeastern Siberia and the Arctic coast of North America south to the mouth of the Yukon and Hudson Bay and east to Baffin Island and northern Labrador; winters from South Carolina and the Gulf of Mexico through the West Indies and Central America to Patagonia; migrates mainly east of the Rocky Mountains.

The Semipalmated Sandpiper is the little 'Sand-peep' of the Atlantic beaches. It runs along the beach, its little blackish legs twinkling over the wet sands, advancing and retreating with the wash of the surf, industriously gleaning its frugal fare from the 'backwash' of that great fecund mother of abundant life, the sea. In August and September it appears in thousands on the sands from Ipswich to Monomoy on the Massachusetts coast, and at many other points along the Atlantic seaboard. It is not confined to the sea-beach, but occurs at low tide on wide sand-flats and muds-flats and in muddy creeks in the salt marsh, all along our coast. Even in the interior in August when lakes, streams and ponds are low it may be found occasionally in small companies along sandy or muddy margins. Its habits are similar to those of the Least Sandpiper, and the two species frequently associate on beach or flat, but the Semipalmated Sandpiper is more a sand bird than its smaller companion.

In northward migration the Semipalmated Sandpiper passes through New England rather rapidly, chiefly in the latter half of May, but on its return it lingers longer. As is the case with many shore birds the adults mostly come first, and the young ones begin to arrive usually after the middle of August.

Dr. C. W. Townsend, in his 'Birds of Essex County, Massachusetts,' well describes the habits of the species as follows:

'Semipalmated Sandpipers are fascinating birds to watch, whether on the wing, when the flocks twist and turn with military precision like one bird, alternately displaying their white breasts and gray backs, or whether busily engaged in feeding on the beach. At such times they occasionally find their small round mouth much out of proportion to the stretch of the end of the bill, and many shakings of the head are needed to get a large morsel past the sticking-point. I have seen one try several times to swallow a large beach flea, and then actually fly off with it in his bill. Their sleep in the daytime is taken at short snatches, standing or squatting for a few minutes at a time with bill concealed in the feathers of the back, not "under the wing" as in poems. They also stand on one leg, even when both legs are intact, for cripples are common. They seem to yawn by stretching lazily one wing over a leg. They also spread both wings above the back as do many other shore birds, and they flirt their tail nervously from side to side, perhaps shaking the head at the same time. When gleaning food in the shallow water, they sometimes immerse their heads completely.

'Their call note is very much like that of the Least Sandpiper but is shriller and less musical. A harsh rasping note and a peeping note are sometimes heard. A low, rolling, gossipy note is often emitted when they approach other birds. This latter note is often imitated with success by gunners. In the spring, however, the bird is delightfully musical on occasions, and his flight-song may be heard on the beach and among the bogs of the dunes. Rising on quivering wings to about thirty feet from the ground, the bird advances with rapid wing-beats, curving the pinions strongly downward, pouring forth a succession of musical notes, a continuous quavering trill, and ending with a few very sweet notes that recall those of a Goldfinch. He then descends to the ground, where one may be lucky enough, if near at hand, to hear a low musical *cluck* from the excited bird. This is, I suppose, the full love flight-song, and is not often heard in its entirety, but the first quavering trill is not uncommon, a single bird, or a member of a flock singing thus as he flies over. I have seen birds chasing one another on the beach with raised wings, emitting a few quavering notes, and have been reminded of a Long-billed Marsh Wren. I have also heard them emit at this time a sharp grasshopper-like sound.'

WESTERN SANDPIPER

Ereunetes maurii CABANIS.

Other names: Western Semipalmated Sandpiper, and other names applied to Semipalmated Sandpiper (page 202).

IDENTIFICATION. — Length 5¾ to 7 inches; spread 11¾ to 13 inches. Similar to Semipalmated Sandpiper; difficult to distinguish from that species in field in summer and autumn, but some adults in July or August may still retain some rich cinnamon on head; in spring, at *close range* with a good glass the rich, rusty cinnamon on sides and top of head and on back may be seen; bill is very noticeably longer, and thicker at base.

On the Atlantic coast the Western Sandpiper is usually seen in company with the Semipalmated Sandpiper, with which it visits the usual feeding-grounds, and it seems to have precisely similar habits. It is a brighter-colored bird in spring plumage, but most of those seen in autumn closely resemble their eastern companions, except for the longer and thicker bill. Therefore, it is quite probable that the western bird is much more common in the East than the records would indicate.

The most remarkable feature in the life of this little bird is the long migrations that many of them are supposed to make from Bering Sea to the Atlantic coast and so on down to South America. Apparently numbers of them cross the Great Lakes and many reach the coast in New Jersey, New York and New England, but more appear to go direct to the Carolinas, Georgia and Florida. In spring they return by a more western route.

BUFF–BREASTED SANDPIPER

Tryngites subruficollis (VIEILLOT).   PLATE 31.

Other names: Hill Grass-bird; Cherook.

IDENTIFICATION. — Length 7½ to 9 inches; spread 15¾ to 17½ inches. Slightly larger than Spotted Sandpiper; rather tawny like Upland Plover but much smaller and not so slender; its short tail does not reach to the tips of its long, pointed, closed wings while the long tail of the Upland Plover projects beyond the tips of its closed wings; frequents fields, pastures and hillsides near coast.

RANGE. — Breeds along the Arctic coast from northern Alaska to northern Mackenzie; winters in Argentina and Uruguay; most abundant in migration in the Mississippi Valley and on the Canadian prairies; occasional on the Atlantic coast in autumn and rare on northern Pacific coasts.

The Buff-breasted Sandpiper resembles the Upland Plover somewhat in appearance and frequents the same localities, sometimes in company with the former or with the Golden Plover or Black-bellied Plover, usually on grassy hills along the sea-coast, sometimes near water, or even on the beach. Formerly it was perhaps not uncommon east of the Mississippi Valley; now it is one of the rarest sandpipers. Mr. E. A. Doolittle, who watched the feeding-habits of a bird of this species, says that the legs were bent, giving the bird a crouching attitude, and that the feet were lifted high at each step, as if 'stepping over and through grass.' Although the bird was on the beach it straightened up every few feet as if peering over grass; showing a decided resemblance, with its extended neck, to the Upland Plover. This bird is unsuspicious and ordinarily may be closely approached.

Professor W. W. Cooke expressed the belief that the majority of this species in its southward migration takes a zigzag route, going first easterly to Hudson Bay (some continuing to the Atlantic coast), thence southerly to the Gulf of Mexico, thence through Central America to the northwestern coast of South America, thence southeasterly to Argentina. Such a peculiar, erratic course is followed by no other North American shore bird. This may explain why the bird is a *rara avis* on the South Atlantic coast of the United States and in the West

Indies. This species, like the Upland Plover, feeds very largely on insects. Its former vast numbers have been greatly reduced by spring shooting in the Mississippi Valley.

MARBLED GODWIT

Limosa fedoa (LINNAEUS). PLATE 29.

Other names: Straight-billed Curlew; Brant-bird; Badger-bird; Marlin; Brown Marlin; Big Marlin.

IDENTIFICATION. — Length 16 to 20½ inches; spread 30 to 40 inches. Distinguished by large size (only Long-billed Curlew exceeds it among shore birds), long straight or slightly upcurved bill, general light reddish or buffy-brown color.

RANGE. — Breeds from southern Alberta and southern Manitoba south to South Dakota; winters from central California, Louisiana, Florida, and Georgia south to Ecuador and Peru; in migration occurs on the Pacific coast north to British Columbia and rarely on the Atlantic coast south to the Lesser Antilles.

There is some reason to believe that the Marbled Godwit, a great, peculiar, handsome shore bird, was not rare on the Atlantic sea-coast in migration early in the last century. Audubon tells of immense flocks passing along the coast from Florida to Massachusetts. Peabody (1839) said that in August they appeared in Massachusetts in large numbers. DeKay (1844) said that they returned in large flocks in August to the coast of New York. So far as we know it always bred in the interior.

Its principal breeding-grounds are believed to have been always near the center of the continent, but in migration numbers formerly appeared on the coast of southern Alaska, on Vancouver Island, in the Maritime Provinces of Canada, and in New England, apparently going almost directly east and west to the two oceans. It has been extirpated from a large part of its former breeding-range, and although it still breeds in some numbers in south-central Canada, it is now an uncommon visitor to the Atlantic seaboard, where it visits the salt marshes along the coast, pools of salt and fresh water, mud-flats, and beaches. Since the stopping of all shore-bird shooting under the Migratory Bird Treaty, it seems to be increasing somewhat in numbers.

In its breeding-range in the interior, the Marbled Godwit is a valuable destroyer of such enemies of farm and ranch as the destructive grasshoppers and locusts, but in the East the economic value of most shore birds, large or small, is very hard to demonstrate, as they frequent habitats which are generally useless to agriculture.

HUDSONIAN GODWIT

Limosa haemastica (LINNAEUS). PLATE 29.

Other names: Spot-rump; White-rump; Straight-billed Curlew; Ring-tailed Marlin; Black-tail; Brant-bird; Godwit; Goose-bird; Red-breasted Godwit.

IDENTIFICATION. — Length 14 to 16¾ inches; spread 25 to 28 inches. Larger than Greater Yellow-legs; in spring gray above with reddish breast; in fall breast is whitish, when it resembles gray autumnal Willet but white upper tail coverts are more conspicuous in flight and it has less white in wing; long, slightly upturned bill distinguishes it from curlews; in breeding plumage much darker than Marbled Godwit, males seeming almost black at a distance.

RANGE. — Breeds from the lower Anderson River, Mackenzie, west to Port Clarence, Alaska, and east to Hudson Bay and Southampton Island; winters in Chile, Argentina, Patagonia, and the Falkland Islands; in migration occurs mainly east of the Great Plains; more common on the Atlantic coast in autumn and in the Mississippi Valley in spring.

The Hudsonian Godwit is one of those interesting shore birds which follows a different line of migration in the spring from that taken in the fall of the year. Its breeding-grounds, so far as known, are in the extreme northwestern part of North America, close to the Arctic Ocean in northern Alaska, Mackenzie and Keewatin; it winters in southernmost South America and in the far Falkland Islands; at the close of the brief breeding period it moves southeast from Hudson Bay to the Atlantic coast, where it is seen for a short period, and then puts out to sea on its journey to the Lesser Antilles and on to South America, continuing on south of the Equator to a second summer in Chile or Argentina. On its northward flight in spring it probably crosses the South American pampas and the great valley of the Amazon River, but its actual course is not well known. Eventually it arrives in the Gulf States and continues its journey up the western part of the Mississippi Valley region, east of the Great Plains, across the western Canadian Provinces, to its breeding-area on the edge of the Barren Grounds and the Arctic Ocean.

While on the Atlantic seaboard in its fall migration, the Hudsonian Godwit seems to have a preference for sandy shores and sandspits, but it also frequents mud-flats, beaches and creeks in the salt marsh, and sometimes goes to the uplands after insects. In its northward migration it is probably largely insectivorous. It is now, unfortunately, one of the rarest of our shore birds. — (J.B.M.)

SANDERLING

Crocethia alba (PALLAS). PLATE 28.

Other names: Beach-bird; Bull Peep; Whitey; Whiting; Skinner; Stib; White Snipe; Beach Snipe.

IDENTIFICATION. — Length 7 to 8¾ inches; spread 14 to 16½ inches. Larger than Spotted Sandpiper; in flight shows a bold white bar along middle of wing in sharp contrast to blackish of flight-feathers; straight, short, black bill and black legs; in spring tawny or ruddy and black above and on *sides of neck and breast;* white below; in fall variable, spotted with black above or pale gray above, continuous *white below;* at this time *whitest* of shore birds.

CALL NOTE. — A short distinctive *chet* or *kip*.

BREEDING. — On Barren Grounds near water. *Nest:* A hollow in ground lined with dried grasses and leaves. *Eggs:* 4, pear-shaped, olive-brown finely spotted with dark brown.

RANGE. — Breeds on the Arctic islands, Southampton, and northern Greenland, also in Iceland, Spitzbergen, and Siberia; winters from central California, Texas, Virginia, and Bermuda to Patagonia, also in the Eastern Hemisphere.

Sanderlings follow the sea. They run over pale sand where storm-tossed breakers roar, for there in the wake of the storm they find their sustenance. The turmoil of the surf stirs up the sandy bottom, and the rush of the waves throws many tiny waifs of sea life upon the shelving beach, where the backwash bears them again to the sea. Here, where breakers thunder down and flying spray obscures the scene, the little Sanderlings, ever on the alert, run nimbly into the returning flood to snatch up many a choice tidbit, and then trip lightly up the slope, ahead of the incoming wave. Sometimes they venture in too far, and must rise on fluttering wings to avoid the onset of the next surge. Real 'children of the sand,' they always may be found in their season along the open sea-coast or on the shores of large bodies of fresh water, where the surf runs high. Elsewhere they are not so common, but they sometimes feed on wide sand-flats at low water. When they are standing still or squatting on the sand their colors so blend with their environment that they become almost invisible; but when they rise and fly out low over the sea they become conspicuous against the dark water. They usually fly in small flocks alongshore, close to the waves, barely rising above the curling tops of the surges, and sometimes disappearing in the hollows between them.

While passing through New England Sanderlings are changing plumage and may be seen in nearly all stages. Such variations are likely to confuse the novice. Some early ornithologists mistakenly described individual Sanderlings in different plumages as distinct species.

In its migrations between northernmost Arctic lands and Patagonia the Sanderling is seen on the North Atlantic coast in greatest numbers during the latter half of May and in September. Its occurrence in midsummer or midwinter is more or less irregular, but in ordinary winters it is not rare as far north as Muskeget Island, Massachusetts.

The food of the Sanderling on the coast consists largely of small mollusks, crustaceans, worms and beach insects. In the interior it feeds largely on insects and is said to eat the buds and seeds of Arctic plants, bits of moss and algae. Dr. Townsend, in his 'Birds of Essex County, Massachusetts,' writes as follows of the feeding-habits of this bird:

'On the hard wet sand of the beaches one may see in places the characteristic probings of the Sanderling without a trace of their foot marks, and these may be the cause of considerable mystery to the uninitiated. While the Semipalmated Sandpiper runs about with his head down dabbing irregularly here and there, the Sanderling vigorously probes the sand in a series of holes a quarter of an inch to an inch apart in straight or curving lines a foot to two feet long. Sometimes the probings are so near together that the line is almost a continuous one like the furrow of a miniature plow. The sand is thrown up in advance, so that one can tell in which direction the bird is going. A close inspection of the probings often reveals their double character, showing that the bill was introduced partly open. The probings are for the minute sand-fleas and other crustaceans in the sand, their principal food. I have seen Sanderlings running about nimbly on the beach, catching the sand-fleas which were hopping on the surface. I have also seen them catching flies.'

AMERICAN AVOCET

Recurvirostra americana GMELIN.

IDENTIFICATION. — Length 15½ to 20 inches; spread 27 to 38 inches. Distinguished from all other shore birds by black and white plumage, brown head and neck, very long light blue legs, and very slender upturned bill.

BREEDING. — In colonies or small groups, near water. *Nest:* A mere hollow on ground, sometimes well lined. *Eggs:* 3 to 8, usually 4, very variable, buff to dark olive profusely spotted with browns and grays.

RANGE. — Breeds from eastern Washington, southern Alberta and southern Manitoba south to southern California, southern Texas, Kansas and northern Iowa; winters from central California and southern Texas to southern Guatemala; rare east of the Mississippi River in migration.

Salt Lake City sprawls over the foothills below the Wasatch Mountains, where once the great post-glacial Lake Bonneville spread its wide waters. High up on the shoulders of the hills are ancient terraces and water-carved cliffs, relics of that long-gone era, while toward the center of the great basin are fertile meadows, and a few sluggish streams find their way through tule swamps to that strange inland sea, Great Salt Lake, at the lowest point of the vast mountain-girt depression. It is a wonderfully interesting country for the bird student, with its bewildering combination of snowcapped mountains, blinding alkali deserts, fertile farmlands, fresh-water marshes, scorched foothills, and tree-filled canyons, all within easy distance of the busy city.

Between the city and Great Salt Lake is a shallow, lake-like widening of the Jordan River, partly open water, but much of it filled with tall growths of tules and other aquatic plants. On my first visit the lake was alive with birds, great rafts of ducks of many species, among them Cinnamon Teal, Blue-winged Teal, Mallards, Pintails, Shovellers, and Baldpates, while flocks of American Coot bobbed and clucked all over the surface of the water. Here and there groups of Wilson's Phalaropes swam gracefully about, and in the shallower parts of the lake were statuesque Treganza's Blue Herons, White-faced Glossy Ibises, Brewster's Egrets, Black-crowned Night Herons, Anthony's Green Herons, and an occasional American Bittern. Where the tiny wavelets stranded bits of flotsam on the beaches between the thickets of tules shore birds were congregated, their sizes ranging from the Long-billed Curlew to the smallest sandpipers. Yellow-headed Blackbirds and Nevada Red-wings called from the tules, while from the near-by sagebrush and alkali flats we flushed the Desert Horned Lark and some unidentified sparrows. Killdeers called in familiar fashion as they circled around, to be joined by noisy Black-necked Stilts and American Avocets, which dove threateningly at our heads, screaming vituperations all the time, while other Avocets, unworried by household cares, waded in the shallow waters or probed in the mud for aquatic insects and other food. The manner of feeding is so well described by Dr. Frank M. Chapman that I quote his words:

'The use of the Avocet's recurved bill is clearly explained by the manner in which the bird procures its food. In feeding they wade into the water and drop the bill below the surface until the convexity of the maxilla probably touches the bottom. In this position they move forward at a half run and with every step the bill is swung from side to side sweeping through an arc of about 50° in search of shells and other small aquatic animals. The mandibles are slightly opened, and at times the birds pause to swallow their prey. It is evident that birds with a straight or a downward-curved bill could not adopt this method of feeding.'

The American Avocet has been practically extirpated from the Atlantic coast, where in the early years of the nineteenth century Wilson reported that he found it breeding on the salt marshes of New Jersey. It was probably never common as far north as New England, and is today a mere straggler in the northeast, and a rather rare visitor on the south Atlantic coast. — (J.B.M.)

BLACK–NECKED STILT
Himantopus mexicanus (MÜLLER).

Other names: Longshanks; Lawyer Bird; Daddy-long-legs.
IDENTIFICATION. — Length 13¼ to 15½ inches; spread 26 to 30 inches. About size of Greater Yellow-legs but much slimmer-appearing, with longer neck, small head, *very long pinkish legs*, plumage black above, white below.
BREEDING. — Similar to that of Avocet but eggs usually darker.
RANGE. — Breeds from central Oregon, to Nebraska and south to northern Lower California, southern Texas, coast of Louisiana and Mexico, and from central Florida and the Bahamas through the West Indies to Brazil and Peru; winters from Lower California, southern Texas, southern Louisiana, and Florida south through Central America and the West Indies to Brazil, Peru and the Galapagos Islands.

The Black-necked Stilt is known in parts of its range as the 'Lawyer' because of its vociferousness, and is also called 'Long-shanks,' 'Long-legs' and 'Daddy-long-legs' in some localities. Despite its apparently unnecessarily long legs, it is a graceful and handsome bird. There is little to say of its habits in the Northeast, as it is a mere straggler here, but there is reason to believe that in the early part of the nineteenth century, when it bred commonly as far north as New Jersey, it was less rare in southern New England than it is today. This bird, probably once common in suitable localities from the Atlantic to the Pacific, seems to be generally rare to accidental now east of the Mississippi Valley. I saw it in great abundance at Lake Harney, Florida, in March, 1878, where it is no longer common. It frequents the margins of grassy ponds, sluggish streams and marshes, both fresh and brackish, and feeds mainly by wading. It can swim and dive at need, but is not so expert a swimmer as the Avocet. In walking, it is a 'high stepper' and when standing the legs are not spread but held parallel. It flies well, with neck somewhat drawn in and long legs trailing behind. Often upon alighting it raises the wings straight up over the back, and in moving about on foot it frequently tosses up the head. It seems to be very suspicious and quite noisy when alarmed by the approach of a human intruder, and is likely to communicate the alarm to other wild denizens of the marsh or shore.

RED PHALAROPE

Phalaropus fulicarius (LINNAEUS). PLATE 24.

Other names: Gray Phalarope; Gray Bank-bird (applied to all phalaropes collectively); Herring-bird; Whale-bird; Jersey-goose; Mackerel-goose; Sea-goose; Sea Snipe.

IDENTIFICATION. — Length 7½ to 9 inches; spread 14 to 16 inches. Size of Sanderling, very unsuspicious, admits close observation; in winter plumage in which chiefly seen at sea, from late July onward, is very white on head, neck and below, with black patches on crown and side head; bill rather short, stout and deep at base; compared with bills of other phalaropes, more like that of Knot or Sanderling; swims buoyantly like a gull and looks larger, stockier and rather grayer above than Northern Phalarope; unmistakable in breeding plumage, with its reddish neck and breast, black crown, white sides of head and yellow, black-tipped bill; a broad white wing-bar in all plumages; uncommon inland on lakes and rivers.

RANGE. — Breeds from northern Alaska, Arctic islands, and Greenland south to the delta of the Yukon, Mackenzie, and Hudson Bay; winters on the oceans from southern California and Florida south as far as the Falklands; migrates along both coasts of North America; mainly well offshore; also found in the Eastern Hemisphere.

Red Phalaropes are shore birds on their breeding-grounds on the Arctic tundra, but sea-birds on the New England coast. In the waning of the summer, far offshore from Cape Ann, Cape Cod or No Man's Land, we may see here and there in the distance on the smooth, glassy surface of the ever restless sea swell a little white speck like a dash of foam — the white breast of the Red Phalarope already taking on its winter plumage. The bird is so tame and gentle that it will hardly get out of the way of our boat until we are nearly upon it, when it flutters away for a few rods and again comes to rest upon the sea, attracted perhaps by some floating food. It rises easily from the water, flies in the manner of a Sanderling, which it somewhat resembles, swims fast and floats as lightly as an autumn leaf.

The idea of 'women's rights' may well have originated with the phalaropes, for among these birds the female, being the larger and handsomer, does practically all the courting, while the male prepares the nest. After she has laid the eggs, her meek and gentle consort incubates them until the young are hatched and then takes upon himself the principal care of the little family while his 'strong-minded' spouse enjoys herself after her own fashion. This species is the most maritime of the phalaropes and breeds near the shores of the sea which it seeks continually. Phalaropes are believed to pass the winter at sea, and it seems remarkable that these delicate creatures should be able to withstand the storms of wide oceans, but after they pass our shores on their southward journey they disappear into the ocean wastes and are rarely seen again by human eyes until they return in spring over the same seas. In its summer home the Red Phalarope feeds largely on insects, but crustaceans, mollusks and jellyfish are eaten, also sand-worms, leeches and small fish. Phalaropes are believed to eat a small quantity of vegetal matter, including some weeds. Far at sea they seek floating masses of seaweed, about which they seem to find quantities of food, and they follow right whales or bowhead whales which feed on small sea animals. The habit has given phalaropes the name Whale-birds or Bowhead-birds. Not infrequently their keen eyes discover a whale before the whalemen see it, and as these little birds hasten toward the gigantic animal they give notice to the lookout at the masthead that his prey is in sight. The rising and spouting of whales assure the birds that food in plenty may be found.

WILSON'S PHALAROPE

Steganopus tricolor VIEILLOT.

PLATE 24.

Other names: Tri-color Phalarope; American Phalarope.

IDENTIFICATION. — Length 8¼ to 10 inches; spread 14½ to 16 inches. Largest of phalaropes; fully as large as Pectoral Sandpiper, but head, neck and bill slimmer than in Red Phalarope; bill longer, needle-like; adults in full plumage unmistakable; in winter plumage or in partial winter plumage they are pale birds, resembling winter Sanderlings, but with longer, slimmer bills; usually seen swimming rather than wading; very young birds are darker, resembling Pectoral Sandpiper but with slimmer, longer bill; unstreaked breast and white rump; *lacks in all plumages broad white wing-bar seen in other phalaropes.*

BREEDING. — Typical sandpiper nest and eggs.

RANGE. — Breeds from southern British Columbia to southern Manitoba and south to central California, Utah, central Iowa, Missouri (formerly), northern Illinois, and northwestern Indiana; winters from central Chile and central Argentina south to the Falkland Islands; in migration occurs on the Atlantic and Gulf coasts from Maine to Alabama, and on the Pacific coast from southern British Columbia to Mexico.

Wilson's Phalarope, one of the most elegant and beautiful of North American shore birds, is a mere straggler on the Northeast coast. Its principal home is in the northern Mississippi Valley and contiguous parts of Canada, and it migrates south mainly through the interior of the United States and along both coasts of Mexico and Central America. Its habits are similar to those of other phalaropes, but it is not so much of a swimmer and diver and seems to prefer land and fresh water to the sea. It feeds in shallow water, spins and bobs like other phalaropes and apparently rarely dives.

The females do most of the wooing. A single male is sometimes chased about by two or more ardent females, but when the nuptials are concluded and the honeymoon is over the henpecked father is said to assume most of the family cares. The young leave the nest soon after they emerge from the egg. The females are very active and vivacious in the breeding season, when it is said a single female often has two mates and two separate families, each presided over by its faithful father.

Wilson's Phalarope feeds more on terrestrial forms of life than do the other phalaropes and destroys many insects. It takes mosquitoes, crane-fly larvae, leaf beetles and bill bugs. It also destroys brine shrimps and alkali flies.

NORTHERN PHALAROPE

Lobipes lobatus (LINNAEUS).

PLATE 24.

Other names: Red-necked Phalarope; Fairy Duck; White Bank-bird. (See under Red Phalarope, page 210.)

IDENTIFICATION. — Length 6½ to 8 inches; spread 13 to 14½ inches. Smaller than Spotted Sandpiper; smallest of phalaropes; distinguished from sandpipers by longer neck and more slender bill; distinguished in breeding plumage by rusty red on sides of neck sharply defined against white throat; in winter plumage (as usually seen in United States) back not pearly-gray as in Red Phalarope but dark gray marked white; compared with Red Phalarope it has an extremely slender head and neck; *a white wing-bar in all plumages.*

RANGE. — Breeds from the Pribilof Islands, northern Alaska, Arctic islands, and central Greenland south to the Aleutian Islands, Prince William Sound, the upper Yukon Valley, northern Manitoba, and northern Quebec

(Ungava), and from Iceland to Siberia and the Commander Islands; winters off the coasts of Peru and West Africa; migrates on the ocean off both coasts of North America and through the interior to Patagonia, and through Eurasia to northern Africa and southern Asia.

The gentle, active, graceful little Northern Phalarope is by no means rare at times in autumn on some of the inland waters of the northern Atlantic States, and rarely considerable numbers are driven into estuaries by severe storms at sea. Sometimes they gather in considerable flocks off outlying points of the coast, and these flocks remain for days at a time only a mile or two offshore. Large numbers have been killed at times by flying against outlying lighthouses, but the species is usually uncommon or rare on the salt marshes, beaches and flats. Sometimes on sunny days a few individuals alight in shallow fresh-water ponds where they spin or circle round and round on the water dabbing their bills into it very rapidly, apparently stirring up the mud or water and catching some minute forms of aquatic life. They pass in greatest numbers about the middle of May, and during August and early September. Anyone cruising offshore at these seasons is likely to see them in numbers from one mile to one hundred miles from land. They flock sometimes with Red Phalaropes, but more often by themselves, and they rest usually on the sea, often fluttering lightly from place to place.

Their food consists largely of small aquatic animals, including mollusks and crustaceans; when ashore they consume many insects, including numbers of mosquito larvae.

POMARINE JAEGER

Stercorarius pomarinus (TEMMINCK). PLATE 4.

Other names: Jiddy Hawk; Gull Chaser.

IDENTIFICATION. — Length 20 to 23 inches; spread about 48 inches. The largest jaeger; dark falcon-like seabirds with two color-phases, all dark, or dark above and light below; adults with elongated central tail feathers twisted so that ends extending beyond rest of tail are set vertically and appear spatulate like the blade of an oar; young indistinguishable from young Parasitic Jaeger except by size.

BREEDING. — Near sea-coast. *Nest:* A hollow in moss of marsh or tundra. *Eggs:* 2 or 3, olivaceous to brownish, spotted with browns and grays.

RANGE. — Breeds from central Greenland to northwestern Alaska, and in Eastern Hemisphere; winters off coast of Virginia and from the Gulf of Mexico southward; common fall migrant off California coast.

Probably the Pomarine Jaeger is not as common on New England shores as is the Parasitic Jaeger but, like all our jaegers and shearwaters, it comes in some numbers when mackerel and bluefish are numerous in August and September off our coasts. When the mackerel fishermen are making great catches, then is the time to look for the Pomarine Jaeger and other jaegers and shearwaters, for the birds follow the fish. In seasons when mackerel-fishing does not pay, few birds are to be found. The fishermen say: 'No fish, no birds.' In autumn when the fish move southward, these birds go with them. This large species is rather less bold and active than the smaller species and a little heavier in flight.

Dr. E. W. Nelson says that whenever a Pomarine Jaeger crosses the path of one of the smaller jaegers, the latter commonly gives chase and beats its antagonist off the field. Regarding this he writes as follows: 'This attack embarrasses the large bird, so that it flinches and dives, and often alights and watches an opportunity to escape from its nimble assailant. One that was driven to alight in the river thrust its head under water at every swoop of its assailant, and exhibited the most ludicrous terror. When on the wing they usually ward off an attack from one side by a half-closed wing, and if above, both wings are used, forming an arched shield above the back.'

Although the Pomarine Jaeger is depicted as a coward in its relations to its smaller and more active congeners, it nevertheless does not hesitate to attack gulls of all sizes, even the great Glaucous Gull and the Black-backed Gull, in its attempts to rob them of their food. The swarming Kittiwakes seem to suffer more than any other species from its persecutions while off our coasts. On its breeding-grounds over the wide and desolate tundra or on its tremendous island cliffs within the Arctic circle this, like other species of the genus, is a notorious nest-robber, taking eggs and young birds alike, but it is constantly on the watch for insects. At sea it has been known to pursue and kill small sea-birds and it continually robs shearwaters of their food. Its evolutions in attacking shearwaters are graphically told by Mr. Walter H. Rich, who says that the 'Gull Chaser,' coveting some dainty morsel which the shearwater has seized, rises against the breeze, turns upside-down, and then, with wings half closed, falls on its victim like a lance. The squealing, choking 'Hag' gulps mightily to swallow its spoil in time; but if the Jaeger has any luck, he may secure a fragment.

The piratical bird is so persistent in its attacks that it often forces the Hag to disgorge. Terns also are pursued by the Pomarine Jaeger, but it is not quite so successful in robbing them as are its smaller congeners.

At almost any outlying point or island from Massachusetts to the Maritime Provinces in September this bird may be seen chasing gulls or terns to make them drop or disgorge food; it is, however, much more common on the fishing-grounds miles from shore. Two or three or even more sometimes join in the chase of a single gull or shearwater, and when the victim disgorges, they fight over their ill-gotten booty. Yet this jaeger does not merely exploit the labor of others; it hunts for itself, sweeping over wide waters with steady flight as it searches the waves for any smaller creature that may come within its ken.

The Pomarine Jaeger may be seen not uncommonly along the Nova Scotia and New England coasts, in its southward migration, but as the shore line of Cape Cod turns and recedes westward toward Long Island Sound, the species grows rare. It seems to move south into the broad Atlantic, and so far as I know has never been recorded from the coast of South America. About May 9 the species again passes northward along our coast. It moves rapidly and a month later appears two thousand miles north of our latitude. A few stragglers return early in July.

PARASITIC JAEGER

Stercorarius parasiticus (LINNAEUS).   PLATE 4.

Other names: Richardson's Jaeger; Jiddy Hawk; Gull Chaser.

IDENTIFICATION. — Length 15½ to 21 inches; spread about 40 inches. Central tail feathers are sharply pointed, not twisted, and extend 3 to 4 inches beyond rest of tail, making best field mark.

BREEDING. — Similar to Pomarine Jaeger.

RANGE. — Breeds in northwestern Alaska, Arctic islands and Greenland and south to the Aleutian Islands, Hudson Bay and northern Labrador; winters from southern California to Argentina and from Florida to the eastern coast of South America; also found in the Eastern Hemisphere.

Dark hawk-like birds chasing terns or smaller gulls may be seen most commonly in August, decreasing in October, on the shores of New England and the Maritime Provinces. They are nearly always common at this season on the fishing-banks. The jaeger singles out some tern that has just caught a fish, perhaps, and darts after it, following every twist and turn of its victim, menacing it with hooked beak and clutching at it with strong, curved claws until the tern either drops or disgorges the fish, when the dashing robber catches its ill-gotten booty in the air. Probably the Parasitic Jaeger is the commonest jaeger off our coast and along-shore when the terns are moving in their autumnal migration. On the fishing-banks the Kitti-wake Gull seems to be the victim most often selected by this species. Jaegers seem to be as well equipped as any tern for swimming and diving, but their powerful, hawk-like pinions, hooked bills and strong hooked claws fit them for a predatory life, and they prefer to profit by the labor of others. At times when food is abundant, however, and easily obtained, they do not rely on the labor of others, but help themselves to anything that they fancy. At such times they so gorge themselves with food as to be unable to fly until they have disgorged at least a part of the feast.

The majority of the birds of this species seen in late summer and early autumn seem to be adults of the lighter phases. Birds of the dark phase are rather seldom seen. At a distance these seem almost as black as a crow.

The Parasitic Jaeger passes northward off the New England coast in May, but is then rarely observed; in the latter part of May or in June it arrives on its breeding-grounds in Arctic regions. Its principal flight along the coast occurs on its southward migration. Now and then one appears in July, but the majority come in late August or September. October usually sees the last of them, but there are November and winter records.

In addition to its fish and shellfish diet this species seeks the eggs and young of gulls and terns, kills small rodents, small birds and large insects; while Chamberlain says that, in ex-tremity, it will feast on crowberries. Also, like all jaegers, it is an ignoble scavenger, feeding on offal, ordure or garbage.

LONG–TAILED JAEGER

Stercorarius longicaudus VIEILLOT.

PLATE 4.

Other names: Buffon's Jaeger; Whip Tail.

IDENTIFICATION. — Length 20 to 23 inches; spread about 40 inches. Small size, slimmer form, and exceedingly long tapering tail distinguish adult from other jaegers; young indistinguishable except by size.

BREEDING. — Similar to Pomarine Jaeger.

RANGE. — Circumpolar in breeding-range, inhabiting Arctic islands and coasts; winters south to Chile, Argentina, Gibraltar, and Japan; occurs on both coasts of North America during migrations.

The Long-tailed Jaeger is the most northerly in range of the jaegers. It breeds largely within the Arctic Circle and perhaps seldom wanders so far south in winter as the others. It is the rarest of the jaegers on the New England coast and keeps mostly well offshore. Its habits are similar to those of other jaegers. In power of flight it rather exceeds its congeners. It is so much superior to the gyrfalcon in the air that in defense of their young a pair of Long-tails will drive off the much larger and more powerful falcon.

It arrives on our coast in September, but authentic records here in the spring migration are rare indeed. In late May and June it reaches its Arctic breeding-grounds.

The Long-tailed Jaeger is almost omnivorous, and takes all sorts of animal food, garbage, insects and even berries.

NORTHERN SKUA

Catharacta skua BRÜNNICH.

PLATE 4.

Other names: Great Skua; Sea-hen; Sea-hawk.

IDENTIFICATION. — Length 20 to 22 inches. Near size of Herring Gull; a robust, dark brown or blackish bird with white at base of primaries conspicuous in flight; broad round-ended wings and short tail.

BREEDING. — On cliffs or tundra. *Nest:* Of grasses, lichens, moss, etc. *Eggs:* 2 or 3, olive to brownish or buffy, spotted with browns.

RANGE. — Breeds locally on Arctic islands, Iceland and to the Orkney Islands; winters on the fishing-grounds off Newfoundland, Nova Scotia, and Massachusetts, and from the British Isles to the Mediterranean Sea.

The Northern Skua is a bird of the wide seas or the fishing-banks far out of sight of land. Chamberlain describes it as a sea-falcon preying upon weaker and smaller birds, robbing those it cannot kill, subsisting on fish and flesh, with a partiality for eggs; piratic, daring, strong and bold; living solitary as the eagle, and defending its nest as few eagles dare; showing so fierce a front in defense of its offspring that few dogs care to close with it. Its attacks in defense of its young are so swift, savage and reckless that even the Golden Eagle is compelled to retreat, and for this reason it is believed to guard from the attack of the king of birds the flocks of sheep on some of its island homes. On the fishing-banks it follows the fishing-fleet and pounces upon any refuse thrown overboard. Powerful of wing, it rides unharmed upon the storm, and so it keeps the sea — a great, dour, somber bird, the embodiment of predatory might. It is not very rare on the fishing-banks off the New England coast.

Mr. Walter H. Rich, who has often observed it, thus excellently describes its appearance in flight:

'When on the wing, which is the greater part of the time, the skua shows in the air hawk-like, rather than like the gulls, with whom we rather expect to find its resemblances. Its appearance in the air is somewhat like the buteonine hawks, except that its wing action, in its seemingly restrained power and forceful stroke, suggests the unhurried flight of a falcon, or, perhaps, more accurately — since the wings are at all times fully opened, employing their full sweep in their action, their primaries slightly separated at the tips and slightly recurved — the majestic flight of an eagle. The wing-spread is ample, the wing well balanced in its proportions of length and breadth, well combined to produce both power and speed. The figure is somewhat burly and chunky as compared with the lighter appearance of the gull and the more racy lines of the yager. The impression of muscularity is heightened by the short, square-cut tail, carried somewhat uptilted, giving the fowl an appearance unmistakable in the eyes of one having once recognized it. This peculiarity of tail, which to me seemed slightly forked instead of having the central feathers lengthened, as in others of this group, together with the broad white patch across the bases of the primaries, furnishes a good field mark for the identification of the species.'

GLAUCOUS GULL

Larus hyperboreus GUNNERUS.   PLATE 5.

Other names: Burgomaster; Ice Gull; Owl Gull; White Minister.

IDENTIFICATION. — Length 26 to 32 inches; spread 57 to 65 inches. Larger than Herring Gull; adult chalky white without black wing-tips; young are cream-colored or buffy and also lack dark wing-tips; bill heavier and longer than that of Iceland Gull.

BREEDING. — See Herring Gull.

RANGE. — Breeds on Arctic coasts and islands from northwestern Alaska to northern Greenland and south to the Pribilof Islands, James Bay, eastern Labrador, and Newfoundland; winters from the Aleutians and Greenland south to California, the Great Lakes, and New York; also found in Eurasia.

The Glaucous Gull or 'Burgomaster' is much on the wing, and apparently does not rest on the water as often as do many other gulls. In the Arctic regions where it breeds it seems to prefer to alight on icebergs and cliffs, but in New England, where it winters, it is sometimes seen along the beaches where fish refuse is thrown into the sea. Even in harbors such as Boston, Gloucester, Rockport and Woods Hole, where such food abounds, this species should be looked for among the many Herring Gulls. Since ornithologists along our coasts have begun to look carefully for it, the bird has been seen during every winter in small numbers on the sea-coast of Massachusetts, which, however, is near its southern limits.

The Glaucous Gull often reaches Anticosti Island in the Gulf of St. Lawrence in August, but does not usually appear in Massachusetts until late November or early December. In spring it reaches southern Greenland and Baffin Land in March or April, and appears in May at the northern limits of its range, though stragglers are still present on the St. Lawrence River as late as the middle of June.

This is one of the largest, most powerful and most predatory of all gulls. It not only robs other gulls, guillemots and other sea-birds of choice morsels and of their eggs and young, but it also actually kills and devours many of the smaller species such as Dovekies. It eats shell-fish, starfish, sea urchins, dead water-birds, dead fishes and other carrion, garbage, and even the droppings of large animals, and is said to feed also on crowberries.

ICELAND GULL

Larus leucopterus VIEILLOT. PLATE 5.

Other name: White-winged Gull.

IDENTIFICATION. — Length 24 to 26 inches; spread about 55 inches. Averages smaller than Glaucous Gull but similar in color; *bill is shorter and less heavy;* usually seems a little smaller than Herring Gulls with which often found.

BREEDING. — See Herring Gull.

RANGE. — Summers from Victoria Island and Boothia Peninsula to Greenland and Jan Mayen Land; winters from southern Greenland to New York, northern New Jersey, and the Great Lakes, and in Europe to France and the Baltic Sea.

The Iceland Gull, like the Glaucous Gull, is a boreal bird, descending to the latitude of Massachusetts or New York during its winter migration only. Comparatively few specimens are seen annually off our coast. Occasionally, though, it is common locally. Wherever along our coast fish-cleaning is done or garbage is thrown into the sea and gulls congregate, this species may be looked for. It is reported each winter at Gloucester, Swampscott and Lynn, and occasionally at Boston. It is seen regularly in small numbers about Block Island and Long Island. White-winged gulls are reported in winter from Cape Cod, and may belong to either this or the preceding species. The bird is not very shy, and I have seen it about the fish wharf at South Boston, seemingly quite as tame and confiding as any Herring Gull. Apparently it is not so predatory as the Glaucous Gull. Its habits are like those of the Herring Gull, as it commonly accompanies many of the latter species and feeds with them. The mottled young birds which greatly predominate here might easily pass unrecognized among young Herring Gulls were it not for their generally lighter hue and their white or whitish primaries.

KUMLIEN'S GULL

Larus kumlieni BREWSTER.   PLATE 5.

Other names: Gray-winged Gull; Lesser Glaucous-winged Gull.

Kumlien's Gull, which is illustrated in Plate 5, was first collected by Kumlien in 1878 and was named for its discoverer by William Brewster, but it is now considered to be merely a hybrid between the Iceland Gull and Thayer's Gull. It is sometimes called the Gray-winged Gull to distinguish it from the white-winged Iceland Gull. It is characterized by dark gray markings toward the tips of the primaries, where the Herring Gull has black markings. Where Iceland and Glaucous Gulls gather, this bird is found with some frequency. — (J.B.M.)

GREAT BLACK–BACKED GULL

Larus marinus LINNAEUS.   PLATE 5.

Other names: Black-back; Saddle-back; Coffin-bearer; Minister; Turkey Gull.

IDENTIFICATION. — Length 28 to 31 inches; spread about 65 inches. Larger than Herring Gull. Adult unmistakable when back is seen in a good light; dark back (much darker than that of other large gulls) contrasts strongly with white head, neck, breast and tail. Young of the year difficult to distinguish at any distance from some immature Herring Gulls, but average larger, are more buffy and less gray, are lighter below and head and bill are larger and heavier; may be distinguished from young Glaucous Gull (which has very light wings and tail) by blackish primaries and wide, dark band near tip of tail.

BREEDING. — See Herring Gull.

RANGE. — Breeds from northern Labrador, Iceland, and central Greenland south to Nova Scotia, Massachusetts (rarely), British Isles, Scandinavia, and Russia; winters from southern Greenland south to the Great Lakes and Delaware Bay (casually to Florida), to the Canaries, Azores and Senegal.

This great, dark-backed, powerful, wary bird is locally common in winter along the New England coast, and a few individuals may be seen for days at a time in all the summer months. Occasionally in June or July scores appear at outlying points on the coast, such as Cape Ann, the tip of Cape Cod or Monomoy, but nearly all these seem to be immature and probably non-breeding birds. The species begins to increase in number in late July and early August and by September it is present in considerable force. Sometimes a hundred may be seen at once, but usually they are much fewer and often appear in the company of the more numerous Herring Gulls. They frequent sand-bars and beaches, rocky ledges and isolated points and take good care to keep out of gunshot. Indeed they are so shy that a powerful glass is needed to make any intimate study of their habits except in places where they are seldom molested, or are protected or fed in winter. On their breeding-grounds they may be watched from a 'blind.' While here their behavior is much like that of the Herring Gull. Commonly they are slow fliers, but when in pursuit of other birds they exhibit both speed and agility. In March or April they begin their return journey to their northern breeding-grounds.

The Black-back feeds on fish or flesh, living or dead. It is a robber among the sea-fowl, sometimes pursuing smaller birds until they drop their prey, which it appropriates. It kills and devours Dovekies and other small birds, young ducklings and the eggs and young of other birds, young mammals such as mice, rats and rabbits, drives other gulls and crows away from their finds upon the beaches, and takes shellfish and crustaceans.

HERRING GULL

Larus argentatus smithsonianus COUES.

PLATE 6.

Other names: Sea Gull; Harbor Gull; Gray Gull; Winter Gull.

IDENTIFICATION. — Length 22½ to 26 inches; spread 54 to 58 inches. Larger than Ring-billed Gull and smaller than Glaucous Gull or Black-back, but size is very deceptive unless species can be compared side by side. Young of these other species resemble young Herring Gulls and all at some age may have (or appear to have) a black band or bar near end of tail; but young Black-backed Gull is more streaked and buffy and lighter below than young Herring Gull, while young Ring-billed Gull is generally lighter in color both above and below, with very distinct blackish subterminal bar on tail; adult Herring Gull may be distinguished from white-winged gulls by black ends of its primaries and from Kittiwake by longer and more irregularly shaped black markings on same, as well as by its flesh-colored feet. This latter character will serve also to distinguish it from Ring-billed Gull, with its yellowish-green feet.

BREEDING. — Typical of the larger gulls. Usually in colonies on islands in sea or in fresh water. *Nest:* On ground, sometimes on a bare shoal or on rocks or cliffs, sometimes in thick vegetation; rarely among or in trees; usually composed of seaweeds when on shore but often of marsh-grasses, weeds, sticks, chips, sometimes a few feathers, shells, and tree-mosses. *Eggs:* 3 to 5, very variable in color and markings — 'light sky blue, dead blue, light blue-gray, light gray-blue, dark lilac-gray, light gray, light pea-green, green, drab, warm drab, ochre drab, pink drab, light brown, and cinnamon,' with spots and blotches of chocolate-brown, rich brown, light brown, snuff brown, asphalt, black, lilac, and mauve (Wm. Dutcher and W. L. Baily); spots and blotches of various shades and many sizes distributed sparsely or thickly as the case may be.

RANGE. — Breeds from south-central Alaska and southern Baffin Island south to northern British Columbia, northern North Dakota, central Wisconsin, southern Ontario, northern New York, Maine, and Massachusetts; winters from southern Alaska south to Lower California and western Mexico, and from the Gulf of St. Lawrence and the Great Lakes south to the Bahamas, Cuba, Yucatan, and the coast of Alabama and Texas.

South of Martha's Vineyard lies a little isle of the sea, a mere sand-bar thrown up by the waves, known as Skiff's Island. It is all that shows above water of a long, dangerous shoal that extends far offshore. Strong tides run swiftly about it and angry waves beat on its sloping sands. It is a place for the mariner to avoid. There are ugly tide-rips about it, and often the pounding surf makes landing difficult. High storm-tides tear it down and rebuild it.

For many years Skiff's Island has been occupied more or less, summer and winter, by Herring Gulls, and in 1919 I found them breeding there. Probably they had been domiciled there for several years. In 1919 they nested in the most primitive manner on the island. The outer beach had been reared high by surf, and usually the sand sloped a little toward the center. Over this outer rampart the sea during storm-tides threw sea-wrack and eel-grass, and in bunches of this stranded seaweed the gulls made their nests. These were mere hollows shaped by the bird in the seaweed and lined with a little of the same material. Young birds that had left the nest squatted and tried to hide from intruders. Larger young ran away over the bare sand until they reached the water, into which they boldly plunged to be washed about by the surf.

Probably the Herring Gull once nested on small islands all along the coast of New England;

but many years ago most nesting sea-birds were driven away from our coasts by continued persecution, and it is only within recent years since protection has had some effect that they have begun to come back. One of the largest colonies is situated on Great Duck Island off Mt. Desert Island in Maine. This is a rocky island sparsely forested with coniferous trees, but there is much relatively open land used as sheep-pasture which supports a good growth of grasses and shrubbery. The sheep probably do no great injury to the gulls' nests, for the birds are well able to defend their eggs and young against these timid creatures. Duck Island is nearly two miles long and perhaps three quarters of a mile wide at its widest part. The gulls build their nests over the greater part of it.

When we approached Great Duck Island in early July, multitudes of white-breasted gulls were seen sitting on stumps or dead branches or on their nests; for in the most thickly settled part of the colony the trees are dead and many have been cut or have fallen, leaving only stumps and dead branches where the forest once stood. Our intrusion disturbed hundreds, if not thousands, of birds, which rose high in air with a continuous, complaining clamor. The avian host presented a wonderful spectacle as they floated on widely extended pinions, some wheeling, others darting downward, and all calling and crying with all their might. Presently many of the more distant birds settled like white doves on the branches of the dark trees, their snowy breasts in bold relief against the blue summer sky. Numerous nests lay scattered about, some in the open, others concealed, some with eggs, others with newly hatched young. Downy young were running about and many more were hiding beneath the weeds or shrubbery.

While the young gulls are small and tender, the parents brood them and protect them from sun, rain and their natural enemies. The parent bird swallows the food intended for its young. On reaching its offspring it bows its head until it succeeds in regurgitating the food, which is either in a fresh undigested condition or partially digested, according to the length of time since it was swallowed. The bowing of the parent sometimes brings up the food at once; at other times it seems as if an emetic would be necessary to produce visible results. In such cases digestion perhaps has gone too far. However, the youngster seems to receive thankfully whatever comes and does not require actually to be fed; for though it receives its food occasionally from the parent's bill, it takes it more often from the ground. The gull chicks as they grow stronger wander about more or less, and some no doubt 'get lost' while the parents are away hunting for food; but the adults seem to be able to find and recognize their offspring. The young, however, do not care by what bird they are fed so long as they get their fill; they beg from any parent that appears near them with food.

About the second week in August when the breeding-season is nearly over and many young are on the wing, the Herring Gulls scatter from their breeding-islands in Maine and the Provinces. Late in July their numbers begin sometimes to increase on the Massachusetts coast and on the fishing-grounds, and before the end of September they have scattered all along the coast of southern New England, and have reached New Jersey. From this point they continue southward, and Herring Gulls banded in New England have been 'recovered' on the coasts of the Gulf of Mexico as far south as Vera Cruz. From late March until well into May flocks may be seen on their return flight along the Atlantic seaboard.

The Herring Gull is a master of the air. It can fly forward or drift backward, veer gracefully in any direction, soar with stiffened pinions or shoot downward like an arrow, sail on steady wing against the wind and perform numberless evolutions with grace and ease. In calm weather it flaps along much like a heron, and ordinarily when traveling this is its mode of progression; but when the wind blows, it sails, wheels, rises and falls with great speed and power. Large flocks sometimes swing in wide circles and rise to immense heights.

Herring Gulls are excellent swimmers; but although commonly seen on the water, they do not swim very far when able to fly. They do not seem to dive commonly or deeply, but in case of necessity they can dive like terns from on the wing. I once saw one at rest on the Wankinco River that dived from the surface in less than six feet of water and apparently brought up some food from on or near the bottom.

Civilization has diminished the natural food for gulls in our harbors and rivers by decreasing the supply of fish and shellfish, but has substituted offal, garbage and sewage which are eagerly sought by these birds. The Herring Gull has become valuable therefore as a scavenger. It gathers in flocks in harbors wherever fish are dressed or thrown away, at canning factories, fish-freezers or fish-wharves, and quickly devours all offal or fish-waste thrown into the water. It flocks in thousands where sewage is discharged and where garbage is dumped at sea, and cleans up much filthy, floating refuse that might otherwise be cast back by winds and tides on beach and shore. Wherever fish, killed in thousands by disease, frost or other causes, are cast up in countless multitudes upon the shore to poison the air with the offensive effluvia of decay, there the gulls gather and in an astonishingly short time succeed in abating the nuisance. Sometimes the zeal of the gulls in disposing of such noisome fare brings them into disfavor with the farmers who, having hauled loads of dead fish to their fields for fertilizer, fail to plow them under, and soon find that they have vanished, the gulls having flown away with them. Not long ago a farmer in Rhode Island bought for fertilizer some tons of starfish that had been dredged up by the oystermen; but he let them lie too long and when he got ready to haul them, they had disappeared. The gulls knew where they went.

RING–BILLED GULL

Larus delawarensis ORD.   PLATE 6.

IDENTIFICATION. — Length 18 to 20 inches; spread 47 to 49½ inches. A little larger than Kittiwake or Crow. Adult black ring or partial black cross-bar on bill, seen only at close range unless with a powerful glass; tarsi and feet greenish-yellow or grayish-yellow-green, instead of black as in Kittiwake, or flesh-colored as in Herring Gull; black of primaries has distinct terminal white spots (see under Kittiwake); back a little lighter than that of Herring Gull. Young not usually so slaty-gray as in Herring Gull but lighter; its lighter color and very distinct, well-defined, dark band on tail should separate it from Herring Gull, immature of which, however, sometimes has, or appears to have, a broad, dark tail-band.

BREEDING. — See Herring Gull.

RANGE. — Breeds mainly on interior lakes from southern Alaska, Great Slave Lake, northern Manitoba, and James Bay south to southern Oregon, North Dakota, southern Ontario, northern New York (casually), and the north shore of the Gulf of St. Lawrence; winters from British Columbia, the Great Lakes and Maine to the Gulf coast, Cuba, and southern Mexico.

The Ring-billed Gull which was described by Aubudon as the 'Common American Gull' is no longer the common gull of New England. It does not breed now very commonly even in Labrador, where formerly it was abundant. It has also forsaken several islands in the Great

Lakes and has retired to regions where it is less persecuted by man. Apparently it cannot stand such persecution as has followed the Herring Gull, and it has been driven to breeding-haunts farther north or in the interior which are remote from thickly populated districts. For many years it has been seen on the northern Atlantic coast only in migration or in winter; but it is still the common gull on the lakes of the prairies and plains of the northern United States and Canada where it far outnumbers the Herring Gull. Since gulls have been given continuous protection under the laws of state and nation, this species seems to have increased in migration, and now it is a common winter resident on the southern Atlantic coast and the Gulf coast of Florida.

In appearance, flight and behavior the Ring-billed Gull resembles closely the Herring Gull. Many of its notes are similar to those of that species; and when seen in flocks of its own kind, it might be (and probably often is) mistaken for its larger congener. It is sociable and gregarious, associating not only with those of its own species but also with other gulls.

The Ring-billed Gull is rarely seen in New England waters before September or early October when young birds appear among flocks of Herring Gulls. Most individuals pass southward and comparatively few winter north of Cape Cod. In March and April they appear on their return; by the middle of April they have reached their breeding-grounds in North Dakota; and during the latter part of the month they arrive in the Canadian Northwest.

This gull frequents the outer bars and beaches where it feeds largely on dead fish and other aquatic animals, small rodents and insects.

LAUGHING GULL

Larus atricilla LINNAEUS.   PLATE 6.

Other names: Black-headed Gull; Black-head; Black-headed Mackerel Gull.
   IDENTIFICATION. — Length 15½ to 17 inches; spread about 40 inches. A medium-sized gull; adults have wings *dark above becoming black at tips and with white hind edge*, white under parts and tail, black head in summer and white head with dark markings in winter; young are dusky gray with a white rump, tail dark with white tip.
   NOTES. — A deep *ha ha ha* followed by rapidly repeated sounds of rippling laughter, complaining cries *ai ai* and *kai kai* (C. W. Townsend).
   BREEDING. — See Herring Gull.
   RANGE. — Breeds from Maine south to Florida, Texas, southern California, the Lesser Antilles, and Venezuela; winters from South Carolina and the Gulf coast to Brazil, Peru, and Chile.

South of the peninsula of Cape Cod lies a sandy island which is now the chief breeding-place of the Laughing Gull in New England. The Indians named this islet Muskeget and it still bears the name. Lying on the boundary of Nantucket Sound and surrounded by treacherous shoals, it is one of the graveyards of the Atlantic and is avoided by mariners. Often its shores are strewn with the timbers and wreckage of lost ships. Strange sea-creatures frequent the deeps and shallows that surround this island. Small fish often abound in the adjacent waters and these are pursued by larger fish and sea-birds. Thousands of gulls and terns breed and rear their young upon the sands of the island. It is one of the largest bird nurseries on the New England coast. Muskeget Island consists mainly of sand built up by wave and wind and appears to be of comparatively recent origin. It is roughly crescent-shaped and is about one and one half miles long. Sandspits rising above the waters near its northwestern face defend it against the sea and provide a harbor for small boats. Tides run fiercely over the shoals about it and in windy weather, particularly at low stages of the tide, foaming breakers roar for miles along the tide-rips and break in fury on the shore. Treeless, Muskeget is a succession of low, rolling dunes and hollows or sandy levels covered more or less with beach-grass, poison-ivy, beach-peas and other low-growing plants and with stunted bayberry and beach-plum bushes. Formerly its vegetation was very sparse; but this has increased in quantity and luxuriance, making conditions more favorable for the Laughing Gulls, which prefer to hide their nests, and less so for the Common Terns, which affect more open sandy land.

When I first visited Muskeget in 1908 with two companions, we were lost in wonder at the enormous numbers of its feathered inhabitants. As we approached the nesting-grounds, we were soon in the midst of a veritable storm of darting, diving, sailing, fluttering, screaming terns, while high above our heads in the blue and cloudless sky floated innumerable black-headed gulls, their clear cries mingling with the harsher sounds given out by the storming terns. Nests were there in thousands; but while those of the terns were usually quite open and unconcealed on the sands, those of the gulls were more often made beneath the shelter of high beach-grass or that of umbrageous plants like the poison-ivy, a path beneath the vegetation leading in at one side of a nest and out at the other. The eggs, therefore, usually were well hidden, and the downy young (which do not remain long in the nest) were mostly lying concealed under the dense foliage. Most of the nests contain eggs by the middle of June; and early in July there are many half-grown young, many of which may be seen running to shelter whenever an intruder appears.

In August, when flying ants are abundant, I have seen these gulls in numbers near shore circling about like swallows over the waters of Buzzards Bay and catching the ants in air or picking them up from the surface of the water. They follow the fishermen for the offal thrown overboard, go far to sea for floating refuse, search river-shores near the sea, and resort to flats and beaches for animal food uncovered by the tide. They often follow steamers and feed upon whatever edible matter is thrown overboard. In summer it is only necessary to toss out a few small pieces of bread or fat to attract numbers from far and near. They hover over or near the stern of the boat, dipping gracefully to the water with extended legs and expertly picking up the fragments. Often they may be attracted in the same way about the wharves of Martha's Vineyard, Nantucket and Cape Cod. When pieces of fish-liver are thrown to them, they become very bold and sometimes will come within a few feet of the observer. With a low sun shining upon their lovely breasts, the wheeling flock makes a very attractive picture, not soon to be forgotten.

In April Laughing Gulls appear all along the Atlantic coast of the United States even to their 'farthest north' in Maine where a few of the birds arrive late in the month. In late August and September they are again on their way southward and October sees most of them in the 'sunny South,' where, with their spotted white heads, they are very different in appearance from the black-headed birds of summer.

The food of the Laughing Gull consists of almost anything edible that it can find on sea or shore. Insects, worms, small fish, crabs and their spawn, various other marine animals, garbage, offal, etc., make up a large part of their food in our waters.

FRANKLIN'S GULL

Larus pipixcan WAGLER.

Other names: Prairie Pigeon; Prairie Dove; Franklin's Rosy Gull.

IDENTIFICATION. — Length 13½ to 15 inches; spread about 35 inches. Similar to Laughing Gull but mantle not so dark, and *black tips of primaries separated by white area from gray of mantle* instead of shading into the gray; the smaller Bonaparte's Gull has primaries largely white.

BREEDING. — Near lakes. *Nest:* A mass of dead reeds, etc., in water, often floating. *Eggs:* 2 to 4, buffy, variously marked with browns and lavender.

RANGE. — Breeds in prairie regions of interior North America from southern Alberta and south-central Manitoba to Utah, South Dakota, Iowa (formerly), and southern Minnesota; winters from the Gulf coast of Louisiana and Texas to Peru, Patagonia, and Chile.

Franklin's Gull in life is one of the most beautiful of all the gulls, for the white of the neck and under parts is suffused with a delicate salmon-pink, varying to a beautiful rose hue, which has given the bird the name of Rosy Gull, but which quickly fades after death, leaving the plumage a dead white contrasting with the very dark head and the gray mantle with its white-framed black patch on the primaries.

Franklin's Gull is a bird of the western prairies which has occasionally wandered to the Atlantic and Pacific coasts. It nests in large colonies in the shallow lakes of western Minnesota, where Dr. T. S. Roberts in 1916 estimated that fifty thousand pairs were breeding at Heron Lake in Jackson County. It is largely insectivorous in its feeding-habits and is a valuable friend of the prairie farmer, devouring immense numbers of grasshoppers, crickets and other destructive agricultural pests. It is a common thing to see numbers of these birds following the plow in spring, feasting on larvae and worms turned up by the share, and later they follow the cultivators and harvesters in their rounds. — (J.B.M.)

BONAPARTE'S GULL

Larus philadelphia (ORD).   PLATE 6.

Other name: Frost Gull.

IDENTIFICATION. — Length 12 to 14½ inches; spread about 32 inches. The 'wing-pattern' is the distinguishing point about our three black-headed gulls (which have white heads in winter, variously blotched with dark); adult Bonaparte's has upper coverts and secondaries largely gray, primaries *largely white* with black tips; young Bonaparte's has narrow black band near tip of tail, white head with dark spot behind eye.

BREEDING. — In forested regions near water. *Nest:* On logs, stumps or bushes but usually in coniferous trees, of sticks, leaves, etc., lined with mosses or down. *Eggs:* 2 to 4, brown, buffy or olive-gray, blotched and spotted with browns.

RANGE. — Breeds in interior from northwestern Alaska and northern Mackenzie south to central British Columbia and central Alberta; winters from Massachusetts to Florida, on the Gulf coast to Yucatan, and on the Pacific coast from Alaska to Mexico; in migration east to Quebec and west to Kotzebue Sound.

With the first warm days of April when the alewives begin to run up our streams comes the lovely, graceful little Bonaparte's Gull. Arrayed in its gay nuptial plumage, with black head and snowy vesture, it wings in graceful flight along the coast or up the great river-valleys of the interior, spurred on by the urge of the reproductive instinct, toward the great forests of the North where it nests in dark coniferous trees. In autumn the immature birds appear — dainty tern-like creatures — with their slender bills, trim forms and long wings; but the rounded tail with the broad black bar near the tip serves to distinguish them at once from the terns. Their flight is airy, buoyant, easy and graceful like that of the terns. They frequently dip down to the water, but I have never seen one go under as terns so often do.

A loose flock of these charming birds wandering alongshore or over river marsh, performing their sprightly evolutions while catching insects, or fluttering poised over the water as they stoop to pick up some tidbit, perhaps a living fish which they secure by a lightning-like dart, adds life and beauty to the landscape. Although this delicate creature seems fitted only to play in the sunlight amid summer zephyrs, it has wonderful powers of flight and is hardy enough to breast the storms and raging seas of winter along our coast. Although it is not often seen during the most inclement seasons on the New England coast, yet it is not uncommon locally during mild winters and a few may be found here irregularly at this season where rivers or estuaries remain ice-free so that the birds can secure food. In winter in our waters it seems to be a rather silent bird; but while feeding in flocks, particularly in spring, individuals sometimes keep up a continual chattering.

Bonaparte's Gull feeds largely on 'small fry,' but during the summer is more dependent on insects than are most gulls. It seeks insects in marshes, on cultivated fields, on seaweed stranded on shore or floating on water; and its stomach is often filled to repletion with such food. Flies, ants, moths and their larvae, and other insects are eaten, also many small crustaceans and marine worms.

ATLANTIC KITTIWAKE

Rissa tridactyla tridactyla (LINNAEUS). PLATE 5.

Other names: Frost-bird; Snow Gull; Winter Bird; Haddock Gull; Winter Gull; Jack Gull; Pinny Owl or Pinyole; Meterick.

IDENTIFICATION. — Length 16 to 18 inches; spread about 36 inches. Similar to Herring Gull but *much smaller*, with black legs and with black tip of wing clearly defined as if dipped in black dye; young resemble young Bonaparte's Gull but with a dark bar across back of head instead of dark spot behind eye and with more black on primaries.

BREEDING. — In colonies on cliffs. *Nest:* Of seaweed, grasses, and mosses. *Eggs:* 1 to 4, similar to those of Herring Gull but much smaller.

RANGE. — Breeds on Arctic islands and south to the Gulf of St. Lawrence; winters from the Gulf of St. Lawrence south to New Jersey; also found in the Eastern Hemisphere.

Out on the heaving sea of the Grand Banks, where dripping bowsprits rise and fall; where plunging bows of fishing-craft throw off the foaming waves and dash aloft sheets of blinding spray which, torn by the wind, descend upon the icy planks in freezing showers; where roaring, foaming crests overleap the bulwarks and flood the rocking decks; there the Kittiwake rides the wind. Where fishing-vessels ride to taut cables, when dories are hoisted aboard and the splitting and cleaning of the fish begins, there our little gulls gather to the feast.

The Atlantic Kittiwake is a sea-bird. It is not so commonly seen in our harbors and estuaries as is the Herring Gull, but keeps more at sea, drinking salt water and sleeping on the waves. It is quite tame, comes close to schooners and dories, and thousands have been caught in the past by fishermen with hooks and lines baited with pieces of fish offal. The birds thus taken were eaten or used for bait. Kittiwakes follow ocean steamers and fishing and coasting vessels, sometimes for long distances. At times, particularly after severe winter storms, they may be seen in harbors like those of Gloucester, Provincetown, and Nantucket where they find food and shelter. At such times they also visit the outer beaches. Kittiwakes fly over the sea in loose flocks or in company with other sea-birds. Their exceedingly long wings and long, broad tails fit them for powerful flight, and they are among the most graceful of the gull family as they circle and glide on fixed and stable wing, or flutter easily above their prey, maintaining always a perfect mastery of the air. The Kittiwake is extremely affectionate toward its mate and young and companions of its own species. If one is shot down, others gather and hover over it and clamorously lament its fate, singularly indifferent to their own peril.

The Atlantic Kittiwake rarely appears in numbers off the New England coast until about the middle of October and sometimes not until well into November. It begins to move northward toward its breeding-grounds in February.

The Kittiwake feeds largely on the smaller fishes of the sea, on crustaceans, mollusks and other marine animals, and like other gulls it is more or less of a scavenger. It follows whales to pick up the fragments that escape the cetacean's jaws.

SABINE'S GULL

Xema sabini (SABINE). PLATE 6.

Other name: Fork-tailed Gull.
IDENTIFICATION. — Length 13 to 14 inches; spread about 33 inches. A medium-sized gull with a *forked* tail; wing-pattern shows three triangles — gray on coverts and tertials, black on primaries, white on hind edge of wing between primaries and tertials; black head in summer only.
BREEDING. — See Herring Gull.
RANGE. — Breeds on Arctic coasts and islands from Alaska to Greenland and in Eurasia; winters on the coast of Peru; migrates chiefly along the Pacific coast; casual on the Atlantic coast and in the interior.

Sabine's Gull is a boreal bird and usually haunts the vicinity of cold seas. It is rarely seen in temperate or tropical regions, except on the coast of Peru to which it migrates in winter. On that coast there is a very cold Antarctic current, and in this current Arctic and Antarctic zoologic forms meet. To this region of cold currents Sabine's Gull annually finds its way over the broad Pacific. As there is no such region of cold waters in the Atlantic, this bird does not migrate in any numbers down the Atlantic coast, and so cannot be regarded as other than a rare or accidental visitant to New England or farther south. It has been recorded in many places in the interior of the continent, which fact may indicate that some individuals normally reach the Pacific coast of South America by the overland route. This bird's habits are much like those of Bonaparte's Gull. According to Mr. F. S. Hersey, the species is usually rather solitary, and at low tide it spends much time feeding on the flats, where it runs about like a plover. In appearance and flight it resembles a tern, and the forked tail adds to the illusion; especially if the bird appears late in September without the hood and in winter plumage.

Toward the end of September Sabine's Gull becomes scarce over its breeding-range as most individuals of the species are then on their way south. In April they begin to move northward and they arrive at their subarctic and Arctic breeding-grounds from the latter part of May until late in June.

In the Arctic regions this species feeds much like other gulls on various aquatic forms of life, and insects. Little is known of its food elsewhere. It picks up much of its food from the surface of the water, not flocking much, but seeking its subsistence singly and attending chiefly to its own affairs. Occasionally two or three are seen together and sometimes they feed with other gulls.

GULL–BILLED TERN

Gelochelidon nilotica aranea (WILSON).

Other names: Marsh Tern; Nuttall's Tern.

IDENTIFICATION. — Length 13 to 15¼ inches; spread 33 to 37 inches. A medium-sized tern, white with gray mantle and black cap; tail shorter and less forked than Common Tern; stout, somewhat gull-like, black bill is diagnostic at short range; feet also black.

BREEDING. — Similar to Common Tern but eggs usually lighter-colored.

RANGE. — Breeds on Atlantic coast from Virginia to Georgia and on the Gulf coast from Mississippi to Texas, also in the Bahamas, Cuba, and at the mouth of the Amazon, and on Salton Sea, California; winters from Texas and Louisiana to southern Guatemala and western Panama, and from Brazil to Patagonia.

The Gull-billed Tern was formerly known as the 'Marsh Tern' because of its fondness for broad tidal marshes both for feeding and nesting purposes, but today it has apparently transferred its nesting activities to open sandy and pebbly beaches a little above high-water mark, where the eggs are well protected by their likeness to the water-worn pebbles and bits of débris with which they are surrounded.

This bird was once a very abundant summer resident on the coastal islands of the Southern States. In 1900 the colony on Cobb's Island, Virginia, was estimated at a thousand birds, though much reduced from its former numbers. In 1901 it was estimated at only 300 birds; in 1903 only eight pairs were counted, and in 1907 Mr. Bent found only two pairs on Cobb's and a few more on Wreck Island a short distance away. That tells the story of their near-extinction for millinery purposes.

The Gull-billed Tern seems to be almost entirely insectivorous in its feeding, and it hawks about over the marshes and tidal channels like a great swallow, turning and darting about with great dexterity and speed, but only rarely dipping to the surface of the water as other terns customarily do when feeding. Its voice is hoarse and its notes are characteristic. Mr. Bent says that on the breeding-grounds they seemed to say '*katydid, katydid,*' or '*kadid,*' accented on the last syllable, or sometimes '*killy*' or '*killy-kadid,*' all quickly uttered, loud, and rasping. — (J.B.M.)

FORSTER'S TERN

Sterna forsteri NUTTALL.

PLATE 8.

Other name: Havell's Tern.

IDENTIFICATION. — Length 14 to 15 inches; spread about 30 inches. Slightly larger than Common Tern but indistinguishable at a distance; whiter below; wings shorter with primaries much lighter than in Common Tern; bill orange-yellow toward base, black toward tip; tail longer and more streaming than in Common Tern and gray like back, while Common Tern has white tail; in winter fore part of head all white and distinct broad blackish stripe along side of head including eye and ear regions.

BREEDING. — Similar to Common Tern.

RANGE. — Breeds in the interior of California, Oregon, Washington, Utah and Nevada, and from southeastern Manitoba to northern Colorado, Minnesota, northeastern Illinois, and southern Ontario, also on the coasts of Texas, Louisiana, and Virginia; winters from central California, the Gulf of Mexico, and South Carolina to southern Guatemala; in migration occurs on the Atlantic coast as far north as Massachusetts.

Forster's Tern is so much like the Common Tern in appearance, habits and behavior that Audubon did not recognize the breeding adult as a different species, though in a quite different winter plumage he named it Havell's Tern. Swainson and Richardson described it as the Common Tern, while Wilson never recognized the species. George N. Lawrence, in 1858, was the first to differentiate the bird in breeding-dress from the Common Tern; and Coues, still later, described for the first time its various plumages. Except by its dissimilar cries the adult in breeding plumage may be distinguished from the Common Tern only at close range; but in the immature and adult winter plumages (in one or other of which it may occur here in late summer or early autumn) the distinct black patch on side of head should enable a close observer with a good glass to recognize the bird.

Forster's Tern is a bird of the interior, nesting commonly about many of the shallow lakes and reed-grown sloughs of the Western and Central States and the prairie provinces of Canada. It is usually found in small colonies, and its nests are placed on masses of floating débris, on flattened reeds and tules, or on old muskrat houses. Sometimes a single muskrat dome will be the site of several occupied nests of the tern. The nest may be merely a slight hollow without attempt at lining, or may be a fairly well-built structure of dead grasses and bits of drift.

Forster's Tern ranges rather widely in its migrations and individuals, or small flocks, may be seen occasionally on the Atlantic coast as far north as New England. It winters from South Carolina to Florida and the Gulf of Mexico, and should be watched for among the other seabirds around the Florida beaches.

This species feeds more on insects than does the Common Tern. It catches them on the wing and picks them up from the water. It also eats fish and frogs (both alive and dead) and other aquatic animals.

COMMON TERN

Sterna hirundo hirundo LINNAEUS.   PLATE 8.

Other names: Wilson's Tern; Tearr; Mackerel Gull; Summer Gull; Sea Swallow; Medrick.

IDENTIFICATION. — Length 13 to 16 inches; spread 29 to 32 inches. Slender white birds with gray mantle and black cap; in summer darker than Roseate Tern; bill bright coral or light vermilion with more or *less black toward end* and longer than that of Arctic Tern; tail usually shorter than in Arctic or Roseate Terns; folded wings reach beyond its tip. Newly fledged young indistinguishable in field from those of Arctic or Roseate Terns except perhaps by an expert.

BREEDING. — On islands in lake or sea or on shores. *Nest:* Varies from a mere hollow in sand or among pebbles, lined with a few bits of shell or small stones to a well-built hollowed mound of grasses and seaweeds; sometimes of fish-bones; usually in the open, sometimes among weeds, grasses, or shrubbery. *Eggs:* 2 or 3 to 6, very varied, from white to pale brown, buff, olive, and green, spotted and blotched with browns, grays, and lilacs.

RANGE. — Nearly cosmopolitan; breeds from Great Slave Lake, northern Manitoba, central Ontario, and the Gulf of St. Lawrence south to southern Alberta, southern Wisconsin, northern Ohio, northwestern Pennsylvania, and North Carolina, also on the Florida Keys, the Bahamas, the Gulf coast of Alabama and Texas, the Dutch West Indies and Venezuela, and in Europe, Asia, and Africa; winters in Florida, on both coasts of South America, and western Mexico, also in Africa and Asia; in migration occurs on Pacific coast from British Columbia to Lower California.

A June morning in 1908 found me marooned on a sandy islet near the elbow of Cape Cod. My skiff had been filled and my oars carried to sea by the surf of the stiffest 'sou-wester' of the season; and with back to the gale and the flying, cutting sand-drift I watched the rising sea gradually march up the streaming strand until the wash began to pour over the seaward bank and race across the sand to my feet. The attraction which drew me that morning to the islet was an immense concourse of birds resting on its sands or hovering above them, most of which proved to be Common Terns. There was nothing to do but await a rescue; so crouching in the stranded boat I watched the birds and the sea. The flying terns soon discovered a 'school' of fish, and then all was wild excitement among them. Instantly the island was birdless, as they all launched upon the gale and rode down to leeward intent upon their prey. When mackerel or bluefish, coming in great hordes, find a school of 'bait,' the larger fish chase the little ones until the latter, in their efforts to escape, break water in all directions and skip over the waves like little flying-fish, or else mill about in a dense mass at the surface. Then the water all about fairly boils under the savage onset of their pursuers. The sharp-eyed terns, too, spying the commotion, flock from afar to feast on the luckless 'fishlings.' To see the terns thus fishing is a sight to stir the blood. High in the sunlight they hover above the surging sea. Below the blue waves roar on, to break in foam on the yellow sand. The whirling, screaming, light-winged birds, strongly contrasted against the smoky murk to seaward, alternately climb the air and plunge like plummets straight down into the waves — rising again and again, fluttering, poising, screaming, striking. So now like birds gone mad the terns flashed from sky to sea. It fairly rained birds; hundreds of them were shooting down into the angry waves. They played with gale and sea. Rising, they shook the brine from their feathers and, towering high, hovered a moment, breasting the gale; then setting their wings like long, barbed spearheads, plunged again and yet again. This was the sight for which I had been waiting. The birds had given the signal to the fishermen to come out from shore. Soon three dories with their adventurous crews had passed out toward the foaming bar, and the men were dropping their lines near where the fishing birds were thickest. I had only to wait for a returning fisherman to take me off. Terns catching fish are a common sight, but that day they furnished a spectacle that illustrated, under stress, their power and address in taking prey — also their utility as guides to the fishermen of our coast.

If one really wishes to see terns *en masse*, he should go in the breeding season to one of the greater tern colonies off the shores of Massachusetts or Maine, such as Muskeget or Machias Seal Island. In years past the human intruder upon the former breeding-ground was surrounded by a confused, gyrating 'snowstorm' of birds and his ears were assailed by an almost deafening chorus of harsh, clashing cries. However, the fitness of Muskeget as a breeding-place for Common Terns is gradually lessening. Perhaps the vegetation over a great part of it is growing too dense for this species, which does not like thick cover, but seems to select the naked sand in preference, especially when nesting on the mainland where it may be disturbed by enemies at night.

Nest building on the open sand is but the work of a moment. The bird alights, selects the spot, crouches slightly and works its little feet so rapidly that the motion seems a mere blur, while the sand flies out in tiny jets in every direction as the creature pivots about. The tern next settles lower and smooths the cavity by turning and working and moving its body and wings from side to side. Occasionally, where nesting-material is abundant, quite an elaborate nest is built — a pile of grass, seaweed or other drift some six inches high. Other nests are mere hollows sparsely wreathed about with a little beach-grass. Sometimes the nests are more or less concealed under beach-grass or other vegetation. When the eggs or young are destroyed, a second set of eggs is commonly laid, and sometimes perhaps a third.

The male constantly attends the sitting female and brings food to her, largely 'sand-eels' or similar small, slender fish which are rarely over five or six inches in length. The food-call of the female is recognizable, and is frequently repeated when the supply arrives, for which she begs with uplifted head and wide-open mouth. Sometimes when the male brings a fish, another bird tries to steal it and seizes one end. Then comes 'the tug of war.' The two pull each other back and forth and sometimes others join in the strenuous struggle, but in the end the owner usually retains his booty. Often he does not feed the female at once, but turning a cold shoulder walks into the grass and drops the much-desired morsel. She follows, begging piteously, and finally picks it up from the ground, and with seeming difficulty swallows it. Now and then as I watched, a male, having fed his mate, stretched his neck to full length, with head horizontal or with bill pointed skyward, and then, with tail jauntily cocked, bowed gravely several times. The males appeared to do most of the fishing. A constant flight of them passed out to sea and returned with fish.

When the parent tern comes in with fish for the family, it utters a peculiar call, somewhat resembling the usual harsh *tee' arr* but higher in pitch and softer in tone. The young beg for food from any incoming fish-laden bird, and give a harsh rattling cry somewhat like the alarm-note of the adult. When a half-grown youngster sees a parent bird fluttering near with food, it cannot contain itself for eagerness. It dances about, flaps or flutters its wings and begs with open mouth in a most appealing manner. The parent, apparently recognizing its offspring while still in air, alights and proceeds unhesitatingly and in the most businesslike and expeditious way to fill the yawning cavity with a small fish. As the day advances and the sun's rays strengthen, any object that provides shade or shelter is sought by the downy young. A bit of driftwood or a dead skate on the beach, a bunch of beach-grass or any weed, will serve. Often under such circumstances I have seen a young tern crowd in between the stems of two plants that afforded it shade and concealment, and then, with flying feet, scoop out quickly a deep cavity for its body in the cooler sand below the surface and lie there hidden and comfortable. As their pinions develop, the young birds frequently stand facing the breeze and flap their wings until gradually, little by little, they become strong enough to raise themselves off their feet. Then it is only a few days before their wings sustain them for considerable flights. Now they make their way to the shore, and the parents feed them on the beach. A little later a parent passes food to its young while both are on the wing, or feeds the fledglings while the latter sit on the water.

The food of the Common Tern varies more or less with locality and circumstance. Along the New England coast small slender fish, never over five or six inches in length, such as the sand-eel or sand-lance (*Ammodytes americanus*), form a large part of their food. Small herrings or alewives are eaten and even menhaden, together with shrimps and other crustaceans, aquatic worms and insects; in addition (in times of scarcity) the offal of fish thrown into the water by fishermen. In August and September the species is observed to catch on the wing such insects as flying ants, butterflies and cicadas.

ARCTIC TERN

Sterna paradisaea BRÜNNICH. PLATE 8.

Other names: Crimson-billed Tern; Long-tailed Tern; Short-footed Tern; Mackerel Gull; Medrick.

IDENTIFICATION. — Length 14 to 17 inches; spread 29 to 33 inches. Grayest of terns; tail longer than in Common Tern, showing beyond wing-tips when perched; bill carmine or blood-red; a white line between the black cap and gray lower part of face is a good field mark at close range; young cannot be certainly identified in the field.

BREEDING. — Similar to Common Tern.

RANGE. — Breeds from northern Alaska to Greenland and south to British Columbia, northern Manitoba, Maine and Massachusetts, and in Arctic Eurasia; winters in the Antarctic Ocean south to lat. 74°; in migration, on the Pacific coast to southern California, and on the Atlantic coast south to Long Island, and on the coasts of Brazil, Peru, Chile, France, and South Africa.

The Arctic Tern is one of the most remarkable birds of the world. It is the long-distance champion of avian migration. It nests at least as far north as the most northern Eskimos live, while in winter its tireless pinions beat along the distant shores of unexplored lands of the Antarctic continent. It sees more hours of daylight and of sunlight than any other creature on earth. On the arrival of the species at its northernmost nesting-site the midnight sun is shining, and it never sets during the tern's stay; while for two months of its Antarctic sojourn the bird sees no sunset. For about eight months of the year it has twenty-four hours of daylight, and during the other four months more daylight than darkness. Says W. Eagle Clarke: 'It has the most extensive latitudinal range to be found among vertebrate animals.'

According to Professor Cooke the Arctic Tern makes a round trip of twenty-two thousand miles between its farthest north and farthest south, and he says that no man knows its pathway on the journey. When it disappears from New England, it seems to be lost in the vast immensity of the Atlantic; but within about seventy days its flocks are seen in the Antarctic Ocean. When summer comes to the Arctic fiords on the coast of Greenland; when the glacial streams begin to flow; when Arctic flowers are budding and the Snow Bunting, the Dovekie and the Burgomaster have returned; then, too, the flocks of Arctic Terns appear at their northern destinations.

Recent bird-banding activities have thrown some light upon the probable course of the Arctic Tern's migration journeys. It had long been recognized that the species, while breeding on the western Atlantic coasts as far south as Massachusetts, was almost unknown along that coast south of Long Island. Its next appearance on the western side of the Atlantic was the coast of Brazil south of the Equator. It was, however, a common migrant on the coasts of western Europe and Africa, and was a visitor to Cape Colony and Natal in South Africa from November to February.

On October 1, 1927, a tern was picked up near La Rochelle, France, which had been banded the previous July in Turnavik Bay, Labrador, latitude 55° 13′ north, by O. L. Austin, Jr. On November 14, 1928, another was found dead on the beach at Port Shepstone, Natal, South Africa, which had been banded at the same rookery on July 23, 1928, and which had made the journey of approximately nine thousand miles air line, in about three months' time. A third tern, banded on the coast of Maine and recorded as a Common Tern but probably an Arctic, as both species bred in the colony and the downy young are practically indistinguishable, had been found near the mouth of the Niger River in western Africa some years previously. These three records suggest that the Arctic Tern, a species of European or Eurasian origin, had gradually extended its breeding range from northern Europe perhaps in successive steps to Iceland, Greenland, Labrador, and finally to New England, but that in its autumnal migrations it returned over its ancestral highway, first east to Europe, then south along the coasts of Europe and Africa, to the South Atlantic and the Indian Ocean (Natal), with stragglers crossing the narrow part of the Atlantic from Africa to South America occasionally.

This species seems to be more of a maritime bird than other common terns. Apparently it breeds in the interior less commonly than the others, and in migration keeps much offshore. The southernmost breeding-place of the species on this coast is Muskeget Island, where it bred formerly in considerable numbers. This is one of the birds that was sacrificed to the millinery interests in the latter part of the last century when it is said that about forty thousand terns were killed in a single year on or near Muskeget. Probably at that time the Arctic Tern was nearly extirpated from New England; now, happily, it is beginning to come back.

ROSEATE TERN

Sterna dougalli dougalli MONTAGU.

PLATE 8.

Other name: Mackerel Gull.

IDENTIFICATION. — Length 14 to 17 inches; spread about 30 inches. Adults in nuptial plumage bill largely black, with red base, gives Roseate Tern different appearance from either of its red-billed associates, Arctic Tern or Common Tern; long, white, streaming, outer tail feathers extending much beyond tips of closed wings help to identify sitting bird; on wing with a low sun lighting up under plumage, Roseate Tern shows *much whiter below* than the others; rosy tint of under plumage usually not noticeable at a distance and not often at close range (but gives a very *creamy* tint to under plumage as bird flies); when so seen exposed primaries are *light*, while those of *Common Tern* are *dark*. Young difficult to distinguish in field from young of Common Tern.

BREEDING. — Similar to Common Tern.

RANGE. — Breeds locally on Sable Island, Nova Scotia, and on the coasts of Maine, Massachusetts, New Jersey, and Virginia, and in the Bahamas, Bermuda, Lesser Antilles, and from the Dry Tortugas to Venezuela and British Honduras, also in Europe, Africa, Ceylon, and China; winters from Louisiana, southern Mexico, and the Bahamas to Brazil.

The Roseate Tern has an elegant form that swells and tapers in lines of grace. Its flight, as it rides at ease upon the gale, exemplifies the poetry of aerial motion. Its lustrous plumage gives back the light in delicate rosy tints. The exquisite blush upon its breast resembles the hue of the inner surface of some rare seashell, but it fades and passes as the love season wanes.

When, in Maytime, spring breezes blow on the shores of New England; when migratory fishes work up along our coast, then, urged on by the universal instinct of reproduction, and sailing upon the free wind as they speed toward their northern haunts, come the Roseate Terns, loveliest of all the graceful 'swallows of the sea.' They glide high over the heaving flood, seeking their native isle; and when Phoebus dispels the mists of morning, they sight the well-remembered shore. Then the glad birds glide gently downward, alight, and rest on wave-washed sands. What a picture they make as they stand in glistening rows, or flutter over the shallows, bringing beauty, action and clamor to the hitherto silent isle! The male birds are a-tremble with amorous ardor — that magic which adds an extra gloss to their plumage, a new fire to their eyes, and fixes the effulgent glow of morning upon their breasts. Soon they begin their wooing. Watch them as they catch little fish which they present to their chosen mates; as they follow them in graceful, wavering flight over land and sea; or as they strut proudly about with upstretched necks, drooping wings and streaming tails held high. Craned necks distended, they wheel with mincing steps and, bowing, exhibit all their graces. There is much caressing, billing and preening of one another's plumage. With it all goes screaming, chattering and much animated vocal exchange. Little time is wasted in house-hunting or building; possessed by the same impulse, hundreds mate and begin their simple nests. At first there are many little hollows made in the sand; next, lining material is added; a day later, many nests have one egg; the next, two; while a little later some have even three. About three weeks later still we may see hundreds of little chicks. Now all is bustle and activity. Parent birds are continually passing to and fro; some flying out to sea and others coming in with fish; while still others remain to brood and shelter the young. Apparently this task falls mainly to the female; but the male occasionally stands guard, repels intruders of his own race and relieves his mate for a time on the nest. I have watched these doings for days; have seen the lovely birds fishing,

233

bathing, mating, incubating and feeding and brooding their young. Their habits at the nesting-place seem to be essentially the same as those of the Common Tern, as hereinbefore described. On the wing, however, they are more graceful than the other species. Their wing-strokes seem a trifle slower, while their long, streaming, spotless tails add much to their aerial grace. On land or water their little feet are of no great service, but their perfect pinions make the air their natural home. At the slightest alarm they spring into their favorite element and give themselves to the winds. They sport tirelessly above the waves and seem fitted for this alone. Often their nests are placed promiscuously with those of the Common Tern, although the tendency of each species seems to be to establish a settlement of its own. Thus in certain parts of a tern colony nests will be mainly of one species; while not far off the other will predominate. The Common Tern seems to seek by preference the more open spaces, while the Roseate Tern seems to favor the tall grass or other vegetation.

So far as my observation goes, the Roseate Tern when nesting in company with the Common Tern feeds on the same sort of food; but I have never known the former to catch insects on the wing as the Common Tern does.

EASTERN SOOTY TERN

Sterna fuscata fuscata LINNAEUS.   PLATE 7.

Other names: Egg-bird; Wide-awake.

IDENTIFICATION. — Length 15 to 17 inches; spread about 34 inches. Unmistakable; larger than Common Tern; adult with white forehead, blackish upper plumage, white under plumage; young smoky-brown all over but lighter below with white marks on back, giving the bird a peculiar spotted appearance.

BREEDING. — In colonies on islands. *Eggs:* 1 to 3, white to buff, sparingly spotted, laid on bare ground but sometimes 'wreathed about' with a few leaves or pebbles.

RANGE. — Breeds from the Dry Tortugas, Bahamas, West Indies, and tropical islands of the Atlantic to Venezuela and west to British Honduras; winters from Louisiana to Brazil and the Falkland Islands.

The Eastern Sooty Tern is found as a breeding species of the United States only on Bird Key in the Dry Tortugas, those isolated islets in the Gulf of Mexico which form the last link in the chain of the Florida Keys, and where a colony estimated at about twenty thousand birds has nested for many years. Though very unlike most of our terns in physical appearance, they are very similar in habits to the Common Tern. They feed almost entirely upon small fishes, but do not dive for their prey, which they pick up from the surface without interrupting their graceful flight as they swoop down in a long curve to the water and up again into the air. They never seem to alight on stakes or pilings as do most terns, but are tireless in flight. They sometimes soar in circles higher and higher until lost to sight. — (J.B.M.)

LEAST TERN

Sterna antillarum antillarum (LESSON). PLATE 8.

Other names: Little Striker; Oyt; Pond Tern; Killing-peter.

IDENTIFICATION. — Length 8½ to 9¾ inches; spread about 20 inches. Our smallest tern; adult recognized by small size, white patch on forehead boldly contrasted against clear black of cap, bright yellow bill with black tip, and orange-yellow feet; young resemble young Black Tern but tail is whitish instead of dark, and under parts pure white not tinged gray.

BREEDING. — Similar to Common Tern but nest a mere hollow in the sand.

RANGE. — Breeds on the Atlantic and Gulf coasts from Massachusetts to the Florida Keys and Texas, on islands of the Mississippi and Missouri river systems to South Dakota and Iowa and west to southwestern Kansas and northern Nebraska, also in Bahamas and West Indies south to Venezuela and British Honduras; winters from the coast of Louisiana along the eastern coast of Central and South America to Argentina, and on the west coast of Africa.

Among the smallest and by far the most delicate and dainty of our sea-birds is the Least Tern. It inhabits sandy islands and barren shores. The south shore of the island of Martha's Vineyard has long been one of its chosen breeding-grounds. Along the stretch of beach extending about fifteen miles from Chappaquiddick to Squibnocket it has reared its young for many years on the 'Great Sands' in such exposed places as it finds suitable.

Chappaquiddick reeks of the sea. Water-fowl and shore birds loiter along its shores or rest upon or about its inner waters. Flotsam of the sea strews the outer beaches — wreck-timbers, the remains of great blackfish, sharks, skates and other sea-creatures. Cape Poge lighthouse, tall and white, rises from a bluff at the northeastern point of the island promontory to mark for mariners the position of this dangerous cape, and to show them the way to shelter in the harbor of Edgartown. From near Wasque Point, at the southernmost end of Chappaquiddick, the great South Beach stretches westward for miles as far as the eye can see until its outline is lost in the misty spray of the distant surf.

Here we visited, on July 15, 1908, one of the few breeding-places of the Least Tern then left in the northeastern United States. My companion and myself sailed from Edgartown across the shallows of Katama Bay, past a little fleet of 'quahoggers.' Steering our boat carefully over bars and along shallow channels, we landed on the beach. This is, in fact, the outer beach, for it lies open to the mighty seas of southeasters that drive in from six thousand miles of ocean. Here the Least Tern nests usually on the wide, open, sandy beach, on a neck of land or point between the ocean and some stream, bay or pond, in situations exposed to the full fury of the gale. This beach is composed entirely of shifting sand and small pebbles held along its low ridge by beach-grass and other sparse vegetation. Very high storm-tides break clear over it. Here, on the barren, seaward sands, in the blinding glare of the sun, without the least cover and exposed to every enemy, this graceful little bird, about the size of a robin, lays its eggs on the sand and rears its tender young.

As we landed that day, a few of the little terns began to fly about, thirty or forty feet above our heads, 'cheeping' complainingly; and by the time we had reached a wide, high, open part of the outer beach, bare of vegetation, fully thirty birds were flying overhead. With angry cries some of them shot down almost to our heads, fearful that their eggs and young were in imminent danger. Menaced indeed they were unless we used the utmost care as we walked, for

235

the color of both eggs and young so closely resembled the sandy beach or the scattered pebbles that it was exceedingly difficult to see them. For this reason they are ever in danger of being stepped on when people walk upon the beach. Usually there were but one or two eggs in each hollow, but occasionally three. The tiny young squatted or lay so flat on the sand that they hardly cast a shadow. Some were yellowish or about the color of the sand, while others were gray and mottled like a beach pebble. This is the simplest form of protective coloration, and as the young ones lie motionless on the least alarm, they are likely to be overlooked by hawks or other winged enemies. Least Terns breed mainly in colonies and a threatening hawk may be attacked by all the enraged parents at once. They follow it in a gyrating, screaming, assailing mob, individuals of which, constantly darting in, strike the enemy from every side.

In attempting to photograph these birds, we found that they were afraid of a device used in photographing birds (the umbrella blind); so we rigged up a less conspicuous place of concealment — with a camera bag, blind cloth and some sticks — and when they had become indifferent to this, I crept within. Near me were two downy young, just hatched and their down hardly dry, yet able to run about a little. Several other youngsters were near-by. As I lay there propped on my elbows, several of the parent birds flitted back and forth, and soon their cheeping cries changed to a musical 'pidink' (somewhat like the tinkling note of the Bobo-link). Then the mother of the two nearest little ones alighted near-by, and running up settled gently upon them and shaded them from the sun's hot rays. Next she turned her gaze upward and answered softly the tender notes of the male which circled overhead. Later he alighted and took her place in shading the young, while she flew away to fish and bathe. Far out over the sunny sea she arrested her flight, and for a few seconds remained poised in the air with beating wings; then suddenly and swiftly she plunged headlong into the waves. Presently she returned with a little 'sand-eel' which she gave to one of the tiny ones who ran to her for it. Again she flew away and plunged into the sea and then returned to her nestlings and relieved the male. She stood over them this time with wet, ruffled feathers, and seemed to shake off some drops of water on their little panting bodies, while she raised her wings a trifle to shade them from the sun. I watched this scene from a distance of about seven feet and photographed some of it, the male meantime standing near-by. He took flight, and she nestled over the chick nearest me, coaxing it gently farther away by using her bill and calling the other, which finally followed and settled by her side. Again the gentle twittering, and the male bird alighted with a tiny, bright, silvery fish. A little one stuck its head out from beneath the mother's wing, the father bird courteously passed the fish to the mother, and she fed the chick which begged with open mouth for it. Again the provider winged his way over the sunny sea to return with another fish. The little ones were now asleep under the breast of the mother. He offered her the fish; she refused it; he flew away, but soon alighted and politely proffered it again, only to be refused again. At last, having full assurance that his family needed no more, he swallowed the fish himself. Where shall we look to find a lovelier picture of happy, harmonious family-relations than that shown here on this sandy beach beside the roaring surf?

ROYAL TERN

Thalasseus maximus maximus (BODDAERT).

PLATE 7.

Other names: Big Striker; Redbill.

IDENTIFICATION. — Length 18 to 21 inches; spread 42 to 44 inches. Nearly size of Herring Gull but typical tern in form and carriage; slightly smaller than Caspian Tern, similarly crested, but with tail forked for half its length (Caspian for one-fourth only); bill more slender and usually lighter in color than Caspian.

BREEDING. — In colonies on sandy islands. *Nest:* A hollow in sand. *Eggs:* 1 or 2, rarely 3 or 4, white to dull yellow, with large and small markings of browns, grays, and black.

RANGE. — Breeds in the Bahamas, West Indies and on South Atlantic and Gulf coasts from Virginia to Texas, also on Pacific coast of Lower California and Mexico; winters from Florida, Louisiana, the Bahamas, and California south to Brazil, Peru, and Argentina.

The Royal Tern is one of the largest species of the family. In eastern North America it is second in size only to the Caspian Tern, which, because of a more deeply forked and longer tail, it nearly equals in length but not in size. This species nests in such massed colonies that in one of the Breton Island Reservations (Louisiana) Mr. Bent counted one hundred nests in a space four yards square. The birds on their nests sat so close together that they could hardly spread their wings without mutual interference. He says that the full black cap seems to be the courtship plumage, and the white forehead is the prevailing nesting plumage. Therefore most of the Royal Terns which wander north in summer may be expected to appear in the latter plumage. The species might be mistaken easily for the Caspian Tern, though it is of lighter and more slender build than the other, while its flight resembles more that of the much smaller Common Tern. It is not improbable that nomadic Royal Terns may reach the northern Atlantic States more frequently than records show.

CABOT'S TERN

Thalasseus sandvicensis acuflavidus (CABOT).

Other name: Sandwich Tern.

IDENTIFICATION. — Length 14 to 16 inches; spread about 34 inches. Slightly larger, paler, and relatively more slender than Common Tern; crown feathers lengthened into a flat crest; long slender *black bill with yellow tip*, and black feet, are diagnostic at close range.

BREEDING. — Similar to other terns.

RANGE. — Breeds on Atlantic and Gulf coasts from Virginia to Florida, Texas, British Honduras, the Bahamas, and West Indies; winters from Florida, the Bahamas and West Indies to Central America, Colombia and Brazil, and on the Pacific coasts of Oaxaca and Guatemala.

Cabot's Tern seems to be the friend and companion of the larger Royal Tern. It breeds in colonies of Royal Terns and lives amicably beside them. In form it appears slender and rather frail, but nevertheless it is strong, swift and daring, a master of the air and capable of battling successfully with wind and storm. Apparently it is not one of the vanishing species. Under protection it seems to be pushing its way northward. Not until recent years has it been known to breed in North Carolina and Virginia.

Cabot's Tern is easily recognized among the wintering birds of the Florida coasts, for its slender black bill with the clearly defined yellow tip is very unlike the heavier coral or orange-yellow bill of the slightly larger Royal Tern with which it is so often associated, and the bird in action gives one the impression of a slenderer, quicker-moving bird. Its habits do not differ materially from those of our other terns. Its nest is usually a mere apology for a home, a slight depression in the sand often without lining of any kind, in which two eggs, or sometimes only one, are laid as a full complement.

CASPIAN TERN

Hydroprogne caspia imperator (COUES).   PLATE 7.

Other names: Imperial Tern; Squawker; Redbill.

IDENTIFICATION. — Length 19 to 23 inches; spread 50 to 55 inches. Our largest tern; head with flat crest; very large bill, blood-red in breeding season, orange-red in winter; tail forked for about one-quarter its length (Royal for one-half); black of crown extends *below* eye in Caspian, *through* eye in Royal Tern; young not separable in the field except by size and heavier bill.

BREEDING. — Similar to other terns.

RANGE. — Breeds locally from Great Slave Lake to Lower California, on the Great Lakes, on the north shore of the Gulf of St. Lawrence, and on the coasts of Texas, Louisiana, Mississippi, South Carolina, and Virginia; winters from central California to Mexico and on the Atlantic and Gulf coasts from South Carolina to Mexico.

The Caspian Tern is the largest and most powerful of the terns. It might well be called the Imperial Tern, since it surpasses in strength the Royal Tern, nearest it in size. Mr. A. C. Bent says of it: 'Among the vast hordes of sea birds nesting in the great colonies of the southern Atlantic and Gulf coasts, this king of terns may be seen climbing the air on its long, strong wings, its big, red bill wide open, yelling out its loud raucous cry of defiance. As the dominant, ruling spirit in tern colonies it scorns the companionship of humbler fowl, holds itself aloof and lives a little apart from the others.'

In its great power of flight and the arrowy velocity of its dive from airy heights above the sea it resembles the great white Gannet of the North Atlantic. Formerly the Caspian Tern must have been rather common along the northern Atlantic coast, on its migrations to and from its summer home in Labrador, but now it is rather rare north of Virginia.

The Caspian Tern flies much like other terns, but on account of its large size, large bill and head, and short tail seems heavier and more gull-like than any of the smaller species. When engaged in fishing it flies swiftly and rather low over the water, with bill pointed downward; when resting on beach or bar it occasionally raises its black crest. Mr. Bent contrasts its note with that of the Royal Tern: 'The cry of the Caspian tern is entirely unlike that of the royal tern and quite different from that of any of the Laridae. Its ordinary note is a hoarse, croaking "*kraaa*" on a low key, loud, harsh and grating. A shorter note sounding like "*kow*" or "*kowk*" is often heard on its breeding-grounds, where it also utters, when angry, a loud, vehement, rasping cry of attack.'

The Caspian Tern feeds on small fish, and it takes various forms of surface-swimming aquatic life, also mussels; it is said to eat the eggs and young of other birds.

BLACK TERN

Chlidonias nigra surinamensis (GMELIN).   PLATE 8.

Other names: Short-tailed Tern; Semipalmated Tern; Sea Pigeon.

IDENTIFICATION. — Length 9 to 10¼ inches; spread about 25 inches. Almost as small as Least Tern; unmistakable in breeding plumage, with its typical tern form, and *black* head, neck and under parts and generally dark plumage; in fall is 'pied' blackish and white; young have back and tail darker than young Least Tern, and dark patch on either side of head.

BREEDING. — See below.

RANGE. — Breeds in interior from central eastern Alaska, central Manitoba, and Ontario south to California, Colorado, northern Missouri, and Tennessee, also to lake shores of northern Ohio, Pennsylvania and New York; winters from Surinam to Peru and Chile; migrates mainly through interior United States but occurs regularly along Atlantic coast in late summer and autumn, and rarely in spring.

The Black Tern is a summer resident of the western prairies with their shallow, reed-bordered sloughs, where its nest is often merely a floating mass of old reed stems and weeds, moored in the water by the growing vegetation, or at other times the nest is a hollow on top of a muskrat house, or a little heap of grasses on a waterlogged plank. The two or three eggs are like those of other terns in the variety of their coloration and markings. This species is quite gregarious and the nests are usually in colonies; in its migrations the birds gather in large flocks. Its winter home is on the coasts of South America, and it appears in considerable numbers on the South Atlantic and Gulf coasts of North America during its periodic migrations, but at all other times it is a bird of the interior.

The Black Tern is much more insectivorous than the Common Tern, and in its prairie home lives chiefly upon aquatic and land insects, including dragon-flies, moths, grasshoppers, locusts and other flying insects, most of which it catches on the wing, pursuing them in zigzag flight after the manner of the Nighthawk; also it follows the plow to pick up grubs and worms. On the Atlantic coast it often catches insects as they fly over fields and marshes. Fish, small mollusks, crustaceans and other small forms of aquatic life are taken.

NODDY TERN

Anoüs stolidus stolidus (LINNAEUS).

IDENTIFICATION. — Length about 16 inches; spread about 31 inches. Slightly larger than Common Terns; tail not forked as in most terns; forehead white shading into pale smoke gray on nape; *rest of body* and wings *fuscous;* bill black, long and slender.

BREEDING. — In colonies on islands. *Nest:* In a bush or low tree, sometimes on the ground, of sticks, grasses, etc. *Egg:* 1, buffy-white sparsely marked with rufous.

RANGE. — Breeds on the Dry Tortugas, Florida, and resident in the Bahamas and West Indies and from British Honduras to Venezuela, also on islands of the South Atlantic.

The Noddy resembles many of our terns in habits, but is absolutely unlike any in appearance. Instead of the usual forked tail, that of the Noddy is rounded, with the middle feathers the longest instead of shortest, and its coloration is a reverse of the common tern pattern of a black cap and light-colored body. As R. T. Peterson has noted, its effect is that of a photographic 'negative' of the usual tern picture.

Like the Eastern Sooty Tern, the Noddy Tern is limited in its breeding range in the United States to the Dry Tortugas southwest of the mainland of Florida in the Gulf of Mexico. It apparently does not ordinarily range very far from these islands during the breeding season, but it is sometimes carried considerable distances to the north by tropical hurricanes. It does not dive for its food like many of the terns but swoops down and picks up small fishes from the surface without checking its flight, or catches minnows which have been driven by larger fishes to jump from the water and skim the surface. Sometimes it lights upon the water and swims easily about pursuing its prey, or rests on the surface. — (J.B.M.)

BLACK SKIMMER

Rynchops nigra nigra LINNAEUS.

PLATE 7.

Other names: Cut-water; Scissor-bill; Shearwater.

IDENTIFICATION. — Length 16 to 20 inches; spread 42 to 50 inches. Larger than Common Tern; upper parts blackish except white forked tail; under parts white; bill long, *flattened vertically, red tipped with black,* and *lower mandible much longer than upper,* making this bird unique.

CALL NOTES. — Peculiar nasal barking or grunting sounds, often suggesting the yelping of hounds.

BREEDING. — In colonies on sand-flats or shell-ridges. *Eggs:* 3 to 5, white to pale greenish-blue or pale buff, boldly marked, laid in a hollow in the sand, pebbles, or shells.

RANGE. — Breeds on Atlantic coast from New Jersey to Florida, the Gulf coast, and Texas; winters from the Gulf coast to northern and eastern coasts of South America.

This most remarkable and highly specialized bird was undoubtedly one of the summer birds of Massachusetts when the Pilgrim Fathers settled in Plymouth. Fifteen years earlier Samuel de Champlain voyaged to Cape Cod and visited what is now Nauset Harbor in Orleans. Dr. C. P. Oles has translated Champlain's 'Voyages' and describes one of the birds observed there, as follows:

'We saw also a sea bird with a black beak, the upper part slightly aquiline, four inches long and in the form of a lancet; namely, the lower part representing the handle and the upper the blade, which is thin, sharp on both sides, and shorter by a third than the other, which circumstance is a matter of astonishment to many persons, who cannot comprehend how it is possible for the bird to eat with such a beak. It is of the size of a pigeon, the wings being very long in proportion to the body, the tail short, as also the legs, which are red; the feet being small and flat. The plumage on the upper part is gray-brown, and on the under parts pure white. They go always in flocks along the seashore, like the pigeons with us.'

Henry A. Purdie quoted old natives of Cape Cod to the effect that 'them cutwater or shearwater birds used to be with us summer times' as proof that the species was found early in the century on our shores. While its plumage was of no great value in the millinery market and its flesh was not valued as food, its eggs were prized on account of their large size. As Skimmers deposit their eggs without concealment on the open sands, the same fate overtook them along the northern coast of the Middle States, where they have been extirpated within recent times. I have never seen them in the North, but on the estuaries and sounds of the South have witnessed their flights and heard their barking cries, particularly in the dusk or at night.

In flight the Black Skimmer is a strikingly individualized bird. Its very long but strong wings give grace and power to its flight and its broad, forked tail lends additional buoyancy. It seems especially adapted for skimming low over the water. The peculiar structure of the bill fits it for picking up fish and crustaceans from the surface while in flight. A. H. Howell asserts that the bird skims over water so near shore and so shallow that its bill strikes the bottom 'every twenty feet or so,' jerking its head back in a most comical manner. If the bird desires to seize anything from the ground, it must turn its head to one side, but it wades into shallow pools and picks up small live fish out of the water. In the young birds the long, projecting lower mandible is not fully developed until after they have reached the flight stage. Therefore, until they are well able to fly, they can readily pick up food from the ground.

GREAT AUK
Plautus impennis (LINNAEUS).

Other names: Penguin; Garefowl; Wobble.

IDENTIFICATION. — Length 28 to 30 inches. Very large bill, as long as head; above black, sides of head and neck, chin and throat dark brown; lower plumage, oval spot before eye, and tips of secondaries white.

RANGE. — Formerly bred on Funk Island, Newfoundland, the Faroes, Orkneys, islands off coast of Iceland, and probably on the coast of Norway; in winter south to Massachusetts, possibly South Carolina and Florida, and in Europe to Denmark, France and Spain. Extinct since about 1844.

The Greak Auk was a large bird, comparing in size with the geese, which in America wandered in its migrations from Labrador and possibly from Greenland, to Florida. It was known to the early explorers and settlers as the 'Penguin,' though not even closely related to that bird, the chief resemblance being that, like the Penguin, the Auk was a flightless swimming bird. At first sight it seems remarkable that this bird could perform such extended migrations by swimming, but fish migrate similar distances and the Great Auk was a faster swimmer than the fish on which it fed.

A flightless bird has little chance against the weapons of civilized man, and so the bird disappeared from the seaward parts of the British Isles so long ago that few records remain of its presence there. The last specimen recorded at St. Kilda was killed in 1821; and the last at Eldey, off Iceland, in 1844. This ended the history of the bird in the Old World and, so far as we know, the history of the Great Auk.

In the meantime the same bird was found in America, where the end came even more quickly. Here, the relations of the white man with this bird began when adventurous French sailors commenced fishing on the banks of Newfoundland, soon after that island's discovery in 1497. As these birds bred on outlying reef-guarded islands, they had not been troubled much on their breeding-grounds by the coast Indians, who at that time had a plentiful supply of other birds along the coast and did not need to take venturesome voyages in their frail bark canoes; but the white fishermen used these birds to provision their vessels and the young were taken for bait. These men, landing at Funk Island, the birds' principal breeding-place off the coast of Newfoundland, killed them with clubs or surrounded them and drove them aboard their boats, where they were killed, taken aboard ship and salted down in barrels. Later, as the demand for feather-beds grew in the United States, the birds were slaughtered by thousands for their feathers alone. Stone enclosures or pounds were built into which the birds when surrounded were driven and there killed with clubs; they were then thrown into great kettles of hot water to scald them so that the feathers would come off easily. Many were salted down, and merchants at Bonavista, Newfoundland, sold them to the poor in the place of pork.

Thus the uncounted hosts of the Great Auk went to their death, and the bird, according to Mr. Michael Carroll of Bonavista, disappeared from Funk Island, its greatest breeding-place and its last refuge in America, between 1830 and 1840. There are about eighty specimens of the birds, about seventy eggs, and many bones and more or less complete skeletons, preserved in the museums of the world.

Little is known about the habits of the Great Auk. The Auk swam with head lifted, but neck drawn in, ready to dive instantly at the first alarm. On its island home it stood or rather sat erect, as its legs were far back. Its notes were gurgles and harsh croaks. It laid but one egg.

RAZOR – BILLED AUK

Alca torda LINNAEUS.   PLATE 3.

Other names: Tinker; Ice-bird; Sea Crow.

IDENTIFICATION. — Length 16 to 18½ inches; spread 25 to 27 inches. Head and upper parts black, under parts white; throat black in summer, white in winter; resemble murres but with compressed, hooked bill; stouter, with larger head and longer tail; vertical white line across black bill; tail often cocked up when swimming.

BREEDING. — In colonies on sea-islands. *Egg:* 1, laid on bare rock or in fissure, bluish- or greenish-white to yellowish, spotted and blotched with browns.

RANGE. — Breeds from southern Greenland and middle Labrador to Newfoundland and New Brunswick (Bay of Fundy), formerly to Maine; winters from southern Labrador and Ontario to New York (Long Island); also found in Europe.

After a long easterly winter storm, in clearing weather when the dark blue wintry seas are stirred by the gusts of a brisk northwester, we may find the hardy 'Razor-bill' riding at ease off the storm-beaten ledges of the New England coast. It swims lightly, swiftly and easily with head sometimes raised but commonly drawn in and often the tail is cocked jauntily upward. It flies with the head held close to the body and level with it and, like murres, it tips from side to side in flight, showing its breast and back alternately. Like auks, murres and guillemots in general it employs its wings in under-water flight, raising them as it dives and using them either partly closed like fins or not quite as fully opened as in flight. It is an expert diver going down to great depths and swimming for long distances under water.

On March 12, 1922, on the beach at Nantucket I surprised a 'Razor-bill' apparently asleep on some seaweed close to the water. In my attempt to catch the bird it menaced me with open bill, flapping wings and strident cries, but before I could seize it, it plunged into the water and swam and dived, opening its wings to nearly full length when under water and moving them backward and forward. The bird moved fast, but the wings were not flapped so rapidly as when used in the air. I could not see the feet; apparently they were hidden by the tail.

Mr. Harrison Lewis sends me the following notes on this species: 'Razor-billed Auks are still quite numerous on some parts of the Canadian Labrador coast, near Cape Whittle. In this region they breed upon islands, where their eggs are deposited in crevices in the solid rock, or under protecting boulders, so that they are usually difficult to reach. Where many birds are incubating together, however, some eggs are almost always in easily accessible situations.

'During the period of incubation, those Auks which are not sitting upon the eggs often stand in groups on rocks from which they can obtain a good view of the surroundings. Upon the approach of an intruder these birds fly away and alight upon the water. Probably, in doing so, they give warning to their incubating mates, for the latter usually scramble hurriedly out from their rocky homes and fly away to join the others. Occasionally, however, an incubating Razor-bill will remain on its egg, in some secure situation, despite the approach of a man to the nearest possible point. In such cases the bird usually faces its unwelcome visitor and opens its mouth very wide.'

'Razor-bills' are staunch and hardy sea-birds, and although many of them in autumn follow the last flights of the scoters as far south as the New England coast, they commonly keep well offshore, even in midwinter. Probably they are far more common off our coasts in winter than the number reported by landsmen would lead us to believe.

This is another of the birds that formerly were abundant from Maine to Labrador and which man's rapacity has reduced in all this territory to a mere remnant of its former numbers. Its habit of nesting in rifts and holes and hiding its eggs in the crevices of inaccessible cliffs has saved it thus far to posterity.

The Razor-billed Auk moves southward to Massachusetts, and occasionally to New York, mainly in November and December, and is most common off our coasts in December, January and February. In March and April it moves north again to its breeding-grounds, migrating mainly at a considerable distance from our shores.

This bird feeds often in the ocean, many miles from land, and its food consists of small fish, crustaceans and other marine organisms.

ATLANTIC MURRE

Uria aalge aalge (PONTOPPIDAN).

Other names: Common Murre; Foolish Guillemot.

IDENTIFICATION. — Length about 17 inches; spread about 30 inches. Slender pointed bill easily distinguishes this bird from Razor-billed Auk or Atlantic Puffin, and less easily from Brünnich's Murre, all which are black or blackish above and white below; larger than Black Guillemot which is black above and below in summer, pied black, gray and white in winter; much larger than Dovekie.

BREEDING. — Similar to Razor-billed Auk but eggs more 'pear-shaped.'

RANGE. — Breeds from southern Greenland, southern Labrador, and the Gulf of St. Lawrence south to Nova Scotia; winters south to Maine and Massachusetts; also found in the Eastern Hemisphere.

Bonaventure Island lies in the Gulf of St. Lawrence only a few miles offshore from the picturesque village of Percé in eastern Quebec. Its slightly tilted strata of red conglomerate alternating with narrow bands of soft sandstone rise from pebbly beaches on the west side of the island, but on the east the weather-worn cliffs drop abruptly a sheer three hundred feet to the restless waters of the gulf, and these colorful cliffs are the nesting-places of thousands of great white Gannets, a few hundred Herring Gulls and dainty little Atlantic Kittiwakes, an occasional Black Guillemot and Atlantic Puffin, and several small colonies of Razor-billed Auks and Atlantic Murres. As one sails past the towering red cliffs their narrow ledges are white with the nesting Gannets, the air is filled with gracefully sailing birds and there is an almost deafening din from their raucous cries. Flocks of smaller birds, black or blackish above and with white breasts, rise from the water and after pattering wildly across the waves, finally get well under way with their feet trailing behind where their tails ought to be. Or we see, on one of the narrower ledges too small for the Gannets to use, a row of queer upright black figures, which suddenly face about and show their white under parts before taking hurried flight, when their small wings beat with astonishing rapidity to support their heavy bodies as they seek safety on the open sea. As they pass near-by, the slender pointed bills and sooty-black upper plumage, head and throat distinguish them from their neighbors the Razor-billed Auks, which are a clear black and white, and we know these birds to be Atlantic Murres.

Lying on a sloping ledge near the top of the great cliff I have often watched the Murres coming in from their fishing-trips to their nesting-crannies, formed by the erosion of a thin stratum of soft sandstone between harder layers of conglomerate. Their wings are so small in proportion to their plump bodies that they have to start against the wind in taking off from the water, or run and flap for some distance before they can rise. Often they clear the crest of one wave only to splash awkwardly into the next, when they must start their run once more. When well under way they travel with considerable speed, so that when about to alight on the almost vertical cliffs they must come in with body erect, webbed feet trailing, and wings furiously 'back-pedaling' to avoid too violent a landing. Frequently as they near the cliff their courage apparently gives out and they swing off into a wide circle and try the landing again time after time before successfully negotiating it.

When one finally alights there is an amusing little ceremony of greeting between the newcomer and its neighbors already on the ledge. Facing each other, two birds extend their bills until the tips almost meet, then bow repeatedly to each other before turning to other birds and continuing the performance. On taking off from the ledge the birds plunge downwards at a steep angle until the wings get properly functioning, and then make off at good speed.

At close range it is sometimes possible to pick out a Murre with a white ring around the eye and a line extending back a short distance from the eye. This is the form known as the 'Ringed Murre,' which is now believed to be merely a color-phase of the Atlantic Murre, though once thought to be a separate species.

The Atlantic Murre formerly bred in immense numbers on the coasts and islands of the North Atlantic, but it has been reduced to an insignificant remnant of its former hosts by the insane policy of slaughter and plunder which has possessed many people in the United States and some of their Canadian neighbors ever since the settlement of the country. While occasionally reported on the southern New England coast, it has become a decidedly rare species there. Doubtless most of the birds winter well offshore, where it is more commonly found than near land. — (J.B.M.)

BRÜNNICH'S MURRE

Uria lomvia lomvia (LINNAEUS).   PLATE 3.

Other name: Thick-billed Guillemot.

IDENTIFICATION. — Length 18 to 19¾ inches; spread 24½ to 32 inches. Distinguished from Atlantic Murre only by thicker, shorter bill and (at very close range) the light flesh-colored stripe on mandible near gape.

BREEDING. — Similar to Atlantic Murre.

RANGE. — Breeds on the eastern Arctic islands, Hudson Strait, Labrador, and northern Greenland south to the Gulf of St. Lawrence and Magdalen Islands; winters from southern Greenland and Husdon Bay to New York (Long Island); also found in the Eastern Hemisphere.

Along the bleak, desolate, rocky and inhospitable shores of the North Atlantic and Arctic oceans, from the Gulf of St. Lawrence to northern Greenland, Brünnich's Murre in migration or in summer is one of the commonest of the water-fowl. It bred formerly in countless thousands on the coasts and islands of Newfoundland and Labrador, but now it is found in such immense numbers only in its far northern retreats where the white man rarely goes.

The egg of a murre is more or less flattened on the sides and pointed at the small end, so that when it is disturbed or displaced, it tends to roll in a circle and stay on the ledge where it lies. When the birds are suddenly alarmed, many eggs are displaced, nevertheless, by the owners themselves and pushed off the rock and into the sea. A murre does not sit upon its single egg like most birds, but stands erect over it like a penguin and pokes it into place with the bill.

Murres can dive at the flash of a gun and are difficult to kill at long range. They use their wings for under-water swimming, at which they are as expert as a loon.

Not many birds of this species arrive before late November off the southern New England coast, where they seem most numerous usually in January and February. Commonly they remain well offshore, but sometimes, particularly during severe easterly storms, they come into open estuaries. They frequent waters off both rocky and sandy shores. They are found most commonly on the coasts of the Maritime Provinces, Maine, and northern Massachusetts, and more rarely on the shores of Long Island. By March they are again moving northward, and in May and June they reach the farthest northern points at which they are known to breed. In some winters a few of these birds are found scattered about the interior as far or farther south than the Great Lakes. Such a dispersal to the interior is believed to be caused in some cases by storms; but Mr. J. H. Fleming gives good reasons for the belief that sometimes the Murres are driven out of Hudson Bay by the freezing of the surface, and so fly southward seeking open water, many of them becoming exhausted and coming to earth in their fruitless search. There have been record flights in the late fall on the lower lakes (Erie and Ontario) when most of the birds die, seemingly of starvation.

245

DOVEKIE

Alle alle (LINNAEUS).

PLATE 3.

Other names. Little Auk; Pine-knot; Knotty; Ice-bird; Little Ice-bird.

IDENTIFICATION. — Length 7¼ to 9 inches; spread 13¾ to 15½ inches. Extremely small size, black back and white under parts, and insignificant tail, distinguish this, the smallest winter sea-fowl on the eastern coast.

BREEDING. — On sea-cliffs or slopes of loose rocks. *Egg:* 1, laid in crevice or horizontal cleft, usually unmarked pale greenish-blue.

RANGE. — Breeds on the north coasts and islands of Greenland, Iceland, Spitzbergen, and Novaya Zemlya; winters from southern Greenland to New York (Long Island), and casually to South Carolina; also from the North Sea to the Azores and Madeira.

In January, 1878, during a great freeze in the north I was on a steamer off the Virginia capes, bound for Florida. We were far offshore as the captain was making a good offing in passing Hatteras, for a great easterly storm was brewing which soon burst in full force and smashed our steering-gear, so that we lay for four hours in the trough of a mighty sea, exposed to the full fury of the cyclone. Before the storm broke, hundreds of Dovekies could be seen scattered on the heaving seas. This was the first time that I had seen the little things alive, and their activities impressed themselves upon my memory. As the steamer's bow approached, some of the birds dipped forward and with partly opened wings flew diagonally downward into the depths. Others pattered along on the surface, some flying from wave-crest to wave-crest and 'skittering' over or through their tops; while still others fluttered into the air and flew along for a short distance, only to alight again or to dip below the surface. All was excitement in their little companies as they fled from the great black, smoking monster, as it rushed furiously on. The impression made on my youthful mind by the sight of these little birds at home far out on that wild sea in the face of a coming storm has never been effaced.

The fishermen call Dovekies 'Pine Knots' or 'Knotties' to indicate their extreme hardiness, for they are indeed as 'tough as a pine knot.' They are rarely numerous near shore, but offshore they fly in small flocks with quick wing-beats close to the waves, or else rest on the sea.

Dovekies seem to be able to weather an ordinary gale, but now and then a protracted storm rising to hurricane force exhausts them and drives many ashore and even into the interior, where some alight in streams or in ponds if these are open. If the ponds are covered with ice, the birds finally fall spent on the snow, ice or frozen ground, from which it is believed they never rise again, since many have been picked up dead under such circumstances.

This Little Auk is a godsend to the Eskimo on its return home to the Arctic regions at the advent of spring. The Eskimos welcome its arrival with joy as we welcome the return of the Bluebird, for its coming means to them not only the recurrence of the vernal season but often the transition from starvation to plenty. Captain Donald B. MacMillan, who has seen, several times, the return of the birds after the dark winter in the North, in his 'Four Years in the White North,' graphically describes the scene as follows: 'But what is that great, pulsating, musical note which seems to fill all space? Now loud and clear, now diminishing to a low hum, the sound proclaims the arrival of the true representative of the bird-life of the Arctic, the most interesting and most valuable of all, the bird which means so much to the Smith Sound native — the dovekie or little auk (*Alle alle*). The long dark winter has at last passed away. The larder open

246

to all is empty. The sun is mounting higher into the heavens day by day. Now and then a seal is seen sunning himself at his hole. The Eskimos are living from hand to mouth. And then that glad cry, relieving all anxiety for the future, bringing joy to every heart, "*Ark-pood-e-ark-suit! Ark-pood-e-ark-suit!*" (Little auks! Little auks!).'

Thus the Eskimos hail these — the first small birds of spring. They come in clouds, like the driving snow, and fill the air with the uproar of their wings. The Eskimos kill them by thousands. The children, expert in stone throwing, knock down many. Some are eaten raw. An Eskimo boy will pick up the quivering body of one of these little birds, tear open its breast and eat the warm and bleeding creature right out of its skin, leaving little else than skin and feathers.

I have heard Captain MacMillan describe the common method of catching Dovekies. An Eskimo woman ascends the steep and rocky slope where the Dovekies have their nests, sits in a hole among the rocks and sweeps with a long-handled dip-net, catching birds as they fly past, as a child catches butterflies. Sometimes as a flock passes she will get several birds at one sweep with her fifteen-inch net. Thousands of these birds are *cached* in the frozen ground to be used in winter for food, and many of the skins are made into birdskin shirts. The eggs also are useful as food, and the children squeeze into the crevices and holes in rocky hillsides to collect them. All this has no noticeable permanent effect on the great abundance of this bird, and as it nests in the Far North where the destructive white man is a rarity, its future seems secure. The Dovekie has many enemies besides man. The Arctic fox seeks its nest and no doubt sometimes catches it there. The Glaucous Gull, the Raven and the Gyrfalcon take their share. The white whale catches it on the sea and no doubt it has other submarine enemies, among them seals and large fish.

Probably Dovekies begin to leave their northernmost breeding-grounds in late July and early August, but many never go much farther south than the edge of the ice pack, and some remain in southern Greenland. Occasionally a few appear on the New England coast in September, but they are seen rarely in abundance until the latter part of November. They migrate at sea, move southward slowly, and seldom appear in great numbers near shore unless driven in by severe storms. Ordinarily they do not winter much south of New England, though they have been found rarely as far south as Florida. They begin to move northward in February, and the migration is at its height in March. In these two months they begin to appear in numbers at their homes beyond the Arctic circle, but they do not reach northern Greenland until about May 15.

BLACK GUILLEMOT

Cepphus grylle grylle (LINNAEUS).

PLATE 3.

Other names: White-winged Guillemot; White Guillemot; Sea Pigeon.

IDENTIFICATION. — Length 12 to 14 inches; spread about 23 inches. Size of our smallest ducks; in summer all black except large white patch on wing *coverts*, red feet and red lining to mouth (often shown in display); in winter irregularly pied black, gray and white, but distinguished by small size, slender pointed bill, and clearly defined white wing-patch as in summer; shorter neck than wintering grebes; young are darker than winter adults.

BREEDING. — On sea-islands or shore-cliffs. *Eggs:* 1 or 2, laid on bare ground, in a hole or crevice, white to bluish- or greenish-white, spotted with browns and lilac.

RANGE. — Breeds from central Labrador south to Nova Scotia and Maine; winters from Cumberland Sound south to Cape Cod and perhaps to New Jersey; also occurs in Eastern Hemisphere.

The sinuous coast of Maine is a little over thirteen hundred miles in length, so many are the islands and so irregular and deeply indented are the rock-ribbed shores. The deep bays, coves and inlets offer some of the finest harbors in the land, and offshore lie scores of little rocky islands and dozens of low sandy islets, many of which are in summer the nurseries of sea-birds. Some of these sea-girt islands, some forested more or less with spruce and fir, are frequented by the handsome little Black Guillemot. Their rocky formation and the loose blocks of stone and boulders piled upon them afford ideal nesting-sites for a bird that seeks a secure place to hide its eggs.

There, above ordinary high-water mark, the 'Sea Pigeon' makes its home, well back under some great stone; or it inhabits the rifts of bare ledges far out at sea. The little domicile requires no furnishing, as the bird is a primitive cave dweller, its roof the sheltering rock, overlooking the heaving sea. Here in their little caves the downy young are fed, and from their rocky fastnesses they go out into a world of water and of sky. Often during cruises along the Maine coast I have watched the Guillemots flying back and forth between their great storehouse, the sea, and their nest-holes in crevices and little caves in the rocks.

Now and then you may see the male in his courtship pursuing the female. He is an ardent lover, but she is coy. She dives and he pursues her. She comes to the surface and he is close at her heels. She swims away and he follows, running and splashing along the water. She flies and he chases after, until finally she seems to accept his attentions as if to be rid of his importunities. The mating over, they hunt for a suitable cavity as remote and inaccessible to their enemies as possible. They are gregarious, and often may be seen in groups sitting on the rocks close to the sea. Normally in many parts of their range they nested in large colonies, but their eggs have been taken for food so constantly throughout the season that the numbers of the species are few compared with its former abundance. In Maine where many island colonies are protected the Guillemots have a better chance for undisturbed nesting; and as they frequently find crevices where their eggs and young are inaccessible, their numbers have not been so reduced as have those of other species whose nesting-places are more conspicuous.

In flight this species progresses swiftly, usually close to the water, its white wing-patches flashing in the sunlight and its bright red feet extended behind. On the water it rides as buoyantly as a Wood Duck. When approached by a boat, it has a trick of lowering the head quickly and repeatedly as if about to go under, but it is more likely to fly than to dive. In rising from the water, which it does easily, it aids itself by striking the surface with its feet. In diving and swimming under water it uses its wings more than its feet and seems to fly rapidly under water.

In New England the Black Guillemot may be looked for in winter (and even in summer) on rock-bound coasts. It leaves its breeding-places when the young are able to care for themselves. Many of this species winter only slightly south of their summer range. It commonly drifts southward along the Maine coast from September until late December. Early in March it turns northward, and its numbers in New England waters begin to decrease.

Small fishes, little mussels and other small shellfish, crustaceans, marine worms and insects seem to form the principal food of the species, but Selous asserts that he has seen it eating seaweed.

ATLANTIC PUFFIN

Fratercula arctica arctica (LINNAEUS).

PLATE 3.

Other names: Sea-parrot; Paroquet; Perroquet.

IDENTIFICATION. — Length 11½ to 13½ inches; spread 21 to 24 inches. A small 'chunky' water-bird that floats high on the water; large head; black above, white below, cheeks white in summer, gray in winter; bill large, compressed, 'triangular,' yellow with red tip in breeding season, smaller and without red and yellow in winter; flight rapid with quick wing-beats of rather small wings for such a plump body.

BREEDING. — In colonies on sea-islands. *Eggs:* 1 or 2, dull white indistinctly spotted and splashed with brown, in a burrow in the soil, or under a rock.

RANGE. — Breeds from southern Greenland and Ungava Bay south to Nova Scotia, Bay of Fundy, and Maine; winters south to Massachusetts and New Jersey; also in Eastern Hemisphere.

'Way down east' on Machias Seal Island, off the easternmost part of the Maine coast, lies the nearest real refuge and breeding-place of the Atlantic Puffin to the United States. Here where the sea dashes heavily against jagged rocks, and the wind blows the white spray high and far, the Puffin now makes its last stand near our shores.

The serio-comic appearance of the little feathered clown is laughable. The bright and handsome colors of its nuptial array are forgotten in contemplation of its peculiar and amazing appearance. Its bright little eyes seem spectacled, while its parrot-like bill like a great, highly colored Roman nose is masked by an outer coating which is mostly shed at the end of the breeding season. The bird stands erect like a little soldier, its red splay feet slightly straddled and planted firmly on the rock, resting not on its tail and tarsi, but standing up high and clear. Add to its ludicrous clownish appearance a voice of deep, sepulchral tones 'full of the deepest feeling' and capable of harsh croakings, and we have a character in feathers — a solemnly comical Mr. Punch among birds.

On the wing the Puffin buzzes about as if upon important business. It tumbles out of its hole, flies down and into the sea, flies around under water, flies out again, and comes back to the rocks, its great 'red nose' pointing the way, its little 'saber-like' wings beating the air like a threshing-machine and its red feet spread out behind. When it comes up from the depths to find that it is being overtaken by a steamboat, it is very likely to 'lose its head' and show the most comical kind of apprehension and indecision. It dips its head under water as if to dive, then raises it and tries to fly, gives this up and finally dives through a wave, comes flying out on the other side and dives again until finally it has blundered and floundered out of the way. When under water it seems to use its wings mainly for progression and its feet chiefly for steering, as it does when flying in the air. The Puffin's wings are so small that it appears to have difficulty in rising from the water, except in a breeze; but they move so fast that it can fly with great rapidity once in the air. On the surface it swims well.

The Puffin usually nests in colonies. A famous one is that on Perroquet Island, visited by many ornithologists since Audubon (1840), whose description is vivid. The burrows are dug in a steep slope or bank of some island and carried inward, downward and upward for an arm's length or more. In some cases the burrow curves so that the nest is close beneath the entrance hole. The nest consists of a little dead grass with sometimes a few feathers. In reaching into a nest I have found gloves very useful, as the Puffin often is at home and will bite and scratch like a cat, or as much like one as a bird can. Its claws and beak are sharp and strong.

Mr. Harrison F. Lewis kindly sends me the following notes on the erratic behavior of the Atlantic Puffin on its breeding-grounds:

'Owing to its grotesque appearance, the Puffin is a most amusing and interesting bird to watch. At Perroquet Island, near Bradore, Canadian Labrador, I found that if I sat nearly motionless, even though fully exposed to view, Puffins at a little distance soon acted as if quite unconscious of my presence. . . . Every few minutes an incubating bird pattered out of its burrow, often apparently for no purpose but to relax its cramped muscles, obtain a breath of fresh air, and view the surroundings. After issuing from the burrow the bird usually stood up very straight, stretched itself, and fluttered its wings for a moment. One could readily imagine it yawning and complaining of the tiresomeness of incubation.

'If I walked slowly toward a Puffin perched on a rock, the bird often alternated for a considerable time between the desire to escape by flight and the desire to avoid the exertion required to get under way. It looked at the advancing human being, apparently decided that it had better depart, crouched for a spring into the air, then at the last instant seemed to find the necessary effort too great, and relaxed to watch the intruder again. As the source of trouble continued to advance, its fears temporarily gained the ascendancy over its indolence, and the performance was repeated. After several repetitions of this behavior the bird finally pitched forward into headlong, clumsy flight.

'Considerable numbers of Puffins were almost always resting on the water near Perroquet Island. I found that if I approached these slowly and quietly, by gently sculling a small rowboat, their curiosity impelled them to swim slowly toward me. When within twelve or fifteen feet of the boat, however, they were likely to be seized with fear and fly hurriedly away.'

Puffins are very hardy birds and do not commonly migrate very far south of their breeding-range. They appear during the latter half of October off the coast of Massachusetts in very small numbers and are believed to go northward in March. Only rarely are they found as far south as Long Island.

Atlantic Puffins feed largely on small fish and other forms of marine life. Doubtless also the powerful bill enables them to crush small crustaceans and mollusks as do the Tufted Puffins on the Pacific coast.

Order Columbiformes. Pigeon-like Birds.

WHITE-CROWNED PIGEON

Columba leucocephala LINNAEUS.

IDENTIFICATION. — Length 13 to 14 inches; spread about 23 inches. General color bluish-slate, crown white in male, drab in female; resembles domestic dove in appearance.

BREEDING. — In colonies. *Nest:* In shrubs or low trees, a crude stick platform. *Eggs:* 2, glossy white.

RANGE. — Breeds in southern Florida Keys, the Bahamas, West Indies, Cozumel Island and islands off coast of Central America to Panama.

The White-crowned Pigeon is a regular summer resident of the Florida Keys, formerly a very abundant bird but now uncommon and local in distribution. It was considered an excellent article of food and was destroyed in great numbers, especially during the breeding season, when the adults were easily shot and the larger squabs were taken, leaving the younger ones to die of starvation. It nested in great colonies, like the Passenger Pigeon, but the remoteness of its breeding-grounds has preserved it in diminished numbers, and now enforcement of conservation measures may keep it from extinction.

The White-crowned Pigeon feeds upon berries and seeds principally, and after the breeding season moves about from place to place in search of an ample food supply. It is occasionally seen near Cape Sable, Florida, in winter, but apparently does not breed there. It almost always travels in flocks, and is most partial to the coastal regions and to the small mangrove islands of the Keys, the Bahamas, and the islands bordering the Caribbean Sea. — (J.B.M.)

ROCK DOVE

Columba livia livia GMELIN.

Other names: Pigeon; Street Pigeon; Blue Rock.

IDENTIFICATION. — Length about 11 inches. Introduced species. The common street pigeon of our cities and towns, escaped from domestication, and showing great variation in color.

The Rock Dove was domesticated in the Old World and introduced into the New. The bird normally bred in caves in rocky precipitous cliffs, and in holes or under overhanging rocks, and was most common near the seashore in localities where caves hollowed out by the sea in great cliffs were numerous. On such cliffs along the coast and on rocky islands of western Europe the Gray Sea Eagle may build her lofty eyrie, the young Peregrine Falcon may nestle on the ledges, or gulls and guillemots may rear their broods — while the dim caves below resound with the cooing of the Rock Doves. In a state of nature all varieties of domestic doves tend to revert to a type resembling the original Rock Dove. Some of those on our streets resemble this dove very closely, but many have lost the white rump. These are the birds known as Blue Rocks, formerly used in pigeon shooting at traps. The species was kept in domestication by the Greeks and Romans, and the birds were used as carriers of messages in very early times.

Not very long after the settlement of this country, doves and other poultry were brought here from England; later, as cities, offering nesting-places about buildings, were established, many doves left the premises of their owners and became habituated to a life of freedom, and their offspring are virtually wild birds. These birds often feed with domesticated birds and sometimes mate and nest with them. Those domiciled in cities are more tame, and some individuals will perch on the shoulder or eat from the hand of anyone accustomed to feed them, but they still possess the normal timidity of the race, and any sudden noise like the firing of a gun, or the backfire of an automobile, or any quick and unusual movement on the part of a spectator is sufficient cause for quick and startled flight. The strutting, billing, and cooing of the male when mating are familiar to everyone. Doves are believed to mate for life, but when one of a mated pair dies, the survivor will mate again. The apparent affection that the mated pair bestow on each other, and the solicitude and loving care with which the young are fed and tended by both parents, have secured the dove an established place in literature, and the bird has become the emblem of peace, notwithstanding the fierce and bloody combats which occur between the males which sometimes result in the complete exhaustion or death of one of the combatants. In the stone, brick and concrete buildings of cities, the doves find sheltered recesses such as occur in the native cliffs of their wild progenitors, and here they build their nests, high up on ledges, under windows, verandas, or porticos, under bridges or wherever they can find reasonable safety, and support and shelter for their nests about any large structure erected by man.

EASTERN MOURNING DOVE

Zenaidura macroura carolinensis (LINNAEUS). PLATE 36.

Other names: Wild Pigeon; Turtle Dove; Carolina Dove; Wood Dove.

IDENTIFICATION. — Length 11 to 13 inches; spread 17 to 19 inches. Length about that of small Sharp-shinned Hawk, smaller than Domestic or Rock Dove; brown head with rather long pointed tail and wings, which have a bluish cast, tail feathers with white tips conspicuous when tail is spread; small black spot below ear coverts; usually rises with twittering whistle from ground in open land, grain-fields, buckwheat fields or weedy gardens and flies swiftly like a small hawk.

NOTE. — A mournful *ooah-cooo-cooo-coo.*

BREEDING. — Almost anywhere. *Nest:* In tree, vine or shrub, occasionally on ground, usually a platform of sticks. *Eggs:* 2, glossy white.

RANGE. — Breeds from Nova Scotia, New Brunswick, southern Maine, Ontario, Michigan and Wisconsin west to eastern Kansas and Iowa and south to the Gulf coast and the Bahamas; winters from Massachusetts, southern Michigan and Iowa southward throughout its range and casually to Panama.

From the meeting of the waters under Punkatasset Height, where the Assabet comes in, the Musketaquid slowly flows on its winding way by the historic grounds of the 'Concord fight' and then, flanked by wide meadows, passes on down to the bridge at Carlisle. With the first blush of day on still May mornings, up from the river valley comes the saddened cooing of the Mourning Doves. All along the valley the sad-voiced birds roam, as they did in the days when Thoreau found a nest in Sleepy Hollow. Formerly this gentle dove was abundant in that part of southern New England best suited to its needs, but it had decreased so much in numbers in the early part of the twentieth century that Massachusetts led the way in 1908 by giving it perpetual protection under the law, to save it from extirpation. Soon its numbers began slowly to increase. Many states now give the species entire protection, and in the Northern States it is protected by Federal law also.

Mourning Doves may be said to belong to the open country. They feed mostly on the ground in grass-fields, gardens, or grain-fields, and are not seen often among forested hills, except in the clearings, though when frightened they often retire to the woods, and sometimes nest there. Nests have been built in peculiar situations, such as on a stump, in a tree cavity, on haystacks, and cliffs, on brush piles, rocks, woodpiles, fence corners, or even on a shed roof, but usually trees are preferred when available. Nests in trees are built mainly on horizontal branches, but often in crotches at heights of five to fifty feet.

The Eastern Mourning Dove like the Turtle Dove is very affectionate; mated pairs seem to remain together during the entire year. The male does not cease his attentions to the female when the eggs are deposited, but often brings sticks and straws for the nest and takes his share of the duties of incubation, feeding and brooding. As a rule, after incubation commences until the young are hatched, one or the other of the parents is continually on the nest. When the adult bird is frightened from the nest by an intruder, it may drop to the ground and imitate so well a wing-broken bird as to lead the enemy away, or it may alight on the ground and flap its wings to draw attention. This is most likely to happen after the young are hatched, and in some cases both parents join in the ruse.

A common performance of the bird during the mating and nesting season is thus well described by W. B. Barrows. 'An individual leaves its perch on a tree, and, with vigorous and sometimes noisy flapping (the wings seeming to strike each other above the back), rises obliquely to a height of a hundred feet or more, and then on widely extended and motionless wings glides back earthward in one or more sweeping curves. Usually the wings during this gliding flight are carried somewhat below the plane of the body, in the manner of a soaring yellowlegs or sandpiper, and sometimes the bird makes a complete circle or spiral before again flapping its wings, which it does just before alighting.' It may glide downward in this way until very near the ground, but more often the soaring dove alights on a limb at a height of twenty feet or more. Its soaring flight increases its resemblance to a small hawk (a resemblance often noted on account of the shape of the wings and the speed of its flight). This peculiar evolution is sometimes repeated several times at brief intervals.

Mourning Doves will live and nest in very dry regions, but they prefer the neighborhood of water, and if not nesting near water they fly long distances to it to drink and bathe, both morning and night. Travelers in the desert in their search for water have learned to follow the morning and evening flight of the doves.

The young of Mourning Doves are fed at first on 'pigeon milk' secreted by the adults, later they are fed worms, insects and seeds. The adults feed very largely on seeds and grains.

Among the grains, buckwheat seems to be their favorite. They are known to eat corn and peas, but on the other hand they destroy enormous quantities of the seeds of weeds.

PASSENGER PIGEON

Ectopistes migratorius (LINNAEUS).   PLATE 36.

Other name: Wild Pigeon.

IDENTIFICATION. — Length 15 to 18 inches; spread 23 to 25 inches. A beautifully colored long-tailed pigeon, considerably larger than Mourning Dove.

RANGE. — Formerly bred from the Canadian Provinces to Kansas, Kentucky, and New York, wintering principally from Arkansas and North Carolina southward; *now extinct*, the last known specimen dying in 1914.

The Passenger Pigeon was a peculiarly graceful and elegant bird, formed for powerful, swift, long-continued flight. It was a native of the great forested region of eastern North America.

It nested in the unbroken forests which covered the land before the advent of the white man, and it fed mainly on the fruits of trees and shrubs. The location of the enormous and wonderful breeding colonies or pigeon cities and the extensive roosts was decided by temporary abundance of mast, such as beechnuts or acorns, either on the trees or beneath them on the ground. The pigeoners believed that the small flocks which first appeared at the sites of these colonies were scouts that reported to the main body, which soon followed. On the appearance of the birds at a nesting-place, they were already mating or mated.

Most of the courtship of the pigeons was conducted in the trees, for the Passenger Pigeon was essentially an arboreal bird. Its legs were short and its tail long and it was not much given to strutting in the manner of the domestic dove. Its usual pose in the trees was quite erect, and in courting the male made use of his vigorous half-closed wings, which were flapped toward the female of his choice. On reaching her he frequently hooked his head over her neck, as if trying thus to embrace her. The male flapped his wings a great deal during the mating and breeding season, while seated on a perch, and often nodded his head with a circular motion as if trying to hook his bill over the neck of the female. The billing between the sexes was not prolonged, but each grasped the other's bill, and with a quick perfunctory shake let go. The males seemed very pugnacious during the breeding season, were very jealous and exhibited the most threatening mien towards a rival, but their fighting was mainly confined to striking out with the wings, which did little injury to the combatants. The nests were crude specimens of bird architecture, often built in one day and occupied the next. Some were so thin and frail that the eggs could be seen through the interstices; others were more strongly built. In most cases hardwood forests seemed to be preferred for the great nestings, but when the pigeons nested in coniferous trees, the number of nests in a tree increased, as these trees provided better support for the nests. As soon as the eggs were laid, incubation commenced, and from that time onward the eggs were carefully guarded, turned and incubated night and day.

Two methods of feeding are described. The first was ground feeding. In picking up mast the flock alighted on the ground with extended front and beating wings, moving rapidly forward, the rear rank continually rising in air and passing over those in front, thus forming the front line until the next rear rank had passed over. Thus, as the flock rolled along with a rotary forward motion, all were fed, and the ground in that place was swept bare of pigeon food. While a flock was feeding, sentinel birds on the watch gave the alarm at the approach of an enemy by clapping their wings together over their backs. This signal was repeated by every member of the great flock as they rose with a thunderous roar of wings.

They drank commonly as other pigeons do, but where steep banks offered them no footing they could light on the water with wings raised and partially extended, drink and rise again on flapping pinions.

Their migrations were not the regular, periodical, long-drawn-out movements that characterize the seasonal flights of most birds. They were undertaken chiefly in search of food. The pigeons were so swift and tireless in flight, however, that they could pass from zone to zone in a day, and a great unseasonable snowstorm in the north, covering their food supply, might send them all south at once, or such a storm in the mountains might drive them to the coast. They migrated *en masse*. That is, the birds of one great nesting rose into the air as one body, and the movements of these immense hosts formed the most wonderful and impressive spectacle in animated nature. There were stirring sights in this and other countries when great herds of grazing mammals thundered over the plains, but the approach of the mighty armies of the air was appalling. Then vast multitudes, rising strata upon strata, covered the darkened sky and hid the sun, while the roar of their myriad wings might be likened to that of a hurricane; and thus they passed for hours or days together, while the people in the country over which the legions winged their way kept up a fusillade from every point of vantage. Where the lower flights passed close over high hilltops, people were stationed with oars, poles, shingles, and other weapons to knock down the swarming birds, and the whole countryside was fed on pigeons until the people were surfeited.

EASTERN GROUND DOVE

Columbigallina passerina passerina (LINNAEUS). PLATE 95.

Other names: Mourning Dove; Moaning Dove; Tobacco Dove.

IDENTIFICATION. — Length 6½ to 7 inches; spread 10 to 11 inches. About size of Bluebird but heavier appearing; a miniature brownish-gray pigeon, with square tail, and *under surface of wings and bases of secondaries rufous*, conspicuous in flight.

CALL. — A soft *coo-oo, coo-oo, coo-oo,* repeated at length.

BREEDING. — *Nest:* On ground or in low bush or tree. *Eggs:* 2, white.

RANGE. — Breeds in South Atlantic and Gulf States from South Carolina to southeastern Texas, mainly near coast.

The attractive little Eastern Ground Dove is a familiar bird throughout most of peninsular Florida, but in Georgia and South Carolina it is found mainly near the beaches and sea-islands, where it may often be flushed from the tall beach-grass upon the seeds of which it feeds. The birds are almost always seen in pairs, or in small flocks of paired birds, for this species apparently mates for life. Its flight when startled is swift but usually not prolonged, the birds often circling about and alighting not far from the place from which they arose. They seem very much attached to their chosen localities, remaining in a suitable area throughout the year. Their nesting period is very much extended, eggs being found from February to late October and a pair of birds rearing from three to four broods (of two young) during a season.

They are very terrestrial in habits, feeding almost entirely on seeds, berries and small insects which they pick up while walking daintily about, heads nodding gracefully and tails held rather high. Their soft cooing notes are a characteristic sound in their Florida haunts and have given the bird the local name of 'Mourning Dove' or 'Moaning Dove,' as it is often pronounced, but when seen the bird should never be confused with the real Mourning Dove, which is much larger and with a long narrowly pointed tail. The Eastern Ground Dove is generally protected throughout its range, because of its friendly disposition (and because it is too small for food), so that it has become a common visitor to barnyards, gardens and fields close to houses, in marked contrast to the wary Mourning Dove. — (J.B.M.)

BAHAMA GROUND DOVE

Columbigallina passerina bahamensis (MAYNARD).

IDENTIFICATION. — Slightly smaller and paler than *C. p. passerina*, the head more ashy and lower parts and wings much less ruddy; the bill is entirely black, not red at base.

RANGE. — Resident in the Bahamas and Bermudas.

This insular race of the Ground Dove is a common and familiar bird in the Bermuda Islands, where it may often be seen about houses and gardens and in open places like the beaches and golf links. It differs in no important essentials of habits from the Eastern Ground Dove. — (J.B.M.)

Order Psittaciformes. Parrots and Paroquets.

CAROLINA PAROQUET

Conuropsis carolinensis carolinensis (LINNAEUS).

IDENTIFICATION. — Length about 13 inches; spread about 22 inches. A small parrot, green and yellow, with red or orange face, powerful hooked beak and long tail.

RANGE. — Formerly ranged from Florida north to southern Virginia and west to Georgia and Alabama, and casually to New York. *Extinct* since about 1904.

The exotic-looking Carolina Paroquet was once a common bird throughout Florida and the near-by states, but it was excellent eating, and it was accused of doing much damage to fruit, so that it was relentlessly killed and its ultimate final extermination was only a matter of time. While the millinery trade contributed its share to this result and scientific collectors may have added the final straw, it was the agricultural interests which had the major part in the extinction of the paroquets, apparently.

Besides eating the products of the orchardist and berry grower, the Carolina Paroquet was fond of many wild seeds and fruits, such as cockle-burs, palmetto berries, cypress 'balls,' wild grapes, papaws, beechnuts, and many others. They stayed in flocks throughout the year, but very little is known about their nesting habits. Apparently they nested in hollow trees and perhaps were communal at this time, but the early accounts differ in details and are rather confusing. — (J.B.M.)

LOUISIANA PAROQUET

Conuropsis carolinensis ludovicianus (GMELIN).

This race was more western in range than *C. c. carolinensis*. Now also extinct.

MAYNARD'S CUCKOO

Coccyzus minor maynardi RIDGWAY.

Other names: Black-eared Cuckoo; Rain Bird.

IDENTIFICATION. — Length about 12½ inches; spread about 16 inches. Very similar to Yellow-billed Cuckoo but a strong yellowish-buff on under parts; blackish-brown stripe under and behind eye.

BREEDING. — Similar to Yellow-billed Cuckoo.

RANGE. — Breeds on the Bahama Islands, Cuba, the Florida Keys, and south and west Florida coast north to Anclote Keys.

Maynard's Cuckoo is a summer resident of the mangrove swamps which border the Bay of Florida and extend northward along the Gulf coast of the peninsula, the species being found as far north as Tampa Bay and the Anclote Keys near Tarpon Springs and Port Richey. It is migratory, however, arriving from the south about the middle of March and departing about the middle of September. It resembles the Yellow-billed Cuckoo in general habits, but according to A. H. Howell its notes are quite different, those which he heard from the Maynard's Cuckoo being 'a sort of clucking note, low and guttural, repeated rather slowly, suggesting the notes of a squirrel rather than a bird.' — (J.B.M.)

YELLOW–BILLED CUCKOO

Coccyzus americanus americanus (LINNAEUS).   PLATE 48.

Other names: Rain Crow; Chow-chow; Storm Crow.

IDENTIFICATION. — Length 11 to 12¾ inches; spread 15½ to 17 inches. Our northern cuckoos are long slender birds, brown above with greenish gloss and white or grayish-white below; this species distinguished from Black-billed Cuckoo by rufous on flight-feathers which often may be seen in the field, and by black tail feathers with their large conspicuous white marks, these white markings much smaller and less conspicuous in Black-billed Cuckoo; yellow of lower part of bill not very noticeable, but may be seen in good light.

CALL. — A throaty *ka-ka-ka-ka-ka-kow-kow, kowp, kowp, kowp, kowp.*

BREEDING. — *Nest:* A flat platform of twigs, etc. *Eggs:* 2 to (rarely) 8, light bluish-green, sometimes slightly clouded with darker.

RANGE. — Breeds from North Dakota, Minnesota, southern Ontario, Quebec, and New Brunswick south to Nuevo Leon, Tamaulipas, Louisiana, and the Florida Keys, and west to South Dakota, Nebraska, eastern Colorado, and Oklahoma; winters in South America to Uruguay; migrates through Mexico, the West Indies, and Central America.

The Yellow-billed Cuckoo is a harbinger of summer. When the woods and orchards have put on their spring greenery; when the blossom-buds of the moccasin flower and the columbine begin to unfold their petals, then the voice of the cuckoo is heard in the land. If the season is early, then a few may appear earlier; but when spring is backward, individuals of the species may be still moving northward on June first. The cuckoo is a graceful, elegant bird, calm and unperturbed, it slips quietly and rather furtively through its favorite tangles and flies easily from tree to tree in the orchard, keeping for the most part under protection of the leaves, which furnish excellent cover for its bronzy, upper plumage, while the shadows of the foliage tend to conceal the whiteness of its under parts. It has a way also of keeping its back with its greenish satiny reflections toward the intruder in its solitudes, and while holding an attitude of readiness for flight it sits motionless, and its plumage so blends with its leafy environment that it does not ordinarily catch the eye. In the meantime it turns its head and regards the disturber with a cool, reserved, direct gaze, looking back over its shoulder, apparently unafraid and giving no indication of nervousness or even undue curiosity; but if the observer approaches too closely, the elegant bird slips quietly away, vanishing into some leafy, cool retreat where it may enjoy the silence and solitude, dear to the woodland recluse. This calm, quiet, secretive bird is far more often heard than seen. Indeed it would be rarely seen were it not for its rather loud unhurried notes. These, frequently repeated, apprise the world of its presence.

Once our cuckoos undoubtedly were birds of the forest and woodland thicket, but they have adapted themselves in some measure to civilization, for the reason, perhaps, that they find an abundant and easily obtained food supply in our orchards. Most fruit trees normally harbor caterpillars of which cuckoos are fond, and in seasons when caterpillars are abundant cuckoos may breed in the orchard or near it, or on occasion they may nest in a village shade tree or even in a city park.

Late nesting is the rule, as nests with eggs are not found very commonly in the latitude of New England until June. The nest is so flat that now and then an egg rolls out or is brushed out by the parent in leaving the nest. Eggs are frequently laid at considerable intervals after incubation has begun, so that young of several sizes may be found in a nest, together with an egg or two, fresh or incubated. The most interesting part of the development of the young is the process of feathering. The nestlings are provided with a black, tough, leathery-appearing skin, and each feather as it grows is encased in a black, pointed sheath, giving the callow youngster the appearance of being clothed in quills like the 'fretful porcupine.' On the day that the fledgling leaves the nest a seeming miracle occurs. In a few hours the sheaths burst open, and the young bird goes forth into the world properly clothed in a plumage resembling that of its parents.

When autumnal caterpillars are scarce about the region where cuckoos have nested, some of them begin to move southward by or before July 20. If fall webworms are abundant, some remain much later in infested regions to feed upon these pests, and cuckoos are seen not infrequently in New England through the month of September. After that they usually become scarce, as most of them are then moving toward South America.

The Yellow-billed Cuckoo feeds very largely on injurious insects. To quote from one of my former works:

'The cuckoos are of the greatest service to the farmer, by reason of their well-known fondness for caterpillars, particularly the hairy species. No caterpillars are safe from the cuckoo. It does not matter how hairy or spiny they are, or how well they may be protected by webs. Often the stomach of the cuckoo will be found lined with a felted mass of caterpillar hairs, and sometimes its intestines are pierced by the spines of the noxious caterpillars that it has swallowed. Wherever caterpillar outbreaks occur we hear the calls of the cuckoos. There they stay; there they bring their newly fledged young; and the number of caterpillars they eat is incredible.'

The chief utility of cuckoos lies in their apparent fondness for hairy caterpillars and their ability to dispose of large quantities of these destructive insects. Many other birds eat such caterpillars when these larvae are very small and others take larger ones, but cuckoos take them at all stages and seem to enjoy it. When, in time, the inside of the bird's stomach becomes so felted with a mass of hairs and spines that it obstructs digestion, the bird can shed the entire stomach-lining, meanwhile growing a new one — a process that would be beneficial to some unfeathered bipeds could they compass it. This species frequently feeds on or near the ground, and there gets an enormous number of locusts and other pests. In summer and autumn it feeds to some extent on small wild fruits, such as the raspberry, blackberry and wild grape.

BLACK–BILLED CUCKOO

Coccyzus erythrophthalmus (WILSON).   PLATE 48.

Other names: Rain Crow; Cow-cow.

IDENTIFICATION. — Length 11 to 12 ¾ inches; spread 15 to 16¾ inches. Size near that of Yellow-billed Cuckoo; lack of both the conspicuous, large, black and white markings on the tail and of rufous, usually, on wing, as well as its black bill, distinguish it from Yellow-billed Cuckoo; the Brown Thrasher resembles it in size and shape, but is more rufous, and has a streaked and spotted breast, where the cuckoo is always unmarked.

CALL. — *Cu cu cu, cucucu, cucucu cucucu,* repeated, and a series of rapid *kuks* all on one note.

BREEDING. — Similar to Yellow-billed Cuckoo but eggs darker.

RANGE. — Breeds from southeastern Alberta, southern Quebec, and Prince Edward Island south to Kansas, Arkansas, North Carolina, and the mountains of Georgia; winters in South America from Colombia to Peru.

The Black-billed Cuckoo is in many respects almost a counterpart of its yellow-billed congener; but it is even more slender and graceful, the markings of the tail differ, the bill lacks any tinge of yellow and the bird is somewhat more retiring and perhaps less vociferous. The present species may be more given to night-wandering, as its voice is heard more frequently at night than that of the 'Yellow-bill.' Otherwise the two are almost identical in appearance and habits and they haunt the same places, and occupy much the same range, except that the Yellow-bill is normally a more southern bird. The development of the 'mailed' young in this species is similar to that of the Yellow-bill.

There is incontestable evidence showing that this bird occasionally drops an egg in the nest of some smaller bird and that the young cuckoo may eventually crowd out the rightful occupants of the nest, but this is exceptional, as our cuckoos as a rule are very faithful parents. Both species incubate, and both care for the young and often will attempt to entice the intruder away from the vicinity of the nest. When once out of the nest, the young before they can fly climb cleverly.

In seasons when caterpillars of any species are abundant, cuckoos usually become common in the infested localities. They follow the caterpillars, and where such food is plentiful, the size of their broods seems to increase. Professor Walter B. Barrows of Michigan is responsible for the statement that in several instances remains of over one hundred tent caterpillars have been taken from a single cuckoo's stomach. The Black-billed Cuckoo, because more common than the Yellow-billed, is the species that most commonly attacks this insect in New

England orchards. The Black-billed Cuckoo seems more inclined to go to the ground than is the other species, though it is rather seldom seen there. It seems to be fond of wet places, and feeds more or less in such localities on aquatic insects and other small aquatic forms of life.

Order Strigiformes. Owls.

AMERICAN BARN OWL

Tyto alba pratincola (BONAPARTE). PLATE 45.

Other name: Monkey-faced Owl; White Owl.

IDENTIFICATION. — Length 15 to 21 inches; spread 43¼ to 47 inches. Size nearly that of Crow but wings longer. If seen sitting, may be recognized by its pale colors, long legs and long, white, nearly heart-shaped face. If seen in flight, may be told by buffy upper plumage, light or white under plumage and long wings; flies very lightly, often reeling from side to side.

BREEDING. — In holes in trees, banks, etc., and buildings. *Eggs:* 5 to 11, white.

RANGE. — Resident from northern California, Colorado, Nebraska, Illinois, southern Wisconsin, southern Michigan, Ohio, western New York, and Connecticut, south to the Gulf States, southern Mexico, and Nicaragua.

Since the dawn of history, owls have been the pitiable victims of ignorance and superstition. Hated, despised and feared by many peoples, only their nocturnal habits have enabled them to survive in company with civilized man. In the minds of mankind they have been leagued with witches and malignant evil spirits, or even have been believed to personify the Evil One. Among these eerie birds the Barn Owl has been the victim of the greatest share of obloquy and persecution, owing to its sinister appearance, its weird night cries, its habit of haunting dismal swamps and dank quagmires, where an incautious step may precipitate the investigator into malodorous filth or sucking quicksands, and its tendency to frequent the neighborhood of man's dwellings, especially unoccupied buildings and ghostly ruins. Doubtless the Barn Owl is responsible for some of the stories of haunted houses, which have been current through the centuries. When divested by science of its atmosphere of malign mystery, however, this owl is seen to be not only harmless but a benefactor to mankind and a very interesting fowl that will well repay close study.

The name Barn Owl has reference to its habit of nesting and hiding in barns which, where both owls and barns are numerous, is a common habit.

The Barn Owl is not really a shy and retiring bird. It has that reputation, perhaps because it seldom is seen abroad in daylight, unless disturbed by some intruder, when it flies off in an uncertain, irregular manner, as if it were unable to see well, and betakes itself to some quiet, dark retreat, where, undisturbed, it can doze away the daylight hours. Where these owls are common they frequent certain roosting-places, and the ground beneath is littered with their pellets and excrement. A number of them may roost in the holes and hollows of some gigantic dead tree, and several have been found during the daytime in a partially covered old well or at the bottom of an old mine-shaft. Some roost in the shade of dense foliage; others on the ground under the shelter of tall, dense reeds or grasses.

Barn Owls frequent almost any kind of territory where mice and other little mammals may be found. In the long days of summer, when their rather numerous young require feeding often, they leave the nesting-place very early in the evening, even considerably before sunset, and at this season or when driven by hunger they hunt sometimes on cloudy days. The female while incubating is steadily supplied with food by the male, but occasionally she leaves the nest, and he takes her place thereon, and probably in some cases he assumes some part of the duties of incubation, as both male and female have been seen sitting side by side on the eggs. As with some other raptorial birds, several days elapse between the laying of each of the five or more eggs in the clutch, and the young generally are of several sizes. The nestlings seem to resemble young vultures more than owls, as they are clothed like the vultures with white or yellowish down and have similar long heads and beaks. When nearly fledged the young (and the parents also), when the nest is approached, are accustomed to lower their heads and sway them from side to side, hissing like a snake, and thus presenting a gruesome and rather fearsome front to the enemy who comes upon them suddenly in the gloom of their retreat.

The American Barn Owl is not a migratory bird in the ordinary sense of the word, but it wanders in winter south of its breeding-places, and in summer or fall individuals straggle northward from their summer homes. There may have been a gradual extension of the species northward in the last fifty years, as the number of records in the north has increased very materially since 1880, but this may be due to the increased number of observers.

Everything indicates that the food of the Barn Owl in the East consists almost entirely of mice and rats, with some other small mammals and a very few birds. In the West it destroys quantities of those destructive pests, gophers and ground squirrels or spermophiles; in the South the cotton rat is one of its chief victims. It is especially fitted to capture such creatures because of its power of night-sight, its remarkably large and sensitive ears, which indicate wonderfully acute hearing, and its superlatively soft plumage, even more light and downy than that of other owls, which enables it to glide silently through the air upon its prey. A mouse is killed by crushing the base of the skull with the beak, and usually food is carried to the nest in the mouth rather than in the talons, the feet trailing backward in flight under the tail.

EASTERN SCREECH OWL

Otus asio naevius (GMELIN). PLATE 47.

Other names: Mottled Owl; Red Owl; Cat-Owl; Shivering Owl.

IDENTIFICATION. — Length 6½ to 10 inches; spread 18 to 24 inches. The only small owl with *ear-tufts;* color generally either light reddish-brown or brownish-gray with streaked breast.

NOTES. — Include a tremulous wailing descending at end; a long tremulous call all on one key; and other low notes.

BREEDING. — In natural or artificial cavity, lined with straw, leaves, feathers, etc. *Eggs:* 3 to 9, white.

RANGE. — Resident in New Brunswick, Maine, northern New York, Ontario, Wisconsin, Minnesota, and southern Manitoba south to the uplands of Georgia, Alabama, Tennessee, eastern Oklahoma, and northern Arkansas.

Out of the wisdom of the ages Pliny produced among other wise sayings the following: 'The Scritch Owl always betokeneth some heavie newes, and is most execrable and accursed. In summer he is the very monster of the night, neither singing nor crying out cleare, but uttering a certaine heavie groane of doleful mourning, and therefore if it be seene to flie abroad in any place it prognosticateth some feareful misfortune.' This dictum was promulgated far away and long ago, but our Eastern Screech Owl has inherited both name and reputation. Many superstitious folk still believe that this little owl is an ill-omened fowl. Its silent, ghostly flight and its mournful night-cries have given it a place among the powers of darkness in the minds of the simple and unlearned. Many still shudder whenever they hear its plaintive, long-drawn-out wail, which, though it seems to carry a note of sadness, is merely a love song, unappreciated, except, perhaps, by the ears for which it is especially intended. Its mournfulness so impressed Thoreau that he characterized the lugubrious lay in his journal as follows: 'It is no honest and blunt *tu-whit to-who* of the poets, but without jesting a most solemn graveyard ditty, — but the mutual consolations of suicide lovers remembering the pangs and the delights of supernal love in the infernal groves. And yet I love to hear their wailing, their doleful responses, trilled along the woodside, reminding me sometimes of music and singing birds, as if it were the dark and tearful side of music, the regrets and sighs that would fain be sung. . . . They give me a new sense of the vastness and mystery of that nature which is the common dwelling of us both. "Oh-o-o-o-o that I had never been bor-or-or-or-orn!" sighs one on this side of the pond, and circles in the restlessness of despair to some new perch in the gray oaks. Then "That I never had been bor-or-or-or-orn!" echoes one on the further side, with a tremulous sincerity, and "bor-or-or-orn" comes faintly from far in the Lincoln woods.'

Many people still believe that this doleful wail is prophetic and foretells disaster, disease or death. The little Southern Screech Owl is known in Louisiana as the 'Shivering Owl'; and along Bayou Lafourche when its notes banish sleep, and the resourceful 'Cajun' wishes to ward off the ills that he believes otherwise sure to follow, he must arise from his couch and turn his left shoe upside down. Then the cries are supposed to be stilled. This charm does not work, however, on the lower Mississippi, where one must turn his left trouser or 'pants' pocket inside out. The latter plan is believed to be effective by many colored brethren on the South Carolina coast, where a piece of iron thrown into the fire also is regarded as efficacious. The belief prevails there that trouble or even death will befall an inmate should one of the owls alight on the roof of the house and utter its prophetic notes. Even in canny, practical New England superstition still lives, for Mr. F. B. White tells us that not many years ago 'one that took up its residence for a few days in a church tower, was credited with foretelling — if not indeed causing — the death of a citizen of dignity, domiciled next door.'

The Eastern Screech Owl lives in an old neglected orchard, often near a brook, where it can find a hollow in the heart of some ancient tree which serves it for a retreat during the hours of daylight; there also is a plentiful supply of food for its young in the shape of mice and insects, with sparkling water for bathing, for this little owl delights in a daily or nightly bath. It was in such an orchard that I first met this bird of darkness. As a small boy it was my custom to spend many hours before and after school in the fields and woods, and so, coming home one night in the gloaming and passing beneath some old apple trees, I was alarmed by a loud snapping just behind my head. I turned quickly and gazed upon empty air. There was nothing to be seen within my field of vision that could by any possibility have produced that sound. Again, but more alertly, I resumed my way when snap-snap-snap sounded once more almost under my hat brim. Turning instantly I saw the form of a little gray owl gliding swiftly and silently on expanded wings to alight near by on a horizontal limb in an opening among the trees. Quick as a flash it turned to face me, and, as the glow from the western sky lighted its fore-front showing its great startled eyes and its broad head and wide-set ears, it seemed like some ancient forest gnome with long, pointed, white beard hanging down between the converging dark stripes on its dappled breast. As I gazed at it in amazement, again behind me sounded a snappy beak as a little red owl charged me from behind. I realized then that this must be a pair of Screech Owls with young which they were trying to defend, and next day I searched the locality for the nest and eggs or young, but did not find them, for, as I learned later, another boy had been before me.

For several years a pair of Eastern Screech Owls raised young in a nesting-box in the pine woods beside my summer cottage. While the young were in the nest, the parents fed them mostly mice and insects and afterwards chiefly insects, as we could see them nightly and watch the feeding in the dusk. The young began to give peculiar calls soon after they were out of the nest, some of which resembled the distant, faint, hoarse squalling of a hen, others were somewhat like the yowling of a tom-cat, others were husky imitations of their parents' usual tremulous call. The old birds meanwhile answered with their wail or called *ou ou*. Such a variety of sounds apparently indicating pain or despair coming from the depths of a dark pine wood at evening would be likely to fill the minds of the ignorant and superstitious with fear or foreboding. The calls of the young gradually lost their husky quality as the fledglings grew older.

Birds of this species appear in autumn and winter in localities where they are not seen in summer, but they may have wandered only a few miles from their breeding-places. Many of the smaller owls are killed and eaten during the winter by larger species, which may account for the reduction in their numbers noticed in spring. I once found in the stomach and gullet of a Barred Owl the greater part of a Long-eared Owl, while in the stomach of the latter were some remains of a Screech Owl.

The Eastern Screech Owl gets its sustenance chiefly from mice and insects. It is very destructive to field mice, house mice, cutworms, grasshoppers, locusts and other pests. It eats many noxious nocturnal moths and many beetles — seems, in short, to have a marked predilection for destructive insects. Usually it seems to kill only small numbers of birds and seldom troubles poultry or game-birds. All one season I watched a pair that were rearing a brood near my cottage. We found in and about their nesting-box feathers from several Blue Jays, others from a male Red-winged Blackbird, and the wing of one Robin. All the pellets and other refuse from their food that season showed only remains of mice, shrews and insects. We concluded that the destruction of the Blue Jays was a benefit, as there were too many of them, and they fed to some extent on the eggs and young of other birds. While the owls were there, the mice did no damage in our young orchard, but two years later their box fell down and was not replaced for the next two years. The second winter mice girdled nearly all our apple trees. The next year a number of boxes were erected. The owls returned and we had no trouble from mice thereafter.

SOUTHERN SCREECH OWL

Otus asio asio (LINNAEUS).

IDENTIFICATION. — This race is apparently intermediate in both size and coloration between the Eastern and the Florida Screech Owls. When the various races of a species can hardly be separated in the museum laboratory, it is not to be expected that they differ in habits markedly.

RANGE. — Resident from Virginia to Georgia and the Gulf States west to Louisiana, north to western Tennessee, southern Illinois, Arkansas, and Oklahoma.

FLORIDA SCREECH OWL

Otus asio floridanus (RIDGWAY).

Other names: Squinch Owl; Death Owl.

IDENTIFICATION. — Much smaller than the Eastern Screech Owl, and colors deeper, especially in the red phase.

RANGE. — Peninsular Florida.

ARCTIC HORNED OWL

Bubo virginianus subarcticus HOY.

IDENTIFICATION. — A very pale race of Horned Owl, with white legs and feet.

RANGE. — Breeds from Hudson Bay and tree limit in the valley of the Mackenzie south to northern Alberta, southwestern Saskatchewan, central Manitoba, and northern Ontario; in winter to southern British Columbia, and the northern United States from Idaho to Nebraska and Wisconsin.

LABRADOR HORNED OWL

Bubo virginianus heterocnemis (OBERHOLSER)

IDENTIFICATION. — A very dark, large race of Horned Owl.

RANGE. — Northern Ungava, Labrador, Newfoundland, and Nova Scotia, migrating in winter to Ontario, and casually to Connecticut.

GREAT HORNED OWL

Bubo virginianus virginianus (GMELIN). PLATE 46.

Other names: Cat Owl; Hoot Owl.

IDENTIFICATION. — Length 18 to 23 inches; spread about 35 to 52 inches. Bulkier than Red-tailed Hawk, with even greater wing-spread; distinguished by conspicuous ear-tufts, generally dark color with white throat-patch, apparently shortened fore parts and lack of visible neck.

CALLS. — Include a deep-toned hoot, a blood-curdling shriek, and many others.

BREEDING. — In dense forests and swamps. Rarely builds its own nest but uses nest of hawk, crow, etc. *Eggs:* 2 to 5, dull white.

RANGE. — Ontario, Quebec, and New Brunswick south to the Gulf coast and Florida, west to Wisconsin, extreme eastern Minnesota, Iowa, southeastern South Dakota, Oklahoma, and eastern Texas.

The Great Horned Owl is not only the most formidable in appearance of all our owls, but it is the most powerful. The Great Gray Owl and the Snowy Owl may appear larger, but the Great Horned Owl exceeds them in courage, weight, and strength. Indeed, it little regards the size of its victim, for it strikes down geese and turkeys many times its weight, and has even been said at times to drive the Bald Eagle away from its aery and domicile its own family therein.

Sometimes when the nest of the Great Horned Owl is disturbed, the bird attacks the intruder and inflicts painful wounds, though usually it is extremely careful not to trust itself by daylight within gunshot of a human being. In my own experiences at the nests of these birds no attack was ever made. The mother bird usually disappeared at once and did not return; but one dull day in early March I had climbed to a nest on a great oak near Lake Quinsigamond in central Massachusetts and had stowed safely in my pocket the two newly hatched young, when the powerful mother, who had been circling the tree, suddenly swooped down, alighted on a limb within a few feet of my face, and, leaning forward until she almost hung head downward, stared directly into my eyes with an expression of such fiendish ferocity that I prepared to defend myself. She soon swept away again, however, and continued her restless circling.

The courtship of the Great Horned Owl is a curious performance. The male goes through peculiar contortions, nodding, bowing, flapping its wings and using, meanwhile, the choicest and most persuasive owl language. One motion which seems common to all owls is a rotary movement of the head, which is raised to the full length of the neck, then swung to one side and dropped as low at least as the feet, and then swung to the other side and raised again, giving the owl a most ludicrous appearance.

Whatever may be said about the fierceness and ferocity of these owls, no one can accuse them of being unfaithful to their young. The mother sits closely on her eggs during the cold days and long nights of late February and early March. Often the snow covers both her and the nest, and then if she is driven away by an intruder, the nest will be found covered with snow surrounding the imprint of her body, showing where she has faithfully outstayed the storm. The young remain in the nest and continue to grow for at least a month, and during all that time they are well cared for and provided with a quantity of food.

In January and February these owls become vocal. Later in the year the birds are less vocal, but now and then, especially in autumn, their hooting may be heard. The following is taken from my notes of September 5, 1904, when I was staying at one of the Brewster cabins on the Concord River in eastern Massachusetts: 'Tonight just after dark as I sat in the cabin a sound came from down river like someone trying to imitate a dog, which was baying on the other shore; then it changed to higher, gabbling tones, gradually coming nearer, and sounding more like the talk and laughter of a boatload of women coming up the river. Soon it was followed by the unmistakable *hŏŏ-hŏŏ, hoo', hŏŏ-hoo'* of the Great Horned Owl. I stepped out of doors and answered it and the bird soon came quite near. I then went indoors, and it alighted on one of the trees above the cabin, where it remained for some time, conversing with me in owl language. That bird made more peculiar and diverse sounds than I have heard from any other owl; for a while its vocalizing was confined to soft cooing tones like *wu woó* and *wu wa*. Then, becoming bolder, it launched forth a volley of interrogative *wahoos* and double hoots that were startling when coming from a distance of less than twenty yards. I answered occasionally and the bird kept up its hooting for half an hour. The upward slide of its loud *waugh-hoo* was inimitable; beginning at C the note *waugh* ran up to F at its ending, followed by the emphatic *hoo* which fell again to C. Also it called *wau-hoo' hoo ooo, oo-oo* without the rising inflection, or *wu waugh?-hoo-hoo-hoo, hoo-hoo, ho, hoo-hoo*, etc. To me this was the principal event of the day.'

The Great Horned Owl is a nocturnal bird, most active in the dusk of the evening and on moonlit nights, but it may be heard hooting at times at midnight in the 'dark of the moon.' It hunts at night, yet it can see perfectly in the daytime. It will hardly allow a man to come within gunshot in daylight, though under the protection of darkness it may come very near him. The best opportunity to see one by day is to advance upon it when it is mobbed by the noisy angry Crows. Then by keeping behind trees and moving up quickly while the Crows are calling, one may rarely get a glimpse of the owl. But it always starts before the Crows, which, as soon as they see the owl go, follow in their usual uproarious pack. The bird often hunts just before dusk on dull days, and on very dark days it may be out before the middle of the afternoon. I remember once looking down from a cliff on the side of a mountain at Mt. Desert upon an owl hunting over the meadows below. This was about 4 P.M. and the view of the owl's back and wings as it quartered over the land like a Marsh Hawk hunting for mice was all that could be desired.

Every living thing above ground in the woods on winter nights pays tribute to the Great Horned Owl except the larger mammals and man. Ordinarily when there is good hunting this owl has a plentiful supply of food, and when there is game enough it slaughters an abundance and eats only the brains; but in winter when house rats and mice keep mostly within the buildings, when woodchucks and skunks have 'holed up,' and when field mice are protected by deep snow — then if rabbits are scarce and starvation is imminent, the owl will attack even the domestic cat, and usually with success. A farmer brought me a Great Horned Owl one winter day that had killed his pet tom cat on the evening of the previous day. The cat was out walking in the moonlight on one of his usual expeditions in search of unattended females, when the farmer heard a wail of mortal agony, and opening the door saw Mr. Cat in the grasp of the owl. Before he could get his gun and shoot the bird the cat was no more.

Great Horned Owls kill and eat many skunks, and seem to care little for the disagreeable consequences of attacking these pungent animals. Many of the owls that I have handled give olfactory evidence of the habit. They kill both wild and domesticated ducks, picking them up skillfully out of the water at night, and no goose is too large for them to tackle. Where hens, chickens and turkeys are allowed to roost at night in the trees, many fall victims to this owl, which is said to alight on the branch beside its chosen prey, crowd it off the limb and then strike it in the air. Usually the owl does not stop to eat his victim on the spot but bears it away.

The Great Horned Owl is no respecter of persons. It kills weaker owls from the Barred Owl down, most of the hawks and such nocturnal animals as weasels and minks. It is the most deadly enemy of the Eastern Crow, taking old and young from their nests at night and killing many at their winter roosts. Game birds of all kinds, poultry, a few small birds, rabbits (especially bush rabbits), hares, squirrels, gophers, mice, rats, woodchucks, opossums, fish, crawfish and insects are all eaten by this rapacious bird. It is particularly destructive to rats.

MONTANA HORNED OWL

Bubo virginianus occidentalis STONE.

IDENTIFICATION. — A pale race of Horned Owl but not as white as *B. v. subarcticus.*
RANGE. — Minnesota, South Dakota, Nebraska, and Kansas, west to Nevada, southeastern Oregon, northeastern California, Wyoming, and Montana, north to central Alberta; south in winter to Iowa.

SNOWY OWL

Nyctea nyctea (LINNAEUS).   PLATE 46.

Other names: Snow Owl; White Owl; Arctic Owl; Great White Owl.
IDENTIFICATION. — Length 20 to 27 inches; spread 54 to 66 inches. Fully as large as Great Horned Owl; largely white, and in flight, seen from below, looks *very* white; distinguished from White Gyrfalcon by apparent lack of neck, larger head and more rounded wing-tips; seen in flight looks whiter than Arctic Horned Owl; some Barn Owls appear very white if seen from below, especially in flight, but the Barn Owl is brown above and much smaller.
BREEDING. — *Nest:* A mere depression in soil or moss in open country or tundra. *Eggs:* 4 to 11, white.
RANGE. — Circumpolar, breeding on the barren grounds of Arctic lands in both hemispheres, south in North America to central Mackenzie, central Keewatin, and northern Ungava; winters south to the southern Canadian provinces and Montana, with periodic and irregular migrations to the Middle States, the Ohio Valley, and New England.

My first acquaintance with the great Snowy Owl came about as follows: Three boys, ages twelve to fourteen, of which I was one, used to go hunting together accompanied by two hounds belonging to neighbors and one muzzle-loading double-barreled shotgun borrowed from an indulgent father. One snowy day Bob came rushing into the house crying excitedly that there was a big white owl on a tree in the old orchard. In the excitement that followed, the gun was loaded somehow and Bill with the deadly weapon at the ready, crept softly through the newly fallen snow toward that owl, keeping well behind the tree trunks. Finally he crouched and sighted the piece, taking long and careful aim. In the silent interval that followed a cap snapped sharply. At that startling sound the owl spread its great white wings and launched its form upon the snow-laden air, followed by the roar of the other barrel, and flapped away into the dim obscurity of the fast-falling snow. In the excitement and haste of loading that gun both charges of shot had been poured into the right barrel and all the powder into the left.

My most satisfactory observation of the Snowy Owl is more recent. The following description is taken from my notebook: 'November 17, 1926. Last Sunday and Monday great flights of Brants came down the Massachusetts coast and small groups of Snowy Owls were seen moving along the shore. All yesterday and the previous night a southerly gale was blowing, and storm warnings were up along the coast. Yesterday in the gale I went to Yarmouthport and at night we drove before the wind across Barnstable Harbor and were washed ashore in a dory at Sandy Neck. All night the gale howled and roared. Rain dashed against the window panes before we slept, but with daybreak the wind 'hauled' to the westward, and the sun rose on one of the most perfect days of the year. The wind, which usually blows there, had moderated somewhat, but still the wind-driven sand swept up the westerly slopes of the taller dunes, streamed off their tops like smoke, and rattled on one's clothing like tiny hailstones.

'What a contrast the bird life of Cape Cod presents at this time of the year to that of the mainland. There it is at its lowest ebb, while here birds are abundant. On the bay, about five hundred yards from shore, gulls may be seen in countless myriads, mile upon mile, as far as the telescope can bring them into view. Up the shore to Sandwich and where the beach curves toward Plymouth their white breasts flash in the sunlight upon the dark blue water. Their presence in such untold multitudes may be accounted for by the vast numbers of squids cast up all along the shore — food for a million gulls.

'Flocks of Brant pass high overhead, bound south toward Muskeget or east toward Monomoy. Bunches of scoters, sheldrakes and Old-squaws speed by before the wind, and now and then a few Black Ducks. Common Loons, Red-throated Loons and Grebes float near the shore. Gannets are fishing in the bay. Among the dunes flocks of Northern Horned Larks and Snow Buntings flit by, and with them, a few Lapland Longspurs. Myrtle Warblers, Flickers and Catbirds move about in the thickets, and a sharp-winged Pigeon Hawk swoops down from the sky on the wings of a driving gale — and is gone. A great flock of Starlings moves on to the southward. Sanderlings run along the shore. Here are more birds than one can often see in one day in Massachusetts, but I disregard them and pass on, for the object of my quest is the Snowy Owl.

'Tramping over the dunes I climb to the tops of the highest and scan the country for patches of white. Most of these prove to be pieces of newspaper that the gale has carried here and lodged among the bushes; but one seen imperfectly through the tracery of little twigs may be an owl. As I tramp toward that suspicious object, there is a flutter of great white wings over the dune top and the bird is gone from my sight forever. It is a wild one, and toil as I will through shifting sands, I search for it in vain. Passing to the northward nearer the beach and on up the interminable sands of the Neck, another suspicious object is seen. It is stationary, but on a nearer approach it spreads great wings, swings over to leeward and alights about one hundred yards away on a low ridge facing me and the sun. The telescope brings the bird up close, and as I am partly hidden by the beach grass of a near ridge, she soon forgets me and sits at ease in the blazing sunshine — a monstrous great female Snowy Owl with her white plumage darkly barred, a face as white as snow, and great yellow eyes wide open and staring as she turns her head from side to side, now forward and now back, watching the birds in the sky. Soon she leaps over the top of the ridge and out of my field of vision. My stalking is a failure, as she has the wind of me and can hear the least motion. Before I have lessened the distance to sixty yards, she is on the wing and away to another dune, where she sits with her great body in profile and her face turned full upon me. Her expression is savage; her eyes have a tigerish glare. At my first forward motion she is up and away, moving with long slow flaps, her ample wings bending well down with each stroke. Occasionally she sails with or athwart the wind. Now she rises high over the bay, and some of the complaining gulls follow her, but although they could easily overtake her, they do not dare to approach too near. Now she swings toward me and from her far height swoops diagonally downward into the wind and straight at my face. She is upon me in a moment, but at my first motion she turns and, passing a few yards to one side, alights on the top of a dune.

'Three cawing, busybody Crows have seen her swoop and have followed her down. As the first one darts at her, she crouches ready to spring at him, but the crafty black rascal has seen the glare of her eyes and sheers wide of that dune top. The Crows continue to plunge at her, but they never come within reach of her spring, and as she disregards them absolutely and entirely, they soon tire of their dangerous game and move on.

'Now she sees something in the sky — probably some great bird — as she begins those curious motions of her head that owls always make when they espy a large hawk or eagle far up in the blue vault. Whatever she sees there is beyond my ken, for I can find nothing there even with the binoculars. Oh, for the eyes of an owl! Those who imagine that owls cannot see in the daytime should watch her now as she follows that phantom shape across the sky far beyond human vision. Twice I have had her within easy gunshot, but had I killed her I would have missed her reception of the Crows and that eery following of that unknown form across that cloudless sky.'

Commander Donald MacMillan informs me that some of these owls remain in northern Greenland all winter, living on northern hares. Wherever food becomes scarce, these owls must leave the region in winter or starve. The Snowy Owl is warmly clad to withstand the cold, and its keen vision serves it well both day and night, as it needs must through the long Arctic summer day.

In the North it subsists largely upon mice and lemmings. It takes many ptarmigans also and sea-fowl along the coast. It captures birds on the wing much after the manner of the Gyrfalcon as its flight is strong and swift. It has been known to catch fish.

The Snowy Owl is a necessary factor in the economy of nature in boreal regions, where its numbers always assemble to check any sudden invasion of those extremely prolific mammals — field mice and lemmings. When these birds arrive in the United States, they seem to prefer mice to any other food when these can be obtained. What we know of the food of the Snowy Owl indicates that it is more beneficial than injurious. It kills few domestic fowls and takes few game-birds in the United States, except in hard winters when mice are sheltered by deep snow.

AMERICAN HAWK OWL

Surnia ulula caparoch (MÜLLER).

PLATE 47.

Other name: Day Owl.

IDENTIFICATION. — Length 14½ to 17½ inches; spread 31 to 34 inches. Size smaller than Crow, about that of Short-eared Owl, but color much darker; *narrowly barred across both breast and abdomen;* wings rather short and pointed; tail rather long for an owl and much graduated; a rather dark, plump bird that usually alights on tops of tall trees and commonly sits not upright as do most owls, but with its body inclined forward, and frequently jets its tail, raising it quite high and lowering it rather slowly; at times, however, this owl sits bolt upright in the conventional owl attitude.

BREEDING. — In coniferous forests. *Eggs:* 3 to 9, glossy white, laid on chips on the hollow top of a stump; occasionally a nest of sticks lined with grass and moss is built in a tree.

RANGE. — Breeds from northwestern Alaska to Hudson Strait and south to southern British Columbia, central Alberta, and Ungava; winters south to Washington, Nebraska, Missouri, Indiana, Ohio, Pennsylvania, and New Jersey.

The American Hawk Owl is a rare and irregular visitor in the northern United States, otherwise it would be reported more often, as it is a conspicuous bird because of its size, its comparative tameness, and its habits of hunting in daylight and perching conspicuously on the very topmost twigs of a tall tree or on the top of a dead stub in broad daylight or before the dusk of evening has obscured the scene. During the great owl flight of 1922–23, when Richardson's Owls were commonly reported, and Snowy Owls were seen all along the coast of the Northern Atlantic States, Hawk Owls were not reported in southern New England, and our only news of them came from correspondents in northern New England and the provinces.

This species follows the rule of the boreal owls in migrating southward in autumn from the most northern part of its range, and when food becomes scarce in its customary winter range, it must necessarily move still farther south. Such scarcity of food probably accounts for its occasional appearance in some numbers in the northern United States. The food of the American Hawk Owl consists mainly of lemmings and mice (sometimes shrews), but it kills weasels also and young hares, and often takes ptarmigans. It has been seen to kill and carry off a Ruffed Grouse.

WESTERN BURROWING OWL

Speotyto cunicularia hypugaea (BONAPARTE).

Other name: Ground Owl.

IDENTIFICATION. — Length 9 to 10 inches; spread 24¼ to 25. Size about that of Screech Owl; a little, long-legged, short-tailed, ground owl, brown spotted with white above and white cross-barred with brown below.

BREEDING. — In burrows in the ground. *Eggs:* 6 to 12, pure white, glossy.

RANGE. — Breeds from Pacific coast of the United States east to Minnesota, western Iowa, and Louisiana, and from British Columbia and Manitoba south to Panama; migratory north of Oregon and northern Kansas.

The comical, slim-legged, little Western Burrowing Owl is a rare straggler in the East, where its occurrence is purely fortuitous, but it was formerly an abundant bird locally in suitable locations throughout the West. It is a winter visitant in northwestern Louisiana (there is only one breeding record for the state), and a summer resident only in Minnesota, where it has apparently become established within the past fifty years. In many parts of its range it is decreasing, owing to its peculiar nesting habits. Although it is called the 'burrowing' owl it does not dig its own burrow, but uses that of some burrowing mammal, especially that of the prairie dog. In many places the prairie dog has been 'eradicated' by poisoning campaigns, as it is considered a serious pest by farmers and cattle raisers, and with the elimination of the prairie-dog holes the owls have been obliged to look elsewhere for nesting-sites. In Minnesota the dens of badgers are used, and skunk and fox holes are also sometimes occupied. Ground-squirrel holes are too small for the owls unless they enlarge them somewhat.

When the young owls are nearly grown they often come out from the burrows and stand around sunning themselves with their parents, for this owl does not seem to object to the light of day. The families are large, eight or ten being the usual number, and one or two are likely to be much smaller than the rest of the brood, as though incubation began as soon as the first eggs were laid. They are amusing-looking youngsters, staring out at intruders like solemn little old men, and occasionally bobbing their heads straight up and down in a most laughable manner. — (J.B.M.)

FLORIDA BURROWING OWL

Speotyto cunicularia floridana RIDGWAY.   PLATE 95.

Other names: Johnny Owl; Ground Owl.
 IDENTIFICATION. — Somewhat darker above than *S. c. hypugaea*, and much less buffy.
 RANGE. — Resident in prairie region of central and southern Florida.

The Florida Burrowing Owl differs from the western race in one habit at least, for it apparently digs its own burrows, while the Western Burrowing Owl almost invariably appropriates a burrow excavated by some other creature, though it may enlarge a hole that is too small for its use without alteration. It is an inhabitant of the broad open prairies of central Florida, and may often be observed while one is driving over the roads of the Kissimmee Prairie region, perched on a fence post or more often standing on the low mound of sand thrown out in digging its tunnel. The nest burrow is from five to ten feet long, but not very far below the surface of the ground, and it frequently has an abrupt turn in its course, or may curve around in a horseshoe shape. If one approach the nest, the watching parent usually flies a short distance, then alights and faces the enemy, bowing once or twice and giving a low warning call. Its mate usually leaves the nest and flies a short distance also before alighting and watching the intruder. Whether it is warned by the note of its partner, or by the sound of the visitor's footsteps, is hard to say, but it is usually difficult to surprise one of the birds in its burrow. — (J.B.M.)

NORTHERN BARRED OWL

Strix varia varia BARTON.

PLATE 46.

Other names: Barn Owl (Maine); Hoot Owl; Black-eyed Owl.

IDENTIFICATION. — Length 17 to 24 inches; spread 40 to 50 inches. Head large, round, without ear-tufts; a dark grayish bird, *barred across the breast* and striped on belly; large *dark eyes;* yellowish bill.

NOTES. — Include hoots, harsh screams, and cackling laughing calls.

BREEDING. — In forests or wooded swamps. *Eggs:* 2 to 4, white, laid in hollow tree or old bird's nest.

RANGE. — Breeds from Saskatchewan, Manitoba, northern Ontario, southern Quebec, and Newfoundland south to Arkansas, Tennessee, Kentucky, northern Georgia, and northwestern South Carolina and west to eastern Wyoming, central Montana, and eastern Colorado.

How strongly strange and striking images are imprinted on the impressionable mind of youth, to remain ineffaceable through the passing years. Thus it is that my first sight of a Barred Owl recurs in my memory to this day. I can see that bird now. Reverberant hooting in the big woods had called me from the roadway to follow the sound for half a mile, when suddenly — there sat the great owl before me, on a horizontal limb, keeping the ready attitude of apprehension, his head turned squarely around so that his dark, solemn eyes stared fixedly at me. They bade me pause, but the moment I stopped, the owl whipped its head about, and springing forward, gave its broad pinions to the air.

The Northern Barred Owl is the most common large owl of New England. Here it is chiefly a bird of the woodland; hunting mostly at night and retiring to some dark retreat by day; but it is by no means confined to the woods. In the West it may be seen on days when the sky is overcast or toward evening, flying low over the prairie grass in search of food, and in New England it sometimes courses over meadows in the dusk of evening with its wings almost touching the grass-tops. In settled regions it likes to nest in wooded swamps where people do not often go, but in heavily wooded districts it seems to live and hoot most on the ridges, while the Great Horned Owl occupies the swamps. Both species become very fond of a certain locality and may continue in it even though the nest is often robbed and the place becomes more or less public. It winters over most of its range, but seems to desert its most northern breeding-grounds in winter, where a southward migration has been reported often. In seasons of deep snow, when mice can keep under cover, and especially when northern hares are scarce, great flights of Barred Owls come from the north. At such times when in search of food this species may be found almost anywhere; many come into towns and cities where they find mice, rats, sparrows, doves and starlings, on all of which they prey.

At one of my lonely wilderness camps in the month of March a pair of Barred Owls came to the trees over my campfire and made night hideous with their grotesque love-making, banishing sleep during the evening hours. Their courting antics, as imperfectly seen by moonlight and firelight, were ludicrous in the extreme. Perched in rather low branches over the fire they nodded and bowed with half-spread wings, and wobbled and twisted their heads from side to side, meanwhile uttering the most weird and uncouth sounds imaginable. Many of them were given with the full power of their lungs, without any regard to the sleepers, while others were soft and cooing and more expressive of the tender emotions; sounds resembling maniacal laughter and others like mere chuckles were interspersed here and there between

272

loud *wha whas* and *hoo-hoó-aws*. These owls call less often after the mating season, but one may hear them occasionally, at times, toward evening or just before daylight in midsummer. The ordinary hooting is considerably higher in pitch than that of the Great Horned Owl.

At sunrise the Northern Barred Owl usually retires to some shady nook, such as a north hillside, shaded by dark hemlock, or the hollow of some old tree, where it remains inert during most of the day. When suddenly aroused from sleep in such a retreat it may appear rather stupid, but it can see perfectly in the daytime. Its large, dark eyes, even though partly closed, will detect a hawk high in the sky, beyond the reach of ordinary human vision.

FLORIDA BARRED OWL

Strix varia alleni RIDGWAY.

Other names: Swamp Owl; Eight Hooter.

IDENTIFICATION. — This southern race is darker than *S. v. varia*, the tail scarcely barred on the basal half, and the bars on the breast narrower and much more distinct; toes entirely bare to extreme base.

RANGE. — South Atlantic and Gulf States from central North Carolina to eastern Texas, north to northern Alabama and Arkansas.

The Florida Barred Owl is an abundant bird in many parts of Florida, where its characteristic notes may often be heard at night and occasionally in the daytime. Like its northern congener, its common call consists of a series of eight notes, with a falling inflection at the end, which has given it its local name of 'Eight-Hooter.' It is well rendered by the old darky's questioning 'Who cooks for you? Who cooks for you-all?' 'who cooks' being given slowly, 'for you' more quickly, and the 'all' dropping abruptly. Arthur T. Wayne gives it as 'I cook today, you cook tomorrow.' The birds also use many other notes and a conversation between two Barred Owls, when heard at close range, is most entertaining. — (J.B.M.)

GREAT GRAY OWL

Scotiaptex nebulosa nebulosa (FORSTER).   PLATE 46.

Other name: Spruce Owl.

IDENTIFICATION. — Length 23½ to 33 inches; spread 48½ to 60 inches. In appearance our largest owl; a dark gray bird without ear-tufts, very large head, and *yellow eyes;* upper *breast not barred* but dappled or vertically streaked.

BREEDING. — In forests. *Nest:* Of sticks, weeds, and mosses, lined with feathers, in tree. *Eggs:* 3 to 5, white.

RANGE. — Breeds from tree limit in north-central Alaska and northwestern Mackenzie south to California, northern Montana, and Ontario; in winter irregularly south to Wyoming, Nebraska, Minnesota, Indiana, Ohio, northern New Jersey, and New England.

Scotiaptex nebulosa, the name which the systematists have given the Great Gray Owl, certainly is descriptive of the bird. Freely translated it runs thus — 'The gray eagle-owl of darkness.'

273

In the Far North where the summer sun hangs in the sky nearly all night, this bird, adapting itself to circumstances, hunts by daylight, but in the more southern parts of its range it prefers dusk or darkness for its hunting. When perched on a limb of some isolated leafless tree, it appears a monstrous fowl, but when taken in the hand its great apparent size is seen to be due largely to feathers. Its head and face seem immense, but its feet are small and it is indeed a light-weight, some weighing less than large Barred Owls. Its long wings and tail increase its apparent size. Its covering of thick down and long fluffy feathers (particularly on breast), which make it seem so large and powerful, are grown as a protection from the cold. It is provided with such a thick non-conducting coat from beak to claws that it is obliged to move southward in winter only by scarcity of food, and it never goes so far south as does that typical Arctic bird, the Snowy Owl. Normally it is a forest bird, living in the wooded wilderness of northern Canada or in the timber on the slopes of immense mountain ranges of the Far West. In winter, however, it moves southward irregularly, and then appears, in most seasons rarely, in the northern United States. Occasionally adverse winter conditions in its usual haunts force it to move southward in unusual numbers. When the northern forests fail to produce cones for winter food of small arboreal birds; when deep snows cover the runways of mice, and grasses and weeds that feed ground-birds, and when bush rabbits and ptarmigan are scarce in the northern wilderness, then we may expect an invasion of Great Gray Owls.

Although it is a forest bird, it may be found almost anywhere in winter outside the cities and very rarely even within city limits, but it prefers deep woods, and as it is here chiefly in winter and moves about mainly at night, it is rarely seen. The Great Gray Owl frequents the woods, and often watches for its prey from a tall tree. It does not always sit erect in the conventional owl position, but often sits with its body inclined forward at an angle of forty-five degrees or more, especially if watching some object on the ground below. The food of this bird is known to consist largely of mice, rabbits and small birds, but we have little information about either the bird or its food.

LONG–EARED OWL

Asio wilsonianus (LESSON).   PLATE 45.

IDENTIFICATION. — Length 13 to 16 inches; spread 36 to 42 inches. Size intermediate between Screech Owl and Barred Owl; if seen sitting, its rather dark colors, rusty-brown face and long 'ears,' rising from near the middle of head, distinguish it; in flight, which is light, wavering and uncertain, ears are not visible, nor all its markings and it may then be distinguished from Short-eared Owl by darker gray coloration (the latter is more buffy); usually seen in or near woods in breeding season, while the other is rarely if ever seen there, but in migration the Long-eared Owl may be found almost anywhere.

BREEDING. — Nest commonly in old bird's nest in tree. *Eggs:* 3 to 7, white.

RANGE. — Breeds from central British Columbia, northern Ontario, southern Quebec, and Newfoundland south to southern California, northern Texas, Arkansas, and Virginia; winters from southern Canada to southern Florida, Louisiana, and central Mexico.

The pretty little Long-eared Owl resembles in color the Great Horned Owl, but is much more delicately formed and its 'horns' are much nearer together. Formerly it was a common bird throughout most of the forested region within its breeding range, and it is more common still than most of us realize. It is so nearly nocturnal that it is seen rarely except when disturbed at its nest, or surprised in some retreat in the daytime. It seems to inhabit dense coniferous woods by preference, where it hides during daylight amid the dark foliage, though at night it often hunts in the open. It is rarely seen hunting in daylight, except on very dark dull days, or just before dusk. During migration, however, it may be found anywhere, and if in a tree-less country will take advantage of such hiding-places in the daytime as a thick bush or the loft of an old barn.

The wings and tail of the Long-eared Owl are so long that in flight the bird looks larger than it really is. Its body is slight and slim, and its feathered feet are small. In winter, num-bers of these birds are accustomed to hunt for field mice along river bottoms in open country where there are few coniferous trees, and to assemble to roost at night in some clump of orna-mental evergreens planted to decorate the grounds of some residence. When in danger of being observed in such a retreat, they draw the feathers close to the body and stand erect so as to resemble the stub of a broken branch. If wounded or cornered and brought to bay, the bird seems to swell to about three or four times its real size, as its wings are partially ex-tended as shields, while the feathers all over its body stand erect. Standing thus with flashing eyes, its ferocious appearance is intended to terrify its enemies. If actually attacked and un-able to escape, it may throw itself on its back and present both beak and talons to the enemy.

Although nesting in trees, this owl, when driven from its nest by a climbing human intruder, sometimes flutters to the ground, where, uttering piercing cries and dragging her wings as if broken, she circles around and around, acting very like that ground-nesting species, the Ruffed Grouse.

There seems to be a general belief that owls do not migrate, but with this species as well as with some others that range far to the north, there is a regular southward movement from the most northern part of the range, a general migration which is evident also for a greater or less distance to the southward of their usual breeding range.

The food of the Long-eared Owl consists almost entirely of field mice and other small mammals with many insects and a few birds. Wherever numbers of this species roost together, as they do commonly in many parts of the country, thousands of pellets may be found upon the ground under the trees, containing the bones and fur of small mammals, mostly mice, which the birds have eaten. I have been unable to find a record indicating that they ever trouble poultry, and most of the few small birds that they eat are seed-eating or forest species, not of great value to agriculture. The Long-eared Owl is a bird to be fostered, and protected.

SHORT-EARED OWL

Asio flammeus flammeus (PONTOPPIDAN).   PLATE 45.

Other names: Marsh Owl; Bog Owl.

IDENTIFICATION. — Length 12½ to 17 inches; spread 38 to 44 inches. A little smaller than Crow; lighter, more yellowish than Long-eared Owl and wings longer, but broad, and chiefly white on under sides with a large blackish mark near base of primaries; wings and tail dark above, spotted and barred dark brown and whitish; keeps in open country, flies much in daytime with light, easy, irregular flight, flapping steadily most of the time with no neck showing; short 'ears' rarely can be seen; eyes completely encircled by black; rests and roosts chiefly on ground.

BREEDING. — In open lands. *Nest:* On ground, with little material added. *Eggs:* 4 to 9, white or creamy.

RANGE. — Breeds locally from northern Alaska, northern Mackenzie, northern Quebec (Ungava), and Greenland south to California, Colorado, Missouri, northern Indiana, northern Ohio, and the coast of New Jersey; winters from British Columbia, Minnesota, Indiana, Ohio, and Massachusetts south to Louisiana, Cuba, and Guatemala; also occurs in Eurasia.

The Short-eared Owl is a bird of the open. Over prairie, marsh, meadow, savannah and even over the sea its tireless dappled wings bear it on and on in soundless wavering flight. In air it exemplifies the poetry of motion. Its pinions press softly on the resistant element and waft the bird gently about over its favorite moors as lightly as a night moth. In the wide savannahs of Florida, bathed in the effulgent moonlight of that subtropical land, it has fluttered noiselessly about my head, its curiosity excited by the strange intruder on its ancient hunting-ground. On the rolling hills of Nantucket and on the bushy plains of Martha's Vineyard, I have watched with delight its daylight hunting, or have had three or four at a time floating erratically about me in the dusk of early evening. In some regions it is called the Marsh or Bog Owl because of its apparent predilection for marsh hunting, and it quarters over marshes as assiduously as a Marsh Hawk; but like the latter it is by no means confined to marshes, for it hunts and even rears its young on high dry plains and desert dunes. Its only requirements are open lands and an abundance of mice — its favorite prey. It nests on the dry plains of Martha's Vineyard in the former Heath Hen country, and on sandy islands in the sea, where there is no fresh water; and it is fond of cruising along sandy beaches and hunting insects over the water, sometimes pursuing them at some distance from land, as does the Laughing Gull. In hunting it may fly only a few feet above the ground, its flight at such times resembling the light and airy progress of the Marsh Hawk, or it may pursue its way from fifty to one hundred feet above the earth, eagerly scanning the surface below. Its aerial movements appear to be effortless. It flaps and hovers about, now and then sailing lightly along. When it sees a favorable opportunity, it may hover for a moment or may drop directly on its prey and remain there to devour it; or if flying low it may snatch the unlucky victim from the ground, and pass on without even checking its speed, so swift and skillful is its stroke. If three or four are cruising about together and one stops to kill and eat a mouse, the others are likely to alight also, either on the ground or on near-by bushes, as if curious to see what their neighbor is doing. If in hunting, one hears or sees a mouse that escapes to its hole or some other concealment, it may alight on a stump, bush or post, where it sits in imitation of a snag, watching, meanwhile, like a cat at a mouse-hole for the appearance of its victim.

In winter, when snow is deep on the ground, this owl is likely to betake itself to some thick evergreen tree to roost, and it seeks shelter in stumps of such trees during storms. Commonly, however, it alights on the ground, where it probably always nests. It is not altogether confined to a treeless country nor to lowlands, as it has been known to breed not only among shrubs but also among scattering trees and even on mountains. It hunts silently for the most part, and much of its vociferousness occurs during the mating season and while breeding, especially when its young are approached or disturbed by an intruder. If one is suddenly startled from the ground during its daylight slumber, it flaps uncertainly away near the surface for some distance, and then drops quickly down and hides in the grass or undergrowth.

This owl migrates both regularly and irregularly; regularly in autumn it moves out of the northern part of its range toward the south; irregularly it remains for two or three years where it finds abundant food; at least it is believed that the same individuals remain without migration. Few of the species winter in the latitude of New England, but in spring the number increases, usually in the latter part of March or in April, as the migrants move northward.

The eggs of this bird are deposited at intervals, usually of about two days, but sometimes longer periods intervene, and as incubation begins about the time that the first egg is laid, the young hatch at different times and there are various sizes in the same nest, as is the case with some other birds of prey. When the young have learned to fly, the family keeps together for a long time, and the parents continue to feed the young, which gradually learn to hunt for themselves. In September, the southward pilgrimage begins.

RICHARDSON'S OWL

Cryptoglaux funerea richardsoni (BONAPARTE). PLATE 47.

IDENTIFICATION. — Length 8¼ to 12 inches; spread 19 to 24 inches. Size of Screech Owl but wings and tail longer; without ear-tufts; darker brown than red Screech Owl; light bill distinguishes it from Saw-whet Owl; facial discs outlined with black; white spotting on forehead.

BREEDING. — In coniferous forests. *Nest:* In holes in trees or in other birds' nests. *Eggs:* 4 to 6 or more, white.

RANGE. — Breeds from tree limit in central Alaska and Mackenzie south to northern British Columbia, Manitoba, Nova Scotia, and the Magdalen Islands; winters south to southern Canada and southwestern British Columbia.

Richardson's Owl is a forest night bird. It lives in dense coniferous forests, where it hides during the daytime, and therefore is seldom seen. In forests within the Arctic Circle during the long days of summer it is obliged to hunt by day to feed its young. As it is not supposed to breed regularly below the upper Canadian Zone, and is not known to nest anywhere within the boundaries of the United States, we may expect to see it only in late fall and winter, and rarely then, but owing to its retiring habits it has been considered far more rare than it actually is. Probably it may be found in the woods of northern Maine and Michigan in most winters in fluctuating numbers, but as ornithologists are far fewer in these winter woods than owls, it is seldom recorded. Now and then there comes a season when deep snow covers the northern country and conceals the mice. When a coincidental lack of food drives the northern arboreal birds southward, then the little owls must follow them or die of starvation, for they are too small to capture northern hares or grouse. Such a combination of circumstances occurred in the winter of 1922–23, when woodsmen in the Maine woods found little owls scattered through the woods, either alive or dead on the snow. The starving birds left the woods in search of food and entered not only farm buildings, but buildings in villages and cities, and many were captured in such situations. The bewildered, weakened birds wandered on until some of them reached the shores of Cape Cod and the valleys of Connecticut. Their exhaustion or their dullness in the daytime enabled some of those who saw them to take them in their hands.

The Eskimos in Alaska, according to Dr. Nelson, believe that this owl cannot see by day, and have named it '*tuk-whe-ling-uk*,' the blind one. Some authors seem to believe that this owl cannot see by daylight. But even if it sees only indifferently well by day, it is the exception among owls, as most of them see remarkably well then.

Apparently there is a more or less irregular migration of this species; otherwise it would not be found so frequently in northern Maine, where it is not known to breed. But the bird apparently never goes as far south as does the Snowy Owl, and rarely is found in considerable numbers within the boundaries of the United States. Little is known of its food which is supposed to consist principally of mice, insects and small birds.

SAW–WHET OWL

Cryptoglaux acadica acadica (GMELIN). PLATE 47.

Other names: Acadian Owl; Saw-filer; White-fronted Owl (young).

IDENTIFICATION. — Length 7 to 8½ inches; spread 17 to 20½ inches. Much smaller than Richardson's or Screech Owl; *no ear-tufts;* lighter-colored than Richardson's and top of head *streaked with white*, not spotted; *bill black.*

BREEDING. — Similar to Screech Owl.

RANGE. — Breeds from southern Alaska, Manitoba, Quebec, New Brunswick, and Nova Scotia south to California, central Arizona, Oklahoma, and the mountains of Mexico to Vera Cruz; also in southern Nebraska, northern Illinois, northern Indiana, and the mountains of Pennsylvania and Maryland; winters south to southern California, Louisiana, Virginia, and casually to the Carolinas and Georgia.

The little Saw-whet Owl, the smallest of all our eastern nocturnal birds of prey, is about the size of a Towhee, but its long, broad wings and its heavy coating of loose downy feathers, which fit it to endure intense cold, give to it a larger appearance. Owing to its nocturnal habits, its reticence and its extremely retiring disposition in daylight, it is not seen often except during those severe winters, when hundreds appear searching for food wherever it may be found. Then they sometimes enter farm buildings for shelter or perhaps in search of mice, and many are captured. The note of this owl, which sometimes is harsh and creaky, resembling saw filing, may be so softly intoned at other times as to bear little resemblance to that nerve-racking sound, and the bird has the power of ventriloquizing so that the softened call seems faint and far away. While its notes frequently are uttered during the mating season in February, March and April, when few people are in the woods, the bird is ordinarily more quiet after the eggs are laid, and even if its voice is heard then, it is commonly attributed to some other creature. It hunts silently at night, and during the day retires to some dark evergreen thicket or a hole in a tree to sleep away the hours of sunlight. Hence it is more common than many a day bird that is more often seen.

Dull and sleepy though it may be in daylight, at dusk it becomes an active, animated forest elf. Its courage is great, as it has been known to attack and kill rats much larger than itself; to kill and devour small squirrels; and even to fly at the head of a man who came near its young.

Wood mice form the principal food of this owl. In winter in the great coniferous forests of Canada much of the snow is upheld on the branches of the trees in such a way that there are spaces here and there close to the trunks where there is little snow. There the wood mice come out at night from their hiding-places under the snow, and there the little owl perched in the branches above them awaits their coming; but if for any reason owl-food is scarce or hard to obtain, as sometimes happens in severe winters with deep snow, the little owls must move south or perish. At such times there is a great influx of these birds from the North. By the time they reach a milder clime, many of them are too emaciated and exhausted to hunt or even to eat. They seem to lose all interest in life, and seek only a quiet retreat in which to die. Others more hardy or less exhausted survive to return, with the advent of spring, to the land of their nativity.

Order Caprimulgiformes.   Goatsuckers and Allies.

CHUCK–WILL'S–WIDOW

Antrostomus carolinensis (GMELIN).   PLATE 95.

Other names: Dutch or Spanish Whip-poor-will.

IDENTIFICATION. — Length 11 to 13¼ inches; spread 24½ to 25½ inches. Resembles Whip-poor-will in coloration but longer and much bulkier; large head and 'neckless' appearance suggest an owl, but usually perches on ground or lengthwise of a limb in a horizontal position, not erect like most owls.

VOICE. — Call is distinctive.

BREEDING. — *Eggs:* 2, creamy white, richly marbled and spotted with grays and browns, laid on dead leaves in forest.

RANGE. — Breeds from southeastern Kansas, southern Missouri, southern Illinois, southern Indiana, and southern Maryland south to central Texas and the Gulf States; winters from Florida to the Greater Antilles, Central America, and Colombia.

While a few Chuck-will's-widows winter in southern Florida, it is a migrant and summer resident in the northern part of that state and in Georgia and the Carolinas. It was among the early avian signs of returning spring at Thomasville, Georgia, where its characteristic notes were first heard in early March. While suggestive of the notes of its smaller congener, the Eastern Whip-poor-will, they are easily distinguished. A. H. Howell gives them as *chuck'*, *will, will*; the last note is sometimes double, giving the 'widow' interpretation in its name, but it is not very distinct.

The mouth of the Chuck-will's-widow is perhaps its most distinctive feature, having an opening 'from ear to ear' of about two inches, with the rather weak beak projecting less than a half inch from the bird's low forehead. The bill is not needed for picking up its food, however, for it flies about catching insects on the wing, and seemingly 'inhaling' them with its huge bristle-beset mouth. It feeds largely upon night-flying moths, but has been known to capture, and swallow entire, such small birds as hummingbirds, warblers and sparrows.

The Chuck-will's-widow furnishes an excellent example of what is termed 'protective coloration.' During the day it is usually resting on the ground in the woodlands, where its mottled-grays, browns and black blend almost perfectly with a background of dead leaves and broken twigs; when perched in a tree it usually sits lengthwise of the branch, its colors shading off into those of the bark so that it looks like a thickening of the limb or the stump of a broken branch. The white on the outer tail feathers of the male, though conspicuous in flight, seldom shows when the bird is at rest. When startled, the bird flutters off like an owl or a gigantic moth, the rather broad wings being quite noticeable. — (J.B.M.)

EASTERN WHIP–POOR–WILL

Antrostomus vociferus vociferus (WILSON).

PLATE 53.

IDENTIFICATION. — Length 9 to 10¼ inches; spread 16 to 19½ inches. A brown bird, easily distinguished from Nighthawk when perched by its shorter wings not reaching tip of *rounded tail*; Nighthawk's wings reach beyond tip of *forked tail* and Nighthawk is darker and more gray and shows large white spot on spread wing; Whip-poor-will usually rises from a dark, shady place on ground in woods, and feeds at night by low, short flights; Nighthawk rises from the open and often flies high by day or night; considerably smaller than Chuck-will's-widow.

VOICE. — See below.

BREEDING. — Similar to Chuck-will's-widow.

RANGE. — Breeds from Manitoba, southern Quebec, New Brunswick, and Nova Scotia south to the northern parts of Louisiana, Mississippi, Alabama, Georgia, and northwestern South Carolina, and from eastern North Dakota, Nebraska, and Kansas eastward; winters from the lowlands of South Carolina and the Gulf States to Central America.

In calm, still summer nights when under the soft light of the full moon the dark plumes of the pines stand motionless against the sky, the loud sweet notes of the Whip-poor-will ring through the forest shades and resound among the fells. On such a night long ago, having addressed an audience in Barre, Massachusetts, I rode through the woods for miles toward Gardner, where another engagement called me the next morning. As the buggy rolled along the darkened roads, Whip-poor-wills were calling from every direction. The air fairly vibrated, and the woods were resonant with their outcries. The dark-eyed French-Canadian driver, listening, shook his head solemnly and peering furtively about as if in apprehension said, 'Ah don' lak' hear dem fellar. Dey say dey breeng bad luck — dem er *woodchuck*.' His words voiced a feeling prevalent among the more ignorant and superstitious of the country folk, some of whom believed that if the Whip-poor-will called on the door-stone, its visit presaged sickness or death. It is natural to suspect those who move silently in darkness; and birds which, like the owl or the Whip-poor-will, fly soundlessly by night from place to place and are so concealed by the shades of evening that they are never seen distinctly are likely to be at least misunderstood. Since man became man he has feared the evil that stalks in the dark, but a creature as harmless as the Whip-poor-will should never be regarded with suspicion or alarm. When one of these birds comes from the woods to alight on the rooftree or on the door-stone, it should be a welcome visitor even though its plaintive calls may banish sleep for a short time.

Whip-poor-wills often appear in the evening about country dwellings in pursuit of nocturnal insects, such as moths, beetles and mosquitoes, which are attracted to the buildings by the lights. While I slept unsheltered nightly for a week in the Concord woods, rolled in my blanket, with only a head-net hung to a branch overhead to protect me from mosquitoes, I noticed each morning upon awaking just before daylight that something fluttered softly about my head. The sound was like that produced by a large night moth, but soon I heard something strike the ground a few feet away, and then a well-known cluck convinced me that my visitor was a Whip-poor-will. The bird came nightly while I remained in the woods, and each morning before daylight it flew around my head-net until it had caught all the mosquitoes there. Never at any other time have I been able to detect a sound from the wings of a Whip-poor-will.

From regions about the Gulf of Mexico the Whip-poor-wills come up by night, arriving in southern New England unheralded in late April or early May. As soon as they have rested from their journey the males announce their presence in the woods or thickets by their calls. The latter part of May sees the mating and nesting at its height.

When the birds have paired, the female chooses some retired spot in the woods or beneath dense shrubbery and usually deposits her eggs on the dead leaves that in such places cover the ground. If the bird is undisturbed, the young are hatched and reared in the same spot, but if too much troubled by visitors the mother may carry either eggs or young to some other location. If surprised with her young she flaps, tumbles and flutters about the intruder with open mouth and whining or guttural cries and feigns a broken wing or other hurt and thus endeavors to draw attention away from her treasures. Often she *clucks* angrily; sometimes in her excitement she seems to forget that a Whip-poor-will should always sit lengthwise on a branch and time after time alights crosswise on a horizontal limb, which merely indicates that birds do not always follow the rules of action that we lay down for them. Apparently the Whip-poor-will rarely if ever hunts food for its young in the daytime, but as the shades of night begin to fall, it rises from the ground or from some horizontal limb along which its body has lain all day, simulating an excrescence of the tree, and begins to flutter and dart about, now low and close along the ground, now just over the shrubbery or among the tree-tops, sailing and wheeling in long graceful curves or doubling and twisting in erratic flight, in pursuit of its favorite insect prey. As the male bird darts and turns, using his quickly spread tail as a rudder, the white of the outer tail feathers flashes sharply for a brief instant here and there, as the tail opens and closes. Now and then he alights, but instead of resting, pours forth his repeated *whip-poor-will* until the woods ring again. This call may be heard occasionally after sunrise, but it is given chiefly in the evening and in the morning on the approach of daylight; yet in full moonlight it may be heard at any time during the night. In the mating season he often continues to enunciate this cry until it would seem that he must drop from exhaustion, turning about occasionally or moving to another perch and sending forth his call to a different point of the compass. When close to the performers we may hear a soft short *cluck* or *chuck*, just before the 'whip.' Provided with a night glass I have watched this bird call at dusk, at a distance of about eight feet. The tips of the wings commonly drop a little below the tail, which is raised slightly. With each *chuck* the head is thrown back, with each note the tail is raised and lowered slightly, and with each complete *whip-poor-will* the shoulders move as if in the effort of expelling the sound, the strongest expulsion coming on the accented *will*. The bill and mouth as I saw them were only slightly opened.

As the season wanes, and the young birds leave the place of their nativity, they soon learn to run and hide. In late summer the calls of the male are seldom heard, though he may be heard again occasionally in September before all depart for the south. A light-colored, flat, open space seems to attract Whip-poor-wills on moonlit nights; they will alight on a bare ledge in a pasture or on the wide farmhouse door-stone. They also alight in the roads at night. Many a driver of a motorcar has been puzzled to see a large red eye glowing in the rays of his headlights and has stopped his car and found a Whip-poor-will sitting in the road. Its eye always shows red in the glare of the light. In daylight in its shaded retreats the Whip-poor-will blends into its surroundings so as to be virtually invisible to the human eye until it moves, which it rarely does, until in danger of being trodden upon, when it flutters along for a few rods and again disappears. In the woods it is fairly safe, though no doubt preyed upon by owls; but when the country becomes thickly settled, Whip-poor-wills are likely to disappear.

The Whip-poor-will is an animated insect trap. Its wide mouth and the long 'bristles' about it fit the bird especially for the capture of the larger nocturnal winged insects, which the smaller day birds cannot eat. It consumes quantities of them. In its food list we find cutworm moths, cranberry moths and practically all the larger moths whose caterpillars destroy the leaves of trees. The bird also takes ants, grasshoppers, potato beetles, May beetles or 'June bugs,' mosquitoes, gnats and many other winged insects and the eggs of insects.

EASTERN NIGHTHAWK

Chordeiles minor minor (FORSTER).   PLATE 53.

Other names: Bull-bat; Mosquito Hawk; Pork-and-beans; Burnt Land Bird; Chimney Bat.
IDENTIFICATION. — Length 8¼ to 10 inches; spread 21 to 23¾ inches. Size about that of Whip-poor-will but wings longer, more pointed, and tail forked rather than rounded; flight usually higher than that of Whip-poor-will and a large *white spot shows in each dark wing* like a hole through it; the white throat band of Nighthawk crosses high on throat while that of Whip-poor-will crosses lower down near upper breast.
CALL. — A harsh *peent*, like note of Woodcock.
BREEDING. — *Eggs:* 2, creamy-white to olive-gray, spotted and blotched with browns, drab, and lilac, laid on bare rock, gravel, etc., or on gravel roofs of buildings.
RANGE. — Breeds from southern Yukon, northern Manitoba, southern Quebec, and Newfoundland south to northwestern Washington, northeastern Oklahoma, northern Arkansas, southeastern Tennessee, northern Georgia, and southern Virginia; winters in South America from Colombia to Argentina; migrates through the Bahamas, Greater Antilles and Central America.

The Eastern Nighthawk is a wonderful bird. It wanders in migration from the islands of the Arctic Ocean to southern South America. It feeds and flies indifferently at any hour of the day or night, being able apparently to see and catch flying insects in brightest sunlight or on clear nights. It has an enormous stomach which requires quantities of food to supply its remarkable digestion, and thus furnish energy to sustain it in tireless flight. Its mouth, like that of the Whip-poor-will, opens far back under its ears and forms a yawning trap to engulf unwary insects, while its long and powerful wings enable it to overtake them with ease. It lays its eggs on the ground, on a ledge or on the flat roof of a building, exposed to the blazing summer sun, where it seems as if the young bird must be roasted alive, but nevertheless it seems to reproduce its kind with fair regularity.

In late April or early May the Nighthawks, coming up from the South, usually appear in the latitude of southern New England. In backward seasons, however, their migration continues until June. In mating the courtship is mostly an aerial performance, for the Nighthawk is pre-eminently a fowl of the air. In the mating season the male often rises to a considerable height and then falls swiftly, head first, with wings partly closed, until near the earth, when, spreading his wings, he turns upward, producing with his vibrating primaries a resounding boom which may be heard at a considerable distance.

The eggs so closely resemble the rock, earth or gravel on which they rest, and the young so simulate in appearance clods or horse droppings covered with mold, that they seem to escape the eyes of their enemies. The mother sitting on her eggs is almost invisible, as her plumage blends into the colors of her environment, and she will sit there with eyes nearly closed until almost trodden upon. Sometimes she will refuse to leave, but with spread wings will make a noise like a spitting cat. If she is brooding young, she may leave them, and rush hissing at the intruder with her great mouth wide open. As she charges forward, almost hidden, as it were, behind that yawning cavity, she must present a fearsome front to any small or timid creature. There is something menacing and snake-like about that swiftly advancing open countenance. But if the bold front fails to daunt the enemy, she may resort to artifice and limp along the ground like a wounded bird, fluttering slowly ahead of her pursuer. If he fails to follow she may fall across the top of a low stump or rock and lie there as if at her last gasp with head down and one wing hanging as if broken, meantime uttering doleful cries, while the young lie flat and motionless.

The Nighthawk usually sleeps during the brighter part of the day, resting upon the ground, a rock, a fence rail or a bough. Often it sits silent on a large limb, where it might be mistaken for an excrescence or a bunch of gray lichens. During the nesting season, however, it keeps very irregular hours; frequently it hunts in daylight, and may sleep in the darker part of the night, but at times it is heard on the wing far into the night. Breeding in cities is a comparatively recent custom and dates from the introduction of flat tar-and-gravel roofs. These arid spaces seem to suit the bird, and it hawks about high over the city roofs, seeking its insect prey.

Late in August the southward movement of the Nighthawks begins, and it continues intermittently through the greater part of September. Unlike the nocturnal migrations of most of our small land birds, the travels of the Nighthawk are made by day. The birds are seen commonly passing southward along some river valley in numbers from a score to a hundred or more in loose scattered flocks, flying about in a leisurely manner at no great height above the ground or water, and catching insects as they go. These flocks sometimes rest during a part of the day, either on the ground or in trees on rough and rocky land, and if undisturbed begin their journey toward evening, first filling their stomachs as they go.

When the flocks are feeding, they do not always move southward, and sometimes they have been observed to travel in exactly the opposite direction. There are certain routes over water which are followed by them, and which often take them far off from the direct southwesterly course. But the general movement trends southward.

The food of the Eastern Nighthawk apparently consists entirely of insects. Its large stomach often is packed with them, and its gullet also and even its mouth may be filled with them when about to feed its young. Its insect food is so varied that it is impossible to enumerate it. Apparently it takes any insect that flies, from tiny gnats to the largest moths.

FLORIDA NIGHTHAWK

Chordeiles minor chapmani COUES.

IDENTIFICATION. — Slightly smaller than *C. m. minor*, with the white and cream-buff markings of the upper parts more numerous.

RANGE. — South Atlantic and Gulf States from central North Carolina to eastern Texas and north to southern Illinois and south-central Arkansas; winters in South America from Colombia to Argentina.

The Eastern Nighthawk, at least in New England, has become very much of a city dweller, being most frequently heard and seen flying over the flat-topped city buildings on which it lays its eggs among the roofing pebbles, but the Florida Nighthawk still haunts its old resorts, open 'piney' woods, old fields and pastures, 'prairies,' marshes and open beaches. Its harsh nasal *peent* is often heard in the daytime, though more commonly toward dusk, and its long wings with their white spots looking like a gap in the flight-feathers, its erratic flight, and occasional downward zooming plunge, which is accompanied by a peculiar booming sound, make it an easily recognized species. Its name, given it because of its habit of hawking about after insects, is unfortunate, for many ignorant people think the bird is a true hawk, and it meets the unnecessary persecution commonly given all hawks, though like most of our true hawks, it is really a very beneficial species and should be encouraged instead of exterminated. — (J.B.M.)

Order Micropodiformes. Swifts and Hummingbirds.

CHIMNEY SWIFT

Chaetura pelagica (LINNAEUS).   PLATE 53.

Other names: Chimney Swallow; Chimney-bird; Chimney Bat.

IDENTIFICATION. — Length 4¾ to 5½ inches; spread 12 to 12¾ inches. A swallow-like but apparently tail-less bird, sooty black all over; usually seen in flight with long, curved, rapidly moving wings and short (occasionally spread) tail suggesting a 'flying cigar'; seen most often in late afternoon or early morning.

BREEDING. — Formerly in hollow trees but now usually in chimneys or vacant buildings. *Nest:* A 'half-saucer' of twigs glued by saliva to a vertical surface. *Eggs:* 4 to 6, glossy white.

RANGE. — Breeds from central Alberta, Manitoba, southern Quebec, and Newfoundland south to Florida and the Gulf coast, and west to east-central Montana and eastern Texas; winters probably in Brazil; migrates across Haiti, Mexico and Central America.

Some people call this bird the Chimney Sweep; but it does not sweep chimneys. It sweeps the skies. There are few farming regions or country villages where any watcher of the sky cannot see the Swifts rapidly drawing disappearing lines across the blue. Zigzags and long curves intersect one another as the merry birds drive through the fresh morning air with quivering wings and shrill twitterings — erratic avian missiles seeking luckless winged insects in the overarching skies.

Swifts are well named. Probably there are no swifter birds. Even the stooping falcon can rarely if ever overtake one. Their speed has been estimated at unbelievable figures, and it has been said that in their ordinary avocations they travel a thousand miles a day. Such statements, however, cannot be verified, and we must be content to watch them with no accurate knowledge of their greatest speed or the length of their daily pathways through the 'illimitable air.'

The Chimney Swift is essentially a fowl of the air. When its growing young are clamoring for food, it keeps the air much of the time, from the first indication of morning light in the east until nightfall. So far as we know, it never rests on ground or tree limb, and it sleeps clinging to a perpendicular wall in chimney, well, cistern, cave, building or hollow tree, or very rarely to a tree-trunk, woodpile or some such upright outer surface. Virtually all its outdoor life is passed in the air. It lives in the air and probably sometimes dies there. The bird is as free as the winds. Even its courtship is an aerial one.

When the birds are mated, they commence breaking dead twigs off the trees for their nest, by flying swiftly against a twig and grasping it in their feet or bills as they pass. Often they are unable to tear the twig loose or even to break it, but each bird perseveres until the nest is finished. Twigs are glued first against the inner wall of tree, cave, chimney, well or building by the copious sticky saliva of the birds, and others are then attached in the same way to these first. Such work is successful only in dry weather and if much rain occurs the building of the chimney nests is long delayed, and sometimes copious rains later dissolve the gluey substance and precipitate nest and eggs or young to the bottom of the chimney. When the young birds are about two weeks old, they leave the nest and usually cling to the chimney wall below it, where they are fed by the parents until they can fly. Swifts prefer large old-fashioned chimneys for nesting-places, and usually occupy such as are unused during the summer.

The Chimney Swift's upward flutterings, downward swoops and quick zigzags commonly are executed in pursuit of fast-flying insects, but these birds are extremely playful and many aerial evolutions appear to be the manifestation of a frolicsome spirit. Once while watching some Cedar Waxwings hawking for insects over a river, I saw a Chimney Swift chase them as if with evil intent. The frightened Cedarbirds quickly sought refuge in the nearest tree. Evidently the Swift was in play, as it could not possibly have swallowed a bird larger than itself, nor could its weak bill have greatly injured the Waxwing. Indeed Swifts seem to be entirely harmless, and so far as I know, they are not in the least quarrelsome and have never been known to injure any other bird. They seem fearless, however, as they pay little attention to hawks and keep the air during the approach of the most violent thunderstorms and tempests. They seem to enjoy riding the storm. If, however, a storm comes on toward night, bringing on premature darkness, the Swifts are very likely to betake themselves to their chimneys as they do at nightfall.

Large numbers of Chimney Swifts roost at night in the capacious chimneys of certain large buildings, such as schoolhouses or factories. The male birds sleep in such dormitories more or less throughout the summer, and when the young are fledged many of them follow their parents to these roosting-places. It is an interesting sight to see a swarm of Swifts retiring at nightfall into such a place of refuge. This happens more or less at the migration periods. Hundreds and sometimes thousands gyrate and play about over the chimney, forming a funnel-shaped flock, and finally one by one they raise their wings and drop quickly into it until the whole swarm is at rest. In some remote places their flocks still descend into great hollow trees to pass the night. Audubon, who effected an entrance into one of these hollow trees and examined the roosting birds by artificial light, estimated that nine thousand were sleeping in that tree. In all their evolutions there seems to be no interference; no collisions occur, and they seem to live in perfect harmony. The first birds to enter arrange themselves in a row near the top, and the later entrants perch in tiers below.

Chimney Swifts are more or less crepuscular as well as diurnal; that is, they go abroad at early morning and evening, seeming to prefer half-twilight to broad day. Therefore dull and cloudy weather suits them well; but they fly in bright sunlight, and may be seen during warm days far up in the sky chasing insects that rise high on such days. At times Chimney Swifts seem to be on the wing far into the night, as their cries come down to us from the darkness. Evidently then their large dark eyes can penetrate the gloom of night. Swifts are believed to feed entirely on flying insects, but my experience in watching them inclines me to the belief that they sometimes take small caterpillars that, spinning down on long threads from the branches of trees, are blown about by the wind, and they may even pick one occasionally from the leaves.

RUBY–THROATED HUMMINGBIRD

Archilochus colubris (LINNAEUS). PLATE 54.

Other names: Hummer; Ruby-throat.

IDENTIFICATION. — Length 3 to 4 inches; spread 4 to 4¾ inches. The only hummingbird found east of the ninety-fifth meridian; easily recognized by size, needle-like bill, and extremely rapid wing-movements; more likely to be confused with a hawk-moth or humming-moth than with any other bird.

BREEDING. — In orchard or woodland trees. *Nest:* A cup of soft felted material saddled on a limb and covered with bits of lichen. *Eggs:* 2, white, about ½ inch long and ⅓ inch in diameter.

RANGE. — Breeds from Alberta, Manitoba, and Cape Breton Island south to the Gulf coast and Florida, west to North Dakota, Nebraska, Kansas, and central Texas; winters from middle and southern Florida and Louisiana through southern Mexico and Central America to Panama.

The Ruby-throated Hummingbird is in some respects the most remarkable bird of eastern North America. When the first settlers landed on these shores, they had never seen a hummingbird. Therefore, some of the chroniclers who set down in ink 'true relations' regarding the New Land included the tiny bird among the marvels of the country. Some of their descriptions are more picturesque than accurate. William Wood, writing in 1634, informs all and sundry that 'The Humbird is one of the wonders of the Countrey, being no bigger than a Hornet, yet hath all the demensions of a Bird, as bill, and wings, with quills, spider-like legges, small clawes: For colour she is as glorious as the Raine-bow; as she flies, she makes a little humming noise like a Humble-bee: wherefore shee is called the Humbird.'

Thomas Morton, writing two years earlier, gives us the following illuminating account: 'There is a curious bird to see to, called a humming bird, no bigger than a great beetle: that out of question lives upon the Bee, which hee eateth and catcheth amongst Flowers. For it is his custome to frequent these places. Flowers he cannot feed upon by reason of his sharp bill which is like the poynt of a Spanish needle, but shorte. His fethers have a glosse like silke, and as hee stirres they show to be of a chaingable coloure: and has bin, and is admired for shape, coloure and size.'

This little bird seems to have few effective enemies. He is too agile and swift for them. At times when he is not feeling truculent, he may allow some of the larger birds to chase him away from their nests, but I have seldom heard of the catching of a hummingbird by another bird. Rarely is he followed far. Now and then an inexperienced Starling will follow one for a long distance, perhaps mistaking it for a moth, but the Ruby-throat easily evades its pursuer.

The tiny hummingbird is a mighty warrior, with greater strength and speed in proportion to its size than any other bird that flies. The flight muscles of its breast are relatively immense, and it is possessed of such spirit that it does not hesitate to attack any bird, no matter what its size, when occasion seems to require it. Kingbird, hawk, crow or eagle, all alike quickly feel the effects of the Ruby-throated Hummingbird's displeasure. It has even been known to drive to cover a pompous Plymouth Rock rooster. Its needle-like bill is an irritating little weapon and not to be despised when driven forward by its sturdy humming wings. Those little wings, beating so fast that eye cannot see their motions nor ordinary camera depict them, carry it on long migrations, as the species ranges from Hudson Bay to Panama. Some of the Ruby-throats must cross wide stretches of ocean. They must pass over at least six hundred miles to reach the Bermudas and five hundred miles to cross the Gulf of Mexico to Yucatan and Central America.

Ruby-throated Hummingbirds appear generally when the cherry trees are in blossom, and sometimes a considerable number may be seen buzzing about one blooming tree — their wings giving forth a sound as if giant bees were swarming. The males come first, and when the females arrive their wooing soon begins. Ruby-throats always are quick, but during the mating season the pugnacious males are so dashing and impetuous that the eye can hardly follow their movements, which in their battles are so rapid that the details are confusing. In courtship the female flees and the male pursues. They vanish like shooting-stars, and the dénouement seldom is witnessed by human eye; but when the male displays his beauties before a female that is sitting demurely on a twig, his movements may be readily descried. He seems able to perform any acrobatic feat in the air. He can charge toward her with amazing speed until almost upon her; then suddenly stop and, hanging in mid-air, back away. His most remarkable feat, however, is to swing before her as if hung from an invisible rod like the 'lob' of a mighty pendulum, swinging from side to side with breath-taking speed in a segment of a vertical circle. The radius of the swing may vary with different individuals from three to forty feet or even more. Some birds rise much higher at one end of the segment than at the other, and often one rises vertically at each end, forming a broad U, or a vertical half circle. Sometimes the male takes only two or three of these swings; or he may execute fifteen or twenty. Usually the female is sitting near the very bottom of his swing or just below it, and as he flashes back and forth close before her or just above, his gorget glows like fire. During the swinging performance the male often makes an unusual humming with its wings and continues chippering or twittering, though some of its notes are so fine that they rarely can be heard by human ears. Now and then a Ruby-throat may be observed to shoot up into the air vertically for fifty feet or more and back again. Probably this also is a manifestation of sexual passion.

After mating, the male apparently becomes a gay wanderer with nothing to do but to enjoy himself or to chase other birds. He spends much time sitting on a particular twig, which he chooses for his watch-tower and resting-place, and dressing his plumage, while his mate builds the nest and rears the brood. Very rarely does the male seem to take any interest in the proceedings, though occasionally one may be seen about the nest. Having once chosen a nesting-site the birds apparently return to the same spot year after year, but I believe that each year a new nest is built. Once I found four nests within a few yards of each other, two of them evidently deserted nests of previous years.

In building the nest the female chooses a limb or twig often sheltered above by leaves or branches, and then collects silky or downy fibers from various plants and trees, such as the down from ferns and milkweed and that from undeveloped oak leaves which she fastens in place with spider's web or that of the tent-caterpillar. With such material she fashions her nest, collecting bits of wet lichens from the trees and attaching them to the outside as the nest rises, so that when finished it appears like a small knot covered with tree lichens. She works expeditiously, flying directly on to the nest with a bit of material, and in another instant off again like a winged bullet.

In building the nest she sits in it, shaping it to her body and working with both bill and feet; often the eggs are laid before the nest is completed, and the female frequently may be seen to add to it even after the young are hatched; in this case, the nest may often appear two-storied on the outside on account of the different-colored lichens used. When the little thing is done, it is the softest, warmest and most lovely cradle imaginable for her tiny white eggs, which are about the size of small white beans. The time required to build it varies much according to the weather, but usually it takes about a week.

The following from my notes taken when standing beside a nest, built about four feet from the ground in an apple tree, describes my impression of the young birds and the manner in which they are fed.

'How perfect are these little fledgling wanderers, in their tiny, moss-covered cup, shaded from the southern sun rays by the green leaves which overhang and surround the nest. Their dainty new feathers, of but a few days' growth, have been touched by the tender mother's breast alone or the gentle dew of heaven. Their inscrutable, brilliant dark eyes flash quick glances all around; no motion escapes them. One leans forward from the nest and attempts to pick a moving aphis from the limb. Their whole bodies throb quickly with the fast-surging tide of hot life pulsing through their veins. Now, with a boom like a great bee, the mother suddenly appears out of the air as she darts almost in my face. I am standing within two feet of the nest, and she hangs on buzzing wing, inspecting me, then perches on a limb just above my head, then on another a few feet away, her head raised and neck craned to its fullest extent. Buzzing about from place to place, she inspects me, until, satisfied, she finally alights on the edge of the nest at the usual place, where her constant coming has detached a piece of lichen and trodden down the fabric of the edge. The little birds raise themselves with fluttering wings, and the parent, rising to her full height, turns her bill almost directly downward, pushes it into the open beak of the young, and by working her gullet and throat discharges the food through the long, hollow bill as from a squirt gun.'

On the day the young Hummingbirds leave the nest, they have learned to strike at insects within reach, and when they go they fly swiftly and surely to some perch not far away, apparently well equipped to care for themselves, but the mother feeds them for a time — sometimes while both are on the wing. During the last part of the nesting period the young are fed more or less with soft insects, not regurgitated, but held in the bill of the parent and passed to that of the young, but probably regurgitation is the rule until the very day of flight. Hummingbirds delight in bathing, but I have never known one to enter the water. They bathe in the

288

rain or in dew by flying and fluttering among the wet leaves on the trees and shaking the drops off on their plumage or by flying in and out of the spray from a waterfall, a fountain, a garden hose or a lawn sprayer. They are quite fearless and often fly into the spray while a person is holding the hose, or feed from flowers held in the hand, and in such cases have been known to alight on an extended finger. They seem particularly attracted by red, orange or pink flowers. By planting these in profusion the presence of hummingbirds may be assured. Anything red, however, seems to have charms. Artificial flowers made of red cloth with small vials of sugar and water concealed at the base of each are used successfully to attract hummingbirds and will lure them even into open windows.

With the first frosts of autumn the Ruby-throats begin to leave us. They can stand but little cold, and now and then in late September one is picked up chilled and apparently dying. If warmed and fed, however, some of them recover. As September wanes most of them depart for the tropics.

NOTE. — The beats of the wings of the Ruby-throated Hummingbird are so rapid that the human eye can only register them in a blur, and at the time when Mr. Forbush wrote the above account, no camera had been devised which was fast enough to catch the movements of its whirring pinions. The hummingbirds as a group are also, as far as I know, the only birds which can actually *fly backwards*, and it had seemed to me that their technique of flying must be entirely different from that of other birds. Ordinary 'slow motion' movies did not tell the story, but in the spring of 1937 I learned of a new type of camera devised by engineers at Massachusetts Institute of Technology, which, by means of an extremely fast electric flash, could photograph the flight of a bullet from a high-power rifle, or the bursting of a soap bubble, and show the movements slowed down to as much as seventy-five times normal speed. If it was possible to photograph hummingbirds with this camera, the mystery of their flight would be solved, but it was a laboratory apparatus, not an easily handled 'candid camera' or home movie machine.

Then I found that my neighbor at Lake Asquam, New Hampshire, Mrs. Laurence J. Webster, had been feeding Ruby-throated Hummingbirds at her home for some years and that possibly fifty of these tiny creatures were visiting her garden daily to feast on the sugar and water solution in her ribbon-bedecked bottles. While photographing some of her birds I described the new camera and its possibilities. Mr. and Mrs. Webster were immediately interested, and it was only a few days before Prof. Harold F. Edgerton and Prof. Charles H. Blake of Technology were at the lake, with a truckful of electrical equipment and cameras. The Websters built a temporary roof over the open porch where the hummingbirds fed, to prevent fogging the very sensitive film, and a high-power line was run in from the street mains to furnish the necessary current for the stroboscopic light machine. The resultant motion pictures, taken at a speed of five hundred and fifty exposures per second, as compared with sixteen exposures for the ordinary movie camera, and with each exposure of an estimated duration of about 1/100,000 part of a second, show the movements of the wings quite clearly. Examination of the film reveals that the Ruby-throat, when hovering and feeding, makes from fifty to fifty-five complete beats of the wings per second, and one bird which flew out of the picture had reached a speed of about eighty beats per second in a distance of about two feet from its hovering position! And the interesting mechanics of the hummingbird's flight is now revealed for the first time to man's observation. — (J.B.M.)

EASTERN BELTED KINGFISHER

Megaceryle alcyon alcyon (LINNAEUS). PLATE 48.

Other names: Kingfisher; Lazy-bird.

IDENTIFICATION. — Length 11 to 14¾ inches; spread 21 to 23 inches. A topheavy-looking bird, with long straight pointed beak and large crested head but very short legs and small feet; upper parts bluish-gray, under parts white; male with a brown 'belt,' female with two; peculiar flight, alternating a few slow and a few fast beats; often hovers over water before diving for food.

CALL. — A loud harsh rattle.

BREEDING. — *Nest:* A burrow in a sand-bank. *Eggs:* 5 to 14, glossy white.

RANGE. — Breeds from Mackenzie, northern Manitoba, central Quebec, southern Labrador, and Newfoundland south to the southern border of the United States, and west to the Rocky Mountains; winters from British Columbia, Nebraska, Illinois, Indiana, Ohio, and Virginia south to the West Indies, Central America, Colombia and British Guiana, and irregularly as far north as New Hampshire and Ontario.

This wild, grotesque 'tousled-headed' bird is a common sight along our waterways. Its nesting-holes may be seen on or near almost any stream with high banks, usually where the bank has been cut away abruptly by the stream, rarely in a low sloping bank covered with sod through which these birds dig easily. A hole in a perpendicular bank or cliff is inaccessible to most of their enemies. The Kingfisher is a fierce fighter and can use its strong bill to good advantage in defending its home, striking out wickedly at an intruder.

The Eastern Belted Kingfisher is a hardy, self-reliant bird, and while most of the species winter from Virginia and Illinois southward, quite a few individuals remain farther north, wherever streams keep open in the interior or small tidal creeks along the coast offer a sufficient supply of minnows to satisfy the voracious appetite of the bird. With the return of the first warm days of spring these birds move around looking for new fishing-grounds, and they are quickly joined by others from a little farther south, for the Kingfisher is an early migrant. It is late April or early May, however, before the bulk of the northward flight of Kingfishers arrives in the latitude of New England. May is the month of mating and nesting. Except during the breeding season the Eastern Belted Kingfisher is a solitary bird. Then, however, he becomes more than chummy, and seeks the society of some double-belted bird who, if he finds favor in her sight, may become the mother of his chicks. When the conjugal arrangement has been satisfactorily completed, the pair begin to dig. Apparently the male is even more diligent at this task than the female, as his beak is usually more scarred by contact with stones and gravel than that of his mate. The time occupied in the task of excavation varies from two to ten days, depending somewhat on the depth of the hole and the character of the soil. Sand or gravel banks are chosen usually, but occasionally a burrow is made in hard clay. The excavation is made by the beaks of the birds, and the soil is removed with their feet, and scratched out to fall where it may. Generally the hole is made near the top of the bank where it is least accessible to four-footed enemies, and it is carried slightly upward, insuring good drainage and a safe sod roof. Apparently the male leaves most of the duties of incubation to the female, while he often utilizes his surplus energies in digging one or two shorter holes near the first. The 'nest' is a rounded chamber at or near the end of the burrow and frequently just beyond where it

290

makes a short turn. When the numerous chicks have hatched, the parents, who are very devoted, must keep busy to furnish sufficient food for so many hungry and rapidly growing mouths. The male takes for his fishing-ground a certain section of the stream, along which he flies from one perch to another in regular sequence while patrolling his demesne. Certain dead limbs along his fly-way are favorite watch-towers from which he scans the stream for fish and the surrounding country for intruders. If any person trespasses upon his bailiwick, he flies before the interloper, passing from station to station, until he reaches the farthest limit of his fishing-ground and then, making a wide detour, he returns to near the starting-point. If another Kingfisher trespasses upon his domain, there is immediate reaction and there ensues literally a rattling fight in the air which continues until the intruder beats an ignominious retreat.

While the Kingfisher seems to love rapid waters, he is by no means confined to their neighborhood, for he lives by large lakes also and along the sea-coast and even upon sea-islands. In fishing, the Kingfisher either dives directly from his perch into the stream below or flies along above the water until he sees his prey, when, hovering above it until satisfied that he can make a strike, he partly closes his wings and shoots down like an arrow, head-first into the water. If successful, he rises with a tiny fish in his bill, turns it head-foremost, and swallows it at once; or if the fish is larger than his usual catch, he takes it to a branch, post or rock and beats it vigorously, holding it first by one end and then by the other, until it has been reduced to a tractable condition, when he takes it by the head and swallows it head first. If the fish is a little too large to be swallowed easily, the bird is compelled to assume a rather strained, uncomfortable position until the extremely rapid process of digestion enables him to engorge and dispose of that part of his meal which at first protrudes from his beak. The indigestible bones and scales of fish are ejected as pellets. Often before the young are fledged, the continual passing of the parents to and fro in their feeding operations wears two grooves, one on either side of the hole, where their little feet have padded down or worn away the soil. The young Kingfishers are naked at first, then covered with bristly feather-sheaths, and finally they become rather comical short-tailed replicas of their parents.

The principal food of the Eastern Belted Kingfisher under ordinary circumstances is believed to be fish, but it does not depend entirely on this diet. In the West when its favorite streams dry up, it readily subsists on other food. It takes some mice, many frogs, lizards and newts, crawfish and other crustaceans, many water-insects and such large terrestrial insects as grasshoppers, crickets and the larger beetles, and it has even been known to eat fruit in times of necessity.

Order Piciformes.   Woodpeckers and Allies.

NORTHERN FLICKER

Colaptes auratus luteus BANGS.   PLATE 52.

Other names: Flicker; Golden-winged Woodpecker; Pigeon Woodpecker; High-hole; Wake-up; Harrywicket; Gaffer Woodpecker; Yellow Hammer, and so forth.

IDENTIFICATION. — Length 12 to 13 inches; spread 18½ to 21¼ inches. A brownish woodpecker, larger than

Robin; large size, bounding flight and black crescent on breast identify it; as it flies up from the ground the white rump is conspicuous; flying overhead the yellow under surface of wings and tail are easily seen.

CALLS. — Include a loud *wick wick wick wick*, a high-pitched *ti-err*, and many others.

BREEDING. — *Nest:* Usually a hole excavated in a tree, about 3 inches in diameter at the entrance and 10 to 24 inches deep. *Eggs:* 3 to 20, usually 5 to 9, glossy white.

RANGE. — Breeds from Canada east of the Rocky Mountains and north to tree limit in Alaska, and throughout northern and central United States south to the northern edge of the Lower Austral Zone; south in winter to the Gulf coast and southern Texas.

The Flicker is the most generally abundant and well known of all American woodpeckers. It is said that it is known in various parts of the country by fully 125 common names. Country people are almost everywhere familiar with the bird.

When the glad vociferous Flickers arrive after a long and severe winter, we feel that surely spring is here. Thoreau recognized the rejuvenating quality in the spring note of the bird. On April 3, 1842, he wrote: 'I have just heard a flicker among the oaks on the hillside ushering in a new dynasty. It is the age and youth of time.' Again he says: 'But how that single sound enriches all the woods and fields ... this note really quickens what was dead. It seems to put life into withered grass and leaves and bare twigs, and henceforth the days shall not be as they have been.'

As the season advances and the wooing of the Flicker begins, his cheery, seductive love notes express the very spirit of the spring. Now comes the season of reproduction and with it the awakening of life in earth, in air, in a million pools, in verdant meadows and slowly greening woods — the teeming vibrant life of coming summer. We hear 'hither and yon' the Flicker's loud, oft-repeated cry, gradually lowering in pitch and often given for an almost unlimited number of times. Next we see the male in the early morning drumming rapidly on some resonant limb or tin roof — too early for the sluggards, who complain of a reveille at such an unseemly hour. The drumming is a long, almost continuous roll, and the bird frequently clings to his drumming-post and continues his music for a long time.

The extravagant courtship of the Flicker is notorious. We see a pair together, the female reluctant and coy, the male following her close by from tree to tree. Slyly he peeks at her from behind a limb; but soon, becoming bolder, sidles up to her, swinging his head about and displaying the beauties of spread wings and tail as he softly calls '*yúcker yúcker yúcker.*' Next a rival male appears. Now all is action and excitement; each vies with the other in exhibiting all his endearing charms to the demure object of his desires. One takes an elevated position on a branch near her side; the other, not to be outdone, mounts to a similar place on the other side, and now begins a superlative effort on the part of each suitor to impress her with the glowing splendors of his plumage and the seductive pleadings of his tenderest tones. With wings open and tails widely spread, they turn and twist about, throwing into their notes the most eager supplication. They bow and nod, advance and retreat and use every art known to Flickers to win the fair one; but she is obdurate, and so the wooing goes on from day to day. If she goes to the ground, he follows. If he presses his suit too boldly at first, she repels him with a sharp jab from her bill. When finally she faces him or stands by his side and reciprocates, by nodding even perfunctorily, the situation seems more encouraging. Then he redoubles his efforts to please, sidling around her, posturing, nodding, tossing his head up or swinging it from side to side, and with spread wings and tail, displaying his charms to perfection. His red nape seems to expand and glow in the sunlight, and his spotted breast swells with renewed ardor. When finally the female accepts a suitor, she acknowledges her submission by returning his courtesies in kind. Later in the season, especially where males are scarce, the females may assume the initiative, two or three seeking the company of a single male. When such an unusual and complicated situation arises, the females have even been known to do battle for the favors of the male; but usually these affairs seem to be settled amicably, the females merely hitching about and bowing to one another and to the male in turn. When the happy twain are united, they soon find a location for their home, and both sexes work at the excavation, relieving each other from time to time. They are so industrious that they sometimes carry on their work far into the night, and soon after daylight their labor begins again. If they choose a hollow tree or a nesting-box for their home, they are likely to hammer away at the inside until they have chips enough in the bottom to make a bed for the eggs. Therefore, it is well to place some fine chips or coarse sawdust with a little dry earth in the bottom of a flicker box when it is put up. They may use the same domicile for years if not molested.

Both sexes take turns in incubation, and the one on the nest is fed by the other. They are very affectionate, continuing their wooing more or less during the nesting season, and both share in caring for the young. As the young in the nest increase in size they become noisy, and if a person taps on the tree, a loud buzzing may be heard from within. In September when the fledglings have grown strong and able to care for themselves, the southward migration begins. This continues through October when, after some severe frost in the north, hundreds may be seen migrating by daylight.

Most of the Flickers that pass the winter in New England seek the vicinity of the sea, though in mild winters an occasional individual may appear anywhere in southern New England. Near the seashore they find bayberries, of which they are very fond, and, other food failing, they get some sustenance from the rows of seaweed along the shore. Usually they retire to some cavity in a tree at night, but during one winter one apparently slept on the wall of my summer cottage under the eaves, clinging to one of the ornamental battens in an upright position as it would cling to a tree-trunk. Commonly in winter Flickers drill holes through the walls of vacant buildings and sleep inside. Sometimes they become confused while exploring the interior of a furnished cottage, and, unable to find the way out, die there.

The Northern Flicker is very fond of ants, which form a large part of its daily food whenever they can be found; hence this bird is often seen on the ground investigating ant-hills, and in autumn while the family keeps together, from five to ten birds may be started from the ground in the same field. While on the ground they run a few steps and stop, run a few more and stop, much in the manner of the Robin, but when they find an ant-hill they spend considerable time there. While thus engaged they often allow a near approach. As they fly off when startled, they are likely to utter a curious purring sound, and they display their white rumps, thus proclaiming their identity.

In late summer and autumn this bird seems to be very fond of wild cherries and the fruit of the Tupelo or sour-gum (*Nyssa sylvatica*). In winter the fruit of the bayberry and that of the poison ivy are favorites.

SOUTHERN FLICKER

Colaptes auratus auratus (LINNAEUS).

Other name: Cotton-backed Yellowhammer.

IDENTIFICATION. — Slightly smaller than *C. a. luteus*, and darker with black bars on back wider.

RANGE. — Breeds in Lower Austral Zone of the South Atlantic and Gulf States from North Carolina to southern Florida and central Texas north to extreme southern Indiana and Illinois, southeastern Missouri, and southeastern Kansas.

NORTHERN PILEATED WOODPECKER

Ceophloeus pileatus abieticola BANGS. PLATE 51.

Other names: Black Woodpecker; Log-cock; Black Cock of the Woods; Woodcock; Woodchuck; Good-god; Lord-god.

IDENTIFICATION. — Length 16½ to 19½ inches; spread 28 to 30 inches. Near size of Crow; dull sooty black with long red crest, slim neck, narrow white stripe on side of head and neck, and conspicuous white patch in wings.

CALLS. — Suggest Flicker but slower and louder.

BREEDING. — In forest of heavy timber. *Nest:* Excavated in trunk or large limb, entrance 3 to 4 inches across, nest 12 to 30 inches deep. *Eggs:* 3 to 6, glossy white.

RANGE. — Resident in Transition and Canadian zones from Mackenzie, Manitoba, Quebec (Gaspé), and Nova Scotia south to Minnesota, Iowa, Illinois, Indiana, Ohio and Pennsylvania, and farther south in the mountains.

This great and striking bird, the Northern Pileated Woodpecker, is not so rare as most people would have us believe, but ordinarily it is shy and keeps under cover of the woods. Its sight and hearing are so keen that it perceives the approach of a man at a distance and slips quietly away before it is seen, and its notes so closely resemble those of the Northern Flicker that few people recognize them, and so the bird escapes notice.

To see this fine bird to advantage one should rise with the lark and embark upon some slow stream that flows through its favorite haunts. Such a place may be found in the lower reaches of Sandy Stream near where it empties into Little Carry Pond, in the great woods of Somerset County, Maine. A slow-flowing watercourse, its borders clogged with duckweed and lily pads, it lies calm and clear at daybreak on a September morning, unruffled by the light breeze that barely fans the cheek. The east foreshore is low and swampy and screened by water-brush. Skeletons of dead trees show bleached and white against the dark green background of the spruces, whose slim spires rise high against the rosy light of coming dawn. The remains of an old beaver-house lie near the low shore. Beyond the farther bank a high ridge looms where grows a forest of spruce, fir, birch, beech and maple, where the trees have clasped great rocks with their gnarled roots and thrust them deep into the crevices of the ledge. Upstream trout leap and play. Deer have waded along the margin, leaving their footprints in the soft earth, and to the east on a low ridge denuded by the lumberman an immense black bear has cleared away the blueberries from many a patch of low bushes. A porcupine comes down to drink at the water's edge. In the woods giant trees lie strewn along the ledge where storm winds have thrown them — their great roots flung high, their tops and branches crushed and torn. Beside these relics of decay springs perennial life from the earth, clothing the rocks in greenery. Here above the murmur of the rising breeze comes the sharp rattle of the great black woodpecker followed by his flicker-like call. Soon the fine bird rises above the tree-tops and alights on a tall slim stub, the remains of a monarch of the primeval forest, towering far above the lesser trees of today. Clearly revealed in the rays of the rising sun the bird erects his blazing crest, and, with head drawn far back, scales his watch-tower to the very top. Once he opens a wing as if to flash its conspicuous white markings. Then he springs away, and with diagonal flight slides easily down the air to a low tree on the eastern shore, showing the great white area under his wings to fine advantage as he passes over the stream. Now he calls to his mate, and she soon rises above the trees, alights on the same tall stub that he has just left, and goes through a performance similar to his own. In flight the wings are spread for a brief instant while the bird sails; then they are struck swiftly far downward for propulsion. They never seem to rise much above the body, and usually the bird does not undulate in flight like other woodpeckers, but steadily keeps to its plane. It can bound through the air, however, at will.

Unless one seeks for a good outlook, he might wander for days in the northern woods without seeing one of these woodpeckers. With the cutting off of the primeval forests and the later increase of gunners this bird decreased rapidly, but now as it has become accustomed to live among smaller trees and as it is more strictly protected than formerly, it is coming back into the region of its former abundance. Within the past five years the increase in numbers of the 'Log-Cock' has been noticeable, and it has become more confiding than formerly, coming into orchards and even to houses where it has been known to help itself to suet hung up for smaller woodpeckers and Chickadees. It has bred in recent years through the northern and western counties of Massachusetts and has even begun breeding rarely again in the hills of northern Connecticut. No doubt the abandonment of many unproductive farms which have since grown up to woods has had something to do with the recent increase of the species here and elsewhere in its range.

In spring the 'Log-Cock' seeks its well-remembered nesting-place. Year after year it returns to the same place to breed. In early spring the bird becomes loquacious, and like other drumming woodpeckers rattles away with its bill on some resonant hollow stub or limb. Its masterly roll is one of the notable sounds of spring, but during the breeding season it is quiet and secretive in the vicinity of its nest.

This woodpecker not only digs out a nesting-hole in a tree but it excavates another for shelter in winter. The bird is so large, swift and strong that it has little to fear from most hawks and its habit of sleeping in a tree-hole at night probably protects it from owls in winter.

Pileated Woodpeckers are such powerful birds that they can split off large slabs from decaying stumps, strip bushels of bark from dead trees, and chisel out large holes in either sound, dead or decaying wood. They like to strip the bark from dead pines, spruces and especially hemlocks. Their size and strength and their long spear-like tongues enable them to penetrate large trees and draw out borers from the very heart of the tree. In a letter to me Mr. Charles L. Whittle describes as follows the work of a bird of this species in a wild cherry tree near Peterboro, New Hampshire, on September 25, 1920: 'I watched a female bird at work for about fifteen minutes. She was directing her attack against a dying and no doubt infested limb.

Chips and bark flew in every direction. She scaled the bark off the limb by powerful tangential blows. Finally a favorable point of attack was uncovered which received sledge-hammer blows in rapid succession, the bird swinging her head through an arc of at least eight inches in length. Her whole body was brought into play at times, the feet only remaining motionless; at last the larvae were uncovered and silence reigned while they were being extracted.'

SOUTHERN PILEATED WOODPECKER

Ceophloeus pileatus pileatus (LINNAEUS).

IDENTIFICATION. — Smaller than *C. p. abieticola;* white markings more restricted; bill shorter.

RANGE. — Lower Austral forests of southern United States from southeastern Pennsylvania, Illinois, and Oklahoma south to northern Florida and the Gulf coast, west to central Texas.

Wherever and whenever one meets the great Log-Cock or Pileated Woodpecker, it is an event to be marked in red letters on the bird student's calendar. I have seen the northern race among the sugar maples of New Hampshire, the yellow birches and spruces of the Gaspé Peninsula, and the hickories of the Litchfield Hills in Connecticut; I have watched the western race working in characteristic manner in the great firs of Yellowstone Park; I have seen the Florida bird knocking great chips from a tall cabbage palm; I have flushed the southern race from a feast of ants in the dense jungle of the sea-islands on the South Carolina coast and have watched a pair of the birds feeding their young in a hole in a towering moss-draped cypress in the heart of a northern Florida egret rookery; and wherever I have been, I have never failed to experience a real thrill over the discovery of this magnificent bird, with its long scarlet crest, its conspicuous white and black markings, and its wild cries which echo through the forests.

The differences in appearance of the four races of Pileated Woodpecker are so slight that they cannot be separated in the field, and their habits vary very little. — (J.B.M.)

FLORIDA PILEATED WOODPECKER

Ceophloeus pileatus floridanus (RIDGWAY).

IDENTIFICATION. — Slightly smaller than *C. p. pileatus;* blacker, less sooty or slaty; bill relatively shorter and broader.

RANGE. — Resident in central and southern Florida north to Orange County.

RED–BELLIED WOODPECKER

Centurus carolinus (LINNAEUS).

PLATE 52.

Other names: Zebra Woodpecker; Guinea Sapsucker; Orange Sapsucker; Cham-chack.

IDENTIFICATION. — Length 8¾ to 10½ inches; spread 15 to 18 inches. About size of Hairy Woodpecker; black and white *barred back* and wings and *gray under parts*, with *scarlet top of head* and nape of male and *scarlet nape* of female, distinguish this bird easily; 'red belly' not usually visible.

BREEDING. — Nest hole about 12 inches deep. *Eggs:* 3 to 5, dull white.

RANGE. — Resident from southeastern South Dakota, southeastern Minnesota, southwestern Ontario, western New York, and Delaware south to central Texas, the Gulf coast and the Florida Keys.

The Red-bellied Woodpecker is a handsome and conspicuous bird. I have seen it only in the South, and there it was usually rather restless, shy and quick to beat a retreat, but in the northern winter, necessity sometimes drives it to feeding-places about houses and it becomes quite domestic, feeding on suet. In Florida it frequently comes into orange groves about the homesteads. In some localities it will pursue its jerky, devious or spiral way up the trunks of the trees utterly regardless of the onlooker; usually, however, when approached it flies away with an undulating motion before the observer is well within gunshot, and it is likely to betake itself to the top of some tall tree at a distance, where it keeps a sharp lookout for danger. There, while hammering away, it utters at intervals a loud and solemn *churr*, always alert and apprehensive. It is rather a noisy bird especially in the mating season. In southern Ontario, at about the same latitude as southern New England, the species seems to be a permanent though not common resident; but in New England the bird is a mere straggler, chiefly during the milder part of the year. It may migrate occasionally, but seems to have no regular migration, and the individuals found outside of the normal breeding range seem to be aimless wanderers. Evidently this bird is another which, like the Red-headed Woodpecker, has retired westward during the last century. Giraud said that formerly it bred on Long Island, and it was once common in the lower Hudson Valley from which it has virtually disappeared. It is now uncommon and local in western New York.

The food of the Red-bellied Woodpecker consists largely of insects, such as beetles, caterpillars and bugs, and still more largely of vegetal matter consisting of wild fruits, seeds, acorns and occasionally a little corn. It sometimes damages ornamental palm trees by excavating large holes in them, and it has a habit of boring into oranges, either on the ground or growing on the tree, and eating both juice and pulp. It feeds somewhat on the ground but does not walk as easily as the Flicker.

RED–HEADED WOODPECKER

Melanerpes erythrocephalus (LINNAEUS).

PLATE 52.

Other names: Red-head; White-wing.

IDENTIFICATION. — Length 8½ to 9¾ inches; spread 16 to 18 inches. Size about that of Hairy Woodpecker; unmistakable; solid masses of color, black (glossed bluish), white and scarlet in adult; white of wings very conspicuous in flight; entire head and neck scarlet; young have grayish-brown heads spotted with blackish.

CALL NOTE. — A loud *tchur, tchur* or *charr, charr*; and a call like that of a Tree-frog.

BREEDING. — *Nest:* Hole 10 to 18 inches deep. *Eggs:* 4 to 6, white.

RANGE. — Breeds from southeastern British Columbia, Manitoba, southeastern Ontario, and southwestern New England south to the Gulf coast and southern Florida, and from central Montana and New Mexico east; irregularly migratory in northern parts of its range.

On the island of Naushon south of Buzzards Bay there exists today one of the last tracts of primeval forest in New England. Great beech and oak trees stand as they have stood through the centuries, while still older trees, now fallen, lie prone on the forest floor. There the deer wander in small bands as they roamed in the days of the red Indian. So abundant are they that they keep the lower leaves trimmed from the trees as high as they can reach and the whole wood presents the appearance of a deer park, practically free of underbrush. There, near the east end of the island, on a cold day in February, with a piercing, cold northwest wind rattling the dry branches, a Red-headed Woodpecker in a sunny nook tapped away as merrily on a dead branch as if summer zephyrs were blowing.

Unlike most woodpeckers the Redhead migrates far and wide. There is a flight southward in autumn, but when the beechnut crop is large the Redheads remain in considerable numbers in the North. They are likely to migrate in any direction toward abundant beechnuts, which are their favorite food. The primeval beech and oak forest on Naushon probably was the attraction that had influenced one hardy bird to remain there alone through a New England winter, while most individuals of the species were enjoying a vacation in a southern clime.

This bird is the most striking of our woodpeckers, clothed in red, white and blue. With the dark blue gloss of its back appearing black at a distance and its colors in masses and strongly contrasted, it is a conspicuous bird. The bird is seen chiefly in open woodlands or among orchard or shade trees. It spends much of its time in the usual woodpecker-like activities and much also in flying to the ground for insects and in fly-catching, for it takes many insects in the air.

It is a rather noisy bird during the breeding season, and often the sexes pursue one another with loud cries and excited flutterings. At times they are active and playful and amuse themselves with drumming on various objects; at other times they are quiet and sedentary. In searching a tree-trunk for wood-boring insects this woodpecker gives it a few smart raps here and there, and then turns the head as if to listen. When apparently satisfied it attacks the bark or wood and drills directly to the lurking grub.

The food of the Redhead consists of about one-third animal and two-thirds vegetal matter, and both are eaten at all seasons of the year as they can be obtained. When acorns or beechnuts are abundant, this bird feeds mainly on them, and in the summer and autumn it eats much fruit and some corn. Occasionally it destroys the eggs or young of other birds, but destructive insects constitute the major part of its animal food. It has a habit of storing beechnuts and acorns for future use, tucking them away under loose bark, in cracks, knot holes and cavities of trees where quantities are stored with, occasionally, a little corn. Sometimes insects such as grasshoppers are similarly stored.

YELLOW-BELLIED SAPSUCKER

Sphyrapicus varius varius (LINNAEUS). PLATE 51.

Other names: Sapsucker; Yellow-bellied Woodpecker; Squealer.

IDENTIFICATION. — Length 7¾ to 8¾ inches; spread 14¼ to 16 inches. Size nearly that of Hairy Wood-pecker; our only woodpecker with forehead and top of head red, and upper breast black. Male distinguish-able from all other eastern woodpeckers by *red crown and throat, large longitudinal patch of white on black wing and black* upper breast. Females and young lack the large crimson patch on throat; young recognized by their yellowish tints; their black wing with longitudinal white patch on coverts, like adults, and their general resem-blance to adults in shape and habits.

BREEDING. — *Nest:* Hole 6 to 18 inches deep. *Eggs:* 5 to 7, slightly glossy, white.

RANGE. — Breeds from central Mackenzie, Manitoba, southern Quebec, and Cape Breton south to central Missouri, central Indiana, northern Ohio, North Carolina (in the mountains), and Massachusetts; winters from Iowa, Wisconsin, Michigan, and Massachusetts to the Gulf coast, Bahamas, Cuba, Jamaica, western Mexico, and Panama.

There seems to be something mysterious about the movements of the Yellow-bellied Sapsucker throughout much of its range. It is a common breeding bird in certain parts of southern Canada and in the northern tier of the States, and it is also common in winter in the Gulf States. Its easily recognized workings on the bark of orchard trees and in other places are often observed, yet the bird itself is not very commonly reported throughout much of its migration routes.

Enough Sapsuckers visit the States to leave their marks on our orchards, however, and very rarely we hear of a tree that they have actually injured by persistently denuding it of small bits of bark. There never are sapsuckers enough to do much harm. My own experience with them would indicate that they are usually hunting insects, going rapidly over the timber and passing quickly from tree to tree, working north or south according to the season. They are addicted largely to the dexterous flycatcher habit and they 'bound,' as it were, through the air from one tree to another.

The Yellow-bellied Sapsucker, like other woodpeckers, is very fond of drumming on some resonant substance, such as a dry limb, tin roof, eaves-trough or conductor. One of its favorite pastimes is to tap on telephone wires and then apparently listen to the sound of the vibration.

In the South I have seen the Yellow-bellied Sapsuckers' work on the southern pine and have examined many fine trees that they have saved from bark beetles. Most of the trees that are marked with their characteristic pits seem not to have been injured thereby. These are chiefly fruit trees, which continue to remain thrifty and bear well. However, these pits, if driven into the sapwood of trees used for lumber or cabinet making, may injure its appearance by provid-ing openings for the entrance of fungous growths, and may result in dark spots which detract from its value for ornamental purposes. But there is another kind of sapsucker work where the bird pecks out larger holes, often roughly rectangular or triangular in shape. In some cases the bird so injures the bark over large areas that the remaining bark between the holes dries out, and if these punctured areas extend entirely around the trunk, the tree is girdled and it dies. Instances of trees killed have been noted in northern New England where it breeds, and also in the South, where the species spends the winter. Sometimes valuable shade trees and timber trees are thus destroyed. It seems that if an individual once gets the habit of visiting a favorite tree, it continues to visit it until the tree either dies or becomes so enfeebled that the bird prefers some more vigorous subject. Sometimes it clings motionless beside a hole it has made on its favorite birch or maple. From this hole or boring the sap usually flows freely, dripping frequently or even running down in a little rivulet. Usually there are several punctured trees in a sapsucker 'orchard,' and the birds, young as well as adults, come to them at frequent intervals throughout the day. Various other creatures, as hummingbirds, chipmunks and red squirrels, and many insects are drawn to the tree to feast on the sap. The Yellow-bellied Sapsucker has been seen to eat ice which had formed where sap had trickled down and frozen.

NORTHERN HAIRY WOODPECKER

Dryobates villosus septentrionalis (NUTTALL).

IDENTIFICATION. — Similar to *D. v. villosus* but larger and whiter.
RANGE. — Breeds from central southern Alaska, northern Manitoba, and southeastern Quebec south to central Ontario, northern North Dakota, Montana, and British Columbia.

NEWFOUNDLAND WOODPECKER

Dryobates villosus terraenovae BATCHELDER.

IDENTIFICATION. — Similar to *D. v. villosus* but slightly larger, black areas of upper parts increased and white areas reduced both in number and size.
RANGE. — Resident in Newfoundland.

EASTERN HAIRY WOODPECKER

Dryobates villosus villosus (LINNAEUS).   PLATE 49.

Other names: Sapsucker; Big Sapsucker.
IDENTIFICATION. — Length 8½ to 10½ inches; spread 15 to 17½ inches. Size slightly smaller than Robin, with much shorter tail; a black and white bird, white below, striped and spotted with white above, wings barred with rows of white spots, a broad white stripe down back; distinguished from smaller Downy Woodpecker (which also has a white stripe down the back) by relatively *larger, longer bill* and unmarked white outer tail feathers; latter cannot be seen unless tail is spread somewhat.

300

BREEDING. — In woods or orchard. *Nest:* Excavated in dead, partly dead, or sound tree. *Eggs:* 3 to 5, shining white, laid on a few chips.

RANGE. — Breeds in Transition and Upper Austral zones from Manitoba, south central Ontario, central southern Quebec, and the Magdalen Islands south to western North Carolina and central Texas, and west to eastern Colorado.

The Eastern Hairy Woodpecker is the embodiment of sturdy energy and persistent industry. Active, cheerful, ever busy, its life of arduous toil brings but one reward, a liberal sustenance. It sometimes spends nearly an hour of hard labor in digging out a single borer, but commonly reaches the object of its quest in much less time. Notwithstanding great and strenuous activity the bird keeps in good condition. It is a bird of verve; even its loud wing-beats (*prut-prut-prut*) are diagnostic. This woodpecker is not very common in Massachusetts, but in the hardwood forests of Maine it may be seen in autumn in considerable numbers. Groups of half a dozen or more birds, each group probably a family party, may be met with at that season scattered through the woods, exploring crevices in the bark and rapping away on the trunks and limbs as if their very lives depended on the success of their undertaking. They are a little shy, but by striking a stick against a tree-trunk, in imitation of their tapping, the traveler may succeed in attracting their attention and causing them to draw near. These family groups often are accompanied by Downy Woodpeckers, nuthatches, or chickadees, all of which are conservators of the forest, as these birds continually search over the trees for insects which destroy the leaves, bark or wood.

As winter approaches many Eastern Hairy Woodpeckers leave their forested breeding-grounds and appear in orchards and villages and in places where they are almost unknown in summer. Their numbers increase considerably also in the southern parts of their range, which indicates a considerable migration. During the winter, in its search for food, the Hairy Woodpecker often becomes a familiar bird about farmsteads, and though normally more shy than the Downy Woodpecker, it may be attracted in winter to any place where people feed the birds.

On bright March days this bird begins to practice what is either a love song, a challenge, a call to its mate, or all combined. This is no vocal music, but instead a loud drumming on some resonant dead tree, branch, or pole. This long roll or tattoo is louder than that of the Downy Woodpecker, not quite so long, and with a slightly greater interval between each succeeding stroke. It takes a practiced ear, however, to distinguish between the drumming of these two species. In courtship the male chases the female from tree to tree with coaxing calls, and there is much dodging about among the branches and bowing to each other before the union is consummated. The tree selected for nesting is often very large and tall, and usually the trunk or branch chosen is dead at the heart, although otherwise apparently sound. Rarely the birds excavate their home from sound live wood.

It is a mystery how woodpeckers are able to tell the exact location of a boring larva beneath the bark or wood. Some of the larger grubs may be heard without difficulty, as they cut away the wood with their strong jaws, but many smaller ones make no audible sound. Maurice Thompson asserted that the Hairy Woodpecker strikes its bill into the wood and then holds the point of one mandible for a moment in the dent thus made. He believed that the vibrations produced by the insect in the wood are conveyed through the beak and skull of the bird to its brain; but this does not explain how the same bird can drill unerringly into the very spot where a grub or ant lies dormant and motionless in winter. The only plausible explanation of this feat seems to be that the delicate sensibilities of the bird enable it by sounding with its beak to fix the exact spot at which the body of its prey fills the burrow. The tapping of the beak may enable the bird to locate the grub by sound, somewhat as the carpenter by striking on the wall of a room with a hammer can find the position of a timber hidden under laths and plaster.

SOUTHERN HAIRY WOODPECKER

Dryobates villosus auduboni (SWAINSON).

Other name: Big Guinea Woodpecker.
  IDENTIFICATION. — Slightly smaller than *D. v. villosus* and with less white in the plumage.
  RANGE. — Breeds in South Atlantic and Gulf States from southeastern Missouri, southern Illinois, and southeastern Virginia to southeastern Texas and southern Florida.

NORTHERN DOWNY WOODPECKER

Dryobates pubescens medianus (SWAINSON).   PLATE 49.

Other names: Downy; Little Sapsucker.
  IDENTIFICATION. — Length 6¼ to 7¼ inches; spread 11 to 12¼ inches. Similar to Hairy Woodpecker but smaller and with proportionately much smaller bill; bill of Downy appears less than one third total length of head, that of Hairy more than one third.
  BREEDING. — Similar to Hairy Woodpecker.
  RANGE. — Breeds from southeastern Alberta, Manitoba, southern Ungava, and Newfoundland south to eastern Nebraska, Kansas, Tennessee, and Virginia.

The sprightly little Downy, smallest of our woodpeckers, is an admirable bird. It sports no gay plumes and sings no song, but it is a model of patient industry and perseverance, and though it may take a little sap from some maple tree occasionally in early spring, the small amount that it requires will never be missed. It is found commonly wherever trees grow in the East, and, unlike the Hairy Woodpecker, it may be seen more often usually in settled cultivated districts than in great forests. It delights in orchards, scattered shade trees, and the borders of woods. It may be found in the lowest swamps or on the mountaintops, though it may become scarce at an altitude of more than three thousand feet.

After a mild winter its courting may begin in March, but if the spring is backward not until late April or early May. Then two males often may be seen following a female about. When one male, with spread wings, and the female have taken up a position on a limb facing each other and ready for the preliminaries, the other male comes in between and interrupts the ceremony, and thus the ancient comedy is re-enacted with small results and little advancement for either ardent suitor. The female may be something of a flirt, and may seem to encourage first one and then the other. In such case the rivals for her affection may be kept in suspense for a week, but when the fickle one finally makes her choice, there is little delay in beginning the domestic arrangements. First, however, there may be rather a protracted hunt for a suitable location. A dead stub or some branch that is decayed at the heart is usually chosen. Often the birds nest in an apple tree, rarely in a building. When a tree that suits the pair has been found, excavation is begun immediately. In a few days a gourd-shaped hole has been dug, provided the wood is decayed enough to be easily excavated, but otherwise a week may be occupied in the task. Occasionally the spot is not well chosen, and progress is stopped by some large, hard knot. In this case the birds give over their task, and begin anew in a more favorable spot. The entrance to the nest is almost perfectly round, and just large enough to enable the occupants to squeeze in and out; not a fraction of an inch to spare is allowed. Here the snow-white eggs are laid and the young are reared until fledged. When hatched they are ugly, blind, naked, helpless and dumb, with an enlargement of the gape, seen in all young woodpeckers. As they grow and their eyes open, they become vociferous, so much so that their insistent cries for food may be heard at a little distance from the tree — a kind of 'shrill twitter, now rising, now dying down like a breath expelled.' When the young are fledged, they follow the parents about until they learn to find food for themselves. Then the family may roam through woods and orchards in company for a time, but finally they separate, and during the winter Downy seems rather to shun its own kind, regardless of family ties. Quite commonly, however, one may be seen with some band of chickadees and nuthatches, and with these birds it is likely to frequent any locality where people are feeding birds with suet or other materials suitable for woodpeckers. As winter comes on, there is more or less migration of the Downy Woodpecker from the northern part of its range to the southward, and from higher to lower altitudes.

Wherever this bird spends the winter, it finds or makes a snug retreat wherein it sleeps on cold winter nights. Often it excavates a cavity in some decayed tree, at the cost of three or more days of hard labor, or it may find an unoccupied nesting hole of some woodpecker, a hollow tree or a bird-house or nesting box in some sheltered situation.

In winter the Downy lives chiefly upon insect enemies of trees. Wherever it works, bits of bark and lichens scattered on the snow give evidence of its diligence. In early spring, however, like several other arboreal winter birds and squirrels it may now and then take some sap from the flowing maples. Hence the popular name Little Sapsucker, which has some foundation in fact, though this bird's work, unlike much of that of the true sapsuckers, seems to cause no injury to the trees.

In searching for and securing the insects on which it feeds, the Northern Downy Woodpecker shows its greatest skill. It is the self-appointed guardian of orchards neglected by their owners, and there its work is most effective. It seems to be especially happy in going over such orchards, perhaps for the reason that the trees always harbor many varieties of insects. It taps on the shaggy bark and locates beneath the scales the cocoons of the codling moth, parent of the apple worm, and drives its bill into the vitals of its victim. The bird lays the side of its head to the bark and apparently listens for the movements of the deadly borer; then with a few smart taps it penetrates the outer bark and hales the fellow forth. It discovers the wingless females of the canker-worm moth crawling up the bark on the way to deposit their eggs; it destroys weevils, caterpillars, ants, plant lice and bark lice. That the Downy can be exceedingly active and swift if necessary can be vouched for by those who have seen him whip round a limb to escape the rush of a hawk. One would think it difficult for him to go down a tree backward with much speed, but he can skip down the trunk in this fashion quick enough to catch a grub that he has dropped.

The Downy Woodpecker searches out the pine weevil which kills the topmost shoot of the young white pine and so causes a crook in the trunk of the tree, unfitting it for the lumber market. It picks into the galls of goldenrod stalks and robs them of their grubs, and works on mullein heads, picking open the brown seed-cases to get at grubs also. It sometimes even goes to the ground to pick up tent caterpillars. It also destroys the corn-borer. The vegetal food of the Northern Downy Woodpecker consists of a few buds and petals of flowers, wild berries and seeds, frozen apples, beechnuts, acorns, hazelnuts, a very little corn, possibly a few cherries and a little cambium.

SOUTHERN DOWNY WOODPECKER

Dryobates pubescens pubescens (LINNAEUS).

IDENTIFICATION. — Similar to *D. p. medianus* but smaller, browner below and with the white more restricted.
RANGE. — Breeds in Lower Austral Zone of the South Atlantic and Gulf states, from Florida to eastern Texas and north to North Carolina and Oklahoma.

RED–COCKADED WOODPECKER

Dryobates borealis (VIEILLOT). PLATE 95.

Other name: Sapsucker.
IDENTIFICATION. — Length 7 to 8 inches; spread 14 to 15 inches. Slightly smaller than Hairy Woodpecker; top of head black, side of head and throat white, back and wings dull black closely barred with white, under parts dull white; the small red 'cockade' on the side of the male's head usually invisible in the field.
BREEDING. — *Nest:* Hole usually in the trunk of a living pine. *Eggs:* 2 to 5, white.
RANGE. — Lower Austral Zone of South Atlantic and Gulf states north to southeastern Virginia, Tennessee, western Kentucky, and southern Missouri.

In the great pineries of the 'turpentine belt' across the Carolinas and Georgia and in the open 'piney' woods of Florida we find the interesting Red-cockaded Woodpecker. It resembles to a certain extent the Downy and Hairy Woodpeckers, but its black is dull and brownish, its head markings are quite different, and its back is liberally crossed with narrow black and white bars. Our attention is usually first drawn to it by its garrulous conversational notes, somewhat suggesting the Brown-headed Nuthatch which haunts the same habitats, but the woodpecker is most often (though not always) on the trunk of the tree, while the nuthatches are usually found exploring the tips of the branches.

The nest of the Red-cockaded Woodpecker differs from those of most small woodpeckers in that it is almost invariably excavated in a living pine tree. Nest holes are easily located by the conspicuous smears of gray pitch extending in a sticky mass from a few inches above the nest opening to perhaps several feet below it. This appears to be a device to keep enemies away from the eggs or young, as it is evident that the bark has been freely punctured around the nest for several inches in all directions, causing the sap to exude freely. How the parents keep themselves clean in this 'tanglefoot' area is hard to understand.

I have watched the Red-cockaded Woodpeckers with a glass at fairly close range and have never been able to distinguish the red 'cockade' on the living and moving bird. But the 'ladder-back' or 'zebra' striping and the prominent black and white areas on the head make this an easily identified species. — (J.B.M.)

ARCTIC THREE–TOED WOODPECKER

Picoides arcticus (SWAINSON). PLATE 50.

Other name: Black-backed Three-toed Woodpecker.
IDENTIFICATION. — Length 9 to 10¼ inches; spread 14 to 16 inches. Slightly larger than Hairy Woodpecker; upper parts black glossed with bluish; under parts whitish narrowly barred at sides with black; male has yellow crown, wanting in female; wings with rows of white spots and outer tail feathers mostly white.
BREEDING. — In coniferous forests. *Nest:* Hole in dead or living tree. *Eggs:* 4 to 6, white.
RANGE. — Breeds from central Alaska, northern Manitoba, and northern Quebec south to Oregon, California, Wyoming, northern Minnesota, Michigan, northern New York, Vermont, New Hampshire, and Maine; casual south in winter.

The dark, sturdy, Arctic Three-toed Woodpecker comes to us in winter from dense coniferous Canadian forests. Comparatively few breed in the evergreen forests of the northernmost states, but occasionally in winter it visits these regions in considerable numbers.

It is difficult to determine exactly what causes these unusual migrations. They are not forced by inclement weather, for one at least has occurred in a mild winter. A scarcity of the seeds of coniferous trees, on which many arboreal birds feed in winter, apparently does not affect them, as they have come in a year of an abundant food supply, when Pine Grosbeaks and crossbills remained in the north. It seems probable that the unusual invasions of the species follow summers when its food has been unusually abundant. An excessive food supply tends to fecundity, and overbreeding naturally compels expansion and induces migration, whether among the lower animals or humankind. On the other hand a scarcity of the usual food supply may cause migration. A wet season with few fires in the woods or a scarcity of insects (such as the spruce bud-moth) that kill trees might, later, cause a migration. When these periodical invasions occur, the species is well distributed far and wide in autumn, but fewer return north in spring, and thus possibly congestion in the north is relieved by the casualties incident to migration, until another particularly favorable breeding season occurs. While with us it seeks white pine woods that have been killed by fire, or isolated dead pine trees. The first or second year after trees have been killed by fire these woodpeckers come into a pine wood in numbers in pursuit of bark-beetles and wood-borers. In winter they usually work quietly, though at times they are vociferous. As a rule they are unsuspicious, and anyone may walk up close to a bird and watch it work. This species very often begins to work on the trunk near the foot of a tree; it sounds the bark with direct blows, and then, turning its head from side to side, strikes its beak slantingly into and under the bark, and flakes it off. It often works long on the same tree and barks the whole trunk in time, only occasionally working on the branches. Thus it exposes channels of bark-beetles and the holes made by borers. When the bird remains motionless, it is well concealed against the blackened bark of the burnt trees. It seems deliberate in its movements and appears to do its work thoroughly, as it often remains five to ten minutes on the same spot and then shifts only a little distance. In early autumn, while the grubs are still at work on the tree, it lays its head against the tree, at times, turning it first to one side and then to the other as if listening.

AMERICAN THREE–TOED WOODPECKER

Picoides tridactylus bacatus BANGS.   PLATE 50.

Other names: Banded-backed Three-toed Woodpecker; 'Ladder-back.'
 IDENTIFICATION. — Length 8 to 9¾ inches; spread 13 to 15¼ inches. Near size of Hairy Woodpecker; distinguished by black and white 'ladder-back' *barring* down middle of black back; crown yellow in male, black in female.
 BREEDING. — Similar to Arctic Three-toed Woodpecker.
 RANGE. — Breeds from Labrador, northern Quebec, northern Manitoba, and southern Mackenzie south to northern Minnesota, northern Michigan, central Ontario, northern New York, New Hampshire, and Maine; casual in winter southward.

The American Three-toed Woodpecker and the Arctic Three-toed are not rightly named, as the latter is a bird of more southern distribution than the former and neither of them are really Arctic birds. They should be known respectively as the Banded-backed Three-toed Woodpecker and the Black-backed Three-toed Woodpecker. These names, even now often used, distinguish them at once. They occupy for the most part the same region, take similar food and have similar habits, except that the American Three-toed Woodpecker is perhaps more closely confined to the spruce growth or its neighborhood than the black-backed species. This may affect somewhat the winter distribution of the American Three-toed Woodpecker in regions like southern New England, where most of the spruce woods have been cut off and replaced by deciduous trees.

There is reason to believe that the American Three-toed Woodpecker once bred more commonly in northern New England than it has since the original spruce growth was cut. There is still some old spruce left on Saddle Mountain and its highest peak, Mt. Greylock, near Williamstown, Massachusetts, where in August, 1919, Mr. William J. Cartwright, a careful observer, reported that he saw a pair of American Three-toed Woodpeckers and two young feeding on a grub-infested tree. The birds were there for several days; the young were nearly full grown but were still fed by the adults. The birds were quite tame, could be closely approached and all their characteristic markings were noted. Their loud rattling notes, uttered frequently, attracted the attention of passersby.

306

IVORY–BILLED WOODPECKER

Campephilus principalis (LINNAEUS).   PLATE 95.

IDENTIFICATION. — Length 19 to 21 inches; spread 30 to 33 inches. The largest woodpecker north of Mexico; blue-black glossed with greenish below; long crest, red and black in male, black in female; white stripe down side of neck to shoulders, and conspicuous white area on wings; bill ivory-white or light horn color, straight and powerful, 2½ to 2¾ inches long.

CALL. — *Kent, kent, kent,* suggesting a tin trumpet.

BREEDING. — In primeval forests and wooded swamps. *Nest:* Hole, oval, high in trunk of a living tree. *Eggs:* 3 to 5, white.

RANGE. — Formerly resident of the South Atlantic and Gulf states from Texas to North Carolina and of the Mississippi Valley States north to Oklahoma, Missouri, southern Illinois, and southern Indiana; now greatly restricted in range and perhaps only persisting in Louisiana, though possibly in South Carolina, Florida, Mississippi, and Missouri; seriously threatened with extinction in the near future.

The magnificent great Ivory-billed Woodpecker was probably never a common bird in its chosen haunts in the extensive cypress swamps of the South, and with the coming of the white man it rapidly decreased in numbers until today it is known to be present in only a few remote fastnesses, where its final extinction is probably a matter of a very few years.

Its disappearance, however, cannot be blamed entirely upon the more 'civilized' white man, for Mark Catesby, more than two hundred years ago, in his 'Natural History of Carolina, Florida, and the Bahama Islands,' published in 1731, wrote this about the Ivory-billed Woodpecker:

'The bills of these Birds are much valued by the *Canada Indians,* who made Coronets of 'em for their Princes and great warriors, by fixing them round a Wreath, with their points outward. The Northern Indians having none of these Birds in their cold country, purchase them of the *Southern People* at the price of two, and sometimes three, Buck-skins a Bill.'

Nearly a hundred years later Alexander Wilson also wrote:

'The head and bill of this bird is in great esteem among the southern Indians, who wear them by way of amulet or charm, as well as ornament; and, it is said, dispose of them to the northern tribes at considerable prices. An Indian believes that the head, skin, or even feathers of certain birds, confer on the wearer all the virtues or excellencies of those birds. Thus I have seen a coat made of the skins, heads, and claws of the Raven; caps stuck round with the heads of Butcher Birds, Hawks, and Eagles; and as the disposition and courage of the Ivory-billed Woodpecker are well known to the savages, no wonder they should attach great value to it, having both beauty, and, in their estimation, distinguished merit to recommend it.'

Audubon also mentions this, saying, 'Its rich scalp attached to the upper mandible forms an ornament for the war-dress of most of our Indians, or for the shot-pouch of our squatters and hunters, by all of whom the bird is shot merely for that purpose.'

In 1893 Arthur T. Wayne wrote: 'This magnificent bird was once very common in this region [on the Wacissa River, Florida] — a country especially adapted to its wants — where it was in a large measure secure, but it is now rapidly becoming extinct on the Wacissa. Everyone is shot by being systematically followed up. They are shot for food, and the people — the crackers — consider them "better than ducks!" The bill is also prized and many fall victims for that reason.'

Recently a few Ivorybills were discovered in a remote district of Louisiana, and that state is co-operating in an endeavor to protect the birds in this, perhaps its last, breeding place. Here it has been studied intensively by scientific ornithologists under the leadership of Dr. A. A. Allen; it has been painted from life, photographed, recorded on sound and motion picture films, and an attempt made to learn more of its habits and especially of any enemies or conditions inimicable to its continued existence. Possibly it is not too late, and the bird may be saved from extinction, but more probably its doom is sealed, and it will soon join the sorry list of recently extinct birds. — (J.B.M.)

Order Passeriformes.   Perching Birds.

EASTERN KINGBIRD

Tyrannus tyrannus (LINNAEUS). PLATE 55.

Other names: Bee-bird; Bee-martin.

IDENTIFICATION. — Length 8½ to 9 inches; spread 14 to 15 inches. About size of Catbird; a dark slaty bird with blackish head, white under parts, and *white tip to tail*.

CALLS. — High rasping notes in considerable variety.

BREEDING. — In open lands, especially near water. *Nest:* Ragged and of coarse materials outside, lined with finer and softer material. *Eggs:* 3 to 5, white with brown and purplish spots mostly at large end.

RANGE. — Breeds from southern British Columbia, central Manitoba, northern Ontario, southern Quebec, and Nova Scotia south to central Nevada, southeastern Texas, and southern Florida; winters from southern Mexico to Bolivia.

Some of the American Indians knew this bird as the 'little chief,' but the English settlers, fleeing from tyranny at home, called him the King Bird. The naturalists dubbed him the Tyrant Flycatcher, but the first name stuck. Nevertheless, the despotic disposition which the bird and some of its congeners exhibit to both greater and lesser fowls has induced ornithologists to name this great American group of birds *Tyrannidae* or Tyrant Flycatchers. The Eastern Kingbird is typical of this group. Savage and fearless, he assails any bird that comes in his way or interferes with his own welfare or that of his neighbors. Hawks, crows, owls, vultures and even eagles feel the weight of his displeasure; about the only birds which he cannot drive away from the vicinity of his domicile are the Ruby-throated Hummingbird and the Duck Hawk. Occasionally a militant Baltimore Oriole with its keen-pointed beak will do battle with the Kingbird. The Catbird sometimes disputes his sovereignty, while the English Sparrow has been known to defeat the Kingbird by force of numbers, but most of the feathered race deem it wiser to leave when the Kingbird hovers above them.

While the female is sitting on the nest, the male stands guard on a tree-top to drive away intruders. He rarely, if ever, attempts to strike a large bird on the ground or on a perch. Therefore, if a crafty Crow slips into a tree unseen by the Kingbird and rifles a nest of its contents, the black robber is safe until he flies; then the avenger strikes. The little tyrant mounts above him in the air and chases him away. Often the Kingbird strikes the Crow, and sometimes even rides on his back while dealing out summary punishment with pointed bill. The little bird is valiant in defense of its young, and may attack a cat or even a birds'⋅ nesting boy if he climbs the nest tree.

When winter has passed, the Eastern Kingbirds move up from Central and South America and usually begin to arrive in the latitude of southern New England about May 10. Kingbirds evidently are fond of water. They often build their nests in low bushes on a river shore or in the water, and they may be seen flycatching along the ocean beach and nesting among the sand dunes, where fresh water is scarce. They bathe either by standing in shallow water and then dipping and fluttering or by flying down to the surface of the water to dip and rise again. As soon as the females arrive, the males begin their courtship, which is carried on largely in the air, where the male can best exhibit his beauties with spread wings and tail, while he seeks the company of the chosen one, fluttering and sailing, rising and falling in an effort to charm her. At this season the males are very pugnacious and some terrific battles are fought.

When union is consummated both sexes engage in the construction of the nest and the care of the young. If the first nest is destroyed they usually rebuild near by. They now become doubly vigilant and truculent, and woe betide the bird that in any way interferes with their domestic arrangements, though they may even allow inoffensive small species to nest in the same tree. In August, the young having been reared, the return flight to the south begins, but some birds, breeding later perhaps than the majority, remain with us until about the middle of September, when they move slowly south. Any birds seen later than September are mere accidental stragglers.

The Kingbird, although primarily a feeder on flying insects, can adapt itself to the pursuit of other food. In flying about it often takes insects by skimming and fluttering over water, or by picking them from the grass or trees.

They sometimes alight on plowed lands, and pick up grubs and myriapods; they will also eat wild berries and seeds. Very large beetles are taken, such as May beetles and *Cetonias*, as well as some of the beneficial tiger beetles and ground beetles. Weevils of both grain and fruit, click beetles, grasshoppers and crickets, wasps, wild bees, ants, and flies are prominent among the food materials of this bird. Among the flies taken are house-flies and several species that trouble cattle; but smaller insects, like mosquitoes, gnats and midgets, are not ignored. Leaf hoppers and many other bugs are taken; and a great variety of caterpillars, mostly of the hairless species, are eaten or fed to the young. This bird is destructive to moths of many kinds, among them the gypsy moth. In two and one-half hours seven of these birds were seen to take seventy-nine male and twenty-four female gypsy moths, and they killed in that time a great many more that could not be positively identified.

The Kingbird, therefore, is particularly beneficial about the garden and orchard, for it eats very little, if any, cultivated fruit. The only bad habit attributed to this bird is that of killing honey bees, and even while catching bees it seems about as likely to do good as harm. On the whole, it seems probable that, while the Kingbirds eat some bees, they confine their bee-eating mainly to the drones, and also protect the bees by killing the moths and flies that prey upon them.

GRAY KINGBIRD

Tyrannus dominicensis dominicensis (GMELIN).

Other name: Pipiry Flycatcher.

IDENTIFICATION. — Length about 9¼ to 9¾ inches; spread about 14½ to 16 inches. Similar to Eastern Kingbird but slightly larger, *much paler above, head gray* instead of blackish; lining of wings yellowish; no white band on tip of tail; bill noticeably longer and heavier.

BREEDING. — Similar to Eastern Kingbird.

RANGE. — Breeds from the coast of southeastern South Carolina and Georgia to southern Florida, the Bahamas, Greater Antilles, Virgin Islands, and Jamaica; winters in northern South America; migrates along the coast of Central America from Yucatan to Panama.

The main automobile highway between Miami and the North skirts the eastern coast of Florida for many miles, though for much of its course it is separated from the waters of the Atlantic by the so-called Indian River and the narrow sea-islands. At times it crosses wide areas of low scrub growth of palmettos, sand pine, shrub oaks of several species, and rosemary; at others it passes low mangrove swamps and islets, or runs for miles through open 'piney' woods. It is in the mangroves and the scrub growths that we find the Gray Kingbird, from April to September. The birds may often be seen from one's car, as they perch in typical kingbird fashion on an exposed branch of a tree or bush or on the telephone wires beside the road, or they may be seen darting after insects or perhaps harrying a passing Fish Crow or a harmless heron. Their notes are much like those of the Eastern Kingbird but perhaps not quite as harsh. Dr. Frank Chapman says that 'its usual call is a vigorous *pitìrri, pitìrri,* which in Cuba, gives it its common name.' — (J.B.M.)

ARKANSAS KINGBIRD

Tyrannus verticalis SAY.   PLATE 55.

Other name: Western Kingbird.

IDENTIFICATION. — Length 8 to 9½ inches; spread 15¼ to 16½ inches. Similar to Eastern Kingbird but much lighter above; tail black but outer tail feathers edged with white and no white tip showing; yellowish belly and gray breast.

BREEDING. — Similar to Eastern Kingbird.

RANGE. — Breeds from southern British Columbia, southern Alberta, and southern Manitoba south to northern Lower California and Chihuahua, east to western Minnesota, western Iowa, central Kansas, and western Texas; winters from western Mexico to Nicaragua; accidental throughout the East.

In comparatively recent years the Arkansas or Western Kingbird has become a common and conspicuous bird throughout much of western Minnesota and Iowa, where fifty years ago it was practically unknown. It seems to prefer inhabited regions, perhaps because of the number of insects found about barns and pastures, and it is much more frequent in the small towns on the edge of the prairies than in natural wooded areas. It may often be seen from the train in crossing this region, the gray-breasted birds perching on the telephone wires near the right of way or darting after insects in typical flycatcher fashion, at which time their yellowish bellies and gray upper parts are easily seen and their black tail with white edges instead of end is diagnostic. In form they are typical kingbirds but in coloration they somewhat resemble the Crested Flycatcher, though the latter has a longer brown tail instead of a white-edged black one. In parts of their range, from Colorado westward, they may be confused with Cassin's Kingbird, which however is darker gray above and with a narrow grayish tip and sides to the tail. Both are noisy, active and quarrelsome birds. — (J.B.M.)

SCISSOR–TAILED FLYCATCHER

Muscivora forficata (GMELIN).

Other name: Swallow-tailed Flycatcher.
  IDENTIFICATION. — Length 11½ to 15 inches; spread 14¼ to 15½ inches; tail 6½ to 12 inches. Unmistakable; extremely long deeply forked tail; light gray above, white below with wing linings and sides pink with a flash of scarlet showing in flight.
  BREEDING. — Similar to Eastern Kingbird; eggs smaller.
  RANGE. — Breeds from southern Nebraska to southern Texas, casually to southwestern Missouri, western Arkansas, and western Louisiana; winters from southern Mexico to Panama.

The Scissor-tailed Flycatcher has a longer tail than any other bird of its size that visits North America except the very rare Fork-tailed Flycatcher. In the air it is one of the most graceful and attractive of birds, flying with extreme lightness and turning with the greatest ease. Rising from the top of some tall tree it flutters and floats through the air and returns to its perch, or it flies easily along low over the grass apparently searching for insects. At other times it rises very high and circles about as if in play. Its notes resemble those of the Eastern Kingbird, and it seems as bold and fearless as the latter in attacking birds of prey, often alighting upon their backs and pecking them fiercely. The Scissor-tail is a great wanderer, and may be found flying over almost any region except a very mountainous country. Cultivated land, prairie and woodland are all visited, though it seems to prefer the more open lands. It is a mere straggler except in the extreme western part of the range covered by this book.

NORTHERN CRESTED FLYCATCHER

Myiarchus crinitus boreus BANGS.   PLATE 55.

Other names: Great Crested Flycatcher; Wheep; Yellowhammer.
  IDENTIFICATION. — Length 8 to 9¼ inches; spread 12¾ to 14 inches. About size of Eastern Kingbird but looks longer; head slightly crested; olive above, throat and upper breast gray, belly yellow; wings with two light bars.
  CALL. — A loud *wheeeeep!*
  BREEDING. — In woodlands and orchards. *Nest:* In a cavity in trunk or large branch, lined with grasses, hair, feathers, etc., and almost always a cast snake skin. *Eggs:* 3 to 8, creamy to reddish-buff with lines and scratches of brown, purple, and lavender.

RANGE. — Breeds from southern Manitoba, southern Ontario, southern Quebec, and New Brunswick south to southern Texas and South Carolina; winters from Mexico to Colombia.

The Northern Crested Flycatcher normally is a dweller in the forest. In the eastern United States, however, most of the ancient forest trees with hollow trunks and branches have fallen before the axe of the woodsman, and now this bird finds nesting places in the cavities of many old orchard trees. For this reason chiefly, perhaps, it is found largely today in open farming country, and especially in neglected orchards near woodland, but the woods were its first love, and often it may be seen perched near the top of some tall forest tree from which it darts forth in pursuit of its insect prey. It is a prominent bird, for it is the largest and in some ways the handsomest of our common flycatchers; it often occupies a conspicuous perch, and its notes are so loud as to compel attention. Its battles in the air are fierce and noisy and it is inclined to bully other birds. It is quick, however, to rush to the defense of feathered neighbors in distress, for on several occasions when I have concealed myself in the woods or underbrush and imitated the cry of a bird in pain or distress this flycatcher has dashed almost into my face before it discovered its mistake. So far as I have been able to observe, this species is solitary, and a lone bird or a single pair keeps guard over a considerable domain.

During the month of April and the early part of May this species migrates northward, flying mostly by day and feeding as it goes. Courtship usually begins here during the latter part of May, when, if two rival males aspire to the favors of one female, a fierce battle ensues which results in one or both combatants losing more or less feathers. When the pair is finally united a search begins for a suitable cavity, and if one cannot be found in some tree, almost any kind of nook may be selected, even a birdhouse or nesting-box. Receptacles for nesting seem to be used without regard to their shape, situation or height from the ground, if only the interior is large enough for the bulky nest and the entrance of sufficient size to admit the birds. Being an active and industrious fowl it may occasionally choose some large, deep cavity when in want of a better place, and fill much of the superfluous space with a mass of rubbish built high, as a foundation to its domicile; or if the hole is too deep for it to fill laboriously, it may block the cavity with sticks and rubbish placed crosswise, and then build its nest on the platform thus prepared.

Many attempts have been made to account for its almost universal habit of adding a cast-off snake skin to the nest. Some believe that this is placed there for the purpose of frightening predatory animals away, but it is often so bestowed as to be invisible from the entrance and it is hardly possible that a dried skin would frighten any animal, unless indeed the scent of the snake still lingers about it. Both sexes engage in nest-building, and when a large cavity requires filling or when the building is interrupted by stormy weather, two weeks may elapse before the nest is complete. The parents feed the young with insects and defend them with great fury against their numerous enemies. In attacking an intruder their swift flight and power of quick turning come into play and are used to great advantage in avoiding retaliation.

SOUTHERN CRESTED FLYCATCHER

Myiarchus crinitus crinitus (LINNAEUS).

IDENTIFICATION. — Averaging slightly smaller than *M. c. boreus* and with a larger bill.

RANGE. — Breeds from peninsular Florida north along the Atlantic coast to southern South Carolina; winters in southern Florida and on the Keys, possibly in Central America.

EASTERN PHOEBE

Sayornis phoebe (LATHAM). PLATE 56.

Other names: Barn or Bridge Pewee; Phoebe Bird; Tick Bird.

IDENTIFICATION. — Length 6¼ to 7¼ inches; spread 10½ to 11¼ inches. Gray-brown above, no conspicuous wing-bars; frequently wags tail when perched.

CALL NOTE. — Most distinctive feature, a spoken, not whistled, *phoe-be*, with accent sometimes on first, sometimes on last syllable.

BREEDING. — Usually near water. *Nest:* Protected under an overhanging rock, upturned root, cut bank, bridge, or building, of mud lined with feathers, grasses, roots, moss, etc., and covered outside with mosses. *Eggs:* 3 to 8, white, sometimes with a few fine brownish spots.

RANGE. — Breeds from Mackenzie, central Ontario, southern Quebec, New Brunswick, Nova Scotia, and Prince Edward Island south to New Mexico, central Texas, northern Mississippi, and the highlands of Georgia, winters in the United States from southern Virginia, southern Kentucky and southern Missouri south to Mexico.

The Eastern Phoebe is an early bird. The chill and blustering winds of March still sweep over fields of frozen snow, when this little feathered wanderer comes from its winter sojourn in more southern lands to its favorite home in the North. Soon its familiar note is heard about the barn, in the orchard or along the rushing stream. Now and then one of these early birds may be seen darting out from its perch in a March snowstorm, apparently catching insects, but Mr. C. J. Maynard told me that he saw one thus snapping up the whirling snowflakes, which may have been one of its ways of securing water. The Phoebe is early also in another sense. In the dusk of morning before the break of day, while Screech Owls and Whip-poor-wills are still abroad, the Phoebe flits silently from mountain cliff, overhanging bank or some other sheltered retreat where it has passed the night and soon its voice may be heard along the river, greeting the first signs of the coming day. It seems to be endowed like the night birds with vision that can pierce the gloom of dusk in shadowy places and so mark down the fluttering insects of the night before they have retired to their daylight retreats. The Eastern Phoebe seeks the waterside because many insects develop early there, and though the little bird can eke out a precarious existence before the insects develop, they are its favorite food. In chill April, for instance, while the days still remain cool and the nights frosty, the Phoebe lives commonly in the woods, flycatching over pools of standing stagnant water, where numerous flying insects flutter when the sun shines. Another reason for the preference for a home near water is that the Phoebe is a great bather and often may be seen flying over the water, plunging in its breast and wing-tips, and afterward shaking the shining drops from its feathers.

The bird also frequently alights in shallow water and bathes by dipping and fluttering in the manner of most perching birds.

Phoebe's choice of a home, however, is not decided so much by proximity to water as by available nesting-sites. She will go far from water to build her nest on a mountain cliff or in some isolated cave in the rocks; but along the many streams of New England, high banks and many bridges furnish her such sites as she most desires for her little dwelling, and along the streams too she can find the mud and moss which go into the construction of the small compact nursery in which the young are cared for and fed.

Sometimes the nest in which the first brood is reared is repaired and used again during the same season. Often, however, a new nest is built for the second brood in a different situation; sometimes several nests are built in the same season. One reason for this is that the fondness which the Phoebe exhibits for poultry houses and her habit of lining her nest with hen feathers tend to infest the little family with those tiny red mites, so abundant where poultry are kept. These and bird lice are sometimes so numerous in the nest of the Phoebe that the young succumb to their attacks. A thorough dusting of the nest with insect powder will dispose of most of these pests.

The Eastern Phoebe nests early and thus lives up to its reputation as an early bird; it sometimes chooses strange situations for its nest. Occasionally one is plastered on a perpendicular wall, but the birds prefer some sort of shelf, as a beam, to support it. One pair built a nest in an old tin colander hung on the wall of a barn, another was placed in an old coffee pot hanging on a nail in a deserted cabin, and more than once I have seen a Phoebe's nest in an uncovered cigar box nailed up on a cottage wall under the veranda roof. Another pair built in a well, five feet below the surface. They reached the nest by passing through a knot hole in the platform that covered the well. Another pair built in an air shaft of a coal mine. Individual Phoebes, which have become accustomed to man and his works, often seem very fearless in their choice of a nesting-site. Bridges over which heavy teams and cars pass daily, railroad culverts over which roll many heavy trains every twenty-four hours, farmhouse sheds and barns where people and animals often pass are chosen.

The Phoebe's first brood often requires six or seven weeks, or even more, from the beginning of the nest until the young have flown; but when the same nest is used for the second brood, a month is ample time, as this brood is reared in warm weather, when food is plentiful and storms usually are few. Both birds often take part in incubation and in feeding the young, and within one or two days after the first brood leaves the nest, the female begins another or starts repairs on the old nest, while the male cares for the first brood.

The Phoebe takes its prey, like other flycatchers, by watching from some prominent perch and darting out at passing insects which it captures mostly in the air, but it also gets more or less food from the ground, especially when the young are being fed. Its tail seems to be very loosely hung and bobs up and down or sweeps sidewise very frequently. It seems a fearless bird, for it often nests in plain sight on cliffs, frequented by the powerful Duck Hawk, but I have noticed that in such a case it seldom flies out far from the cliffs into the open, and that in passing down to its nest from the top of the crag it shoots down like a plummet, close to the rock, and exposes itself as little as possible. Not many feathers of the Phoebe are found around the Duck Hawk's nesting-place, although the hawk gets one rarely. Phoebes let the Duck Hawk severely alone, but sometimes, like the Kingbird, chase other hawks or crows.

They usually live at peace with the smaller birds, except when two rival males contend for the favors of the same female, when a spirited contest ensues.

During his mating days the male may be seen, at times, fluttering about ecstatically in a circle and pouring forth what no doubt passes for a flight-song with his indulgent mate. Sometimes the bird rises high repeating his usual notes with some twittering variations, but it can hardly be called a musical triumph. Often this is an early morning performance.

In studying the food of the Eastern Phoebe one wonders how such an insectivorous bird can exist in New England in February and March and how it can withstand the storms of this period. During severe snowstorms this bird betakes itself to some shelter such as a shed, a barn cellar or a poultry house. I have seen it in February on the ground with Tree Sparrows apparently picking up small seeds. In late winter and early spring the bird subsists more or less on seeds and wild berries, but it prefers animal food and especially insects.

YELLOW–BELLIED FLYCATCHER

Empidonax flaviventris (BAIRD AND BAIRD).   PLATE 56.

IDENTIFICATION. — Length 5 to 5¾ inches; spread 8 to 8¾ inches. Olive green above and *more decidedly yellow below* than any other small flycatcher of eastern North America; has an olive shade across breast and yellow eye-ring; should be unmistakable in spring as it is then the *only small flycatcher that is distinctly yellow below, including the throat;* our other small flycatchers have the throat white or whitish; Acadian Flycatcher is only *yellowish* below; in autumn when others are yellowish below, identification is more difficult.

NOTE. — A weak *per-wee* or *pse-ek*, rising on the last syllable.

BREEDING. — In coniferous swamps. *Nest:* On ground, sunk in moss or under a stump or upturned root, of rootlets, moss and grasses. *Eggs:* 4 or 5, white or creamy, spotted with browns and purplish.

RANGE. — Breeds from northern British Columbia, central Manitoba, central Quebec, and Newfoundland south to northern Minnesota, northern Michigan, northern Pennsylvania, southern New Hampshire, and Nova Scotia; winters from southern Mexico to Panama.

The flycatchers of the genus *Empidonax* are thus dubbed the kings or rulers of gnats, or at least that is what the Greek name signifies, but they are really destroyers of the gnat tribes. The one now under consideration seems to seek out places infested by many mosquitoes, and seems to delight in reducing the number of these pests. According to my experience the Yellow-bellied Flycatcher is always, even in migration, a bird of wet or swampy woods, particularly amid rather low undergrowth, along streams or about borders of swamps. In the northern wilderness it breeds in sphagnum bogs among coniferous forests. There in the moist, gloomy, insect-infested morass the little bird is happy, well fed and perfectly at home. More or less silent in migration, it becomes quite loquacious in its summer home, accompanying its frequent remarks with fluttering wings and a quick jetting of its rather brief caudal appendange.

Usually its principal spring migration comes late in May, and in some backward seasons the flight continues well into June. Thus the bird's greatest numbers appear at a time when it can easily hide amid the umbrageous thickets of its chosen retreats, for the well or fully developed leaves and the swarming mosquitoes in its haunts render calm and uninterrupted observation difficult. The bird itself is secretive and quiet and has no trouble in keeping out of sight. Also its return migration is at its height while the trees are still in full leaf in August and before most people begin to watch for returning wood birds. Thus the bird very often escapes observation by all except keen and expert bird watchers and collectors.

The Yellow-bellied Flycatcher is a great ant-eater, as flying ants make up a considerable proportion of its food. Apparently it eats very few useful insects and it takes many harmful beetles, moths and caterpillars and some garden and orchard pests.

Dr. Jonathan Dwight, Jr., in Chapman's 'Handbook of Birds,' wrote of the notes of the Yellow-bellied Flycatcher:

'The song is more suggestive of a sneeze on the bird's part than of any other sound with which it may be compared. It is an abrupt *psĕ-ĕk*, almost in one explosive syllable, harsh like the deeper tones of a House Wren, and less musical than the similar but longer songs of the Alder or the Acadian Flycatcher. It is hardly surprising that the birds sing very little when we see with what a convulsive jerk of the head the notes are produced. Its plaintive call is far more melodious — a soft, mournful whistle consisting of two notes, the second higher pitched and prolonged, with rising inflection, resembling in a measure *chū-ē-ē'-p*.'

ACADIAN FLYCATCHER

Empidonax virescens (VIEILLOT).   PLATE 56.

Other name: Green-crested Flycatcher.

IDENTIFICATION. — Length about 5½ to 6¼ inches; spread about 9 to 9½ inches. The greenest of our small flycatchers of the *Empidonax* group; appears dark grayish above, but the green tinge appears in strong light; pale under plumage has sulphur-yellow tinge with a shade of grayish or greenish on upper breast; *two wing-bars buff or pale buffy-whitish;* yellow below resembling that of Yellow-bellied Flycatcher, but paler and *throat white* or whitish while that of the latter is yellow; Acadian Flycatchers are quite yellow below in autumn.

BREEDING. — In woods or thickets. *Nest:* Near end of low branch, of rootlets, moss, grass, etc., lined with finer material. *Eggs:* 2 to 4, pale cream to buffy, with a few brownish spots.

RANGE. — Breeds from northeastern Nebraska, central Iowa, southern Michigan, southeastern Ontario, New York, southern Vermont (casually), and Massachusetts (casually) south to southern Texas, the Gulf States, and central Florida; winters in Colombia and Ecuador; migrates through Yucatan and Central America.

Owing to the close resemblance borne by the Acadian Flycatcher to the Alder Flycatcher or even to the Least Flycatcher, especially in the autumn, it is difficult to get accurate information regarding its distribution, status or habits. Both this and the Alder Flycatcher are mostly silent in migration, and appear so much alike in the field that only those who have known both species for years are capable of surely distinguishing them.

The Acadian Flycatcher is first of all a bird of the wilderness, nesting in the deep woods, in a well-watered country, either in swamps or on drier lands. It does not sit on the top of tall trees as does the Olive-sided Flycatcher, nor is it as often found in low shrubbery as is the Alder Flycatcher. It loves the shady woods and usually takes its stand on a rather low limb to watch for its prey. It is a bird of the lower and more open spaces of the woodland, but occasionally builds its nest on some low limb by a roadside. The bird may be easily over-looked and may be less rare than the paucity of our present information would indicate. Even in the Southern States in localities where it is the commonest of flycatchers, it is often passed by unnoticed, as it is rather shy and usually keeps well within the shadows of the trees. From southern Illinois and West Virginia southward it is a very common bird. Like most of the flycatchers it is somewhat arrogant and pugnacious.

ALDER FLYCATCHER

Empidonax trailli trailli (AUDUBON).   PLATE 56.

Other name: Traill's Flycatcher.

IDENTIFICATION. — Length 5¼ to 6 inches; spread 7¾ to 9 inches. The brownest *Empidonax;* difficult to identify, however, except by its notes, and these vary considerably in different localities.

BREEDING. — In swampy meadows and thickets. *Nest:* Compact but not neat, of vegetable fibers, lined with fine grass, hair, etc. *Eggs:* 2 to 4, creamy to buffy with brownish spots.

RANGE. — Breeds from central Alaska, northern Manitoba, northern Ontario, central Quebec, and Newfoundland south to southern British Columbia, northeastern Colorado, central Arkansas, and Kentucky, and to the mountains of West Virginia, western Maryland, and Pennsylvania, also in Connecticut and northern New Jersey; winters from Yucatan to Colombia and Educador.

When the first half of May has passed, when the new, tender, bright green leaves of spring have expanded enough to form a forest screen, when nearly all the birds have come and summer is at hand, the Alder Flycatcher appears. On some warm still morning in the waning of the Maytime the bird watcher notes here and there in the edge of the woods, on a pasture fence, in a small tree by the bog or even in the orchard, a small flycatcher usually on a rather low perch, sitting quite erect, silent and watchful, occasionally dashing out in pursuit of a flying insect or flitting from one point of vantage to another. This is the Alder Flycatcher in migration — quiet, watchful and discreet. Unlike the Least Flycatcher Chebec, it rarely appears until summer is at hand and if the season is late, its migration is delayed and may continue until the tenth or twelfth of June.

This bird resembles the Chebec so closely and comes so late that it is likely to be overlooked, as on its breeding grounds it is inclined to keep much under cover of the foliage. It breeds in wet, bushy meadows, flies rather low and is very inconspicuous, and as its autumnal migration takes place mostly in August, when few people observe fall migrants, it is rarely noted. No sooner are its young able to fly well and feed themselves than both old and young begin to depart for the south. The Alder Flycatcher is not, as its name seems to imply, confined to alders. It usually nests near but not on them, and may be found about them as they grow along the watercourses and the swampy borders of the more open bushy marshes and meadows in which it breeds, but in migration it may be found almost anywhere, even in city parks.

LEAST FLYCATCHER

Empidonax minimus (BAIRD AND BAIRD).

PLATE 56.

Other name: Chebec.

IDENTIFICATION. — Length 5 to 5¾ inches; spread 7½ to 8½ inches. The smallest and grayest *Empidonax;* a *conspicuous eye-ring* and *two light wing-bars;* its call *chebec'* or *se-bic'* is its best identifying distinction.

BREEDING. — In open woods, orchards, etc. *Nest:* A neat compact cup of soft vegetable fibers, hair, etc. *Eggs:* 3 to 6, white, rarely dotted faintly with reddish brown.

RANGE. — Breeds from west-central Mackenzie, southern Quebec, and Cape Breton Island south to central Montana, western Oklahoma, Missouri, Indiana, northern Pennsylvania, northern New Jersey, and in the mountains to North Carolina; winters from Mexico to Panama.

The Least Flycatcher or 'Chebec' may be characterized by superlatives. It is the smallest, earliest, tamest, smartest, bravest, noisiest and most prominent member of its genus in the East, and many ladies will agree that it is the dearest. The bird arrives in spring before the other small flycatchers. A few individuals are here ere the end of April, and when a thousand orchards burgeon with the bloom of spring, when the first misty green begins to screen the woodlands, a host of these little feathered warriors spreads over the Northern States and into Canada. At first, in migration, they are rather silent and appear wherever open spaces among the trees or along the edges of thickets give them fly-room. At this time they may be mistaken for the Alder Flycatcher, as they may frequent alders along a brook and may even appear among the tall bushes at the edges of meadows. Later, when the females come, the males are the most vociferous and pugnacious of their kind, and nearly every orchard resounds with their cries. Although usually their relations with other birds are amicable, they fight fiercely among themselves in the mating season. When rival males meet, the issue is decided at once by combat. The loud unmusical *chebéc* is uttered with the utmost vim and vigor, accompanied by an upward jerk of the head and a flirt of the tail, as if to call attention to the little bird's superior musical abilities, while some of his softer notes are given with a characteristic trembling of the wings, as if he were rendering ecstatic melodies. His emphatic call is sometimes repeated almost incessantly by the male, who stands guard over the nest while the female is incubating. The male has a so-called flight song which consists of a jumble of notes uttered in a kind of ecstasy while he flutters about in a circle. The nest-building is an interesting operation. Mr. A. A. Cross, who watched a female at this work, sent me a letter from which I append the following graphic description:

'It so chanced that in June, 1916, following a shower which had thoroughly dampened vegetation, I stepped from a clump of small pines facing an alder run. My eyes almost instantly focused upon the nest of a Least Flycatcher. About one half of the upper edge seemed literally torn to pieces, the frayed fragments projecting in all directions. The work of some robber, I thought. Such was not the case, for presently the owner appeared with her beak full of building material which, a piece at a time, she thrust into the edge of the nest, leaving the loose ends free. Watching her, I noted that she was gathering the inner bark from the dead and broken stems of last year's goldenrod. She made many trips, working rapidly, and disposing of the material as in the first case. In about twenty minutes she had finished, causing the edge of the nest to look like a miniature hedge. She then settled herself solidly in the nest, hooked her head over the edge and pivoting on her legs ironed out the rough brim with her throat, putting considerable energy into the work and working first one way and then the other. In this manner she was able to take in about one third of the circumference of the nest before changing her position. Then readjusting herself, she continued the process until the nest was finished. This was the last step in the building of the nest, the following morning it contained one egg. Had the material used not been rendered pliable by the rain it would not have stayed in place readily.'

The Chebec, unlike the other small flycatchers of its genus, has gradually become accustomed to man and his works and prefers his neighborhood to more retired localities. While orchard and shade trees are its favorite breeding-places, it may be found nesting in village and city streets. Stakes, bean poles, dead limbs in orchards, clothes-lines and the poles which uphold them are favorite perches for this little bird, from which it marks down flies, moths and other small winged game, which it pursues and captures with snapping bill, returning to its perch to devour them.

The Least Flycatcher feeds chiefly on insects, most of which it gets on the wing, but it takes some from plants and trees, and may even go to the ground for them in case of necessity. As it comes in close contact with agriculture it takes many farm pests, such as cotton-boll weevils, squash beetles, cucumber beetles, clover weevils, plum curculios, ants, moths (including gipsy moths), caterpillars (including cutworms), bark beetles and the fly of the railroad worm.

EASTERN WOOD PEWEE

Myiochanes virens (LINNAEUS).   PLATE 56.

Other names: Pewee; Dead-limb Bird.

IDENTIFICATION. — Length 6 to 6¾ inches; spread 9¾ to 11 inches. Slightly smaller than Phoebe; dusky olive-brown above, whitish below, with two conspicuous wing-bars; does not wag tail; lacks eye-ring.

NOTE. — A drawling, slurring, whistled *pee-wee* or *pee-a-wee*.

BREEDING. — In woods or orchards. *Nest:* A shallow cup saddled on a branch, of bark, rootlets, etc., covered with bits of lichen. *Eggs:* 2 to 4, creamy white with ring of spots at large end.

RANGE. — Breeds from southern Manitoba, southern Ontario, southern Quebec, and Prince Edward Island south to southern Texas and central Florida, west to central Nebraska; winters from Nicaragua to Colombia and Peru.

'When the tide of spring migration is at its height, and the early morning woods are bursting with melody, a pensive stranger, clad in soberest olive, takes his place on some well-shaded limb and remarks *pé-a-wee*, in a plaintive voice and with a curious rising inflection at the end. Unlike his cousin, the Phoebe, who came too early in March, and who felt aggrieved at the lingering frosts, the Wood Pewee has nothing that he may rightly complain of. The trees are wreathed in their tenderest greens; the fresh blossoms opening to the waving breeze, are exhaling their choicest odors; the air hums with teeming insect life. But the Wood Pewee takes only a languid interest in all these matters. His memory is haunted by an unforgotten sorrow, some tragedy of the ancestral youth, and he sits alone, apart, saying ever and anon as his heart is freshly stirred, *pê-a-wee, pê-a-wee.*' Thus William L. Dawson in his 'Birds of Ohio,' aptly characterizes the Wood Pewee and its pensive lay.

The sad or dreamy nature of its call, however, is in harmony with its environment among the whispering trees. Its plaintive tone is deceptive, for the Wood Pewee evidently is a happy bird. Dallas Lore Sharp says that 'not much can be said of the Flycatcher family except that it is useful — a kind of virtue that gets its chief reward in heaven.'...'a duck,' he says, 'seems to know that it cannot sing. A flycatcher knows nothing of its shortcomings. He believes he can sing and in time he will prove it.'

It is true that, as a family, flycatchers are not singing birds, but the Wood Pewee comes nearer to being a songbird than any other flycatcher with which I am well acquainted. It has the sweetest and most pleasing voice of them all. In spring and early summer the male often attempts at early morning and occasionally at evening a song of some length which is really quite a creditable effort for a flycatcher. The bird seems to show little of the irritability and pugnacity that renders most of our flycatchers quarrelsome and even tyrannical. When on the lookout for its prey it does not take up a position at the top of a tree, like some of the other members of the family, but sits upright on some dead limb in the cool shades of the forest where light and shadow fleck the leafy ground, and from this perch sallies forth from time to time in pursuit of ill-fated insects, which with snapping bill it captures unerringly. Like the Phoebe, the Wood Pewee is abroad even before daylight, and seems to be able to pursue and capture its winged victims before it is light enough within the woods for the human eye to perceive the little bird. Where woodlands are numerous the Wood Pewee breeds mostly within their shades, although it occasionally nests in an orchard tree near the woods; in more open parts of the country its nest is not infrequently to be seen in orchard and shade trees. Usually it is saddled on a dead limb at no great distance from the ground. The adults are devoted to their offspring and have been known to defend them courageously by darting at a man's head, though they are not brave enough actually to attack a human being. They feed the young for quite a long time after the fledglings have left the nest, and while they still continue to call on their parents with a mouse-like squeak.

OLIVE–SIDED FLYCATCHER

Nuttallornis mesoleucus (LICHTENSTEIN). PLATE 55.

Other names: Three-deer; Pitch-pine Flycatcher.

IDENTIFICATION. — Length about 7 to 8 inches; spread 12¼ to 13½ inches. Slightly smaller than Eastern Kingbird; large head and heavy bill; dark patches at sides of chest separated by white stripe, are diagnostic.

CALL. — Resembles *three-cheers* or *hip-three-cheers!*

BREEDING. — Similar to that of Wood Pewee.

RANGE. — Breeds from central Alaska, central Manitoba, northern Ontario, southern Quebec, and Cape Breton Island south in coniferous forests to Lower California, New Mexico, and western Texas, also in northern Michigan, New York, northern New Jersey, and Massachusetts, and south in the mountains to North Carolina; winters from Colombia to Peru; migrates through Mexico and Central America.

The Olive-sided Flycatcher is a forest recluse. Normally it lives and breeds about unfrequented swamps, lonely mountain lakes and ponds or mountain streams, where coniferous forests grow.

It is by no means confined to the mountains, however, and may even breed on lowlands near the sea, but in such cases it nests near water or wet lands. It seems fond of the spruce in the northern part of its range, and in the southern part seems to prefer pitch pine. It breeds locally in orchards and open groves and in old fields grown up to red cedars (Virginia junipers), but this is a departure from its usual habits. It seems to prefer some lone swamp or lake, where fire or flood has killed some trees, or where the settler has girdled them, and left them standing bleak and bare to be used by the bird as watch-towers on which it sits very erect and from the tall tops of which it shoots straight up into the air and then stoops hawk-like or else darts off most gracefully at varying angles in pursuit of its insect prey. Our recluse is pugnacious, his mate is company enough, and he defends an exclusive territory against any interloping male of the same species. When another male appears the two often battle in the air until both are completely exhausted.

The Olive-sided Flycatcher usually arrives in New England in May, and always alone. During the period of migration one may appear anywhere, usually perched in or near the top of some tree on the edge of the woods or in the orchard, silent and watchful, except that on its breeding grounds its loud cries frequently are heard. The shallow nest is placed well out on some rather slender limb, often high from the ground in a coniferous tree where it is difficult to reach.

The birds are very brave in defense of their eggs or young. As the climber nears the nest, they become miniature furies, darting close to one's head and snapping their bills like owls, but behaving far more bravely than most birds of prey. In August when the young are strong on the wing, both old and young start on their long journey to South America.

HOYT'S HORNED LARK

Otocoris alpestris hoyti BISHOP.

IDENTIFICATION. — Similar to *O. a. alpestris* but upper parts generally paler and more gray; yellow of head and neck replaced by white except forehead, which is dirty greenish white, and throat, which is distinctly yellow.

RANGE. — Breeds from the mouth of the Mackenzie to the west shore of Hudson Bay and south to northern Alberta and northern Manitoba; winters south to Nevada, Kansas, Michigan, Ohio, New York, and Connecticut.

NORTHERN HORNED LARK

Otocoris alpestris alpestris (LINNAEUS).

PLATE 57.

Other names: Shore Lark; Snow Lark.

IDENTIFICATION. — Length 6¾ to 8 inches; spread 12¼ to 14 inches. About size of Bluebird; brown above and on sides; face and throat yellow with black marks across top of forehead, on side of head back of and below eye, and across lower throat.

SONG. — Given in flight, a long tinkling twitter.

BREEDING. — On open lands. *Nest:* Sunk in ground or moss, of grass lined with plant down and feathers. *Eggs:* 4 or 5, drab or grayish, spotted with browns.

RANGE. — Breeds from Hudson Strait south to the head of James Bay, Labrador, southeastern Quebec (Gaspé), and Newfoundland; winters south to the Ohio Valley and Georgia, and west to Manitoba.

Along the winter beaches the Northern Horned Lark runs. Where restless rolling surf has piled up blocks and cakes of ice and hardened snow, in open spots where the snow has melted, or on the bare and open sands left by the receding tide, the larks in merry companies industriously seek their sustenance. Their tracks may be seen almost anywhere along the beaches of New England and the Central Atlantic States in the fall and winter months, and in migration they sometimes penetrate far into the interior. Dr. Charles W. Townsend, in his 'Birds of Essex County, Massachusetts,' gives the following excellent description of the habits of the species along our coast:

'The old term, Shore Lark, is a most appropriate name for this bird, as it is generally seen near the shore. Here it is equally at home on the beach, among the dunes, and in the salt marshes, as well as on the hills and in the cultivated fields. It occurs in small or large flocks, sometimes to the number of two hundred. It is found alone or associated with Snow Buntings and occasionally with Longspurs.

'The Horned Lark is a swift walker, and, considering its short legs, takes long strides. It picks at the grass-stalks from the ground, never alighting on them as do the Snow Buntings and Longspurs. It sometimes flies up from the ground, seizing the seeds on the tall grass or weed-stalks, at the same time shaking many off onto the ground, which it picks up before flying up to repeat the process. Horned Larks are frequently found in roads picking at the horse-droppings, especially when much snow has covered the grasses and weeds. They also come into the farmyards for scraps of food.

'Although a ground bird, the Horned Lark occasionally alights on the extended roots of old tree stumps two or three feet from the ground and on stone walls. I have never seen it in trees. It is a persistent fighter or extremely playful, whichever you will, and is constantly engaged in chasing its fellows. I have seen two face each other for a moment, with heads down like fighting cocks, the next instant twisting and turning in the air, one in hot pursuit of the other. When in flocks with the other winter birds, they more frequently chase them, especially the smaller Longspurs. I have also seen them chase Snow Buntings, and often Ipswich Sparrows that were feeding with them, and once, what appeared to be a Prairie Horned Lark.

'Horned Larks fly in scattered flocks with an undulating motion. Their flight is often at a considerable height from the ground, and their call notes appear to come from out of the depths of the sky. These notes may be written *tssswee it, tsswt*, the sibilant being marked. At times the notes are almost trilled. They are emitted as the birds fly and occasionally from the ground.'

Northern Horned Larks are hardy birds. In midwinter they take snow baths. When the snow is crusted they may be seen feeding at times with Snow Buntings, while both species are exposed to the freezing wind. Sometimes as the little birds hop up to peck seeds from the weeds they are blown sidewise along the smooth surface before they can recover their footing and again face the gale.

PRAIRIE HORNED LARK

Otocoris alpestris praticola HENSHAW.

PLATE 57.

IDENTIFICATION. — Smaller and somewhat paler than *O. a. alpestris*, with forehead and line over eye white instead of yellow, and throat either white or slightly tinged with yellow.

RANGE. — Breeds from southern Manitoba and south-central Quebec to eastern Kansas, central Missouri, Ohio, West Virginia, Maryland, and Connecticut; winters south to Texas, Tennessee, Georgia, and Florida (rarely).

This hardy bird is the first of all the songbirds in vernal migration to push on toward the frozen north. Long before the Northern Horned Larks leave us, even before the first Eastern Bluebirds appear, amid the lingering snows of February the bold and restless Prairie Horned Larks are on their way. They reach New York, Massachusetts, Vermont and southern Ontario usually during the first thaw in February, and it is quite possible that a few may remain all winter along the Massachusetts coast, as they do on Block Island. In nesting also they antedate all our other small birds. Many of these larks are mated by March 1, and most of the nests for the first brood are built before the snow has entirely disappeared. They usually are located on the east or south side of some little rise of land where the sun has melted all the snow and the snow water has drained away. The nest is made beside some object or vegetation that will shelter it somewhat or render it inconspicuous. Sometimes a heavy snowstorm forces many of the birds to desert their unfinished nests or their incomplete sets of eggs, but if incubation has begun, so long as the bird can reach up and clear away the snow which covers her, just so long will she continue to impart warmth to the little speckled eggs. Thus, after a storm, nests have been discovered at the bottom of a deep little hole in the snow. When approached, the female ordinarily leaves the nest while the intruder is at some distance, and sneaks off quietly along the ground before she rises, but sometimes when the eggs are near hatching, and she is suddenly surprised while incubating, she may act like a crippled bird to deceive the enemy and entice him away. Commonly, however, neither bird exhibits much of that anxiety which often leads some birds to betray the situation of the nest.

My experience with this bird in the breeding season has been confined to two localities, one in Manitoba and the other in Massachusetts, where I have not heard such extended flight-songs as are described elsewhere by others. After the young are hatched, the old birds manifest their anxiety by voice and action, but usually at a distance from the nest. Both parents assume the care of the young, but as soon as they are able to fly the female begins to prepare for a second brood, leaving the young chiefly if not entirely to the care of the male, who faithfully feeds and guards them. If all goes well, two and even three broods may be safely reared. The song of this lark like that of the Skylark of Europe is not a remarkable performance (for, by the way, the vocal efforts of the latter will not compare as bird-music with the jingle of our Bobolink), but the flight that often accompanies the song is (as is the case with the Skylark) truly remarkable. How exhausting the effort that must be required of a small bird to rise both flying and singing up into the zenith beyond the range of human vision.

Prairie Horned Larks are birds of the open country. They seek the treeless lands. I have

323

never seen one in a tree, but now and then one may alight on a rock, a stone wall or stump or even a fence post or rail. Seen in the fields and pastures they walk or run about or squat in the grass. If a hawk appears, they will disappear from sight (thanks to their protective coloration) until the danger is past. I have never seen one hop or jump along as the Robin does. In summer they are fond of dust-baths in the country roads, but I have never known one to bathe in water, though they may do so. As autumn comes on they live in a land of plenty as their grain crop, the abundant seeds of weeds and grasses, is ready for the gathering. They now renounce their family ties and assemble in loose flocks, sometimes with other races of the Horned Lark or with Snow Buntings, and forage over the land. As the frost begins to congeal the soil, and the snows of winter cover much of their food, they seek wind-swept, bare spots or weed patches or feed on undigested grain from horse droppings in the roads, but most of them drift southward, though sometimes in winter a few may be found with the Northern Horned Larks along the coasts of southern New England.

TREE SWALLOW

Iridoprocne bicolor (VIEILLOT).

PLATE 77.

Other names: White-bellied Swallow; White-breasted Swallow.

IDENTIFICATION. — Length 5 to 6¼ inches; spread 12 to 13¼ inches. Steely green-black or blue-black above, white below; tail slightly forked.

BREEDING. — *Nest:* In a natural cavity in a tree, old woodpecker's hole, birdhouse, etc., of straw and feathers. *Eggs:* 4 to 10, white.

RANGE. — Breeds from northwestern Alaska, northern Manitoba, and northern Quebec to southern California, Kansas, northeastern Arkansas, and Virginia; winters from central California, coasts of Gulf and South Atlantic States to North Carolina south over Mexico to Honduras and Cuba.

The Tree Swallow is quite as common as the Barn Swallow in some localities, and more numerous in others. When the country was first settled, it nested in hollow trees and abandoned holes of woodpeckers, but now probably most individuals utilize birdhouses and nesting-boxes, or crevices about buildings. It is not so communal in its breeding-habits as are the other species, but where numerous nesting-places are available, colonies of from ten to fifty pairs may be seen. It is fond of the water and many still nest in woodpeckers' holes in the dead trees killed by water in overflowed swamps.

The Tree Swallow is the first of its tribe to arrive in the North and the last to depart for the South. It is so constituted that it can subsist on berries, and, therefore, is not so closely confined to an insect diet as are other swallows. In the East it follows the coast largely in migration, where it can feed on the numerous bayberries which grow there, and where it can sustain life much earlier in spring and later in autumn than it could in the interior. Usually Tree Swallows do not appear in the highlands of New York and western New England much before the middle of April, though in the river valleys stragglers may be seen earlier. With rising April temperatures and balmy airs, they appear at their breeding-grounds and become interested in their former nesting-places. They flutter and dart happily about in pursuit of awakened insects and all is merry until a cold storm or a sudden drop in temperature occurs,

324

when they suddenly disappear and are not seen again until the next warm wave. The question often is asked, 'Where do the swallows go?' Usually on cold days they go to sheltered places on the coast or to lakes or rivers where hills and trees give shelter from cold winds, and where the sun shines more warmly — where they can still find some flying insects or can pick up benumbed ones from the water or the ice along the shore. During a long, cold storm in the breeding season they crowd together in some sheltered tree cavity, or in a birdhouse with entrance turned away from the stormy wind, and there they stay until the storm has passed.

Like Barn Swallows, Tree Swallows seek feathers for lining their nests, and seem to prefer white ones, for they have been known to go to a distance for white feathers, when only colored ones could be found near-by. During the nesting season these birds will come for white feathers tossed in the air for them, and often one will try to carry several feathers at once, only to lose one or more at each attempt to snap up another. Where suitable white feathers are scarce, spirited combats for their possession often occur. This swallow is very pugnacious, and in the nesting season furious, long-continued battles may be seen between rival males, as well as struggles between Tree Swallows, English Sparrows, Bluebirds and Purple Martins, for the possession of nesting-boxes, in which the Tree Swallow often is successful.

Most of the adults have finished rearing their broods and have left the nesting-boxes by the tenth or fifteenth of July, having reared their single brood. But some of the less mature birds, more tardy in coming and in mating than the adults, linger until later. The young usually are strong and well able to fly when they leave the nest, and never return to it, but in cases where they leave too soon, they may come back to it with their parents for several nights. At first young swallows alight on some dead limb where the adults feed them. Later, as they become more proficient, they are fed on the wing by the parents, but they soon learn to catch their own insects, and then they course much over water, flying very low in cool weather, so that their wings almost touch the surface, and now and then one is caught by a large pickerel, which leaps at it from the depths below.

In August, thousands of Tree Swallows, with other species, arrive at the seashore, where they roost in the marshes. They scatter about in the daytime, feeding on insects and berries. Their numbers continue to grow by accessions from the interior, until many thousands are gathered along the coast. Sometimes they alight on telegraph wires, covering them for miles, or they may light on the beaches until the sand is black with their hosts. When ready to migrate they sometimes rise to great heights, even beyond the reach of human vision and follow the coast southward, but if they encounter strong head winds they fly close to the ground or water to escape the full force of the blast.

This is the only swallow that habitually winters in the United States. Great numbers spend the winter near the Gulf coast, where they roost at night in large marshes and scatter over the country during the day. One of the most remarkable sights that I have witnessed was that of a vast concourse of these birds going to roost in southern Florida. Twilight was falling when, with one companion, I approached a great marsh in lower Brevard County, not far from Indian River, in what was then an unbroken wilderness. As we came nearer, a huge black cloud drifted rapidly in from the west, and as it came over the marsh it began to roll and gyrate as if tossed about by strong, erratic winds. Then we knew that it must be a vast flight of birds. As the mass veered about over the center of the marsh, there shot down from near its center a long black tongue, forming a column which, when it reached the reed-

325

tops, spread out with a terrific roar of wings until the whole phenomenon resembled a great black cloud connected with a black sea by a waterspout of equal blackness, and down this spout the cloud itself discharged into the marsh. When the last of the birds were down, I waded far into the marsh until I came to the edge of the roosting flock, and found the tops of the reeds covered with Tree Swallows. The next morning I was there before daylight to see them go out, but there was nothing spectacular about their departure. They merely spread out over the ground, flying low in every direction, each bird hunting insects for himself; hardly a chirp broke the silence of the morning, and in a few minutes the great flock was gone, but all that day, wherever we went, Tree Swallows could be seen in the air.

The food of the Tree Swallow differs from that of other swallows by including more vegetal matter, mainly wild berries and seeds. The fruit of the bayberry or wax myrtle is its chief reliance when insects are hard to find, but it takes some blueberries and a few other berries including those of the Virginia juniper or red cedar and the woodbine or Virginia creeper, with a few small weed seeds and grass seeds. It takes some of the same insect pests as does the Barn Swallow, and it seems not improbable that this bird ranks second only to the Barn Swallow in usefulness. The Tree Swallow is of great value about cranberry bogs and about mosquito-infested marshes.

BANK SWALLOW

Riparia riparia riparia (LINNAEUS). PLATE 77.

Other names: Sand Martin; Sand Swallow.

IDENTIFICATION. — Length 4¾ to 5½ inches; spread about 10 to 11 inches. Our smallest swallow, brown above and on sides; brown *band across lower throat* separating white upper throat and belly; wings and tail darker than back.

BREEDING. — In colonies. *Nest:* A burrow in a sand-bank, excavated by the birds, and lined with grass and feathers. *Eggs:* 3 to 7, white.

RANGE. — Breeds from northern Alaska and northern Quebec south to southern California, Texas, central Alabama, and Virginia; winters in Brazil and Peru; migrates through Mexico and Central America; also occurs in Eurasia and northern Africa.

The little brown Bank Swallow is not only the smallest of our swallows, it is the only one that has not learned to nest about man's buildings or other structures. It prefers to dig its own hole. Like the Tree Swallow it often arrives much earlier along the coast than in the interior. From the coast it follows up the rivers, usually arriving in their valleys before it appears on the higher lands, for the high shores of the ocean and the cut banks along river shores are its normal breeding-places. When the birds arrive they retire at night to sleep in their last year's holes, or they quickly excavate new ones, far enough into the bank to give them shelter for the night. In delving into the bank they cling to it, and peck the dirt out with their bills, but when the holes are deep enough for them to enter, they use both bills and feet. When a hole becomes too deep to throw dirt out with the feet, it is carried out in the mouth. In sandy, friable soil only a single row of holes is made near the top of the bank, and each hole runs slightly upward, so that the nest is just beneath the sod, which keeps the roof from caving in. In clayey soil, however, the bank may be honeycombed with several irregular rows of holes. When a bank is formed of stratified layers of clay, sand and gravel, the nests may appear spaced almost as regularly as the windows of a factory, as only certain strata are used by the birds. Some Bank Swallows burrow in great heaps of sawdust, left by lumbermen, but these heaps must be unsafe nesting-places.

The holes usually approach a circle in section and are about two inches in diameter, but some are much wider than their height, as if both the mated birds who excavated the apartment had worked side by side. Usually they work into the bank only two or three feet, but in gravelly soil they have been known to go in eight or nine feet to find a place without small stones, which might fall on the nest. When they find stones too large for them to dig around, they abandon the attempt and try again elsewhere. The Rev. F. O. Morris, who has watched the work of this species in England, says that a pair of these birds will remove about twenty ounces of sand in a day and that they can move pebbles two ounces in weight. The time occupied in making the burrows depends upon the kind of soil, the obstructions encountered and the length of the burrow, and may therefore vary from a few days to a few weeks. In favorable localities where they are undisturbed hundreds of pairs may nest in company.

Notwithstanding the apparent inaccessibility of their nests, there are enemies that are able to enter them. Sometimes an entire colony is destroyed by a mink or a weasel which somehow succeeds in climbing to their burrows. Those foreign interlopers, the English Sparrow and the Starling, sometimes drive out the Bank Swallows and utilize the burrows for their own nests. Occasionally a river in flood undermines a bank, and the nests go down in an avalanche of sand, or when, as is frequently the case, the Bank Swallows utilize a sand-pit for their nesting place, teamsters carting out sand may destroy their home, and bird-nesting boys must be reckoned with; then there is that danger that all swallows must face at times — the continued prevalence of cold rains in the nesting season. Many colonies have been exterminated at such times where the rains have been heaviest. The poor birds then huddle together in their holes, and being unable to find food, they perish.

ROUGH–WINGED SWALLOW

Stelgidopteryx ruficollis serripennis (AUDUBON).　　　　　　　　PLATE 77.

Other names: Sand Martin; Gully Martin; Rough-wing.

IDENTIFICATION. — Length 5 to 5¾ inches; spread 11½ to 12¼ inches. Slightly larger than Bank Swallow, brown above more uniform; throat brownish shading into white of belly, without throat-band.

BREEDING. — *Nest:* In a hole in a bank, cliff, tree, or building, of grasses, rootlets, leaves and (rarely) feathers. *Eggs:* 4 to 8, glossy white.

RANGE. — Breeds from southern British Columbia, Montana, Minnesota, central Wisconsin, southeastern Ontario, southern New York, and Massachusetts south to southern California, central Mexico, and southern Florida; winters from southern Arizona to Costa Rica.

The Rough-winged Swallow is the rarest of the six species of *Hirundinidae* found in New England. While it probably breeds in every state of the Union except possibly Maine, it is not considered common in any of the Northeastern States. Forty years ago there was only one authentic record of this species north of Connecticut, that of a couple of pairs which Mr. Walter Faxon found breeding at North Adams, Massachusetts, in 1895. Since that time, however, either the species is increasing in numbers and extending its range to the northeast, or it is being identified more frequently because there are more good field observers studying our birds than in former years. It requires a quick eye to detect, as the birds wheel and pass in rapid flight, the slight differences which distinguish the Rough-winged Swallow from the Bank Swallow or the immature Tree Swallow.

The Rough-wing may be recognized in its chosen haunts by a careful observer, as it courses rather slowly over a stream, pond, marsh or field, seeming to follow an established route over and over, its direct flight showing little of the rapid zigzagging characteristic of the slightly smaller Bank Swallow. It is not as communal in its nesting habits as the latter bird, and it is seldom that more than a few pairs occupy any given locality. It is also much more catholic in its choice of a nesting-site than is the Bank Swallow, the latter always excavating its own nest burrow, while the Rough-wing sometimes digs its own tunnel, sometimes uses that of a Bank Swallow or a Belted Kingfisher, often nests in the crannies of a ledge or in the crevices of a bridge or mill foundation, and even at times uses an open tile drain in a river bank.

My first experience with the Rough-winged Swallow was at Clark's Pond in Ipswich, Massachusetts, on May 21, 1916, while watching a mixed flock of swallows hawking about over the pond, which included two birds we recognized as Rough-winged Swallows. They were seemingly following a clearly defined aërial pathway, down a shallow gully to the pond, out over the water, then back across a swampy field to the upper end of the gully, and repeating this trip over and over. By crouching in the gully we could watch the birds as they passed close overhead, and were able to identify them beyond question, and to compare them with the somewhat similar Bank Swallows.

About six weeks later, as I was paddling my canoe down the Asquam River in Ashland, New Hampshire, my attention was drawn to a pair of swallows zigzagging back and forth across the swamp close by. I decided they were Rough-wings, but it was impossible to follow them among the flooded thickets of the marsh, and they soon disappeared from sight. Exactly a year later, two birds were again seen at the same place, and this time they very accommodatingly perched on a dead twig in good light only a few yards from my canoe. The brownish throat, shading off into grayish below, was plainly visible, and in flight the back and wings were a nearly uniform brownish color, while the wings of the Bank Swallow are noticeably darker than its back.

I immediately began a search for a nesting-site and soon located it in a low under-cut bank just across the narrow stream. The nest was in a burrow a foot or so from the top of the bank, apparently an unfinished and abandoned Kingfisher's hole. The entrance was very different from the small opening made by Bank Swallows, and was large enough to admit my hand readily. By reaching in until my elbow was within the hole I could just touch the nest lining, which was made principally of grasses, but I could not reach the eggs without digging out the hole which would probably have caused the birds to abandon the nest.

A week or so later I returned to the locality, armed with a camera and a small dip-net used in fishing. Both parents were busily engaged in feeding their young, entering the burrow at frequent intervals, their throats distended with insects. After watching them for some time, I allowed one parent to enter the burrow and then slipped the dip-net over the opening, easily catching the bird when it started to leave the nest. Its mouth was filled with long-legged insects which it was feeding to the young when disturbed. Holding the bird in one hand and the camera in the other I took several portraits, then examined the stiff barbs on the first primary feather, which give the bird its distinctive name, and which are very easily felt by running the finger along the feather-edge. The next summer the river was unusually high, the bank was undermined and the nesting-place destroyed, and I never identified the birds again in that nieghborhood.

In many of the Central and Western States the Rough-winged Swallow is an abundant bird, much more common than the smaller Bank Swallow, the reverse of the condition in New England. — (J.B.M.)

BARN SWALLOW

Hirundo erythrogaster BODDAERT.   PLATE 76.

IDENTIFICATION. — Length 5¾ to 7¾ inches; spread 12½ to 13½ inches. Our only swallow with a *deeply forked tail; forehead and throat chestnut;* no brown on rump.

BREEDING. — Originally in caves and under cliffs, now usually inside barns and other buildings. *Nest:* Of mud, and straw, lined with grasses and feathers. *Eggs:* 3 to 6, white, lightly spotted with browns and purplish.

RANGE. — Breeds from northwestern Alaska, southern Manitoba, and central Quebec south to southern California, southwestern Texas, northern Arkansas, Tennessee, northern Alabama, and North Carolina, and in Mexico; winters from Mexico to Brazil, northern Argentina, and central Chile; migrates through the Bahamas and West Indies.

No bird in North America is better known or more truly the friend and companion of man than the swift and graceful Barn Swallow. It nests within his buildings, and with a flight that seems the very 'poetry of motion' it follows the cattle afield or swoops about the house dog as he rushes through the tall grass, and gathers up the flying insects disturbed by his clumsy progress. When the mowing machine takes the field, there is a continual rush of flashing wings over the rattling cutter-bar just where the grass is trembling to its fall. The Barn Swallow delights to follow everybody and everything that stirs up flying insects — even the rush and roar of that modern juggernaut, the motor-car, has no terrors for it.

The Barn Swallow is a truly admirable bird — well-beloved for its excellent disposition and its altruistic behavior. It is brave, but not quarrelsome. Many nest side by side in the same building with little friction, although occasionally two pairs clash over the same nesting-site, and the battle lasts until one or the other gives up the fight. It is said that as many as two hundred sometimes occupy the same barn. In my experience, however, forty nests in one building is the maximum. All join in attacking the common enemy. The appearance of a strange cat, a weasel or a Sharp-shinned Hawk, when the swallows have young, is the signal for a concerted assault. I have even seen a lone pair of breeding birds drive both cat and weasel from the neighborhood of their helpless young.

When the first settlers came to this country, the Barn Swallows nested in caverns and crevices and under projecting shelves along our 'rock-bound coast' as well as on the high rocky shores of certain lakes and rivers, in great hollow trees, or in caves and recesses of mountain

329

cliffs. They must have left the primal nesting-places early to consort with mankind, for now they are not known to use such nesting-places, except in the northern wilderness and on the Pacific coast. Old residents of Lynn, Massachusetts, who were still living in the latter part of the nineteenth century, could remember when Barn Swallows in numbers nested in the 'Swallow Caves' at Nahant, situated on the south side of the rocky peninsula known as Little Nahant.

As the country was settled they forsook their grottoes in the rocks for barns, sheds, bridges, boat-houses, wharves and abandoned or unoccupied dwellings. There is no more skillful mason among the feathered tribes than this same Barn Swallow. Years ago I encamped in an abandoned house on the inner shore of Sandy Neck, Barnstable, Massachusetts, where Barn Swallows had built their nests. The walls of the room were plastered and smoothly finished, but the little feathered artisans had affixed their nests to the smooth, upright, plane surface of human masonry and had attached it so firmly and well that they could rear their young in perfect safety, for no climbing animal could scale that sheer wall. Since then lightning has riven the old house and vandals have destroyed it, leaving to me only a pleasant memory of the little colony of twittering birds. This is the only case known to me where Barn Swallows have built nests on such smooth walls without support, and there may have been a concealed supporting nail or two projecting from the wall unobservable by me. Swallows often avail themselves of such a foundation. A pair of projecting nails or a small block of wood nailed to a sheer wall may be utilized by them in situations where, otherwise, they would not attempt to build.

During the latter part of April the pioneers of the Barn Swallow host usually appear in New England. Sometimes they come too early and are met by cold and storm and so, unable to obtain food, they seek shelter in some building or huddle together behind a closed blind or windowsill on the south side of a house until the sky clears and the temperature moderates. By snuggling together in their nests, some of these birds have been able to survive two or three cold days, when morning outdoor temperatures were as low as fifteen degrees above zero mark, but such temperatures may be fatal, even when the birds are well protected.

The courtship of the Barn Swallow takes place largely on the wing, she flying, he pursuing, but its culmination often occurs on a building. Nest-building is an absorbing occupation. In a dry time mud may be scarce near by, and some farmers go to the trouble of mixing some for the swallows. Where this is done the alert birds find it immediately, and some may even hover happily about while the mixing is going on. Having fashioned their mud-built habitations, they readily find dried grass or hay for lining, but feathers are always in demand. Some people put out feathers for them, and take delight in watching their aërial evolutions in pursuit of the elusive things. In a high wind the feathers are hard to catch and are frequently blown out of the swallow's beak after she has seized them. Or if a bird holds firmly to a large feather, she may be blown to one side or even turned about when she endeavors to breast the gale.

As the mud nests are strengthened with straw, and usually plastered on rough boards or rafters, or on a small support, as they are under cover, they rarely fall, as those of Cliff Swallows often do, and the young are fairly safe. Therefore as the birds usually rear two broods each year, they are perhaps the most numerous of our swallows. If all goes well the young birds leave the nest in about sixteen days. They first exercise their wings within the building and then try them out of doors. When the young are able to fly well, they do not desert the old home entirely, but often spend several nights in or near the nest. Now and then they return

330

later to the same neighborhood, and some have been known to join the parents in feeding young of the second brood. Most of the individuals of the first brood probably leave for the sea-shore in August, where they flock with other swallows in preparation for their southward journey. The male usually cares for the first brood after they are well able to fly and until they learn to catch their own food; meanwhile the female prepares for the second brood.

Barn Swallows are children of the aërial spaces. They spend a great part of each long summer day on the wing. They eat and drink on the wing, as they drink and also bathe by dipping down to the surface of the water. Thus they are exposed to some danger from large frogs and swift fishes, which sometimes jump at them.

Barn Swallows seem to be better equipped to fight for life during long, cold storms in the breeding season than Purple Martins or Chimney Swifts. In flooded areas they fly close to the surface of the rising waters, and pick off insects that have been driven to the tops of reeds and grasses, or they go to the ground and pick up dead or benumbed insects, and they even eat berries or seeds. Thus, in the disastrous storm of June, 1903, many of them came through alive, though most of the young in the nests perished, while at the same time the Purple Martins in eastern Massachusetts were almost exterminated and the Chimney Swifts were sadly reduced.

Barn Swallows are very industrious birds, working many hours daily, and missing no chances. I have seen them flying along the margin of a river, where mosquitoes were abundant, until the moon rose and the bats came out, and have seen them on the same river when it was so dark that they could be recognized only by their notes. Farmers often, with some reason, predict the coming weather by the flight of these and other swallows. When the air is warm and the sky clear, many small insects rise very high with the upward currents and the swallows follow them. In cool, cloudy weather, with no upward movement of heated air from the ground, insects fly low, and the swallows then sweep close to the water or the grass tops.

Before the middle of August, the different species of swallows in the interior, preparing for migration, gather to roost in the river marshes. They begin to collect there before dark, fluttering lightly down and alighting so gently on the tops of wild rice, sedges, reeds and bulrushes that their footing rarely gives way. Sometimes hundreds so gather to pass the night. From these roosts they start early some fine morning, hawking about low down at first, picking up their breakfasts and then, rising high, pursue their flight to the coast, where they join hundreds or thousands more, and all move gradually southward, feeding as they go.

NORTHERN CLIFF SWALLOW

Petrochelidon albifrons albifrons (RAFINESQUE).   PLATE 76.

Other names: Eaves Swallow; Cliff Swallow.

IDENTIFICATION. — Length 5 to 6 inches; spread 12 to 12½ inches. Resembles Barn Swallow but with shorter, nearly square tail, *whitish forehead,* and *pale brownish rump.*

BREEDING. — In colonies, under cliffs and eaves of buildings. *Nest:* Of mud, often shaped like a bottle with opening on one side, lined with grass and feathers. *Eggs:* 4 or 5, white, rather thickly marked with browns.

RANGE. — Breeds from central Alaska, north-central Mackenzie, northern Ontario, southern Quebec, Anticosti Island, and Cape Breton Island south over entire United States except Florida and the Rio Grande Valley, also in western Mexico; winters probably in Brazil and Argentina; migrates through Florida and Central America.

The early history of the Northern Cliff Swallow is involved in obscurity. We hear of it first in an account published in 'Philosophical Transactions' in 1772, where John Reinhold Forster, in an account of birds sent from 'Hudson's Bay,' refers to it as *Hirundo No. 35*, but gives it no name. Audubon says that he saw the bird at Henderson, Kentucky, on the Ohio River in 1815, and that he saw it again at Newport, Kentucky, in 1819; but it was first described and named as a new species by Thomas Say, in the account of Long's 'Expedition to the Rocky Mountains,' compiled by Edwin James in 1823. The belief was quite general at one time that the Cliff Swallows, finding both shelter and strong points of attachment for their nests under the eaves of the rough buildings of the early settlers, gradually moved eastward from the Rocky Mountains and so settled in the Northeastern States and the southeastern provinces. Probably, however, they were already established in this area on some of the rather infrequent cliffs of the eastern country, which they forsook later to take up their residence under the protection afforded them about the dwellings of mankind, wherever clay or mud could be found sufficiently plastic and adhesive to answer their purposes.

As the land was cleared for fields and pastures, and as barns with wide eaves were erected, we may suppose that the Cliff Swallows finding abundant food and good shelter on the farms, deserted their inhospitable rocks for the new type of refuge afforded by buildings and, multiplying exceedingly, spread from place to place over the land. It is not improbable also that there was an eastward movement later from the bluffs and cliffs west of the Mississippi. Thus the 'Cliff' Swallows under man's protection became 'Eaves' Swallows and waxed fat and numerous until the decade beginning in 1870, when the English Sparrow began to increase and spread over the Eastern States. Then the nests built by the industrious Cliff Swallows were appropriated, after a struggle, by the swarming and ubiquitous Sparrows, whose clumsy and bustling occupancy soon resulted in the destruction of their stolen domiciles. Another factor in the diminution of the Cliff Swallows was the substitution of modern, painted barns for the rough, unpainted buildings which formerly predominated. Swallows' nests will not adhere long to the side of a freshly painted building, and it is only when the paint has become much weathered and worn that these birds can find safe attachment for their nests.

During my childhood, double rows of Cliff Swallows' nests under the wide eaves of some great unpainted barn were commonly seen in Massachusetts. I remember well such a colony within the present city limits of Boston, and the swarm of birds that played about this barn during the nesting-time. They did not arrive in spring until after some of the Purple Martins had come, but when the Cliff Swallows came their numbers about their chosen resorts were even greater than those of the Martins.

The Northern Cliff Swallow, unlike the Barn Swallow, makes 'bricks without straw.' Usually it does not use dried grass or hay to hold its plastic building material together. Therefore it must have clay or clayey mud for building material. If there is too much sand in the mud the nests, when dry, will fall. As they cannot build without mud, an exceedingly dry time may delay their home-making far beyond the usual date. They are so adept at gathering their material that they can hover over the bottom of a miry ditch that offers no secure footing, and dexterously snatch up mouthful after mouthful of viscid mud, but they prefer to stand on the edge of a puddle and work at their leisure.

The first pellets are plastered on the barn where the base of each nest is to be, and the birds cling to the rough boards, bracing themselves with their tails like woodpeckers, and hold the mud in position until it has dried sufficiently to adhere and retain its form; from this foundation a base is built in the shape of a very shallow half-cup. On this the back wall is erected and then the sides are built up. The builders usually work at the nest only a few hours each day. They do not seem to be in great haste, and four or five days may be occupied in fashioning each structure. If heavy rains or cold days come, the work of construction may be still further delayed, and then the nest-building period may extend to ten, fifteen or even twenty days. Driving storms sometimes destroy many nests, but the optimistic birds persevere. Often the female is obliged to deposit eggs before the nest is finished, but still the work goes on.

Dr. Coues, in his 'Birds of the Colorado Valley,' writes entertainingly of this communal effort, as follows: 'It is pleasant to watch the establishment and progress of a colony of these birds. Suddenly they appear — quite animated and enthusiastic, but undecided as yet; an impromptu debating society on the fly, with a good deal of sawing the air to accomplish before final resolutions are passed. The plot thickens; some Swallows are seen clinging to the slightest inequalities beneath the eaves, others are couriers to and from the nearest mud-puddle; others again alight like feathers by the water's side, and all are in a twitter of excitement. Watching closely these curious sons and daughters of Israel at their ingenious trade of making bricks, we may chance to see a circle of them gathered around the margin of the pool, insecurely balanced on their tiny feet, tilting their tails and ducking their heads to pick up little "gobs" of mud. These are rolled round in their mouths till tempered, and made like a quid into globular form, with a curious working of their jaws; then off go the birds, and stick the pellet against the wall, as carefully as ever a sailor, about to spin a yarn, deposited his chew on the mantelpiece. The birds work indefatigably; they are busy as bees, and a steady stream flows back and forth for several hours a day, with intervals for rest and refreshment, when the Swallows swarm about promiscuously a-flycatching. In an incredibly short time, the basement of the nest is laid, and the whole form becomes clearly outlined; the mud dries quickly, and there is a standing place. This is soon occupied by one of the pair, probably the female, who now stays at home to welcome her mate with redoubled cries of joy and ecstatic quivering of the wings, as he brings fresh pellets, which the pair in closest consultation dispose to their entire satisfaction. In three or four days, perhaps, the deed is done; the house is built, and nothing remains but to furnish it. The poultry-yard is visited, and laid under a contribution of feathers; hay, leaves, rags, paper, string — Swallows are not very particular — may be added; and then the female does the rest of the "furnishing" by her own particular self.'

The Doctor goes on to say that he has seen in the West many nests of Cliff Swallows built among the outer sticks of Great Blue Herons' nests, and has even seen them attached about the cliff-built nests of the Prairie Falcon. In each case the larger birds attended to their own duties, apparently not molesting their little tenants. Some nests are built of such lasting material and are so firmly attached and so well sheltered that they are used year after year, probably by the same birds. The usual shape of a Cliff Swallow's nest when built on the exposed face of a cliff resembles that of a retort or a gourd with the stem projecting outward and slightly down-curved. But many nests built under the shelter of wide eaves or under the roof of a building lack the neck, and some are merely cup-shaped, much like those of the Barn Swallow. In such sheltered situations the protection afforded by the enclosed, vestibule type of construction is unnecessary. Occasionally a pair of Cliff Swallows will build a nest on and over an abandoned nest of the Barn Swallow, Robin or Phoebe.

PURPLE MARTIN

Progne subis subis (LINNAEUS).   PLATE 76.

Other names: Black Martin; House Martin; Martin; Gourd Martin.
IDENTIFICATION. — Length 7¼ to 8½ inches; spread 15½ to 16¾ inches. Largest of our swallows; tail forked but not deeply; male dark blue-black all over; female and young not so dark, mottled gray and whitish on throat becoming whiter on belly.
BREEDING. — In colonies, in holes in cliff, or in birdhouses. *Nest:* Of twigs, grass, leaves, feathers, etc. *Eggs:* 3 to 8, white.
RANGE. — Breeds from west-central Alaska, southern Manitoba, northwestern Ontario, New Brunswick, and Nova Scotia west to Vancouver Island, and south to central Mexico, the Gulf coast, and Florida; winters in Brazil; migrates through Central America, Venezuela, and Guiana.

Formerly the Purple Martin was an abundant bird in the Eastern States. It was always local, however, and probably it was never an inhabitant of the great forests that covered so large a part of the country in aboriginal times. Then it must have been confined mostly to open, grassy valleys along the lower reaches of rivers, and to shores of lakes and possibly also to the vicinity of marshes along the sea-coast, where it nested in the abandoned habitations of woodpeckers.

The bird has been a favorite with mankind from time immemorial. The Indians were accustomed to trim up a few saplings about their crude dwellings and hang from the stub of each limb a gourd or calabash, hollowed for the convenience of their feathered visitors. Where saplings were not conveniently situated the Indians set up poles, fastened crossbars to them and hung the gourds to these crossbars. Later, the Southern negroes followed their example.

What can add more in life, color and action to a country place than a handsome martin box with a great colony of Purple Martins? Their loud and cheerful voices, their rapid, aërial evolutions, and their swift massing for attack on an enemy of the flock always attract attention. When domiciled in the yard of a farm home, they protect the chickens by attacking hawks and crows *en masse* the moment these marauders appear in the vicinity.

Purple Martins are fond of wide river valleys, where slow streams flow, flanked by broad meadows, but they have nested on highlands, and even on the high roofs of city blocks, or in recesses and holes about the roofs of buildings on busy city streets. They may be attracted almost anywhere in open unforested country by erecting suitable nesting-boxes. If such houses are put up on tall poles and not too near trees or occupied dwellings, the Martins are likely to find them. But no martin house should be erected (or if erected the entrance should be kept closed) until the Martins arrive. It is well to have the pole hinged, so that the box may be readily taken down.

The Purple Martin usually flies at moderate speed, but at need it can fly very fast. It easily

334

catches fast-flying dragonflies and butterflies that are such expert dodgers that comparatively few birds get them. It takes nearly all of its food on the wing. Nevertheless some individuals learn in cases of emergency to go to the ground, where they walk about and pick up or catch insects. In severe weather such birds might survive by thus obtaining dead or benumbed insects from the ground. Some have been seen to flutter over rose bushes and pick off rose beetles, but such habits may be individual and exceptional. A colony of Martins will scour the country far and near, meantime catching hosts of flying insects.

A flock of these birds, all gathering material for their nests, is a pretty sight. Nest-building is shared by both sexes, and occupies several days. Most nests that I have examined have been protected in front of the entrance by a wall of mud. When the young are hatched both parents care for them and feed them, and at the end of from twenty-four to twenty-eight days they are about ready to leave the nest. This feeding period is a time of great activity. I have never been so much impressed by the number of insects required by young birds as when, perched at the top of two braced ladders, I watched the parent birds feeding their young in a large martin box. Every few seconds a bird struck that box, alighting at an entrance with its gullet or its bill full of insects. Among the insects brought were some large dragonflies; some were brought by the wings, and the young bird leaning forward snatched the insect and swallowed it, often with difficulty, leaving the wings in the beak of the parent. Some were held by the body in the beak of the adult bird and were swallowed wings and all by the young bird, though the ends of the wings stuck out of its mouth for some time afterward. In some cases small snails and eggshells are fed to the young along with their insect food.

Usually when the young leave the nest they fly quite readily, but many of them return to the nest night after night for a week or ten days, especially if the weather be windy and stormy. In the meantime they learn to alight on trees and on the wires of telephone or telegraph lines. In the latter part of August or early in September the Purple Martins begin their southward migration. Usually old males are the first to go. They have been gradually assembling in large flocks which roost together at night, usually in trees with dense foliage. Then a day comes when at daybreak all is excitement and commotion. Soon the flock circles and rises to a great height, and off they go, commonly heading southwest. The young birds follow a little later in the season.

CANADA JAY

Perisoreus canadensis canadensis (LINNAEUS).   PLATE 58.

Other names: Whiskey Jack; Whiskey John; Moose-bird; Grease-bird; Meat-bird; Camp Robber; Meat Hawk.

IDENTIFICATION. — Length 10¾ to 12 inches; spread 16 to 17½ inches. Size of Blue Jay; a gray bird with a darker cap and white throat; young are dark slate-color.

BREEDING. — In coniferous forests and swamps. *Nest:* Of twigs, bark, moss, grass, etc., warmly lined with mosses and feathers. *Eggs:* 3 to 5, grayish, profusely speckled.

RANGE. — Breeds from tree limit in northern Mackenzie, central Quebec, Labrador, and Newfoundland south to central British Columbia, central Alberta, northern Minnesota, Michigan, New York (the Adirondacks), New Hampshire, northern Maine, New Brunswick, and Nova Scotia; casually south in winter.

The Canada Jay is an inhabitant of the northern wilderness where it consorts with the mighty moose. Its home is in boreal coniferous forests and swamps where civilized man seldom penetrates. In these wilds it shows little fear of mankind. Its principal characteristic is its boldness. Probably most people who have camped in the forests of Maine or of southern Canada have experienced the attentions of this jay. It follows the hunter, and the sound of a gun attracts rather than repels it, as it has learned to associate that sound with meat. It trails after the trapper, and robs traps of their bait and even eats small animals caught in them. Camp is no more than established when the Canada Jays or Moose Birds 'rally round' eager to snatch any bit of meat or other edible substance. They learn to go into tents and even into buildings; they have dropped into canoes for food, while the occupants were paddling, and in winter have been known to feed from the hand. In the winter, especially, when life in the North is hard, these birds will steal anything apparently edible and eat it, if possible, or carry it off to hide in some crevice of the trees. By this method of storing food they are enabled to sustain young in early spring before vegetation and animal life have developed, and their nests are made and the eggs laid while snow still lies deep in the woods, and when night temperatures often run below zero. Small articles like pieces of soap, plug tobacco and matches left lying about soon disappear from the camp, and sometimes other articles which could never by any possibility be of use to the birds go in the same way; any meat or fish left exposed in the open is soon carried off piecemeal by these Camp Robbers, as they are called.

The name 'Whiskey Jack' is said to have been derived from the Indian name of 'Wiss-ka-chon' or 'Wis-ka-tjon' which was corrupted by the whites to 'Whiskey John' and then to 'Whiskey Jack,' but Professor F. G. Speck states in his 'Myths and Folk-Lore of the Timiskaming Algonquin and Timagami Ojibwa' that the trickser-transformer *Wiskedjak*, Meat Bird, is the personified Canada Jay or 'Whiskey Jack'; also he says in his 'Bird-Lore of the Northern Indians' that among the Indians north of the St. Lawrence the name *Wiskedjak*, from which the English name 'Whiskey-Jack' has been derived, is the common term applied to the Canada Jay (and its various races) from Labrador to the Rockies.

In its choice of food the Canada Jay is even more omnivorous than the Blue Jay. It attacks almost anything that seems edible, and in winter it is said at times to feed on the lichens that caribou eat. Probably it is fully as destructive to the eggs and young of other birds as is the Blue Jay. It subsists largely on insects in summer, and later on berries. There is no reasonable limit to its appetite. Any bird that will consume quantities of soap probably will take almost anything eatable. Indians say that it will eat moccasins and fur caps, but its food habits have never been the subject of exhaustive investigation.

NORTHERN BLUE JAY

Cyanocitta cristata cristata (LINNAEUS). PLATE 58.

Other names: Jay; Jaybird.

IDENTIFICATION. — Length 11 to 12½ inches; spread 15¾ to 17½ inches. Unmistakable; mostly blue above and gray below but with white on wings and tail, black blotch on breast, and conspicuous blue crest.

VOICE. — A noisy bird with a great variety of notes, the commonest a harsh slurring *jay* or *jeeah*.

BREEDING. — *Nest:* In tree, of twigs and rootlets lined with bark, leaves, feathers, etc. *Eggs:* 3 to 6, variable, creamy, or buffy to greenish, irregularly marked with browns and lavender, etc.

RANGE. — Breeds from southern Alberta, northern Manitoba, Quebec, New Brunswick, Nova Scotia, and Newfoundland south to central Illinois, Tennessee, and Virginia, and west to eastern Colorado and central Texas; ranges south in winter irregularly.

The handsome, active Northern Blue Jay is an engaging rascal. Where there are Blue Jays, there always is action and usually noise, for jays, like crows, are fond of hearing their own voices. Often a great uproar in the woods may be traced to a dozen or more Blue Jays in the tree-tops, screaming as if in great terror or pain, and apparently for no earthly reason except to keep up the excitement, which seems to be of the hair-raising kind, and to exercise their lungs; in autumn they seem to delight in gathering near some woodland dwelling and 'yawping' in a raucous chorus, apparently with no particular object in view except to wake the sleepers; but let them find a Screech Owl dozing the day away close to the trunk of some tall pine — then we shall see real excitement! The woods ring again with the screaming chorus, and blue flashes to blue as the crested birds converge to the attack. In their excessive agitation the jays seem to lose their habitual caution, and it appears as if the mob would annihilate the despised and hated imp of darkness. Surely the poor little gray owl will be torn in shreds! But no! After half an hour of ceaseless clamor hardly a feather of the drowsy one is ruffled. The onset of the Blue Jays consists mainly of fuss and feathers — bluff and bluster. Occasionally, how-ever, the mob becomes so numerous and aggressive as to drive the owl out of the woods, but having thus rid themselves of his presence they do not follow far. The jays take good care to keep out of the owl's reach, for many a Screech Owl's nest is lined with the feathers of such as they.

Now and then the jays will attempt to badger a Sparrow Hawk, a Red-shouldered Hawk or even a Sharp-shinned Hawk. With the latter, however, they are playing a dangerous game and they know it and always keep a line of retreat open where they can quickly plunge into some thicket, for if the hawk is either hungry or angry, he may rush suddenly upon one of the mock-ing crew and strike his victim down. The jay, now at bay, fights to the last gasp, but it avails him little, as the courage of his companions evaporates, and they fly, screaming, away to cover. Though the Blue Jay shows courage in defense of its young, it evidently prefers the rôle of a live coward to that of a dead hero and takes the very best of care of its own precious skin.

The Northern Blue Jay is regarded as a resident bird, wintering wherever it breeds; never-theless it migrates more or less. Its migrations are of two kinds: (1) regular southward move-ments in autumn or winter from the more northern parts of its range and return movements in spring to its breeding-places; (2) irregular movements in autumn or winter from those parts of its range where food is scarce to those where it is abundant. Migrations of the first class prob-

337

ably take place every autumn from the extreme northern parts of the range and extend to the Middle States at least. Those of the second class usually occur from some region where beech-nuts, chestnuts or acorns are not plentiful to some other region where some of them are abundant. Wherever beeches fruit in profusion, jays assemble in numbers in winter, becoming very scarce in other sections. These migrations take place in the daytime, but we get fewer observations of the spring flight than of the autumnal one, possibly because while jays usually travel in noisy flocks in the fall, they are seen in spring commonly singly or in pairs, and throughout most of the month of May doubtless work slowly and rather silently northward day after day, and so pass unnoticed.

Many jays remain in the Northern States all winter. Some of these may be migrants from farther north, but others seem to be birds that nest here. During the colder part of the year, many leave some of the higher and more exposed parts of the country and betake themselves to the valleys or to the more southern seacoasts, where the cold is not so severe and the snow less often covers the ground. Occasionally large flocks are seen in winter, apparently indicating local movement. By the middle of April some jays have paired and a few have begun their nests. Indeed they have been seen carrying sticks at much earlier dates. This early desultory occupation may have given rise to the saying of the southern negro that 'the jaybird carries sticks to the devil.'

Although I have lived among Blue Jays and watched them much, I have never seen any special mating antics, but the Blue Jay is so prone to action of some peculiar kind whenever it opens its mouth to squall that special antics of the mating season may have been overlooked. The males follow the females around, and now and then there is an ardent disagreement between two rival males, but that is all that I have noticed. Usually a new nest is built each year, both birds working upon it, but rarely an old nest is slightly repaired and used. When the stick-carrying begins, every stick that goes into the nest is tested with care. The jay does not pick up dry sticks from the ground for the structure that is to hold its young, but breaks twigs and small branches from the tree; strong dead twigs are used, and they even attempt to break green twigs which they seize with their bills in the tree-tops. Thus they secure a strong and lasting framework for the nest. When nesting in the woods, forest materials alone are used, but if near human habitations string, paper, cotton and other products of civilization may be interwoven with the woodland material. The nest finished, an egg is laid daily. Then the hitherto noisy and loquacious bird becomes silent and furtive. When coming to the nest he glides silently in among the lower branches and hops from limb to limb near to and around the trunk, watching on all sides, and thus, climbing a spiral stairway, reaches unobserved the nest on which his beloved partner sits waiting for him to bring the morsel which he politely tenders her. Both sexes share in the duties of parenthood and both exhibit great bravery in defense of their young.

When the young have left the nest and learned to provide for themselves, the family roams through the woods, reveling in plenty that nature has provided for them; they are joined by others and it is a noisy rollicking crew. In the woods in September or October one may hear most of the notes that jays commonly utter — from the clear clarion ring of the trumpet to the soft conversational chattering, meant only for the ears of their companions, and now they not infrequently imitate the soft 'whisper songs' of smaller birds, for the Blue Jay as a mimic is second only to the Mockingbird, though most of his imitations are given in secret, and, apparently, are not meant for human ears. On one occasion while concealed in the woods watching for deer (though without a rifle), I heard a full, loud, clear song of a Baltimore Oriole in the trees overhead. As it seemed a strange place for an oriole at that season I scanned the tree-tops carefully and saw the singer — a Blue Jay. One day in October I heard and saw a jay imitate the mew of the Catbird, and on the same day in another wood, another jay sang the 'whisper song' of the Catbird many times. Either bird would have deceived the most discriminating listener. It is still a question in my mind whether mimicry and ventriloquism are gifts shared by all Blue Jays or are practiced only by a select few. I have heard these birds much, when entirely concealed from them, and have rarely heard them imitate the songs of others, though giving a great variety of soft notes peculiar to themselves. They do, however, imitate the cries of several hawks, reproducing them exactly. It is easy for jays to imitate some notes of hawks, for there is a similar quality in the strong, wild notes of both. Thoreau, writing of the jay in winter, says: 'You hear the lisping tinkle of chickadees from time to time and the unrelenting steel-cold scream of a jay, unmelted, that never flows into a song, a sort of wintry trumpet, screaming cold; hard, tense, frozen music, like the winter sky itself....' True, but in the winter woods it is a heartening sound of vigorous, wild nature, and the bird itself is a brilliant spectacle amid the bare limbs or on the white carpet of the snow. The most remarkable thing about the jay in winter is the ease with which it hides its azure beauty. Among bare and snowy limbs you see it fly, a most conspicuous, lovely object — its handsome wings and tail wide-spread — and then, as it alights, it disappears. It has merely slipped behind a limb which conceals its brilliant colors or has turned to face you behind a dead leaf or two and so becomes virtually invisible. Jays are such adepts at hiding that when the leaves are still on the trees they may be all about a person and yet escape observation. They may be circumvented, nevertheless, by the quiet sitter or by a person lying still on the ground. Their curiosity is then their undoing, and they will soon be heard conversing in very low tones, or they may approach and examine the intruder in silence. Curiosity often induces the jay, while keeping mostly concealed, to follow a man for a considerable distance through the woods; and a person concealed in shrubbery or thick trees may attract several of these birds by imitating a jay's cry of distress, as they seem to sympathize with the unfortunate. Unfortunately for the Blue Jay, he has acquired an unsavory reputation among men, a part of which he deserves, if the killing of smaller birds can be considered a crime. He has been seen to kill young pheasants and even chickens. In winter he has been known to attack and kill birds as large as the Downy Woodpecker, but the Hairy Woodpecker seems able to defend itself against its larger antagonist. There is a valid excuse, however, for the jay's so-called cannibalism, as it is his natural prerogative to eat the eggs and young of smaller birds or even the adults in case of necessity, if he can catch them. His right to thus comport himself is quite as clear as that of the little birds to eat flies or caterpillars; moreover, from his point of view it is ethical for him to steal corn, for he does not know the grain is not his. It is only when judged by human standards that we find him lacking in virtue.

FLORIDA BLUE JAY

Cyanocitta cristata florincola COUES.

IDENTIFICATION. — Slightly smaller than *C. c. cristata*, upper parts grayer, white spots more restricted.
RANGE. — South Atlantic and Gulf States from the coast of North Carolina to northern Florida, and west to Louisiana.

SEMPLE'S BLUE JAY

Cyanocitta cristata semplei TODD.

IDENTIFICATION. — Generally paler and duller colored than *C. c. cristata*.
RANGE. — Central and southern Florida.

FLORIDA JAY

Aphelocoma coerulescens (BOSC).

PLATE 95.

Other name: Scrub Jay.
IDENTIFICATION. — Length about 11½ inches; spread about 17 inches. About size of Blue Jay but appears slimmer, and with longer tail; *crestless;* nape, rump, wings and tail dark blue; back light drab; under parts smoke gray; *no white or black markings.*
COMMON NOTE. — A loud harsh *churr.*
BREEDING. — Similar to Blue Jay.
RANGE. — Resident on peninsula of Florida.

The slender and crestless Florida Jay is restricted to the 'scrub' lands across central Florida and along the east and west coasts, where it is found in the dense growths of low oaks, myrtle bushes, sand pines, palmettos and similar growths. It is not ordinarily as noisy as its congener the Blue Jay, though it can be very clamorous at times. In fact it is rather easily overlooked by the casual observer who is not searching carefully for birds.

As we drive southward along the Atlantic highway from St. Augustine toward New Smyrna, Florida, we pass through a region of low dunes bordering the blue waters of the Atlantic, the sandy soil supporting a scanty growth of bushes and low trees, with here and there a clump of palmettos, yuccas, or prickly pears. Offshore, gulls are circling, an occasional string of Eastern Brown Pelicans may pass by, and perhaps in the distance we see Gannets diving or an Osprey hovering briefly before its plunge downwards. White-eyed Towhees, a few warblers and sparrows, Loggerhead Shrikes, Eastern Mockingbirds, and Gray Kingbirds are found in the scrub oaks and myrtles, and it is a chosen haunt of the Florida Jay. You see these Jays, not in flocks, but here a single bird and there a pair, perched on the top twigs of low sand pines or dense-growing scrub oaks, not very conspicuous unless outlined against the sky or the restless Atlantic, or you catch a brief glimpse of their blue wings and tails and brownish-drab shoulders, quite different in effect from the white-spotted blue of the Florida Blue Jay, as they drop out of sight in the thick chaparral. Much of their time is occupied on the ground, where they feed about equally on animal and vegetable matter, acorns and seeds being taken in season, with a great variety of insects, an occasional small lizard, and even mollusks and crustaceans from the near-by beaches. — (J.B.M.)

AMERICAN MAGPIE

Pica pica hudsonia (SABINE).

IDENTIFICATION. — Length 17 to 22 inches; spread about 24 inches. A striking black and white bird with short wings and a very long graduated tail; the black is glossy with steel-blue, brassy, and violet iridescence; lower breast, sides and patches on wings showing in flight, white; bill black.

BREEDING. — *Nest:* A globular mass of sticks with opening on one side, surrounding a mud cup lined with rootlets, grass, etc. *Eggs:* Usually 7, grayish, heavily marked with browns.

RANGE. — Breeds from the Alaska Peninsula, central Saskatchewan, and southern Manitoba south to northern Arizona and New Mexico, and from eastern Washington and the eastern slope of the Sierra Nevada to western North Dakota and New Mexico; casual eastward in winter when often seen in Minnesota.

How well I remember my first view of the American Magpie! We had crossed the flat country of western Nebraska during the night and our train was nearing Denver. Ahead of us the mountains rose, blue against the western sky. We had left behind us the almost desert-like plains and on either side were beginning to appear scattered ranches, each with its windbreak of cottonwoods or box-elders and a few green fields under irrigation. Then from a thicket beside the gravel bed of a nearly dry river, several strange birds flew a short distance and dropped into another clump of bushes. The glimpse was brief but it was enough, for the Magpie is impossible to confuse with any other North American bird. Conspicuously marked with iridescent black and gleaming white, its short rounded wings flashing their semaphore message with each stroke, its long kite-shaped tail trailing behind, and seeming to constitute more than half of the bird's total length, it is striking and unmistakable.

Like the Northern Blue Jay, the American Magpie is inclined to be a very noisy bird, though at times it slips around silently enough. P. A. Taverner, in his 'Birds of Canada,' writes of it: 'It is most often seen retreating up the coulee, chattering as it glides from bush to bush, its broad showy color surfaces in brilliant contrast with the dark green background. At other times a small flock or family party will be seen passing noisily along the tops of the hills, from brush clump to brush clump. Again, they steal silently into camp or about the farm buildings intent on any mischief that may present itself, but flee away in consternation when disturbed, and talk the matter over in loud raucous voices in the nearest safe shrubbery.' — (J.B.M.)

NORTHERN RAVEN

Corvus corax principalis RIDGWAY.   PLATE 59.

IDENTIFICATION. — Length 21½ to 26½ inches; spread 46 to 56 inches. Much larger than Eastern Crow; entire plumage glossy black; bill longer and heavier looking; tail distinctly wedge-shaped; narrow throat feathers may give the appearance of a 'mane'; hawk-like flight, with much soaring.

NOTE. — A hoarse prolonged *crauk* or *cr-r-r-cruk*.

BREEDING. — In coniferous tree or on rocky ledge. *Nest:* Of sticks lined with grass, seaweed, bark, etc. *Eggs:* 5 to 7, similar to those of Crow.

RANGE. — Resident from northwestern Alaska to northern Greenland and south to Washington, central Minnesota, Michigan, Virginia, and in the mountains to northern Georgia.

'When the thick, white fog hangs like a pall over the Magdalen Islands, quite obscuring the surrounding water and causing the steep, conical, grass-covered hills near at hand to look like dim, greenish clouds suspended in mid-air; when nothing is to be heard save the monotonous, never-ceasing sound of waves beating at the base of the high cliffs, and the east wind, coming fresh from the icebergs which float in the mighty ocean not far away, is as chilly as a breath from the tomb; when all objects appear so distorted and unreal in the misty light that one seems transported to another world; then a harsh croak is heard sounding out with such sudden distinctness as to be startling.

'One who is unaccustomed to the locality gazes about in amazement, for there is not a living thing in sight, and the cry was so weird and coincided so perfectly with the gloomy surroundings as to suggest that it was of supernatural origin. Again the uncouth note is repeated but nearer, harsher and more real, and then the eye guided by the sound sees a black shape gliding through the mist. Then another appears and still another, followed by half a dozen more, while the air is filled with dismal croakings. One can by this time discern that the mysterious sounds are produced by Ravens which are returning from a predatory excursion to some neighboring island, for these black pirates take advantage of the obscuring fog in order to rob the nests of various sea birds which breed near.' So writes that ornithologist of great field experience, Mr. C. J. Maynard, in his 'Birds of Eastern North America.'

The Northern Raven is an inhabitant of great forests and mighty cliffs. Its rugged form and hoarse, weird cries belong to the wilderness, far from the works of man, but the bird is so quick to take advantage of its opportunities that where not molested it is even more bold than the Crow. It comes about the dwellings of Eskimos and Indians for food, and has even fed with domestic fowls near the white man's dwelling. It is peculiarly fitted, because of its size, strength, cunning and endurance, to survive where weaker birds cannot live. In case of need it is not in the least fastidious about its food. My friend, Captain Donald MacMillan, tells me that it is the only bird, except perhaps the Snowy Owl, that is known to live through the long, dark winter in Northern Greenland, where if other food fails it can subsist on the ordure of the Eskimo dogs.

My only opportunities to watch the habits of the Northern Raven were on Vancouver Island off the Pacific coast and on the rocky forested islands and shores of Maine. In both regions the bird was extremely cautious. Along the Maine coast it usually nests in trees, while from Grand Manan northward it is far more likely to be found breeding on cliffs along the shore. Were it not for its strange notes this bird might be mistaken for a Crow, for it keeps at a distance from the observer. When seen with Crows it seems about twice as large as the ordinary Eastern Crow. Occasionally, however, an unusually large Crow appears among its companions and might be mistaken for a Northern Raven.

The Raven has a habit of sailing and soaring, at times, high in the air, which I have never observed in the Crow. It seems to delight in sailing thus when a storm is breaking, and to enjoy the fury of the elements while it calmly breasts the gale. Ordinarily its flight, though heavy, does not differ greatly from that of the more common Eastern Crow.

The Raven is said to feed its young largely by regurgitation. It is extremely devoted to its callow offspring, and sometimes will risk its life in protecting them. The parents remain with their young throughout the entire summer and feed them for a long time after their charges have mastered the art of flight.

The Northern Raven is indiscriminately voracious. Its food consists of anything edible, alive or dead, which it can catch, kill, disable or pick up; carrion, offal, garbage, filth, birds, mammals, reptiles, fishes; the lower forms of life found along the seashore, and particularly shellfish, the shells of which it breaks by carrying them to a height and dropping them on rocks. It takes many insects and worms. It destroys many eggs and young of the larger birds. The large gulls band together to attack it when it encroaches on their breeding-grounds, but when these birds are driven from their nests by human intruders, the Ravens are quick to take advantage of the opportunity to steal many eggs and hide them away for future food. Ravens have been known to depopulate the nests in a heronry and compel the herons to seek quarters elsewhere. Regarding the vegetal food of the Northern Raven — it can subsist on many kinds of fruit and grain, but it seems to prefer animal food.

EASTERN CROW

Corvus brachyrhynchos brachyrhynchos BREHM.   PLATE 59.

IDENTIFICATION. — Length 17 to 21 inches; spread 33 to 39½ inches. Indistinguishable from smaller Fish Crow in the field except by notes; all black, tail rounded.

NOTES. — Very varied but *caw* is typical.

BREEDING. — *Nest:* Of sticks lined with bark, rootlets, leaves, grass, moss, etc. *Eggs:* 3 to 9, pale bluish-green to olive-green or olive-buff, and variously marked with browns and grays.

RANGE. — Breeds from southwestern Mackenzie, northern Manitoba, southern Quebec, and Newfoundland south to northern Texas, the northern part of the Gulf States, and Maryland; winters from northern border of United States southward.

The Eastern Crow 'knows a good thing when he sees it.' He seeks and finds for his home a land of plenty. Arctic regions with their 'icy mountains' are not for him; he leaves them to the Northern Raven, and inhabits temperate climes and fertile lands where the fruits of the earth are spread before him. He seeks the bounty of the fields.

On September 23, 1913, while sitting on a moss-grown ledge near the brow of a precipitous side-hill just east of the village of Stowe, Vermont, I viewed a splendid panorama of mountain, valley and sky. Below me lay the village, nestling amid its environment of autumnal foliage like a gem in its setting or a bird on her nest. The neat well-painted houses and well-kept yards, the tall white church spire pointing toward the sky and the American flag flying from its staff on the cupola of the public hall typified much that is best in American village life. The eye roved to wide meadows stretching down the valley, clothed in plush-like green. There the winding course of the stream was marked by a double border of green shrubbery, with here and there a row of willows, and some scattering elms and maples glowing in the sunlight with the rich primal colors of the season. Then the eye, lifting, passed on over bordering fields to upland pastures with their soft and changing tints, interspersed with groups and groves of trees — the whole a great park laid out as if by the hand of a master. Beyond the pastures on either hand rose the hills, and in the background towered mighty Mount Mansfield, the giant of them all, its slopes darkened and blued by distance. Over the landscape flamed the red and gold of autumn, toned and darkened here and there by drifting shadows, and above all arched the blue dome with its fleecy clouds. The warmth and peace of summer brooded gently over all. Crows cawed in the valley, where substantial farmhouses and well-filled barns attested the prosperity of the people. This is indeed a country of the blest. Such are the favorite haunts of the Eastern Crow in New England. Such fertile valleys are chosen by the wise old birds when in March they begin to push northward, and in autumn many crows from the hills come down to them, some remaining all winter in mild seasons or as long as they can find food.

Unfortunately for the Crow he has a bad reputation, and it must be admitted that there is some reason for the low regard in which he is held among men. First he is black, the color of evil; then, he knows too much; his judgment of the range of a gun is too nearly correct. If Crows could be shot oftener they would be more popular. Henry Ward Beecher once remarked that if men wore feathers and wings a very few of them would be clever enough to be Crows. Also, as Dr. N. A. Cobb says, 'The Crow rises too early.' We have to get up very early in the morning to get ahead of the Crow. Most of us rarely see the sun rise, and while the sluggards still slumber, the early Crow is up to some abominable mischief in the back yard. It irritates us to have this disreputable fowl take such a mean advantage of us, especially as we know that it would not have happened had we been up and about, as we know we should have been. Then, according to human standards, the Eastern Crow is a thief and a robber. He steals eggs, chickens, corn; he robs songbirds of their eggs and young, and so he is vilified and anathematized, pursued and destroyed, at every opportunity; but all to little purpose, for we may well believe that there are more Crows in the country now than there were when the Pilgrims landed on Plymouth Rock. Today, then, the Crow is the great American bird. Everybody knows him. How many people have ever seen the American Eagle except on the silver dollar? But who has not seen the Crow? If a person knows only four birds, one of them will be the Crow. The bird is well known because he is large, black, ubiquitous and noisy. He is well worth knowing. Each Crow is a character. There is more difference in Crows than appears as they fly over.

Some individual Crows are superior in vocal powers, or in the imitative faculty, to most of their race. The Crow is not generally regarded as a songbird; although as a member of the order *Oscines* it is provided with the syrinx of a singer, it seems to lack a tuneful voice; yet some Crows, if not all, are capable of producing unusual, tuneful or pleasing sounds. As an example of the musical attainments of the species, mention may be made of a Crow that I

344

saw on the banks of the Musketaquid, August 10, 1906, which uttered a series of exceedingly melodious, soft, cooing notes unlike any others within my experience. I have heard from Crows a varied assortment of notes, some of which apparently were imitations, such as the cry of a child, the squawk of a hen, or the crow of a young rooster. The cooing notes mentioned above were similar to sounds uttered by the male in courtship. At that season the male pursues the female through the air in swift flight, and both fly erratically, rising abruptly, plunging downward, and at times turning almost complete somersaults as they go. The male now becomes very excitable. His behavior at this interesting period includes spreading the tail, drooping the wings, strutting with head held high, and neck curved like that of a prancing horse. When the female responds to his advances, there is much lover-like contact of bills and more cooing. Sometimes one bird apparently performs for the benefit of two others, sitting on a near-by perch while he bows, and sways back and forth on the limb; the others seem to be interested observers.

Crows take the best of care of their young and defend them valiantly against their enemies. In some cases the young, when nearly fledged, climb out of the nest and perch on branches during the day. The parents attend them, guard them and feed them for a long time after they are fully fledged. After the young have left the nest, they keep their parents exceedingly busy for some time, as the condition of the stomach of a young Crow seems to approximate that of a bottomless pit. They require to be fed almost constantly.

In October before the frosts of autumn begin to form thin skims of ice around the shores of lakes in the northern woods, the Eastern Crows, which have been drifting down from the highlands into the valleys, form into great migrating flocks, not in any regular formation, though occasionally columns or ring-shaped flocks are seen. More often the birds fly southward in irregular masses, usually in daylight, as they rarely move about at night. These great flocks continue to pour southward in November, leaving behind only a remnant of the vast summer Crow population. However, many Crows remain through mild winters wherever food is plentiful. A piggery with its daily supply of garbage attracts a multitude. A corn-field from which not all the grain has been removed, the salt marshes along the seacoast, a crop of beechnuts or any large space of ground bare of snow will attract many winter Crows.

At night these Crows assemble, sometimes from a distance of forty miles around, to a common roosting place. In New England, white pine groves are favorites for crow roosts. Farther south deciduous trees may be chosen. In recent years many crow roosts have been broken up by gunners and the birds composing them have scattered to roost in smaller colonies from which persecution continually drives them; nevertheless some of the larger roosts still remain to be reckoned as among the most wonderful assemblies of birds to be seen now on the continent of North America. Occasionally during severe winters considerable numbers of Crows are found dead in the woods. Sometimes they are the victims of a disease resembling roup, but possibly in some cases some are starved and frozen — victims of strong attachment for their winter home. Crows swallow the hard parts of their food, and, after digestion has had its way, eject through the mouth such substances as hard seeds, fur, bones and teeth in the form of pellets, such as are regurgitated by birds of prey.

The food of the Eastern Crow consists of almost anything edible alive or dead which it can seize in bill or claws — all animals of every kind that it can catch and kill except some of the very small ones such as the smaller insects. Birds' eggs and young birds, mammals,

345

reptiles, fishes, batrachians, insects, crustaceans, worms, etc., all pay tribute to the Crow. Dead animals of all sizes furnish food for the sable bird.

Its vegetal food is confined largely to seeds, nuts, acorns, grains and fruit (both wild and cultivated) of nearly all native kinds. Corn is the principal vegetal food of the Crow. Perhaps the greatest visible damage by Crows results from their habit of pulling sprouting corn, but that may be prevented by tarring the seed before planting; there are various devices that usually will keep them away from corn-fields, and poultry may be safeguarded from their attacks by wire netting. They are a serious menace, however, to a game farm or game preserve and their numbers about estates devoted to such purposes must be reduced. We are not likely to exterminate the Crow, although by taking advantage of the bird's weaknesses many may be killed, and sometimes such killings are justifiable. Thoreau says: 'This bird sees the white man come and the Indian withdraw, but it withdraws not. Its untamed voice is still heard above the tinkling of the forge. It sees a race pass away but it passes not away. It remains to remind us of aboriginal nature.'

SOUTHERN CROW

Corvus brachyrhynchos paulus HOWELL.

IDENTIFICATION. — Slightly smaller and with a more slender bill, otherwise like *C. b. brachyrhynchos.*
RANGE. — Resident from the lower Potomac and Ohio valleys south to southern Georgia and the Gulf Coast (except Florida) and west to eastern Texas.

FLORIDA CROW

Corvus brachyrhynchos pascuus COUES.

IDENTIFICATION. — Similar to *C. b. paulus* but wings and tail shorter and bill and feet slightly larger.
RANGE. — Resident of the Peninsula of Florida.

FISH CROW

Corvus ossifragus WILSON.   PLATE 59.

IDENTIFICATION. — Length 15 to 21 inches; spread 30 to 43 inches. Smaller than Eastern Crow but best distinguished by voice.
COMMON CALL. — A short nasal *car* or *ca* almost exactly like a common note of a young Eastern Crow.
BREEDING. — Similar to Eastern Crow.
RANGE. — Atlantic and Gulf coasts from southern Massachusetts, Connecticut, the Hudson and Delaware valleys south to Florida, Louisiana, and eastern Texas.

346

The Fish Crow, a smaller species than the common Eastern Crow, resembling it very closely but having a rather weak, undeveloped voice, is rather closely restricted in its range to the seaboard, and the lower valleys of rivers. Its haunts and habits are similar to those of the Eastern Crow, except that it is more strongly attracted by water, and that its food consists more largely of fishes and crustaceans. It is more destructive to the eggs of wild birds than is the Eastern Crow, and less injurious to crops and poultry. Its flight is similar to that of other Crows, except that it hovers, much like a gull, when it discovers food in the water below it. When, in early spring, a small crow is seen which cries like a young one, the presumption is that it is a Fish Crow. Some Fish Crows breed here and there on Long Island and in southern Connecticut, and in early spring when the alewives begin to run up the streams of Plymouth and Barnstable Counties, Massachusetts, a small number of Fish Crows, migrating eastward, follow the alewives up to the head of Buzzards Bay and along the coast of Cape Cod. Now and then one may stray up the Connecticut Valley into central Massachusetts. In the Low Country of the Carolinas, in Louisiana, and especially in Florida, the Fish Crow is an extremely abundant species, and in some places it is a very serious menace to nesting birds. In one of the large egret rookeries in Florida, a careful study resulted in the estimate that two thirds of the nests were robbed by Fish Crows. Great numbers of the Crows are always present, waiting in the rookeries for the brooding birds to leave their nests even briefly, when the black hordes swoop down and hastily devour or carry away eggs or helpless downy young. The same conditions prevail on some of the sea-islands where terns of several species, Black Skimmers, Oyster-catchers, and other ground-nesting birds are robbed systematically. The Clapper Rail is another species which suffers badly from the depredations of the Fish Crow. Florida Cormorants, Water-turkeys, and Eastern Brown Pelicans are also listed among the victims of these marauders. These are all colony-nesting birds, where the marauders' work can be easily observed, but the losses of other species can only be surmised.

BLACK–CAPPED CHICKADEE

Penthestes atricapillus atricapillus (LINNAEUS). PLATE 90.

Other names: Black-capped Titmouse; Eastern Chickadee.

IDENTIFICATION. — Length 4¾ to 5¾ inches; spread 7½ to 8½ inches. Easily recognized by calls, form and actions; distinguished from Acadian Chickadee by black cap, wider black throat-patch, and whiter under parts.

NOTES. — Include a gurgling *chick-a-dee-dee-dee; day-day-day;* and a clear, high, whistled *phe-be* or *phe-be-be.*

BREEDING. — Usually in forests, sometimes in orchards, etc. *Nest:* In natural cavity, woodpecker's hole, or bird box, but usually excavated in a rotten stub, lined warmly with plant fibers and down, fur, feathers, etc. *Eggs:* 5 to 10 or more, white with fine reddish-brown spots.

RANGE. — Breeds from northern Ontario, central Quebec, and Newfoundland south to southern Missouri, Illinois, northern Indiana, Ohio, Pennsylvania, northern New Jersey, and in the mountains south to North Carolina; irregularly farther south in winter.

The little Black-capped Chickadee is the embodiment of cheerfulness, verve and courage. It can boast no elegant plumes, and it makes no claims as a songster, yet this blithe woodland sprite is a distinctive character, and is a bird masterpiece beyond all praise. It is spruce and smart in its plain black, gray and white livery; and its cheery, cordial notes are the 'open sesame' to woodland secrets. Follow the call of a Chickadee and it will introduce you to its brethren and to a sociable gathering of kinglets, nuthatches, a Downy Woodpecker or two, and possibly a Brown Creeper. In the proper seasons migrating warblers may also join the group.

Let the north winds howl, let the snowstorm rage — it may be bitter cold, but Chickadee worries not as he hustles about to keep his little stomach filled with insects. Only the ice storm which envelops the trees and conceals the insects beneath its crystal cloak is likely to have an intimidating effect on Chickadee's otherwise deep-rooted self-confidence. Then it will come to human friends for food and care, or else hie away to some snug refuge in a hollow limb or deserted bird's nest, there to abide till the storm has run its course.

At this season Chickadees are roving the woods in small bands. Move quietly now; imitate their '*phe-be*' call, or suck in gently on the back of your hand, which will give rise to low, squeaky sounds. This ruse will not fail to attract our little friends, for they are innately inquisitive. Soon they flit and flutter about the twigs right over your head, come close at arm's length and peer down at you with their keen bead-like eyes and scold you or mock you with a voluble chattering of *chic-chic-a-dee-dee*.

When the blustering winds of March have followed the passing of winter, Chickadee acquires new notes, high pitched, sweet and plaintive, consisting of two or three notes which sound like *phe-be* or *phe-be-be*, or, as it has been translated, '*Spring's come*.' The first note is protracted and the others fall one or two tones lower.

As April approaches the roving flocks disperse and the birds separate into scattered pairs. Then they become more shy and retire to secluded spots in the woods to nest. Occasionally a deserted woodpecker's home is appropriated, but normally the birds elect to excavate their own chamber in the decaying punky stump of a birch or pine. In such cases they often take advantage of the pit made by some woodpecker in its efforts to get at a grub. Soon the pit is enlarged to a sizable cavity and furnished to accommodate a whole family of five to ten future Chickadees. Unlike the Downy Woodpecker who flirts the chips out upon the ground beneath its hole, the Chickadee invariably carries the tell-tale chips to a safe distance to be dropped. The bird is not known to penetrate sound wood.

The male Black-capped Chickadee is a devoted father, assisting his mate in all the tasks of home-building, incubation and the raising of their offspring; and the birds exhibit a tender affection and constant solicitude for the care of their eggs and young.

The first few days after the young Chickadees have left the nest are ones of anxiety and great exertion for the old birds. So many children require an enormous amount of food, and constant care must be taken lest they fall into the clutches of marauding hawks, owls, crows or the destructive house-cat. They are handsome, fluffy little bunches of black, gray and white feathers, and already display the tempered dispositions of their parents. By the end of August the fledglings have attained strength and wisdom, and are able to shift for themselves. A month later the family begins to wander, and perhaps to unite with another friendly family.

The Chickadee is one of the most valuable of our orchard, woodland or forest birds. Throughout the year Chickadee wages warfare on infinite hosts of insect pests, and in effectively reducing their numbers renders invaluable services to agriculture and forestry. This versatile bird has learned to procure its sustenance from trunk and bough, from tree-top and ground, and every crack and cranny in which insects hibernate or lay their eggs. No bug is too small to escape its penetrating eyes. It is as much an acrobat as any nuthatch and is a skillful flycatcher as well, catching insects on the wing with remarkable facility.

During cold weather the little Black-capped Chickadee may easily be attracted to any farmyard or orchard, and sometimes to suburban dwellings. By hanging up here and there among the trees, scraps of suet, pork rind or bacon, and maintaining some sort of feeding shelf amply supplied with sunflower seeds and split squash or pumpkin seeds (of which it is very fond), shelled nuts and meats, the Chickadees and other birds will come day after day to feast on the provided food, while their almost ceaseless activity keeps them gleaning the insects from the surrounding trees; thus such favored localities are apt to be freed from the ravages of insect pests. If the Chickadee has become habituated to a certain place during the winter, it may be induced sometimes to stay and breed in a suitable nesting-box if conditions are favorable. — (M.B.)

CAROLINA CHICKADEE

Penthestes carolinensis carolinensis (AUDUBON).

IDENTIFICATION. — Length 4 to 4¾ inches. Similar to Black-capped Chickadee but smaller; greater wing coverts *not* margined with whitish; wing and tail feathers with *less white* on their outer vanes.

BREEDING. — Similar to Black-capped Chickadee.

RANGE. — Breeds from central Missouri, Indiana, central Ohio, southwestern and southeastern Pennsylvania, and central New Jersey south to southeastern Louisiana and the Gulf Coast.

In general habits the Carolina Chickadee and its subspecies, the Florida Chickadee, are much like the slightly larger and more northern Black-capped Chickadee. Their most noticeable difference, perhaps, is in their calls. Instead of the latter's clear whistled *phee-bee* or *phee-bee-bee*, the southern species repeats three or four rather querulous notes and its *chick-a-dee* call is higher pitched and more hurriedly given. — (J.B.M.)

FLORIDA CHICKADEE

Penthestes carolinensis impeger (BANGS).

IDENTIFICATION. — Length 4 to 4¼ inches. Slightly smaller than *P. c. carolinensis*, and darker above.

RANGE. — Resident on the peninsula of Florida.

HUDSONIAN CHICKADEE

Penthestes hudsonicus hudsonicus (FORSTER).

IDENTIFICATION. — 'Similar to *P. h. littoralis* but more rufescent; crown averaging lighter; difference between back and crown more pronounced; flanks averaging brighter rufous; size somewhat larger, bill averaging slightly heavier.'

RANGE. — Breeds from Alaska, central Mackenzie, and northern Manitoba south to central Manitoba and central Ontario; in winter casually to Illinois.

ACADIAN CHICKADEE

Penthestes hudsonicus littoralis (BRYANT).   PLATE 90.

Other names: Hudsonian Titmouse; Brown-capped Chickadee.

IDENTIFICATION. — Length about 5½ inches; spread about 8½ to 9 inches. A typical Chickadee but brown above with a grayish-brown cap, smaller black throat-patch, and more reddish on sides.

VOICE. — '*Chick-a-dee*' note harsher and more prolonged than that of *P. a. atricapillus*, 'a nasal drawling *tchick, chee-day-day.*'

BREEDING. — Similar to Black-capped Chickadee but limited to coniferous forests.

RANGE. — Breeds from Labrador, central Quebec, and Newfoundland south to Nova Scotia, Maine, the mountains of central New Hampshire and northern Vermont, and the Adirondacks of New York; in winter casually south to northern Pennsylvania, northern New Jersey, and southern New England.

The Acadian Chickadee seems to prefer cone-bearing trees to the broad-leaved hardwoods and in my experience, the little bird seems loath to leave the coniferous woods. I have never seen it far from its natal spruces, firs, cedars or pines. Otherwise in its habits it closely resembles our common Black-capped Chickadee, though its color is quite different and the black cap is replaced by grayish-brown. It seems perfectly at home in cedar swamps and apparently prefers moist lands and shady sheltered woods the year round. Its habits and behavior are very similar to those of the Black-capped Chickadee, with which it is often associated after the breeding season. It is just as acrobatic and as cheerful in the face of the severest weather.

The bird is an irregular and rare straggler into southern New England, as it is not a migratory species and seldom wanders far from its northern breeding-grounds. In the White Mountains, the Adirondacks, northern Maine, and southeastern Canada, it is a common and characteristic bird of the woodlands. There are many years in which it is not recorded at all but occasionally a few appear here and there.

The food of this species consists largely of caterpillars, moths and beetles and the eggs and hibernating forms of many small insects, among them many of the greatest enemies of coniferous trees. Little is known of the exact character of its food, but the food of all our northern titmice is of the same general character, and only varies according to the kinds of trees that they frequent, and also in accordance with the climatic character of their range.

350

TUFTED TITMOUSE

Baeolophus bicolor (LINNAEUS).

PLATE 90.

Other name: Crested Titmouse; Tomtit; Peter-bird.

IDENTIFICATION. — Length 5½ to 6½ inches; spread 9¼ to 10¾ inches. Larger than Black-capped Chickadee; crested head, large dark eye, gray upper plumage, whitish lower parts rusty on flanks; blackish forehead contrasted with white fore face.

COMMON CALL. — *Peto, peto* repeated several times, and many other notes.

BREEDING. — Similar to Black-capped Chickadee.

RANGE. — Breeds from Nebraska, Iowa, Illinois, Indiana, Ohio, southern Pennsylvania, and New Jersey south to central Texas, the Gulf coast, and southern Florida.

As I have never had a good opportunity to study the habits of the bird I must refer the reader to the writings of others. Mr. Arthur T. Wayne says, in his 'Birds of South Carolina': 'This species deposits its eggs in natural cavities of trees or in deserted holes of the smaller woodpeckers and does not appear to excavate a hole for itself. It seems to have a preference for hollows in chinquapin and dogwood trees, and the hole ranges from four to forty-five feet above the ground. While nest-building, the birds carry large quantities of material at every trip and one generally accompanies the other to and from the site. The nest is composed of wool, cotton, hair, leaves, fibrous bark and snake skins, the last article being indispensable to this species, as it is to the Crested Flycatcher.... The birds are the closest of sitters and have to be removed from the nest before it can be examined. Only one brood is raised and these follow their parents for many months.

'Although this species is supposed to breed only in cavities of trees, I found a pair breeding in festoons of the Spanish moss and herewith transcribe the account which I published in the "Auk":

'On April 23, 1896, I noticed a Tufted Titmouse with its mouth full of building materials, and upon following it closely saw it fly into a very large mass of Spanish moss (*Tillandsia usneoides*). When it appeared again after depositing the nesting materials I was very much surprised to find that there was no hollow whatever where the moss was growing. It was followed by its mate, and made ten trips to the tree in less than fifteen minutes. Having had a good deal of experience with this species when nesting I knew it was characteristic of this bird to carry building materials to the nest even *after* the eggs were laid. I resolved to climb the tree with assistance later in the day, but a violent rainstorm prevented my doing so.

'The next day, however, to my sorrow, I counted five eggs upon the ground and the nest completely blown out. Undismayed, the female began work again in the same bunch of moss, but was not encouraged at all by her mate, who would fly into a hollow near at hand and whistle for her, but she paid no attention to the hollow — just looked in and left. She worked rapidly and carried huge mouthfuls at every trip. Upon climbing to the nest on May 3 I found that it contained three eggs, and left it for a full set. I was doomed to disappointment again, however, for the next day was very stormy, and upon visiting the tree I saw all the eggs on the ground and the nest, which was composed of dry leaves, hair, sedge, feathers and snake skins, blown down in a mass. The fact of the Tufted Titmouse breeding in Spanish moss is certainly a surprising departure for this bird.'

The habits of this bird seem much like those of the Black-capped Chickadee. It evinces similar curiosity. A good imitation of its common call is enough to entice it down from the tree-tops to within a few feet of the person who calls. Sometimes it becomes quite tame and confiding.

The Tufted Titmouse is not migratory in the true sense of the word, although after the breeding season it wanders about somewhat and unmated birds are prone to wander at any season of the year.

WHITE–BREASTED NUTHATCH

Sitta carolinensis carolinensis LATHAM.   PLATE 90.

Other names: White-bellied Nuthatch; Sapsucker; Devil-down-head; Topsy-turvy-bird.

IDENTIFICATION. — Length 5 to 6¼ inches; spread 9¼ to 11½ inches. Size larger than Song Sparrow, but tail very short; a rather stout, compact, flattened bird, light bluish-gray above with black cap, *white sides of head and neck* (no dark line through eye), *white chin, throat and breast;* creeps up and down the trunks and limbs of trees, often head downward.

CALL. — A nasal *ank ank ank.*

BREEDING. — Similar to Black-capped Chickadee.

RANGE. — Resident from southern Manitoba, northern Minnesota, central Ontario, and southern Quebec south to northern Texas, central Illinois, and South Carolina.

No other bird can compete with the nuthatches in running up and down a tree-trunk. They are so often seen creeping head downward that some country people call them 'Devil-down-heads' or 'Upside-down-birds.' They seem to have taken lessons of the squirrel, which runs down the tree head first, stretching out his hind feet backward and so clinging to the bark with his claws as he goes down; but the nuthatch, having only two feet, has to reach forward under its breast with one and back beside its tail with the other, and thus, standing on a wide base and holding safely to the bark with the three fore claws of the upper foot turned backward it hitches nimbly down the tree head first — something that other birds hardly attempt — and it runs around the trunk in the same way with feet wide apart.

White-breasted Nuthatches are called resident birds; that is, they are found both winter and summer in the latitude where they breed, but in winter they are wide rangers and at that season often appear in localities or regions where they never breed. At this time they usually travel about singly or in pairs. Their winter movements are governed largely by the abundance or scarcity of food such as appeals to a nuthatch. Nevertheless there is a winter movement out of the northern part of their range and a return to it in spring of the individuals that breed there. They seem to be quite regular in returning to the same wintering grounds, as birds banded in autumn or winter have returned to the places where they were banded at about the same time in succeeding years.

As spring approaches the male begins his courtship. He becomes very gallant and attentive to the female and even shells seeds for her and passes her the freed kernels. He often displays his plumage by ruffling up his feathers and spreading the wings partly and tail fully so as to show their black and white markings, and then slowly oscillating. This flashing display of quickly increased size and conspicuous colors is used also to drive other birds away, for the male nuthatch is a brave little bird; one alone defeated and drove away a pair of pugnacious English Sparrows.

When nesting-time comes the birds usually find a cavity in a tree for a nesting-place. Occasionally a pair dig out a hole in a decaying trunk. Deciduous trees are commonly chosen. More rarely they find some aperture like a knot hole in some rough building and nest on a beam or between the inner and outer walls.

The female usually does most of the nest building but the male brings considerable material which he passes into the hole for her to use, and he also brings food and feeds her, particularly while she is incubating her eggs.

When the young have hatched both parents tend them assiduously. While the female broods them the male hurries about to find food, which he gives her to eat or to feed to the young as she sees fit. Evidently she is the mistress of the home. For some time after the young leave the nest the little family keeps together, only to scatter in the end and roam the winter woods with little companies composed of chickadees, woodpeckers and a creeper or two. Occasionally, however, where food is plentiful, a small band of White-breasted Nuthatches will remain together throughout the inclement season. In winter the nuthatches have a habit of storing food in the crevices of the bark of trees or in cracks of poles, under loose shingles, clapboards, etc. I have seen quantities of chestnuts thus stored by them under the flakes of the bark of a shag-bark walnut tree. Seeds and acorns are often so stored and are used by the birds in time of want when ice storms coat the trees, if the jays and squirrels have not already stolen them. They often come to feeding-stations and stow away sunflower seeds or bits of suet in near-by crevices.

Nuthatches do not commonly hold seeds and nuts with one foot and crack them with the bill after the manner of the Blue Jay; they push the food into a crack or crevice and there hammer it until they come to the kernel. This habit has given nuthatches their name. They 'hatch' the nut or break its shell with the bill as with a hatchet, but they can do this only on shells that are soft or thin like those of pine seeds, some acorns and chestnuts.

FLORIDA NUTHATCH

Sitta carolinensis atkinsi SCOTT.

IDENTIFICATION. — Similar to *S. c. carolinensis*, but slightly smaller, wing coverts and quills but slightly or not at all edged with whitish; female with top of head and nape black.

RANGE. — Breeds in the Lower Austral Zone of Georgia and Florida and along the Gulf coast, north in the Mississippi Valley to Kentucky, southern Illinois, and southeastern Missouri.

RED–BREASTED NUTHATCH

Sitta canadensis LINNAEUS.

Other names: Red-bellied Nuthatch; Canada Nuthatch; Devil-down-head; Topsy-turvy-bird.

IDENTIFICATION. — Length 4 to 4¾ inches; spread 8 to 8½ inches. Smaller than White-breasted Nuthatch and even more 'chunky'; darker bluish-gray above and buffy or brownish below with a *black or dark stripe through eye;* moves up or down a tree trunk head first; a very nimble, active, nervous bird.

CALL. — Higher pitched, more nasal than that of White-breasted Nuthatch; *yna, yna, yna.*

BREEDING. — Similar to Black-capped Chickadee but entrance to nest hole often smeared with pitch.

RANGE. — Breeds from the upper Yukon Valley, northern Manitoba, southern Quebec, and Newfoundland south to northern Minnesota, Michigan, Indiana (casually), mountains of New York, and Massachusetts, south in the mountains to California, Arizona, and New Mexico, and in the Alleghanies to North Carolina; winters from southern Canada south to southern California, New Mexico, the Gulf coast, and northern Florida.

The dumpy little Red-breasted Nuthatch when seen among our other feathered tree-climbers seems like a small boy at play among his elders. Nevertheless it is quite as interesting as any. In winter it consorts more or less with other nuthatches, chickadees, woodpeckers and creepers, but during migration is often seen among the branches and foliage with the warblers. It prefers pine and other coniferous trees, but often may be seen in deciduous trees. When the cone trees of the Northland fail to produce a crop of seeds and those of southern New England produce abundantly, we may expect a multitude of Red-breasted Nuthatches. In such years some begin to appear in southern Maine by the second week in July, and the forerunners of the flight reach Massachusetts in the latter part of that month, becoming rather common by late August or early September, and continuing farther south in unusual numbers. Usually, however, the migrants come later and in smaller numbers and in some years very few birds go as far south as the latitude of Massachusetts. At first, on their arrival, they may be found in all sorts of places; on barren rocky islands where they climb rocks, cliffs, fence-posts or roofs, and fly off into the air after flying insects or search about in the long grass for them; in orchards and gardens, and along tree-bordered streets as well as in the woods; but soon they are attracted to cone-bearing trees, spruces, white pines and pitch pines, all of which are favorites in this latitude and it is in woods composed of these trees that they are most commonly found. Usually by November most of them have moved on but where food is plentiful many linger for the winter.

Those that remain and mate in the spring, usually dig out holes in decaying stubs with much labor, penetrating sometimes to a depth of nearly a foot. They usually excavate for a nesting-place a hole in a dead stub, fifteen or twenty feet high, in either hard or soft wood and commonly among cone-bearing trees. They first mark out the entrance by a series of small holes which form a circle about an inch in diameter, then they work inward for an inch or two and then downward as woodpeckers do. Professor O. W. Knight says that he has known them to begin and complete a nest and lay an egg within a week, while some nests required two or three weeks to finish, and sometimes two months passed after a beginning had been made before the nest was completed and eggs laid. The habit of smearing pitch below the entrance hole or around it persists, even when the bird builds in a nesting-box. The origin of this habit and its possible utility have never been explained satisfactorily.

354

The Red-breasted Nuthatch is an exceedingly active little bird and is at home on any part of a tree. It climbs freely also about rocks and buildings, and like the White-breasted Nuthatch occasionally goes to the ground. Its flight is undulating and it seems to fairly bound through the air. Despite its short tail it seems to turn rather readily while pursuing insects in the air. Usually it is very tame and confiding — some individuals are exceedingly so.

We know very little about the food of the Red-breasted Nuthatch. Most of its life is spent in northern cone-bearing forests where it feeds on the seeds of spruces, balsam fir, and probably other coniferous trees. In southern New England it takes seeds of Norway spruce, white pine and pitch pine. It is known to take a considerable toll of insect life, particularly beetles, including some wood-borers, plant-lice, scales, caterpillars, hymenoptera and spiders.

BROWN–HEADED NUTHATCH

Sitta pusilla pusilla LATHAM.   PLATE 94.

IDENTIFICATION. — Length about 4½ inches; spread about 8 inches. Smaller than Red-breasted Nuthatch; crown and nape grayish-brown, a whitish patch on nape, no line over eye.
BREEDING. — In hole in tree or stump. *Nest:* Lined with feathers, hair, down, grass, etc. *Eggs:* 5 or 6, white or creamy, heavily spotted and blotched with browns.
RANGE. — Resident from eastern Arkansas, southern Missouri, and southern Delaware south to the Gulf coast and eastern Texas.

GRAY–HEADED NUTHATCH

Sitta pusilla caniceps BANGS.

IDENTIFICATION. — Similar to *S. p. pusilla* but back slightly, and head distinctly paler.
RANGE. — Resident on the peninsula of Florida.

The little Brown-headed and Gray-headed Nuthatches differ but slightly in appearance or in habits. I first made the acquaintance of this interesting species at Thomasville, Georgia, where the birds observed were probably intermediates between the two races. I have since then studied the Brownheads near Charleston, South Carolina, and the Grayheads at Clearwater, Florida, and wherever I have seen them they are the same cheerful, talkative, intriguing little creatures. They are about two thirds the size of our well-known northern White-breasted Nuthatches, and also noticeably smaller than the Red-breasted Nuthatch. They are easily distinguished by their grayish or brownish caps, their grayer under parts, and their many frequently reiterated call-notes, which are quite different from the loud nasal *yank yank* or *yna yna* of their larger cousins. One of their twittering calls is a rapidly repeated *pit pit pit* in a very conversational tone, and another suggests the repetition of the name *Keokuk, Keokuk.*

Their favorite feeding-places are the open 'piney' woods, those park-like tracts of long-leaf

355

pines which are so characteristic of much of the Southeastern States, and are broken here and there with dense thickets of magnolias, gum trees, swamp maples, bamboos and thorny smilax which hide a small stream or 'branch,' and with scattered areas of cultivated ground, cotton fields or corn patches. The nuthatches are often associated with birds of several other species, with which they seem to be on the most friendly terms. They are perhaps most frequently seen feeding near the tips of the branches, where they are pretty well hidden among the sprays of long needles, as they explore the very heart of the clusters for their tiny insect food, or pick the seeds from the big cones. At times they may clamber around the trunks or larger branches in typical nuthatch fashion, but they more frequently resemble the titmice and kinglets in their predilection for the terminal clusters of the long-leaf pines. — (J.B.M.)

AMERICAN BROWN CREEPER

Certhia familiaris americana BONAPARTE.

PLATE 90.

IDENTIFICATION. — Length 5 to 5¾ inches; spread 7 to 8 inches. A small slender bird, brown above with whitish spots and streaks, whitish below; a slender curved bill; tail long, graduated, each feather sharply pointed.
  NOTE. — A thin high *seeee.*
  BREEDING. — In deep woods or swamps. *Nest:* Usually behind a piece of partly detached bark, sometimes in a hole in a tree, of twigs and bark strips lined with feathers, hair, cocoons, etc. *Eggs:* 5 to 9, grayish-white sparsely covered with reddish-brown and purplish spots.
  RANGE. — Breeds from southern Manitoba, central Ontario, and southern Quebec south to eastern Nebraska, northern Indiana, New York, and Massachusetts, and in the mountains to North Carolina; winters south to central Texas, southern Alabama, and southern Florida.

The little American Brown Creeper is nothing if not thorough; he goes to the bottom of things; and having reached his objective, he climbs. He seems to be actuated by the motto 'Excelsior,' which is a good one for man or bird. For climbing purposes he prefers tree-trunks. He climbs straight up the trunk or spirals around, and having neared one tree-top or its first branches he glides down to the bottom of another and begins all over again. The process is much like that followed by the flying squirrel, who climbs a tree and then sails down to the next.

  For his purposes the Brown Creeper evidently prefers trees and 'the more the merrier,' and that is why we usually find him in the woods, but where there are no trees he still needs must climb and so he climbs the rocks, a sand-bank, the brick wall of a city house, a fence post or a man's leg as the case may be. Down on Block Island, Rhode Island, Miss Elizabeth Dickens saw one climbing a cow's tail for want of a more promising prospect.

  The bird does not 'back down' as often as a woodpecker, and its few attempts at descending head-first are ill directed and awkward but if it finds a favorite food on a horizontal branch it may follow that out to the end, usually keeping to its lower side suspended upside down like a fly walking on the ceiling, thus varying its usual practice. Mr. C. E. Bailey spent an hour in watching a Brown Creeper and found that in that time it inspected forty-three trees, beginning on each about two feet from the ground, which is about as high as a Ruffed Grouse could reach, and ascending for about twenty feet or about as far as it seemed to find its favorite food, going all the time around and around the trunk in a very thorough manner, after which

356

it flew to another tree. It appeared to prefer the white oak to any other tree, probably because the oaks in that vicinity were infested with numerous insects. In that hour it progressed only about one hundred yards and at night a Creeper, probably the same one, was still in the woods near-by.

To see the Brown Creeper hitching his near-sighted way up a tree might lead one to wonder at the incessant labor of the task and to pity the poor bird, condemned to a lifetime of monotonous toil, but this feathered Brownie is evidently happy and contented with his lot, and occasionally in March or April I have heard one burst into a long and ecstatic song bearing some resemblance to the finer song of the Winter Wren. While with us in winter the Brown Creeper often tags along with a little group of woodland birds, chickadees, kinglets, nuthatches and woodpeckers, but he is often solitary, and though he may be with the winter birds he is not of them. He is so protectively colored that he has only to remain motionless on the bark of a tree to escape detection, but when observed he is very likely to retreat to the other side of the trunk.

We see the greatest number of creepers when they are migrating in April and October and only a few remain to breed in cool swamps in the latitude of eastern Massachusetts. The nest is usually concealed behind a partly detached strip of bark on the trunk of a good-sized tree. The female is the nest builder. The male, however, is very attentive and may sometimes assist. She also apparently performs all the duties of incubation and brooding, but the male is assiduous in feeding the young, which remain in the nest about two weeks.

EASTERN HOUSE WREN

Troglodytes aedon aedon VIEILLOT.   PLATE 89.

Other names: Jenny Wren; Wood Wren.

IDENTIFICATION. — Length 4¼ to 5¼ inches; spread 6 to 7 inches. Smaller than Chipping Sparrow; tail much shorter and often cocked up; a little unstreaked brown bird with sharp bill and faint, narrow, blackish bars on wings and tail; resembles the Winter Wren, but is larger, tail longer, and plumage usually lighter, especially below, than in the Winter Wren; it does not bob its head in the manner characteristic of that bird; also the House Wren is rather seldom seen in the woods which the Winter Wren inhabits. Bewick's Wren, sometimes called 'House Wren,' is larger, with longer tail. Marsh Wrens are almost never seen away from open marshes and meadows, which the House Wren does not frequent.

SONG. — A stuttering, gurgling outburst, repeated at very short intervals.

BREEDING. — On edge of woods and in towns. *Nest:* In almost any kind of hole of suitable size, of twigs, roots, grass, bits of wire, etc., lined with grass, feathers, hair, cocoons, etc. *Eggs:* 5 to 12, pinkish-white, thickly spotted with browns and lavender.

RANGE. — Breeds from Michigan, southern Ontario, southern Quebec, and New Brunswick south to Kentucky, Virginia, and the uplands of South Carolina; winters in eastern Texas, northeastern Mexico, and the South Atlantic and Gulf States.

The Eastern House Wren is a modestly colored, cunning little elf, but true modesty is not in him. His is a character that makes its mark. He is a bold and happy warrior, and wherever he is there is 'action.' Let an enemy appear and Mr. Wren becomes a perfect spitfire, while his mate nobly seconds his efforts, and when there is no enemy in sight he whiles away his time by building another nest or by fighting with his mate. When the young are hatched he should find business enough while filling the hungry little mouths in the nest, but even then he snatches time to sing and to poke his bill into the business of his neighbors and sometimes into their eggs. Nevertheless on the whole he is a fairly good citizen, a good provider and a devoted parent.

House Wrens usually arrive in the North during the latter part of April. Almost immediately after his arrival the male begins to sing. Next he commences to fill up with sticks such suitable nesting-places as he finds in the neighborhood. When he has mated with a female, she usually throws out the sticks from one of his chosen nests and begins all over again. Between them a real nest is finally finished. Wrens have so much to do singing, squabbling, courting, and policing about the grounds of their chosen residences that it is usually late in May or June before the nest is finished and the eggs laid.

Almost any kind of cavity will do for the reception of the nest. Among those which have been used are a hanging fish basket, a clothes-pin bag hanging up on a house, the pocket or sleeve of an old coat hanging in a shed, the fold of an unused horse blanket, the pocket of a broken-down carriage, an old felt hat on the head of a scarecrow, a leather mitten on a shop shelf, the skull of an ox or a cow stuck up on a pole or a tree, and even a human skull in the house of a doctor.

Some House Wrens may mate for life, others certainly do not. Mr. S. Prentiss Baldwin, who has many House Wrens breeding in nesting-boxes on his estate, and who has attached numbered bird bands to the legs of each bird, says that one male mated with a certain female and while she was sitting on her eggs he left her and mated with another female, joining her in nesting in another box. The first female hatched her brood, fed them for a while, and then apparently became enamored of another male, brought the first male back to attend to her brood, and went away with her new lover and started another family while her first mate fed and reared her first brood. Such actions would constitute a scandal in polite society. I have heard of several instances where a male House Wren was mated with two females, each with a brood, and domiciled in nesting-boxes near each other. In these cases the male divided his attentions between the two, sang mostly where both could hear him, and 'all was merry as a marriage bell.'

Sometimes a male, being disappointed perhaps in securing a mate, continues nest-building on his own account, and mated males often use what little leisure time they have in building one or two nests in the neighborhood of the one where the female is incubating her eggs. These nests are rough affairs, composed chiefly of sticks or sometimes of pieces of wire poultry netting, but occasionally one may be finished by a female and used for a second brood. In any case the entrance is usually well barricaded with sticks to keep out larger birds.

Long ago this little bird left its forest dells to be the companion of the white man. Some when kindly treated become very tame, and one has even been known to take suet from a person's hand. But in isolated localities some still breed in the woods, where they retain much of their natural wildness.

When the young have been reared, most of the wrens leave the vicinity of houses and go into the 'bush' in the last half of August. In the autumn they frequent the southern woods or their borders. In September they have a song somewhat different from the spring song, and their color is somewhat deeper than in the breeding season. Then our old friend the House Wren becomes the 'Wood Wren' of Audubon, described by him as a distinct species.

The Eastern House Wren lives almost entirely on animal food, which made up 98 per cent of the contents of 88 stomachs of the species examined at the Bureau of Biological Survey. The material contained in these stomachs was composed of insects and spiders with the exception of 2 per cent of vegetal food, apparently taken accidentally with the insects. Grasshoppers and beetles made up half of the stomach contents, the remainder was caterpillars, bugs and spiders. Crickets and locusts are eaten by the House Wren, which is very constant and diligent in its search for insects to fill its own stomach and to feed its numerous young.

WESTERN HOUSE WREN

Troglodytes aedon parkmani AUDUBON.

IDENTIFICATION. — 'Similar to *T. a. aedon* but grayer, bars above usually more distinct; black bars of tail usually more or less margined posteriorly with grayish or buffy; flanks less rusty.'

RANGE. — Breeds from southern British Columbia, central Alberta, southern Manitoba, and northern Wisconsin south to Lower California, central-western Texas, southern Missouri, and southwestern Kentucky; winters from California and Texas south to central Mexico, and occasionally in northern and central Florida.

EASTERN WINTER WREN

Nannus hiemalis hiemalis (VIEILLOT).   PLATE 89.

IDENTIFICATION. — Length 3½ to 4¼ inches; spread 5½ to 6½ inches. Smaller than House Wren; a dark bird with a very short tail; almost continually bobs head, often cocking up its stubby tail; mouse-like in actions.

SONG. — A sustained, tinkling warble.

BREEDING. — Usually in damp woods and near water. *Nest:* In hollow of a log, under upturned roots or a bank, or in a brush heap, etc. *Eggs:* 4 to 10, white spotted with browns and purplish.

RANGE. — Breeds from southern Alberta, southern Manitoba, northern Ontario, central Quebec, and Newfoundland south to central Minnesota, northern Wisconsin, central Michigan, Rhode Island, and Massachusetts, and through the mountains to northern Georgia; winters south to Texas and central Florida.

When October wanes we may look with confidence for the Eastern Winter Wren. When the trees are bare and the north wind of November has drifted their scattered leaves in thicket and fen, this little Brownie of the forest creeps like a woods mouse under the roots of trees standing on banks overhanging the water, in and out of brush heaps and wood piles along river bottoms and on the banks of woodland brooks, cautious and furtive — an absurd little creature, its stub tail turned up over its back at the least provocation, until it seems as if the bird would tumble forward, pushed over by the efforts of its own tail, or overbalanced by the bobbing of its head.

It flies little and only to move from cover to cover, where most of the time it keeps concealed. Driven from one cover it dives into the next. If unduly alarmed it may peer out for an instant in an apprehensive attitude, *chirr* or chatter once or twice, and disappear. Quick, active and extremely wary, the Winter Wren is well equipped to secure its own safety. Mr.

A. C. Bagg relates the following observation: 'As I was watching, a branch high above the bird came loose and fell a short distance. Quick as a flash the wren swung under the small branch he was on, suspended upside down. It was all over in an instant, but it showed me how constantly they are on the alert for the slightest movement.' Sometimes, however, the little bird's propensity to run into hollow logs, holes about the roots of trees and other dark holes results in misfortune. On two different occasions Winter Wrens entered camp buildings at Squam Lake, New Hampshire, through knot holes in the walls, and, unable to find their way out again, perished, their shriveled bodies being found in the buildings the next spring.

In spring the Winter Wren appears in April and most of its numbers pass north to breed. They breed chiefly in dark forests, near mountain torrents, about tamarack swamps and in other wild and silent places. A strip of 'down timber' or a windfall where a tornado has passed is sometimes alive with them, for such tangles they seem to admire. The nest is artfully concealed under a cut bank or the roots of an overturned tree.

In the breeding season the male, losing much of his usual timidity, often ascends to a tree-top or a dead stub, from which he pours forth his loud melodious song; he sings much also while close to the ground and even in thick cover. There is considerable difference of opinion in respect to the rank of this bird as a songster. There is much variation individually in the excellence of the bird's songs, but the best of them rank high among our sylvan melodies. Thoreau says of the song: 'It reminded me of a fine cork-screw stream, issuing with incessant lisping tinkle from a cork, flowing rapidly, and I said that he had pulled out the spile and left it running.... The note was so incessant that at length you only noticed when it ceased.' The song harmonizes well with the sound of babbling brooks heard in the wild mountain glens and ravines where so often the bird breeds. At its best it is a much finer song than that of the House Wren, which it does not resemble. Nuttall says: 'This wren has a pleasing warble, and much louder than might be expected from its diminutive size.' Commenting on this statement Montague Chamberlain says: 'Had Nuttall ever met with the Winter Wren in its summer haunts; had he heard its wild melody break the stillness of the bird's forest home, or known of the power controlled by that tiny throstle and of its capacity for brilliant execution; had he but once listened to its sweet and impassioned tones, and the suggestive joyousness of its rapid trills; had Nuttall, in short, ever heard the bird sing — he could not, surely, have damned it with such faint praise.'

In migration the Winter Wren is usually silent, and even on its breeding-grounds, though its charming song may quickly attract attention, you see the bird usually as a mere passing shadow in the underbrush and then it is gone. It will go into a knot hole and come out at the other end of the log. It keeps its own secrets. Although I have searched assiduously where I felt sure a nest must be, I have never been able to find one. While migrating it sometimes frequents parks, and even the grounds about residences, but always with some cover near-by to which it may retreat at the least alarm.

BEWICK'S WREN

Thryomanes bewicki bewicki (AUDUBON).

Other name: Long-tailed House Wren.

IDENTIFICATION. — Length 5 to 5½ inches; spread about 7 to 7¼ inches. Slightly larger than Eastern House Wren, with a *long white-tipped tail; line over eye buffy-white*, not whitish as in slightly larger Carolina Wren.

VOICE. — See below.

BREEDING. — Similar to House Wren.

RANGE. — Breeds from southeastern Nebraska, southern Illinois, southern Michigan, and central Pennsylvania south to central Arkansas, northern Mississippi, central Alabama, central Georgia, and the highlands of South Carolina; winters southward to the Gulf coast and central Florida.

Bewick's Wren is even more attracted to the vicinity of man's dwelling than is the House Wren. Indeed the bird is often called House Wren or Long-tailed House Wren. It resembles somewhat the Long-billed Marsh Wren, though larger, and it is not improbable that some of the sight records of this marsh wren in winter in the North should be credited to Bewick's Wren, as it is a hardy bird.

I have never had an opportunity to study its habits, and therefore quote as follows from 'Birds of Illinois,' by Robert Ridgway, one of the foremost of American ornithologists: 'No bird more deserves the protection of man than Bewick's Wren. He does not need man's encouragement, for he comes of his own accord and installs himself as a member of the community, wherever it suits his taste. He is found about the cow-shed and barn along with the Pewee and Barn Swallow; he investigates the pig-sty; then explores the garden fence, and finally mounts to the roof, and pours forth one of the sweetest songs that ever was heard. Not a voluble gabble, like the House Wren's merry roundelay, but a fine, clear, bold song, uttered as the singer sits with head thrown back and long tail pendant — a song which may be heard a quarter of a mile or more, and in comparison with which the faint chant of the Song Sparrow sinks into insignificance. The ordinary note is a soft low *plit*, uttered as the bird hops about, its long tail carried erect or even leaning forward, and jerked to one side at short intervals. In its movements it is altogether more deliberate than either *T. ludovicianus* or *T. aëdon*, but nothing can excel it in quickness when it is pursued.'

Mr. Arthur H. Howell speaks of the musical powers of this wren compared with those of other birds as follows: 'I have listened many times to the songs of the Texan Bewick Wren, whose musical talents apparently are fully equal to those of the eastern subspecies. The songs given by the Texas birds resembled in form and tone quality the finest song heard from the Petworth Wren, and there was an almost endless variety in the construction of the songs.'

CAROLINA WREN

Thryothorus ludovicianus ludovicianus (LATHAM).

PLATE 89.

Other names: Great Carolina Wren; Mocking Wren.

IDENTIFICATION. — Length 5 to 6 inches; spread 6¾ to 7¾ inches. A reddish-brown bird, lighter below; whitish stripe over eye; barred wings and short barred tail; back plain, unbarred; a rather long curved bill.

VOICE. — A great variety of calls. SONG. — *Tea-kettle, tea-kettle, tea-kettle; wheedle, wheedle, wheedle;* etc.

BREEDING. — Similar to House Wren but eggs more heavily spotted.

RANGE. — Breeds from southeastern Nebraska, southern Iowa, Ohio, southern Pennsylvania, and the lower Hudson and Connecticut valleys south to central Texas, the Gulf States, and northern Florida.

From time immemorial the word 'wren' has been used in the Old World to denote one of the smallest of birds. The settlers of New England, finding a similar little feathered friend in this country, recognized and named the bird described by Darius Green as 'the little, chatterin' sassy wren.' Larger wrens were discovered later, and one was so much larger than the other members of the family then known that it was named the Great Carolina Wren, with the emphasis on the *great.* Exploration in the South and West brought to light still larger wrens, so finally the word 'great' was dropped, and the bird became the Carolina Wren, with races in Florida and Texas.

Though much larger than other eastern wrens, the Carolina Wren is a typical or even a superlative member of the wren family, full of nervous energy, remarkably quick and active, almost always in motion, consumed by curiosity, an adept at concealment, and shy or confiding according to circumstances and individual caprice. Its flight is short and rather ragged, but its little wings seem to vibrate almost as rapidly as those of a hummingbird. Normally it is a bird of primeval forests; low moist woodlands and alder swamps are suited to its tastes, and it nests largely along the branches of streams in holes in the ground, among the upturned roots of fallen trees, or in lowly cavities of trunk or limb.

With the coming of settlements, and the introduction of roaming cats, dogs and hogs, many wrens sought safer nesting-places higher up in the trees and in the outbuildings of the settlers. Naturally devoted to brush heaps, tangles, thickets, fallen timber and the dells of deep woods, where it can hide away at the least alarm, such a complete change of location as the environment of farm buildings, with a nest in some barn or other outbuilding, must have been made with many misgivings, many advances to reconnoiter, and many quick retreats to the shrubbery or the woodpile, where the little creature can vanish like a mouse, but its curiosity must be satisfied. The wren, energetic, tireless, with tail on end, must explore every nook and cranny of the outbuildings and observe surreptitiously or otherwise the strange creatures that inhabit them.

This wren is so furtive and secretive that when seen in a bush in the open field or pasture, often it will disappear on close approach of the observer by dropping to the ground and running rapidly but unseen, under cover of weeds and grass, to the shelter of some other bush or clump, rather than expose itself by flight through the air.

Although it gets most of its food on or near the ground, it sometimes climbs the trunks of trees like a creeper in its search for insects or their eggs, and it goes over rough buildings inside and out, peering into cracks, crannies and recesses for insects or spiders that may be lurking there.

The Carolina Wren is one of the few birds in North America that sing in every month of the year. The song is remarkably loud and clear, and the singing bird is very likely to come out of hiding and carol boldly from the top of bush or tree. In uttering it the bird often squats a little and jerks its body as if putting all its energy into its voice. Some of its common notes have been represented by the words *wheê udel*, *tea-kittle* or *twi-pity*, etc., according to the imagination of the listener, the words being repeated two or three times. Dr. A. W. Butler says that a boy represented two of its phrases with the words '*kick'er mother, kick'er mother.*' In the South, where the bird is common, it is supposed to sing *sweetheart sweetheart sweetheart*, sometimes adding the word *sweet*. A great number of phrases are attributed to it, for it is really a very accomplished musician, a ventriloquist also, and something of a mocker. Some of the notes resemble closely those of the Cardinal Grosbeak. On account of its apparent imitative powers, it is known locally as the Mocking Wren. Some good judges believe, however, that its notes are all its own. This wren is a persistent singer; it sings more or less in every winter month.

The Carolina Wren is non-migratory. It stays throughout the year in its chosen location, but it is not a very hardy bird, and a severe winter will destroy most of the individuals in the northern part of its range. Thus its northern distribution is limited, like that of the Eastern Mockingbird. During the summers succeeding mild winters, the number of Carolina Wrens increases in the Middle States and northward and many young or unmated birds wander into northern states. During the next severe winter most of these birds succumb to cold and starvation. As the Carolina Wren gets most of its food on or near the ground, deep snow is fatal, but a succession of mild winters will favor another increase.

FLORIDA WREN

Thryothorus ludovicianus miamensis RIDGWAY.

IDENTIFICATION. — Slightly larger than *T. l. ludovicianus*; above darker and below more richly colored.
RANGE. — Peninsular Florida except northern portion.

LONG–BILLED MARSH WREN

Telmatodytes palustris palustris (WILSON).   PLATE 89.

Other names: Marsh Wren; Cattail Wren.
IDENTIFICATION. — Length 4¼ to 5½ inches; spread 5 to 7 inches. Size, between Carolina Wren and Short-billed Marsh Wren; somewhat like Bewick's Wren but tail shorter and Bewick's Wren has no black and white stripes on back; distinguished from Short-billed Marsh Wren by larger size, longer bill, *conspicuous white stripe over eye* and blackish top of head; usually found in or near cattail marshes or salt marshes.
SONG. — A series of gurgling notes of reedy quality.

BREEDING. — In cattail marshes, etc. *Nest:* A ball of grasses, rushes, etc., lined with down and feathers. *Eggs:* 5 to 10, brown thickly dotted with darker.

RANGE. — Breeds in the Transition and Upper Austral zones of the Atlantic slope from Rhode Island to the Potomac Valley and the coast of Virginia; winters from southern New Jersey to South Carolina and sparingly to Florida.

The Long-billed Marsh Wren is well named. It is not, like the Short-billed Marsh Wren, a bird of the meadows or the upper marsh. It is a real *marsh* wren, a bird of the cattail swamp, the quaking bog, and the oozy slough. It frequents the shores of tidal creeks, salt and brackish marshes and the marshy borders of sluggish rivers, the home of Bitterns, Soras, Swamp Sparrows and bullfrogs. It seems to be normally a bird of coastal regions, following up the river valleys as its numbers increase.

The Long-billed Marsh Wren usually arrives in the latitude of New England before the middle of May. The birds soon commence their singing and nest building, and where there is a large colony the number of nests rapidly increases. The nest used for the brood usually appears old and weather-worn when compared with the extra nests that the male builds of green fresh material. Most of these nests are never used unless the males sleep in them, but their construction gives the birds an outlet for their superabundant energies. Though usually attached to reeds, rushes, wild rice or flags, they have been found in bushes, and Mr. Robert Ridgway tells of nests that he found in a tide-water region of the Potomac River, that were built in small willow trees at 'heights varying from six to fifteen feet above high tide.'

The songs of the Long-billed Marsh Wrens seem to bubble forth irresistibly, though as musical efforts they do not rank high. Wilson likens their lays to the sounds produced by air bubbles 'forcing their way through mud or boggy ground when trodden upon.' Dr. P. L. Hatch thinks them little more than an indistinct rasping or grating sound like that produced by 'a sliver on a fence rail vibrating in the wind,' but in the still and peaceful night, when the full moon of June rose grandly over the river marshes and the full chorus of the wrens was at its flood, sounding from far and near, I have listened with much pleasure to the sound. They often sing from the rushes or cattails, sometimes from the water brush, and frequently rise in brief flight straight up into the air for six to twelve feet, singing as they flutter down. The male cannot resist the urgent impulse to sing while on his way to the nest with a billful of cattail down for the lining. He sometimes sings two or three times on the way, thus losing his down and having to pick it all up again.

Dr. C. W. Townsend well describes the song as follows: 'The song begins with a scrape like the tuning of a violin followed by a trill which bubbles, gurgles, or rattles, depending no doubt on the skill or mood of the performer; at times liquid and musical, at other times rattling and harsh, but always vigorous. It ends abruptly but is generally followed by a short musical whistle or a trill, as if the Wren were drawing in its breath after its efforts. I have heard one sing fifteen times in a minute. The bird often reminds me of a mechanical musical toy wound up to go off at frequent intervals. Their scolding notes at times resemble those of their neighbors, the Red-winged Blackbirds.'

They travel along over the water by grasping the rushes or flags with their feet, and often with tail erected and slanting forward over the back they chatter their disapproval at the unhappy mortal who braves treacherous ooze and swarming mosquitoes to pay them a visit. The best way to observe them at close quarters is to float silently in a canoe along the marshy shores of a sluggish river. It is easy then to call the wrens to the margin of the stream. It is useless to look for them outside the marsh except on the occasion of a sudden flood in late May or June. Such floods submerging the entire marsh drive them to near-by upland fields and gardens. In the floods of June, the nests of Marsh Wrens in river marshes are sometimes ruined and all the eggs or young destroyed.

NOTE. — When Mr. Forbush wrote the above account, naming a marsh-haunting wren in the Northeastern States was a comparatively easy matter. It was either a Short-billed or a Long-billed Marsh Wren. Now the 'Check-List' of the American Ornithologists' Union recognizes nine races of *Telmatodytes palustris*, five of which come within the scope of this book. But their habits differ very little, wherever they are found. — (J.B.M.)

WORTHINGTON'S MARSH WREN
Telmatodytes palustris griseus (BREWSTER).

IDENTIFICATION. — The grayest of the Marsh Wrens; under tail coverts barred.
RANGE. — Lower Austral Zone in the South Atlantic coast region from South Carolina to northern Florida.

MARIAN'S MARSH WREN
Telmatodytes palustris marianae (SCOTT).

IDENTIFICATION. — Smaller than *T. p. palustris*; upper parts darker, sides and flanks more heavily washed and about color of rump; under tail coverts barred or spotted with black.
RANGE. — Gulf coast from Charlotte Harbor, Florida, to Mississippi.

LOUISIANA MARSH WREN
Telmatodytes palustris thryophilus OBERHOLSER.

IDENTIFICATION. — Similar to *T. p. marianae* but much paler and more grayish above.
RANGE. — Coast district of Louisiana and Texas.

PRAIRIE MARSH WREN
Telmatodytes palustris dissaëptus (BANGS).

IDENTIFICATION. — Slightly larger than *T. p. palustris*, with coloration much more rufescent.
RANGE. — Breeds from the Great Plains and Prairie district of the central Mississippi Valley east to Ontario, New York, and New England; winters along Gulf coast from western Florida to central Mexico.

SHORT–BILLED MARSH WREN

Cistothorus stellaris (NAUMANN).

PLATE 89.

IDENTIFICATION. — Length 3¾ to 4½ inches; spread 5¼ to 6 inches. A very small wren with a short bill; *no distinct stripe over eye;* throat white or whitish.

SONG. — Wren-like but not very musical; *tip tip tip a trrrrrrrr,* descending in pitch and increasing in tempo.

BREEDING. — In wet grassy meadows. *Nest:* A ball of grass attached to growing grass or sedges. *Eggs:* 4 to 10, pure white.

RANGE. — Breeds from southeastern Saskatchewan, southern Ontario, and southern Maine south to eastern Kansas, central Missouri, central Indiana, and northern Delaware; winters from southern Illinois and southern New Jersey to southern Texas, the Gulf coast, and southern Florida.

The little Short-billed Marsh Wren is a bird of the fresh-water meadows, where grasses and sedges grow. If it nests in a marsh it will be found in its higher parts or near the edge, and not usually among the cattails. If it goes to the salt marsh, as it does sometimes in its southern journey, it keeps chiefly to the drier parts of the marsh near the uplands. For breeding purposes it prefers a grassy meadow drained by a sluggish brook, creek or river and it breeds, so far as my experience goes, in such places only. If the meadow be over-drained the bird deserts it, or if it be converted into a marsh by damming its waters, the result is the same.

This wren seems to spend most of its time close to the ground, hidden in the grass. When flushed it flies feebly with fluttering wings for a short distance and tumbles down into the grass again. One who wishes to observe its habits will usually find it a very unsatisfactory subject for study, for it is hard to find. It is a great nest builder. Just how many unlined nests one ambitious male will build nobody seems to know, but where there is a large colony of these wrens, the nests are legion, and where few birds are breeding the occupied nests are difficult to find. Usually the nests are built while the grass to which they are attached is growing, sometimes not far from the grass tops, and as it grows they are gradually raised higher from the ground. The birds themselves are so secretive and unobtrusive that it is a common experience for an ornithologist who knows them and their haunts to find them nesting in places where the local observers, who have been passing the location for years, are entirely ignorant of the presence of the birds.

The males in song take up stations on small bushes, weeds, or grass stalks in the meadow or near the edge of a fresh-water marsh, but even while singing they are usually quite shy, and will not allow a close approach; when the apprehensive bird finally dives into the grass it is all over, for he can creep off unseen through the grass. The species is active in early morning and at night, and its notes may be heard in the meadows as twilight falls; like the Long-billed Marsh Wren it sings more or less at night. After the breeding season the bird is not entirely confined to wet meadows, but sometimes may be found in July in upland fields where the grass has not been cut. When it retires southward it frequents marshes and fields of broom grass.

EASTERN MOCKINGBIRD

Mimus polyglottos polyglottos (LINNAEUS).　　　　　　　　　　PLATE 88.

Other names: Mock-bird; Mocker.

IDENTIFICATION. — Length 9 to 11 inches; spread 13 to 15 inches. Size, near that of Robin or even longer, but more slender, tail longer; brownish-gray above, whitish or grayish below, with a large patch of white in lower wing, conspicuous in flight, and long, slender, rounded tail with much white in outer feathers; may be distinguished from shrikes by lack of the *broad* striking *dark* stripe through eye which both shrikes show.

SONGS. — A sweet thrasher-like medley, often with many imitations, and a rapturous flight-song; many calls; often sings at night.

BREEDING. — On edge of woods or about towns. *Nest:* In bush, vine, tree, etc., a bulky mass of twigs and miscellaneous matter lined with fine rootlets, etc. *Eggs:* 3 to 6, varied from pale greenish or buffy to dark green or bright blue and covered with spots and blotches of yellowish-brown to dark brown and purplish.

RANGE. — Resident from eastern Nebraska, southern Iowa, Illinois, Indiana, Ohio, and Maryland south to eastern Texas, the Gulf coast, and southern Florida, and sparingly north to New York and Massachusetts.

I have written in the 'Nature Lovers' Library' as follows regarding the Eastern Mockingbird as a songster: 'The Mockingbird stands unrivaled. He is the king of song. This is a trite saying, but how much it really means can be known only to those who have heard this most gifted singer uncaged and at his best in the lowlands of the Southern States. He equals and even excels the whole feathered choir. He improves upon most of the notes that he reproduces, adding also to his varied repertoire the crowing of chanticleer, the cackling of the hen, the barking of the house dog, the squeaking of the unoiled wheelbarrow, the postman's whistle, the plaints of young chickens and turkeys and those of young wild birds, not neglecting to mimic his own offspring. He even imitates man's musical inventions.

'The Mocker is more or less a buffoon, but those who look upon him only as an imitator or clown have much to learn of his wonderful originality. His own song is heard at its best at the height of the love season, when the singer flutters into the air from some tall tree-top and improvises his music, pouring out all the power and energy of his being in such an ecstasy of song that, exhausting his strength in the supreme effort, he slowly floats on quivering, beating pinions down through the bloom-covered branches until, his fervor spent, he sinks to the ground below. His expanded wings and tail flashing with white in the sunlight and the buoyancy of his action appeal to the eye as his music captivates the ear. On moonlit nights at this season the inspired singer launches himself far into the air, filling the silvery spaces of the night with the exquisite swells and trills, liquid and sweet, of his unparalleled melody. The song rises and falls, as the powers of the singer wax and wane, and so he serenades his mate throughout the livelong night. One such singer wins others to emulation and, as the chorus grows, little birds of the field and orchard wake just enough to join briefly in the swelling tide of avian melody.'

Dr. T. Gilbert Pearson says: 'In those states which border on the Gulf of Mexico, Mockingbirds sing at intervals throughout the winter months, and by March 1 are in full song. In that semi-tropical climate they abound, and in many sections are the most abundant species. I have sometimes thought that they must be conscious of the power of their numbers, from the bold defiant manner in which the music will often come from a dozen or more throats within hearing at one time, drowning in its volume the notes of all other denizens of the fields and shrubbery. The bird revels in the glory of his vocal strength, and shouts his ringing challenge to the trees, the flowers, the very sky itself. Watch the Mockingbird some spring morning, as with ruffled feathers and drooping wings he sits on the topmost bough of a neighboring tree and pours out the beautiful story of his love. At times, the very intensity of the music within his breast seems to lift him many feet in the air. With dangling legs and carelessly flopping wings, he drops again to his perch, singing the while. Anon he descends to the earth for a moment, a few rapid hops in the grass, and he bounds again into the air with scarcely an intermission in his song. Music high and low, loud and soft, hilarious and sad, with never a hesitation, never a false note, is what falls upon your ears as you hearken to this wonderful, masterful fellow, the music-prince of the southern highways and groves. However, it is at night that the Mockingbird is at his best. If he is the music-prince of the grove by day, he is the song-king of the lawn on moonlight nights, when at times his singing may be heard until dawn.'

The courtship performances of the Mockingbird are unique. As spring approaches the male often pauses for a moment in his song and stretches his wings high above his head, like a great butterfly, thus exposing in a flash his large, white wing-markings; this may be repeated two or three times. The courting or mating antics include a nuptial dance during which a pair face one another, with heads held high and tails cocked up, then *chassez* solemnly and silently from side to side, or circle one about the other. Mrs. Alice B. Harrington describes as follows the nuptial dance as she saw it at Dallas, Texas: 'We saw the dance of the Mockingbirds on two different days in June.... It was a curious and most interesting performance. The first time they danced exactly opposite each other. They faced each other about a foot apart, hopped up and down, moving gradually to one side, then back again, and so on. A second pair began their dance in the same position, but first one hopped twice to one side, then the other followed the first, which hopped again sideways and the other followed, always facing each other, then they moved back in the same manner to where they started and repeated the performance. After each dance was finished the birds flew off a short distance in opposite directions.'

The nest building is largely the task of the female, but the male often assists by bringing material, and in some cases at least seems to select the site and start the nest building. The nest itself is a coarse, rather bulky affair, and is usually placed in the center of a dense bush or low tree. The young usually remain in the nest about ten days, but even then they cannot fly well, and are likely to come to the ground where they are quickly picked up by prowling cats, which are perhaps the Mockingbirds' worst enemy.

The Mockingbird is a masterful creature. He lords it over the lesser birds, and does not hesitate to attack larger ones. In winter at feeding-stations the other birds seem to fear the Mocker as they do a shrike, and most of them leave the feeding-place when he comes. If the Northern Flicker remains to face the newcomer, the Mockingbird descends upon his back, knocks him off the perch and swoops at him, as the discomfited woodpecker retreats. A single Mockingbird has been seen to drive three Blue Jays away from a feeding-table. There is, however, much individuality in Mockers. Some will never attempt to molest a Blue Jay at a feeding-tray, and others rarely seem to peck or strike any other bird in winter, but during the breeding season while the young are in the nest, most of them are pugnacious and do not hesitate to attack any cat or hawk that appears about the premises, and they have been known even to alight on the back of a person meddling with their nest. The Kingbird, however, often is more than a match for the Mockingbird, and has been known to give one of the truculent fellows a sound drubbing.

In spring and early summer, the Mockingbird feeds largely upon insects such as ants, flies, wasps, harvestmen, bugs, caterpillars, beetles (including curculios) and grasshoppers; it has been known to eat the cotton-boll weevil and the moth of the cotton boll-worm, and it takes many spiders. In late summer and autumn it feeds chiefly on wild fruit, swallowing the fruit and ejecting later the indigestible seeds. People who supply food to Mockingbirds in winter find that they will eat at that season cut or sliced apples, chopped figs, dried raspberries, currants and blueberries, chopped seeded raisins, nutmeats, suet and bread crumbs mixed, and doughnuts. The small fruits given them are mostly canned fruits dried; dead insects are eaten eagerly.

CATBIRD

Dumetella carolinensis (LINNAEUS). PLATE 88.

Other name: Black Mockingbird.

IDENTIFICATION. — Length 8¼ to 9¼ inches; spread 11 to 12 inches. Smaller and slimmer than Robin; slaty-gray, with black cap and chestnut under tail coverts.

SONG. — A medley of short phrases often interrupted by harsh 'mewing' note.

BREEDING. — In thickets and swampy woods. *Nest:* Similar to that of Mockingbird but eggs are deep glossy greenish-blue, unmarked.

RANGE. — Breeds from central British Columbia, southern Manitoba, southern Ontario, southern Quebec, and Nova Scotia south to western Washington, northeastern New Mexico, southeastern Texas, central Alabama, central Georgia, and northern Florida; resident in Bermuda; winters from the Southern States to the Bahamas and Cuba, and through Mexico to Panama.

The Catbird is a busybody. He is consumed with curiosity. Let anyone but imitate the scream of a frightened or wounded bird, and all the Catbirds in the neighborhood will appear in full cry; some will almost project themselves into the very eyes of the offender, as they protest with open mouths and hanging wings. Their continual outcry soon results in an anxious assembly of all the small birds in the vicinity. As I have said elsewhere, 'The bird's moods are many. It is in turn a merry jester, a fine musician, a mocking sprite, and a screaming termagant — but always an interesting study.'

Let the facile pen of Dr. Elliott Coues, in his 'Birds of the Colorado Valley,' describe the prying habits of the Catbird about the farm and garden: 'Explain him as we may, the Catbird is inseparable from home and homely things; he reflects, as he is reflected in, domestic life. The associations, it is true, are of an humble sort; but they are just as strong as those which link us with the trusty Robin, the social Swallow, the delicious Bluebird, or the elegant Oriole. Let it be the humble country home of toil, or the luxurious mansion where wealth is lavished on the garden — in either case, the Catbird claims the rights of squatter sovereignty. He flirts saucily across the well-worn path that leads to the well, and sips the water that collects in the shallow depression upon the flag-stone. Down in the tangle of the moist dell, where stands the spring-house, with its cool, crisp atmosphere, redolent of buttery savor, where the trickling water is perpetual, he loiters at ease, and from the heart of the greenbrier makes bold advances to the milkmaid who brings the brimming bowls. In the pasture beyond, he waits for the boy who comes whistling after the cows, and follows him home by the blackberry road that lies along

369

the zigzag fence, challenging the carelessly thrown stone he has learned to dodge with ease. He joins the berrying parties fresh from school, soliciting a game of hide-and-seek, and laughs at the mishaps that never fail when children try the brier patch. Along the hedge row, he glides with short easy flights to gain the evergreen coppice that shades a corner of the lawn, where he pauses to watch the old gardener trimming the boxwood, or rolling the gravel walk, or making the flower bed, wondering why some people will take so much trouble when everything is nice enough already. Ever restless and inquisitive, he makes for the well-known arbor, to see what may be going on there. What he discovers is certainly none of his business; the rustic seat is occupied; the old, old play is in rehearsal; and at sight of blushing cheeks that respond to passionate words, the very roses on the trellis hang their envious heads.'

Few North American birds excel the Catbird in the quality or variety of its song. It is the equal of the Brown Thrasher's song, except in volume, and often excels it in sweetness; the notes resemble those of both Brown Thrasher and Mockingbird, and were it not for the cat-like mews and other harsh sounds that mar his utterances, the Catbird might rank as a songster with either of these competitors. As a mimic the Catbird falls far short of the Mockingbird, but excels the Thrasher. It is somewhat startling at times to hear the Catbird's sweetest song interrupted by a perfect imitation of some harsh cry such as that of the Northern Crested Flycatcher, the squawk of a hen, the cry of a lost chicken, or the spitting of a cat.

Like the cat, the Catbird sings much at night. Never perhaps quite all night, but often most of the latter part of the night, or from about midnight until morning. At certain times his carol is almost continuous for hours. While the female is confined to the nest by the duties of incubation, the male sings as if in an ecstasy of delight, but at the least alarm he interrupts the flow of music with a cat-like *mew*. As with most songbirds, so it is with the Catbird; some are indifferent songsters, while others are highly gifted. Some, at least, are able to ventriloquize, and probably all can reduce the volume of their song until it seems far away. On a fine Indian summer day in the long ago, I listened to the song of a Catbird that seemed to come from the distant swamp, when a slight movement in the bush by which I was standing caught my eye, and there sat the little scamp singing his faraway 'whisper song,' about six feet from my face. The bird commonly sings in this manner on warm October days. It is a characteristic of some Catbirds to sing in concealment, as it is of the Brown Thrasher to choose a conspicuous post in the top of some sapling. Others, apparently more bold, repair to the top of a bush or the end of a limb, 'as the spirit moves.'

The Catbird at times seems to pour out his very soul in song! Nevertheless he also sings frequently in a matter of course, conversational, fragmentary way, and with little effort, as he goes about his daily avocations.

The Catbirds do not announce their coming, for they migrate at night and are rather quiet upon their arrival, as they are tired, hungry and looking for food. But within a day or two, or even within a few hours, their songs are heard and they are repeated day after day until July begins to wane. In autumn I have never heard the full-voiced song, but the whisper song, audible only a few yards away, is given on warm days as long as the birds remain.

Not long after the males arrive in spring, the females appear, and then courtship begins. This is carried on largely in the seclusion of the thickets. There is much flight and pursuit, and an outpouring of song. The male with plumage raised and tail lowered bows until his bill touches the ground, and sidles about in a curious manner, or struts with lowered wings and tail erected, wheeling about and exhibiting the chestnut patch on his under tail coverts. When finally the nuptials have been celebrated, the nest building begins. At this some males become capable assistants; others leave this task entirely to the female, while still others assist in nest-building but not in incubation or brooding. Perhaps there is as much individuality in this respect among birds as among men. The nest is usually well hidden in dense shrubbery, and is a coarse mass of twigs, dried leaves, etc., lined with rootlets. The eggs are unmarked, deep glossy greenish-blue.

The Catbird has earned a place as the characteristic bird of the country home. Around him cluster memories of childhood's days. Dr. Witmer Stone, recognizing the claim of the bird on our bounty, says: 'Let us bear in mind the needs of the Catbird when we care for our grounds, and leave him a corner in which he may find a shady thicket sufficiently dense to be congenial. It would be to me a poor garden indeed that did not have some retreat from which I could hear that harsh complaining cry of the Catbird, when I chanced to stroll by. Every bird note brings back to us some association, some memory of the past, and with the cry of the Catbird there comes before my mind's eye the old garden with which, as a boy, I was so familiar. I see the thicket of lilacs and mock-oranges, and the gooseberry bushes bordering the path, the spreading boughs of the apple trees with the sunlight filtering through; the smell of ripening fruit is in the air, and the stillness of a quiet summer afternoon is broken only by the hum of insects and the complaining voice of the Catbird from his shady retreat.'

The Catbird's food in spring consists almost entirely of both land and water insects. As wild fruits begin to ripen it turns largely to these or to the small fruits of the garden, and wintering Catbirds subsist almost entirely on persistent wild fruits, which are retained on the stem throughout the inclement season. At feeding-stations they have learned to take boiled potato, cold mush, fried fish, beef stew, chopped peanuts, moist bread, bits of beef scraps, suet, raisins, apples cut in halves and hemp seed.

BROWN THRASHER

Toxostoma rufum (LINNAEUS). PLATE 88.

Other names: Brown Thrush; Red Mavis; Planting Bird; Sandy Mocker.

IDENTIFICATION. — Length 10¼ to 12 inches; spread 12½ to 14½ inches. A rusty-red thrush-like bird with a long rounded tail; breast darkly streaked; bill long and curved; two prominent wing-bars.

SONG — A succession of phrases of two to four syllables, rich, musical, and varied, with an interval between phrases.

BREEDING. — Similar to that of Mockingbird but eggs white to pale green, thickly dotted with reddish-brown.

RANGE. — Breeds from southern Alberta, southern Manitoba, northern Michigan, southeastern Ontario, southwestern Quebec and northern Maine south to central Florida and on the Gulf coast to eastern Louisiana, and from the base of the Rocky Mountains in Montana, Wyoming and Colorado eastward; winters from southeastern Missouri and North Carolina to southern Texas, central Florida, and casually northward.

As April wanes the Brown Thrasher comes. Silent at first, and furtive, he reconnoiters the land. We may hear him scratching among the fallen leaves of yesteryear, but if approached he retires into the thickets, there to lurk and perhaps to mope silently for a few days if the face of the sun be hidden. He prefers dry thickets to the swampy ones so often sought by the Catbird. Bushy pastures, sproutland, brier patches and tangles are his favorite haunts. He is more shy and retiring than the Catbird, but nevertheless may be found occasionally about farmyards, or even lawn shrubbery. In late April or early May in sunny hours, especially when the south wind blows, the Thrasher mounts some sapling and pours forth his song. For the time he seems to have lost his shyness, for he sits aloft for all to see and his song is loud, clear, eloquent and sweet. It must attract attention to the singer, for under favorable circumstances it may be heard for half a mile. Nevertheless let some one approach him too closely and he dives down into the cover of his favorite thickets and steals away to hide from curious eyes. This shyness is characteristic of the bird. Unlike the Catbird or the Mockingbird that frequently build their nests about the habitations of mankind, the Brown Thrasher prefers to retire to bushy pastures or thickets, and only an occasional pair becomes bold enough to nest in the shrubbery about the lawn or garden.

He pays little attention, however, to the plowman or the busy farmer, for at planting time he sits near by on some tree-top and sings — at least so the country people say — 'Drop it, drop it, cover it, cover it, I'll pull it up, I'll pull it up,' and so some of the country people call the singer the 'Planting Bird.' The song is so bold and emphatic, its phrases so abrupt, that it annoys some people, while others believe that it has few rivals among bird songs. Simeon Pease Cheney thus describes his actions: 'On a fine morning in June, when he rises to the branch of a wayside tree, or to the top of a bush at the edge of the pasture, the first eccentric accent compels us to admit that the spirit of song has fast hold on him. As the fervor increases, his long and elegant tail droops, his whole plumage is loosened and trembling, his head is raised, and his bill is wide open; there is no mistake, it is the power of the god. No pen can report him now; we must wait till the frenzy passes.' William L. Dawson says: 'Now and then he lapses into mimicry, but for the most part his notes are his own — piquant, incisive, peremptory, stirring. There is in them the gladness of the open air, the jubilant boasting of a soul untamed.'

Curiously enough there is disagreement among authors regarding the imitative powers of the Brown Thrasher. Wilson, Nuttall, Brewer, Samuels, Nehrling, Minot and Simmons seem to believe that it never imitates the notes of other birds; while Maynard, Knight, Dawson, Judd, E. A. Brooks, and Bradford Torrey all give the bird credit for successful imitations. I am inclined to agree with the latter gentlemen, as I do not believe that the clear call of the Whip-poor-will which I have heard some Brown Thrashers give and repeat is a natural Thrasher song, nor can I believe that the notes of the Bobolink which are sometimes attempted by the Thrasher are an integral part of his own native song.

In early spring the song of the male is delivered from an elevated position, apparently to attract the female. When the females arrive courtship proceeds mostly on or near the ground, under cover of the sheltering foliage, and so it is rarely observed. During the building of the nest, which requires from six to ten days, and in which both birds take part, the song of the male is heard more from cover. Thus during love making and nest-building, the male is not very conspicuous. But when the nest is completed he again sings occasionally from the tree-tops, though he usually takes some part in incubation until the young are hatched, after which he takes his full share of their care and protection.

The bulky nest is usually built in a bush or low tree, often on the ground, and is composed largely of twigs and roots and lined with fine rootlets. The three to six eggs are whitish or greenish-white profusely marked with reddish dots.

The young remain in the nest about twelve days, unless frightened out of it by some enemy, when they hide in the underbrush. Brown Thrashers pass the greater part of their time on or near the ground. They run or hop and when running in great haste partially spread and even flutter their wings to help themselves along. Their flights usually are short, low and not very rapid. They frequently come out to dust in dirt roads and they are fond of bathing. In August when the young of the second brood have been reared they all go into retirement during the molt and gradually slip away toward the south. They are said to migrate by stealing from thicket to thicket, and this may be true as their migrations are very slow. A few are left behind to winter in New England, and although the numbers of those wintering there are less than those of either the Catbird or the Mockingbird, they seem to be scattered more widely through the interior, whereas the others winter chiefly along the coast.

The constituents of the food of the Brown Thrasher vary of course with the season and during its migrations, as in the case with most of our migratory birds. In spring it subsists almost entirely on insects, spiders and worms, but in summer and autumn the greater portion of the food is fruit (chiefly of wild varieties), mast (chiefly acorns) and corn (chiefly waste grain picked up from the ground).

EASTERN ROBIN

Turdus migratorius migratorius LINNAEUS.   PLATE 93.

Other names: American Robin; Robin Redbreast.
IDENTIFICATION. — Length 9 to 10¾ inches; spread 14¾ to 16½ inches. Our familiar black-headed, gray-backed, red-breasted 'Robin Redbreast.'
BREEDING. — Almost anywhere. *Nest:* A mud cup on a foundation of coarse grass and rubbish, lined with finer grass. *Eggs:* 3 to 6, greenish-blue, rarely with faint brown spots.
RANGE. — Breeds from the limit of trees in northwestern Alaska, northern Manitoba, northern Quebec, and Newfoundland south to Cook Inlet, Alaska, central Alberta, Kansas, Illinois, Indiana, Ohio, Pennsylvania, and New Jersey; winters from central Kansas, the Ohio Valley, and eastern Massachusetts to the Gulf coast and southern Florida, and to Mexico.

On every vernal morning a wave of Robin song rises on the Atlantic coast to hail the coming day, and so, preceding the rising sun, rolls across the land until at last it breaks and dies away upon the distant shores of the Pacific Ocean. All through the Northern States the Robin ushers in the day with song. Hot or cold, wet or dry, the Robin sings. He makes himself at home in the back yard; he hops about on the lawn; he knows all the folks and they all know him. Why then should one write about his haunts and habits, which should be well known to everybody? In answer to this it may be said in truth that most people really know very little about him.

To begin with he is not a robin and never was one. The real 'Robin Redbreast' is a native of the Old World — a little bird formed much like our Eastern Bluebird with a dark brown back and a reddish-orange throat and breast. This is the 'Robin' that appears so often in European literature and folklore — the one that covered with leaves the 'Babes in the Wood.' Our so-called Robin is a large migratory thrush with a reddish-brown or tawny breast, but our forefathers named him Robin in remembrance of the beloved English bird and despite the protests of naturalists the name sticks.

Another thing about this bird that most people do not know is that many Robins spend the entire winter in the latitude of New England, where they roost among the evergreens in swamps, feed on winter berries and come out into the fields occasionally when the snow has vanished during a thaw. This common habit is so little known that nearly every winter the newspapers publish articles predicting an early spring because the 'first robin' has appeared or because 'the robins have arrived early.' In some winters when persistent berries are abundant in the North hundreds of Robins pass the winter in New Brunswick and Nova Scotia, but this is unusual. Most of our Robins, however, go south in winter and probably all those that winter in the Northern States are hardy birds that nest in Ungava or Labrador, and even some of these perish of privation and cold in severe winters.

The New England breeding birds go south, and in severe seasons many of them go to the extreme tip of the peninsula of Florida. Large flights sometimes reach Key West. In Brevard County, Florida, I have seen Robins in one continuous stream crossing the sky from horizon to horizon for an entire forenoon, all traveling southward, and in the afternoon many were seen retracing their flight. There they feed much on palmetto berries in winter. They seem to have no particular destination in the south but wander about, stopping where food is plentiful as was the case with the Passenger Pigeon, and like the pigeons they roost in immense numbers in favorite places.

Apparently the northward movement of Robins begins before spring opens. Not infrequently Robins appear in considerable numbers in January. Large flocks have been seen at that season in Maine and many in Nova Scotia, but we cannot assume that such birds are on their way north. More likely they are late migrants from the north or from the interior; but in late February and early March there is evident some northward movement.

On bright warm mornings in early spring the Robins sing their well-known carols. The songs vary considerably; the meter and rhythm of one song is imitated by the well-known words *kill'em, cure'em, give'em physic.* Later, in the season of summer showers, the more copious 'rain song' is given. Now and then a Robin appears to imitate some other sound beside his own. Thus, one may render the song of the Blue-headed Vireo, another whistles like a boy calling a dog, but in most cases the Robin adheres closely to his own characteristic but somewhat varied repertoire.

As spring advances the Robins begin their wooing. Everybody in the rural districts whose eyes and ears serve them has seen it, for it is by no means carried on in private. The pursuit, the battles of the jealous rival males and the apparent lack of interest shown by the demure females are apparent to all. Courtship often begins while some snowbanks still remain in shady places and while morning temperatures are below the freezing point.

When a pair of Robins have chosen their nesting-place for the season, the male drives off other Robins that encroach on his domain. If one of them comes close to a house and sees his reflection in a cellar window he is likely to fly at it and to continue to attack it day after day. In some cases where the nest is on the building or on a branch near it the male attacks his image in an upper window and continues to do so intermittently for weeks. Then occasionally a Robin has what seems like a mania for nest building. One season a Robin built three nests over my cottage door, and as many as ten nests or partial nests have been built by one bird in a season on some beam of an outbuilding.

In nest building Robins normally use mud, with a foundation of coarse grasses and stems, and a lining of fine dry grass. Occasionally in a dry time and in a locality where mud is unobtainable a Robin builds a nest without it. Often after the mud cup of an April nest is finished, from four to seven days elapse before the lining is put in, and in rainy weather long delays occur before the nest is completed, probably to give the mud time to harden. In fact these copious early rains sometimes wash more or less mud away so that the nest must be rebuilt more than once, but in the warmer, drier weather, when the nest for the second brood is built, it is begun, completed and dried out ready for the eggs in from two to three days. The eggs are the well-known 'robin's egg blue,' and unmarked.

Usually the nest is built chiefly or entirely by the female, who sometimes sits in it as if to enjoy it and rest. In building she uses both bill and feet at the same time, working the lining into place on one side with her feet and smoothing the edge on the other side with her bill and throat. She smooths and shapes the lining also with her breast.

Robins will use almost any pliable, fibrous material for nesting purposes. I once supplied a pair with cotton batting, which, barring mud, was almost the only material used in building their nest. When finished the nest looked like a patch of snow on the high fork of a limb in a dark pine tree.

As soon as young Robins leave the nest they are exposed to manifold dangers, and cats get a very large proportion of them. Many Robins' nests are built in trees along river banks on branches overhanging the water, and young birds in their first flight not infrequently land in the water, where they may become the prey of large fish, turtles or frogs. They do not remain long in the water if they escape these dangers, for the mother bird calls from the shore and the little ones flutter and scramble over the surface until they reach her.

Robins are very fond of bathing, and the young birds begin to bathe soon after they leave the nest, and while in their juvenal dress; after the bath some of them find a secluded warm and sunny place and lie in the sun to dry, usually on one side with partly spread wings and tail. When the first brood leaves the nest they are guarded and fed by both parents, but soon the mother bird leaves them to be cared for by her mate and prepares for another brood. In some cases the fledglings return to the nest for a few nights to sleep; other broods never return to it. The young birds do not at once learn to feed themselves, but follow the male about with plaintive cries as if famishing.

Robins not only resort to community roosting places in winter, but also establish summer roosts to which some of the old males begin to go nightly even in June. In July they are joined by young birds of the first brood, and when the last brood has been reared, old and young, male and female, all resort to the roost at night. The numbers at these roosts increase greatly in August, and thousands of Robins continue to occupy these roosts nightly until the middle of September, when their southward migration begins.

As soon as the last brood of young has been reared, the Robins change both haunts and habits. They assemble in flocks and range over the country, searching for wild cherries and wild berries on which they subsist for the rest of the year. When the wild cherries, wild grapes, and mountain ash berries are gone they feed on berries of the red cedar or Virginia juniper, bayberry, bittersweet, buckthorn, etc., or move on to the south.

What American bird is as adaptable as the Robin? Normally a bird of the great primeval forests, it has seen them disappear but it still remains. As trees have been planted on the prairie it has extended its range over the whole country, and where there are no trees it nests in bushes, on stone walls, in buildings or on fences, or even in some cases on the ground. Trustful in a wisely discriminating way, it comes into our yards and builds its nests in fruit gardens and even in sheds and outbuildings, ever watchful and alert for prowling cats. It penetrates into the cities and even raises its young in street trees and city parks.

As for food, there is hardly a wild fruit of any kind produced in the North that Robins do not eat, swallowing pits and seeds of the smaller fruit with the pulp and ejecting the undigested parts through the mouth. They thus become distributors and planters of nearly all our wild fruits — which need such agencies to scatter them widely so that not all will be found beneath the trees by those animals which feed upon the seeds. Its percentage of vegetal food is larger than that of any other American thrush. This vegetal matter is mainly fruit, which constitutes over fifty per cent of the entire aliment for the year, but more than four fifths of this is wild fruit. In farming regions, especially where clean and intensive cultivation gives little room for wild fruit, Robins take a heavy toll from the cultivated varieties, chiefly from cherries and other small fruits. Their animal food consists chiefly of insects — among them some of the greatest pests of the farm, garden, orchard and forest.

People often ask whether there is any food that they can feed to Robins in time of need, especially in unseasonable snowstorms in early spring. Robins at such times may be induced to eat cottage cheese or ordinary curds. Some people gather elderberries and sumac berries in the autumn for this purpose. The food should be placed on some natural object such as a rock or a log or on the ground.

SOUTHERN ROBIN

Turdus migratorius achrusterus (BATCHELDER).

IDENTIFICATION. — Slightly smaller than *T. m. migratorius*, and colors in general much duller and lighter.

RANGE. — Breeds from southern Illinois and Maryland south to northern Mississippi, central Alabama, northern Georgia, and upper South Carolina.

WOOD THRUSH

Hylocichla mustelina (GMELIN).

PLATE 92.

Other names: Swamp Angel; Wood Robin; Eeolee.

IDENTIFICATION. — Length 7½ to 8½ inches; spread 13 to 14 inches. Size between Robin and Bluebird; largest and most robust of our true thrushes; bright brown above, becoming more olive-brown on rump and tail; white or whitish below with large rounded black or blackish spots on breast and sides; readily distinguished from the Brown Thrasher, by *smaller size, much shorter tail, round spots on breast* and large dark eye; the Thrasher has a yellow eye.

SONG. — A series of tripled phrases, the middle note lower pitched than the first, the last note highest and trilled; *ee-o-leé*, etc.

BREEDING. — In moist woods and thickets. *Nest:* Of leaves, grass, bark fibers, bits of paper, etc., lined with fine rootlets. *Eggs:* 3 to 5, greenish-blue.

RANGE. — Breeds from southern South Dakota, central Minnesota, central Wisconsin, southeastern Ontario, central New Hampshire, and southern Maine south to eastern Texas, Louisiana, southern Alabama, and northern Florida; winters from southern Mexico to western Panama, and occasionally in Florida.

The Wood Thrush usually arrives in the latitude of New England between the fifth and the fifteenth of May. Soon after the males arrive the females also appear, and there is much swift flight on their part and swifter pursuit as the ardent males follow all their twistings and turnings through the forest shades. Then, too, these woodland minstrels tune their lyres, and their music is excelled by few North American birds. It has an ethereal quality that sets the thrush apart from all others. As we listen we lose the sense of time — it links us with eternity. Thoreau says of it: 'The thrush alone declares the immortal wealth and vigor that is in the forest. Here is a bird in whose strain the story is told. . . . Whenever a man hears it he is young, and Nature is in her spring; wherever he hears it, it is a new world and a free country, and the gates of heaven are not shut against him.'

As I have written elsewhere: 'Among all the bird songs that I have ever heard, it is second only in quality to that of the Hermit Thrush. It is not projected upon the still air with the effort that characterizes the bold and vigorous lay of the Robin, or the loud and intermittent carol of the Thrasher. Its tones are solemn and serene. They seem to harmonize with the sounds of the forest, the whispering breeze, the purling water, or the falling of raindrops in the summer woods. As with most other birds, there is a great difference in the excellence of individual performers, and, while some males of the species can produce such notes as few birds can rival, this cannot truly be said of all. At evening the bird usually mounts to the higher branches of the taller trees, often upon the edge of the forest, where nothing intervenes to confine or subdue his "heavenly music." There, sitting quite erect, he emits his wonderful notes in the most leisurely fashion, and apparently with little effort. *A-olee*, he sings, and rests; then, unhurried, pours forth a series of intermittent strains which seem to express in music the sentiment of nature; powerful, rich, metallic, with the vanishing vibratory tones of the bell, they seem like a vocal expression of the mystery of the universe, clothed in a melody so pure and ethereal that the soul still bound to its earthly tenement can neither imitate nor describe it. The song rises and falls, swells and dies away, until dark night has fallen.'

The Wood Thrush is ordinarily a denizen of cool woodlands, where rushing streams dally on their way among the moss-grown rocks, where rank ferns and lush mosses hide the oozy ground, and great swamp maples cast their shade.

When the pairs have mated and settled down for the summer we find most of them in low swampy woodland or near the wooded banks of lake or stream, though some choose dry wooded hillsides or thickets near the edge of the woods for their abode. Some even forsake the retirement of their woodland retreats to dwell in parks or about the abodes of man, where they nest in ornamental trees or shrubbery and forage like Robins on the lawns. In suburban New York and New Jersey they have become familiar inhabitants of gardens and shrubbery about houses.

Most authors assert that this bird uses mud in building the nest, which is doubtless true in some cases, but so far as my experience goes the substance actually used is wet leaf-mold which, when gathered from swamp or stream and dried in place, makes a firm layer similar to that of the actual mud in a Robin's nest. The materials used in the nests vary greatly. Sometimes they are composed largely of sticks, at other times of moss or lichens, and I have seen two that were ornamented with a mass of long strips of paper, but usually the foundation is mainly dried leaves and the lining fine rootlets. The eggs, like those of the Veery and Hermit, are unmarked greenish-blue.

The young thrushes grow very rapidly and in eight or ten days are able to fly and seek food for themselves. The Wood Thrush gets a large part of its food on the ground, where it scratches much about the roots of the shrubbery. When disturbed it is likely to fly up and light upon a limb, where it gives utterance to its alarm notes and flirts its wings, though I believe that it rather seldom jets the tail in the manner so characteristic of the Hermit Thrush. The song usually continues until mid-July, or if the season be not too dry a little longer. Then the birds become silent and retiring and finally slip away to the south almost unnoticed.

EASTERN HERMIT THRUSH

Hylocichla guttata faxoni BANGS AND PENARD.   PLATE 92.

Other names: Swamp Angel; Swamp Robin.

IDENTIFICATION. — Length 6½ to 7½ inches; spread 11 to 12 inches. The thrushes of the *Hylocichla* group are easily separated by the color of their backs; the Hermit has *brown tail* and rump, and *olive head* and shoulders; the Wood Thrush *reverses* these colors; the Veery is *all tawny* above; the Olive-back and Gray-cheek are *all olive* above, and we must look at their cheeks closely; the Wood Thrush has the most distinctly marked breast, the Hermit next, the Veery the least clearly marked.

SONG. — A series of strains of different pitch; usually each phrase starts low and ascends to a high fine note, and succeeding phrases are higher until the climax, when after a pause, the song starts low again.

BREEDING. — In cool woods and swamps. *Nest:* On or near ground, of moss, twigs, bark, leaves, ferns, etc., lined with rootlets, pine needles, etc. *Eggs:* 3 to 5, greenish-blue.

RANGE. — Breeds from Yukon, northern Manitoba, and southern Quebec south to central Alberta, central Minnesota, northern Michigan, Ontario, the mountains of Pennsylvania, Maryland and Virginia, and to Long Island; winters from Massachusetts and the lower Delaware and Ohio valleys to Texas and Florida.

When October comes with its clear, crisp, exhilarating weather, when fading leaves begin their brief flights through space, and squirrels scurry about garnering acorns and other delicacies on which to nibble during the long winter months, the Eastern Hermit Thrushes slip silently southward. Then we need not penetrate the heart of the woodland to find these celebrated anchorites of dim forest sanctuaries, but instead, during our country rambles we flush them, alone or in small groups, from wayside thickets, from orchards and coppices. And arriving home at our own garden plots we find these quiet, unobtrusive birds there also! At our approach, perhaps, a Hermit turns about and wings a silent retreat to the nearest covert, but another is just as likely to fly up to the low limb of a near-by tree or fence, where, regarding us with deep hazel eyes, it utters a low *chuck*, slowly tilting its tail. This is the manner in which the Hermit Thrush introduces and identifies itself to us.

Again in the early spring the Hermits are met with commonly for a few weeks, as they advance towards the northern forests with the hosts of other birds. These supposedly shy thrushes sometimes stop off even in the noisy city during their journeys to and from their breeding-grounds. Rarely do they sing while migrating, for they reserve their solemn lays for their summer haunts.

The Eastern Hermit Thrush is the hardiest member of the *Hylocichla* group, coming north a month earlier than any of the other thrushes, and departing south long after the last Graycheek has left our borders. While other thrushes are disporting in tropic glades and wildernesses, the Hermit is reluctant to leave our Eastern States, and is found during winter as far north as Massachusetts, but rarely beyond this state.

It is indeed strange that so exquisite a vocalist as the Hermit Thrush should have been but little known to the pioneers of American ornithology. Audubon and Wilson, evidently confusing this bird with the other species of thrushes, fell into extraordinary errors in their accounts of it, agreeing, for example, that this thrush is a summer resident in the Southern States, and that its eggs are sprinkled with dark spots toward the end. Audubon states that it has no song! while Wilson, making some allowance for its singing, also says that in the spring it has 'an occasional squeak like that of a young chicken.' Nuttall gives the bird full credit for its musical talents, but repeats some of the errors of his contemporaries. Thoreau seems never to have had a clear conception of the vocal differences between the Wood and the Hermit Thrushes, and confused the two.

The ineffable charm and sweetness of the Hermit's song has been the inspiration of many a gifted writer. Poets have lauded it above all other North American birds, and its genius is declared by some to surpass even that of the Nightingale. Indeed, one of the names which the Hermit has earned is 'American Nightingale.' Mr. F. Schuyler Mathews describes its song as 'the grand climax of all bird music,' and says that 'the passionate and plaintive notes of the Nightingale apparently have no place in the Hermit's song; our gifted Thrush sings more of the glory of life and less of its tragedy, more of the joy of heaven and less of the passion of earth.'

It is to the genius of John Burroughs that we owe this inspiring passage, so expressive of the mysterious, elevating character of the emotions with which the Hermit's song infuses us: 'Mounting toward the upland again, I pause reverently as the hush and stillness of twilight comes upon the woods. It is the sweetest, ripest hour of the day. And as the Hermit's evening hymn goes up from the deep solitude below me, I experience that serene exaltation of sentiment of which music, literature and religion are but the faint types and symbols.'

The Hermit pours out his soul in these tender, stirring hymns at all hours of the day, and sings from the time of its arrival at its breeding-grounds until late August. The songs of the Hermit and Wood Thrushes bear such close similarity in quality that among the uninitiated it is always a matter of much difficulty to distinguish them. Ralph Hoffmann writes: 'The song of the Wood Thrush begins with a phrase which suggests the syllables *ee-o-lee*, and continues with phrases, often containing notes separated by great intervals.' There are no great gaps in the Hermit's song, and as Mr. Hoffmann further points out, the song of the Wood Thrush contains bass notes, of which there are none in the Hermit's voice.

In selecting its nesting-site the Hermit is partial to the proximity of bogs and swales and the sloping banks of brooks or streams, and evergreen woods seem to be a necessary concomitant. Its habits are quite similar to those of the Olive-backed Thrush, with which it is often associated. The female chiefly is concerned with the care of the young, attending to most of the brooding and the greater part of the feeding. The Hermit does not use mud in constructing its domicile, after the manner of the Robin, but fashions it with moss and other material, into a deep cup-shaped structure, lined with pine needles.

During spring and summer the food of the Eastern Hermit Thrush consists principally of insects such as beetles, caterpillars and ants, with spiders and worms of various kinds. In the fall and winter the bird's food becomes mainly vegetal, consisting of a considerable amount of small fruit and a negligible proportion of seeds, including those of poison ivy, which, however, it does not destroy. Berries of the mountain ash, staghorn sumac and barberry are favorite items, while checkerberries, privet berries, dogwood and arrowwood berries, and even wild grapes and juniper berries, are eaten, all in their season. — (M.B.)

OLIVE–BACKED THRUSH

Hylocichla ustulata swainsoni (TSCHUDI). PLATE 92.

Other names: Swainson's Thrush; Swamp Robin.

IDENTIFICATION. — Length 6¼ to 7¾ inches; spread 10½ to 13 inches. A rather large thrush all olive above; *stripe over eye* and faint eye-ring, *buffy*; cheeks have a buffy tinge which may be seen in good light; spotting of breast not so heavy as in Wood Thrush, and the bird is nowhere tawny; occasionally raises its tail slowly but not so habitually as does the Hermit Thrush.

SONG. — An ascending phrase, repeated at intervals without changing; suggests a Veery song *reversed*.

BREEDING. — *Nest:* In bush or low tree in deep woods, similar to that of Hermit Thrush but eggs spotted and blotched with browns and lilac.

RANGE. — Breeds from northwestern Alaska, northern Manitoba, central Quebec, and Newfoundland south to Kenai Peninsula, Alaska, northern California, Colorado, northern Michigan, New York, northern New England, and in the mountains to Pennsylvania and West Virginia; winters from southern Mexico to Brazil and Argentina.

Among the hills of western Massachusetts there remain a few isolated remnants of the spruce growth that clothed them in the days of yore. There today in the murmuring forest, tall, straight columnar trees still stand, their serried ranks extending far up the mountain sides. As they fall in death, succumbing to age or the axe of the woodsman, the sun streaming in between the remaining trunks stimulates the seeds buried by birds and squirrels in the soft mold of the forest floor and starts a dense miniature forest of beautiful little spruces. In time these cover the ground to replace the ancient wood and hide the great, moss-covered, decaying trunks on the ground. Here and there young trees of moosewood and black birch are growing, and little brooks fringed by overshadowing ferns prattle noisily down over their beds of age-old moss-grown rocks. Here the winds whisper the secrets of the forest and here the Hermit Thrush, with time and eternity all his own, sings his unhurried, ethereal lay. Jays call mournfully from the distant tree-tops, and at the foot of the slope we hear the strange chant of the Olive-backed Thrush.

The Olive-backed Thrush is a bird of the Canadian fauna, a bird of the spruce and fir, and its presence in the breeding season seems to be mostly confined to the region of these coniferous trees, but like many other birds it frequents both mixed and deciduous woods during migration, also orchards, gardens and parks where there are trees and shrubbery. Occasionally it searches for grasshoppers, locusts and other insects in open fields near the borders of woods. I have seen a small flock scattered about like Robins in such a field. The bird seems to feed more in the trees, however, than most thrushes and is especially active in catching tree insects. Although the Olive-backed Thrush usually is rather shy, it seldom manifests the extreme caution so often observed in the Gray-cheeked Thrush, and some individuals become quite tame when unmolested.

The Olive-backed Thrush seldom appears in any numbers in southern New England much before the middle of May, though some stragglers may come early in the month. The comparatively few individuals that nest here seem to prefer moist or swampy spruce thickets or spruce woods near streams. In its northern wilds it may be found generally in spruce woods wet or dry, and often in mixed or deciduous woods, usually, however, nesting among spruce, hemlock, fir or pine woods.

The Olive-back is the most common thrush in the woods of northern and eastern Maine. Years ago in the great woods of eastern Maine, I saw an irruption of bud-moths among the spruce trees and there from every direction came the song of the Olive-backed Thrush and that of the Hermit Thrush, about five of the former to one of the latter. The birds were so abundant in the moth-infested region in July that it seemed that they must have gathered there especially to feed upon the moths, which they often pursued through the air in the manner of flycatchers.

GRAY–CHEEKED THRUSH

Hylocichla minima aliciae (BAIRD). PLATE 92.

Other name: Alice's Thrush.

IDENTIFICATION. — Length 7½ to 8 inches; spread 12¼ to 13½ inches. Entirely olive above; *sides of head olive-grayish,* eye-ring whitish and very inconspicuous; whiter below than Olive-back.

SONG. — Drops down like that of Veery, then rises abruptly at end.

RANGE. — Breeds in the Hudsonian Zone in a narrow belt just below tree line from Siberia through Alaska, Mackenzie, and Manitoba to central Quebec, and in Newfoundland; winters from Colombia to Peru and British Guiana; migrates through eastern North America and eastern Central America.

BICKNELL'S THRUSH

Hylocichla minima minima (LAFRESNAYE).

PLATE 92.

IDENTIFICATION. — Similar to *H. m. aliciae* but slightly smaller; length 6¼ to 7½ inches.

BREEDING. — Similar to Olive-backed Thrush.

RANGE. — Breeds in Nova Scotia, the mountains of northern New England, the Catskills and Adirondacks in New York, and probably in western Massachusetts; winters in Haiti and Venezuela; migrates through the Southeastern States and the Bahamas.

The two races of *Hylocichla minima*, the Gray-cheeked Thrush and Bicknell's Thrush, may well be treated together here, since their haunts and habits are practically identical. It is practically impossible to distinguish them in the field as there is no recognizable difference in color between them. Their notes and songs are essentially the same. They may even intergrade in size, overlooking the fact that we have established measurements which usually will determine the race of an individual. If we see one of these birds in the latitude of New England early in May it is probably *minima*, for this race begins to migrate earlier than the Gray-cheeked Thrush. So also if we find one in the breeding season on any New England mountain we may assume that it is *minima*. Otherwise I know of no way to differentiate the two birds in the field, especially as they are both normally shy and resort largely to shady places where fine points are not easily determined except perhaps with the best of eyes and glasses. It may be possible also that some of the birds that breed on the mountains of extreme northern New England are referable to *aliciae*, though the Gray-cheeked Thrush is not supposed to breed south of the St. Lawrence River. *Aliciae* breeds north to the Arctic Ocean and west to Bering Sea, while *minima* is merely a smaller, more southeastern race of the Canadian-Hudsonian fauna.

William Brewster says of these birds in migration, referring to both races, 'Like most of the spotted-breasted Thrushes belonging to the genus *Hylocichla* they dislike strong sunlight, which, no doubt, is trying to their fine, large, dreamy-looking eyes. In the spring, they frequent, for the most part, upland woods and thickets where there are crowded growths of young pines or other evergreens or where the ground is deeply carpeted with fallen leaves, among which they search industriously for worms and the larvae of insects. In autumn, when they subsist largely on berries, they are found oftenest in dense, moist thickets, such as those in the Fresh Pond Swamps, [in Cambridge, Massachusetts], where they eat the fruit of the cornels and of the deadly nightshade. They may also be seen along country roads and lanes bordered by woodland, where they feed on the berries of the barberry, spicebush, wild grape, woodbine and poison ivy. When met with in retired places they are almost invariably silent and so shy that it is difficult to approach them closely; but in our garden, where they occur very regularly late in May and more or less frequently in October, and where they often linger for days in succession, they soon become accustomed to our presence and comparatively tame. Indeed we often see them hopping about over the flower beds, along the garden walks, and on the turf under the trees, almost as boldly and familiarly as the Robins. In this garden, moreover, they sometimes sing a little, usually at morning or evening, or during rainy weather.'

On their breeding-grounds both of these thrushes are so shy that it is of little use to follow them as ordinarily they will not permit a close approach. They will come close, however, to a quiet sitter, especially if he imitates the cry of a bird in distress, but even then they usually keep well concealed behind the foliage, and quiet sitting on the part of a watcher is somewhat difficult where black flies and mosquitoes are rampant.

In my opinion the songs of these thrushes cannot compare with those of the Hermit Thrush, the Wood Thrush or even the Veery. They may be ranked between the song of the Veery and that of the Olive-backed Thrush — a rather inferior thrush song.

In the breeding season Bicknell's Thrush may be found among the stunted spruces and firs near the summits of the Adirondacks and the New England mountains, mostly about three thousand feet altitude or higher to timber line, often in the same woods with the Olive-backed Thrush. The bird is more loquacious than the Olive-backed Thrush and usually more shy, and therefore will be heard much more often than it is seen.

VEERY

Hylocichla fuscescens fuscescens (STEPHENS). PLATE 92.

Other names: Wilson's Thrush; Tawny Thrush.

IDENTIFICATION. — Length 6½ to 7¾ inches; spread 11¼ to 12½ inches. A slender light tawny-brown bird, whitish below with tawny-brown V-shaped spots on a buffy breast, least distinct spotting of any of the thrushes; no eye-ring.

SONG. — A descending liquid 'spiral,' repeated frequently without variation in phrasing.

BREEDING. — *Nest:* Usually on ground, similar to that of Hermit Thrush. *Eggs:* 3 to 5, greenish-blue.

RANGE. — Breeds from Michigan, southern Ontario, southern Quebec, and Anticosti Island south to northern Indiana, northern Ohio, and New Jersey, and in the mountains to northern Georgia; winters in Colombia, Brazil and British Guiana; migrates through Yucatan and Central America.

Usually the Veeries or Wilson's Thrushes begin to arrive in the latitude of southern New England during the first or second week in May. They come in silently in the night and unlike most of our local summer residents, rarely begin to sing until at least a week after their appearance. However, when walking through deciduous woods, which they chiefly affect, one may now and then see them running along on the ground or hear their alarm notes.

They are fond of low moist woodlands, wooded swamps and the banks of streams, but they often live during the summer in woods of mixed oak and pine, on dry hillsides or even on the summits of low hills, though they are seldom seen at any great height on the mountains of New York or New England. Usually they are rather shy and retiring, but in migration some of them visit city parks and gardens and become quite tame.

I consider the Veery one of the finest of our songsters and have formerly written of it: 'The song of this thrush, one of the sweetest sounds of the woodland, is among the earliest notes of the morning, and is often heard during the day and in the dusk of evening. It consists of several ringing phrases or triplets, which its name Veery describes fairly well. It is not so full-toned as the songs of other thrushes, but has an attenuated sound. Robert Ridgway expresses the quality of the phrases by the syllables "*taweel'ah, taweel'ah, twil-ah, twil-ah.*" The last two phrases are lower in tone than the first, and end with a vibrating chord which suggests the vanishing of the note into ethereal space. The melody often has a muffled sound when heard near by, but at a distance it seems to ring out clear. To be fully appreciated, this song must be heard when one is alone in the deep woods, among the falling shades of the coming night. It breathes the spirit of the dying day. Sometimes at evening these thrush songs reply to one another like echoes in the moonlight.'

That brilliant and versatile ornithologist Dr. Elliott Coues says of this bird: 'I rate the bird as one of the sweetest of our songsters of whose "clear bell-like notes, resonant, distinct, yet soft and of indescribable sadness," I have spoken on a former occasion.' The same author thus graphically describes the bird's nesting-place: 'The heavy growth of timber that fringes the streams includes many nooks and dells, and broken ravines overgrown with thick shrubbery, from out the masses of which the tall trees tower, as if stretching forth their strong arms in kindly caressing of the humbler and weaker vegetation, their offspring. In such safe retreats, where the sombre shade is brightened here and there with stray beams of sunlight, in the warmth of which myriads of insects bathe their wings and flutter away their little span of life, humming a quaint refrain to the gurgle of the rivulet, the Veery meets his mate — the song rises — the wooed is won — the home is made. Should we force our unwelcome presence upon the bird who is brooding her newly found treasures with the tenderest solicitude, she will nestle closer still, in hope of our passing by, till we might almost touch her; when, without a word of remonstrance or reproach, she takes a little flight, and settles a few yards away, in silent appeal. If the time, the place, the scene, suffice not for our forbearance, with what poor words of hers may we then be moved?'

Mrs. Richard B. Harding, who spent a large part of a summer watching nests of this species in New Hampshire, is positive that the bird usually rears two broods there. The building of the nests required from six to ten days, depending on the weather. Both parents joined in guarding and defending the young. The male was most aggressive in driving other birds away from the nesting area and attacked red squirrels and chipmunks which trespassed upon his precincts, flying at them with great fury. The young were not fed by regurgitation on the first day, but with small hairless caterpillars together with soft white grubs and other small insects, all of which had been thoroughly bruised between the mandibles of the parent bird. This diet was continued for about four days. On the fifth day dragonflies and slugs were added and a day or two later black swallow-tailed butterflies were added. The capture of many dragonflies and butterflies indicates that this thrush is a skillful flycatcher as such insects are swift, erratic fliers. The Veeries having raised their young begin to depart for the south in August and most of them have left the Northern States by the tenth of September.

WILLOW THRUSH

Hylocichla fuscescens salicicola RIDGWAY.

Other name: Newfoundland Thrush.

IDENTIFICATION. — Similar to *H. f. fuscescens* but upper parts slightly darker.

RANGE. — Breeds from southern British Columbia, southern Manitoba, and Wisconsin (and apparently in Newfoundland), south to central Oregon, northern New Mexico, and central Iowa; winters in South America to Brazil.

EASTERN BLUEBIRD

Sialia sialis sialis (LINNAEUS). PLATE 93.

IDENTIFICATION. — Length 6¼ to 7¾ inches; spread 11½ to 13¼ inches. Only *blue* bird in the East having a *brown* breast; female duller than male; young have spotted breast and blue only on wings and tail.

SONG. — A short soft warble, *cheuery, cheuery,* often repeated.

BREEDING. — On edge of woods and about towns. *Nest:* In natural or artificial cavity or bird box, lined with fine grasses, occasionally other materials. *Eggs:* 3 to 7, light blue, rarely white.

RANGE. — Breeds from southern Manitoba, northern Ontario, southern Quebec, and Newfoundland south to central and southeastern Texas, the Gulf coast and southern Florida; resident in Bermuda; winters most commonly south of the Ohio Valley and the Middle States, casually farther north.

Who does not welcome the beloved Bluebird and all that his coming implies? His cheery warble, heard at first as a mere wandering voice in the sky, heralds returning spring. There must be something wrong with the man who, hearing this brave and happy bird and seeing him fluttering and warbling in his lovely vernal dress, does not feel a responsive thrill. Snow may still lie in patches or drift in flurries; storm clouds may gather, and winter may retreat with slow and sullen steps, but when the Bluebird comes we know that spring is near.

In mild seasons a few Eastern Bluebirds appear in central Massachusetts by the twentieth of February. Probably these are birds that have passed the winter in southern New England. Usually a considerable migration appears by the middle of March and continues well into April.

The earliest birds ordinarily are males and sometimes a flock of males is seen, but many birds are paired when they arrive. There are many combats among the rival males, and occasionally a pair of females will fight long and fiercely for the favor of a particular male. Now and then as the mating season advances an enthusiastic male will leave a tree-top and flutter up into the air for a hundred feet or so and then sail down again to his tree-top, singing all the way. The pretty flutterings and flitterings of the Bluebird in courtship are well known, and most of its habits are matters of common observation, since it has become a tenant of the yard and orchard. Often the male is very gallant and sometimes is seen proffering food to his mate which she readily accepts.

The Bluebird likes to choose a nesting-site near some open field or in a grass-grown orchard where it finds a hollow branch or an old woodpecker's hole, which it lines with soft dried grasses. The eggs are plain light blue, or occasionally pure white. In the search for suitable nesting-places Bluebirds sometimes enter water conductors and being unable to fly out are drowned in cisterns. Occasionally one has entered a stovepipe in an unoccupied building and died in the stove.

Like most of our farm birds the Bluebird is devoted to its young, which remain in the nest about fifteen to nineteen days. Both parents feed them and keep the nest clean. Usually when the first brood is out of the nest the male takes charge of it, while the female prepares a nest for the second brood.

Young Bluebirds as well as the young of other birds that nest in hollow trees are sometimes killed by the larvae of a bloodsucking fly of the genus *Protocalliphora.* In some localities these larvae, which bear a superficial resemblance to a tick, wipe out about seventy-five per cent of the young birds. In such cases the nests and all the dirt in the nesting-box or cavity should be burned to prevent the larvae which hide there from maturing.

Most of the late broods of Bluebirds are out of the nest in August, and by the tenth of that month small flocks, probably mostly young birds, may be seen moving southward. Birds that raise several broods, however, are sometimes much later, as very young fledglings are seen occasionally in September and large flights of Bluebirds go south in October.

The few birds that remain through a New England winter, mostly along the southern coastal plain or in the river valleys leading north from it, feed largely in thickets of Virginia juniper or red cedar, where they are somewhat protected from the cold winds, and they roost in companies in hollow trees or nesting-boxes, but there are some exceptions to this rule.

The food of the Eastern Bluebird is of especial interest to the farmer and fruit grower, as next to the Robin it is one of the most domestic of birds and nests freely about the farmstead and orchard. Almost seven tenths of its food is derived from the animal kingdom, chiefly from insects, and the balance is vegetal, mainly wild fruit.

GREENLAND WHEATEAR

Oenanthe oenanthe leucorhoa (GMELIN).

IDENTIFICATION. — Length about 6¼ inches. In summer upper parts light gray; forehead and upper tail coverts white; cheek and wings black; basal two-thirds of tail white, end black; under parts whitish, washed with buffy. In winter upper parts cinnamon-brown, under parts yellowish-buffy, light edgings to feathers of wings and tail.

BREEDING. — *Nest:* Usually in crevices among rocks, of moss and grasses. *Eggs:* 4 to 7, bluish-white.

RANGE. — Breeds in the Arctic Zone from Ellesmere Island and Boothia Peninsula east to Greenland and Iceland and south to northern Quebec; winters in West Africa; migrates through the British Isles and France; casual in winter in Canada and the United States.

The Greenland Wheatear is a bird of most unusual and interesting range. While its principal breeding-grounds are in the Western Hemisphere, it winters in the Old World, the only small land bird which has such a distribution. Evidently the species originated in the Eastern Hemisphere and our race still breeds in Iceland, but it has extended its nesting area to Greenland, Ellesmere Land, Boothia Peninsula and northern Ungava, and there is even evidence that it has bred near Godbout in Canadian Labrador. Instead of migrating south in autumn along the coast of North America, it travels back over its old ancestral route, visiting the British Isles, France, Holland and Germany, to spend the winter in western Africa. Occasionally individuals straggle to points in Canada and farther south, and the bird has been recorded from Keewatin, Ontario, Quebec, New Brunswick, New York, Louisiana, Bermuda and Cuba.

BLUE–GRAY GNATCATCHER

Polioptila caerulea caerulea (LINNAEUS).   PLATE 91.

IDENTIFICATION. — Length 4 to 5 inches; spread 5¾ to 6½ inches. A tiny long-tailed bird, not much larger than kinglets and much more slender; blue-gray above, grayish-white below, with white eye-ring, black tail showing white outer feathers in flight.

SONG. — A thin lisping warble.

BREEDING. — *Nest:* Saddled on limb of large tree, of vegetable fibers, covered with lichens, a deep cup. *Eggs:* 3 to 5, greenish-blue to bluish-white, spotted with browns and grays.

RANGE. — Breeds from eastern Nebraska, Iowa, and southern parts of Wisconsin, Michigan, Ontario, southwestern Pennsylvania, Maryland, and southern New Jersey south to southern Texas, the Gulf coast, and central Florida; winters from southern Texas, southern Mississippi, and the coast of South Carolina to the Bahamas and Cuba, and through eastern Mexico to Guatemala.

The Blue-gray Gnatcatcher is a fidgety little midget. Tiny, slender and frail in appearance, with shape and manners that resemble those of the much larger active and fussy Catbird, nevertheless its littleness and defenselessness and its air of innocence and artlessness at once enlist our sympathy and interest.

Normally a wood bird, it may be looked for wherever trees and thickets grow. It seems to have a preference for tall trees. It is exceedingly active and graceful and may be seen dashing and skipping about amid the underbrush with twitching body, lifted wings and expanded tail, only to appear a moment later amid the topmost branches of some tall tree, from which it launches into the air like a flycatcher in pursuit of some passing insect or hovers before some spray to peck off some small creature hiding there. Every dart after an insect is punctuated with a sharp snap of the bill which signalizes the end of some tiny life.

Mr. C. J. Maynard says of its song: 'I never imagined that any bird was capable of producing notes so soft and low, yet each one given with such distinctness that the ear could catch every part of the wondrous and complicated song' which he describes as a 'silvery warble which filled the air with sweet continuous melody.'

Both birds labor together in the construction of the beautiful nest, after the hummingbird's, the daintiest in the woods, but the female is the more assiduous nest builder. She often sits in the uncompleted nest and rounds its rim, pressing her breast against the inside wall and reaching over, smoothing the outside with her throat and bill in the manner of a warbler. The lichens with which the outside is covered and beautified are fastened down with spiders' webs or caterpillars' silk, and the whole fabric when finished resembles a knot on a limb covered with tree lichens.

This species seems to fluctuate much in numbers from year to year. In the years of abundance small numbers reach New England, but in years of scarcity the bird is exceedingly rare or absent from this region. It is a fairly common bird near Washington and in the Southern States.

Most of the active life of the Blue-gray Gnatcatcher is spent in catching small insects, many of them in flight. What little we know of the food of this bird indicates that it is a decidedly useful species.

EASTERN GOLDEN–CROWNED KINGLET

Regulus satrapa satrapa LICHTENSTEIN.

PLATE 91.

Other names: Golden-crested Wren; Gold-crest.

IDENTIFICATION. — Length about 3¼ to 4¼ inches; spread 6½ to 7 inches. A tiny olive-green and gray bird, smaller than any American wood warbler; lives largely among the twigs and branches of trees, especially cone-bearing trees with thick foliage; shows two light wing-bars and *a white stripe over eye* bordered above by a black stripe; a yellow or yellow and orange crown-patch bordered with black; has a habit of flipping out the tips of its wings above its back frequently.

COMMON CALL. — A high, sibilant *tsee-tsee-tsee.*

BREEDING. — In coniferous woods. *Nest:* Globular and usually pensile, of green mosses, lichens, bits of bark, etc., lined with feathers. *Eggs:* 8 to 10, whitish thickly spotted with brown and larger spots of lavender.

RANGE. — Breeds from central Alberta, central Manitoba, southern Quebec, and Cape Breton Island south to Minnesota, Michigan, New York, the highlands of Massachusetts, and in the Alleghenies south to North Carolina; winters from Iowa, Ontario, and New Brunswick to northern Florida and northeastern Mexico.

This tiny dainty birdlet, whose long soft plumage and remarkable vigor enable it to withstand the rigors of a northern winter when much larger birds leave us for the South, is not uncommon at that season in the dense pine woods of southern New England. In summer, however, I have found it only in or near the spruce growth where it retires to breed. Old residents say that it has disappeared since the spruce and pine were cut from a large part of the region in western Massachusetts where it formerly bred. It is to be found occasionally, however, where spruce still grows. In migration it may be found almost anywhere where trees grow or even in bushes and thickets, in orchards or in sproutlands, but in summer or winter it prefers the cone-bearing trees. If seen in winter its little nervous trick of flirting up the wing-tips, like a flash, will identify it at once, as then it is the only bird that habitually does this except the Ruby-crowned Kinglet, and the latter is almost accidental in winter in the Northern States. It feeds much near the ends of the limbs among the small twigs and during the warmer part of the year it often flutters there in the air like a hummingbird before a flower.

Usually the orange central part of the crown of the male is concealed by the yellow feathers, so that a male is easily mistaken at times for a female, but whenever he becomes in the least excited the orange blazes forth. On the breeding-grounds this bird might be overlooked among the dark evergreen trees were it not for the song of the male which, in nest building time, will lead the observer to his consort. The female does most of the nest building while the male stays with her and encourages her with song. It is useless to attempt to find a nest except when the female is building or later when the parents are carrying food for the young. When a nest is found no one should go near the tree until a week or two after building is finished, as any near approach to the nest before the eggs are laid probably will cause the birds to abandon it.

The nest is a very dainty affair, globular with the opening on one side, often pensile, and composed largely of usnea or other mosses, and lined with feathers. The tiny eggs, eight to ten in number, are whitish with many fine reddish and lavender dots.

The young ones having donned their winter dress and learned to care for themselves, as autumn wanes the kinglets work their way southward in little companies though a few remain all winter, wandering through the winter woods where food is plentiful, often in company with chickadees, nuthatches and other winter wood birds, but not infrequently by themselves. Although I have watched these birdlings many times at dusk, I never could tell where they slept throughout the long winter nights except that they gathered in dense pine woods. It is probable that these tiny things find some old deserted squirrels' nest or some hollow tree as a shelter in which to pass the cold windy nights of winter. Although their plumage is long, thick and fluffy for so small a bird, doubtless a bleak exposure at night would be more than they could bear. Probably kinglets, like nuthatches, chickadees and the smaller woodpeckers, are obliged to find snug quarters on cold nights.

Eastern Golden-crowned Kinglets in summer feed chiefly on small flying insects, many of which they catch on the wing. In winter they feed largely on scale-insects and the eggs of plant-lice and other small tree pests. Among the insects eaten are small grasshoppers and locusts, weevils, leaf-hoppers, plant-lice and caterpillars.

EASTERN RUBY-CROWNED KINGLET

Corthylio calendula calendula (LINNAEUS). PLATE 91.

Other names: Ruby-crowned Wren; Ruby-crested Wren; Ruby-crown.

IDENTIFICATION. — Length 3¾ to 4½ inches; spread 6¾ to 7½ inches. Smaller than smallest warbler; has nervous manner of the Golden-crown and similar flirting of wing-tips; may be distinguished by absence of light and dark stripes on head and of *yellow crown patch; conspicuous white eye-ring enclosing black eyelid and large dark eye* give the bird a startled staring expression unlike that of any other bird near its size; plain greenish-olive fading to whitish below; two pale wing-bars; *the red patch usually concealed.*

BREEDING. — Similar to Golden-crowned Kinglet, but markings on eggs finer and fainter.

RANGE. — Breeds from northwestern Alaska, northern Manitoba, and west-central Quebec south to southern Arizona, central New Mexico, northern Ontario, New Brunswick, and Nova Scotia; winters from southern British Columbia, Iowa, and Virginia south over the United States and the Mexican tableland to Guatemala, and in Lower California.

The Eastern Ruby-crowned Kinglet is a lively, nervous little creature, quite as active as a wren. Its behavior, however, much more resembles that of the Golden-crowned Kinglet than that of any wren. Soon after it arrives in spring it becomes conspicuous, announcing its coming by its wonderful song. Dr. Elliott Coues says of it, in his 'Birds of the Colorado Valley':

'One of the most remarkable things about the Ruby-crown is its extraordinary powers of song. It is really surprising that such a tiny creature should be capable of the strong and sustained notes it utters when in full song. The lower larynx, the sound-producing organ, is not much bigger than a good-sized pin's head, and the muscles that move it are almost microscopic shreds of flesh. If the strength of the human voice were in the same proportion to the size of the larynx, we could converse with ease at a distance of a mile or more. The Kinglet's exquisite vocalization defies description; we can only speak, in general terms, of the power, purity and volume of the notes, their faultless modulation and long continuance. Many doubtless have listened to this music without suspecting that the author was the diminutive Ruby-crown, with whose common-place utterance, the slender wiry "*tsip*," they were already familiar. Such was once the case even with Audubon, who pays a heartfelt tribute to the accomplished little vocalist, and says further — "When I tell you that its song is fully as sonorous as that of the Canary-bird, and much richer, I do not come up to the truth, for it is not only as powerful and clear, but much more varied and pleasing."

'This delightful rôle is chiefly executed during the mating season, and the brief period of exaltation which precedes it; it is consequently seldom heard in regions where the bird does not rear its young, except when the little performer breaks forth in song on nearing its summer resorts. . . .

'To observe the manners of the Ruby-crown, one need only repair, at the right season, to the nearest thicket, coppice, or piece of shrubbery, such as the Titmice, Yellow-rumps and other warblers love to haunt. These are its favorite resorts, especially in the fall and winter; though sometimes, in the spring more particularly, it seems to be more ambitious, and its slight form may be almost lost among the branchlets of the taller trees, where the equally diminutive *Parula* is most at home. We shall most likely find it not alone, but in straggling troops, which keep up a sort of companionship with each other as well as with different birds, though each individual seems to be absorbed in its particular business. We hear the slender wiry note, and see the little creatures skipping nimbly about the smaller branches in endlessly varied attitudes, peering in the crevices of the bark for their minute insect food, taking short nervous flights from one bough to another, twitching their wings as they alight, and always too busy to pay attention to what may be going on around them. They appear to be incessantly in motion — I know of no birds more active than these — presenting the very picture of restless, puny energy, making "much ado about nothing."'

The favorite haunts of the Ruby-crowns in spring are swampy thickets along the borders of some little streamlet, ditch, brook, pond or meadow. In autumn they are commonly found in low woods or among birches on the hills, usually in small parties, or singly or in pairs with small warblers in the shrubbery along swampy streams. Some authors assert that they sing only in spring, but on warm autumn days they frequently sing a low whisper song and sometimes a carol almost equal to their best vernal efforts. Little seems to be known of their nesting habits though many nests have been found in the great forests of the Rocky Mountains and a few in eastern Canada.

AMERICAN PIPIT

Anthus spinoletta rubescens (TUNSTALL). PLATE 88.

Other names: Titlark; Wagtail; American Skylark.

IDENTIFICATION. — Length 6 to 7 inches; spread 10 to 11 inches. Slightly larger than Song Sparrow, but more slender, with *slender bill;* a brown or brownish-gray bird, buffy below, inconspicuously marked; walks or runs on the ground with tail constantly tilting or see-sawing; flight erratic, wavering, often showing white on two outer tail-feathers on each side, and thus might be mistaken for a Vesper Sparrow. Pipits are smaller and more slender than Horned Larks, and in flight show more white on tail.

BREEDING. — On barren open lands. *Nest:* On ground, of grass. *Eggs:* 4 to 6, bluish-white to light brown, thickly spotted with chocolate, and streaked with black.

RANGE. — Breeds from northeastern Siberia, northern Alaska, the west coast of Davis Strait, and the west coast of Greenland, south to Great Slave Lake, northern Manitoba, Quebec (Gaspé), and Newfoundland, from the Aleutian Islands to Prince William Sound, and in the mountains south to Oregon, Colorado, and New Mexico; winters from northern California and the Ohio and lower Delaware valleys to the Gulf coast, Lower California, and Guatemala.

Down from the wastes of Greenland, the rocky coast of Labrador and the barrens of New-foundland come the American Pipits in September to the windswept hills and pastures along the New England shores. Marsh and moor are enlivened by their restless vacillating hosts, until the frosts of late October and November send them on their way. Again we may see a few individuals here and there in April, but the majority seem to pass northward west of the Alleghanies, and the bird is not common in the East in spring. Its two-syllabled call-note is supposed to resemble the word *pip-it*, and so has given the bird its name.

This modest little wanderer is not a conspicuous bird. Seen in the short grass with Savannah Sparrows and other small birds of the fields, it might be taken for one of them and overlooked. It has no bright colors, no conspicuous markings, except the white in the tail, which is con-cealed when that member is closed, and no striking notes. When it rises, its flight is undulating and erratic, like that of sparrows, and then only the white in the outer tail feathers serves to distinguish it from all but the Vesper Sparrow. When it alights on plowed ground (a common habit) it so closely matches the soil in color that it is almost invisible. It walks or runs, while sparrows usually hop.

The Titlark, as it is often called, is a bird of the open spaces. Barren rocks, sand-dunes, beaches, salt marshes, wide meadows and cultivated lowlands are some of its favorite resorts. It is fond of the water, and frequents the seacoast and the valleys of streams or the shores of lakes. In the interior a plowed meadow with a small brook running through it often attracts a flock of Pipits. Their actions about the water somewhat resemble those of a Northern Water-thrush, as they walk into the water with teetering tails, but they are never heavily streaked on the breast like the Water-thrush. In the lakes, they sometimes alight on large rocks, where they find food amid the moist rock vegetation at the water's edge. Usually while feeding they run or walk along the ground, searching for insects and other small forms of animal life, almost constantly moving the tail. A flock in flight resembles a flock of Northern Horned Larks, having a similar undulating movement, and similar notes, but the birds show more white in the tail. They fly in loose order and rather fitfully, but they are powerful fliers and their evolu-tions in flock formation often are graceful and sweeping. When moving about singly in flight, they seem always uncertain what to do next, whether to go here or there, to alight or go on. When they alight, as they do occasionally, on the ridgepole of a building, a telegraph wire, or a naked tree, they become conspicuous and may readily be distinguished from sparrows by their slender bills. They fly in flocks of from ten to one hundred or more, but often scatter over a wide area to feed, and when approached under such conditions jump up from the grass singly or a few at a time.

SPRAGUE'S PIPIT

Anthus spraguei (AUDUBON).

Other name: Missouri Skylark.

IDENTIFICATION. — Length 6¼ to 7 inches; spread 10 to 11 inches. Similar to American Pipit in appearance but upper parts distinctly streaked and under parts paler; much like a slender Vesper Sparrow but with slender, not sparrow-like, bill.

BREEDING. — *Nest:* On ground, of grasses. *Eggs:* 3 to 5, grayish-white thickly and finely speckled with purplish and blackish.

RANGE. — Breeds from west-central Saskatchewan and southern Manitoba south to western Montana and North Dakota; winters from Texas, southern Louisiana, and southern Mississippi through eastern and central Mexico.

Sprague's Pipit is a bird of the wide treeless prairies which probably finds its most easterly breeding range in western Minnesota, where it is a common summer resident. In winter it is found on the Gulf coasts of Louisiana and Mississippi, and occasionally as far east as Georgia and South Carolina.

Of this species on its breeding-grounds Dr. T. S. Roberts, in his 'Birds of Minnesota,' says: 'Sprague's Pipit is a bird that may be easily overlooked. It should be looked for high overhead rather than on the ground. In the nesting season the characteristic song of the male, floating down from far up in the sky, is the surest indication of its presence. The performer may not be easy to locate, but the song can belong to no other bird. On the ground it disappears completely in the prairie grass, walks or runs nimbly away without showing itself and, if flushed, flies quickly off, appearing much like a Vesper Sparrow.'

P. A. Taverner, in his 'Birds of Canada,' furnishes the following description: 'Its flight song is unmistakable. Flitting around in wide circles, so high in the air as to be an all but invisible speck, it repeats over and over again in a sweet voice its simple little song, a *"ching,-ring,-ring,-ring,-ring,-ring,-ring,-ring"* on a steadily descending scale, dropping about an octave in all and lasting about five seconds. This may be repeated a hundred times or more with only a few seconds' interval between. Sometimes it keeps steadily at it for twenty minutes, then it comes to earth in a straight dive like a falling stone and vanishes from sight in the short grassy covering of the prairie. It has much the sound of a very distant Wilson's Thrush song, but is longer, less rich, and silver rather than golden in tone.' — (J.B.M.)

BOHEMIAN WAXWING

Bombycilla garrula pallidiceps REICHENOW.   PLATE 78.

Other name: Chatterer.

IDENTIFICATION. — Length 7½ to 8¾ inches; spread 13¼ to 14¼ inches. Similar to Cedar Waxwing but larger; white markings on wings, chestnut under tail coverts, and gray below where Cedarbird is yellow, distinguish it.

BREEDING. — Similar to Cedar Waxwing.

The Bohemian Waxwing is circumpolar in its distribution, its several races breeding in the more northerly parts of Europe, Asia, and North America. It is very erratic in its migratory movements and apparently is influenced much more by the food supply than by the rigors of the climate. Its appearance in eastern Canada and the United States is purely sporadic, many winters passing without more than a few scattered occurrences along the Atlantic coast, and then some years bringing a very definite influx of these wanderers.

In the East the bird is usually found in company with wintering flocks of its smaller congener, the Cedar Waxwing, and it feeds on the same food, mainly such berries as the mountain ash, the hawthorns and wild crabs, and the sumacs. With us it is usually a very silent bird and its European name, the 'Chatterer,' seems badly misapplied, but in its northern breeding area it is more vocal. At Carcross on the headwaters of the Yukon River, I watched a number of Bohemian Waxwings busily engaged in flycatching from the tops of small evergreens, and they frequently gave their calls while watching for insects. T. S. Roberts says of this bird: 'Its only utterance is a series of rather fine but rather penetrating notes, which has been called a "chatter" and from which comes one of its names, "Chatterer." It is an unmusical, beaded call, which can hardly be dignified by the name of song. The syllables *te-e-e-e-e* may suggest the character of the notes.' The name 'Bohemian,' as applied to this bird, is said to refer to its wandering or bohemian disposition, rather than to its being a native of Bohemia. — (J.B.M.)

CEDAR WAXWING

Bombycilla cedrorum VIEILLOT.   PLATE 78.

Other names: Cedar-bird; Cherry-bird.

IDENTIFICATION. — Length 6½ to 8 inches; spread 11 to 12¼ inches. Slightly larger than Eastern Bluebird; long-crested, brownish birds, very sleek in appearance; yellow below on flanks; tip of tail dark yellow; black about eyes and on chin; under tail coverts whitish; sometimes red wax-like appendages on tips of secondaries and less often on tail quills.

BREEDING. — *Nest:* Bulky and rough, of twigs, roots, bark-strips, leaves, scraps of paper and rags, string, etc., lined mostly with fine rootlets and bark shreds. *Eggs:* 4 to 6, dull pale bluish, greenish-slate, or yellowish-gray, spotted with blackish and brown and with 'under-markings' of purplish.

RANGE. — Breeds from central British Columbia, central Manitoba, northern Ontario, southern Quebec, and Cape Breton Island south to northwestern California, northern Arkansas, North Carolina, and northern Georgia; winters south to Cuba, Mexico and Panama.

Who can describe the grace and elegance of this bird? What other common bird is dressed in a robe of so delicate and silky a texture? Those shades of blending beauty — velvety black brightening into fawn, melting browns, shifting saffrons, quaker drabs, pale blue-gray and slate, with trimmings of white and golden-yellow, and little red appendages on the wing-quills not found in any other family of birds — all, combined with its symmetrical form, give it an appearance and distinction peculiarly its own. Its erectile crest expresses every emotion.

When lying loose and low upon the head it signifies ease and comfort. Excitement or surprise erect it at once, and in fear it is pressed flat.

'At any time of the year,' writes Dr. Coues, 'in almost any part of the country, one may hear some curious wheezing, lisping notes, and, on looking about him, may see a dozen or a hundred little birds in sight, flying in an easy, rather undulating course, to alight in a compact body on the nearest tree, where they remain silent and motionless for a few moments, drawn up to their full heights, displaying their long top-knots; then they begin to move about and feed, unless some alarm sends them off to another tree. When the cedar ripens its glaucous-blue berries, these same birds are sure to be found there, gorging themselves on this fruit till they are literally choke-full — the last few berries sticking in their capacious throats for want of room below.'

Cedar Waxwings are such gluttonous birds that they sometimes become so surfeited as to be unable to fly, and have been known to fall helpless on the ground. At least one instance is on record where a bird of this species was supposed to have died from overfeeding. Whether in such cases the victims are suffering from gluttony or from intoxication, caused by the fermented juices of over-ripe fruit, does not always appear, but in the following account sent to me by my young friend John Willison, the behavior of the birds was attributed to the latter cause:

'One warm day last fall, I was walking with a chum through the fields and woods at Manomet Point, Plymouth, Massachusetts. Suddenly my friend, who knew nothing about birds, pointed to a twenty-foot chokecherry tree, which was loaded with birds, and asked what those birds were. I told him that they were Cedar Waxwings. As we drew closer the birds looked as though their feathers had been drawn or brushed the wrong way, and I realized that something was wrong with them. The birds did not seem to notice us and we soon came near enough to easily catch them with our hats. All the while the birds were eating the berries ravenously. My companion was soon in a fit of laughter. "Why, they're drunk!" he exclaimed. Sure enough, the birds were evidently intoxicated by the over-ripe chokecherries. Their actions were very comical, for they were helpless. One fellow bobbed up and down even after we had secured him under my hat. Their crests were erect and in the excitement of seeing us they all tumbled around. Some tumbled to the ground where with outspread wings they attempted to run away; still others tottered on the branches with wings continually flapping, as though for balance. All the time we were there they kept up a continual hissing noise, as a family of snakes might do. We caught several to inspect, and finally left them in peace.'

All through the spring the Cedar-birds loiter about with nothing on their minds and nothing to do but to eat and grow fat. Many of them even allow early summer to pass before they begin to prepare for family cares. They are rather slow in mating, but at nest building are very diligent. They will use cotton, rags or string in place of the ordinary vegetal fibers; usually when string is accessible they prefer white and sometimes blue to other colors of twine or yarn. Usually there is considerable grapevine or cedar bark used, and the lining is fine black rootlets. Both male and female work together at their loving task, taking material wherever they can find it; sometimes they even steal some from the nest of some other bird.

Like some other plump and well-fed personages, the Cedar Waxwing is easy-going, happy, and blessed with a good disposition. It is fond of good company. When the nesting season is past each harmonious little family joins with others until the flock may number from thirty to sixty individuals. They keep well together through the winter and spring until the nesting season again arrives. Their manner of flight is quite their own. They fly in close order, and often they suddenly wheel, as if at command, and plunge swiftly downward, alighting in a compact band on the top of some leafless tree.

The seasonal movements of the Cedar Waxwing appear to be rather erratic. There seems to be a southward movement in August and September, when the majority of the species leave the latitude of New England, but if there is a bountiful supply of wild fruit of the kinds which persist during the winter many birds remain here, associating in flocks of various sizes, and so perhaps, in the white days of winter, you may see a little flock sitting upright upon some leafless tree, the birds calling softly to one another in their high-pitched, lisping, sibilant monotone.

Usually during the latter part of the winter there is an early northward movement of these birds, most of which disappear before the end of April, but the main flight does not appear before May and sometimes quite late in that month.

'So,' says Dr. Coues in his 'Birds of the Colorado Valley,' 'they lead their idle, uneventful lives — these *debonnaire* birds, sociable but not domestic, even a trifle dissipated, good-natured enough to a friend in a scrape, very reliable diners-out, and fond of showing off their dressy top-knots, on which so much of their mind is fixed.'

The food of the Cedar Waxwing consists very largely of fruit, but most of it is wild fruit of no value to man. The animal food consists mainly of insects. When Cedar Waxwings first come in spring, they may be seen pecking at the blossoms of fruit trees and scattering the petals broadcast, but when their stomach contents have been examined, quantities of insects that infest blossoms have been found, with very few petals or stamens. They are fond of small moths, leaf-eating beetles and curculios, and devour quantities of the Colorado potato beetle and the pernicious elm-leaf beetle, which has proved very destructive to elms recently in the Eastern States. The young are fed quantities of insects and as they grow older the parents give them some fruit. The food is usually carried in the gullet of the parent until regurgitated into the open mouths of the little ones.

I watched the Cedar Waxwings in a canker-worm year, when all through the orchards the little 'inch-worm' caterpillars began to cut holes in the leaves. Then came the eager birds in flocks and there they stayed, often whispering to one another and always catching worms. Such gourmands as they were! They ate until they could eat no more, only to sit about on the branches or play with one another awhile, and then eat again. The canker-worms stripped a few of the old trees, but the Waxwings cleared most of them and saved the leaves, thereby saving the fruit also. When the cherries were ripe these birds always found them. They stayed in the cherry trees with the same persistence that they showed in their work with the canker-worms. They have a habit, when satiated, of sitting together, sometimes five or six on the same limb, all facing the same way, and at such a time I have seen a cherry or a caterpillar passed from one to another until it had passed up and down the line before one would eat it.

In late summer and early fall the Cedar Waxwing turns to flycatching, and taking its post on some tall tree, usually near a pond or river, launches out over water or meadow in pursuit of flying insects. Birds taken at such times have been found crammed with insects to the very beak. In late summer, autumn and winter their vegetal food consists largely of wild cherries, blackberries, raspberries, mulberries, pokeberries and such other wild fruit as that of the

Virginia juniper or red cedar, mountain ash, buckthorn, hawthorn, barberry, privet, bush cranberry, sassafras, flowering dogwood, nightshade, honeysuckle, mistletoe, black gum and hackberry. Like some other birds the Cedar Waxwing seems to enjoy the sweet sap of the sugar maple, from which it takes an occasional drink. It takes sap from the birch also, when opportunity offers.

NORTHERN SHRIKE

Lanius borealis borealis VIEILLOT.   PLATE 78.

Other names: Great Northern Shrike; Butcher-bird.
  IDENTIFICATION. — Length 9 to 10¾ inches; spread 13½ to 16½ inches. A large-headed, thick-set, rather long-tailed bird, somewhat resembling Mockingbird but heavier appearing and with a broad black stripe through or behind eye and less white showing on wings and tail.
  SONG. — Suggests that of Brown Thrasher but more harsh.
  BREEDING. — In forests. *Nest:* Bulky, of twigs and leaves thickly lined with fur, feathers, etc. *Eggs:* 4 to 7, whitish, bluish- or greenish-gray, marked with greenish, light brown, purple or grayish.
  RANGE. — Breeds from northern Ungava to southern Ontario and southern Quebec, west at least to east side of Hudson Bay; winters southward to Kentucky, Virginia, and North Carolina.

A lonesome bird, more solitary than the eagle, this 'Butcher of the North' comes to us in the wake of the smaller land birds, when increasing frosts denote the approach of winter. While here he hunts alone, frequenting broad uplands, sparsely wooded swamps, orchards and fruit gardens — in fact any place where small birds or mice congregate. He enters villages and cities in pursuit of the English Sparrow and Starling, and he follows the winter birds wherever they may be found. His usual watch tower is the top of some tall tree, telegraph pole or wire, or even the top of a small tree or a post, where he often sits upright like a hawk, scanning the ground below. Any unfortunate mouse, bird or insect hiding there is then in danger from this sharp-eyed butcher, who, on perceiving his prey, descends like a plummet, rarely missing his aim. Sometimes he leaves his perch and hovers over his prey for a few seconds, as does the Sparrow Hawk. He occasionally jets his tail while sitting, or even in flight, which usually is slightly undulating, but is very direct when in pursuit of birds.

  Apparently he has no love for his own kind, and is sufficient unto himself, and though we may deplore his attack on the smaller birds, we can but admire his self-reliance, audacity and courage. Though ordinarily rather wary, when in pursuit of his prey he is as fearless as a Goshawk. He attacks birds as large as himself, and even larger. Blue Jays, Robins, Pine Grosbeaks and the redoubtable Starling are among his victims, though the Blue Jay does battle with him, and oftentimes escapes when aided by its companions. The Starlings mob the invader with enthusiasm tempered by caution, following in a compact flock above him, using the same tactics as with a hawk, but the undaunted butcher usually carries off his selected prey.

  If the victim is a bird, the Shrike usually goes with it to the ground, kills it by a few blows on the head and then commonly takes it to some tree or bush, where he either hangs his victim on a thorn, suspends it by the head in the crotch of a branch, or places it between two contiguous branches, where it is held by twisting one leg among forked twigs. The evident objects of this habit are to fasten the bird so that the Shrike, whose feet are not so strong relatively as those of a hawk, can tear off its food with its stout bill, and in case it does not need the victim at once for food, can preserve it 'for future reference.' Many times, however, the rapacious bird kills and suspends more victims than it can use, as insects, birds and even mice are sometimes left to desiccate or decay.

The Northern Shrike usually catches its birds on the wing, either by rising above them and plunging swiftly downward or by sheer persistent speed. While following a bird on the wing it follows every twist and turn of the victim, whose only chance is to outspeed its pursuer and climb higher and higher. In this way some small birds escape. Others get away safely by being able to dodge at sharp angles to their line of flight, when the eager pursuer, having attained its best speed, has its prey almost within its grasp. Then its superior weight and momentum carry it so far past the fleeing quarry that the latter obtains a good lead, and by repeating this maneuver may gain some sheltering thicket, impenetrable to the larger bird.

In bearing away its prey the Shrike uses either bill or claws, whichever are most useful, and sometimes in conveying unusually heavy game, it fastens on it with both bill and claws, and laboriously flutters off with it. In pursuit of its quarry it is so fearless that it often dashes against windows or into rooms to attack caged birds.

Shrikes frequently attack small birds at feeding-stations at the very windows of houses and often in pursuit of their prey enter the traps of bird banders. In such cases they are so fearless that they are driven away with difficulty. Usually when the small birds see a Shrike, they remain motionless, if not perceived by him, until the danger is past. But once I saw a Northern Shrike in a bush surrounded by a small band of complaining Chickadees. The Shrike had been singing previously and its peculiar notes may have attracted the little birds.

Notwithstanding all the above, the food of this species consists very largely of mice and insects. It is true that in winter, when deep snow covers and protects the mice, and when the larger insects are mostly unobtainable, it feeds chiefly on birds — but this occurs only during a few months of the year. All through the spring, summer and autumn, so long as insects are abundant they are the chief food of the Northern Shrike.

LOGGERHEAD SHRIKE
Lanius ludovicianus ludovicianus LINNAEUS.

Other names: French Mockingbird; Butcher-bird.

IDENTIFICATION. — Length $8\frac{1}{2}$ to $9\frac{1}{2}$ inches; spread $12\frac{1}{4}$ to 13 inches. Smaller than Northern Shrike and with a wide black stripe from bill through eye and extending narrowly across base of forehead where Northern Shrike has whitish forehead; darker above and usually unbarred below.

BREEDING. — In farming country. *Nest:* In thick bush or tree, especially thorny ones, bulky, of twigs, rootlets and other miscellaneous material, lined with feathers, wool, etc. *Eggs:* 4 to 8, similar to those of Northern Shrike.

RANGE. — Lower Austral Zone of the Atlantic and Gulf States from southern North Carolina to southern Florida and west through southern Georgia and Alabama to central Louisiana.

397

The Loggerhead Shrike is an extremely common bird along the roadsides in Florida, where in winter every third or fourth telephone pole seems to serve as outlook point for either a Mockingbird, a Sparrow Hawk, or a Loggerhead Shrike. While there is considerable apparent resemblance between the Shrike and the Mocker, they are really very easy to distinguish, the Mocker having a smaller head, a longer tail, and more conspicuous patches of white on wings and tail, which show plainly in flight. The Shrike is heavier looking, with a large head and heavy bill, and darker wings and tail with less white on them.

The Loggerhead is an indefatigable destroyer of grasshoppers, for which it seems ever on the watch. Occasionally it catches small birds, and mice pay toll to its appetite more frequently. It also catches lizards and small snakes. Mr. Archibald Rutledge told me of seeing a Loggerhead Shrike carry some prey to a small holly tree in front of Hampton, his historic plantation house near Charleston, South Carolina, and examination revealed a young cottonmouth moccasin snake. A few days later a second cottonmouth was captured and impaled on the same tree. As he expressed his feelings, 'My opinion of the Loggerhead went up a long way,' for the poisonous moccasin is a decidedly dangerous neighbor in the Southern woods. — (J.B.M.)

MIGRANT SHRIKE

Lanius ludovicianus migrans PALMER.   PLATE 78.

Other names: Butcher-bird; Grasshopper Hawk.
   IDENTIFICATION. — Similar to *L. l. ludovicianus* but paler above and somewhat grayer below.
   RANGE. — Breeds from southeastern Manitoba, southern Ontario, southern Quebec, Maine, and New Brunswick south to northeastern Texas, Louisiana, Mississippi, Kentucky, western North Carolina, and the interior of Virginia; winters chiefly in the Mississippi Valley and Texas, irregularly north to New England.

My chief recollections of the Migrant Shrike picture a gray bird sitting on a telephone wire where he could scan the scenery and from which he occasionally descended swiftly to pick up an unlucky grasshopper. The Migrant Shrike is a bird of the farm, the orchard and the hedgerow. It prefers the neighborhood of thorny trees or bushes on which it can transfix its victims. When hungry, of course, it eats them at once, but when its appetite is satiated it hangs them on thorns, nails or barbed wires, and leaves them there, sometimes for future reference, but often for good. Its habits are much like those of its larger relative, the great Northern Shrike, except that it is not so destructive to small birds. Its notes and song also resemble somewhat those of the larger species. The Migrant Shrike is the only one of the family that is known to breed in the northeastern United States.

Although two broods in a season have been recorded often, the species does not seem to increase and spread rapidly, yet it follows clearing and settlement to a certain extent, and appears to be disseminating slowly in the East. Probably many individuals are shot by people who have observed shrikes killing small birds.

The food of the Migrant Shrike consists very largely of mice and the larger species of destructive insects, such as grasshoppers, crickets and caterpillars, moths, butterflies, large beetles and cicadas. The bird also kills some small birds, shrews, frogs and snakes.

STARLING

Sturnus vulgaris vulgaris LINNAEUS. PLATE 62.

Other names: English Starling; European Starling.

IDENTIFICATION. — Length 7½ to 8½ inches; spread about 15½ inches. About as heavy as Robin but *shorter*. Adult in summer a black bird with short tail and yellow bill; iridescence of plumage seen at close range or in good light; light spots not noticeable at a distance. Young in summer a rather dark, grayish-brown bird, like female Cowbird, but larger with longer, slimmer *dark* bill, and short tail. Adults and young in winter similar to summer plumage, but light spots more noticeable and bill showing little or no yellow, becoming more yellow as winter wanes; bustles about with a quick, nervous, erratic *walk* while looking for food on the ground.

CALLS. — Many and varied; an excellent mimic.

BREEDING. — Usually in villages and cities, sometimes in woods. *Nest:* In any cavity of proper size, of grass and straw, corn husks, etc., lined with feathers, etc. *Eggs:* 5 to 8, pale blue, or whitish.

RANGE. — Native of western and central Europe, wintering south to Africa. Introduced in the United States in 1890 and has spread north to New Brunswick, southern Quebec, and southeastern Ontario, west to Iowa, Kansas and Oklahoma, and south to Texas, Mississippi, and Florida.

The European Starling is a trim and handsome bird. It haunts by preference grass fields, pastures and lawns, but it feeds more or less also among cultivated crops, fruit trees and to some extent in the woods. It has become somewhat of a parasite on man, depending much on his agricultural industries for its food supply and increasing to excessive numbers in a cultivated, fertile country. Therefore it haunts farms, villages and cities wherever grass grows, and is more rarely seen in unsettled regions. It seems particularly fond of lawns and pastures where the grass is short, the walking good and the ground easily gotten at. In pastures it follows the cattle or sheep, catching the insects that the animals stir up, or actually alighting on their backs in search of ticks or other insects. A flock of Starlings so occupied might be mistaken for Cowbirds as the adult males appear black at a distance, thus resembling male Cowbirds, while the young Starlings are about the color of females and young of the Cowbird. Starlings, however, may be distinguished from Cowbirds at a considerable distance by their short tails and their quick, nervous, erratic walk. They zigzag about over lawns or pastures, stopping only long enough to pick up food or to fly away with it. In villages and cities where no shooting is allowed, Starlings feed largely on lawns and in parks where people are constantly passing; the birds seem to exhibit no fear of them, but let one stop to watch the birds and the moment they feel that they are under observation, they become restive and soon fly. In flight the Starling is spindle-shaped, the rather long bill and short tail giving it a somewhat similar shape at both ends. It moves through the air by alternately flapping and sailing on fixed wings, much in the manner of the Meadowlark, which it somewhat resembles in shape. Its flight appears fluttering, slow and feeble, but it can attain great speed at need.

The song of the Starling, so far as I have heard it, seems to consist largely of imitations of the notes of other birds. It begins to sing in winter or even in autumn and continues throughout a great part of the year. Its vocal performances seem to reach their climax in early spring. While family cares take up its attention, its tuneful lays are more in abeyance, though even in the height of the breeding season it sings occasionally a 'whisper song' (with bill closed) interspersed, as usual, with softly whistled imitations.

The Starling nests in hollow limbs, old woodpecker holes, bird-boxes, and about buildings. The eggs resemble those of the Robin in size and color.

Many Starlings' nests for the first brood are completed in April, and by early May the young are crying for food. The parents are very industrious and devoted. They search the grassy lands almost constantly for food, and carry great numbers of worms and insects to the young. By late May or early June many young of the first brood are out of the nest. These gather in small flocks which frequent pastures and other grass lands, and pay regular visits many times a day to cherry trees when the fruit begins to ripen. Few if any adults now flock with them in the daytime, but some roost with them at night. (Many are engaged with their second broods.) The small flocks roost at night in trees or buildings or among the reeds in marshes. Second broods are commonly fledged in July or August, and as summer wanes these flocks continue to increase. By late August and early September they contain many adults and also many molting young, some of which have acquired winter plumage with the exception of their heads, which are still brown. At that time many roost nightly in large marshes, in river valleys or near the sea-shore. I once visited a great marsh near the Hudson in New York State to see the Starlings come in. As the sun set and the shades of evening began to fall, birds appeared, coming from every point of the compass in twos or threes or in small flocks. All converged on the great marsh, plunging down into it and alighting on the reeds. They continued to come in increasing numbers until thousands had assembled at the roosting place. Now and then flocks rose, swept rapidly back and forth for a time, turning like a flash, all in exact concert, and then gradually settled again in the marsh. This animated scene continued until night shut down. Another type of roost, which attracts many thousands, consists of the rows of street trees in southern cities.

In winter, Starlings gather wherever they can find food. They visit barnyards, poultry-yards, garbage dumps, etc. Many are fed by humane people who put out food for birds in winter; but whenever the thermometer goes far below the zero mark with cold winds or storms, some are frozen, for, hardy and fit as they undoubtedly are, many of them cannot endure the extreme cold and privation of a very severe winter.

In the matter of food the Starling is nearly omnivorous, though its food materials are not quite so varied as are those of the Blue Jay and the Crow. Its vegetal food consists largely of fruit, both cultivated and wild. A flock of Starlings swings into a cherry tree, there is a rain of cherry stones and the flock is away again, only to return later unless the flock is large enough to strip the whole tree at once. It takes practically all grains, including corn, and digs up the seed in planted or sowed fields. It takes the young sprouts of garden vegetables and young flowering plants as well. The food of nestling Starlings is nearly all animal, largely insects. The largest animal item consists of caterpillars, including many cutworms, and the largest vegetal item consists of cultivated cherries.

WHITE–EYED VIREO

Vireo griseus griseus (BODDAERT).

PLATE 79.

Other names: Hanging Bird; White-eyed Greenlet.

IDENTIFICATION. — Length 4½ to 5½ inches; spread 7½ to 8½ inches. Smallest of our common vireos; size near that of Chipping Sparrow; a well-rounded, portly little olive-green bird with yellow 'spectacles,' two yellowish-white wing-bars, and white below with yellow sides and flanks; a bird of shrubbery and thickets.

SONG. — Loud and energetic, *chip-whee-oo,* or *chick-per-wee-oo-chick,* etc.

BREEDING. — In lowland thickets. *Nest:* All vireos' nests are suspended cups below a horizontal crotch of a branch, and are made of pliable vegetal fibers, usually decorated outside with lichens, cocoons, bits of birch or other barks, scraps of hornets' nests, bits of old newspapers, etc. *Eggs:* Usually 3 or 4, sometimes 2 or 5, white, marked, chiefly around larger end, with a few spots of browns, purplish, or blackish.

RANGE. — Breeds from southeastern Nebraska, southern Wisconsin, Ohio, New York, and Massachusetts to central Texas and southern Florida; winters from Texas, southern Alabama, southern Georgia, Florida, and South Carolina through eastern Mexico to Honduras.

'Now leaving the ornamental park, the mantling woodland of deciduous trees, and the perpetual robe of green that the mountains wear, and losing as we go the band of Greenlet musicians that sing in these shades, let us push into more lowly places — for we have not done with the Vireos yet. Indeed, the species of this group might be classed according to their life's station, almost as well as by those technicalities which the ornithologist discovers in beak and wing. One set of Greenlets are large and emulous birds — the Red-eye, the Yellow-throat, the Solitary, Plumbeous, and Warbling Vireos — living in woodland high above the level of the ground; and these we have already seen in their native haunts. With the White-eyed Vireo we enter upon a group of smaller species, whose surroundings we shall find to be quite different; for these live in the thickets, down among the Catbirds, Thrashers, Sparrows, Chats and Wrens. This group of nearly-related, bush-loving species includes the Black-capped, the Least, and Bell's Vireos, besides the more familiar White-eye, whose turn comes first.' Thus that brilliant ornithologist, Dr. Elliott Coues, painted the haunts of the subject of this sketch.

In southern New England, which is the northern limit of the White-eyed Vireo's range, it is found chiefly in the coastal regions and in the lowlands of the river valleys, about swamps and ponds, and nearly always among the umbrageous foliage of bosky thickets. In the South it may be found also in the highlands, wherever its favorite thickets abound. Not many of this species reach New England until about the second or third week in May, and most of them move southward in late August and early September. Though while with us this bird keeps largely hidden in thickets, it is not exceedingly shy. It is noted for its irascible temper whenever an intruder nears its nest, and in its excitement frequently approaches the invader, scolding him soundly meanwhile and jetting its tail. It is an inquisitive bird and shows its inordinate curiosity by stealing very near a person seated in its resorts and peering at him, much in the manner of the Catbird, when hardly more than an arm's length away.

The most remarkable and noticeable characteristic of this bird is its song, which is loud for the size of the singer, very emphatic, so ventriloquial as to deceive the listener as to its locality, and not infrequently interrupted by, or interlarded with, fairly good fragmentary imitations of songs or notes of the Song Sparrow, Robin, Flicker, Catbird, House Wren, Goldfinch, Whip-poor-will, Yellow-breasted Chat, English Sparrow, Towhee, Carolina Wren, Warbling Vireo,

Summer Tanager, Wood Thrush and others, and although its imitations are not as accurate as those of the Mockingbird, or even as those of the Starling, they are easily recognizable.

Often the nest is located near a spring, for the bird is fond of water, or in a thicket or brier-patch at the edge of the woods. The parent birds are very devoted to their young and may even imperil their own lives in defense of their treasures. But they are frequently the victims of the Cowbird and are excellent foster parents for her young.

KEY WEST VIREO

Vireo griseus maynardi BREWSTER.

IDENTIFICATION. — Averaging somewhat paler and less yellow below than *V. g. griseus,* and with a larger bill.
RANGE. — Resident in the Florida Keys.

BERMUDA VIREO

Vireo griseus bermudianus BANGS AND BRADLEE.

IDENTIFICATION. — General coloration grayer, less yellow and olivaceous, than *V. g. griseus.*
RANGE. — Resident in Bermuda.

The Bermuda race of the White-eyed Vireo is an abundant resident of the islands, where it is familiar to everyone. It has earned the local name of 'Chick-of-the-village' from its song, which is also rendered as *chick-choo-willie.* It differs little if any in habits from its continental forms. S. G. Reid, in his 'Birds of Bermuda,' mentions an enemy of this bird, which the other races do not have to contend with, however. He says: 'It is on record that the newly-fledged young of this species have been found entangled in the meshes of the web of the "silk" spider, *Epiera clavipes.* These webs are of great size and strength, extending for many feet between adjoining cedars, and the number of them among the woods in summer and autumn is almost incredible.' — (J.B.M.)

BELL'S VIREO

Vireo belli belli AUDUBON.

IDENTIFICATION. — Length 4¾ to 5 inches; spread 7 to 8 inches. Similar to White-eyed Vireo, but smaller; crown and nape grayish-brown; line above eye yellowish and broken or imperfect; iris dark; one or two pale wing-bars; more yellow below.
BREEDING. — See White-eyed Vireo.
RANGE. — Breeds from northeastern Colorado, southern South Dakota, northern Illinois, and northwestern Indiana to eastern Texas, and northeastern Mexico; winters from Mexico to northern Nicaragua.

The home of Bell's Vireo is the prairie regions of the West. It is similar to the White-eyed Vireo in habits but even more addicted to thickets and brier-patches. Its song is similarly emphatic but more 'sputtering' and wren-like.

Mrs. M. M. Nice in her 'Birds of Oklahoma' says: 'There is no music in the Bell's Vireo refrain, but it possesses a quaint charm in its air of enthusiasm, in the rapid jumble of it all. It may be phrased *whillowhee, whillowhee, whee;* sometimes there are three *whillowhees.* Either song may end with a rising or falling inflection. When the bird is thoroughly in the mood, his rate is a song every three seconds, but this rapid pace is seldom kept up as long as a minute, fifteen, sixteen and seventeen songs a minute being the highest numbers I have recorded, while eight to twelve are more commonly heard. . . . These birds seem to sing all day long and all summer long, although in August their zeal diminishes; the last songs are heard from the thirteenth to the twenty-first of September. . . . Although not strikingly colored, nor blessed with a fine voice, this little bird will win a secure place in the affections of anyone who comes to know him well.' — (J.B.M.)

YELLOW–THROATED VIREO

Vireo flavifrons VIEILLOT.   PLATE 79.

IDENTIFICATION. — Length 5 to 6 inches; spread 9½ to 10 inches. Olive-green above, with bright yellow breast and throat, yellow line around eye, and white wing-bars; the only vireo with *bright* yellow breast.

SONG. — A series of short phrases, lower in pitch than Red-eye and more musical.

BREEDING. — Similar to other vireos but eggs rather heavily marked.

RANGE. — Breeds from east-central Saskatchewan, southern Manitoba, southeastern Ontario, southwestern Quebec, and Maine south to central Texas, central Louisiana, central Alabama, and northern Florida; winters from Yucatan to Venezuela.

The Yellow-throated Vireo is a summer bird. Most individuals of the species arrive in the northern United States after the middle of May and leave for the South in late August or early September. Very early and very late birds are mere stragglers. They are here mainly while the woods are in full leaf, keep usually in the tops of the larger trees and might be overlooked but for their loud, rich, distinctive song, coming as it does, not only from the woods, but from shade trees, orchards and gardens near our dwellings; for although this vireo is normally a forest bird, it has learned to trust the New England folk, so that it seeks rather than shuns their neighborhood. If it fails to bring up a brood, however, it is likely to leave the neighborhood, and thus it sometimes disappears from a locality, changing its place of residence in a quest, perhaps, for safer quarters. It is a favorite, and in this region is so confiding that it often hangs its nest from a low limb of an apple tree near some farmhouse. The nest is one of the most beautiful pieces of bird architecture to be found in this region. Gracefully shaped and lightly covered with tree lichens, it vies with the nests of the Ruby-throated Hummingbird and the Wood Pewee, though not so neatly lined as either of these. Nest building occupies the mated pair for about a week.

Like all our vireos the male is a good father, taking on his share of the home duties, and he often sings while on the nest. Like other vireos also, the sitting bird will sometimes stay

403

on the nest (especially when the eggs are about to hatch) until one can almost place a hand upon its back. I watched one (apparently the male) that would actually allow a person to place the tips of the fingers upon his back before he would leave the nest. When the camera was mounted a few feet away and two persons and two dogs were on the ground immediately beneath the nest, this bird remained calmly sitting there.

When the single brood has been raised the parents take them to the berry pastures, and they pass the molting season amid the fruiting thickets and are ready for their long southward journey by September, if not before.

BLUE–HEADED VIREO

Vireo solitarius solitarius (WILSON). PLATE 79.

Other name: Solitary Vireo.

IDENTIFICATION. — Length 5 to 6 inches; spread 8½ to 9¾ inches. A rather dark-colored vireo, with slaty-gray head, white eye-ring, and white wing-bars.

SONG. — Similar to Red-eye but more deliberate, higher in pitch, and clearer.

BREEDING. — Similar to other vireos but nest often lined with pine needles.

RANGE. — Breeds from southern Mackenzie, northern Ontario, southern Quebec, and Cape Breton Island south to central Alberta, central Minnesota, Michigan, the mountains of southern Pennsylvania, and Rhode Island; winters in the Gulf States from Texas to Florida and from eastern Mexico to northern Nicaragua.

As I have written in the 'Nature Lovers' Library': 'He whose ears are attuned to the harmonies of nature may find the Blue-headed or Solitary Vireo on warm April days or in early May in the wooded regions of most of the Northeastern States. It may be recognized by its bluish head, the white ring around the eye, and the pure white throat. It heralds its presence at this time by its wild sweet song, a charming cadence of the wooded wilderness. Its notes seem more spiritual and less commonplace than those of the familiar vireos of village and farmstead.'

Bradford Torrey says: 'In form its music resembles the Red-eye's, the Philadelphia's, and the Yellow-throat's; but to me it is more varied and beautiful than any of these, though some listeners may prefer the Yellow-throat for the richness and fullness of its 'organ tone.' The Solitary's song is matchless for the tenderness of its cadence, while in peculiarly happy moments the bird indulges in a continuous warble that is really enchanting.'

On August 19, 1907, in Concord, Massachusetts, I watched a Blue-headed Vireo sing beautifully in a subdued tone — almost a 'whisper song.' The bird apparently was molting, but still it sang. The song resembled in some respects the subdued autumnal music of the Catbird. It was interspersed with a very soft chattering like that of the Ruby-crowned Kinglet. The bird meanwhile searched about in a leisurely manner, scanning the under sides of the leaves, from which it took hairy caterpillars, eating a part of each and discarding the rest.

This is a bird of the white pine woods. On lowland or highland, mountain, valley or plain, it seeks the shade of columnar, sighing pines. It rarely breeds except amid its favorite pines or near them, though its nest is sometimes hung on a birch or even on an apple tree near the woods. Although this vireo has the reputation of a recluse, and usually retires to the woods to breed, it is by no means solitary, as one of its common names implies, nor is it shy as a rule, though some individuals are more so than most. Usually the incubating or brooding bird may be closely approached, whether male or female, and some have even allowed a visitor to touch them.

The male bird is an attentive husband and father. He assists in building the nest, though often he only brings the material and sometimes very little of that, but he assists in incubation, in brooding and in the care of the young, and guards the nest jealously; like other vireos he frequently sings while on the nest. Thus one or the other of the parents usually may be found on or near the nest. When incubating one remains on the nest until the other returns and does not leave it unless its mate is ready to step in. Both parents are devoted to their young.

The food of this bird consists largely of destructive bugs, beetles and caterpillars; sawflies, ants, two-winged flies, dragonflies, grasshoppers, crickets and spiders are taken in much smaller numbers.

MOUNTAIN VIREO

Vireo solitarius alticola BREWSTER.

IDENTIFICATION. — Similar to *V. s. solitarius* but back generally with more or less slaty blue, and bill much larger.

RANGE. — Breeds in the Canadian and Transition zones of the Alleghenies from western Maryland to eastern Tennessee and northern Georgia; winters in the lowlands from South Carolina to Florida.

BLACK–WHISKERED VIREO

Vireo calidris barbatulus (CABANIS).

IDENTIFICATION. — Length about 6 inches; spread about 10 inches. Similar to Red-eyed Vireo but bill larger; *a short narrow stripe of sooty-drab on each side of throat;* iris cherry-red or wine color.

BREEDING. — In mangroves often over water; otherwise like other vireos.

RANGE. — Breeds on west coast of Florida from Anclote Keys south to Key West, Dry Tortugas, Cuba, Haiti, Little Cayman, and the Bahamas; winters in Colombia.

The Black-whiskered Vireo is a denizen of the mangrove islands of the Bay of Florida and similar regions in western and southern Florida. It resembles the Red-eyed Vireo in appearance and habits, with the change from northern woodlands to southern mangrove swamps taken into consideration.

Its song, according to A. H. Howell, 'resembles that of the Red-eye rather closely, but is shorter, less smooth flowing, and distinguished by the recurrence of two rather abrupt phrases, suggesting a trill.' — (J.B.M.)

RED–EYED VIREO

Vireo olivaceus (LINNAEUS).

PLATE 79.

Other names: Red-eyed Greenlet; Preacher.

IDENTIFICATION. — Length 5½ to 6½ inches; spread 9¾ to 10¾ inches. Olive-green above, gray crown, and *black-bordered white line over eye*, white under parts, no wing-bars, red iris seldom visible in the field.

SONG. — A monotonous series of short phrases, suggesting the name *vireo* with varying inflections and emphasis — *vireéo, vireó, veério*, etc.

BREEDING. — Normally in woods of mixed growths, often in orchard or shade trees. *Nest and eggs:* Similar to other vireos.

RANGE. — Breeds from central British Columbia, central Manitoba, central Ontario, Anticosti Island, and Cape Breton Island south to northern Oregon, eastern Wyoming, western Texas, southern Alabama, and central Florida; winters in Colombia and Venezuela south to Ecuador and southern Brazil; migrates through eastern Mexico and Central America.

Throughout the long hot summer days the Red-eyed Vireo sings. He begins with the Robin at early dawn, but in time the Robin tires. Not so the Red-eye. His singing is a part of the game. He sings as a matter of course, with little apparent exertion, almost unconsciously, thus expending his pent-up energy in a most pleasing and cheerful manner. He uses short phrases intermittently, but continually, from morn till night unless interrupted, and he sings much of the time from spring to autumn. The song is so continuous, so much like the Robin's in quality, and harmonizes so well with the murmur of the breeze among the trees, and the bird is so well hidden by the leaves, that it is commonly passed, unnoticed, by the uninterested observer, though it is one of **our** most common birds, and its song may be heard during the summer more often than that of any other.

Wilson Flagg named it the 'Preacher,' because of its elocutionary powers and continuous discourse, with short pauses, as if to give the listener time to reflect. He seemed to hear it say: 'You see it — you know it — do you hear me? Do you believe it?' and these words really give some idea of the *tempo* and style of the bird's 'preaching,' if we remember that each phrase is given with a rising inflection at the end. Let no one imagine, however, that our bird sits and prates in idleness. My attention was first drawn to the food of birds and their usefulness to agriculture and forestry when, in my early boyhood, I watched a Red-eyed Vireo singing in a swampy thicket. I recorded the incident in the following words: 'He sang a few notes, his head turning meanwhile from side to side, his eyes scanning closely the near-by foliage. Suddenly the song ceased; he leaned forward, sprang to another twig, snatched a green caterpillar from the under side of a leaf, swallowed it, and resumed the song. Every important pause in his dissertation signalized the capture of a larva. As the discourse was punctuated, a worm was punctured.' The seeming carelessness and idleness of the bird are deceptive. Deliberately and carefully he scans leaf and twig, searching out protectively colored insects which some other bird might pass unnoticed, but never he. It is astonishing to see him detect and capture caterpillar after caterpillar where the human eye fails to discern them. Caterpillar hunting, not singing, is his serious business. Rarely some flying insect tempts him to leave his perch, and he launches forth and captures the fleeing creature with all the address of a flycatcher.

Now and then the Red-eyed Vireo utters a peculiar song resembling that of some other bird.

I have record of one that added to its own song notes similar to those of the White-eyed Vireo, and of another that sang in September a very faint imitation of the song of the Catbird. In singing the bird keeps mainly to the upper part of trees, but sometimes descends to the shrubbery.

This is by all odds our most common vireo of the woodlands. As farms and villages have taken the place of primeval forests, however, the bird has adapted itself to the new conditions, until it has become common wherever trees grow, even in cities. It was a common bird in Boston streets in my boyhood days, before the English Sparrow came.

The Red-eyed Vireo is not likely to become common in the latitude of southern New England until after the middle of May. The males arrive first, some few very early in the month. Courtship begins as soon as the females arrive, but I have observed no unusual antics, although the males exert themselves to please the females with song and attention. There is much chattering and fluttering about in pursuit of prospective mates. The male is a good husband and father, not infrequently assisting in nest building, commonly relieving the female on the nest, singing quite constantly while attending to the duties of incubation, and when the young arrive, bringing at least his share of the food, and often the larger part.

The nest is a neat and handsome little basket and very durable. Like that of the other vireos, it is a shallow cup suspended from a horizontal crotch. It is constructed of strong but pliable vegetable fibers, lined with finer fibers, and decorated on the outside with lichens, bits of birch bark, scraps of hornets' nests, or shreds of old newspaper. The three or four eggs are white with a few tiny brown spots ringing the larger end, typical of the family. Nest building ordinarily requires about a week, but if storms intervene, or if the birds must go a long distance to secure the material, or if the summer days are unusually hot, more time may be required. When much exposed to a hot sun in securing material for their nest, the birds may work only during the cooler part of the day. In the heated hours they prefer the woodland shades. If the nest building is too long delayed the female may be compelled to deposit her eggs and begin incubation before the nest is completed. Then the male attends her gallantly, bringing nesting material which she arranges and weaves in place as she sets upon the eggs. Deposition of the eggs before the nest is finished is not uncommon among birds, but not every male bird will assist the female in such an instance.

Among the chief enemies of the vireos we must reckon the Blue Jay and the Cowbird. The Cowbird sometimes deposits several eggs in the nest of the Red-eyed Vireo, and where Cowbirds are plentiful the first brood often consists of one or more Cowbirds, so that if they are to raise any young of their own, they must nest again late in the season.

When the eggs are hatched, the parents are very attentive in their care, whether the young are Cowbirds or their own offspring. During a tempest, accompanied by torrential rains, a male Red-eyed Vireo was seen to join his mate on the nest, and there the devoted pair sat side by side in that driving, tempestuous downpour, sheltering the tender young beneath their wings.

When the young are able to fly well, and when in late summer the berries in pastures and swamps are ripening, the whole family resorts to these localities, and early in September the migration south begins.

PHILADELPHIA VIREO

Vireo philadelphicus (CASSIN).

PLATE 79.

Other name: Brotherly-love Vireo.

IDENTIFICATION. — Length 4½ to 5 inches; spread 8 to 9 inches. Smaller than Red-eyed Vireo; head less distinctly striped; yellowish below; no wing-bars.

BREEDING. — In sparsely wooded country, and second-growth woods.

RANGE. — Breeds from northern and central Alberta, southern Manitoba, northern Ontario, New Brunswick, and Maine south to northern North Dakota, northern Michigan, and New Hampshire; winters from Yucatan and Guatemala to Panama.

Probably the trim little Philadelphia Vireo in not so rare a bird in the Northeast as it is believed to be, but it is seldom seen south of Canada except in migration, when it is not usually in song. Its song is so like that of the Red-eyed Vireo that no one not familiar with the songs of both species would question it, and amid the leaves the bird easily escapes notice. Even if seen, its colors and movements are so like those of the Warbling Vireo that it is likely to be mistaken for that bird. As Bradford Torrey says, 'It looks like one vireo and sings like another.' It may occur almost anywhere in migration. I have seen it in the spring of the year three feet from the ground in a bush beside a city street, and from thirty to forty feet above ground in the woods. But probably it is most often seen in shrubbery or among the lower branches of trees, where it is not difficult to observe it. When seen it may be mistaken for a warbler, but not for another of our native vireos if its colors and their arrangement are noted carefully at short range, in good light.

Mr. Ludlow Griscom says of it: 'This species is tame, inactive, and prefers low or medium levels, and a good study of it is not particularly hard to obtain. Such a study simply *must* be obtained, however; identifying this bird on brief glimpses will not do. If really well seen, the uniformly yellow under parts, the whitish line over the eye, and the absence of any dusky stripes on the side of the head are readily observable.' The ordinary observer who goes a-birding chiefly at week-ends and on holidays will not be likely to identify this bird satisfactorily more than three or four times in a lifetime — at least that has been my experience. But in southern Canada, northern Maine or extreme northern New Hampshire, where it breeds, it is not difficult to find.

EASTERN WARBLING VIREO

Vireo gilvus gilvus (VIEILLOT).

PLATE 79.

IDENTIFICATION. — Length 5 to 6 inches; spread 8½ to 9¼ inches. Head indistinctly striped; no wing-bars; under parts whitish.

SONG. — Resembles that of Purple Finch; a long, rather deliberate warble, unlike song of any other vireo.

BREEDING. — Often in shade trees in village streets.

RANGE. — Breeds from Saskatchewan, central Ontario, and Nova Scotia south to northwestern Texas, southern Louisiana, eastern Kentucky, North Carolina, and Virginia, and west to North Dakota; winters south of the United States but place not definitely known.

The Eastern Warbling Vireo is a tree-top bird. Most of its daylight hours are spent in the tops of tall elms or other trees that stand along the streets or roads or in city parks, and there from its retirement in the concealing verdure the male sends forth his tender, soft and liquid strains. He is a remarkably persistent singer. Ralph Hoffmann estimates that the bird sings more than four thousand songs a day during the breeding season.

Dr. Coues with lavish rhetoric characterizes the bird as follows, in his 'Birds of the Colorado Valley': 'Neither disposed to undue familiarity, nor given to overconfidence, these urbane birds move in a quiet circle of their own, in slight contact with less polished members of society, quite apart from the vulgarity of the street and market-place, and always with the easy self-possession that marks the well-bred. We seldom see them, indeed; they are oftener a voice than a visible presence — just a ripple of melody threading its way through the mazes of verdure, now almost absorbed in the sighing of foliage, now flowing released on its grateful mission. Theirs is a tender, gentle strain, with just a touch of sadness, borne on the same breath that wafts us the perfume of April's early blossoms; and these are all the sweeter for the installation of such song. From the poplar that glances both silver and green as its tremulous verdure is stirred — from the grand old halls of the stately, splendid-flowered liriodendron — from the canopied shade-weaving elm, and the redolent depths of magnolia — issues all summer long the same exquisite refrain, while the singers glide through their hermitage unseen. Who would know these *spirituelle* musicians better must be quick to catch a glimpse of a very small sober-colored bird whose tints are those of its leafy home, and whose course in the heart of the trees is as devious as the play of the sunbeam itself.

'The Warbling Vireo is no less agile a bird than his cousin the Red-eye, and equally tireless in the pursuit of his insect prey; both these birds sing as they go, with an unconscious air, as if in a reverie; but the easy and wonderfully skillful modulation of the former's flowing song contrasts to great advantage with the Red-eye's abrupt and somewhat jerky notes. Both are among the most persistent of our musicians; in the Middle States, for example, their notes are heard from the latter part of April until far into September, and at all hours of the day.'

The male bird is a good provider, and a good husband and father. He relieves the female on the nest, feeds her while she is sitting, and like all our vireos sings while taking his turn on the nest, and he assumes his full share of caring for the young.

The feeding habits of the bird are such that it takes principally the insect enemies of shade trees and orchard trees. As it is rather a skillful flycatcher, it takes both crawling and flying insects, among them horse-flies, crane-flies, mosquitoes, caterpillars, plant-lice — which constitute its largest food item — beetles, especially leaf-beetles, and the twelve-spotted cucumber beetle. Few useful insects are taken, and the fruit eaten seems to be chiefly wild, and worthless as human food.

The Eastern Warbling Vireo is regarded by ornithologists generally as a beneficial bird. Says Dr. Elliott Coues: 'But much as we may admire Gilvus in the agreeable sentiment which his song inspires, we owe him a higher and more respectful consideration for the good services he renders us in a very practical way. Inhabiting by choice our parks, lawns and orchards, and even the shade-trees of our busiest streets, rather than the untried depths of the forest, these birds collectively render efficient service by ridding us of unnumbered insects, whose presence is a pest, as well as a continual annoyance to sensitive persons. They take a foremost place among the useful birds for whose good services in this regard we have reason to be grateful, being much more beneficial than the European Sparrows, which we have imported for the same purpose, and against whose insolent aggressions these tender birds should be protected.'

BLACK AND WHITE WARBLER

Mniotilta varia (LINNAEUS).

PLATE 80.

Other names: Black and White Creeping Warbler; Black and White Creeper.

IDENTIFICATION. — Length 4½ to 5½ inches; spread 8¼ to 9 inches. A striped black and white warbler; wide white central stripe through black cap distinguishes it from Blackpoll with solid black cap; female and young similar but duller.

SONG. — A thin, high-pitched *teesee, teesee, teesee, teesee.*

BREEDING. — *Nest:* On ground in mixed woodlands, of grasses, rootlets, leaves, mosses, etc., roofed over, and lined with finer material. *Eggs:* The eggs of all the group of wood warblers follow one general pattern of coloration. The ground color is *light* — white, creamy, pale bluish- or greenish-white. They are more or less spotted with browns, lavender, and lilacs, chiefly around the larger end where they form a 'wreath.'

RANGE. — Breeds from central western Mackenzie, northern Ontario, New Brunswick, Nova Scotia, and Newfoundland to eastern Texas, Louisiana, central Alabama, and northern Georgia, west to South Dakota; winters from Mexico to Venezuela, and in Florida, the Bahamas, and West Indies.

In the last days of April or in early May, when the buds on deciduous trees are swelling and when tiny, light green leaflets appear on the shrubbery, in sheltered sunny spots we may find a little black and white striped bird hopping along the lower limbs in the woodlands, turning this way and that, searching over the branches from one side to the other, often head downward, closely scanning the bark, silently gleaning the insect enemies of the trees. This is the Black and White Warbler. A day or two later we may hear his attenuated wiry song as he industriously searches over his favorite trees for the wherewithal to nourish him and sustain his manifold activities of climbing, flight and song. When with the opening of the leaves his favorite insect food becomes more plentiful, his spirits rise, and occasionally he adds a few more musical notes to his song. When the females arrive there is much agitation, and often a long-continued intermittent pursuit, with much song and fluttering of black and white plumage, and much interference from rival males before the happy pair are united and begin nesting. The nest is on the ground, often at the base of a tree and well hidden, sometimes under roots or a fallen log. The female is the chief builder, and attends to the duties of incubation, but the male assists in caring for the young. When the female, who is a very devoted parent, is surprised on her carefully hidden nest by an intruder, she is likely to attempt to lead him away by pretending to be crippled and by fluttering painfully in his path, using every artifice to induce him to follow her.

When the young in the nest are more than half-grown it is well not to handle or disturb them, as they are then likely to spring out and run away, beating their little wings in a fruitless attempt at flight. The general color of the nestlings is almost exactly the same as that of the forest floor, where they readily hide, and once out of their snug home, they are not likely to return to it.

When the frosts come in September the Black and White Warblers that breed in southern

New England depart for the South, but others continue to come from the North until October nights grow cold.

PROTHONOTARY WARBLER

Protonotaria citrea (BODDAERT).   PLATE 80.

Other name: Golden Swamp Warbler.

IDENTIFICATION. — Length 5¼ to 5½ inches; spread 8½ to 9 inches. A large warbler with rather large bill; head and lower plumage yellow or with orange tinge; back olive-green; wings and tail steel-gray; female duller.

BREEDING. — Usually in wooded, swampy lands. *Nest:* In a hole in a tree or stump, occasionally in a bird-box or about buildings. *Eggs:* 3 to 7, creamy-white, profusely spotted and blotched.

RANGE. — Breeds from northeastern Nebraska, southeastern Minnesota, southern Wisconsin, southern Michigan, Ohio, central Delaware, and eastern Maryland to eastern Texas, southern Alabama, and northern Florida; winters from southern Mexico to Venezuela; migrates across the Gulf of Mexico.

The Prothonotary Warbler is normally a bird of swamps or overflowed lands, and in the North willows growing in or near water seem to attract it. In full sunlight it is a remarkably beautiful bird. Its brilliant breast seems to glow like a torch when seen against the dark background of the swamp.

In courtship the male makes a wonderful display, swelling and partially erecting his plumage and spreading his wings and tail. At this season he is very irascible and there are frequent combats between two males, during which both of the combatants sometimes fall into the water.

This is the only warbler in North America that is known to nest habitually in holes in trees. The male apparently renders some assistance to the female by bringing nesting material, and he joins her in feeding the young, but the female usually does most of the nest-building.

Mr. P. A. Taverner tells of a pair that chose a very unusual situation for their nest. They utilized a letter box on the front of a piazza of a house situated in a busy city street and close to traffic. First the female (apparently) came into the house at the back door and was let out at the front. Three days later a nest partly built was found in the letter box and thrown out, but the nest-building continued; again the nest was thrown out and later replaced by the residents, and the birds were allowed to raise young in the box.

When the young of the second brood have become strong on the wing, the birds of this species breeding in the Middle and South Atlantic States start southward. Apparently, according to Dr. Frank M. Chapman, they fly then to northwest Florida and from there go straight out to sea, flying seven hundred miles across the Gulf of Mexico to southern Yucatan, instead of following down the peninsula of Florida and then passing over Cuba on their way, as a human flier naturally would do, as a matter of precaution. Doubtless many lose their lives in the crossing.

SWAINSON'S WARBLER

Limnothlypis swainsoni (AUDUBON).   PLATE 94.

IDENTIFICATION. — Length about 6 inches; spread about 9 inches. Resembles Worm-eating Warbler but has whitish line over eye and lacks blackish lines on head; olive-brown above and dingy white below, with cinnamon-brown crown.

BREEDING. — In or near canebrakes. Nest in bushes, canes, etc., 3 to 10 feet up.

RANGE. — Breeds from northeastern Oklahoma, southeastern Missouri, southern Illinois, southern Indiana, and southeastern Virginia south to Louisiana and northern Florida; winters in Jamaica and southern Yucatan; migrates through Cuba and the Bahamas.

This secretive and little known warbler has an interesting history. It was first discovered by the Rev. John Bachman in 1832, near Charleston, South Carolina, and was described by Audubon from a specimen sent him by Dr. Bachman. Only four more specimens were collected until 1878, when it was studied in Alabama. In 1884 William Brewster and Arthur T. Wayne made a more detailed study of the bird, and much of our present knowledge of its habits is based on their observations, for comparatively few ornithologists have ever seen this species in its native haunts.

Swainson's Warbler is a denizen of swamps and river bottoms of the Southern States. William Brewster described its haunts clearly when he wrote, 'Briefly, four things seem indispensable to his existence, viz., water, tangled thickets, patches of cane, and a rank growth of semi-aquatic plants.' It is almost invariably associated in the breeding season with the tall cane, *Arundinaria tecta*, which makes such impassable thickets of great areas of the swamplands which compose so much of the low country from the Carolinas to Louisiana. This difficult and inhospitable terrain, together with the inconspicuous colors of the bird and the ventriloquial quality of its song, have combined to keep Swainson's Warbler a much-sought but seldom-found species. When not singing the bird spends most of its time on the ground searching among the dead leaves and other débris for its food, which is probably almost entirely insectivorous, walking about with a graceful gliding motion. Brewster calls it 'a rarely fervent and ecstatic songster ... also a fitful and uncertain one.' — (J.B.M.)

WORM–EATING WARBLER

Helmitheros vermivorus (GMELIN).   PLATE 80.

Other name: Forest Chippy.

IDENTIFICATION. — Length 5 to 5¾ inches; spread 8 to 8¾ inches. A very plain olive-green warbler without wing-bars or other markings except four black stripes on buffy head; under parts buffy.

SONG. — Much like that of Chipping Sparrow.

BREEDING. — In dense undergrowth of damp woods. Nest on ground.

RANGE. — Breeds from southern Iowa, northern Illinois, western New York, southern Pennsylvania, and the Hudson and Connecticut valleys south to southern Missouri, northern Alabama, northern Georgia, Tennessee, Virginia, and the mountains of South Carolina; winters from Mexico to Panama, in Cuba and the Bahamas, rarely in Florida.

This modest and rather shy and secretive bird may be quickly recognized, whenever plainly seen, by its well-marked, striped head and large bill. In the North it frequents wooded hill-sides. 'In such a country,' says Ludlow Griscom, speaking of the New York City region, 'a Chipping Sparrow song almost certainly can be traced to this species. A practiced ear can distinguish the two songs, however, the sparrow having a "rattle" in its effort, rather than the "buzz" of the warbler.'

Often the Worm-eating Warbler may be seen on the ground, walking about rather slowly, bobbing its head as it steps, and habitually carrying its tail quite high. When in the trees, which it sometimes ascends to a considerable height, it may be seen at times searching about the trunk and branches, much in the manner of a Black and White Warbler. It feeds largely in low, damp, bushy places where it can easily avoid observation, and as it is very inconspicuous it escapes the notice of the ordinary observer. Its nest is built on the ground, most often near a stream or swamp.

GOLDEN–WINGED WARBLER

Vermivora chrysoptera (LINNAEUS). PLATE 81.

IDENTIFICATION. — Length 5 to 5¼ inches; spread 7¾ to 8¼ inches. Adult male gray or bluish-gray above with bright yellow patch on forehead and crown and on wing coverts; throat black, black patch from bill through and below eye; below whitish; female duller, gray replacing black on head and throat.

BREEDING. — See below.

RANGE. — Breeds from central Minnesota, southeastern Ontario, and Massachusetts south to southern Iowa, northern Illinois, northern Indiana, northern New Jersey, and in the mountains to northern Georgia; winters from Guatemala to Venezuela; very rare in Florida and southern Georgia, crossing the Gulf of Mexico in migration.

The Golden-winged Warbler is a beautiful and graceful little bird that nests on the ground or very near it, but often may be seen in tall tree-tops. It is a red-letter day when one sees one of these bright wood sprites for the first time. I remember well my first specimen as I saw it creeping out to the end of a nearly horizontal limb of a tall tree. I had never been able to find one in the shrubbery that they usually inhabit, and here was the bird in a tree, where I had never expected to see one. Mr. H. O. Green sent me this account of its breeding habits in Massachusetts:

'The Golden-winged Warbler arrives about the second week in May, but nest-building is seldom commenced until after the middle of the month. For their summer home these birds prefer the border of deciduous woods, where tall trees give plenty of shade, to an adjacent clearing with a growth of briers, bushes and grass, and the nest is usually placed just outside the line of the forest proper, but within the shade of the trees. A meadow wholly surrounded by woods is frequently selected. The ideal place to search for a nest of the species is in one of those woodland meadows, which has a clear brook flowing through it, with briers, tussocks of grass and a fresh growth of goldenrod scattered around in profusion, with birch trees and wild grapevines growing near the edges where the meadow meets higher and drier ground, — and all this bordered by tall oak, chestnut and maple trees which furnish an abundance of shade to the vegetation of the meadow itself.

'In such a place during the latter part of May and the earlier days of June will your ear be most likely to catch the notes of this warbler's song, a simple *zee, zee, zee, zee*, or sometimes this is shortened to *zee, zee, zee*, — in either case the first note being slightly longer than those which follow. Once the note is heard and recognized it is generally easy to locate the singing male bird, and the chances are that he will soon be discovered on some near-by tree, exploring the tips of the branches searching for food, and occasionally stopping on some twig, standing quite erect, and giving forth his little song, — and frequently he will perch in one place long enough to repeat the song several times before going on his way.

'If the date is not earlier than May 20th nor later than June 15th you may reasonably expect that somewhere on the ground in the immediate vicinity there is a nest of the species, for these birds do not ordinarily wander far from their home during the breeding season.

'The site chosen for the nest varies somewhat, but is generally where it will be in the shade most of the day. The nest is always placed either on the ground, or just slightly above it, and is almost invariably built where a fairly firm support to the sides is supplied by the surrounding vegetation, and frequently the nest is well hidden from view.

'When clusters of fresh goldenrod stems are easily available the Golden-wings seem to prefer this plant to all others in which to place their homes. At the time the nest is built it is frequently possible to see it from a distance of several feet, although from even a short distance it looks simply like a bunch of very dark colored leaves, and in wet weather the leaves look nearly black. But by the time the full clutch of eggs has been laid, the goldenrod has sometimes grown so dense that it is impossible to see the nest without carefully separating the stems of the plant and looking down between them, for the nest is usually down in the center of the cluster.

'The nest of the Golden-wing usually has a bottom layer of coarse dead leaves on which is placed a ring of large dry leaves, arranged with the points of the leaves downward, so that the leaf stems stick up noticeably around the edges of the nest proper, which is built within and upon this circular mass of leaves, and is made of rather wide strips of coarse grass or rushes, and usually has considerable grapevine bark interwoven in it. The nest lining is coarse and rough, sometimes the eggs being laid on the rough grapevine bark, and in some nests other coarse fibers are used. A very characteristic feature of the nest lining is fine shreds of light reddish-brown vegetable fiber, which at first glance might easily be mistaken for dry needles from the pitch pine, — but careful examination shows it to be the inner layers of the bark from the grapevines. The nest is very bulky for the size of the bird and is rather loosely put together by crossing the materials diagonally, so that it slightly resembles a rather coarse basket-work. I never saw a nest of this species which had a soft lining, such as many other warblers use, — the eggs are apparently always deposited on rough material.'

In feeding, the actions of the Golden-winged Warbler often more resemble those of a titmouse than the ordinary fluttering activity of a warbler. It searches and peers about around twigs and branches, often hanging back downward at the end of a limb and performing many acrobatic feats.

Soon after mating occurs, the nest is hurriedly put together, within two or three days in favorable weather, though should a long storm intervene it may be abandoned and a new one started in another situation. Often the nest seems unfinished, lacking a completed lining and having ragged edges, but it is home to the little female, who lays an egg daily until the set is complete.

When the eggs have been laid the female begins at once to incubate. While she is thus engaged the male passes from tree-top to tree-top, where with upraised head he gives forth what she doubtless regards as a fine musical effort. In about ten days after hatching the young birds are ready to leave the nest.

BLUE–WINGED WARBLER

Vermivora pinus (LINNAEUS). PLATE 81.

Other name: Blue-winged Yellow Warbler.

IDENTIFICATION. — Length 4½ to 5 inches; spread 6¾ to 7½ inches. Adult male has top and fore part of head, and lower plumage (except under tail coverts), yellow; back olive-green; wings and tail chiefly bluish-gray, two white or yellowish wing-bars; black stripe through eye narrowing behind; female similar but duller.

BREEDING. — Similar to Golden-winged Warbler.

RANGE. — Breeds from southeastern Minnesota, southern Michigan, western New York, southern Massachusetts, and Rhode Island to northeastern Kansas, central Missouri, northern Alabama, northern Georgia, Maryland and Delaware; winters from southern Mexico to Guatemala; migrates across Gulf of Mexico and is very rare in southeastern United States south of Virginia.

The Blue-winged Warbler is a shy, retiring species, which commonly keeps near the ground and under cover, and its so-called song is so much like that of a grasshopper or a Grasshopper Sparrow that the bird usually escapes notice.

It frequents low shrubbery, brier patches, bushy fields, neglected pastures, thickets in or near the edges of woodlands, and the edges of open fields near such situations, often on the drier lands, but also on low, swampy or moist lands near swamps and streams, in rank growths of bushes and weeds, and in ravines with running water. It is chiefly a ground warbler, but it visits orchards and gardens when the apple trees and pear trees are in bloom. I have not seen it more than fifteen feet from the ground in a tree, but when the male is in full song on his breeding-grounds he frequently takes a higher position in a good-sized tree. He flies occasionally from one tree to another, now and then going a considerable distance, but usually keeping within about one hundred and fifty feet of the nest. The female is a close sitter and will almost allow the searcher to touch her before she will desert her charge. When the female is surprised on her nest she usually slips quietly away without any attempt to deceive the intruder and lure him away from her treasures.

The young remain in the nest eight or ten days and then leave it, never to return, although for a time, until their wings grow strong, they remain in the immediate vicinity.

Little is known definitely of the food of this species. Small insects, such as caterpillars and other larvae, beetles, ants and spiders are taken, and doubtless many others.

LAWRENCE'S WARBLER

Vermivora lawrencei HERRICK

PLATE 81.

BREWSTER'S WARBLER

Vermivora leucobronchialis BREWSTER.

PLATE 81.

These two birds, which are illustrated in Plate 81, are now known to be merely hybrids of the two preceding species, the Blue-winged and Golden-winged Warblers, and as a result are no longer listed in the 'Check-List' of the American Ornithologists' Union.

There is a detailed description, by Mr. Maurice Broun, of the long controversy over these confusing hybrids, in Mr. Forbush's 'Birds of Massachusetts and other New England States,' to which any interested reader is referred. — (J.B.M.)

BACHMAN'S WARBLER

Vermivora bachmani (AUDUBON).

PLATE 94.

IDENTIFICATION. — Length 4¼ to 4½ inches; spread about 7 inches. A small warbler with *yellow face* (forehead, eye-ring and chin), and yellow belly; crown gray with fore part spotted with black; black patch on breast; back olive; no wing-bars; female similar but lacks black on crown and breast.

BREEDING. — See below.

RANGE. — Breeds in southeastern Missouri, northeastern Arkansas, western Kentucky, northern Alabama, and near Charleston, South Carolina, and probably in southern Indiana and eastern North Carolina; winters in Cuba; migrates across Gulf States from Louisiana to Florida.

The history of this bird is much like that of Swainson's Warbler. It was discovered near Charleston, South Carolina, in 1833, a year later than Swainson's Warbler, also by Dr. John Bachman, and was named for him by Audubon. Then for about fifty years it remained unknown except for a few specimens of migrating birds, and it was not until 1897 that the first nest was found, in Missouri.

Bachman's Warbler is a resident of the deep-shaded cypress swamps and of the river bottoms with their heavy growth of hardwood trees, in a limited area across the Southeastern States from South Carolina to Missouri. In parts of its range it is quite common, though it is easily overlooked. In the cypress swamps it haunts the highest branches, and its small size and quiet ways, and the fact that its song is very much like that of the Worm-eating Warbler or the Chipping Sparrow, prevent its being as well known as many of its congeners. The nest, however, is usually built in low bushes one to three feet from the ground, of fine grasses, leaves, etc.

During migration Bachman's Warbler apparently crosses the Florida peninsula in some numbers, being fairly common both in the Suwannee River region and on the Keys, and it winters in Cuba. — (J.B.M.)

TENNESSEE WARBLER

Vermivora peregrina (WILSON). PLATE 81.

Other name: Swamp Warbler.
IDENTIFICATION. — Length 4½ to 5 inches; spread 7½ to 8¼ inches. Adult male a plain colored warbler, distinguished by gray crown, white stripe over eye (resembling Philadelphia Vireo but with more slender bill); in autumn resembles Orange-crowned and Nashville Warblers but has no eye-ring and under tail coverts are white.
BREEDING. — Usually in boggy lands, sometimes in bushy clearings. *Nest:* On ground, often arched over.
RANGE. — Breeds from the upper Yukon Valley, northern Manitoba, central Quebec, and Anticosti Island south to southern British Columbia, southern Manitoba, northern Minnesota, northern Michigan, Ontario, New York, New Hampshire, and northern Maine; winters from Mexico to Venezuela; migrates chiefly through Mississippi Valley and rare in spring on the Atlantic slope.

The Tennessee Warbler is a very unassuming little bird, with no bright colors or showy spots and no very conspicuous markings. I have found it mostly in damp, somewhat swampy woodlands, but in migration it goes wherever there are trees, in yards, orchards, cemeteries, parks, villages and the suburbs of cities. In spring it may be identified readily by its loud, noticeable and unmistakable song, which is no more musical than that of the Chipping Sparrow. It begins in a rather slow and hesitating manner and ends in a rapid succession of *chips*, like those of the Chipping Sparrow.

Its habits are similar to those of the Nashville Warbler. It is an active insect hunter, feeding on grasshoppers, locusts, caterpillars, grubs, beetles, including weevils, flies, plant-lice, spiders, etc., the eggs of insects and a certain proportion of fruit.

ORANGE–CROWNED WARBLER

Vermivora celata celata (SAY). PLATE 81.

IDENTIFICATION. — Length 4½ to 5¼ inches; spread 7 to 8¼ inches. A very plain bird lacking any conspicuous markings; orange crown usually hidden; distinguished from Nashville Warbler by greenish-yellow under parts with faint dusky streaks.
BREEDING. — In thickets and undergrowth. *Nest:* On ground, or in low bushes.
RANGE. — Breeds from Kowak River, Alaska, southeast to northern Manitoba; winters in the Gulf and South Atlantic States north to South Carolina, casually to Ohio and Massachusetts, also on Pacific coast from southern California south to central Mexico; migrates mainly through Mississippi Valley and rare on Atlantic slope.

The plainly colored and unobtrusive Orange-crowned Warbler has a very misleading name, for the feathers on the top of its head, which gave it its name, are not a true orange but are tawny, and at their base only, so that the 'crown' is hidden from view unless the greenish tips of the feathers are separated. Possibly this concealed patch of color is displayed by the males during their courtship or perhaps when disputing a nesting territory with other males, like the somewhat similarly hidden but much more brilliant crest of the Ruby-crowned Kinglet, but ordinarily it is invisible in the field. On one occasion I was watching an Orange-crowned Warbler, a rare migrant near my home in eastern Massachusetts, when another rare visitor, an Acadian Chickadee, lit in the cedar tree within a few inches of the warbler. All three of us were mutually surprised, and for just a second I caught a glimpse of the reddish crown of the warbler, before the titmouse departed in haste. Apparently the flash of color either marked fright on the part of the warbler, or was used in an attempt at intimidation.

The principal migration route of this species from its summer home in the far north to its winter residence in the Southern States is through the Mississippi Valley, and the bird, while fairly common in Florida in winter, is rare on the Atlantic coast north of South Carolina. Occasionally a bird appears in autumn in New England and lingers late after all the other warblers except the hardy Myrtle Warbler have departed for a warmer climate, but it is almost unknown in that region in the spring. In Florida it may be looked for among the live-oaks and water oaks, and in the thickets of dense bushes, where it hunts assiduously for its tiny insect prey. In the North it must eat berries at times. Its call-note is a sharp chip, easily recognized after it is once learned. — (J.B.M.)

NASHVILLE WARBLER

Vermivora ruficapilla ruficapilla (WILSON).

PLATE 81.

IDENTIFICATION. — Length 4½ to 5 inches; spread 7¼ to 7¾ inches. Back olive-brown; head ashy-gray with veiled reddish crown-patch and white eye-ring; lower plumage chiefly unstreaked bright yellow; female and young duller, eye-ring buffy.

SONG. — *Wee'-see-wee'-see, wit'-a-wit'-a-wit'*.

BREEDING. — In moist woods, old bush-grown pastures, and swampy thickets. *Nest:* Sunken in ground and well concealed.

RANGE. — Breeds from central Saskatchewan, central Ontario, southern Quebec, and Cape Breton Island south to Nebraska, northern Illinois, northern Pennsylvania, northern New Jersey, and Connecticut; winters from central Mexico to Guatemala and casually in Florida and southern Texas; migrates across Gulf of Mexico and is rare on Atlantic slope south of Chesapeake Bay.

This beautiful, bright and sprightly little bird was named the Nashville Warbler by Alexander Wilson, who first discovered it in 1808 near Nashville, Tennessee. How inappropriate is the name when we realize that the bird is not known to breed in Tennessee. Its specific name *ruficapilla* or 'red-haired' is much more fitting.

Wilson found the bird very rare in the Southeastern States, where it always has been rare, because when it leaves its northern breeding-grounds for its southern journey, it follows down the western side of the Alleghenies, and then turns toward Mexico, returning by the same route in spring.

This bird rarely arrives in the northeast until the first week in May, and its principal numbers come later in the month. In migration it may be found at times in places where trees and bushes grow. Among its favorite haunts are the bushy edges of woodlands, whether along roads, railroads or streams, or about ponds, lakes, marshes, swamps or open fields. It may often be found among willows, alders, birches or poplars. Old neglected fields and pastures, with scattered growths of birches and bushes, are favorite feeding-grounds, but the bird also visits orchards, gardens and shade trees, even in city parks. It may be found on dry lands where scattered pitch pines grow, and on moist lands with rank shrubbery.

Soon after arrival the males are in full song, a simple ditty which some have likened to the songs of the Yellow Warbler and the Chestnut-sided Warbler, but I have never traced to the Nashville Warbler any song which to my ear resembled that of either of the former birds.

The birds are very active. For about two weeks they are common and then most of them pass northward, leaving comparatively few of them to mate and nest in extreme southern New England, where they are common only locally in the breeding season. June is the principal nesting-time, and the female is the principal nest builder. The nest is on the ground, in clearings or bush-grown pastures, and it is usually so well concealed and the female sits so closely that it is only by watching the female carrying building material or by quietly sitting down until she goes to the nest, that it is ever found, unless one chances upon it suddenly in such a way as to drive the sitting bird off.

While the female is incubating, the male occupies a large part of his time in singing from near-by tree-tops, though in one case he was seen to feed his mate on her nest. Both parents feed the young, which are ready to fly in about ten or eleven days. As soon as they can fly well the whole family, keeping together, explores the ground, the grass, weeds and shrubbery, and when in August all have molted, the southward migration begins. They join with small bands of other warblers and all follow the retreating sun southward.

NORTHERN PARULA WARBLER

Compsothlypis americana pusilla (WILSON). PLATE 80.

Other names: Blue Yellow-backed Warbler; Usnea Warbler.

IDENTIFICATION. — Length 4¼ to 5 inches; spread 7 to 7¾ inches. Smallest of eastern warblers; blue above with inconspicuous yellowish saddle; throat and breast yellow crossed by dark band; broad white wing-bars; female duller, washed with greenish above.

SONG. — A buzzing, beady twittering or a sizzling trill, with several variations.

BREEDING. — Most commonly in wooded coniferous swamps. *Nest:* In tree and usually composed of a bunch of hanging *Usnea* moss with entrance on one side.

RANGE. — Breeds from eastern Nebraska, northern Minnesota, central Ontario, Anticosti Island, and Cape Breton Island south to Texas, Louisiana, and Maryland; winters in the Bahamas and West Indies, and from central Mexico to Nicaragua.

The Northern Parula Warbler is the smallest warbler in the East. It seems to be a happy little creature, much given to singing in a characteristic weak, high-pitched, drawly, buzzy voice, which may be heard almost anywhere in our deciduous woods about apple-blossom time or later in May. The singer usually keeps well up in the trees, often near their tops or out at the ends of branches, where, when not engaged in giving his peculiar music to the world, he may be seen climbing, reaching or fluttering among the leaves in pursuit of insect quarry. While the bird is found at times during the migration wherever trees grow, it seems fond of the woods, especially about the shores of lakes and rivers.

When the nesting season comes the Parula Warbler may be found wherever the bearded *Usnea longissima*, which grows largely in low wet land, hangs from the trees. The bird turns up some of the ends of the lichen so that it forms a pocket , and conceals the eggs. The nest appears much like other bunches of moss hanging all about it on the trees. Though it usually shapes its nest from the hanging bunches of *Usnea*, several instances are on record where the nest was built of grass and afterward decorated or covered with *Usnea*. I once discovered a female building a nest saddled on a horizontal branch of an oak tree which overhung a highway near Dartmouth, Massachusetts. The foundation of the nest (nearly completed) was chiefly of grass and the bird had begun bringing *Usnea* from the swamp in an apparent attempt to conceal the nest, but there was very little of this material to be seen in the vicinity.

In the latter part of August when the young have been reared and have grown strong, the leisurely southward migration begins; then these warblers may be seen in company with the ubiquitous Black-poll Warblers, and both may be found among gray birches during fall migration, if the birches, as is often the case, are infested with plant-lice. The food of this warbler is similar to that of other warblers that spend much of their time in the trees. It feeds much on small hairless inch-worms, such as the fall canker-worm and the spring canker-worm, and on the younger and smaller hairy caterpillars, such as the gypsy and the tent caterpillar.

SOUTHERN PARULA WARBLER

Compsothlypis americana americana (LINNAEUS).

IDENTIFICATION. — Similar to *C. A. pusilla* but with less black about the lores; throat of male more yellow, blackish throat band very narrow and poorly defined; females and young indistinguishable.

BREEDING. — 'Spanish moss' (*Tillandsia*) usually takes the place of *Usnea* in nest construction.

RANGE. — Breeds from District of Columbia south to Alabama and Florida; winters in Florida and the Bahamas.

Dr. Frank M. Chapman, in his 'Warblers of North America,' writes of this race: 'About March 1, in northern Florida, when the blossoming cypress, maple and red-bud announce the coming of spring the quaint sizzling trill of the newly arrived Parula Warbler is one of the characteristic bird voices of the season. Possibly among these migrants there may be representatives of the more northern form of this bird, but if the singer's drowsy little lay appeals to you as it does to me you will not stop to inquire the exact shade of his coat but will greet him as the author of one of the most welcome bits of bird music in the Florida spring.

'The abundance of the Spanish "moss" (*Tillandsia*) in which this southern Parula nests is accountable for its being a more common and uniformly distributed bird than the northern Parula. When migrating it is often found feeding amid the blossoms of the cypress, while the quantity of "moss" usually pendant from these water-loving trees makes them a favorite summer home. The Parula also frequents the deciduous "hammocks" but not, so far as I have observed, the pines.' — (J.B.M.)

EASTERN YELLOW WARBLER

Dendroica aestiva aestiva (GMELIN).

PLATE 82.

Other names: Yellow-bird; Summer Yellow-bird; Wild Canary.

IDENTIFICATION. — Length 4¾ to 5¼ inches; spread 7 to 8 inches. Only northeastern warbler chiefly yellow; male streaked with reddish on breast; female and young darker above and paler below, unstreaked breast.

SONG. — *Wêe-che, chee, chee, chêe-wee,* or *weê-chee weê-chee weê.*

BREEDING. — Chiefly about farms and roadsides and near ponds or streams. *Nest:* In bush or low tree, a dainty but firm cup of soft vegetal fibers lined with plant down and finer fibers. *Eggs:* 3 to 5 or 6, grayish- or greenish-white to green, marked with varying shades of browns, purplish, blackish, and grays, all over or mainly around larger end.

RANGE. — Breeds through North America east of Alaska and the Pacific slope from tree-limit south to Nevada, northern New Mexico, southern Missouri, northern Alabama, northern Georgia, and northern South Carolina; winters from Yucatan to Peru, Brazil and Guiana.

The Eastern Yellow Warbler usually comes to us with the apple blossoms. Its coloring is so rich that neither artist nor lithographer can do it full justice, and its song is louder and more melodious than that of many among the warbler tribe. It is a bright and happy creature of the sunshine, shunning deep woodland shades but frequenting gardens and orchards and the trees and shrubbery about open spaces, water courses and bodies of water; it favors brush-grown fences, hedgerows, roadside thickets and open brushy swamps. Habitually it keeps to shrubbery, low trees and the lower parts of larger trees and is rather seldom seen in tall tree-tops. It seems particularly fond of willows and alders that grow near the water, but it nests often in orchards and fruit gardens and in village shade trees.

The male bird is a persistent singer, singing every minute or two throughout most of the day. He is particularly vociferous while paying court to the female and while she is building the nest, a labor in which he sometimes joins his mate. In many cases, however, he seems to leave the nest-building chiefly or wholly to her. In building their nests most warblers use the bill, throat, wings and tail to smooth down the edges, meanwhile sitting in the nest and turning around from side to side arranging the lining behind with the feet and smoothing it in front with the breast, thus utilizing all their members in building, smoothing and shaping the nest. Mr. Paul Morris, who watched a female Yellow Warbler building her nest, says that she commenced by weaving a small ring about two inches in diameter out of coarse gray fibers of the milkweed, by way of foundation, and then built up the nest by taking fine fibers in her bill and weaving them into the foundation, meanwhile turning around and around and pushing and felting it together. Mr. F. H. Mosher also watched a female building her nest. He says: 'She first laid a foundation of a few straws and placed upon them the cotton or down from fern fronds. These she bound together with the silk from a tent caterpillar's web. Then she went alternately for the cotton and the silk, stopping occasionally at an apple tree and feeding for a moment or two on canker-worms. When I went past the nest at night I found she had it nearly complete; the lining only was lacking.' Sometimes the nest-building occupies a week or more.

The Yellow Warbler often is victimized by the Cowbird, and is likely then to build another nest on top of the first, thus burying the Cowbird's egg. This manner of disposing of the Cowbird's egg may be repeated until four or even five nests are built, and in one case a six-

421

storied nest was built, with a Cowbird's egg in every one. The young usually remain in the nest from eleven to fifteen days. Their juvenal plumage, like that of nearly all our warblers, is worn but a short time and by the middle of July most of them have donned their winter dress.

The Yellow Warbler is rather a tender bird and starts south very early. By the middle of July some individuals, probably from the southern part of their range, begin to cross the Gulf of Mexico, and by the fifteenth of August most of the local breeding birds of this species have left the Northern States. Stragglers are still going in early September, and by the latter part of the month all have disappeared.

It would be hard to find a summer bird more useful among the shade trees or in the orchard and small-fruit garden than this species. Almost entirely insectivorous, it feeds on many of the greatest pests that attack our fruit trees, vines and berry bushes. Whenever the cater-pillars of which it is fond are plentiful, they form about two thirds of its food. It is destructive to the small caterpillars of the gypsy moth and the brown-tail moth, and is inordinately fond of canker-worms and other measuring-worms. Tent caterpillars are commonly eaten. Small bark-beetles and boring beetles are eaten, among them the imago of the currant-borer. Weevils are greedily taken. A few useful beetles are sacrificed; among them ground-beetles, soldier beetles and small scavenger-beetles. The Yellow Warbler has some expertness as a flycatcher among the branches, and seizes small moths, like the codling-moth, with ease, but apparently does not take many parasitic hymenoptera, though some flies are taken. Plant-lice sometimes form a considerable portion of its food. No part of the tree where it can find insect food is exempt from its visits, and it even takes grasshoppers, spiders, and myriapods from the ground, grass, or low-growing herbage. It attacks none of the products of man's industry, so far as our records go, except the raspberry, of which it has been known to eat a few occasionally.

MAGNOLIA WARBLER

Dendroica magnolia (WILSON). PLATE 83.

Other name: Black and Yellow Warbler.

IDENTIFICATION. — Length 4¼ to 5 inches; spread 7 to 7¾ inches. Male has upper parts largely blackish, crown gray, black cheeks, white patch on wing coverts, *yellow under parts streaked with black,* yellow rump, *tail largely white with conspicuous black end;* female has back olive-green, less white in wings, duller yellow; adults and young in fall duller, more brown above, but tail much as in spring.

SONG. — Very variable but suggests a short song of Yellow Warbler.

BREEDING. — In coniferous growths on edge of forest.

RANGE. — Breeds from central British Columbia, southwestern Mackenzie, central Manitoba, central Quebec, and Newfoundland south to central Alberta, Minnesota, northern Michigan, and northern Massachusetts, and in the mountains of New York, Pennsylvania, Maryland, West Virginia, and Virginia; winters from southern Mexico to Panama, and rarely in Haiti and Porto Rico; in migration west to the base of the Rocky Mountains.

The Magnolia Warbler is to my mind the most strikingly beautiful warbler that makes its home in New England. The Blackburnian Warbler with its orange front may be preferred by many, but that bright front is its chief glory, while the Magnolia Warbler's beauties are dis-tributed to every part of its graceful little form. Seen from above or below with both wings and tail partly spread while flitting from branch to branch in eager pursuit of its insect prey, or while engaged in paying court to its prospective mate, the male of this species is a wonderfully beautiful creature. Active and vivacious, he seems to take little rest throughout the livelong day.

This warbler is most common in the latitude of southern New England for a few days about the middle of May, though in some seasons a small flight occurs during the first week in May. Like other Canadian warblers of the coniferous woods, it can subsist and find shelter in such woods before the leaves have developed on the broad-leaved trees. Later, however, when the deciduous trees are clothed with young leaves, it may be found in migration almost anywhere in the woods and even in orchards.

Wherever spruce trees grow in western and northern New England this warbler is likely to breed. Spruces, hemlocks and balsam firs of the Canadian flora seem to be its favorite trees at this season.

Both male and female labor at nest-building, though the female is the real builder, while the male's part seems to be largely that of bringing material, although he often enters the nest. Miss Cordelia J. Stanwood, who watched a pair while they were nest-building, gives the following account of the progress of the work: 'First bits of spider's silk were laid in the shape of the nest on the brush-like needles of the fir. The bird seemed to secure the spider's floss by rubbing it against the twigs with her breast. Later bits of hay or cinquefoil stems were bent in the shape of a loop or swing and secured by the silk. The next step was to bend the material in the shape of a circle around the top, always pressing it into shape with the breast and securing it at intervals with knots of spider's silk. A frame similar to this seems to be constructed by the Magnolias always before filling in the foundation.'

June and July are largely given to the nesting and to the care of the young, which must be fed and attended for some time after they leave the nest. Early August is spent in wandering about while the young develop more fully and grow fat and strong in preparation for their southern journey, which begins about August 15, and most of them have left their breeding range before the last of September.

So far as is now known the Magnolia Warbler feeds entirely upon insects and other small forms of animal life. During the spring migration it may often be seen feeding on small caterpillars and plant-lice in the maples planted along village streets. In the orchards it feeds to repletion on such geometrids as the canker-worms.

CAPE MAY WARBLER

Dendroica tigrina (GMELIN). PLATE 82.

IDENTIFICATION. — Length 4¾ to 5¾ inches; spread 7½ to 8½ inches. Only eastern warbler with *chestnut cheeks and sides of neck bright yellow;* crown black; under parts yellow, narrowly striped with black; rump yellow; females and young lack chestnut cheek and are duller generally, but with a diffused spot of yellow behind ear.

SONG. — A monotonous *zee-zee-zee-zee* or *zee-zee-zee*.

BREEDING. — In coniferous forests and more open land.

RANGE. — Breeds from southern Mackenzie, northern Ontario, New Brunswick, and Nova Scotia south to southern Manitoba, New Hampshire and Maine; winters in the Bahamas and West Indies; in migration west to North Dakota and Kansas.

In the years of my boyhood the brilliant Cape May Warbler was so rare that it was considered a lucky day if one were seen, and a real red-letter day when a specimen was taken. In the spring of 1873, if my memory serves me, I met the first bright male of this species that my eyes had rested upon, and that bird, nicely mounted, is before me now. For nearly one hundred years at least this species had been considered very rare in New England, but about 1909 it seemed to become more common. Since that time Cape May Warblers have been not uncommon transients in certain years, and they have never been so rare as they formerly were.

In migration they may be found in trees and shrubbery about dwellings and along village streets almost as commonly as in woods or in swampy thickets, where at this season they find many insects. Occasionally a few may be seen in blossoming orchards. They appear more rare in autumn because they are more seldom observed, as they pass through while the trees are fully clothed with leaves, and they are likely to keep concealed more or less in the tree-tops. They also frequent dense thickets and brier-patches, and at that season in their dull fall plumage are seldom noticed. They are not extremely active but are very diligent in the pursuit of insects.

Little is known about the mating or nesting habits of this warbler, and its food has not been carefully studied. We know now that it often nests near the ground in coniferous trees, but there are indications that it may also nest much higher at times. It seems to prefer for this purpose rather open lands with scattering small trees, yet it undoubtedly nests also in northern forests.

BLACK–THROATED BLUE WARBLER

Dendroica caerulescens caerulescens (GMELIN). PLATE 82.

IDENTIFICATION. — Length 4¾ to 5½ inches; spread 7 to 7¾ inches. Male plain slaty-blue above, without wing-bars but conspicuous white spot on wing; throat and sides black, breast and belly white; female and young quite different, brownish-olive above, yellowish below, small whitish spot on wing, and light streak over eye.

SONG. — *Wee-wee-wee-weep* with downward inflection on first three and rising on last note.

BREEDING. — In second-growth woodlands and near deep woods, especially near water.

RANGE. — Breeds from northern Minnesota, central Ontario, and southern Quebec south to central Minnesota, northern Michigan, southern Ontario, Pennsylvania, and northern Connecticut; winters from Key West, Florida, to the Bahamas, Greater Antilles, Cozumel Island, and casually to Guatemala and Colombia.

This is a real woods warbler. It loves the woods. 'Its typical haunts,' says Herbert K. Job, 'are the densely shaded second-growth on the sides of wooded hills, either well to the north, or else to the corresponding faunal altitude. To suit its fastidious taste there should be rather dense undergrowth, with more or less fallen branches, and more particularly where mountain laurel luxuriates. It might well have been named the "Laurel Warbler."' In southern New England it often nests in laurel thickets, but in northern New England, according to Brewster, the yew is its favorite.

The male of the Black-throated Blue Warbler may be recognized at once, for his name describes him. The female, however, is an obscure, inconspicuous bird, though she may be recognized if the small white patch in her lower mid-wing can be seen, for its situation is the same as in the male. They arrive in the latitude of New England from the South by the middle of May, if not before, and frequent deciduous or mixed woods, though in migration they often visit farms, orchards and even villages, but they breed in or near the woods. Often the males are seen high in the trees where they are active, though less so than those of the American Redstart. Like the latter they catch many insects on the wing. Their colors are striking rather than bright, and their peculiar buzzing songs guide the observer to them. For breeding purposes this bird seems to prefer woodland clearings, hill pastures with young spruces, hemlocks and deciduous shrubbery, wooded ridges where the lumbermen have taken out the larger deciduous trees, or the bushy edges of woodlands. It is fond of mountain laurel thickets and second-growth of beeches and maples. It often nests near streams, or wood roads, preferring small openings to dense timber.

When a nest is discovered the female may fluff out the feathers of her sides so as to cover the whole top of the nest in an apparent effort to conceal it and her young. Mr. J. A. Farley gives me the following notes on this habit: 'A female Black-throated Blue Warbler whose nest I found in Rowe, Massachusetts, made a unique display of herself as a close-sitting bird. The nest, a beautiful and elaborate structure, was three feet from the ground in a hemlock sapling, which was one of a thick clump of the same sort that bordered a wood road. The female was off the nest when I found it. But when I returned, a quarter of an hour later, she was on. I got within two feet of her, but she would not fly.... But it was not her bravery that made this close-sitting bird unique, it was the unusual way in which she protected her young from my gaze. She had spread the white feathers of her lower parts out so completely over her young that there was not a vestige now visible of the four young birds that I had found a short time previously filling the nest so full. She "fluffed" herself out so as to hide all traces of the young. For a moment I even thought that during my absence of a few minutes she had brought a great deal of some soft stuff additional lining for the nest, as breeding birds sometimes do. To quote from my journal: "She made a beautiful picture. The whole effect was wonderful. The bird seemed to be sitting in a billowy mass of eider down, or cotton wool, that swelled, or rather bulged, up all around her, a regular bed of down."'

Some females when startled from the nest attempt by every artifice to draw the intruder away; others seem to be exceedingly shy and conceal themselves as if more fearful for their own safety than for that of their young. When the female utters her alarm note, the male may appear or he may not; usually if he comes he seems not greatly perturbed.

When the young leave the nest they soon shed their juvenal plumage and molt into their winter dress, and as August wanes they are ready for their southward migration. Most members of this species leave the Northern States during September.

CAIRN'S WARBLER

Dendroica caerulescens cairnsi COUES.

IDENTIFICATION. — Similar to *D. c. caerulescens* but back always more or less spotted with black, the center of the back being sometimes entirely black; adult female generally darker than *D. c. caerulescens*.

RANGE. — Breeds locally in the Canadian and Transition zones of the southern Alleghenies from Maryland to Georgia.

Mr. John S. Cairns, for whom this race was named by Elliott Coues, recognized a difference in its habits even before it had been separated from the northern form by the systematists. He wrote of it in the North Carolina mountains: 'These birds are a local race; breeding from one generation to another. They arrive from the south nearly ten days earlier than those that pass through the valleys on their northward migration. It is common to observe migrants through the valleys while breeders on the higher mountains are already nest-building and rearing their young.' — (J.B.M.)

MYRTLE WARBLER

Dendroica coronata (LINNAEUS).   PLATE 82.

Other names: Yellow-rumped Warbler; Myrtle-bird; Yellow-rump.

IDENTIFICATION. — Length 5 to 6 inches; spread 8 to 9½ inches. Adult male in spring a bluish-gray bird streaked with black; white below with *much black* on breast and sides; *four bright yellow patches*, one on top of head, one on rump and one on each side; two white wing-bars; white spots showing in spread tail. Adult female in spring a brownish bird with yellow markings placed as in male, but duller and with less black; wing-bars less prominent. Adults and young in autumn and winter similar to adult female in spring, but browner, showing less black and less yellow; all, however, have a white or whitish stripe over eye, *a distinct white or whitish throat*, two white wing-bars and a yellow patch on rump. Magnolia and (usually) Cape May Warblers also have a yellow rump, but are yellow below where the Myrtle Warbler is mainly white or whitish with dark streaks.

BREEDING. — Usually in coniferous woods, sometimes in mixed woods, in small tree.

RANGE. — Breeds from tree-limit in northwestern Alaska, northern Manitoba, and central Quebec south to northern British Columbia, southern Alberta, northern Minnesota, northern Michigan, central Ontario, New Hampshire, and Maine, and in the mountains of New York and Massachusetts; winters from Kansas, the Ohio Valley, and New Jersey (locally in southern New England), south to the Greater Antilles, Mexico, and Panama, and on the Pacific coast from central Oregon to northern Lower California.

This gentle warbler is an early migrant. In March and April there is a great flight of Myrtle Warblers up the Atlantic coast of the United States, following the coastal belt of wax myrtle and bayberries. Their average arrival at Prince Edward Island is April 26, thirteen days ahead of eleven other species of warblers, and nearly a week earlier than at certain interior stations of Pennsylvania, six hundred miles to the southwest. This early migration is possible along the coast largely because of the food supply furnished them by the bayberry which grows chiefly in the coastal region, as far north as Prince Edward Island.

In the latter days of April or very early in May when the south wind blows, when houstonias and violets begin to bloom on sunny southern slopes, when the wild cherry and apple trees and some of the birches, sumacs and the shrubbery in sheltered sunny nooks begin to put out a misty greenery of tiny leaflets, then we may look for the Myrtle Warblers, the males lovely in their nuptial dress of blue-gray, black, white and lemon-yellow. Then they may be found fluttering about in sheltered bushy bogs, catching the early insects that dance in the sunshine along the waterside. All through early May they move northward, or westward toward the mountains, migrating by day or night indifferently as the case may be.

As summer approaches the males begin their courtship of the females, following them about and displaying their beauties by fluffing out the feathers of their sides, raising their wings and erecting the feathers of the crown, so as to exhibit to the full their beautiful black and yellow markings. After much time spent in courting they mate, and at once look about for a nesting-place. The nest is usually in a small conifer, and is rather bulky for a warbler.

The nest-building usually is the work of the female, though in some cases the male helps a little, bringing some material, and usually encourages her by his companionship and song. The nest-building may occupy six to ten days. Incubation ordinarily begins when the first egg is deposited, and some males assist their mates briefly in this task. The young remain in the nest about two weeks. As in all our wood warblers, the juvenal dress is worn for a brief period only, and by early August the young birds have acquired their first winter plumage.

In September and early October, when all our forested hills are red and golden, our Myrtle Warblers come back to us again. Then they may be found where plant-lice swarm upon the birches in sheltered situations, where they feed diligently until the insects are gone, when they take wing again and wend their southward way, clothed now in modest vesture, each little bird retaining, however, a yellow spot just above the upper tail coverts, by which, whenever his wings are spread or lowered, he discovers his identity to those who know his secret.

Even before the first of September some of the birds have begun to move southward or toward the coast, where many remain all winter or until the bayberry crop is exhausted, when they must move on or starve. Thus they disappear in late winter from many localities where they were common earlier in the season. Now that thousands of European Starlings remain on our seacoast in mild winters, these alien interlopers devour the bayberries earlier in the season than would be the case were the berries left to the native birds alone; and we may expect the wintering Myrtle Warblers gradually to disappear from our coastal regions if the Starlings continue to increase at their present rate.

The Myrtle Warbler is one of the few warblers that can subsist for long periods upon berries and seeds, although undoubtedly it prefers insects when it can get them. Along the coast during the milder winters there are many flies rising from the seaweed in sheltered spots on mild days even in January, and there are eggs of plant-lice and some hibernating insects to be found on the trees, but the principal food of the Myrtle Warbler on the eastern coast during the inclement season is the bayberry. It can exist, however, on the berries of the Virginia juniper or red cedar and these seem to form its principal food when wintering in the interior; berries of the Virginia creeper or woodbine, those of viburnums, honeysuckle, mountain ash, poison ivy, spikenard and dogwoods also serve to eke out the birds' bill of fare. In the maple sugar orchards in early spring they occasionally drink sweet sap from the trees. In the Southern Atlantic States they take palmetto berries. North and south they also eat some seeds, particularly those of the sunflower and goldenrod. During spring and summer they destroy thousands of caterpillars, small grubs and the larvae of saw-flies and various insects, leaf-beetles, bark-beetles, weevils, wood-borers, ants, scale insects, plant-lice and their eggs, including the woolly apple-tree aphis and the common apple-leaf plant-louse, also grasshoppers and locusts, bugs, house-flies and other flies including caddice-flies, crane-flies, chalcid-flies, ichneumon-flies and gnats, also spiders.

AUDUBON'S WARBLER

Dendroica auduboni auduboni (TOWNSEND).

PLATE 82.

IDENTIFICATION. — Length 5 to 6 inches; spread 8¾ to 9¼ inches. Adult male similar to Myrtle Warbler in size with similar yellow patches on top of head, sides of body and rump, but also a *yellow chin and throat* and more white on wings and tail; *gray cheeks* and a *large white patch or double patch on fore wing* in place of two separate wing-bars. Female similar to female of Myrtle Warbler, and *with two wing-bars;* but throat usually yellow though paler than in male. Young much like adult female in autumn; throat slightly tinged yellow, or nearly as white as in young of Myrtle Warbler; those with white throat not recognizable in the field.

BREEDING. — Similar to Myrtle Warbler.

RANGE. — Breeds from central British Columbia, central Alberta, and west-central Saskatchewan south to the mountains of southern California and northeastern New Mexico, and east to South Dakota and western Nebraska; winters from northern California and the Rio Grande to Guatemala.

Apparently this western warbler frequents regions similar to those visited by the Myrtle Warbler and has similar habits. In fly-catching ability it exceeds the latter and it is even more showy, as the deep black of its breast contrasts strongly with its yellow throat and sides, and it shows more white in wings and tail than does its common congener of the northeast. As the Myrtle Warbler in autumn may sometimes have a slight yellowish tinge on the throat and as Audubon's Warbler seems to have been actually taken but twice to the eastward of the Mississippi, sight records, especially in autumn, should be distrusted.

BLACK–THROATED GRAY WARBLER

Dendroica nigrescens (TOWNSEND).

PLATE 84.

IDENTIFICATION. — Length 4¼ to 5¼ inches; spread 7½ to 8½ inches. A black and white warbler with a gray back; black cap, wide black patch through and behind eye, black throat; female with less black especially on crown and throat.

BREEDING. — Among low growths of scrub oaks, manzanitas, etc.

RANGE. — Breeds from southern British Columbia, Nevada, and northwestern Colorado south to Lower California, southern Arizona and southern New Mexico; winters in Mexico.

The Black-throated Gray Warbler is a bird of the Pacific coastal region and the western mountain ranges, and is entirely accidental east of the 95th meridian. There seem to be individual birds, as well as men, that are obsessed with the *wanderlust,* or else they simply go astray and having once lost the way keep on wandering. Thus we may account for the accidental occurrence of western species in our territory. Eventually most of the birds of North America may be recorded here.

This warbler seems to be normally a bird of dense thickets or chaparral, an inhabitant of heavy but stunted mountain tree growths. It frequents both pine and oak, particularly the low-growing scrub oaks. It is not a remarkably active bird, and is likely to keep well within the foliage, as normally it is rather shy.

BLACK–THROATED GREEN WARBLER

Dendroica virens virens (GMELIN). PLATE 84.

IDENTIFICATION. — Length 4¼ to 5¼ inches; spread 7 to 8 inches. Adult male unmistakable in spring with its bright yellowish-olive-green back, *bright lemon-yellow sides of head and pure black throat*, black streaks on sides, two broad white wing-bars, white belly, and much white in tail. Adult female resembles male but is duller, and has only traces of the black throat. Female and young in autumn similar but lack the black throat, though black, gray or dusky traces of it are often seen in autumnal adult females or young males.

SONGS. — *Zee zee zu zi* and *zi zi zi zi zee zu zi*, sometimes rendered 'trees, trees, murmuring trees.'

BREEDING. — Among coniferous trees. *Nest:* Usually 15 to 70 feet up in a conifer, a deep cup on a horizontal limb, of twigs bound with spider or caterpillar webs, lined with fine grasses, pine needles, bark shreds, etc.

RANGE. — Breeds from central Alberta, central Ontario, central Quebec, and Newfoundland south to southern Minnesota, southern Wisconsin, northern Ohio, northern New Jersey, and Connecticut, and in the mountains south to northern South Carolina, northern Georgia, and northern Alabama; winters from Mexico to Panama; in migration west to eastern Texas; occasional in the Florida Keys and the West Indies.

The Black-throated Green Warbler was the bird that first led me to follow him and his companions into the dark pines. As a boy I early learned to know the common birds of farm and orchard, but I had never seen a flight of wood warblers until one still, bright morning in May I entered an old pinery near Worcester, Massachusetts, and, listening carefully, heard strange notes on all sides and caught glimpses of little forms darting and flitting among the branches. Then there came into view close by in a little opening, where the sun shone in, a brilliant male of this species, his green back, yellow cheeks and black throat fairly gleaming in the morning sun, and the white markings of his wings and tail flashing in and out as he moved among the dark branches. I thought it the most beautiful bird in the world and longed to possess it. It was my first real introduction to the wood warblers — a day never to be forgotten — and since then I have always had an affection for the gentle bird.

Like all the wood warblers it is fond of bathing, its bathtub often some pool in a mountain trout brook. One day as I stood beside such a brook, a very lovely male, disregarding my presence, alighted on a stone at my feet, and at once hopped into the clear spring water and performed his ablutions, dipping into the stream and throwing off the sparkling drops in little showers. As he stood there in the sunlight which streamed through an opening in the tree-tops, he left an enduring picture in my memory.

The Black-throated Green Warbler usually arrives from the South early in May. In migration it may be found among all kinds of trees, where it searches for insects from the lower branches to the tree-tops. It rarely goes to the ground except to drink, bathe or gather nesting material. As the breeding season comes on it seeks the coniferous evergreens, particularly the white pines, in which it commonly nests. If the trees are tall it spends much of its time among the higher branches. When nesting in dense spruce woods, it frequents trees near the edge of the forest. The male now sings at intervals through a large part of the day, its song harmonizing well with its surroundings and the gentle breeze in the tree-tops. It is typical of quiet, peaceful, woodland scenes. 'His voice is suggestive of the drowsy summer days, the languor of the breeze dreamily swaying the pines, spruces, firs and hemlocks. It recalls the incense of evergreens, the fragrance of the wild strawberry, the delicate perfume of the *Linnaea*. No other bird voice is so potent to evoke that particular spell of the northern woods,' writes Miss Cordelia J. Stanwood.

I have watched the nest-building of this warbler and seen both male and female carrying nesting material, but if their attention is called to the watcher, they are very likely to leave their real nest and start building a sham nest in another location. One pair that I watched, seeing that their activities were observed, started a nest in an empty fruit can that had lodged on a limb of a white pine, but ceased carrying nesting materials there as soon as I left them. Many of the nests built among the pines come to grief, for always there are rapacious jays or red squirrels hanging about the pine woods.

The young birds remain in the nest from eight to ten days. Both parents care for their young with devotion. The female sometimes will throw herself in the path of an intruder and simulating a wounded bird, endeavor to entice him away. Soon after the young leave the nest they take to the tree-tops. Most of them are strong on the wing by early July. In August they have molted and are ready to start for the South. In autumn some of the young males attempt to sing, and their songs usually are more like those of the Cape May Warbler or the Bay-breasted Warbler than those of their parents. Most of them have left before the middle of October. Frosty nights hurry them along.

WAYNE'S WARBLER

Dendroica virens waynei BANGS.

IDENTIFICATION. — Like *D. v. virens* but black areas on throat and sides of breast averaging smaller, yellow of sides of head paler, and bill more slender.
RANGE. — Resident in the coastal region of South Carolina.

This race of the Black-throated Green Warbler is indistinguishable in the field to the ordinary observer, but it differs in habits in one important detail; it is a year-round resident in its restricted range, while the more northerly race migrates annually to Mexico and back again. — (J.B.M.)

CERULEAN WARBLER

Dendroica cerulea (WILSON).   PLATE 83.

IDENTIFICATION. — Length 4 to 5 inches; spread 7¼ to 8 inches. Male blue above with black streaks, white below with a bluish band across upper breast and black streaks on sides; female bluish-gray to olive-green above; young distinctly greenish above.
SONG. — Resembles that of Parula Warbler; *see-see-seep*, ascending at end.
BREEDING. — On heavily wooded lands and swampy woods, or in tall southern pines.
RANGE. — Breeds from southeastern Nebraska, southeastern Minnesota, southern Wisconsin, southern Michigan, southern Ontario, western New York, western Pennsylvania, and West Virginia south to northeastern

Texas, Louisiana, central Alabama, and northern Georgia, and locally in the Hudson Valley, central Delaware, eastern Maryland, and western Virginia; winters from Venezuela to Peru, migrates through Central America.

The little Cerulean Warbler is the bluest of eastern warblers. It is almost sky-blue. It is considered extremely rare east of the Appalachian ranges. Probably it has visited the Atlantic States many times, but as it is a bird of the tree-tops it is difficult to identify. Especially so are the females and young, as they are inconspicuous and obscurely marked. In the North they frequent the tops of such tall trees as maples, lindens, walnuts and elms. They resort to upland woods and wooded hillsides, where they dart out like flycatchers in pursuit of flying insects, search about leaves, twigs and blossoms like vireos, and creep about on the large limbs like the Black and White Warbler. They seem to prefer the more open woods, where they sometimes come down from the tree-tops and work more in the manner of a chickadee or a creeper; in nest-building the female comes to the ground for much of her material, working very busily and paying little attention to spectators.

In May, while mating, the males are very pugnacious and fight furiously and persistently. However, these combats are soon settled and the nest-building, defense of the nest and care of the young take their attention. Early in July when the young are out of the nest, the males stop singing and molting begins. In August they are off on their southern journey.

BLACKBURNIAN WARBLER

Dendroica fusca (MÜLLER). PLATE 84.

Other names: Hemlock Warbler; Torch-bird; Orange-throated Warbler.

IDENTIFICATION. — Length 4½ to 5½ inches; spread 7½ to 8½ inches. Mainly black above with orange on crown, over eye, behind ear, and on throat and breast; in autumn back is more brownish, orange more yellow, and white wing-patch has become two wing-bars.

SONG. — Extremely thin, very variable, a common form *wee, see, see, see, zi, zi, zi.*

BREEDING. — In coniferous or mixed woods, especially hemlocks, spruces, and pines. *Nest:* Commonly of coniferous twigs lined with fine rootlets or hair.

RANGE. — Breeds from central Manitoba, central Ontario, Quebec, and Cape Breton Island south to central Minnesota, Wisconsin, central Michigan, Massachusetts, and Connecticut, and in the Alleghenies from Pennsylvania to Georgia and South Carolina; winters from Yucatan to Peru.

This little bird is the most brilliant of all our warblers. It has not that perfection of beauty in all its parts which characterizes the Magnolia Warbler, for its rump and tail are rather commonplace, but its front is a brilliant and intense flame-color. Dr. Elliott Coues says there is nothing to compare with the exquisite hue of the chin, throat and upper breast and he calls it 'Prometheus, the Torch-bearer.' When the low morning sun shines full upon its gorgeous frontlet, backed by the dark recesses of the pines, it flashes out like a burning flame as the bird turns its breast suddenly to the light. Sometimes its front seems to change almost to a brilliant pink, and again it disappears, as the bird turns a 'cold shoulder' to the looker-on. Probably no artist or engraver can represent in its full intensity the beautiful flame-color of this warbler's throat as its lambent sheen reflects back the sunlight, but neither can we depict in their full beauty the colors of any of the brighter warblers as seen in the light of the orb of day and in their natural environment. To appreciate them we must see the living birds against the vital background provided by the Creator.

This warbler is a type of arboreal bird. The whispering forest is its home. It dwells among the tall timber, and in migration often passes much of its time near the very tops of trees. It is generally regarded as rare in migration in Massachusetts, though probably untold numbers pass over the state every year, but only a few stop here. It is not when the birds are migrating that we see them, but when they *stop* to rest.

At sunrise one morning in early May, many years ago, when the tiny green leaves were just breaking forth on the tall trees of the woods near Worcester, Blackburnians were everywhere in the tree-tops. They swarmed in the woods for miles. Years later, in Amesbury, on another May morning, the night flight, having met a cold wave from the north with a light frost, had come down to earth and the birds were busily looking for food; many Blackburnians and many other warblers were in the low shrubbery, in the grass, and even on plowed fields in every direction all through the village and about the farms. The sudden cold had stopped them. A few hours later as the day grew warmer they disappeared and were not seen again.

Probably the number of birds of this species breeding in the Northern States is much greater than the records indicate. They breed chiefly in dense woods among pine, spruce and hemlock trees. The female is inconspicuous, and the male spends most of his time amid the branches where he is seldom seen or heard, or if heard his song is mistaken for that of some of the more common warblers whose notes resemble it. The nest is often high in the trees and hard to find. I have seen the birds in the breeding season in nearly all parts of Massachusetts. Sometimes the song of the male has been the only indication of his presence, the bird keeping well concealed in thick pines or in tall spruces, hemlocks or deciduous trees, but usually a search led to the discovery of the singer and sometimes the pair appeared.

The bird is quite active. It catches insects in the air occasionally, but spends most of its feeding time in searching among the branches. Like other warblers it takes many moths and caterpillars, and both adult forms and larvae of beetles that feed on trees.

YELLOW–THROATED WARBLER

Dendroica dominica dominica (LINNAEUS).   PLATE 84.

Other name: Yellow-throated Gray Warbler.

IDENTIFICATION. — Length 4¾ to 5¾ inches; spread 8 to 8¾ inches. A gray-backed warbler with throat and upper breast lemon yellow; yellow line from bill to near eye changing to white and passing into a white patch on side of neck; young browner above, yellow of throat paler.

BREEDING. — In pine and deciduous woods where 'Spanish moss' is found.

RANGE. — Breeds from southern Maryland, Delaware, and southern New Jersey to central Florida; winters in southern Florida, the Bahamas and Greater Antilles.

The Yellow-throated Warbler is a handsome, well-marked species. On its southern breeding-ground it often keeps mainly to the tops of tall pines, and as its creeping gait along the branches resembles that of the Pine Warbler, it is commonly overlooked, but when it comes down into low shrubbery it is easily identified. I have seen the bird only in Florida, where it kept in thick woods exploring the lower branches of trees and the tops of shrubbery. It also frequents open piney woods and mixed growths containing some pine trees. Its song has a ringing quality, resembling that heard in the songs of the Water-Thrush and the Indigo Bunting.

Mr. Arthur T. Wayne, who was very familiar with the bird in the coastal region of South Carolina, says that there it is seldom found in the breeding season except where the Spanish moss grows, and its nest is almost invariably built in festoons of that moss.

SYCAMORE WARBLER

Dendroica dominica albilora RIDGWAY.

IDENTIFICATION. — Adults are distinguished from Yellow-throated Warbler by absence of yellow between bill and eye, and possibly by shorter bill.

BREEDING. — Generally in sycamores near water.

RANGE. — Breeds in the Mississippi Valley from southeastern Nebraska, southern Wisconsin, southern Michigan, Ohio, West Virginia, and western North Carolina south to central Texas and Louisiana; winters from Mexico to Nicaragua and Costa Rica.

This Mississippi Valley race of *Dendroica dominica* resembles the Yellow-throated Warbler very closely in coloration, habits and haunts, so that outside its breeding range it is very difficult to distinguish between the two forms. It has the same fondness for tall trees near streams, especially for the great sycamores which have given it its name. — (J.B.M.)

CHESTNUT–SIDED WARBLER

Dendroica pensylvanica (LINNAEUS).   PLATE 83.

IDENTIFICATION. — Length 4½ to 5¼ inches; spread 7½ to 8¼ inches. The only warbler all white below except for broad chestnut stripe on each side; yellow crown; female duller; fall adults and young have white eyering and lack yellow cap.

SONG. — Suggests that of Yellow Warbler but more emphatic; two main songs with much variation.

BREEDING. — In sproutlands, shrubbery, in or near edges of woodlands, in bushy fields and pastures, along brooks and roadsides. *Nest:* In low bush, sapling or brier patch 1 to 6 feet up.

RANGE. — Breeds from central Saskatchewan, central Ontario, southern Quebec, and Newfoundland south to eastern Nebraska, Illinois, Indiana, northern Ohio, northern New Jersey, and Rhode Island, and in the mountains to Tennessee and South Carolina; winters from Guatemala to Panama.

The common and familiar Chestnut-sided Warbler was once a comparatively rare bird in the Atlantic States; Audubon met with it but once; Wilson saw little of it; Nuttall, who considered it rare, evidently knew little about it, and saw very few. Since his time, however, its numbers have increased until it has become one of the commonest of eastern warblers. Its increase was favored by the destruction of the primeval forest and the continued cutting away of subsequent growths, and later by the increase of neglected fields and pastures with their growths of bushes and brambles, for it is not a frequenter of deep woods, nor yet of well-kept gardens, orchards or farmyards, but prefers neglected or cut-over lands, with a profusion of thickets and briers. So we may find it usually away from houses, in low roadside and brookside thickets, or in sproutlands rather recently cut over. As the coppice grows up the bird retires to other quarters or to the edges of the woods. It is not shy, nor does it seek the company of man, but seems rather indifferent to his presence, unless he too closely approaches its lowly domicile.

It is not, perhaps, so beautiful as some of the more retiring warblers, but as Professor Lynds Jones says, it impresses one as an exquisite, and there is something about it which makes the 'day brighter, the wearing field work easier and the hours of fasting forgotten,' when it flies into view. Perhaps its dainty, immaculate white vesture, with its clean-cut chestnut stripes, so unique among the small birds, together with its jauntiness and trimness, set it apart from and above all its fellows.

Normally it is a bird of the shrubbery and lower branches, a bird of the open and sunlight. It rarely penetrates the deep woods though sometimes it may be found traveling through them with other warblers in migration. It sings from tree-tops but more often from bush-tops, and anyone walking or driving slowly along country roads will have many opportunities to see and hear it. In migration it may be seen with other warblers gleaning insects well up in the trees even in town or city parks.

The Chestnut-sided Warbler commonly appears in New England during the first or second week in May — a joyous, tuneful bird conspicuous among the nearly naked trees and shrubbery. As the days grow warmer it is seen hunting amid the thickets, often with slightly drooping wings and jaunty cocked-up tail. As the foliage develops, courtship is rife and nest-building begins. Five or six days suffice for the building of the nest, if the weather continues favorable. My former assistant, the late F. H. Mosher, watched a pair throughout the building of the nest. The female did all the actual work. She laid straws and plant fibers in a fork of an arrowwood bush, then went to a tent caterpillar colony and tearing off some of the web bound the forking branches about with it, thus tying them together and forming a deep cup-like framework for the habitation; she also bound the foundation firmly in place with more of the same web, then brought dried grasses or straws and placed them around to form the sides of the nest and bound them to the branches with more caterpillars' webs. Having finished the sides, she put in a lining of soft grasses, fine rootlets and plant fibers. This nest when completed at the end of five days was much less bulky than the usual nest of the Yellow Warbler, and much firmer, with walls not more than one fourth as thick. When the nest is finished care should be taken not to disturb it or handle the eggs, as the birds are then extremely likely to desert it.

The young remain in the nest about nine or ten days. When they have learned to fly well, the family retires to bushy lands, where they begin molting in July, and in August they are ready for their southward journey. Before the month closes most of them have left New England, but some are still passing until the last days of September.

The food of the Chestnut-sided Warbler is such that the bird must be exceedingly useful in woodland and shrubbery, and in orchard and shade trees as well, whenever it frequents them. It is probable that at times it destroys considerable numbers of parasitic hymenoptera, as it is rather expert as a flycatcher; but it is very destructive to many injurious beetles and caterpillars, being one of the most active consumers of leaf-eating insects. Small borers or bark-beetles, plant-bugs and plant-lice, leaf-hoppers, ants and aphids are eaten.

In seasons of great want it eats a few seeds. Audubon says that he once shot several birds in Pennsylvania during a cold spell and snowstorm in early spring, and that the only food in their stomachs was grass seeds and a few spiders, but the birds were emaciated and evidently half starved. It not only takes hairless caterpillars but it eats numbers of the hairy larvae of the gypsy moth and brown-tail moth, as well as tent caterpillars and the forest tent caterpillars. In autumn it takes some wild fruit.

BAY–BREASTED WARBLER

Dendroica castanea (WILSON).   PLATE 83.

IDENTIFICATION. — Length 5 to 6 inches; spread 8¼ to 9¼ inches. A large dark warbler; grayish back streaked with black; black face with buffy patch on side of neck; chestnut crown, throat, upper breast and sides; female, chestnut much restricted; adults and young in autumn, olive-green above, dingy buffy-yellow below, two white wing-bars.

SONG. — A high thin *teesi teesi teesi*, perhaps the highest and squeakiest of all the warblers.

BREEDING. — In northern coniferous or mixed forests often on low land near ponds and lakes.

RANGE. — Breeds from east-central Alberta, central Manitoba, and Newfoundland south to southern Manitoba, northern Maine, the mountains of New Hampshire and Vermont, and the Adirondacks in New York; winters in Panama and Colombia; irregular in migration on the Atlantic slope and rare south of Virginia; regular migrant across Gulf of Mexico and through Guatemala to Panama.

This large, dark, gentle warbler is usually considered a rare bird in New England. It seems to be more common in migration from the Connecticut Valley west than it is in eastern New England. With us it is a late spring and early fall migrant, not arriving in numbers until after the middle of May and beginning to move southward in the last half of August. It may be more common in autumn than it is believed to be, as it is very difficult to distinguish it at that season from the autumnal Black-poll Warblers, when both are moving through the tree-tops together.

The Bay-breasted Warbler may be looked for in fall before the Blackpoll comes; usually in the spring migration the Baybreast is seen in dense woods of coniferous or mixed trees. It spends most of its time amid the foliage of trees, moving about rather deliberately after the manner of the vireos, and searching among the leaves and twigs for its insect prey. It is by no means confined to the tree-tops or to dense forests, as it is seen at times in low scattered trees and occasionally a few may be seen in the more suburban parts of cities.

This warbler breeds chiefly in northern forests. The nest is not very artfully concealed, though usually well hidden from below by thick spruce foliage. The male feeds the female and both feed the young. The young leave the nest in about ten days. Most members of this species pass southward in late August and September, largely through the Mississippi Valley region, which may account for their usual rarity along the Atlantic seaboard.

435

BLACK–POLL WARBLER

Dendroica striata (FORSTER).

PLATE 84.

IDENTIFICATION. — Length 5 to 5¾ inches; spread 8¼ to 9¾ inches. A striped gray warbler with a black cap and white cheeks; female lacks black cap and is less heavily streaked; autumn birds very different, olive-green above, dingy white below, two white wing-bars.

SONG. — A high, thin, monotonous *zi-zi-zi-zi-zi-zi-zi*, all on one pitch or swelling in volume in the middle.

BREEDING. — Among conifers, often in swampy groves. *Nest:* Usually low in an evergreen tree, sometimes on the ground.

RANGE. — Breeds from tree-limit in northwestern Alaska, northern Manitoba, northern Quebec, and Newfoundland south to northern British Columbia, Manitoba, Michigan, northern Maine, and the mountains of New York, Vermont, and New Hampshire; winters from Guiana and Venezuela to Brazil; migrates through the Bahamas and West Indies.

The Black-poll Warbler arrives in the latitude of New England on the crest of the great spring wave of bird migration; a few may appear early in May, but when their sibilant insect-like songs come from orchards, shade trees and woodlands on every hand we hear them in sadness, for they signify that the great vernal flight of the beautiful wood sprites soon will pass — that spring wanes and summer is at hand. Usually they are about the last of the wood warblers to appear and although they come in multitudes they keep mostly in leafy tree-tops, where they are lost to view, and where their thin voices are noticed only by those who have learned to listen for the warblers and to distinguish their faintest chirp from that of the insects which now swarm in woods and fields.

The Black-poll Warbler breeds in the dark evergreen forests of the north. Its home is among the spruces and firs. It nests in the wilderness of Labrador and Alaska, penetrating well into the Arctic Zone wherever it can find its favorite stunted evergreens, and southward throughout most of the forested regions of Canada. It is, perhaps, the most abundant and wide-spread of all the American wood warblers, and yet we seem to have learned little about its breeding habits or its food.

It migrates from the borders of the Arctic Zone to South America. Its autumnal migration begins usually in September. It is difficult for the beginner in bird study to believe that the little green birds that come trooping down from the north in autumn are the same that went north in their black and white vesture in the spring; silently they pass or with only a faint lisping chirp in place of the songs of the spring migration. From far-off Alaska, from the great Northwest Territories, from Hudson Bay and Labrador, the Blackpolls come down toward the peninsula of Florida and steer their course across Cuba and the West Indies to South America. In spring their hosts return by the same route. Mr. C. J. Maynard, who landed April 27, 1884, on a small key in the Bahamas, says: 'We found this little spot of land, which consisted of two acres, fairly covered with warblers, which were constantly arriving and departing. Of all the thousands which we saw, by far the greater number were Blackpolls.' He also says that the numbers of these birds that came and passed were countless, even beyond estimation, and that for two days more the flight continued with numbers somewhat abated. Some of these birds died apparently from exhaustion. They are supposed to fly several hundred miles across the Caribbean Sea before they reach land. When we consider that this key was only a tiny spot in the wide belt that must have been covered by this migration, we can only wonder at the vast numbers that pass northward. While migrating this warbler may be found wherever trees grow, and often also along fences and stone walls in fields and pastures, and in autumn even along weedy roadsides. Its motions are rather deliberate for a warbler, and it is usually unsuspicious and approachable.

NORTHERN PINE WARBLER

Dendroica pinus pinus (WILSON). PLATE 85.

Other name: Pine-creeping Warbler.

IDENTIFICATION. — Length 5 to 5¾ inches; spread 8½ to 9½ inches. Olive-green above, yellow below dimly streaked, two white wing-bars; female varies from whitish to dull yellow below, dull olive above, sides faintly streaked.

SONG. — A simple 'trill,' slightly more musical than that of Chipping Sparrow.

BREEDING. — In pine, hemlock or cedar groves, in open woods or near edge of woods.

RANGE. — Breeds from northern Manitoba, northern Michigan, southern Ontario, southern Quebec, and New Brunswick south to east-central Texas and the Gulf States; winters from southern Illinois and the coast of Virginia to Florida, eastern Texas, and Mexico.

The Northern Pine Warbler is the gentle, modest minstrel of the pines. Dry, sandy land that has been much burned over and supports a sparse growth of pitch pines and scrub oaks is its chosen home. It is a common bird wherever pitch pines grow, as on the wastelands of Cape Cod and Martha's Vineyard, and New Jersey, and it breeds locally also among red or Norway pines and white pines, and rarely among red cedars and hemlocks. Its sweet monotonous song harmonizes well with the sighing of the summer wind through the branches, while shimmering heat-waves rise from the sandy soil. Its song is usually described as a trill, but is really a succession of soft notes, all delivered on the same pitch. (A trill is a rapid rendering of two differently pitched notes alternately, not separated by more than the width of a whole tone.) When the song is followed to its source, the bird usually will be found sitting on a pine limb, occasionally lifting its head to sing, or stealing quietly along the limb like a creeper, or hopping from twig to twig like any other warbler searching for its insect prey, or even fluttering out after some flying insect.

The Pine Warbler usually comes to the Northern States in the waning of the month of April (though stragglers may come even in March), and it may appear almost anywhere in migration, frequently with Yellow Palm Warblers, keeping mostly to the trees or shrubbery and occasionally alighting on the ground. As the breeding season comes on it will be found most of the time among pines. It mates very early, and at that season the males, influenced by jealousy, become pugnacious and often do battle for the favor of the modest, dingy female, making the woods resound with their angry chirps.

By the last of October most of the Northern Pine Warblers have left the latitude of New England for their winter home in the Southern States or northern Mexico, but now and then one is seen in winter as far north at least as Massachusetts. While migrating in October they gather in flocks and associate with other birds. I remember seeing a mixed flock of about one hundred birds, composed mainly of Pine Warblers and Bluebirds, upon the ground, bushes and trees about a large nearly empty tidewater pool. The blue backs of the Bluebirds and the yellow breasts of the Pine Warblers seen in sunlight against the dark bottom of the pool and the overhanging shadowy pines made a charming picture to carry in the memory.

FLORIDA PINE WARBLER

Dendroica pinus florida (MAYNARD).

IDENTIFICATION. — Indistinguishable from *D. p. pinus*, in field, but bill longer and upper parts slightly more yellowish.

RANGE. — Resident throughout the year in southern Florida from Citrus, Lake, and Volusia counties south to Homestead and Long Pine Key, in the southern Everglades.

The Florida Pine Warbler is a common resident of the extensive pine forests of southern Florida north to about the region of Gainesville, where the Northern Pine Warbler replaces it. Being non-migratory it stays in this area while the more northerly race is passing through on its annual migration flights, and some of the northern birds join it for the colder season. Otherwise their habits are apparently identical. — (J.B.M.)

KIRTLAND'S WARBLER

Dendroica kirtlandi (BAIRD).   PLATE 94.

Other name: Jack-pine Warbler.

IDENTIFICATION. — Length 5½ to 6 inches; spread about 9 inches. Gray above and yellow below, with coarse spotting in breast and sides; two light wing-bars; blackish spot on cheek of male, grayish in female.

SONG. — A clear *wichi chee chee — cheer-r-r*.

BREEDING. — *Nest:* On ground, of strips of bark and other vegetal fibers, grass, etc., lined with finer grass, pine needles, and hair. *Eggs:* 3 to 5, speckled and wreathed with umber.

RANGE. — Apparently limited in breeding season to Oscoda, Crawford, and Roscommon counties in Michigan; winters in the Bahamas; recorded in migration from Minnesota to Ontario, and south to Missouri, Georgia, Florida, and Virginia.

Kirtland's Warbler is probably the rarest warbler in the eastern United States, and it certainly has the most restricted breeding range. Not only is it limited in the breeding season to a few counties in Michigan, but it is very locally distributed in those counties, nesting in small scattered colonies in the sandy plains grown up to the jack pine, *Pinus banksiana*, where its nest is usually located on the ground at the foot of a pine or a scrub oak in a thicket. Its habit of wagging or bobbing its tail as it *walks* about on the ground is quite distinctive as it is the only gray-backed warbler which has this trait. — (J.B.M.)

NORTHERN PRAIRIE WARBLER

Dendroica discolor discolor (VIEILLOT). PLATE 85.

IDENTIFICATION. — Length 4¼ to 5¼ inches; spread 6¼ to 7¼ inches. Yellowish-olive-green above with chestnut spots on back, lower plumage and sides of head yellow, sides of head and sides of body streaked with black; female duller; young similar but chestnut not apparent and side streaks narrower.

SONG. — Very distinctive, a high thin *zee zee zee zee zee zee zee*, ascending regularly in pitch.

BREEDING. — On dry, open, brushy plains, with scattering trees, not far from water, also rocky bushy pastures. *Nest:* In bush or low tree.

RANGE. — Breeds from eastern Nebraska, eastern Kansas, southern Ohio, southwestern Pennsylvania, southern New Jersey, southern New York and southeastern Massachusetts, south to Arkansas, southwestern Missouri, northern Mississippi, southern Alabama, central Georgia, and the Bahamas, and north locally to central Michigan, southern Ontario, and New Hampshire; winters from central Florida through the Bahamas and West Indies and islands of Central American coast.

The handsome little Northern Prairie Warbler is remarkable only for its song. Its ascending series of whistling creaks when once well heard and memorized is not likely to be mistaken for that of any other of the warbler tribe.

The bird is not, as its name indicates, an inhabitant of grassy plains. Never was bird more ineptly named. We find the Northern Prairie Warbler mostly on dry brush-covered lands, amid the scrub, upon the barrens, in stony, rolling, bushy pastures and fields, and even in the bushy borders of woodlands. Such localities in Massachusetts, Long Island, New Jersey and Virginia, as dry, sandy, burned-over lands, overgrown with bushes, shrub oaks and scattering pitch pines, or rocky pastures, are the chosen haunts of this pretty warbler. On these lands, or on such bushy tracts as are frequented by the Chestnut-sided Warbler, it builds its nest. It is a clannish little fowl, and often assembles in small colonies to breed in its favorite localities. It is seldom seen about cultivated lands or grassy fields, or in deep woods.

Although it breeds occasionally in colonies, the nests are widely scattered, and each male seems to patrol a certain small territory to which he lays claim, and where he is always ready to give battle to any rival who encroaches on his section; but if danger in the shape of some enemy threatens the family of any one of them, the entire colony soon joins in protesting the invasion or threatening the invader. Usually they are somewhat deep and secretive, but they are consumed with curiosity, and if a visitor sits down quietly or conceals himself in a colony, most of the birds in it will be inquisitive enough to come prying about him.

While the female is sitting on her eggs the male wanders from bush to bush and tree to tree, often stopping to sing with lowered tail and upraised head, as if praising his Creator, but rarely going very far away from his patient mate. Both parents feed the young and care for them for some time after they have left the nest. In July they wander about, often in berry pastures, and some of them begin their southward journey during that month. Others go in August and by September few remain in the north though stragglers may be seen even later.

FLORIDA PRAIRIE WARBLER

Dendroica discolor collinsi BAILEY.

IDENTIFICATION. — Similar to *D. d. discolor* but upper parts (especially in females) more grayish and less greenish; reddish marking on back less pronounced, sometimes absent.

RANGE. — Breeds in mangrove swamps on Florida coasts from New Smyrna and Anclote Key southward; winters, in part at least, in Florida.

The chosen habitat of the Florida Prairie Warbler is very different from that customary with the Northern Prairie Warbler. As Mr. Forbush wrote of the northern race, it is not an inhabitant of prairies, but this southern subspecies goes even farther in making its name misleading, for it is a dweller on the low mangrove islands growing in the shallow coastal sloughs and marshes of southern Florida. A. H. Howell says of it: 'The birds are rather shy during the nesting season; the males sing from near the tops of small mangrove trees and manage to keep well hidden in the foliage. The song sounds to my ear essentially like that of the northern birds — a series of drawled, shrilling notes on an ascending chromatic scale, uttered rather rapidly with the bill pointing nearly straight upward.' — (J.B.M.)

WESTERN PALM WARBLER

Dendroica palmarum palmarum (GMELIN).

PLATE 85.

Other name: Red-poll Warbler.

IDENTIFICATION. — Length 4½ to 5½ inches; spread 7½ to 8½ inches. See below.

BREEDING. — In swampy lands, among or near bushes or small trees. *Nest:* Concealed in a tussock on the ground.

RANGE. — Breeds from southern Mackenzie and northern Manitoba south and southeast to northern Minnesota; winters from southern Florida and the Bahamas to the Greater Antilles and Yucatan; occurs casually in migration on the Atlantic slope mainly in autumn.

The two geographical races of the Palm Warbler differ but little in appearance or habits; their breeding ranges are different but in migration and in winter they are sometimes found together. The Western Palm Warbler averages slightly smaller and has less yellow on its under parts especially than the Yellow Palm Warbler, the contrast between the pale belly and yellow under tail coverts of the western race being very noticeable, while the corresponding region of the eastern race is almost uniformly colored yellow; in winter the line over the eye of the Western Palm is whitish, while in the Yellow Palm it is yellow. — (J.B.M.)

YELLOW PALM WARBLER

Dendroica palmarum hypochrysea RIDGWAY.   PLATE 85.

Other name: Yellow Red-poll Warbler.

IDENTIFICATION. — Length 5 to 5¾ inches; spread 8 to 8½ inches. See Western Palm Warbler.

RANGE. — Breeds from Ontario, central Quebec, and Newfoundland south to southern Nova Scotia, New Brunswick, and Maine; winters from Louisiana to Florida, casually north to Massachusetts.

Mid-April has passed and there is still some snow in the deep woods, when, walking by some bush-bordered wayside, we see what might well be called 'a little yellow wagtail.' It has a red cap and an olive-gray back, but its lower plumage is practically all bright yellow. It flits from bush to ground, sometimes accompanied by several companions, or in a scattered group of Northern Pine Warblers or Myrtle Warblers, with its loose-hung tail almost continually wagging 'with methodic regularity,' not from side to side like that of a dog, but up and down like that of an Eastern Phoebe, and with the same easy unhurried motion. This is the Yellow Palm Warbler.

As the late W. L. Dawson said of the Western Palm Warbler, 'in the careful husbandry of nature this bird alone of the wood-warbler kind has been assigned to a station unmistakably humble.' Other warblers inhabit low bushes, but perhaps no member of the genus *Dendroica* spends so much of its time on the ground as the two races of *D. palmarum*. The Yellow Palm Warbler often associates with sparrows in the field, where it scratches or hops about as they do, and is a typical bird of the undergrowth of thin open woods. Nevertheless it is no stranger to trees, though seldom ascending them to any great height from the ground, which is its favorite nesting-place. In early spring it picks out the most likely places for the early development of insects, such as sunny sheltered shores of ponds and streams, or bushy swamps, or an old orchard on the south side of a hill, near water. In pursuit of its prey it flits from branch to branch, and often to the ground, and captures flying insects in the most active manner, though its ordinary movements, especially those of the tail, may seem rather indolent and lackadaisical.

It sings more or less during migration. Its common song is generally termed a trill, as its short notes are uttered rapidly. It is not very loud, but rather soft and sweet, resembling slightly the song of the Northern Pine Warbler. It also has another song, and both have variations.

On the return south in autumn, the Yellow Palm Warblers scatter over fields, pastures and swamps, and often assemble where gray birch saplings are infested with plant-lice, of which they seem particularly fond. Thus they pass through in late September and early October, and a few stragglers continue to pass in November; occasionally some are reported in winter. During the autumnal migration a pale-bellied Western Palm Warbler may sometimes be recognized among the commoner Yellow Palms, but this race normally migrates west of the Alleghenies, and it is almost unknown on their eastern slopes in the spring migration.

The food of the Yellow Palm Warbler is almost entirely insects and seeds. Along the northern Atlantic coast in winter it apparently eats bayberries, like the Myrtle Warbler.

OVEN–BIRD

Seiurus aurocapillus (LINNAEUS).

PLATE 85.

Other names: Golden-crowned Thrush; Teacher-bird; Accentor; Nightwalker.

IDENTIFICATION. — Length 5½ to 6½ inches; spread 8¾ to 10½ inches. Bright olive-green above, below white streaked with blackish, crown with broad, black-margined brownish-orange stripe; walks on ground, jetting tail frequently.

BREEDING. — Usually in deciduous or mixed woods, but often among pines. *Nest:* Sunken somewhat in ground and arched over with dead leaves of the forest floor.

RANGE. — Breeds from southwestern Mackenzie, northern Ontario, central Quebec, and Newfoundland south to southern Alberta, Colorado, Arkansas, southern Missouri, northern Alabama, northern Georgia, and eastern North Carolina; winters from northern Florida and islands off Louisiana coast through the Bahamas and West Indies, and from Mexico to Colombia.

The Oven-bird was one of the first birds to attract my attention when in May dawns I first began to wend my way to the shades of the wonderful leafy woods. Then all the wood birds were new. It was as if they had just been created and loosed in those dim sequestered shades for my edification and delight. Among them all, the most common and conspicuous was the Oven-bird. Its staccato song with its crescendo ending rang through the woods, seemingly the loudest of them all, and when I saw the pretty bird walking with its alert air along a log, putting its little head forward at each dainty step in the manner of a diminutive chicken, I was utterly captivated. One sunny day as I trod a woodland path a tiny bright object, glistening like a dewdrop flashing in the sunlight, caught my eye; pausing to examine it, I saw that a sun ray was reflected from the eye of a bird sitting upon her nest. She sat there until almost trodden upon, and then fluttered out and trailed pitifully away like a cripple with a broken wing, but I had guessed her secret and, parting the leaves, looked into her cunningly concealed nest and saw for the first time the pretty speckled eggs.

Many moons passed and my knowledge of the notes and calls of the bird seemed to be complete, but I had still much to learn. One evening when I had lingered in the loved woods until twilight came, I heard in the air a wild outburst of intricate rapturous melody ascending far above the tree-tops, and saw the little singer rising against the glow of the western sky, pouring out his passion song to the slowly rising moon. When the song was done and the exhausted singer fell from out the sky, his final notes were those of the common song of my little friend, the Oven-bird, who at the end shot down with wings nearly closed and dropped to earth almost at my very feet. Many times thereafter I heard this song, with its accompanying variable flight, which years later was hailed as a new discovery by John Burroughs. Probably every field ornithologist had heard it, but Burroughs was the first to describe it *at length*. Nuttall speaks of the night song and Brewer mentions it. Thoreau speaks often of this mysterious 'night warbler,' but apparently never identified it. His anxiety to know the source of the night melody was so great that Emerson warned him to cease trying to find out what it was lest he should succeed and 'thereafter lose all interest in life.' Samuels also heard and described the flight-song briefly when I was still a small child. It is, as Dr. Chapman says, 'a wild outpouring of jumbled notes over which the bird seems to have no control, and is often concluded with the common *teachêr* song.'

Although its flight-song is usually uttered at dusk on moonlit nights, it is given occasionally in the daytime or just before daylight, and sometimes from a perch. Usually the *teachêr* song is uttered from the ground, from a prostrate log or from a low branch of a tree; as I have heard it commonly, it might be rendered as *cher-têa cher-têa*, etc., but sometimes *têacher* or *teachêr*, etc.

The Oven-bird most commonly inhabits dry deciduous or mixed woods, but it is sometimes found in white pine or spruce groves and often in rather low swampy ground. Like its congeners, the water-thrushes, it walks and runs much upon the ground, but keeps mostly out of the water (although fond of bathing) and does not, like them, habitually wave its tail up and down, though the tail is jetted or waved more or less, in the manner of the Hermit Thrush. Often it is held rather high with wings drooping below it, as the bird steps daintily along on its pretty pink feet.

Our little woodland songster usually arrives during the first ten days of May, and when the females come, courtship soon begins. The male, now all ardor and animation, flies and dashes about the female, hops, struts and postures, raising tail and crest, lowering wings and singing with great vigor and abandon. Sometimes he flutters up into the air and shows his devotion by revolving in flight about the demure and retiring female. If rivals appear there is much swift chasing through the air, and withal numerous outbursts of song. When the happy pair is finally united, nest-building begins. Both birds labor lovingly together, burrowing into the forest floor to round out an aperture for their lowly nest, which often is completed in fair weather in two or three days. As soon as the newly hatched young are ready for food, both parents begin to feed them. They are cared for not only in the nest but until they are able to fly strongly and feed themselves.

When the female is startled from the nest, she drags herself along the ground fluttering as if sorely wounded, in an effort to lead her disturber away from her home. However, as in the case of many other ground-nesting birds, frequently the first brood is destroyed by enemies, and it is difficult to get accurate information regarding the actual rearing of two broods in one year.

Most of the insects with which the young birds are fed are taken from the ground, but they also take some from the shrubbery and from the lower parts of trees, and they sometimes pursue flying insects and capture them in the air.

This little wood bird manifests much interest in what is going on about him and curiosity seems to dominate his actions. If we imitate his call or the cry of a wounded bird, we may soon see three or four Oven-birds hastening toward the sound. If we sit quietly down on a log in the woods, one or more of these prying little creatures may soon appear, to inspect the novelty.

During August many Oven-birds wander about with small flocks of other warblers — with the tree warblers but not of them — for although they may keep near the more arboreal birds, they rarely mix with them in the trees, but stay mostly on or near the ground. Early in September most of the local breeding birds are on their southward way. During migration they are seen occasionally in parks and in the shrubbery of gardens in village or city.

NORTHERN WATER–THRUSH

Seiurus noveboracensis noveboracensis (GMELIN).

PLATE 85.

Other name: Water Wagtail.

IDENTIFICATION. — Length 5 to 6¼ inches; spread 8½ to 10 inches. Above dark olive-brown, buffy stripe over eye, below buffy-yellow or greenish-yellow spotted with dark olive.

SONG. — A loud ringing *ching-ching-ching, chee-chee-chee, ch-ch-ch-ch*; also a flight-song.

BREEDING. — In wooded swamps and bogs, along wooded watercourses, or low wooded shores of a pond. *Nest:* In cavity in the ground, under a mossy log or the roots of a tree, or side of a bank, largely of green moss.

RANGE. — Breeds from northern Ontario, northern Quebec, and Newfoundland south to southern Ontario, northwestern New York, and northern New England, and in the mountains to Pennsylvania and West Virginia; winters from the Valley of Mexico to Colombia and British Guiana and from Florida through the Bahamas and West Indies; in migration west to Minnesota, Iowa and Missouri.

Though not really a thrush, the Northern Water-Thrush is well named. It is a large wood warbler disguised as a thrush and exhibiting an extreme fondness for water. Like the Oven-bird it walks, and seems fond of walking on a log, but prefers to pass down a slanting log, the lower end of which enters the water. It is unlike the Oven-bird, however, in its almost continuous teetering of the body and wagging of the tail, which it seems to move up and down almost as unconsciously and regularly as it draws the breath of life; this action is accompanied by a springy motion of the legs. It is so fond of the water that it is never seen far from it, except when, in the exigencies of migration and in search of food, it may alight and feed for a time away from its beloved element. Thus, in the fall migration, it occasionally visits gardens, the trees and shrubbery about buildings, and groves at some distance from water. But in spring and summer it usually may be found along woodland brooks, in dark and shaded swamps and bogs, or along the low and swampy wooded shores of lakes and rivers. It delights to wade in shallow waters much after the manner of the sandpipers, but is much more retiring than they, and at the first real alarm it seeks cover. Although its activities are largely terrestrial or even aquatic, it is at home amid the tree-tops as well.

Dr. Elliott Coues, in his 'Birds of the Colorado Valley,' thus describes the haunts and habits of the Northern Water-Thrush:

'Should you force your way — perhaps by paddling in a light canoe beneath the overhanging mysteries of the dank morass — perhaps by clambering among the fallen logs that jut from treacherous black depths of ooze and slime — you may even catch a glimpse of this coy songster as he dashes onward into yet more secret fastness of his watery and seldom sun-lit home. His song is still now; silence broods, or else a sharp short note of anger and anxiety betrays the presence of the timid bird, too restless and too nervous in his vague alarm to hide in safety, but rather dallying with danger as he leaps and balances on log, moss-heap, or branch-let. But this is only when he feels the cares and full responsibilities of home and family. Later in the season, when these things are off his mind, he is quite another fellow, who will meet you more than half-way should you chance to find him then, with a wondering, perhaps, yet with a confident and quite familiar, air of easy unconcern. Anywhere by the water's edge — in the *débris* of the wide-stretched river-bottom, in the flowery tangle of the brook, around the margins of the little pools that dot the surface where tall oaks and hickories make pleasant shade — there rambles the Water-Thrush. Watch him now, and see how prettily he walks, rustling

444

among the fallen leaves where he threads his way like a mouse, or wading even up to his knees in the shallow miniature lakes, like a Sandpiper by the sea-shore, all intent in quest of the aquatic insects, worms, and tiny molluscs and crustaceans that form his varied food. But as he rambles on in this gliding course, the mincing steps are constantly arrested, and the dainty stroller poises in a curious way to see-saw on his legs, quite like a Titlark or a Spotted Sandpiper. All of his genus share this gait, quite different from the hopping movement with which the *Sylvicolidae* in general progress — but see! he catches sight of us, and quite breaks off the thread of such reflections as he casts his bright brown eye upon us with a coquettish turning sideways of the head. Let the pretty picture be — we leave him to resume in peace his morning's walk, bidding good-speed.'

The ordinary song of this bird, ringing through a dark, shaded swamp, is so loud as to be somewhat startling. It is wild, ringing and melodious, exceeding in power that of the Winter Wren, and occasionally when the passionate creature rises above its lowly habitat in its flight-song, it eclipses all its mundane efforts in a burst of enraptured music which is heard only in the retired precincts of its breeding haunts, where the song mingles with the murmur and splashing of cool waters or wells up from leafy swales.

When the young have left the nest they may be found with their parents about the shores of ponds, along streams, or in bushy hollows until the latter part of August, when the southern migration begins.

GRINNELL'S WATER–THRUSH

Seiurus noveboracensis notabilis RIDGWAY.

IDENTIFICATION. — Slightly larger than *S. n. noveboracensis* and bill longer; upper parts darker, less olive, under parts and line over eye whiter.

RANGE. — Breeds from limit of trees in northwestern Alaska to northern Manitoba, south to southern British Columbia, central Montana, northwestern Nebraska, northern Minnesota, and northwestern Michigan; winters in Cuba, Haiti, Porto Rico, the Bahamas, Mexico and northern South America; in migration through the Mississippi Valley and along the Atlantic coast from South Carolina southward.

This western race goes even farther north in the breeding season than the so-called Northern Water-Thrush, and migrates diagonally across and down the Mississippi Valley, so that it is found on the southern Atlantic seaboard at this time. — (J.B.M.)

LOUISIANA WATER–THRUSH

Seiurus motacilla (VIEILLOT). PLATE 85.

Other names: Large-billed Water-Thrush; Southern Water-Thrush; Water Wagtail.

IDENTIFICATION. — Length 5¾ to 6½ inches; spread 9¾ to 10¾ inches. Above dark olive-brown; conspicuous pure white stripe over eye; below white tinged buffy and heavily streaked.

BREEDING. — Usually in the wooded valley of a rocky brook or small stream, sometimes in a swamp. *Nest:* In an excavation in a brook bank or among upturned roots of a fallen tree, of grass, dry leaves, rootlets, and moss.

The haunts of the Louisiana Water-Thrush are even wilder and more retired perhaps than those of its northern relative. It is fond of rocky glens in deep woodland shades, where the rushing waters of a brook tumble and splash over a stony bed. This bird arrives in New England in April and departs in July, both surprisingly early dates, much earlier both in spring and fall than its northern congener. It is interesting to note that both species are found in the same localities where their respective ranges overlap.

As a songster the Louisiana Water-Thrush is nearly or quite the equal of the northern bird. Some ornithologists, having heard both, regard it as superior to the other, but perhaps they have heard particularly gifted individuals. Often it is so difficult to get a fair view of the bird that though its wild ringing song may be readily followed through the shrubbery and tangles in which it delights, the would-be observer is puzzled regarding which species he is following. Fleeting glances of a teetering bird, or a flitting form darting low and fast through the undergrowth, are all that may be vouchsafed the vexed pursuer.

The bird seems usually even more shy than the Northern Water-Thrush. Nevertheless, when this bird has young in the nest or fledglings that have recently left the nest, it forgets its caution when a human intruder seems to menace their safety. The female, though shy, sits very closely on her nest, and will allow a hand to be placed almost on her back sometimes before she will desert her charge. She seems to be aware that as long as she keeps still she is well concealed. A pair that I watched while they were feeding newly fledged young seemed to care little for their own safety when their young appeared to be in danger.

Mr. W. Lindsay Foxhall says that when the bird is surprised on the nest it will tumble out of it and into the water in the most surprising and startling manner, and then it will flutter and roll over and over for several yards downstream, as if its head were severed from its body.

KENTUCKY WARBLER

Oporornis formosus (WILSON). PLATE 86.

IDENTIFICATION. — Length 5 to 5¾ inches; spread 8 to 9¼ inches. Plain olive-green above, bright yellow below, partial yellow eye-ring, black patch extending from eye down side of throat, black forehead; female duller, with less black about head and throat.

SONG. — Loud, frequently repeated, suggesting that of Carolina Wren, *turtle, turtle, turtle,* or *tweedlé tweedlé tweedlé.*

BREEDING. — In open, bushy swamps, moist hillsides, wooded bottomlands, sproutlands, and ravines. *Nest:* On or near ground in thick growth, among roots of a tree, etc.

RANGE. — Breeds from southeastern Nebraska, southern Wisconsin, northern Ohio, central western Pennsylvania, and the Hudson Valley south to eastern Texas, Louisiana, southern Alabama, and northern Georgia; winters from Mexico to Colombia.

The Kentucky Warbler habitually feeds on or near the ground, but it usually sings in the trees. It is extremely active and usually shy and suspicious. As it commonly keeps in rather thick cover it might escape notice were it not for its habit of loud and persistent singing. Regarding this habit Dr. Chapman says 'in the height of the breeding season this warbler is a most persistent singer. On one occasion, at Englewood, New Jersey, I watched a male for three hours. During this period, with the exception of five interruptions of less than forty-five seconds each, he sang with the greatest regularity once every twelve seconds. Thus, allowing for the brief intervals of silence, he sang about 875 times, or some 5250 notes. I found him singing, and when I departed he showed no signs of ceasing.'

During its stay in the North the bird seldom flies far, but keeps rather closely to the cover of trees, shrubbery and the rank plants that grow in moist or swampy land. On the ground it walks very prettily in the manner of the Oven-bird, and often tilts its body and wags its tail up and down, though not so much addicted to this habit as are the water-thrushes. It frequents boggy woodlands, especially their bushy borders, deep, dark, gloomy swamps and shores of bush-bordered streams and ponds, and delights in dark boggy tangles where the way is obstructed with fallen logs or uprooted trees. The nest, which is on the ground in open bushy swamps, and in the construction of which both sexes share, is so well concealed that it is seldom found except by accident or by watching the birds while engaged in building it, or in feeding the young, a task which occupies both parents. When the female is incubating she uses great care in entering and leaving her little domicile not to betray it to any enemy. The young are ready to leave the nest in about eight days from the date of hatching. Probably but one brood is reared in the northern part of its range, as the species begins to move southward in August. In migration it sometimes may be found along the edges of fields and in other situations where one would hardly expect to find it. In autumn it is silent, keeps well under cover, and is likely thus to escape notice.

CONNECTICUT WARBLER

Oporornis agilis (WILSON).   PLATE 86.

IDENTIFICATION. — Length 5¼ to 6 inches; spread 8½ to 9 inches. Above olive-green, below pale yellow; most of head, throat and upper breast gray; complete white eye-ring; female duller, pale brownish on throat and upper breast, eye-ring tinged buffy.

SONG. — Suggests that of the Oven-bird, but without changing pitch or emphasis.

BREEDING. — In tamarack swamps. *Nest:* Of grass, sunk in swamp moss.

RANGE. — Breeds from Alberta and Manitoba to central Minnesota and northern Michigan; winters in Colombia, Brazil and Venezuela; migrates through South Carolina, Florida, and the Bahamas; rare in spring east of the Alleghenies but common in the Mississippi Valley; in autumn rare in the Mississippi Valley but common east of the Alleghenies.

Mr. William Brewster, who was very successful in finding this species in Massachusetts during its migrations, wrote of his experiences as follows: 'We used to find the Connecticut Warblers oftenest among the thickets of clethra, *Andromeda ligustrina*, shad-bush, and black alder, which formed a dense undergrowth beneath the large maples that shaded the wooded islands of this swamp, and in the beds of touch-me-not (*Impatiens*) that covered some of its wetter portions. They were also given to frequenting the banks of the numerous intersecting ditches, especially where the deadly nightshade, clinging to the stems of the bushes, trailed its gray-green foliage and coral-red berries over the black mud or coffee-colored water. In such places they often literally swarmed, but so retiring and elusive were they that by anyone unacquainted with their habits they might easily have been overlooked. They spent most of their time on the ground under or among the rank vegetation, where they would often remain securely hidden until nearly trodden on. Indeed we learned eventually that the only certain method of starting all the birds that a thicket contained was to beat the place closely and systematically many times in succession. When flushed they would usually fly up into the low bushes and sit there motionless in thrush-like attitudes, gazing at us intently with their large dark eyes. If further disturbed, they were nearly sure to take long flights to distant parts of the swamp. During cloudy weather we sometimes found them feeding with the Black-poll Warblers in the tops of large willows, fifty or sixty feet above the ground. The earliest date on which they were ever seen by us was September 7 and the last stragglers usually departed for the south before the first of October. They never appeared in spring, nor is there a single record in which I have full confidence of their occurrence at that season in any part of Massachusetts.'

In migration the Connecticut Warbler frequents swampy, bushy, moist lands, or weed patches and brier patches along the edges of moist fields and pastures, keeping usually well within thick cover, near the ground, where it remains for the most part silent. It is generally so secretive that its habits and food are little known.

MOURNING WARBLER

Oporornis philadelphia (WILSON).   PLATE 86.

IDENTIFICATION. — Length 5 to 5¾ inches; spread 7½ to 8¼ inches. Above mainly olive-green, under parts yellow; a gray hood encircling head and neck becoming black on upper breast; no eye-ring or wing-bars; female lacks hood but shows some gray on throat.

BREEDING. — In clearings grown up to weeds, bushes, etc., along bushy roadsides, borders of woods, or swampy clearings. *Nest:* Among weeds or sprouts, near ground, of weed stalks, leaves, and rootlets.

RANGE. — Breeds from east-central Alberta, central Saskatchewan, central Manitoba, Nova Scotia, Newfoundland, and the Magdalen Islands south to central Minnesota, Michigan, central Ontario, and in the mountains of Massachusetts, New York, Pennsylvania, and West Virginia; winters from Nicaragua and Costa Rica to Venezuela and Ecuador; in migration mainly west of the Alleghenies and to eastern Texas, rare in the lowlands of the Gulf States.

The Mourning Warbler is a striking and beautiful bird, though frontally 'veiled in crêpe.' This crêpe-like marking about the breast is the only thing about the bird that would suggest mourning, for it seems as happy and active as most birds, and its song is a paean of joy.

It has always seemed to be one of the rarest of warblers in the Northern States, but its apparent extreme rarity is due in part to the fact that although a straggler may appear very rarely early in May, the main spring migration does not arrive until late May and early June, when most observers are not looking for migrating warblers, and the foliage has become so dense that the bird can skulk most of the time in cover. On its breeding-grounds the male, when undisturbed, will sit on the branch of a dead tree for all the world to see, giving out intermittently his full-voiced song, but upon the appearance of a human intruder he is likely to dive into the brush and conceal himself so effectually that his occasional song will be the only indication of his whereabouts. In migration the bird skulks silently from thicket to thicket and rarely makes its presence known. An unusual noise, like the imitation of the cry of a wounded bird, may so stimulate its curiosity as to cause it to show itself for a moment, only to disappear for good and all. Such, at least, is my own experience with this elusive little feathered biped. During migration it seems to haunt dense thickets along the streams, especially in swampy localities where it consorts with other warblers.

Ordinarily we seldom see it in the States south of its breeding range until late May, when it arrives from South or Central America, and in September it appears again in company with Maryland Yellow-throats, Palm Warblers, Myrtle Warblers, White-throated Sparrows, Swamp Sparrows and other birds of the thickets, that make up the little wandering groups of the fall migration. The Mourning Warbler is not, however, confined to swampy localities, and may be found occasionally far from water, but seldom far from good cover. Sometimes it betakes itself to some tall tree-top where it can survey its surroundings.

In the breeding season I have found it in high, dry clearings overgrown with underbrush and briers. The nest is usually in a thicket or clump of weeds quite near the ground.

When the female is flushed from the nest, she slips quietly away under cover and therefore it is difficult to identify her. When the young have been reared the parents remain with them near the place of their nativity until the molt is finished, and before September ends most of them have left for the South.

NORTHERN YELLOW–THROAT

Geothlypis trichas brachidactyla (SWAINSON). PLATE 86.

Other names: Yellow-throat; Ground Warbler; Black-masked Warbler.

IDENTIFICATION. — Length 4½ to 5¾ inches; spread 6½ to 7¼ inches. Male with bright yellow throat and *black 'domino' mask* is unmistakable; female and young lack black mask and are plain olive with yellow throat and breast, but *whitish belly.*

BREEDING. — In wet bushy meadows, swampy thickets, the edges of damp woods, near ponds or streams, in cattail bogs, etc. *Nest:* On or near ground among weeds, sedges, ferns or shrubs, or in a tussock of grass.

RANGE. — Breeds from Quebec, southern Labrador, Newfoundland, Nova Scotia, New Brunswick, and Maine south to northern New Jersey, southern New York, and northern Pennsylvania, and west to Ontario and North Dakota; winters in the Bahamas and West Indies and through eastern Mexico to Costa Rica.

Dear to the heart of every bird lover is that engaging warbler with the bright yellow bib and black domino, the Northern Yellow-throat. To make his acquaintance one has only to visit his favorite haunts — tangled shrubbery by the brookside and dense coverts that margin swampy woodland, or matted reeds and sedges of the swamp — when presto! up bobs that masquerading scrap of animated feathers, nervously voicing his alarm with a variety of scolding chirps and chattering notes, his black eyes sparkling with excitement. Suddenly he explodes in a vigorous outburst of song, as if to inquire '*whatcha-see, whatcha-see, whatcha-see*' and darting impatiently here and there in the low undergrowth, plainly announces that his privacy has been

449

disturbed; but his curiosity and indignation are soon over, and, scurrying to the shelter of his retreat, he leaves the cause of his disquietude flooded with emotions of surprise and delight. The Yellow-throat captivates one's fancy. His attractive plumage and winsome, wren-like manners give him a marked individuality which few birds possess, and such traits being decidedly uncommon in a warbler, account for his great popularity. Far less handsomely attired is the object of his affections; but despite the subdued colors of the female, she is always recognizable by the distinctive Yellow-throat personality.

By no means is this lively little favorite wholly partial to swampy localities, for we often find it in the woods and orchards, and even in bushy pastures. Seldom does it mount to the tree-tops, but even during migrations it may be found in the lower branches. From its habit of breeding and spending most of its time on or very close to the ground, it has obtained the name of Ground Warbler. This title, however, is perhaps more fittingly applied to the Oven-bird than to the subject of this sketch.

During the breeding season the Yellow-throat is strongly attached to the immediate neighborhood of its domestic activities, where it restlessly skulks and hops about the bushes and brambles, much in the manner of a wren. It is very resentful of intrusion, and will give vent to its displeasure with vigorous protests of harsh, rasping notes, and sometimes a peculiar snarl.

Although rather bulky, the nest is so well concealed that it is usually found only by flushing the female. Occasionally nests are found well above the ground, in bushes or tangles of briers, and I have seen one about a foot up, lodged in a thick mass of spruce foliage.

Nest construction is accomplished solely by the female in a little over a week, and to her also fall the cares of incubation. She is a fearless, devoted mother, and zealously guards the contents of her nest. Often while she is brooding one can almost stroke her back. The male is not wholly idle, however, for when the young hatch, he is a faithful, assiduous worker in feeding them. If everything goes well, after two weeks the young birds follow their parents into the wide world.

Of considerable variability is the Yellow-throat's song; still it is one of the easiest to learn, by virtue of its peculiar swing and loud, pleasing notes. Soon after the male arrives at its summer home from southern climes, its rollicking medley is heard. It sings constantly until the latter part of July, when the almost universal lull in bird song takes place; then, however, it may continue to sing more or less, but with diminished spirit, until the first few days in September, when its voice is seldom heard.

The Yellow-throat also has a flight-song, which is really nothing more than a silly little outburst of ecstasy, consisting of a brief utterance of confused and spluttering notes as it springs a few feet into the air. It is heard throughout the breeding season and into late summer.

Of all the useful warbler clan, the Northern Yellow-throat is one of the most beneficial to the agriculturist. In its habit of frequenting a variety of situations, its feeding range is perhaps wider than most warblers, and this, coupled with its abundance, adds to its economic importance. It is particularly fond of canker-worms, for which it scours the orchard; it eagerly eats fall web-worms, and destroys immense numbers of many other destructive caterpillars, including those of the gypsy moth; grasshoppers and leaf-hoppers bring the bird to the fields, where it makes of these insects important articles of diet, while plant-lice, flies and beetles help to appease this bird's voracious appetite. Its menu contains also such delicacies as grubs, small moths, spiders, ants and the larvae of many insects, all of which it consumes in considerable quantities. — (M.B.)

MARYLAND YELLOW–THROAT

Geothlypis trichas trichas (LINNAEUS).

Other names: Yellow-throat; Ground Warbler.

IDENTIFICATION. — This southern race of Yellow-throat is slightly smaller than the Northern Yellow-throat and its colors are somewhat paler or duller, but it is indistinguishable in the field, and its habits are similar to those of its northern relative.

RANGE. — Breeds from southern Pennsylvania south to eastern Texas, northern Alabama, and northern Georgia; winters from North Carolina and Louisiana to Florida, the Bahamas, and Haiti.

FLORIDA YELLOW–THROAT

Geothlypis trichas ignota CHAPMAN.

IDENTIFICATION. — Similar to *G. t. trichas* but yellow of under parts deeper and of greater area, flanks much darker, upper parts browner; black mask wider and ashy border slightly paler but wider; bill, tarsus and tail longer.

RANGE. — Breeds from Dismal Swamp, Virginia, coast region of South Carolina, central Georgia and central Alabama south to Florida and along the Gulf coast to Louisiana; winters from the coast of South Carolina to southern Georgia and southern Alabama.

Dr. Frank M. Chapman, who first described and named this race, says that it is usually found in dense growths of scrub palmetto and that its song differs recognizably from that of the Maryland Yellow-throat. A. H. Howell says that it resembles that of the Northern Yellow-throats in general, but 'has a peculiar turn in it that appears to be a local variation.' — (J.B.M.)

YELLOW–BREASTED CHAT

Icteria virens virens (LINNAEUS).   PLATE 86.

IDENTIFICATION. — Length 6¾ to 7½ inches; spread 9 to 10 inches. Larger than Bluebird; olive-green above, bright yellow on chin, throat and breast and abruptly white on belly; white eye-ring but no white on wings or tail.

SONG. — Very varied, a mixture of clear whistles, harsh notes, and soft crow-like *caws*, etc.

BREEDING. — Chiefly in bushy pastures, thickets, or brier-patches. Nest in bush, small sapling, or tangle of grapevine, smilax, briers, etc. *Nest:* Coarse and bulky, of leaves, grasses, bark-strips, etc., lined with finer grasses.

RANGE. — Breeds from southern Minnesota, Wisconsin, Michigan, Ontario, central New York, and southern New England south to southeastern Texas, southern Alabama, and northern Florida; winters in Mexico and Central America.

My first meeting with the Yellow-breasted Chat occurred when as a boy, wandering idly through an old pasture overgrown with bushes near the shore of Lake Quinsigamond in central Massachusetts, I was assailed by a medley of strange sounds which seemed to move from place to place in the bushes about me, while their author kept well concealed. There were turkey calls, whistles, mews and a rapid succession of notes and phrases, musical and unmusical, and all attempts to identify the singer or even to get a fair look at him were unsuccessful. Finally I sat down quietly among some bushes and began to imitate the cry of a bird in distress. At once a Yellow-breasted Chat dashed almost into my face — caution thrown to the winds. Later I found that this eccentric character was breeding there, as well as at other stations about the city of Worcester, and farther north in the country towns.

They sometimes appear in the North after the leaves in their favorite retreats have developed sufficiently to furnish excellent cover, of which they immediately avail themselves. They are so furtive at first that their arrival passes unnoticed and how they get there nobody knows. Their ordinary flight is so short and desultory that it would seem that they are not fitted for the extended movements incident to a migration from South America to the northern parts of the United States. Audubon believed that in migration they merely skulked from bush to bush, as is their habit on their breeding-ground, and that they traveled night and day.

'However this may be,' says Dr. Coues, in his 'Birds of the Colorado Valley,' 'no sooner is the ardor of the occasion stimulated by the presence of the females than the gay and gaudy Chats develop those eccentricities that make them famous. They grow too restless to abide the covert they have chosen for their home, and are seen incessantly in motion, flitting with jerky movement from one bush and brier-patch to another, giving vent to long-pent emotions in the oddest notes imaginable. Such a medley of whistling, chuckling, barking and mewing sounds proceeds from no other bird, unless it be the Mockingbird itself, to whom all possibilities of song are open. During such performances, the Chats seem sedulous to keep concealed, displaying ingenuity and perversity in thwarting our best efforts to catch them at their tricks. The notes, in all their infinite variety, come now from this and now from that spot in the bushes, shifting from point to point as we peer eagerly into the tangled underbrush to catch a glimpse of the tantalizing musician. Such restlessness, and all this variation in the rendering, have much the effect of ventriloquism, and we have not seldom to acknowledge that the Chat has fairly beaten us. But his coloring is brilliant; he has, moreover, a fancy to return again to some particular spot already chosen as his stage; so that if we discover it, and keep so still as not to cause the bird anxiety, nor yet to arouse his ire, we shall most likely see him take his stand again to swell his golden throat afresh with the fantasy of song.

'His nuptial song, I should observe, is something very different from the medley of sounds, not all of which are pleasing, that are heard when each Chat, as one performer in an orchestra, first tunes his curious pipe. Such prelude, after several days' essay, is changed into the rich, voluminous ode with which the bird inaugurates a new order of events, in bursts of almost startling eloquence and fervor. For the nesting-place is fixed upon, the fabric hastens to completion; and the exultant bird, no longer constrained to the lowliness of the coverts, mounts buoyantly from bough to bough of some tall sentinel that guards the leafy undergrowth, to sound his exultation from the very tree-top. Yet once more: the nest now bears its precious burden; the brooding bird assumes her patient place, and presses down her golden breast upon her hopes. Then this strange bird goes fairly wild with joy; he spurns the ground, the favorite singing-post no longer bids him welcome, he rises on the wing, and in mid-air above the nest, with fluttering pinions, down-stretched legs and open beak, he poises, hovers, and performs a thousand antics in the sheer abandon of his eccentricity.

'Such are the Chat's most characteristic actions during the heyday of his life; and when we see him cutting such capers, we may be sure that the nest is not far off.'

HOODED WARBLER

Wilsonia citrina (BODDAERT).   PLATE 87.

IDENTIFICATION. — Length 5 to 5¾ inches; spread 8 to 8½ inches. Adult male unmistakable with *yellow mask, black hood*, olive-green upper parts, yellow under parts, white inner vanes on outer tail feathers; female with less black or none, and *yellow forehead*.

SONG. — A loud musical *weeta weeteo* with a downward slur at the end.

BREEDING. — In bushy, swampy lands or woodlands with dense undergrowth and in hillside thickets of laurel, etc. *Nest:* In bush or sapling 1 to 5 feet above ground or water.

RANGE. — Breeds from southeastern Nebraska, northern Iowa, southern Michigan, central New York, and the lower Connecticut Valley south to the Gulf coast of Louisiana, Alabama, and Georgia, and in northern Florida; winters from Mexico to Panama.

In the Hooded Warbler we have a peculiar and striking combination of black, green and gold, as well as a lively and engaging bird. Normally it is an inhabitant of the lowlands, preferring well-watered woodlands and swampy lands overgrown with bushes, for it is largely a bird of the undergrowth and the lower levels of the trees. My chief experience with it has been in southern Connecticut, where it nests in small numbers, but after the breeding season some individuals in their wanderings reach Massachusetts, where I saw one once in the Boston Public Garden; at that season of the year the bird is likely to appear in unexpected places, as well as in the spring migration.

In migration it does not seem shy, but usually on its breeding-grounds it keeps largely under cover. While searching its native thickets its presence is often revealed as it flutters up above the bush-tops, or darts out after some passing insect. Its sweet song, which it utters frequently during the daylight hours, carries far, and reveals its presence to the passer-by. It has at least two main songs, very unlike, and some variations. While singing it frequently opens its tail and when in the air it opens and closes it, thereby 'flashing' the large white terminal spots.

The home life of this warbler seems to be little known, and I have never had an opportunity to observe it sufficiently. Both parents are devoted to their young and to one another, and sometimes will approach very close to a person disturbing the nestlings, and attempt to lead him away.

In late July when the young have been reared and have donned their winter plumage, most of the Hooded Warblers begin to leave their northern homes for the long journey to Mexico or Central America; some individuals continue to wander about in the North through August, and some of the males have a second song period during that month.

WILSON'S WARBLER

Wilsonia pusilla pusilla (WILSON).

PLATE 87.

Other names: Wilson's Black-cap; Black-capped Yellow Warbler.

IDENTIFICATION. — Length 4¼ to 5 inches; spread 6¾ to 7 inches. A small warbler, yellow with a *black cap* in male; female and young may lack black or have only a trace, but have *sides of head yellow and ear region olive-green.*

BREEDING. — Usually in a tamarack bog or a swampy run. *Nest:* On ground or sunken in it, among bushes, and composed mainly of grass, lined with finer grass and a few hairs.

RANGE. — Breeds from tree limit in Mackenzie, northern Manitoba, central Quebec, and Newfoundland south to southern Saskatchewan, northern Minnesota, central Ontario, New Hampshire, Maine, and Nova Scotia; winters from Guatemala to Costa Rica; migrates mainly along the Alleghenies, and is practically unknown in Lower Austral Zone from North Carolina to Louisiana, apparently crossing this region and the Gulf of Mexico in a continuous flight.

Among the least and lowliest of our warblers, the pretty little Wilson's Warbler is a marked bird, because of its black cap. Both adult male and female show this cap, though in spring females it is not usually so prominent as in the male, and the young in autumn show little if any trace of it. The bird is quick, active and energetic, nearly always busy in excited pursuit of its small game, which it often follows and catches on the wing, snapping its bill in the manner of a flycatcher. The little bird has spells of excessive tail-twitching, with a sort of rotary motion, which perhaps expresses its emotion, as it does not sing very much in migration; this is sometimes accompanied by much flipping of the wings, such as is common with kinglets.

I have found it almost invariably in bushes near water, where dense willows grow, on roads leading through swamps or on swampy, shrubby lands, but at this season it may be found elsewhere occasionally, in upland deciduous or coniferous woods, in orchards or even in city gardens or parks. It is normally a bird of the shrubbery, the weed patch, and the lower branches of trees near woodland waters and in bushy bogs. The alder copse is one of its favorite haunts. It usually arrives in New England about the middle of May, and departs for the North before the end of the month. The southward migration begins in August, and all but a few delayed stragglers have left before September ends.

CANADA WARBLER

Wilsonia canadensis (LINNAEUS).

PLATE 87.

Other names: Canadian Warbler; Canada Flycatcher.

IDENTIFICATION. — Length 5 to 5¾ inches; spread 8 to 8¾ inches. Plain gray above; male with well-defined necklace of black spots across yellow breast; female duller and necklace less distinct; young with upper plumage more or less tinged with brownish and necklace barely visible.

BREEDING. — In cool woodlands or wooded swamps, of deciduous or mixed growth. *Nest:* On or near ground, among ferns, in grassy tussocks, beneath bushes or logs or upturned roots or banks, and mossy situations in general.

RANGE. — Breeds from southern Alberta, central Manitoba, central Ontario, central Quebec, and Newfoundland south to central Minnesota, central Michigan, southern Ontario, central New York, and Connecticut, and along the Alleghenies to northern Georgia and Tennessee; winters in Ecuador and Peru; in migration to eastern Mexico.

This charming little bird is one of the most handsome and most musical of our warblers. It is not as strikingly colored as some of the others, but its simple beauty consists in the exquisite ornament of a heavy jet necklace across its yellow breast. The Canada Warbler vents its good spirits in lusty, rippling, much reiterated warbling notes that have scarcely any semblance to the sibilant utterances of most of its congeners, but suggest rather the songs of the Goldfinch and Canary.

During migration this sprightly bird consorts freely with other warblers, but upon reaching its breeding grounds in the North, it becomes rather solitary, and resorts to the cool, deep, moisture-laden forests, carpeted and draped with mosses, and abounding in dense tangles and coverts. Here it fulfills nature's requirements, erecting and concealing its loose, bulky nest in some depression in the ground among clumps of lush ferns or other vegetation.

The Canada Warbler habitually forages among shrubbery and the lower limbs of trees, seldom venturing to the higher tree-tops. In this and in many other habits it resembles its nearest relative, the Wilson's Warbler. Early writers always referred to it as the 'Canada Flycatcher,' because of its expertness in catching insects on the wing. Its flycatching propensities are often manifest, but the bird also gleans its prey from leaf and twig, and occasionally from the ground. — (M.B.)

AMERICAN REDSTART

Setophaga ruticilla (LINNAEUS).

PLATE 87.

IDENTIFICATION. — Length about 4½ to 5¾ inches; spread 7¾ to 8¾ inches. Adult male with striking pattern of black, orange-red and whitish is unmistakable; female and young male with black replaced by grayish and olive, and orange-red by yellow in same pattern.

BREEDING. — In orchards, woodlands, the borders of pastures, even in shade trees and garden shrubbery. *Nest:* In an upright crotch, a firm deep cup of vegetal fibers lined with fine grass, fern-down, bark-strips, hairs, and a few small feathers.

RANGE. — Breeds from northern British Columbia, central Manitoba, southern Quebec, and Newfoundland south to Oregon, Colorado, Arkansas, southern Alabama, northern Georgia, and North Carolina; winters in the West Indies and from central Mexico to Ecuador and British Guiana.

Every bird lover has at some time been asked 'Of all the warblers, which one is your favorite?' And he has probably answered — the Redstart! Of all that brilliant galaxy of warblerdom, dainty little birds, prim in form and kaleidoscopic in plumage, the American Redstart stands pre-eminent. Though some may choose that animated sunbeam, the Yellow Warbler, the Maryland Yellow-throat because of its quaint manners and captivating domino, the gorgeous Blackburnian, or any other of the gaily clad tribe, none of these possesses the distinctiveness of the '*Candelita.*' As Dr. Frank M. Chapman tells us, this is the happy title the Cubans have conferred upon the Redstart, in distinction from most of our warblers, which are known simply as '*Mariposas*' — butterflies. The pleasing harmony of black and flame color in this 'little torch' is a delight to the eye, and as one writer has expressed it, the bird is 'a constant source of pleasure to even the most blasé observer.' A pent-up bit of feathered energy, ever nervous and vivacious, the Redstart darts and flutters about the sylvan verdure like a tongue of flame. As it whirls and dashes up and down, around and about, in skillful pursuit of its fated insect victims, one is not only fascinated by its wild antics, but also by its vivid display of orange-red, as the wings and tail spread, contract and flash.

Like a few other warblers, the Redstart exhibits a superficial affinity to the flycatchers. It has prominent bristles about its mouth, and like these last-named birds, it is expert in pursuing and capturing insects in the air. But the Redstart could never sit sedately and wait for some obliging gnat to pass by ere it tickled the bird's gullet. No, he is a restless, harum-scarum sort of fellow, and could hardly keep his wings folded twenty seconds. His mate, however, is constrained to some degree of inactivity when it is necessary that she incubate her beautiful gem-like eggs. Not only from the air does the bird glean insect sustenance, but from bole and bough and leaves, and sometimes from the ground.

Although this bird has a preference for low sapling growths in which to nest, it is just as much at home in more or less heavily wooded areas, chiefly deciduous, and sometimes comes to nest in orchards and about dwellings. The nest is customarily built in an upright crotch, and is daintily made of fine plant fibers such as the silky bark of last year's milkweed stems, and lined with fern-down and similar soft materials.

The tasks of home-building and incubation are executed by the mother bird, but when the young hatch, the father shares interest, and both parents become ceaselessly engaged in filling the hungry mouths of their offspring. The American Redstart is one of the most frequent victims of that insidious parasitic scourge of many of our warblers and other small birds, the Cowbird. Consequently each year much time and effort is uselessly expended by this bird in nesting developments, made abortive by the intrusion of a Cowbird's egg. Either the whole affair is abandoned, or else the poor little mother adopts the unwelcome addition to the family, which proves a perfect glutton in consuming most of the food brought to the nest, and often actually crowds out the rightful progeny.

Many a bird student has racked his brain in an endeavor to discriminate between a song of this species and that of the Yellow Warbler. The Redstart's song is so constantly varied that it would be difficult indeed to catalogue the several variations, whether reduced to musical notation or syllabification. But the keen ear soon learns to detect the normal differences between the songs of the two species. Young males sing rather crudely until the first autumn, when, garbed like their mothers, they sing with the same ease and flexibility as their fathers. — (M.B.)

ENGLISH SPARROW

Passer domesticus domesticus (LINNAEUS).   PLATE 74.

Other name: House Sparrow.

IDENTIFICATION. — Length 5½ to 6¼ inches; spread 9½ to 10 inches. Near Song Sparrow size, but tail shorter and slightly forked, bird much stouter and head larger. Adult male recognized by gray or grayish cap and black throat-patch extending down middle of upper breast. Female and young similar in shape to male, but brown without black and gray areas.

BREEDING. — See below.

RANGE. — Resident throughout Europe and the British Isles except Italy, east to Siberia. Introduced in the United States about 1850, now thoroughly naturalized wherever settlements extend, in this country and Canada.

The European House Sparrow, or English Sparrow as it is commonly called, has been known in the Old World from time immemorial. For ages it has been considered typical of the sparrow tribe, and has been the most prominent of all passerine birds, because of its intimate parasitic relation to mankind. This is the 'sparrow' mentioned in the Bible and other ancient literature, but now we are told by Professor Peter P. Sushkin, who has studied its habits, anatomy and osteology, that it is not a sparrow at all but a weaver-bird, which probably spread over Europe long ago from Africa. The name 'English Sparrow' is a misnomer, as the species inhabits the greater part of Europe (and is not a sparrow), but the name was derived from the fact that most of the individuals brought to this country came from England.

In 1850 eight pairs were introduced at Brooklyn, New York. The birds did not thrive, and in 1852 many more were imported, and those that survived the winter in confinement were liberated in Greenwood Cemetery. These multiplied, and they and their progeny spread over the country. In 1854 some were introduced at Portland, Maine. Others were liberated at Peacedale, Rhode Island, and Boston, Massachusetts, about 1858, and at New Haven, Connecticut, in 1867. The birds, finding a plentiful supply of food in the undigested seeds in horse droppings, multiplied exceedingly, and spread with amazing rapidity into the farming districts, especially in grain-raising sections, where, because of their attacks on ripening grain, they soon became a serious pest. Before 1875 the species is said to have reached the Pacific coast at San Francisco, and then it rapidly over-ran the inhabited regions of the United States and Canada.

For about 50 years the English Sparrows continued to increase and spread, until nearly every village and hamlet in the greater part of North America was occupied by them. In recent years, however, they have decreased in numbers in the cities at least, especially in the northern parts of the country, where their chief food supply in winter formerly was found in the street droppings. With the invention of the automobile and its introduction in place of other vehicles, horses began gradually to disappear from city life, and as motorcars increased, Sparrows starved in winter. Ordinarily there is not much nourishment for Sparrows about a motorcar, though sometimes when May-flies are abundant they accumulate on the radiators, and Sparrows have been seen to glean them from parked cars. Many English Sparrows left the cities for the South or the farming districts, where they became a pest on poultry farms, subsisting largely in winter on 'chicken feed.' Many are said to have contracted fatal diseases from poultry. Since the decrease of Sparrows began there has been a corresponding increase in House Wrens, which are now fairly well distributed through a large part of New England.

The English Sparrow has been introduced into many countries, and wherever it has appeared it has been stigmatized as injurious, pernicious, disreputable, salacious, quarrelsome and even murderous. It has been branded as thief, wretch, feathered rat, etc. etc., but whatever may be said about it, the bird certainly is important. During the cycle of its increase in the United States much ink was spilled in denouncing it. Dr. Elliott Coues in 1879 gave a list of more than two hundred titles or articles, most of which were unfavorable to the bird, and many were written in succeeding years. Nevertheless the bird has many friends who feed it and

457

believe it to be a useful species. In any case, it is here to stay and we must make the best of it. It prefers to stay in the neighborhood of human dwellings, for it gets its sustenance chiefly from the products of man's labors in agriculture. Therefore it is almost never seen in great forests or anywhere at any great distance from settlements.

It is a sturdy, upstanding little fowl, aggressive, pugnacious and active. As spring approaches, even while snow still covers the ground, a few Sparrows may be seen carrying straws to their nesting-places. Their mating is an occasion for clatter and strife. Three or four males will often attend a single female, fluttering about with spread wings and discordant shrieks, chattering and fighting, both on the ground and in the air, until finally the most vociferous and pugnacious bird secures the prize. The female often shows her regard for the accepted suitor by seizing him by one wing and pulling him about, but he is tough and hardy and seems to like rough treatment, coming from such a source.

Both sexes engage in the nest-building and in feeding the young. The nest, unlike those of our native sparrows, is often built in roughly globular form — a great mass of heterogeneous materials, largely grass and lined with feathers. It often presents a filthy appearance by the time the young leave it, and it naturally swarms with vermin. When the young become strong on the wing many go into the country districts, where they subsist largely on weed seeds, grass seeds, grain and fruit. Their injurious habits are emphasized in summer and autumn, but they eat grain at any season of the year wherever they can find it. As winter approaches the Sparrows gather into towns, villages and cities. Some find refuge during the severest weather in barns or sheds. They usually roost in sheltered places, such as an open shed, an unoccupied building or among thick ivy vines on large buildings, and in various holes and crevices about buildings and trees. There is more or less migration during the winter, but as a rule the species is rather sedentary, clinging persistently to the locality of its chosen home, and in severe winters many perish in the North from starvation and exposure.

The food of the English Sparrow includes many substances, ranging from fruit and grain to garbage, and undigested grain and seeds in horse droppings. It eats greedily all the small grains and bird seeds, crumbs of bread, cake and other foods of mankind, small fruits and succulent garden plants in their tender stages. It destroys young peas, turnips, cabbage and nearly all young vegetables, and it often eats the undeveloped seeds of vegetables. When numerous it attacks apples, peaches, plums, pears, strawberries, currants and all other common small fruits. During the early part of the season before seeds ripen, it takes many insects, and feeds many more to its young. Its insect food includes several injurious caterpillars such as are eaten by most native birds and some destructive moths and beetles.

EUROPEAN TREE SPARROW
Passer montanus montanus (LINNAEUS).

IDENTIFICATION. — *Both* the male and female European Tree Sparrow are similar in general appearance to the *male* English Sparrow, but they have chestnut on the crown and back of the head, a large black spot behind the eye, and two white wing-bars, which identifies them.

RANGE. — Resident of Europe, the British Isles, and Siberia. Introduced about 1870 near St. Louis, Missouri, where it has become established.

Fortunately the European Tree Sparrow has not increased and spread with the rapidity of the English Sparrow, or it might have proved to be equally objectionble. It is never wise to experiment with the introduction of alien animals or plants, for, though perhaps harmless in their native habitat, they may prove decidedly undesirable in their new surroundings.

W. H. Hudson, in his 'British Birds,' writes of this species in its native haunts: 'In its habits it is more active and lively than its more domestic relation, and is more at home on trees, and may be seen moving about among the lesser branches and twigs with much freedom, after the manner of the siskin and redpoll; but it feeds principally on the ground. It can scarcely be called a song-bird, its most song-like sounds being composed of a few chirruping notes uttered in the pairing season. Its voice, both in its attempted singing and in its ordinary chirp and call-notes, is much shriller than that of the common sparrow.' — (J.B.M.)

BOBOLINK

Dolichonyx oryzivorus (LINNAEUS).   PLATE 60.

Other names: Reed-bird; Rice-bird; Skunk Blackbird; Oat Bird.

IDENTIFICATION. — Length 6¼ to 8 inches; spread 10¼ to 12½ inches. Male in breeding plumage unmistakable, with 'coat on upside down,' a black bird with white patches on wings and lower back, and buff on back of head and neck; male in autumn, female and young, sparrow-like birds yellowish-buff below and streaked brown above; tail rounded and quills pointed.

SONG. — An indescribable bubbling medley, often given in flight. CALL NOTE: A metallic *chink*.

BREEDING. — In grass or clover fields, grassy tracts near streams, and lowland pastures. *Nest:* On ground among tall grasses, usually in a depression, rarely above ground attached to grass stems, of grasses, weed-stems, and rootlets. *Eggs:* 4 to 7, grayish-white with umber and olive-brown markings.

RANGE. — Breeds from southeastern British Columbia, southern Manitoba, southern Ontario, southern Quebec, and Cape Breton Island south to northeastern California, Colorado, northern Missouri, Illinois, Indiana, central Ohio, West Virginia, Pennsylvania, and New Jersey; winters in South America to northern Argentina; migrates through the West Indies and along the east coast of Central America.

The Bobolink is a distinctive bird; he is unlike all the rest. If there exists anywhere on earth another bird like it, I have yet to see it. His song is entirely his own. I have never yet heard the Mockingbird, the Catbird, the Starling or the Blue Jay even try to imitate it. His finest livery and his sweetest music are reserved for northern fields and for a brief period only. He is at his best in May and early June. As I have written elsewhere:

'The Bobolink is the harlequin of the spring meadows. He is a happy-go-lucky fellow, with his suit on wrong side up, the black below and the white above; a reckless, rollicking sort of a fowl, throwing care to the winds, and always bent on a lark. His spirits are of the effervescent kind, and his music bubbles irrepressibly forth at such a rate that half a dozen notes seem to be crowding upon the heels of every one uttered. Indeed, this is about the only bird that completely baffles the latter-day "interpreters" of bird music. His notes tumble out with such headlong rapidity, in an apparent effort to jump over each other, that it is next to impossible for the scribe to set them down in the proper sequence of musical notation. Nevertheless, this harum-scarum expression of irrepressible joy is of the most pleasing character, and ranks among the finest music of the fields.'

About the second week in May the male Bobolinks usually arrive in some numbers in the Northern States, and they continue to come all through the month. They have run the gauntlet of the guns in the South and they are now among friends. Care and caution they throw to the winds and usher in the day with a revel of flight and song. A little later when the females arrive the merry fellows seem to go mad with joy in pursuit of their fleeing inamoratas. They chase their prospective mates about the fields, pouring forth a perfect torrent of song. Dr. C. W. Townsend gives the following account of the behavior of the wooing male. 'The courtship song of this bird bubbles over with joy and merriment. Not only from the air but from the tops of trees and from the ground the song is given, but its ardor almost always carries the bird through the air. Especially is this the case when the courting season is in full sway. When the birds first come, before the arrival of the females, they often sing in trees, sometimes as many as a dozen together, making a splendid chorus. One may see a male courting a female on the ground. He spreads his tail and forcibly drags it like a Pigeon. He erects his buff nape feathers, points his bill downward and partly opens his wings, gurgling meanwhile a few of his song notes.'

My old friend, the late Edward A. Samuels, in his 'Birds of New England,' has written thus of the nesting: 'When the birds are mated, usually early in June, they commence the structure in which their family is to be reared. Selecting a thick tussock of grass in a field or meadow, through which, or near which, a brook prattles of cool and delicious draughts and sweet and refreshing baths, beneath the bending and concealing leaves, they entwine fine grasses and rootlets into a loose and not deeply hollowed nest, which they line with softer pieces of the same material.

'The position is so well chosen that, nine times out of ten, if you walk the meadow over again and again, knowing it to be there, you will not discover the nest; the male bird flies over your head, chiding and complaining at your presence, and his mate skurrying off through the thick grass, rises away from the nest, that you may not discover its locality.'

The female takes entire charge of the eggs, while the male enjoys himself, but he is likely to be near enough to give the alarm when an enemy appears and to draw the attention of the intruder to himself at some spot distant from the nest. Samuels says: 'As soon as the young birds are hatched, the father, hitherto full of song and merriment, becomes more quiet, spending a great part of his time in family cares. The young birds are fed on grasshoppers, crickets, and various other insects; and this food is the chief sustenance of the parents as well, at this period, for the seeds of the wild grasses are not yet ripened. . . . When the young birds leave the nest, the parents provide for them for a few days, and then turn them away to shift for themselves; this is in about the middle of July. The old birds then pass a comparatively idle season — roaming through the country, recuperating from the cares of parentage, and exchanging their nuptial dress for one more in accordance with their matured, respectable, old folks' condition; the male assumes the sober, and lately more sober, attire of his mate, and dropping his song, contents himself with repeating her simple "*chink*."'

By the middle of July most of them have left the higher lands and after that date their songs are rarely heard. By the last of July most of the males have assumed their modest autumnal garb and both old and young have assembled in flocks. In August they begin to move slowly southward, frequenting river marshes, coastal lands and grain-fields, taking toll of the seeds as they go. By the middle of August they are abundant in the marshes of southern

New Jersey, Delaware and Pennsylvania, where thousands formerly were shot by gunners, and by the second week of September their flocks have assembled in the rice fields of South Carolina.

Normally the Bobolink is a bird of the river valleys of eastern North America. When the country was forested, the bird must have been confined to grasslands in these valleys and to marshes along the coast, for there only could it have found its favorite foods — the seeds and insects of the grasses and weeds. In autumn it followed the Atlantic coast southward and fed largely on the seeds of wild rice, wild oats and other reeds. When the white man came, cleared the land and sowed grass and grain, the food supply of the bird was vastly augmented in the North, as well as the area suitable for its breeding purposes, and so it increased greatly in numbers and spread westward. It still follows, however, its old migration route down the Atlantic coast. While settlement and clearing went on in the North the same process continued in the South, but not so rapidly. However, the coastal regions and the river valleys soon were settled and here grain and rice were sown, the rice mostly in marshes along the coast, thus supplanting the native seeds and grasses, on which the Bobolink fed formerly, with a larger and more productive seed, and so increasing its food supply beyond anything known in aboriginal times. The rice industry increased and during the first half of the nineteenth century brought great wealth to the Low Country planters. And the Bobolinks and other 'rice-birds' waxed fat and abundant. With the shifting of the important rice-growing center to Louisiana, Arkansas and Texas, the Bobolinks concentrated on the few small rice plantations left in the Southeastern States, causing serious losses to the planters.

There is no question about the economic value of the Bobolink in New England, where it is decidedly insectivorous in its feeding habits, the small amount of grain which it takes being negligible, but in the South it has without doubt caused damage amounting to millions of dollars So the bird that Lowell called 'gladness on wings' in New England, is 'that —— —— rice-bird' in the Carolinas and Georgia.

EASTERN MEADOWLARK

Sturnella magna magna (LINNAEUS).   PLATE 61.

Other names: Marsh Quail; Old-field Lark.

IDENTIFICATION. — Length 9 to 11 inches; spread 13½ to 17 inches. A plump brown-streaked bird with yellow under parts and a broad black crescent on the breast, short tail with outer tail feathers largely white showing conspicuously in flight; walks much in grassy fields, flies low with alternation of fluttering and sailing, often spreads tail quickly flashing white at sides.

CALLS. — A guttural chatter, a shrill whistle.   SONG: A plaintive, variable, slurring whistle.

BREEDING. — In open country and meadows. *Nest:* On ground, in grass and arched over, of grasses and weeds. *Eggs:* 4 to 6, white spotted with reddish-browns.

RANGE. — Breeds from eastern Minnesota, southern Ontario, southern Quebec, and New Brunswick south to northern Texas, Missouri, and North Carolina, and west to western Nebraska, Kansas, and northwestern Texas; winters regularly from the Potomac and Ohio valleys to the Gulf States and north locally to the Great Lakes and southern Maine.

The Eastern Meadowlark is a bird of the fields. There it greets the spring while the meadows are still brown. Often it mounts to the top of some tall tree on a grassy hilltop and with brilliant yellow breast turned to the rising sun welcomes with song the coming day. The male is a persistent singer and continues to sing more or less from March to November. The Meadowlark is not a lark; it is a meadow starling. The name of the genus *Sturnella* is an irregular diminutive of *Sturnus*, the Starling, and one can see at a glance that the bird bears a close superficial resemblance in form to a Starling, and its flight is similar to that of the latter. Our Meadow Starling is rather a shy bird and keeps to the open lands where it can command a wide view and perceive from afar the approach of an enemy. Along the seaboard it frequents meadows and salt marshes and there it is known as the Marsh Quail, and though protected by law it sometimes is the victim of youthful gunners.

About the second week in March the flight of Eastern Meadowlarks reaches southern New England. It continues into April. More and more birds come from the South until the fields are sparingly populated with them. Here their courtship begins in late April or early May and nest building quickly follows. Dr. T. Gilbert Pearson tells of the nesting:

'If you want to find a Meadowlark's nest you must look for it on the ground. It is usually made entirely of dead grasses, although at times a thin lining of horsehair is added. Most of the nests I examined possessed a dome-shaped roof of grass, thus allowing inspection from one side only. This snug little house is hid under the edge of a clump of grass or weeds. Sometimes one finds it in a field of corn, or concealed by a stump around which grass is growing, or elsewhere protected by an overhanging grassy clod left unbroken at the spring plowing.

'It is something of an adventure to find one of these stationary cradles built for the comfort of the wee Larks to come. Usually it is discovered quite by accident as one pursues his way across a meadow or field. So closely do the colors of the feathers on the head and back of the bird resemble its surroundings that if it could restrain its fear one might pass within a foot of the spot with small chance of discovering the secret. The bird seems to be conscious of this fact, and often will permit one almost to step on it before fluttering away. One day, after a forenoon spent in a marsh with two other bird-lovers, we came out on a dry meadowland for lunch. After spending half an hour lunching and lounging on the ground we rose to go, when suddenly up flew a Meadowlark from her nest with its five speckled eggs not over twelve feet from where our lunch had been spread. There she had been sitting all that time, and probably would not have moved when she did had I not stepped within a foot of her hiding-place. It is a very discouraging task to attempt to find a Meadowlark's nest by watching the birds go to it, for the reason that when one of them wishes to approach the spot, it alights on the ground many yards away and walks quietly through the grass to its destination. Ordinarily it leaves its home in the same careful manner. Certain well-defined paths of travel may often be noted radiating from the nest.'

While the female is incubating, the male sings to her as she sits on the nest. At that time the listener may hear, rarely, the jingling flight-song, as the bird flies high, pouring forth a bubbling medley not unlike that of the Bobolink, but louder and not so hurried. The young remain in the nest for ten days or two weeks, and then wander about in the grass until their wings grow strong, attended by their solicitous parents. Dr. Pearson says:

'Late in the summer the birds assemble and in more or less straggling companies go foraging about over the fields. Sometimes one may find only half a dozen together, but in crossing meadows I have at times seen fifty or a hundred at a time. They do not fly in compact flocks like Blackbirds, nor do all the members of a company spring into the air at once as is the custom with Quails. Their flight is leisurely and rather slow, which renders them an easy mark for the amateur gunner.'

When the frosts begin to nip the meadow grasses, the Eastern Meadowlarks gather in small flocks each containing several families, and fly southward or toward the seacoast. A few may winter regularly for a series of winters in the interior of the New England States or near the Great Lakes, until some very severe season destroys most of them. This occurs not infrequently. Along the coast many winter in flocks about the salt marshes and old fields, but even there exceptionally severe seasons kill many of them.

SOUTHERN MEADOWLARK

Sturnella magna argutula BANGS.

IDENTIFICATION. — Similar to *S. m. magna* but smaller and darker.

RANGE. — From southern Illinois, southwestern Indiana, and South Carolina south to Florida and the coast of Louisiana and southeastern Texas.

WESTERN MEADOWLARK

Sturnella neglecta AUDUBON.

IDENTIFICATION. — Similar to the Eastern Meadowlark but lighter colored and the yellow of the throat extends more or less up onto the cheek.

BREEDING. — Similar to that of Eastern Meadowlark.

RANGE. — Breeds from southern British Columbia, central Alberta and southern Manitoba south to northwestern Lower California, northern Mexico, and central Texas; winters from southern British Columbia and Iowa south to central Mexico.

The Western and Eastern Meadowlarks can only be distinguished by a careful field observer, when they are silent. The western bird is lighter colored, especially above where the heavier black markings of the eastern species give it a generally darker appearance. In habits and haunts they are almost identical, in fact in some regions they breed together in the same fields, and their principal difference lies in their songs and call notes which are easily recognized, the western species being much the better musician and having a longer, louder, lower pitched and more musical song than its eastern congener. Even the call notes are different. Dr. Frank Chapman describes this latter distinction thus: 'The call of the Western Meadowlark is a *chuck, chuck* followed by a wooden, rolling *b-r-r-r-r-r*, wholly unlike the sharp *dzit* or *yert* and metallic twitter of the eastern bird.' — (J.B.M.)

YELLOW–HEADED BLACKBIRD

Xanthocephalus xanthocephalus (BONAPARTE).

Other names: Yellow-headed Troupial; Saffron-headed Maizo Bird.

IDENTIFICATION. — Length 8¾ to 11 inches; spread 14 to 17 inches. Male a black bird with yellow head and neck and white patch on wing; female, smaller, duller colored; young like female but head dark brown.

BREEDING. — Similar to Red-winged Blackbird.

RANGE. — Breeds from southern British Columbia, central Manitoba, northern Minnesota, and the east side of Hudson Bay south to Lower California and central Mexico, and east to central Iowa, southern Wisconsin, northern Illinois, and Indiana; winters from southwestern California and southwestern Louisiana south to central Mexico.

The Yellow-headed Blackbird is a conspicuous feature of the swamps and sloughs of the western and prairie provinces and states, where it is likely to be associated in summer with Red-winged Blackbirds, Black Terns, Pied-billed Grebes and other grebes, and ducks of various sorts. The striking yellow head and neck of the male attract attention, and its harsh, rasping notes forbid its being overlooked. Of its attempts at song Dr. Frank M. Chapman has this to say:

'If result were commensurate with effort, the Yellow-head would be a world-famed songster; but something besides unbounded ambition and limitless muscular exertion is required to produce music. In vain the Yellow-head expands his lungs and throws out his chest, his widespread tail testifying to the earnestness of his endeavor; sound he produces in volume, but surely such a series of strained, harsh calls, whistles, like escaping steam, grunts, groans and pig-like squeals never before did duty as a song! In his youth he does far better, the note of the young bird being a wooden-rolling call as different from the voice of the parent as is that of a young Baltimore Oriole.'

Soon after the females arrive on their western breeding-grounds in spring, the males begin their wooing. Dr. Alexander Wetmore thus describes one of their mating displays: 'In the most common display the male started towards the female from a distance of thirty or forty feet with a loud rattling of his wings as a preliminary. The head was bent down, the feet lowered and the tail dropped while he flew slowly toward his mate. The wings were brought down with a slow swinging motion and were not closed at all so that the white markings on the coverts were fully displayed, the whole performance being reminiscent of a similar wing display of the Mockingbird.' Professor F. E. L. Beal says of this bird: 'Its breeding habits are much like those of the Red-wing, but it is usually less abundant than that bird. It is gregarious and resorts to marshes to build its nest, which is very similar to that of the Red-wing, and similarly placed. Although it breeds in marshes, it does not by any means confine itself to them in its search for food, but forages far afield, visiting corncribs, grainfields, and barnyards. The writer's first experience with the Yellow-headed Blackbird was on the prairies of Nebraska, where flocks visited the railway then in process of construction, running about among the feet of the mules and horses in search of grubs and worms exposed by the plow and scraper, and all the time uttering their striking guttural notes (almost precisely like those of a brood of suckling pigs). In their habit of visiting barnyards and hog pastures they resemble Cowbirds much more than Red-wings. When the breeding season is over they often visit grainfields in large flocks, and become the cause of much complaint by Western farmers.'

EASTERN RED-WING

Agelaius phoeniceus phoeniceus (LINNAEUS).

PLATE 60.

Other names: Swamp Blackbird; Marsh Blackbird.

IDENTIFICATION. — Length 7½ to 9½ inches; spread 12 to 14½ inches; female smaller than male. Male all black in breeding plumage, except red shoulders with (often concealed) buffy after border; after breeding season much like female but red shoulder may be detected; female and young mottled and striped above and below with dusky and whitish or buffy.

SONG. — *Quong-ker-eee* or *okalee*; various clucks and whistles.

BREEDING. — Often in communities, in swamps, marshes and meadows, sometimes in grassy fields. *Nest:* In reeds, cattails or a tussock of grass or in a bush near or over water, of grasses, sedges, rushes, etc. *Eggs:* 3 to 5, pale blue, oddly streaked, spotted and scrawled with purple and black.

RANGE. — Breeds from Ontario, Quebec, and Nova Scotia south to the northern parts of the Gulf States; winters mainly south of the Ohio and Delaware valleys but locally north to Massachusetts.

The Eastern Red-wing is a typical marsh blackbird. It loves the marsh and waterside and seldom nests far from water. Its very notes carry a suggestion of boggy ooze, and its *chuck*, like that of other blackbirds, is frog-like. It has a strong predilection for the oozy slough and the 'floating island,' where the treacherous soggy turf gives beneath the incautious footstep and precipitates the adventurer into the dark and watery depths below. Nevertheless Red-wings sometimes choose other places for nesting. We may find an isolated pair, here and there, nesting on some beach ridge among the dunes by the sea, and where their favorite marshes have been filled or drained, or are insufficient in area for their numbers, they sometimes build on the ground in a hayfield.

Although these birds nest near water they are not by any means confined to its vicinity. They may go half a mile from their nests to an orchard to secure an abundance of caterpillars for their young, while in migration they often swarm on the upland and in the corn-fields. From late February to late March, according to the season, Red-wings appear in the Middle States, moving up a little later from the South in enormous flocks. If the season is early, the advance guard (very few in number) reaches southern New England about the twenty-second of February. When the main flight arrives there, from the middle of March to the first part of April, the flocks have become much smaller, as many have fallen out of the ranks on the way. Sometimes in their early northward movement, they meet a blizzard from the frozen North, and then some of them turn and drift before the storm toward the shores of Long Island Sound or the sand dunes of Cape Cod.

The early flights consist of males alone; the females follow later. The males are now perfecting their bright nuptial dress and are full of vigor and song, and when a flock alights on some lone tree, blackening it with their sable plumage, the air is resonant with blackbird music. The spring movement of the flocks seems orderly and directed as if at the command of a leader. If there really is a leader, when he turns, all the rest turn at the same instant. They choose certain trees about some swamp or body of water which they use regularly as stopping places and from which they sing for about ten to fifteen minutes at a time even while the swamps are still ice-bound. Some small flocks increase in numbers as the days go by until they number hundreds (including Cowbirds and Starlings), but after the females appear they begin to scatter and mate. Now the males actively pursue the females, or perching before them they raise the fore part of the wings well out from the shoulders, bowing with lowered head to show the beauties of their epaulets, spreading their shining black tails, and pouring forth their finest music. Their song does not sound very fascinating to our ear, but it seems to be effective with the gentler sex, as some males secure two or three mates, all living happily together with nests near one another in the same bog or meadow. While their modest consorts attend to their wifely duties, the brilliant male stands guard over his numerous progeny. Perched high on the top of some tree or bush he watches for intruders. Let a crow appear and the blackbird is after him. He will chase a Marsh Hawk, a Bittern or even an Osprey in his anxiety to protect those dependent upon him, and sometimes his mates lend a hand in driving the enemy from the field. At sight of a man approaching he becomes hysterical, and goes out to meet him, fluttering overhead and uttering blackbird maledictions or lamentations as long as the intruder remains in the vicinity of his charges. Some of the males are devoted to their offspring and assist in feeding them. Others seem to leave this duty mostly to their mates. The males are not all polygamists, as some, apparently less vigorous or less willing to accept the responsibility which devolves on the father of several families, have but one mate. It may be that polygamy results from a disparity of the sexes.

Red-wings often breed in communities in swamps, marshes or meadows, though sometimes in grassy fields. The nest is usually built among reeds, rushes or cattails or on a tussock of grass, occasionally in a bush or small tree, and is composed of dry grasses and rushes woven into a deep firm basket. The eggs are pale bluish-green variously marked with spots, blotches and scrawls of black, browns and purplish.

The young often leave the nest before they are able to fly, and climb about among the reeds or bushes, moving actively from place to place. Where blackbirds nest in large colonies, the marsh soon becomes alive with moving young. Some fall into the water, but usually get out again unless snapped up by frogs, fish or turtles. Blackbirds have their full share of enemies and many of the eggs and young fall victims to them before the flocks gather for the fall migration.

Although the Red-wings almost invariably breed in the swamp or marsh, they have a partiality for open fields and plowed lands; and most of the blackbirds that nest in the smaller swamps adjacent to farm lands get a large share of their food from the farmer's fields. They forage about the fields and meadows when they first come north in spring. Later, they follow the plow, picking up grubs, worms and caterpillars. They eat comparatively little grain, although they get some from newly sown fields in spring, as well as from the autumn harvest; but they feed very largely on the seeds of weeds and wild rice in the fall. In the South they join with the Bobolink in devastating the rice-fields, and in the West they are often so numerous as to destroy the grain in the fields; but in the Northeast the good they do far outweighs the injury, and for this reason they are protected by law.

FLORIDA RED-WING

Agelaius phoeniceus mearnsi HOWELL AND VAN ROSSEM.

IDENTIFICATION. — Similar to *A. p. phoeniceus* but bill longer and more slender; female has upper parts browner, lower parts more buffy with dark streaks browner.

RANGE. — Greater part of the Florida Peninsula, south to the lower Kissimmee Valley and the Caloosahatchee River, north to Putnam County and Anastasia Island, and west on the Gulf coast to Apalachicola.

MAYNARD'S RED-WING

Agelaius phoeniceus floridanus MAYNARD.

IDENTIFICATION. — Size of *A. p. mearnsi*; upper parts of female paler, under parts more whitish.

RANGE. — Florida Keys and southern portion of Florida peninsula, north to Lake Worth and Everglade, Collier County.

GULF COAST RED-WING

Agelaius phoeniceus littoralis HOWELL AND VAN ROSSEM.

IDENTIFICATION. — Darkest of eastern Red-wings; bill slightly more slender in profile than *A. p. phoeniceus*.

RANGE. — Gulf coast from Choctawhatchee Bay, Florida, west at least to Galveston, Texas.

GIANT RED-WING

Agelaius phoeniceus arctolegus OBERHOLSER.

IDENTIFICATION. — Similar to *A. p. phoeniceus* but larger and with a larger bill.

RANGE. — Breeds from Mackenzie and Keewatin south to Montana, North Dakota, Minnesota, Wisconsin, and northern Michigan; in winter to Kansas, Texas, Louisiana, Alabama, and Illinois.

Of the fourteen races of *Agelaius phoeniceus* listed in the fourth edition of the 'Check-List' of the American Ornithologists' Union, five are found regularly east of the ninety-fifth meridian, but they are all essentially alike in habits, and call for no special discussion. — (J.B.M.)

ORCHARD ORIOLE

Icterus spurius (LINNAEUS).

PLATE 61.

Other name: Swinger.

IDENTIFICATION. — Length 6 to 7¾ inches; spread 9¼ to 10¼ inches. Male similar to Baltimore Oriole but slightly smaller, and chestnut substituted for the orange and yellow; female and young yellowish-olive above, olive-yellow below, wings dusky with two wing-bars greener than similar Baltimore Oriole; young male has throat black.

SONG. — 'Like glorified song of Purple Finch,' given with great abandon.

BREEDING. — In orchards and gardens, on farm-lands, among shade trees, and in timber along streams. *Nest:* Sometimes among twigs but usually suspended, a short, purse-shaped structure woven of green grasses, etc., with lining of plant-down. *Eggs:* 4 to 6, bluish-white, blotched, spotted and scrawled with browns, purplish and lavender.

RANGE. — Breeds from North Dakota, northwestern Minnesota, Wisconsin, Michigan, southeastern Ontario, central New York, and Massachusetts south to southern Florida, the Gulf coast to southern Texas, and to central Mexico, also west to central Nebraska, northeastern Colorado, and western Kansas; winters from southern Mexico to northern Colombia.

The Orchard Oriole has been a rare bird wherever I have had an opportunity to observe it and I have watched it only briefly here and there, so I know little about its habits in the Northeastern States. I can do no better than to quote a part of Audubon's life history of the bird, which is more nearly complete than any other that has come to my notice: 'The migration of the Orchard Oriole from south to north is performed by day, and singly, as is that of its relative the Baltimore Oriole, the males appearing a week or ten days sooner than the females. . . . No sooner have they reached the portion of the country in which they intend to remain during the time of raising their young, than these birds exhibit all the liveliness and vivacity belonging to their nature. The male is seen rising in the air for ten or twenty yards in an indirect manner, jerking his tail and body, flapping his wings, and singing with remarkable impetuosity, as if under the influence of haste, and anxious to return to the tree from which he has departed. He accordingly descends with the same motions of the body and tail, repeating his pleasant song as he alights. These gambols and carolings are performed frequently during the day, the intervals being employed in ascending or descending along the branches and twigs of different trees, in search of insects or larvae. In doing this, they rise on their legs, seldom without jetting the tail, stretch their neck, seize the prey, and emit a single note, which is sweet and mellow, although in power much inferior to that of the Baltimore. At other times, it is seen bending its body downwards, in a curved posture, with head greatly inclined upwards, to peep at the under parts of the leaves, so as not to suffer any grub to escape its vigilance. It now alights on the ground, where it has spied a crawling insect, and again flies towards the blossoms, in which many are lurking, and devours hundreds of them each day, thus contributing to secure to the farmer the hope which he has of the productiveness of his orchard.

'The arrival of the females is marked with all due regard, and the males immediately use every effort in their power to procure from them a return of attention. Their singings and tricks are performed with redoubled ardour, until they are paired, when nidification is attended to with the utmost activity. They resort to the meadows, or search along the fences for the finest, longest, and toughest grasses they can find, and having previously fixed on a spot either on an apple tree, or amidst the drooping branches of the weeping willow, they begin by attaching the grass firmly and neatly to the twigs more immediately around the chosen place. The filaments are twisted, passed over and under, and interwoven in such a manner as almost to defy the eye of man to follow their windings. All this is done by the bill of the bird, in the manner used by the Baltimore Oriole. The nest is of a hemispherical form, and is supported by the margin only. It seldom exceeds three or four inches in depth, is open almost to the full extent of its largest diameter at the top or entrance, and finished on all sides, as well as within, with the long slender grasses already mentioned. Some of these go round the nest several times, as if coarsely woven together. This is the manner in which the nest is constructed in Louisiana; in the middle districts it is usually lined with soft and warm materials. ... The young follow the parents for several weeks, and many birds congregate towards autumn, but the males soon separate from the females, and set out by themselves as they arrived in spring.

'Although the food of the Orchard Oriole consists principally of insects of various kinds, it is not composed exclusively of them. They are fond of different sorts of fruits and berries. Figs are also much relished by them, as well as mulberries and strawberries, but not to such a degree as to draw the attention of the gardener or husbandman towards their depredations.'

BALTIMORE ORIOLE

Icterus galbula (LINNAEUS). PLATE 61.

Other names: Oriole; Golden Robin; Fire-hang-bird; Hang-nest; Fire Bird.

IDENTIFICATION. — Length 7 to 8¼ inches; spread 11¼ to 12½ inches. Adult male, head, neck, back, wings and tail mainly black, one white wing-bar, breast, rump, and outer tail feathers orange; female and young olive above, yellower on rump and under parts, wings dusky with two wing-bars.

SONG. — A succession of clear, wild, rounded notes easily imitated by whistling but difficult to describe. CALL NOTES: Clear short whistles.

BREEDING. — Similar to Orchard Oriole but nest deeper and woven of vegetable fibers instead of grass, and sometimes made largely of string, yarns, etc.

RANGE. — Breeds from central Alberta, southern Manitoba, Ontario, New Brunswick, and Nova Scotia south to southern Texas, central Louisiana, northern Alabama, and northern Georgia and west to eastern Montana, Wyoming, and Colorado east of the Rocky Mountains; winters from southern Mexico through Central America to Colombia.

The coming of the Baltimore Oriole to the North is always an event to be welcomed with joy. The winter now is past, April showers have fallen and May is here. Again we see the annual miracle of the spring awakening. Where but a few weeks since the 'white death' covered all and the brook was fettered by the frost, now a velvety carpet of tender grasses and green mosses clothes the earth. Dandelions, cowslips and violets are in bloom, and the stream prattles noisily over its stony bed. The wonderful old earth, swinging the Northern Hemisphere again toward the sun, responds as ever to his cheering warmth and clothes herself in beauty. A thousand orchards are in bloom, and among their tinted blossoms the resplendent Orioles with songs of joy weave in and out. Ever in New England this beautiful, elegantly formed bird is associated with blooming apple orchards, and with peach and cherry blossoms.

Baltimore Orioles almost always arrive in the latitude of New England about the tenth of May, though some arrive earlier, and they continue to come and pass for two or three weeks. The males usually precede the females by several days, but when their modest consorts arrive, the ardent birds soon begin their wooing. In displaying his charms before the object of his affections the male sits upon a limb near her, and raising to full height bows low with spread tail and partly raised wings, thus displaying to her admiring eyes first his orange breast, then his black front and finally in bright sunlight the full glory of his black, white and orange upper plumage, uttering, the while, his most supplicating and seductive notes. A pair once mated appear to be very affectionate and constant during the season. The males rarely assist the females in nest-building, but most of them keep close to their consorts while nest-construction is going on, cheer them with song and evidently take much interest in the proceeding. Some males bring nesting material, but so far as I have observed the female alone builds the nest. In fashioning her swinging domicile she displays great skill in weaving. She first hangs long strands over the twigs which support the nest, fastening them in place until she has a hanging framework, then she loops and weaves them together, frequently hanging back downward on the suspended fabric while she works. The happy bird while building sometimes chatters or sings a bit while in the nest.

The material normally used for the framework is vegetal fiber, gathered chiefly from dried or decaying stalks of plants of the previous year; fibers of tree bark also are used by some females. Birds building (as most of them now do) near the habitations of men use also string, yarn, horsehair, strands of hemp or flax and other similar materials gleaned from dooryards, farmyards or roadsides. The birds usually select white or light grayish tints, similar in color to the natural materials used for ages by their forbears; but I have seen one nest chiefly composed outwardly of jet-black hair from the manes and tails of horses. This nest, placed low down in a pear tree, was very conspicuous among the green leaves. The nest of this oriole, whatever its color, usually is more conspicuous than that of the Orchard Oriole, which is built largely of green grasses which, shaded by the leaves, retain for a long time some resemblance to their primal tints and so are easily concealed amid the foliage. Many attempts have been made by putting out brightly colored yarns in conspicuous places to induce the Baltimore Oriole to build a nest of the gayest hues, but usually with little success. Apparently they prefer white yarn or twine to any of the brighter colors.

The completion of the external part of the nest occupies two to six days. While the female is incubating the male wanders back and forth in the immediate neighborhood, singing and calling to her, and she sometimes answers from the nest as if to assure him that all is well. While she seems to perform most of the labor of incubation, the male in some cases relieves her, taking her place upon the nest, and usually he does his full share of brooding and feeding the young. Both birds exhibit an attachment to the nesting-site and return to it year after year. Occasionally such a nest of the preceding year is repaired in spring and used again, but commonly a new nest is fashioned each year, and so lasting and durable are these fabrics that one may see nests of three successive years upon the same tree, if not on the same branch. Sometimes material is taken from an old nest and incorporated in a new one.

The male sings loudly and cheerfully through May and June or until the young have left the nest, which in most cases occurs in late June, and soon thereafter the melodies of the male are hushed. Now, with few exceptions, the Baltimore Orioles leave the scene of their nativity, and in early July the broods with their parents betake themselves to the woods, pastures and thickets where wild berries are ripening; now the swamps and thickets resound with the cries of the feeding young, and there most of them remain until late August. In some localities, even in city streets, a number of them remain at this season, molting, shy and silent, keeping largely in the tops of tall elms and maples where they escape notice. The males usually have a second song period when from about the middle of August to its last week they reappear in their former haunts in winter plumage, singing more or less. Occasionally a young male will attempt a snatch of song at this time. Early in September most of them disappear on their southward migration, and by the end of September they are well on their way to their winter haunts in Mexico and Central or South America.

RUSTY BLACKBIRD

Euphagus carolinus (MÜLLER). PLATE 62.

Other names: Rusty Grackle; Thrush Blackbird.

IDENTIFICATION. — Length 8¼ to 9¾ inches; spread 13 to 15 inches. Male in spring a black bird with a light eye; in autumn male has head and body feathers edged with rusty; female in spring slaty; female and young in autumn rustier than males and a broad light stripe over eye.

SONG. — Like the creaking of ungreased wheels.

BREEDING. — In swamps or on borders of ponds and streams. *Nest:* In thickets near water, of sticks, mosses, leaf-mold, and grasses, etc. *Eggs:* 4 or 5, bluish-green, blotched and spotted with browns and grays.

RANGE. — Breeds from the Kowak River, Alaska, northern Manitoba, and northern Quebec south to central British Columbia, central Manitoba, central Ontario, New York, northern Vermont, northern New Hampshire, northern Maine, New Brunswick, Nova Scotia, and Newfoundland; winters mainly south of the Ohio and Delaware valleys to the Gulf coast; west in migration to the Great Plains.

The Rusty Blackbird is not so widely known as other blackbirds, as it breeds only in rather inaccessible places in the northern parts of the United States and in Canada, and generally is rather shy, when, as a migrant, it passes through on its migrations. It is the most nearly aquatic of our blackbirds, and in spring it frequents lowlands, swamps, woodland pools and the margins of ponds and streams. When it first appears in small groups or flocks, its *chuck* so nearly resembles that of the wood frogs which frequent its favorite woodland pools that it is rather difficult to tell at a distance whether the frogs or the birds are responsible for the noisy chorus; but when the blackbirds begin to sing, their notes at once distinguish them, not only from frogs, but from all other birds. Their chorus then is a mixture of chuckling and shrill squeals or whistles unlike any other sound in nature. When once heard it will always thereafter be recognized. In spring they like to feed in shallow water where they find insect larvae and probably some small crustaceans or other forms of life. At times they may be seen wading quite deeply in the water and plunging in not only their bills but their whole heads in the manner of the Solitary Sandpiper and very likely finding similar food. If disturbed they usually fly up into a tree all together and all facing the same way, and after some preliminary chucks and tail-flirts give the listener one of their free concerts. In autumn they are not so closely confined to the water, and they often frequent weedy gardens and cornfields, where they walk

471

quietly about, turning over dead leaves, etc. They flock at times with other blackbirds or Starlings.

Dr. C. W. Townsend says that their courtship display 'is produced with apparent great effort, wide-open bill and spread tail, resulting in a series of squeaking notes suggestive of an unoiled windmill — *wat-cheê e.*' This note represents very well its usual song, and, he says, 'at times a sweet lower note, often double, is heard.'

Mr. F. H. Kennard writes as follows of its nesting habits in northern New England:

'The female usually starts incubation with the laying of the first egg, particularly in the early spring, when the weather is cold, and sits pretty close, flying off only upon one's near approach. Particularly shy birds may, when disturbed, disappear without uttering a note, but the great majority that I have observed will remain in the vicinity of the nest, uttering their loud "chips" of alarm, becoming more and more distressed, when disturbed, as incubation progresses, until after the hatching they are particularly vociferous. During incubation the male is very assiduous in his attentions to the female, feeding her frequently, and seldom flies far from the nesting locality. The female at this season is usually seldom in evidence, but by watching the male, one can soon determine by his actions the approximate locality of the nest. He has the very conspicuous habit of sitting on the top of some tall dead stub or tree, often with a nice fat grub in his bill and calling to the female. This call note is a two-syllabled "conk-ee," very similar to the three-syllabled "conk-a-ree" of the Red-wing, but clearer and more musical, and usually distinguishable from the notes of the other blackbirds.

'If disturbed by the proximity of watchers, he may delay for a while, uttering an occasional "chip" of alarm, but sooner or later he will fly close to the nest or to the top of some near-by stub, when the female will fly out to him, and with low "chucks" and much fluttering of wings, partake of the delicious morsel he has brought her.'

BREWER'S BLACKBIRD

Euphagus cyanocephalus (WAGLER).

Other name: Blue-headed Blackbird or Grackle.

IDENTIFICATION. — Length 8¾ to 10¼ inches; spread 14 to 16 inches. A slim blackbird with square-ended tail; male all black with greenish gloss on body and violet on head and neck; female smaller, dark brownish black with faint purplish gloss; young duller than female.

BREEDING. — Around ranches and farms, on the edge of marshes, etc. *Nest:* In a bush or low tree, of sticks, plant stalks, grass, roots, etc. *Eggs:* 4 to 6, grayish or greenish, variously marked with browns and lavender.

RANGE. — Breeds from central British Columbia, and central Manitoba south to Lower California, New Mexico and western Texas, and from the Pacific to northwestern Minnesota, Wisconsin, and northern Illinois; winters from southern British Columbia, Kansas and Wisconsin south to Guatemala.

Brewer's Blackbird is a very common bird in suitable localities throughout its western range. It is a rather slim and sleek-looking bird, all black at a little distance but showing violet reflections on its head and neck, and greenish iridescence on its body plumage when seen in a good light. It is considerably smaller than the Bronzed or Purple Grackles but in the spring it may be hard to separate from the Rusty Grackles, with which it often associates for a season.

It is quite gregarious, usually nesting in small colonies and later joining the Red-wings and Rusties in large congregations, when the assembled hosts may do considerable damage to ripening grain.

The courtship of the Brewer's Blackbird is a simple affair. The males walk around on the ground slowly, occasionally raising the head and neck almost straight up in the air and holding them so for a brief interval. Every little while they pause and spreading the wings slightly, puff out the body feathers something like a miniature turkey cock.

The nests are frequently built on the ground in meadows, though in some regions the birds prefer low trees or bushes. Soon after the young leave the nest the flocking begins, and as the Red-wings assemble in similar regions, the two species unite and later are joined by the Rusty Grackles from their more northerly breeding-grounds. — (J.B.M.)

BOAT–TAILED GRACKLE

Cassidix mexicanus major (VIEILLOT).

Other names: Jackdaw; Salt-water Blackbird; Cowbird (female).

IDENTIFICATION. — Length of male 15½ to 17 inches, spread 21 to 23½ inches; length of female 12 to 13½ inches, spread about 18 to 20 inches. A large, slim, long-tailed blackbird; adult male all black with glossy violet-blue reflections on head and throat, and greenish-blue on body; wings and tail brownish-black; females much smaller, upper parts clove-brown, under parts buffy-brown, throat paler, wings and tail brownish.

BREEDING. — In colonies, in bushes near water. *Nest:* Bulky, of grasses, seaweed, etc., with a mud core. *Eggs:* 3 to 5, pale bluish-white, spotted, scrawled and blotched with purplish and blackish.

RANGE. — Lower Austral Zone of South Atlantic and Gulf States from southern Delaware to the Florida Keys and west to the eastern coast of Texas.

The male Boat-tailed Grackle looks like a big, overgrown, long-legged Purple Grackle, with a proportionately longer tail, but his mate is a very different looking creature, about a fifth shorter, and entirely unlike him in coloration, being a rich dark brown above and buffy-brown below. They are common birds in the coastal region of the Southeastern States, but are seldom found far from salt water except in Florida, where they are pretty generally distributed. They are easily recognized from their size, the extra long and strongly graduated and keeled tail of the male, and the very different coloration of the female. They are quite gregarious, nesting in loose colonies and moving about throughout the year in flocks sometimes numbering several hundred individuals. They are very conversational at times, their notes, according to A. H. Howell, being 'varied and interesting, though not very musical. The "song" of one I observed sitting on a telephone pole at Jupiter in March sounded like *churr-churr; cheep-cheep-cheep,* faster and sweeter toned, then a coarse *chuck,* followed by a peculiar guttural, clattering sound that seemed to be of vocal origin, though accompanied by a fluttering of the wings.'

The Boat-tailed Grackle may often be seen walking and jumping around on the beaches looking for crustaceans which are a favorite article of food, or any bits of animal or vegetable matter which is edible. They are also common around the borders of the many shallow ponds in central Florida and in the wide marshes, where they find an abundance of insects, snails, and other aquatic or semi-aquatic creatures on which they feed. They walk about on floating veg-

473

etation almost as expertly as the gallinules and rails, and they also wade in shallow water when occasion demands. At some seasons they feed largely upon seeds and sometimes damage growing grain, especially rice. At St. Petersburg, Florida, where the tourists feed the Scaup Ducks from the seawall, the big Boat-tailed Grackles have learned to gather in the rustling palm trees above the sidewalks and to get their share of the rice or other food brought for the ducks. A handful of rice tossed onto the ground will quickly bring a small flock of hungry Boat-tails to the scene, walking rapidly about and jumping from place to place, as they hastily pick up the grains of food, the showy black males in striking contrast to the smaller brown and buff females. — (J.B.M.)

PURPLE GRACKLE

Quiscalus quiscula quiscula (LINNAEUS).   PLATE 62.

Other names: Crow Blackbird; Crow-billed Blackbird.

IDENTIFICATION. — Length 11 to 13½ inches; spread 17 to 18½ inches. Slim blackbirds with rather long and graduated tails, females duller than the glossy black males with their metallic reflections; head, neck, throat, and upper breast brilliant metallic purple to bluish-green or steel-blue; back and rump varying from bottle green to metallic purple or brassy green, *the feathers with iridescent bars.*

SONG. — Has been likened to the squeaking of an oilless wheelbarrow.

BREEDING. — In coniferous groves, open and swampy woods, city parks, swamps, and reedy marshes. *Nest:* Of grass, weed-stalks, seaweed, etc. *Eggs:* 4 to 6 or 7, vary from pale greenish-white to light reddish-brown, and variously marked with browns and lavender.

RANGE. — Breeds from the north shore of Long Island Sound and the lower Hudson Valley west to the Alleghenies and south to northern Georgia, northern Alabama, and eastern Tennessee; winters mainly south of the Delaware Valley.

FLORIDA GRACKLE

Quiscalus quiscula aglaeus BAIRD.

Other name: China-eyed Blackbird.

IDENTIFICATION. — Slightly smaller than *Q. q. quiscula*; feathers of back with *more or less concealed iridescent bars.*

RANGE. — South Atlantic coast from South Carolina to Florida, and west in the southern part of the Gulf States to southeastern Texas.

474

BRONZED GRACKLE

Quiscalus quiscula aeneus RIDGWAY.

PLATE 62.

Other names: Crow Blackbird; Crow-billed Blackbird.

IDENTIFICATION. — Back metallic seal-bronze, the feathers *without iridescent bars*.

RANGE. — Breeds from Great Slave Lake, northern Manitoba, Nova Scotia, and Newfoundland south to Montana and Colorado (east of the Rocky Mountains), and southeast to northwestern Georgia, Pennsylvania (west of the Alleghenies), New York, western Connecticut, and Massachusetts; winters from the Ohio Valley south to southern Texas.

The three races of *Quiscalus quiscula* found in eastern North America are so alike in habits and haunts that, with some slight allowance for difference in habitats north and south, the following description of the Bronzed Grackle should apply to any race.

As winter nears its end grackles begin to move up the Atlantic coast from the South. Some day in March or early April when the brown earth has partly emerged from the receding snows of winter and while snowdrifts still linger in shady places, we may see a flock of blackbirds whirl into the top of some tall, lone, leafless tree. They may be too distant to identify by sight, but soon the twanging of their 'loose-strung harps' floats down the wind and then we know that they are grackles. If in the northern United States or southern Canada the singers presumably are Bronzed Grackles; if in extreme southern New England or farther south or west they are likely to be of the purple race. Both are known to the people as Crow Blackbirds.

Evidently Grackles believe that they can sing, and they apply themselves to song with enthusiasm, industry and perseverance, but from our point of view their performance is not harmonious music. The outpourings of a flock of these birds have been likened to a 'wheelbarrow chorus,' but the sound might be better represented by a number of iron gates swinging, creaking and clanging on rusty un-oiled hinges. Musical or not, it is one of the sounds of nature which is worth the hearing.

Later in the season you may see one or a pair in the backyard or on the lawn. The male is trim and handsome. As his iridescent plumage flashes in the sun he appears as a creature cast in polished bronze and blued steel. He walks with head held nearly level, taking not short, quick, nervous steps like the Starling, but longer, more labored strides. With each step his head is pushed forward and one shoulder is raised a trifle, and as he walks, his long tail swings a little from side to side. In the mating season he carries the tail rather high, and in flight, which is rather heavy, the upturning of the outer tail feathers is very noticeable. Dr. C. W. Townsend gives the following account of the display of the male:

'The courtship of the Bronzed Grackle is not inspiring. The male puffs out his feathers to twice his natural size, partly opens his wings, spreads his tail and, if he is on the ground, drags it rigidly as he walks. At the same time he sings his song — such as it is — with great vigor and abandon. That this vocal performance should be classed as a song from a scientific point of view there is no doubt, but such it would not seem to the ordinary observer. It is harsh and disagreeable, a squeaking, saw-filing explosion of notes. It varies considerably and sometimes suggests the sound of a jet of escaping steam. I have written it down *er wheet, dam that*, but my interpretation may have been influenced by my mental attitude induced by the performance.

475

'During the period of courtship the male in flight depresses the central feathers of its tail, forming a V-shaped keel. I was at first inclined to think that this was of use in flight like a rudder, but I am inclined to think that it is in the nature of courtship display, for this arrangement of tail feathers is not seen when a bird is actively engaged in flight for the purpose of obtaining food. Under these circumstances the tail is spread in the ordinary manner.'

Normally our Crow Blackbirds are birds of the marsh and waterside in forested regions. As settlements and clearings took the place, in part, of the primeval forests, these birds found a new food supply in the corn crop of the settlers, and multiplied exceedingly. In colonial days Crow Blackbirds were known far and wide as 'Maize Thieves,' bounties were paid for their heads, and in some Cape Cod towns a young man was forbidden by law to marry until he had turned in to the town clerk a certain quota of blackbirds' heads. The war against the birds was so successful that in 1749 locusts, cutworms and other grass-destroying pests so completely ruined the grass crop of the New England States that the farmers were obliged to send to England and Pennsylvania to obtain hay enough to feed their cattle through the winter. The Swedish traveler Kalm tells us that after this occurrence the people 'abated' their enmity against the 'Maize Thieves' as they thought that they had observed the birds feeding on the pests which destroyed their crops. Owing to the widespread sentiment for the protection of the birds we have now again an excessive multiplication of Grackles in New England with accompanying complaints of serious damage to the corn crop.

The Grackle is a wise bird and, like the Crow, the Blue Jay and the Starling, soon recognizes a place of safety. It has learned to come into villages and cities and to nest in trees in parks and cemeteries and in grounds of the larger estates, where it prefers the white pine as a nesting tree. A few Bronzed Grackles came into the Boston Public Garden before the year 1900, and then they began to breed there regularly and in some numbers, and although their favorite pine trees are not grown in the garden they have continued to nest there, meantime waging war on the English Sparrows, which are now reduced to minimum numbers. Thus far, also, the Grackles have held their own with the Starlings.

Grackles are extremely interesting birds; they rank high in intelligence. They are excellent judges of the extent of the danger zone surrounding the man with a gun. They destroy the eggs and young of other birds, and not only do they take young birds from the nests but they catch, kill and eat them after the little things are fledged and able to fly, and at times they kill adult birds. This has been observed repeatedly. As a water bird the Grackle is by no means a failure. It is fond of the water and bathes in it even in a Massachusetts winter. It walks about in shallow water with tail elevated to keep it dry. It often catches small fish by dipping down like a gull or a tern, though I have never seen one go entirely under water. Several observers have seen grackles take dry, hard pieces of stale bread and soak them in water until softened.

Like Crows, Grackles are more or less omnivorous. Among their vegetal food we can list all common grains, most wild and cultivated fruits that are eaten by man and a few that are not, acorns, beechnuts, chestnuts and the seeds of many noxious weeds, small bulbs, plant galls, grass and leaves. In spring a large part of their food consists of noxious insects, and when feeding the young the destruction of insects increases rapidly, as the young are fed a considerably larger proportion of insects than that taken by the adults. The adults are so fond of insects that they sometimes clumsily pursue them in the air and occasionally catch one, though they are not fitted to do the work of flycatchers; but in autumn when grain, fruit, nuts and seeds begin to develop, this species turns largely to vegetal food. Before the end of August, Grackles assemble in flocks and these flocks increase in size until some contain thousands of birds. When such flocks roost in thickly settled localities they become a nuisance because of their noise and droppings. They sometimes ruin many early apples and pears pecking them as Starlings do, and eating only a little from each fruit. Such vast bodies of birds can do immense damage to cornfields, and they attack the corn when it is in the milk. As they move south the flocks grow to enormous size.

A great flight of these birds passed over Concord, Massachusetts, on October 28, 1904. From my post of observation, on a hilltop, an army of birds could be seen extending across the sky from one horizon to the other. As one of my companions remarked, it was a great 'rainbow of birds'; as they passed overhead, the line appeared to be about three rods wide and about one hundred feet above the hilltop. This column of birds appeared as perfect in form as a platoon. The individual birds were not flying in the direction in which the column extended, but diagonally across it; and when one considers the difficulty of keeping a platoon of men in line when marching shoulder to shoulder, the precision with which this host of birds kept their line across the sky seems marvelous. As the line passed overhead, it extended nearly east and west. The birds seemed to be flying in a course considerably west of south, and thus the whole column was gradually drifting southwest. As the left of the line passed over the Concord meadows, its end was seen in the distance, but the other end of this mighty army extended beyond the western horizon. The flight was watched until it was nearly out of sight, and then followed with a glass until it disappeared in the distance. It never faltered, broke, or wavered, but kept straight on into the gathering gloom of night. The whole array presented no such appearance as the unformed flocks ordinarily seen earlier in the season, but was a finer formation than I have ever seen elsewhere, among either land birds or water-fowl. It seemed to be a migration of all the Crow Blackbirds in the region, and there appeared to be a few Rusty Blackbirds with them. After that date I saw but one Crow Blackbird. It was impossible to estimate the number of birds in this flight. My companions believed there were 'millions.'

EASTERN COWBIRD

Molothrus ater ater (BODDAERT). PLATE 60.

Other names: Cow Blackbird; Cow Bunting; Lazy Bird; Tick Bird; Brown-headed Blackbird.

IDENTIFICATION. — Length 7 to 8¼ inches; spread 11¾ to 13¾ inches. Male all black except brownish head; female and young grayish-brown; bill short and thick suggesting a finch.

SONG. — A squeaky, bubbly *glug-glug-gleeee*. CALL: A high whistled *phee de de*.

BREEDING. — Eggs, white or whitish, speckled thickly with browns and grays, laid in nests of other birds.

RANGE. — Breeds from southern Ontario, southern Quebec, Nova Scotia, and New Brunswick south to central Virginia, southeastern Kentucky, central Tennessee, south-central Arkansas, Louisiana, and central Texas, and west to Minnesota, northeastern Iowa, southeastern Nebraska, southwestern Kansas, and New Mexico; winters from the Ohio and Potomac valleys south to Florida and the Gulf coast.

Cowbirds are free lovers. They are neither polygamous nor polyandrous — just promiscuous. They have no demesne and no domicile; they are entirely unattached. Their courting is brief and to the point. In this pleasant pastime the male usually takes the lead. He erects his feathers until he is all 'puffed up' and struts with spread tail, and wings drooping or partly extended, in the meantime making the most farcical attempts at song. At times he opens and closes his wings in his excitement and stretches up his neck to its full length with bill pointing upward. One spring day I observed a male on the ridgepole of a house, attitudinizing for the benefit of his consorts. His attempts at song were peculiar and probably unusual. With each swelling of his throat he produced a soft rather musical sound in two syllables like that of the cuckoo of Europe, but with the accent on the last syllable thus — *cook-oo'*, but several seconds elapsed between the calls. At times a male performs before several females, at other times males are in the majority. Sometimes a popular female will have three or four males in attendance. There seems to be little jealousy, and few combats occur between either males or females; the courtship is a happy-go-lucky affair. It is 'off with the old love and on with the new,' and the results of this brief union of congenial natures are surreptitiously deposited, not on the nearest available doorstep — but in the nests of other birds which are relied upon as good foster-parents to rear the foundlings, while the care-free Cowbirds wander at their own sweet will with nothing to do but 'eat, drink and be merry.' The saddest part of the life-history of the Eastern Cowbird is that the introduction of its egg or eggs into the nests of smaller birds usually dooms the eggs or young of their foster-parents. Apparently in most cases the birds so imposed upon do not seem to realize the danger that threatens their own brood through the introduction of the interloper; though now and then a Cowbird's egg is found broken beneath the nest of another bird.

Occasionally a warbler or some other small bird will build a new nest on top of the Cowbird's egg, thus burying it for good and all. In some cases nests three stories in height have been thus built, each of the upper stories with one or more cowbird's eggs buried beneath it. If the Cowbird cannot wait until there are eggs in the nest which she has chosen, and therefore deposits her egg first, or if several Cowbirds' eggs are deposited in the same nest, the owner may desert it. But many birds having one or more Cowbird's eggs thus foisted upon them proceed to incubate it or them with their own. The Cowbird commonly deposits but one egg in a place, and in most cases that is left in the nest of some bird which already has one or two eggs of its own. A pregnant Cowbird, desiring to be rid of an egg, sneaks quietly through orchards, woods or thickets searching for an unguarded nest in which to deposit her leavings. This must be done surreptitiously in the absence of the owners, as they would make it very unpleasant for this unattached female should they discover her in the act. She is not always able to find an unoccupied and unwatched domicile at the right moment, and sometimes is obliged to deposit her treasure on the ground.

Once in the nest, the Cowbird's egg, being usually larger than those of the bird chosen to incubate it, gets more heat from her body than the other smaller eggs; therefore it often hatches first. The young bird being larger than the other occupants of the nest reaches higher and gets most of the food, so that while he or she waxes fat and lusty, the legitimate nestlings remain weak and stunted, and usually either die in the nest or are thrown or crowded out alive by the young Cowbird. Cases where any of the 'rightful heirs' survive are rare indeed. The Cowbird now has the nest to itself and all food brought by its foster-parents goes into its capacious maw, which seems to be ever ready for more. In about seven days the youngster is strong enough to climb out of the nest, and in a few days more essays its first flight; but its faithful foster-parents guard and feed it for many days thereafter. It is a common sight to see a young Cowbird tended and fed by a little warbler so much smaller than the great clumsy foundling that in feeding it the little bird seems almost in danger of being swallowed alive. The number of species imposed on by the Cowbird considerably exceeds one hundred, ranging in size from the Blue-gray Gnatcatcher to the Mourning Dove. It seems to make little difference to the Cowbird where the nest is built in which her eggs are left, but nests on the ground or in the lower branches of trees are commonly chosen. Domiciles in hollow trees are entered freely and even the redoubtable Kingbird occasionally is victimized. As soon as the young Cowbird has learned to feed itself, it seeks others of its kind or is sought by them, for Cowbirds are always gregarious and flock more or less the year round.

During the summer, Cowbirds gather about pasturing cattle and search for the insects stirred up by the beasts, or, as the cows lie tranquilly chewing their cud, the birds may be seen walking about upon their backs, engaged in ridding them of flies and other pests, or merely resting quietly there in perfect security. In September the flocks begin to move southward; they often associate with other blackbirds and with Starlings, and at times the mixed flocks are enormous, but so far as I have observed Cowbirds usually roost by themselves; often they choose thick coniferous trees or other thickets in the shelter of which they pass the night in great numbers. Another favorite roosting place is in the grass and reeds far out on wide meadows. These moving flocks drift southward until November when most of the Cowbirds have reached their wintering grounds. During mild winters considerable flocks remain on the coast of southern New England and the Middle Atlantic States.

WESTERN TANAGER

Piranga ludoviciana (WILSON).   PLATE 75.

Other name: Louisiana Tanager.
IDENTIFICATION. — Length 6¾ to 7½ inches; spread 11 to 12 inches. Adult male, face and more or less of head red, wings and tail black, two light wing-bars, rest of plumage yellow; female and young above dull green, below yellowish, with dusky wings and light wing-bars; winter male like female but with blackish wings and tail.
BREEDING. — Similar to Scarlet Tanager.
RANGE. — Breeds from northwestern British Columbia, southwestern Mackenzie, and southwestern South Dakota to the mountains of southern California, Lower California, southern Arizona, and central western Texas; winters southward from central Mexico to Costa Rica.

The Western Tanager is a handsome, showy bird, given to singing from the tree-tops along the edge of great forests, or in rather open forest glades. It was discovered in Idaho during the memorable expedition of Lewis and Clarke in 1808. It was named the Louisiana Tanager because it was a native of that great and formerly unexplored land beyond the Mississippi then known as Louisiana, but today the name Western Tanager is much more appropriate, for it is a typical western bird. When, on first visiting the Pacific coast, I heard the song of this striking bird, it seemed almost exactly to duplicate the well-known strident, hoarse carol of the Scarlet Tanager of the eastern United States, and it has the same ventriloquial quality, so that often it is difficult to locate the direction of the singer. However, his habit of singing at the very top of tall trees gives the observer every opportunity when once the bird is located. The female is inconspicuous, and the nest so well hidden that it is seldom found.

This bird feeds largely on insects, which it takes from the foliage or pursues through the air in the manner of a flycatcher. It is a mere straggler east of the Rocky Mountain region.

SCARLET TANAGER

Piranga erythromelas VIEILLOT.   PLATE 75.

Other names: Black-winged Red Bird; Fire Bird.

IDENTIFICATION. — Length 6½ to 7½ inches; spread 11 to 12 inches. Male bright scarlet with black wings and tail; female and young olive-green above, yellow below; male in winter like female but with wings and tail black; *no wing-bars*.

SONG. — Like Robin, but hoarse. CALL: A low *chip-churr*.

BREEDING. — In high open woods, low thick woods, or old orchards. *Nest:* On a horizontal branch, flat and thin, of roots, twigs, bark-strips, weed-stems, and grasses, lined with rootlets. *Eggs:* 3 to 5, greenish-blue heavily spotted with browns.

RANGE. — Breeds from southern Saskatchewan, southern Ontario, southern Quebec, New Brunswick, and Nova Scotia south to southern Kansas, northern Arkansas, northern Alabama, northern Georgia, and the mountains of Virginia and South Carolina; winters from Colombia to Peru and Bolivia; migrates through Cuba, Jamaica, and Yucatan and along the east coast of Central America.

The Scarlet Tanager is one of the most gorgeous birds in eastern North America. Its encrimsoned body and sable wings and tail stand out in strong relief against the greenery of tender May-time foliage. This striking bird has been the inspiration of many a facile pen. Mrs. Florence Merriam Bailey says of it: 'High among the tree-tops of the cool green woods the Tanager sings through the summer days. Hidden by the network of leaves above us we often pass him by; but once discovered he seems to illuminate the forest. We marvel at his color. He is like a Bird of Paradise in our northern landscape.'

Here is a common bird that passes most of his life in the woods, hidden by the foliage where he is seldom seen by the uninitiated, who look upon him as a *rara avis*, and count it a redletter day when once they glimpse the brilliant bird. His consummate ventriloquism adds to the difficulty of the search. The novice hears the song apparently far away, when in reality the bird may be just overhead, but concealed by dense foliage. He may be located, however, by going past the sound and then returning to it, and when the elusive singer is once discovered the sight of his scarlet vesture is well worth the trouble. This bird has the distinction of being the first among the feathered races to fix the attention of that brilliant ornithologist, Dr. Elliott Coues, who says: 'I hold this bird in particular, almost superstitious, recollection, as the very first of all the feathered tribe to stir within me those emotions that have never ceased to stimulate and gratify my love for birds. More years have passed than I care to remember since a little child was strolling through an orchard one bright morning in June, filled with mute wonder at beauties felt, but neither questioned nor understood. A shout from an older companion — "There goes a Scarlet Tanager!" — and the child was straining eager, wistful eyes after something that had flashed upon his senses for a moment as if from another world, it seemed so bright, so beautiful, so strange. "What is a Scarlet Tanager?" mused the child, whose consciousness had flown with the wonderful apparition on wings of ecstasy; but the bees hummed on, the scent of the flowers floated by, the sunbeam passed across the green-sward, and there was no reply — nothing but the echo of a mute appeal to Nature, stirring the very depths with an inward thrill. That night the vision came again in dreamland, where the strangest things are truest and known the best; the child was startled by a ball of fire, and fanned to rest again by a sable wing. The wax was soft then, and the impress grew indelible. Nor would I blur it if I could — not though the flight of years has borne sad answers to reiterated questionings — not though the wings of hope are tipped with lead and brush the very earth, instead of soaring in scented sunlight.'

In my own earliest childhood in Massachusetts the Scarlet Tanager was a bird of which I dreamed, but which I never saw. However, as soon as I became familiar with its note, I found it a common woodland sound. There was a wood of giant white oaks in southern Worcester County, and there during the spring migration the trees were peopled with the scarlet males, all in full song. That grove became the destination of an annual spring pilgrimage. It has vanished long since with all the other big timber of the region, but every year the Tanagers appear in the coppice growth that succeeded the old trees. They prefer white oak woods, but may be found anywhere in deciduous woods, and in mixed growths, especially in a well-watered country.

We see few Scarlet Tanagers in the North until the foliage develops somewhat upon decidu-ous trees, and most of them do not arrive until the leaves are large enough to afford them some measure of concealment. They are warm weather birds, fond of sunshine, though often some-what oppressed by an excessively hot sultry atmosphere. June 24, 1904, was an extremely hot, humid day at Concord, Massachusetts, and as I moved along a woodland path, the more tender plants were beginning to droop with folded hanging leaves and wild strawberries were drying on the stem. Thunderclouds were rolling up in the north, and a distant rumbling warned me to hasten toward the shelter afforded by the cabin on the river. As I passed hurriedly along, a beautiful Scarlet Tanager flew up from beside the path and alighted a few feet away. His bill was wide open as he panted, almost gasping for breath. He reached forward, picked an insect off an oak twig, flew along a few feet, fluttered over an oak leaf, and took another insect from that, all the while panting violently. In hot weather the males of this species often may be seen with the wings drooping and tail cocked up, which gives them a jaunty appearance. This posture is exaggerated during courtship by dragging the wings and fluffing up the scarlet plumage, which may add to his attractiveness in the eyes of his expectant consort.

This species does not sing so often nor so regularly as the Indigo Bunting or the Red-eyed Vireo, but when one is silent and hidden it may be startled into song by a sudden shout or by a noisy vehicle coming along the road, or if it fails to sing it may give a sharp *chip* or *chip-churr*, which may betray its location.

Most of the motions of the Scarlet Tanager are leisurely, except in love or war, but in case of necessity it can move very fast. While not particularly active as a flycatcher, it is a premier caterpillar hunter. It destroys not only hairless larvae of many species, but also such hairy ones as those of the gypsy moth and the forest tent caterpillar as well. Once my attention was called to a bush partly defoliated by a swarm of the latter caterpillars. Soon a Scarlet Tanager alighted there, and continued to come and go until he had taken every caterpillar from that bush. This species destroys enormous numbers of tiny newly hatched caterpillars before the little pests have any opportunity to commit their depredations upon the foliage. But this bird does not confine its attentions to caterpillars alone; it eats their parents, the nocturnal moths. Even the giant *polyphemus* and the *luna* are not safe from its attacks. The larvae of these species are very destructive to trees, where arboreal birds are lacking. Among the first-class pests eaten by this tanager we find the Colorado potato beetle, many wood-boring beetles, bark beetles, leaf-eating and leaf-rolling beetles, click beetles, grasshoppers and locusts; it takes ants also, but destroys some useful ichneumon-flies and some spiders. It is said to take some wild berries and seeds, but insects seem to form its principal food.

SUMMER TANAGER

Piranga rubra rubra (LINNAEUS).   PLATE 75.

Other names: Crimson Tanager; Summer Red-bird.

IDENTIFICATION. — Length 7 to 7¾ inches; spread 11¼ to 12¼ inches. Adult male rosy or brick-red all over (not scarlet); female and young dark olive-green above, dull yellow below; no wing-bars.

BREEDING. — Similar to Scarlet Tanager.

RANGE. — Breeds from southeastern Nebraska, southern Iowa, southeastern Wisconsin, central Indiana, central Ohio, Maryland, and Delaware south to southern Florida and northeastern Mexico; winters from central Mexico and Yucatan to Ecuador, Peru, and Guiana; migrant in western Cuba.

The rosy-tinted Summer Tanager is called the 'Summer Redbird' in the South to distinguish it from the Cardinal or 'Winter Redbird.' The latter winters where it breeds, but the Summer Tanager passes the winter in tropical America. This bird need never be mistaken for the Scarlet Tanager, as its wings and tail are not black, and it is not so richly colored as the scarlet beauty.

The bird seems to be attracted by tall open woods with scrubby oak underbrush. It likes to sing in the tops of tall trees, but it usually nests rather low in the oaks. Its loud, clear notes are commonly heard before the bird is seen, for in the tree-tops it often is concealed by the foliage from an observer on the ground below. This bird is an expert flycatcher and sometimes it may be seen darting about like a Kingbird in pursuit of flying insects, such as bees, wasps and beetles. Its habit of taking bees has given it the name of Red Beebird in some parts of the South.

The Summer Tanager is an early spring arrival in the Southern States. Its presence is announced by its characteristic call notes, a clearly enunciated *tshicky-tukky-tuk*, very different from the familiar *chip-churr* of the Scarlet Tanager. It is most often found in the rather open pine woods, especially when they have an undergrowth of oaks or other deciduous trees. The song suggests that of the Scarlet Tanager, but it is a soft melodious whistle, less resonant and without metallic quality.

The rather shallow nest of the Summer Tanager, like that of the Scarlet Tanager, is usually placed near the end of a horizontal limb and is made of grass-stems, leaves, and bark-strips, lined with rootlets. The eggs are bluish-green heavily marked with browns and purplish.

EASTERN CARDINAL

Richmondena cardinalis cardinalis (LINNAEUS).   PLATE 73.

Other names: Cardinal Grosbeak; Virginia Red-bird; Kentucky Cardinal.

IDENTIFICATION. — Length 7½ to 9¼ inches; spread 10¼ to 12 inches. A crested, short-winged, long-tailed bird with a very heavy bill; male chiefly vermilion-red, face and chin black; female not so full crested, yellowish-brown with some red especially on wings and tail.

BREEDING. — In thickets or among saplings. *Nest:* Loosely built of twigs, leaves, bark-strips, rootlets, weeds, and grasses, lined with fine grass and hair. *Eggs:* 3 or 4, white to greenish- or bluish-white, variously marked with browns, etc.

RANGE. — Breeds from southeastern South Dakota, southern Iowa, northern Indiana, northern Ohio, southern Ontario (locally), southwestern and southeastern Pennsylvania, and the southern Hudson Valley south to the northern parts of the Gulf States, and in Bermuda; winters throughout its range.

Cardinals are abundant birds in some of the Southern States, where they seem to be almost ubiquitous, for we find them in the gardens about houses, in bushy thickets everywhere, in the heavy growths along swampy streams, and in the mixed woodlands.

The song of the male Cardinal is a series of loud but melodious whistles, each phrase usually repeated several times. One of its common notes is very much like a whistle used in calling a dog, and dogs are frequently deceived by the bird's calls. The female also sings a softer song than that of her mate. The Eastern Cardinal is one of those rare songsters that breaks into music in every month of the year.

The nest of the Eastern Cardinal is usually in a thicket of dense bushes, or in a brush heap, sometimes on top of a bush-grown fence or vine-covered stump, and is a bulky, loosely built structure of leaves, bark-strips, twigs, rootlets, weed-stems, and grasses, lined with fine grasses or hair. The three or four eggs are quite variable in coloration, the ground color being white, grayish, bluish or greenish, and they are blotched, spotted and dotted with various shades of brown, purplish, and lilac. The birds are prolific, often raising two broods and sometimes three in a single year.

The male is very attentive to his mate, following her while she is building the nest and singing in his most melodious strain, and while she is performing the duties of incubation he brings her choice morsels of food whenever she calls for nourishment. Both parents assume the care of the young, which remain in the nest for nine or ten days. When the young birds are out of the nest and able to fly, the mother bird leaves them to the care of her mate, who guards them for three weeks or more, while the female is bringing up another brood.

While most abundant in the extreme South, the Cardinal is resident throughout the year as far north as the region about New York City, and in southern Ontario, and when in winter a thick carpet of snow lies on the ground, its plumage seems to shine with unusual brilliancy in the reflected light from the snow and it stands out in marked contrast to the wintry background. — (J.B.M.)

FLORIDA CARDINAL

Richmondena cardinalis floridana (RIDGWAY).

IDENTIFICATION. — Slightly smaller than *R. c. cardinalis*, male averaging deeper red, female darker and richer in color especially on breast.

RANGE. — Resident of the Florida peninsula.

LOUISIANA CARDINAL

Richmondena cardinalis magnirostris (BANGS).

IDENTIFICATION. — Red of head and under parts of male not so dark as in *R. c. floridana*; bill largest and heaviest of the six races of *Richmondena cardinalis*.

RANGE. — Southern Louisiana and eastern Texas.

ROSE–BREASTED GROSBEAK

Hedymeles ludovicianus (LINNAEUS).   PLATE 73.

Other names: Throat-cut; Potato-bug Bird.

IDENTIFICATION. — Length 7 to 8½ inches; spread 12 to 13 inches. Bill very large, thick and powerful, white in male, darker in female; male strikingly black and white with rose-red breast and pink under wings; female much like female Purple Finch but larger and bill proportionately heavier.

SONG. — A sweet mellow warble. ALARM NOTE: A metallic *ick*.

BREEDING. — In thickets, woodlands near water, on farms, and in gardens and orchards. *Nest:* Loosely made of twigs, vegetable fibers, grass, etc., lined with finer material, rootlets, or pine needles. *Eggs:* 3 to 5, very variable, bluish-green to grayish-white, spotted and blotched with browns, purplish, and lilac.

RANGE. — Breeds from south-central Mackenzie, central Ontario, southern Quebec, and Cape Breton Island south to central Kansas, southern Missouri, central Ohio, central New Jersey, and in the mountains to northern Georgia; winters from southern Mexico and Yucatan to Venezuela and Ecuador.

Nearly sixty years ago there stood, some half a mile from my father's house, near Worcester, Massachusetts, a tract of heavy timber shading a living spring, from which ran a little brook meandering down to the lake two miles away. There one bright June day on the bank of the stream occurred my first meeting with the Rose-breasted Grosbeak. A beautiful male bird sat upon the frail nest, about ten feet from the ground in a tall shrub. When I saw that black bird with a large white bill, I hailed it as a new species, thinking it to be a female, not knowing that the male grosbeak relieved the female on the nest. Those great woods were cut off long ago, and the spring has disappeared along with the stream that flowed from it, but I still recall the very look of that bird as from the nest he regarded my approach with bright startled eyes, his head cocked on one side. Since then frequently I have seen the male bird performing his share of the duties of incubation. At Concord, Massachusetts, by the riverside, there was at one time a nest in a tree that hung over the roof of the cabin, and the male bird sitting there commonly sang while on the nest. When a hawk flew overhead he continued to sing, but so reduced the volume of the song that it seemed to come from far away, raising his voice again when the hawk had passed on. Singing on the nest and ventriloquizing are common habits of the male.

The Rose-breasted Grosbeak is an admirable bird. It is beautiful, tuneful and useful, which from a human standpoint is about all that could be desired. The male assumes his full part of the family duties, and is very devoted to his partner, and their young. While the female is incubating he feeds her, and when not incubating himself, stands guard over his mate and home, and cheers her with his wonderfully sweet song.

Normally the Rose-breasted Grosbeak is a forest bird, nesting usually in thickets about swamps, lakes and streams. Deciduous or mixed woods are as one to him. He inhabits birches and alders, and the low growth near the water, but usually sings from tall trees. He may be looked for early in May in the latitude of southern New England. The males usually come first, and when the modestly attired females arrive they are pursued with fierce rivalry. Sometimes from four to six males may be seen paying attentions to one female. They dart from twig to twig, pouring forth their sweetest songs, or hover about her in the air, both singing and fighting at the same time. Their battles sometimes are sanguinary as the beak of the bird is a powerful weapon. I have seen such a fracas but once, but it is well worth seeing. When the battle is won the female, though apparently indifferent during it all, accompanies her conquering hero as he leaves the scene. Having won her he seldom leaves her for long until the young are able to care for themselves.

Fifty years ago the bird was far less common in New England than it has been since the twentieth century came in. Once it nested only in the woods. Now its breeding-grounds have been extended to the farm and village, while it still occupies the woodland breeding-grounds. Its numbers, however, fluctuate; it may appear commonly for a few years in a section, and then suddenly become rare.

The destruction of the buds of forest trees by this Grosbeak is only a form of natural pruning which ordinarily never injures the trees, and the blossoms destroyed are principally the sterile, staminate flowers which are unproductive. The bird occasionally raids garden peas, corn and sprouting wheat, but the damage done in this way is far more than compensated by the service of the bird in destroying noxious insects. It is an inveterate enemy of that pernicious pest, the Colorado potato beetle. This is now a well-recognized habit of the bird which has been known in some places as the 'Potato-bug Bird.' The vegetal food consists largely of wild seeds and wild fruit. It takes many weed seeds and tree seeds, and also in spring many buds and blossoms of trees. A small quantity of grain is taken, and sometimes rather an excessive number of peas.

EASTERN BLUE GROSBEAK

Guiraca caerulea caerulea (LINNAEUS).   PLATE 74.

IDENTIFICATION. — Length 6¼ to 7½ inches; spread 10½ to 11½ inches. Size of Bluebird; only the Indigo Bunting can be mistaken for this bird in a good light, and the Blue Grosbeak is much larger, has a relatively larger bill, and has two *brown* wing-bars, the forward one being *very wide* and rich chestnut-brown. Female and young similar in shape to male, but brown with two wing-bars resembling those of male.

BREEDING. — In low trees or thickets or on edges of woods. *Nest:* Of bark-strips, rootlets, grass, dry leaves, etc., lined with rootlets, and usually contains a cast snakeskin. *Eggs:* 3 to 5, light blue.

RANGE. — Breeds from western Nebraska, Missouri, southern Illinois, and Maryland south to eastern Texas, southern Alabama, and central Florida; winters from southern Mexico to Honduras.

The Eastern Blue Grosbeak is a haunter of bush-grown fields, swampy thickets, and the edges of woods, where it exhibits a rather shy and retiring nature, especially at nesting-time. Its song is a pleasing warble but not as mellow and full-toned as that of the Rose-breasted Grosbeak and in fact is more suggestive of that of the Purple Finch, though not usually as sustained or given as frequently.

The nest of the Blue Grosbeak is usually near the ground, often being suspended between a few upright stems of tall weeds, in a bush, or on a low branch of a small tree. It is built more firmly than the rather thin nest of the Rose-breasted Grosbeak, of bark-strips, dried grass, a few dead leaves in the foundation, and a lining of fine rootlets, and this grosbeak resembles the Crested Flycatcher in its predilection for using a cast snakeskin in the construction of its nest. — (J.B.M.)

INDIGO BUNTING

Passerina cyanea (LINNAEUS).   PLATE 74.

Other name: Indigo-bird.

IDENTIFICATION. — Length 5¼ to 5¾ inches; spread 8 to 9 inches. A small finch; male in summer blue all over with darker wings and tail; in autumn brown with wings and tail as in summer; female plain brownish, indistinctly streaked; blue of adult male quite different from that of adult Blue Grosbeak, but both look black in certain lights.

SONG. — A series of warbled phrases, each group given in a high pitch, then repeated in a lower pitch, the song finishing *diminuendo*.

BREEDING. — In bushy pastures, briery hillsides, and sproutlands. *Nest:* In bush or brier-patch, of twigs, grass, leaves, etc. *Eggs:* 3 or 4 or more, pale blue or greenish, rarely mottled with brown.

RANGE. — Breeds from central eastern North Dakota, central Minnesota, northwestern Michigan, southeastern Ontario, southern Quebec, and southern New Brunswick south to central Texas, southern Louisiana, central Alabama, central Georgia, and northern Florida; winters from Yucatan through Central America to Panama, and in Cuba.

How came this brilliantly garbed little creature to make its home in the North? Dressed in changeable, tropic blue, it nevertheless breeds as far north as Ontario, northern New England and New Brunswick. It is the only one of the little 'painted' buntings to range so far to the northward; the others are all typically southern birds, but this one being virile and prolific may have gradually worked toward the Pole, to find more room for its increasing numbers, until it finally reached its present farthest north. Even now it has not grown hardy. We rarely see it until the May days grow warm, and most of the northern members of its race are on their southward way before the middle of September. In spring the males come several days before the females appear. Soon they start to sing, and when the females come pairing begins. Then the male follows his prospective mate hour after hour in full song. When the union has been consummated, the nest built and the eggs laid, the mated pair seem to dwell in different zones. The female quietly incubates or keeps largely to the bushes near the ground, where, modestly clad and unobtrusive, she is seldom seen; while the brilliant male sings conspicuously, high in the tree-tops or from roof or chimney top; nevertheless he sometimes relieves the female on the nest. His plumage is so changeable that in one position it appears blue and in another or in a different light it seems green, while at a distance it appears quite black.

When as a boy I was on my way home from a morning woodland excursion, under the hot sun of a June noon, the gay Indigo Buntings were always conspicuous songsters, as they perched on the telegraph wires along the way, but I rarely saw a female unless I began exploring the bushes in the neighborhood of the nest. Then her nervous chipping apprised me of her whereabouts and soon she was joined by the male as she protested with twitching wings and tail against the rude invasion of her humble domain. The male seems to delight in singing during the hottest part of the summer days, when other birds are resting in the shade. He will sing his way from the bottom of a tree to the top, going up branch by branch until he has reached the topmost spire, and there, fully exposed to the blazing sun, he will sing and sing and sing. His song period often continues well into August or until a second brood is under way. The male often seems to do little but enjoy himself and sing to the female, while she is incubating the eggs and caring for the young in the nest, but when the little brood is ready to leave the nest, he begins to show more interest in his progeny. In late summer when the corn has 'tasseled out,' the Indigo Buntings seem to find some food about the corn tops and often may be found in cornfields. When the young have waxed strong and fat, and the male has donned his sober brown fall dress, they are all ready to depart, and by the time they have reached South Carolina in October they have gathered in considerable numbers.

PAINTED BUNTING

Passerina ciris (LINNAEUS).   PLATE 94.

Other name: Nonpareil.

IDENTIFICATION. — Length 5 to 5½ inches; spread 8 to 8½ inches. Adult male, head and nape dark violet-blue, back and scapulars golden-green, rump 'dragon's-blood red,' wings dusky glossed green and red, tail purplish-brown, under parts scarlet; female and young male, upper parts green, under parts yellowish-green shading to amber on belly, wings and tail dark drab shaded with green.

SONG. — A low pleasing warble.

BREEDING. — Similar to Indigo Bunting but white or bluish-white eggs with numerous brown markings.

The gorgeous little Painted Bunting or 'Nonpareil,' as it is commonly called, is the most exotic and 'tropical-looking' of all our eastern birds. I well remember my first view of this gaily colored bit of feathered animation. It was April and we were visiting one of the famous old estates on the Ashley River near Charleston, South Carolina, where masses of hundred-year-old azaleas of many colors spread a painter's palette under the great moss-draped live-oaks and glossy-leaved magnolias. It was a little late for the azalea display and the ground under the bushes was covered with fresh fallen blossoms, though they seemed to have thinned the masses of blooms but little. Suddenly from one sun-flecked bush a red flower detached itself, but instead of dropping to the ground fluttered off toward another clump of bushes, with the flash of green wings and a glint of the violet-blue head and blood-red rump of the little Nonpareil.

In many of its traits the Painted Bunting resembles its close relatives, the Indigo Bunting of the North, and the Lazuli Bunting of the West. It haunts similar brushy places, its mate is a very plainly colored little home-body, its nest is hidden in low bushes or dense clumps of weeds, and its song is much like that of the Indigo Bunting, though less energetic. — (J.B.M.)

DICKCISSEL

Spiza americana (GMELIN).   PLATE 74.

Other names: Black-throated Bunting; Little Meadowlark.

IDENTIFICATION. — Length 5¾ to 7 inches; spread 9 to 11 inches. Somewhat smaller than Bobolink. Adult male a light colored sparrow with a yellow line over eye, white throat and yellow breast, with large black patch just below throat; seen in front view, with its yellow breast and black, often crescentic, patch *below* throat, resemblance to Meadowlark is striking. Female and young have less yellow, breast more or less streaked, and lack the black patch on throat; they resemble female and young of Bobolink, but fore wing near bend bright reddish-brown (nearly chestnut).

SONG. — A staccato, clinking strain, *dick-dick-dickcissel*; sometimes merely *dickcissel* or *dick-dick*.

BREEDING. — In meadows, grain fields, pastures, and prairies. *Nest:* On or near ground, of leaves, grasses, hair, etc. *Eggs:* 3 to 5, bright greenish-blue.

RANGE. — Breeds from northeastern Wyoming, northwestern Minnesota, southern Michigan, and southeastern Ontario south to southern Texas, southern Mississippi, central Alabama, and northern Georgia; winters from Guatemala to Colombia, Venezuela, and Trinidad; migrates through Mexico and Central America.

Early American ornithologists found the Dickcissel abundant in the Middle Atlantic States, and Thomas Nuttall, writing in the early part of the last century, said that the bird was not then uncommon along the coast of Massachusetts in the fields near the salt marshes. The bird virtually disappeared from the Atlantic slope before the beginning of the present century. Dr. Witmer Stone says that 'up to 1860, and locally later, the bird was of regular occurrence on the Atlantic coastal plain, but during the next twenty years it practically disappeared from this region, and now is restricted to the Mississippi Valley, except in the case of occasional stragglers.' This well summarizes the case. The cause of its disappearance here must be left

488

to conjecture, but similar disappearances of the species in other parts of the country have been followed by reappearances, and the time may come when these birds will be common again on the Atlantic coast.

In the spring of 1873, if I mistake not the date, I was roaming over a hill pasture near Worcester, Massachusetts, one bright morning, in my hands a sawed-off Belgian musket containing a small charge of powder and dust shot, when I heard a bird-song new to me. The little singer sat upon the top of a tall mullein stalk and sang his metallic notes for all the world to hear. Having listened to his simple lay and marked it well, I saw that he had a bright yellow breast and a black, somewhat crescentic, patch upon it, and I knew him at once for a male Dickcissel (for I had handled specimens of the bird in the museum), and, being in quest of rare specimens, thought to take him home. But the bird had other plans, and before the lumbering, clumsy piece could be brought to bear, he was off and away to the south at express speed before the wind. High he went and far before he faded from my sight and vanished in the dim and hazy distance. Many a time thereafter I lugged that old musket to that hill pasture, but I have not seen that bird since.

Mr. Robert Ridgway writes as follows of this bird in his 'Ornithology of Illinois': 'While some other birds are equally numerous, there are few that announce their presence as persistently as this species. All day long, in spring and summer, the males, sometimes to the number of a dozen or more for each meadow of considerable extent, perch upon the summits of tall weed-stalks or fence-stakes, at short intervals crying out: "*See, see — Dick, Dick-Cissel, Cissel;*" therefore "Dick Cissel" is well known to every farmer's boy as well as to all who visit the country during the season of clover-blooms and wild roses, when "Dame Nature" is in her most joyous mood.

'Perhaps the prevalent popular name of this species is "Little Field Lark" or "Little Meadow Lark," a name suggested by his yellow breast and black jugular spot, which recall strongly the similar markings of the *Sturnella*, and also the fact that the two frequent similar localities. The name "Black-throated Bunting" is probably never heard except from those who have learned it from the books.

'The location of the nest varies much with locality, though probably not more than in the case of many other species. At Mount Carmel, all that I found were in clover fields, and built upon or very close to the ground. In Richland county they were almost invariably built in small clumps of coarse weeds, at a height of about a foot above the ground.'

EASTERN EVENING GROSBEAK

Hesperiphona vespertina vespertina (COOPER).   PLATE 63.

Other name: English Parrot.

IDENTIFICATION. — Length 7 to 8½ inches; spread 13 to 13¾ inches. Catbird size but stouter. Great, stout, pale yellowish-green beak and striking contrast of colors (black, white and yellow) distinguish adult male at once from any other winter bird; large white patches in black wings of male show distinctly. Female and young resemble male closely in size and shape, have no streaks and little yellow, but show much pale gray or whitish on black wings; the large pale bill is diagnostic; flight somewhat undulating.

Song. — A brief warble.

Range. — Breeds from western Alberta east to northern Michigan; winters in the interior of North America south of the Saskatchewan and east of the Rocky Mountains, and irregularly to Quebec, New England, and south to Delaware, Kentucky, and Missouri.

The Evening Grosbeak resembles the common Grosbeak or Hawfinch of Europe, but is quite distinct from it. It was regarded until within the past fifty years as typically a bird of the far Northwest. Its generic name is derived from the Greek, referring to the *Hesperides*, 'Daughters of Night,' who dwelt on the western verge of the world where the sun goes down. It was discovered in 1823 by Henry R. Schoolcraft and named in 1825 by W. Cooper from a specimen taken at Sault Ste. Marie, Michigan. It was called the Evening Grosbeak as it was then observed to sing only at evening. Whatever may have been its distribution and habits then, it is no longer a distinctively western bird, nor does it sing only at sundown.

That gifted writer, Dr. Elliott Coues, says of the Evening Grosbeak: 'In full plumage this is a bird of distinguished appearance, whose very name suggests the far-away land of the dipping sun, and the tuneful romance which the wild bird throws around the fading light of day; clothed in striking color-contrasts of black, white and gold, he seems to represent the allegory of diurnal transmutation; for his sable pinions close around the brightness of his vesture, as night encompasses the golden hues of sunset, while the clear white space enfolded in these tints foretells the dawn of the morrow.'

Seen for the first time amid the snows of winter and against a background of darkling pines, these strange and beautiful waifs of the northland seem somehow out of place, as would some rare and singular exotic plant blossoming in a New England winter. Their presence appears almost miraculous. They usually come without warning very late in autumn, and as suddenly disappear in spring. They are swift of flight, and when on the wing thread their way easily through the branches of the forest. Where food is plentiful, they are quiet and sedentary, gentle and unafraid, though they soon become cautious if molested. Where people feed them and use them well, they return winter after winter, and often spend a part of each forenoon at the feeding place. Some of them at times become so tame under good treatment that they will almost eat from the hand. During their stay with us they feed almost entirely on vegetal matter and chiefly on seeds. They are fond of bathing even in winter, and visit unfrozen parts of swift streams at this season to bathe and drink, and, like several other birds, they drink the sap of maple trees wherever they find it.

As spring approaches there is some attempt at song and courtship on the part of the most vigorous adult males, and now and then one may be seen prancing before a female with wings and tail opening and closing to exhibit his charms to the utmost, but probably the full courtship display is witnessed seldom in this region.

Usually their favorite food at feeding stations is sunflower seeds, and where these are to be had other food seems not to interest them much, except perhaps the seeds of their favorite box-elder. They feed also on the seeds of coniferous trees, on the seeds and buds of many deciduous trees, also on a considerable number of winter fruits. They also eat the tender leaves of succulent plants. Some of these birds, kept in confinement, refused all insects offered them, though probably they consume insects in the breeding season and feed insects to their young.

EASTERN PURPLE FINCH

Carpodacus purpureus purpureus (GMELIN).   PLATE 63.

Other names: Red Linnet; Linnet.

IDENTIFICATION. — Length 5½ to 6¼ inches; spread 9¼ to 10½ inches. Size of Song Sparrow but with much thicker bill, more robust, and tail shorter, sharply forked. Adult male suffused largely with rosy-red, usually brightest on top of head and conspicuous on rump, throat and upper breast; a wide stripe of this red over eye; wings and tail mostly brownish or dusky, with no very prominent pale marks. Female, immature and young, brownish-gray or grayish-brown above streaked darker, grayish below also streaked darker; large bill of female prevents confusion with other streaked sparrows.

SONG. — A lively and prolonged warble, often given in flight.

BREEDING. — Usually in conifers, occasionally in apple, etc. *Nest and Eggs:* Similar to those of Chipping Sparrow.

RANGE. — Breeds from northwestern British Columbia, northern Ontario, southern Quebec, and Newfoundland to southern Alberta, central Minnesota, northern Illinois, Maryland (mountains), northern New Jersey, and New York (Long Island); winters from its southern breeding area to the Gulf coast from Florida to Texas.

This favorite bird is one of the most melodious of American finches. He pours out his gushing, ecstatic warble from the top of some tree, and when performing before his mate his musical efforts transcend his ordinary notes and he launches into the air, fluttering about with quivering wings in lowly emulation of the Skylark, pouring forth a continuous melody until, exhausted with this most remarkable vocal effort, he floats down with uplifted pinions toward the object of his affections.

By nature the Eastern Purple Finch is a forest bird, and although it adapts itself readily to civilization it prefers the neighborhood of coniferous trees, and shuns open plains. Before the advent of the English Sparrow in the United States, Purple Finches nested in abundance in the region about Boston, building their nests chiefly in Norway spruces and Virginia junipers. The sparrows in time apparently drove a large part of these finches out of the region and kept them out, as they never have returned in their former numbers. Those who wish to keep these birds about both summer and winter should plant coniferous trees and should feed sunflower seeds, of which these finches are very fond.

Purple Finches are hardy birds and, if well fed, will live through rather severe winters. They bathe in brooks with the temperature below freezing point and some have been known to sing in the clearing weather directly after a blizzard. Nevertheless a few are overcome by starvation and cold, as occasionally one has been picked up from the snow helpless or dead. If well fed, some males may be heard singing more or less almost daily in mild seasons during the latter days of February. Purple Finches spend winter nights in dense evergreen trees or thickets, or even in some open building or under the shelter of a cupola roof.

Some of the wintering young males begin to show a little red in their plumage in March. Migrants from the south continue to arrive in Massachusetts through April and early May, and by apple-blossom time, or even before, some begin their courtship. The male in his nuptial antics, clad in his brightest, rosiest plumage, dances erect before the female, facing her with quivering wings fully extended, raised at an angle and vibrating so rapidly that they seem of gauzy texture, and with crown feathers erected, displaying his colors as he swings from side to side about her. Sometimes his excess of ardor carries him up into the air on fast-beating wings, pouring out either soft continuous twitterings or the full, loud clear mating song, while she usually seems indifferent to his wooing. But if she is at all responsive he may drop down in front of her and they may touch bills time after time. If she grows more complaisant and flutters before him with open bill, their passion soon reaches its climax and the united pair fly away together. The wooing antics may occur on the ground, on top of a large rock, in a tree-top, or wherever the female happens to be.

The nest is built in most cases by the female, the male sometimes assisting. When the eggs are laid the mother bird incubates, while the male watches, feeds her and sings to her. Both parents feed the young, and when the young birds can fly well the family group begins its wanderings. In September and October there is a movement of the species out of the northern part of the range, and there is a general shifting about even in winter to places where food may be found in abundance. The feeding of a flock in the trees usually is accompanied by a continuous sound of fluttering wings.

In spring and summer the Purple Finch feeds largely on insects, buds and blossoms; in summer on insects and wild fruit, though it takes some cherries, blackberries and raspberries; in autumn and winter on wild fruits, on weed seeds, and also on seeds of trees (especially those of white pine and white ash), and the pulp or seeds of frosted crabapples and hawthorns. It is fond of the seeds of millet, hemp and sunflower, and has been known to eat dried currants and privet berries in winter. It seems to relish the fruit of the dogwoods, elders and viburnums very much. The stamens of the ash, red maple and elm are eaten by this bird. In spring it destroys the most succulent parts (stamens and pistils) of apple, cherry and peach blossoms, but this fruit tree pruning is not excessive, and, though sometimes viewed with alarm by the orchardist, has never been known to do material harm to the fruit crop.

CANADIAN PINE GROSBEAK

Pinicola enucleator leucura (MÜLLER). PLATE 63.

Other name: Canadian Grosbeak.

IDENTIFICATION. — Length 9 to 9¾ inches; spread 13¾ to 15 inches. Approaches size of Robin, but more robust; short, thick, blackish bill; general rosiness of most adult males noticeable especially on head, rump and breast; black wings and tail, with two conspicuous wing-bars, and olive-yellow of females where males are red distinguish the species from other winter birds; lacks large white or pale gray area in upper wing shown by Evening Grosbeak. Flight usually undulating and accompanied by calls.

SONG. — A clear melodious whistle, two or three notes in a descending series, *tee-tee-tew*.

BREEDING. — In coniferous forests. *Nest:* Of moss and twigs lined with hair. *Eggs:* 3 or 4, light greenish, marked with purple and purplish-brown.

RANGE. — Breeds from northwestern Mackenzie, northern Quebec, Labrador, and Newfoundland south to Manitoba, the mountains of New Hampshire, Maine, central New Brunswick, southern Nova Scotia, and Cape Breton Island; winters irregularly south to eastern Nebraska, Iowa, Indiana, Pennsylvania, northern New Jersey, and southern New England, and west to Manitoba, North Dakota, and Kansas.

The robust, brilliantly colored Pine Grosbeak is an arboreal bird, living in northern forests around the world. It is seen in the United States principally as a winter visitor, and its numbers are often so small that it escapes general notice. Occasionally, however, it appears in considerable numbers, and large flocks become more or less common. The accepted belief is that they are driven south by 'hard winters,' but such winters can have only a secondary effect on birds so warmly clad and so well sheltered by coniferous forests, and deep snow is no hardship for birds that feed principally on buds, seeds and fruits of tall shrubs and trees. Severe winters may have a minor effect, but considerable flights of these birds arrive here occasionally in mild winters. When there is a heavy crop of beechnuts in northern Maine and the southern Canadian forests, the Pine Grosbeaks sometimes swarm in those regions but a lack of wild fruit, cones and seeds in northern forests might compel these birds to seek food to the southward.

When Canadian Pine Grosbeaks come here in numbers from their northern solitudes, some of them, especially the younger birds, having had little experience with the wiles of man, are so unsuspicious that they may be taken by a noose on the end of a pole, or even captured by hand. Nevertheless when persecuted by man the Pine Grosbeak, learning by sad experience, becomes more shy.

Usually when these birds arrive in the northern United States, those in the plumage of the females and young largely predominate. This may be accounted for in part by the fact that when the birds breed well the young always outnumber the adults in the autumnal migration; also most of the young birds apparently do not get their full plumage until the postnuptial molt in their second year, or even later, and it may be possible that some of the males never acquire high adult plumage but continue to wear a dress similar to that of the adult female, with yellow and orange largely replacing the red of the normal male.

The song of this bird has a ventriloquial quality, in that sometimes when near-by it seems to come from a distance. As bird music goes it is very fine, full of warbles and trills, and often is given very softly with many tender notes. Sometimes the males sing in winter, even when the thermometer falls well below zero, 'singing of the northern summer — clear and cool like the wind among the fir trees.' Thoreau refers to their song and their 'dazzling beauty' and terms them 'angels from the north.'

Pine Grosbeaks rarely appear in New England in any considerable numbers before November. During their stay they are seen usually in small parties, although occasional flocks of from thirty to three hundred birds have been reported. The few birds that appear early in autumn are mere stragglers. Their number increases in November somewhat, but usually no great numbers are seen until December, and often an increase occurs in January. On bright days in early February with the thermometer below the zero mark, some of the males, stirred by the approach of spring, may give forth a tender bit of song. About the tenth of February the northward movement usually begins and only stragglers are seen after March.

During their stay with us they frequent pine, hemlock and deciduous woods, and orchards and also hill pastures where many red cedars grow, and when very numerous they may be seen often in villages and cities, where they feed on the buds and seeds of street trees. When they come in large numbers they quickly strip from the trees the fruit and seeds left upon them and so they constantly wander from place to place seeking food.

William Brewster presents the following graphic picture of the feeding of a flock and its results:

'When I first saw them they were assembling in a large white ash which overhangs the street. This tree was loaded with fruit, and with snow clinging to the fruit-clusters and to every twig. In a few minutes it also supported more than a hundred Grosbeaks who distributed themselves quite evenly over every part from the drooping lower, to the upright upper, branches and began shelling out and swallowing the seeds, the rejected wings of which, floating down in showers, soon gave the surface of the snow beneath the tree a light brownish tinge. The snow clinging to the twigs and branches was also quickly dislodged by the movements of the active, heavy birds and for the first few minutes it was incessantly flashing out in puffs like steam from a dozen different points at once. The finer particles, sifting slowly down, filled the still air and enveloped the entire tree in a veil-like mist of incredible delicacy and beauty, tinted, where the sunbeams pierced it, with rose, salmon, and orange, elsewhere of a soft dead white, — truly a fitting drapery for this winter picture, — the hardy Grosbeaks at their morning meal. They worked in silence when undisturbed and so very busily that at the end of the first hour they had actually eaten or shaken off nearly half the entire crop of seeds. Some men at work near-by afterwards told me that this tree was wholly denuded of fruit by three o'clock that afternoon when the birds descended to the ground and attacked the fallen seeds, finishing them before sunset.'

During the winter these birds bathe in the soft snow, standing in it, either on the ground or on the thick foliage of coniferous trees, fluttering their wings and throwing the snow-spray over their plumage in the same manner in which many birds bathe in water.

BRITISH GOLDFINCH

Carduelis carduelis britannica (HARTERT).

IDENTIFICATION. — Length about 5 inches; spread about 8 inches. Head of adult varied with crimson, black and whitish; wings and tail varied with yellow, black and white; back brown lighter on rump; under parts whitish shaded with brown on sides; bill white; young lack crimson mask, and yellow and black of wings and tail.
BREEDING. — In orchards, etc. *Nest:* Of fine twigs, roots, grass, leaves, moss, and wool. *Eggs:* 4 to 5, white with a few brown and purple spots.
RANGE. — Native of the British Isles. Introduced unsuccessfully in the United States, but well established as a resident in Bermuda.

The British Goldfinch is about the size of our Eastern Goldfinch but is a very different-appearing bird, the face markings being very distinctive, crimson-red around the bill, a white stripe in the sides of the head and across the throat, and a black stripe outlining the white from the forehead down the sides of the head. There is more yellow on the wings than with our American bird, but no yellow in the body plumage, and the colors remain about the same summer and winter. W. H. Hudson in his 'British Birds' writes of this species: 'Among our passerine birds . . . the goldfinch, in his pretty coat of many colours . . . is regarded as the most beautiful of all. . . . It is charming to watch a small flock of these finches in late summer, busy feeding on the roadside, or on some patch of waste land where the seeds they best love are abundant, when they are seen clinging in various attitudes to the stalks, deftly picking off the thistle seed, and scattering the silvery down on the air. They are then pretty birds prettily occupied; and as they pass with easy undulating flight from weed to weed, with musical call-notes and lively twitterings, bird following bird, they appear as gay and volatile as they are pretty. . . .

'As a vocalist the goldfinch does not rank high; but his lively, twittering song, uttered both on the perch and when passing through the air, and his musical call-notes, have a very pleasing effect, especially when the birds are seen in the open country in bright, sunny weather.' — (J.B.M.)

HORNEMANN'S REDPOLL

Acanthis hornemanni hornemanni (HOLBOELL).

IDENTIFICATION. — Similar to *A. h. exilipes* but larger and with proportionately thicker and less acute bill.
RANGE. — Breeds in Greenland north to Lat. 70°, and in Iceland; winters in its breeding area and southward to Ungava.

HOARY REDPOLL

Acanthis hornemanni exilipes (COUES).   PLATE 65.

Other name: Coues' Redpoll.
IDENTIFICATION. —Length 4½ to 5½ inches; spread about 9 inches. A gray and white bird narrowly streaked dusky; male has top of head red, breast pink and rump white; female and young show no pink; distinguished from Common Redpoll by *whiter* appearance, white unstriped rump, and white lower plumage.
BREEDING. — Similar to Common Redpoll.
RANGE. — Breeds from western Alaska to Ungava, and in northeastern Siberia; winters occasionally southward to British Columbia, northern Minnesota, Michigan, Illinois, Ontario, southern New York, Connecticut, and Maine, also in Asia to northern Japan.

COMMON REDPOLL

Acanthis linaria linaria (LINNAEUS).   PLATE 65.

Other names: Mealy Redpoll; Lesser Redpoll.
IDENTIFICATION. — Length 4½ to 5½ inches; spread 8 to 9 inches. Similar to Hoary Redpoll but browner; male has rump tinged with pink.
BREEDING. — In northern forests, grasslands, or tundra. *Nest:* 'Of any available material.' *Eggs:* Greenish-blue with wreath of spots.
RANGE. — Breeds from northwestern Alaska, northern Mackenzie, and northern Quebec south to northern Alberta, northern Manitoba, and islands in the Gulf of St. Lawrence; winters in northern United States irregularly southward to California, Kansas, Alabama, and South Carolina; also occurs in Europe and Asia.

This little wanderer drifts into the most northerly of the United States every winter in considerable numbers, but rather irregularly as far south as the latitude of New York City.

It appears here in companies varying from small groups to flocks of hundreds, frequenting old fields, pastures and swamps where birches or alders grow, and often feeding in patches of weeds about farms and villages. As the flocks may be found not infrequently also among pines and other coniferous trees, one who is often abroad in winter can hardly fail to see them.

They come with the snowflakes out of the dun sky of November and leave as spring approaches. They are such hardy, boreal birds that probably they leave the northern wilderness in great numbers only when driven south by lack of food. As they are near the size of Goldfinches and resemble them in their undulatory flight it is difficult to discriminate between the two species at a distance, but on nearer approach the pink on the breasts of the males, their blackish chins and their red caps distinguish them at once from either Goldfinches or Pine Siskins.

The feeding flocks may be startled by any sudden noise or violent movement. Then they rise and wheel in concert, but after going through their usual evolutions they may return to the very place from which they took flight. In winter they spend most of the brief days in searching for food and in consuming it, and at night they may retire to some dark thicket of coniferous trees to sleep. I have never heard any song from this species, but their lay is said to resemble that of the Goldfinch.

The food of the Redpolls while with us consists largely of the seeds of birches and alders and those of common grasses and weeds. At feeding stations they eat greedily the seeds of sunflowers, millet and hemp, also hayseed and 'rolled oats.' They take seeds of pines, elms and lindens and the buds of various trees and shrubs, including those of the larch and lilac. During the brief summer in their northern homes they feed largely on insects.

HOLBOELL'S REDPOLL

Acanthis linaria holboelli (BREHM).   PLATE 65.

IDENTIFICATION. — Slightly larger than *A. l. linaria* and bill longer.
RANGE. — Breeds on Herschel Island, Siberia; south in winter to Germany, Japan, and southeastern Siberia; occasional in northwestern Alaska and southeast to British Columbia, Iowa, Illinois, Massachusetts, Maine and Quebec.

GREATER REDPOLL

Acanthis linaria rostrata (COUES).   PLATE 65.

IDENTIFICATION. — Larger than *A. l. linaria*, bill shorter and stouter, upper parts darker.
RANGE. — Resident in Greenland; irregularly in winter southward through Manitoba, Ontario, Quebec and Ungava to Montana, Colorado, northern Illinois, Michigan, northern Indiana, southern New York, Massachusetts, and Connecticut.

The Greater Redpoll is rather rare in the Northeastern States except along the seaboard, where in certain winters it appears with the Common Redpoll. It visits the same localities as the latter, and its food and habits seem not to differ materially from those of its smaller companions. Only close inspection of the winter flocks of redpolls will enable one to distinguish this larger race. Even more rare than the Greater Redpoll, but occasionally found, are the Holboell's Redpoll, and the two light-colored races of *Acanthis hornemanni*. — (J.B.M.)

NORTHERN PINE SISKIN

Spinus pinus pinus (WILSON). PLATE 66.

Other names: Pine Finch; Gray Linnet; Pine Linnet.

IDENTIFICATION. — Length 4½ to 5¼ inches; spread 8½ to 9 inches. A small, sharp-billed, dark-streaked finch, with two light wing-bars and some yellow showing on edges of flight-feathers and tail; similar to Goldfinch in flight, habits and song.

BREEDING. — In coniferous forests. *Nest:* Of twigs, moss, bark-strips, etc., warmly lined with down, fur, hair, feathers, etc. *Eggs:* 3 to 6, pale greenish-blue, spotted with browns, purplish and black.

RANGE. — Breeds from central Alaska, central Manitoba, and central Quebec south through the higher mountains of the western United States to southern California and southern New Mexico, also to southeastern Nebraska, northern Minnesota, northern Michigan, northwestern Pennsylvania, the mountains of North Carolina, northern New Hampshire, northern Maine, New Brunswick, and Nova Scotia; occurs in winter over most of the United States south to southern Florida and northern Mexico.

The Northern Pine Siskin is almost as erratic as the crossbills. During every month in the year small flocks wander about as if there were no such thing as a breeding season, and individuals may be seen occasionally in summer far south of their usual breeding-grounds. They may breed one year in a certain region and far away the next, and in migration or in winter they may visit a locality in great numbers in one year and pass it by the next. Apparently they migrate southward regularly in autumn and northward in spring, but probably they take long flights and without stopping. They cannot be expected in great numbers more than once to three times in a decade. Along our Atlantic seaboard the greatest flight apparently takes place in autumn. The Pine Siskin comes almost invariably in flocks searching for food in weedy fields and among birches and alders, like the Goldfinch and Redpoll. It is difficult to distinguish these three species one from another at a distance, as their flocks, flight and notes are somewhat alike and they sometimes intermix.

The Northern Pine Siskin frequents pines (especially pitch pines) and spruces of various kinds. Siskins are very active birds. A large flock settles in a tree, springs up again, swirls back and forth and round about, and settles again in about the same place. When hundreds rest thus in the trees, uttering their 'z-ing' calls, a humming, buzzing sound fills the air.

Their southward migrations in unusual numbers doubtless are caused chiefly by lack of their usual food in the North. They feed on the seeds and buds of coniferous trees and the seeds of birches and alders, maples and elms; in winter, they eat berries, such as those of the Virginia juniper and honeysuckle, and the seeds of many weeds and grasses. The seeds of the northern white cedar or *Arbor vitae* are favorites with these birds, and they seem fond of the aphids that breed on willows.

EASTERN GOLDFINCH

Spinus tristis tristis (LINNAEUS).

PLATE 66.

Other names: Thistle-bird; Yellow-bird; Wild Canary.

IDENTIFICATION. — Length 5 to 5½ inches; spread about 9 inches. Male in summer, yellow body, black cap, wings and tail, white wing-bars, tail coverts and tips of outer tail feathers, bill yellowish; male in winter, dull olive-yellow with brownish edges to black wings and tail, yellow shoulder patch; female and young, like dull winter male but with olive shoulder patch.

CALL. — *Per-chic-o-ree.* SONG: Canary-like but lacking long trills.

BREEDING. — In open country among scattered trees. *Nest:* Neat, cup-shaped, of fine soft vegetal fibers, lined with thistle-down, etc. *Eggs:* 4 to 6, bluish-white, unspotted.

RANGE. — Breeds from southern Manitoba, southern Quebec, and Newfoundland south to eastern Colorado, central Arkansas, northern Alabama, and northern Georgia; winters over most of its breeding range and southward to the Gulf coast.

'Panoplied in jet and gold' the merry, carefree Goldfinches in cheery companies flit in the summer sunshine. They wander happily about, singing, wooing, mating, eating, drinking and bathing until July or August without family worries. As Dr. Chapman says: 'Few birds seem to enjoy life more than these happy rovers. Every month brings them a change of fare, and in pursuit of fresh dainties the nesting-time is delayed almost until summer begins to wane. ... Their love-song is delivered with an ecstasy and abandon which carries them off their feet, and they circle over the fields sowing the air with music.'

This vivacious little finch is one of the most interesting and conspicuous birds of village, farm and field. Its flashing yellow, its undulating, bounding flight and its canary-like song have given it the name of Wild Canary among the country people.

Although many Goldfinches winter in the northern United States, their winter dress is rather dull in color, and except at close range it is difficult to distinguish them from other small finches, but when spring greenery tints the woods and fields, the males in their bright nuptial dress, in full song and increased in number by accessions of migrants from the south, become very conspicuous. As the season advances the attentions of the males to the females become more marked and their songs more frequent and ecstatic. Often a little company may be heard singing together. Like many other birds the Goldfinch can reduce the volume of its song until it seems far away, but it is capable of remarkable bursts of melody, sweet and long-continued.

The Goldfinch delays its nest-building until the seeds of weeds begin to ripen and until it can find thistle-down, with which almost universally it lines its nest. So it is not until most other birds have young that the Goldfinch begins to fashion its pretty fabric. Often the nest is not built until July or August, and young birds recently fledged are not uncommon in September.

The nest is built chiefly or wholly by the female, while the male accompanies her in her labors, caresses her and cheers her with song. When the nest is finished (it, by the way, is often so compactly built as to hold water), and the pretty eggs are laid, the mother bird sits closely while her mate supplies her with food. She quickly recognizes his voice among the notes of other Goldfinches and with anticipatory flutterings answers him from the nest. When the birdlings are hatched they are fed by both parents, sometimes chiefly by the female, though her mate continues to feed her assiduously. The young are fed largely by regurgitation and probably in some degree on partly digested vegetal food, as in such cases the feeding does not occur as often as when insect food is supplied. However, there is evidence that many insects also are fed to the young. As the little ones grow the parents leave them much to themselves and never seem to manifest such fussy anxiety about them as is displayed by the Robin or the Catbird, nor are they so assiduous in cleaning the nest, which often presents a rather slovenly appearance before the young are ready to leave. They remain in the nest about fifteen or sixteen days and finally leave it with fluttering but typically undulating flight.

Goldfinches love companionship. They gather the year round in companies ranging from small groups to large flocks. Even in the breeding season those birds not engaged for the time being in the actual duties of homekeeping gather with others of their kind. As soon as the young are on the wing all assemble in their usual companies, and after a few weeks spent in seeking the good things of the autumn harvest of weed seeds and other dainties, they begin to move southward. Later, others come from the North to take their places, and such movements continue until the rigors of winter are here. Then when the brown earth is covered deeply with billowy drifts of newly fallen snow, the flocks of Goldfinches in their dull winter dress sweep from weed patch to weed patch, or swirl and circle about among the pasture birches, seemingly intent only on feasting. Probably the flocks return at night, like the redpolls, to some coniferous thicket where, screened from the cold wind by the dense foliage, they may sleep in comfort.

The food of the Goldfinch consists largely of a great variety of seeds, from which it skillfully extracts all nourishment, leaving only the husk. It splits the envelope of the dandelion and extracts its contents so nicely that only by careful examination can one discover the loss of the seed. It is a great destroyer of weed seeds, and two or three birds often may be seen hanging to the topmost branches of a slender weed until it bends to the ground under their weight, when they stand upon it and proceed to rob it of its fruition. It is so fond of the seeds of thistles that it is often called the Thistle-bird. Among other seeds of uncultivated plants, it takes those of the goldenrod, asters, wild sunflowers, wild clematis, mullein, evening primrose, dandelion, chicory, burdock and catnip.

The fondness of the little bird for burdock seeds now and then costs one its life, when it is caught and held by the strong hooks of the plant and, unable to break away, starves to death. The bird is so small that its strength is not sufficient to disengage itself when entangled by caterpillar silk.

Among cultivated plants the Goldfinch eats the seeds of zinnia, coreopsis, bachelor's button, cosmos, millet, hemp, salsify, turnip, lettuce and sunflower, and some other garden plants. It takes the seeds of birch, alder, sycamore, spruce, hemlock, larch and perhaps a few other coniferous trees. Occasionally it eats a few tender buds, and now and then takes a nip from a succulent leaf of lettuce or some other garden plant, while drinking from its leaves the morning dew. In spring Goldfinches eat many insects at times, among them young grasshoppers, beetles, inch-worms, plant-lice and their eggs, and eggs of that imported wheat pest, the Hessian fly.

RED CROSSBILL

Loxia curvirostra pusilla (GLOGER).

PLATE 64.

Other name: American Red Crossbill.

IDENTIFICATION. — Length 5½ to 6½ inches; spread 10 to 10¾ inches. Male brick-red with carmine rump: female and young grayish-olive, streaked with dusky, and yellowish on rump and breast: much variation in young males in transition plumage.

CALL. — *Yip* or *pip* like cry of young chicken. SONG: '*Too-tee too-tee, too-tee, tee, tee*,' also a flight-song.

BREEDING. — In coniferous forests. Nest of twigs, rootlets and bark lined with moss, hair, grasses, etc. *Eggs:* 4 or 5, pale greenish spotted with browns and lavender.

RANGE. — Breeds from central Alaska, and central Quebec south to Michigan, and irregularly in the Alleghenies to northern Georgia; winters irregularly south to northern Texas, Louisiana, and Florida.

It is winter in the woods of the Pine Tree State. Broad the white mantle lies over field and farm, hill and dale. Every tuft and branch of spruce, pine and hemlock bears its fluffy burden of soft, pure snow crystals. All the air is misty with the driving snow. On distant hills the trees, no longer darkly green, stand white and ghost-like against the gray and lowering sky. The view is circumscribed by the thickening storm which shuts us into an ever-narrowing circle as daylight wanes. Despite the storm the happy, carefree Red Crossbills shake the snow in showers from each heavily laden tuft as they seek the cones from which they glean their sustenance — and so the twilight comes.

The handsome Red Crossbill is a strange, erratic, and seemingly irresponsible bird. It may start nesting either in January or in midsummer, placing the nest in a dense coniferous tree or on a bare leafless limb. It may pass one winter in the forests of the frozen north, and the next it may be found in the sunny south. Having had a taste of a milder climate it may give up all idea of nesting in the far north and carelessly remain away from the country of its nativity for a whole season. In a region where its native food is scarce, it will try almost anything else that is edible. Salt, which is anathema to many birds, seems rather to please the Crossbill, as it eats almost anything that is well salted. The bird, however, may not be such a happy-go-lucky individual as it seems. The migration of the species, especially when the birds move south in large numbers in winter, probably is caused by a lack of their favorite food in their usual winter habitat, or by very deep snow which cuts off their supply of grit, which is necessary to aid digestion. Their extremely erratic breeding dates may be due to an abundance of some favorite food at these times in the region in which the birds happen to be. If in a certain season, for example, seeds of coniferous trees and wild fruits are very abundant in the Maine woods, we may expect great numbers of Crossbills to breed there, particularly if a dearth of such food prevails farther north. The next year with opposite conditions hardly a Crossbill will be found in these woods.

Crossbills normally are absolutely unsuspicious. I have lain on the ground under a tree watching Crossbills feeding among the low branches only a few feet away, and they completely disregarded my presence. It is extremely interesting to watch their feeding habits. The peculiar bill seems a poor tool for picking out seeds, but the birds use it largely for wrenching off the scales from the cones, and then pick out the seeds with their tongues. They climb about among the twigs and sprays like little parrots, using both bills and feet. A Crossbill may hang easily by its beak, or by one foot while reaching with the other, and an individual when suddenly frightened may swing underneath a twig and hang there head downward, where, partially concealed by the foliage, he might be mistaken for a cone.

Crossbills commonly move south more or less in winter. They frequent pitch pines, many of which grow on the sandy lands of Cape Cod and the Elizabeth Islands, and so those regions are favorite resorts for Crossbills. Occasionally the birds remain very late, and summer invasions have occurred rarely. While here in winter they are always attracted to fruiting larches or spruces growing on lawns, and will frequent such trees until the cones are stripped of seeds.

Crossbills, though specialized for feeding on the seeds of cones, are by no means confined to such food. They feed on the seeds of white pine, pitch pine, Norway and native spruces, balsam fir, larch, hemlock, ailanthus, maple and elm, beechnuts, seeds of sunflower, dandelion, evening primrose and other weeds, the buds of a number of coniferous trees, and some wild fruit, including that of the sweet gum. In late spring and summer they eat insects such as gall-insects, ants, plant-lice and caterpillars of various species, but their food has not been carefully studied.

NEWFOUNDLAND CROSSBILL

Loxia curvirostra percna BENT.

IDENTIFICATION. — Similar to Red Crossbill but larger, with a much larger and heavier bill, 'red deeper and more brilliant and greenish-yellow richer and brighter.'

RANGE. — Resident in Newfoundland and Nova Scotia; south in winter to the District of Columbia and northern Virginia.

This race of the Red Crossbill seems to have similar habits to those of the more common bird. In New England it frequents the same localities, and feeds on the same food. Mr. Harry S. Hathaway says that the birds of this race that he saw in Rhode Island were far more wild than the common Crossbill, and that their calls seemed much louder. They were easily alarmed in all cases, and difficult to approach.

WHITE–WINGED CROSSBILL

Loxia leucoptera GMELIN.   PLATE 64.

IDENTIFICATION. — Length 6 to 6¾ inches; spread 9½ to 10½ inches. Adult male; rose-red with black wings and tail and two broad white wing-bars: female and young: olive-gray with yellowish rump, wings brownish with wing-bars similar to male.

CALLS. — *Cheep*, and *wheet, wheet, wheet*. SONG: A very fine series of loud whistles, trills and twitters, suggesting that of Goldfinch.

BREEDING. — In coniferous forests. Nest and eggs similar to Red Crossbill.

— Breeds in boreal zones from the limit of trees in northwestern Alaska, northern Manitoba, and northern Quebec south to southern British Columbia, central Ontario, New York, New Hampshire, southern Maine, and southern Nova Scotia; winters in much of its breeding range and southward irregularly to northern Oregon, Kansas, southern Illinois, southern Ohio, and North Carolina.

The White-winged Crossbill is a bird of coniferous forests, leaving them only when food is scarce in its favorite regions. Its distribution is slightly more northern than that of the Red Crossbill, and it does not go far south in its irregular migrations.

In my youth, much time was spent unsuccessfully in searching for this bird about Worcester, Massachusetts. One bright morning, however, a pair appeared, feeding on weed seeds by the roadside in front of a neighbor's house, the last place I would have looked for them. Like the Red Crossbill this species keeps mostly in flocks at all seasons of the year. The male leaves the flock to feed the female on the nest, feeding her as the young are fed, by regurgitation. Having fed her he flies in wide circles above her, pouring forth an ecstatic song.

The habits of this bird are much like those of the preceding species, and it partakes of similar food, which consists largely of buds and the seeds of trees, shrubs and weeds and many berries and insects; but it seems to prefer the seeds of the Norway spruce and hemlock to those of the pitch pine, and is more likely to be found where these trees are grown on cultivated grounds than in the wild pitch pine lands much frequented by the Red Crossbill.

RED-EYED TOWHEE

Pipilo erythrophthalmus erythrophthalmus (LINNAEUS).   PLATE 73.

Other names: Chewink; Ground Robin.

IDENTIFICATION. — Length 7½ to 8¾ inches; spread 10 to 12¼ inches. Male: black above and on throat and breast, with chestnut sides and white belly and much white in wings and tail; iris red; female and young, similar but duller and black replaced by brown.

CALL. — *Towhee* or *chewink*. SONG: *Chuck-burr, pill-a-will-a-will-a.*

BREEDING. — In bushy lands, open woods, and clearings. Nest on ground or near it, of leaves, bark, twigs, grass, etc., lined with finer material. *Eggs:* 4 to 6, white, finely dotted all over with brown and some lilac.

RANGE. — Breeds east of the Great Plains from southeastern Saskatchewan, southern Manitoba, southern Ontario, and southern Maine south to central Kansas and northern Georgia; winters from southeastern Nebraska, Wisconsin, and the Ohio and Potomac valleys to central Texas, the Gulf coast, and central Florida.

The active, strong Red-eyed Towhee is a bird of striking appearance. He is noisy and conspicuous whether on the ground or in the air. He rustles the dry leaves like some animal twenty times his size, scratching like a Fox Sparrow with both feet, and even his wing-strokes in flight are noisy, while his flashy tail advertises his progress.

He is a ground bird — an inhabitant of bushy land. No other sparrow in the East seems to be so wedded to life in thicket and tangle. He is rarely seen high in a tree, unless drawn there by some alarm, for his curiosity is great and he follows the crowd that gathers when cries of distress are heard in the grove. He spends most of his life in thicket, 'scrub' or sprout land. He is not a dooryard bird except in winter, when necessity now and then drives one to a feeding-station, but even then he spends most of his time in the shrubbery, coming out only to secure food. He may be found along bushy fences and roadsides, and often finds food or sand in country roads.

The male arrives in southern New England late in April. He comes in advance of his mate, and after a short time of rest and recreation following the fatigue of the journey, he mounts to the top of some bush or small tree, and gives to the wide world all the music he has. Dr. Frank M. Chapman thus aptly characterizes this bird: 'There is a vigorousness about the Towhee's notes and actions which suggests both a bustling, energetic disposition and a good constitution. He entirely dominates the thicket or bushy undergrowth in which he makes his home. The dead leaves fly before his attack; his white-tipped tail feathers flash in the gloom of his haunts. He greets all passers with a brisk inquiring *chewink, towhee,* and if you pause to reply, with a *fluff-fluff* of his short, rounded wings he flies to a near-by limb to better inspect you. It is only when singing that the Towhee is fully at rest.'

Not long after the females arrive, the males begin their wooing, pursuing their brown inamoratas about among the thickets, with a great display of black, white and chestnut plumage. The wings and tails are opened and closed rapidly, so that the white patches of both sexes flash frequently.

While the female is incubating, the male waits upon her and occasionally relieves her on the nest. As the nest is exceedingly well concealed, and the female dull-colored, she can sit until almost trodden upon before she leaves the nest; when finally driven from it she is likely to act as if disabled, thus attempting to lure the intruder away. The young usually remain in the nest ten or twelve days, if not disturbed, until their wings grow strong, but if disturbed they may leave it before they are able to fly. When the young have learned to fly, the family keeps together for a time, but seldom, even in migration, is anything like a close flock formed, for Towhees are not normally gregarious. During and after the molt in August they are rather quiet and shy. When severe frosts come most of them disappear in the night on their southward migration.

The Towhee feeds chiefly on seeds, wild fruit and insects. Its food is obtained mainly from the ground, the shrubbery, and as high up the tree-trunks as it can reach or jump. While scratching and digging among the leaves in early spring it unearths many dormant insects, and disposes of them ere they have an opportunity to propagate their kind. Weed seeds, grass seeds, and a little grain are eaten. The only cultivated fruit I have known one to take was now and then a gooseberry or two that had dropped off the bush.

ALABAMA TOWHEE

Pipilo erythrophthalmus canaster HOWELL.

IDENTIFICATION. — Similar to Red-eyed Towhee but with larger bill and longer tail; white markings less extensive, sides and flanks paler; female grayer; *iris red.*

RANGE. — Resident in Alabama and central Georgia.

WHITE–EYED TOWHEE

Pipilo erythrophthalmus alleni COUES.

Other names: Joree; Brush Robin; Bull Finch.

IDENTIFICATION. — Similar to *P. e. erythrophthalmus* but less white on wings and tail, rufous areas paler; *iris yellowish or white.*

RANGE. — **Resident of** coast region from about Charleston, South Carolina, southward to and including Florida.

LARK BUNTING

Calamospiza melanocorys STEJNEGER.

Other names: White-winged Blackbird; White-wings; Prairie Bobolink; Buffalo Bird.

IDENTIFICATION. — Length $5\frac{1}{4}$ to $7\frac{1}{4}$ inches; spread 10 to $11\frac{1}{2}$ inches. A plump thick-billed sparrow: male in summer, a striking black bird with large white patch on wing and white edges to flight feathers and tail quills; male in winter, female and young, grayish-brown streaked upper parts, lightly streaked breasts, and conspicuous white or creamy patch on shoulder.

CALL. — A soft *hoo-ee.* SONG: A rich, varied flight-song.

BREEDING. — On plains and prairies. *Nest:* On ground, of grasses, fine roots, etc., lined with finer grasses, plant down, or hair. *Eggs:* 4 or 5, light bluish-green, rarely lightly spotted with reddish-brown.

RANGE. — Breeds from southern Alberta, and southwestern Manitoba south to southeastern New Mexico and northwestern Texas, and east to Nebraska and west-central Minnesota; winters southward to southern Texas and central Mexico; in migration to Wyoming and California and east occasionally to Ontario, southeastern Minnesota, and western Iowa.

The afternoon of June 9, 1907, was a fine sunny Sabbath as my wife and I drove along the country road leading from Duxbury, Massachusetts, to the part of Marshfield known as Green Harbor. Just after we had crossed the 'Dyke Meadow Bridge' and were nearing the seashore, my attention was attracted to an unknown bird which was feeding by the roadside with a small flock of English Sparrows. My first thought was that it was a partial albino Red-winged Blackbird or a freak Bobolink. The bird was quite tame and allowed a prolonged observation, with glasses, at the width of a country road, and we were able not only to take note of all the plumage markings but to see the shape of the bill very clearly, so that the bird was recognized as a finch of some kind. The bird was feeding avidly upon the seeds of wayside dandelions, which it procured by jumping up from the ground and nipping, with its powerful beak, through the base of the ripening flower heads, each time alighting with a beakful of white pappus. After we had watched it for some time, during which it was frequently interrupted by passing carriages and autos, it flew off across the grassy meadows and disappeared behind a knoll. It was an adult male Lark Bunting in full breeding plumage.

The Lark Bunting is a characteristic bird of the great western plains. When the birds first arrive on their breeding-grounds from their southern wintering places, the flocks of black and white males form a striking and pleasing addition to the open grassy or weed-grown stretches of prairie land. There is much twittering and cheery warbling as the birds select their mates from the dull-colored females and the courtship is soon culminated. Much of the singing is done while on the wing, the male birds rising obliquely 'with a tremulous fluttering motion of the wings' from a lowly perch on a prairie weed, to perhaps fifteen feet in air, hovering a moment on rapidly beating pinions, then descending again to the ground, all the time giving utterance to a sweet and lively, modulated warbling.

At the end of the mating and nesting season the male quickly becomes a quiet, sparrow-like, dull-colored imitation of his modest mate, very much as the Bobolink changes at the same season. And like the Bobolinks, the Lark Buntings now gather in good-sized flocks, feeding together in grassy places, weed patches or grain-fields, the entire flock often rising and wheeling in unison, to alight again like a well-trained battalion. They are birds of strong flight and will often struggle against a gale which forces other birds to seek shelter. — (J.B.M.)

IPSWICH SPARROW

Passerculus princeps MAYNARD.   PLATE 68.

Other names: Gray Bird; Pallid Sparrow; Maynard's Sparrow; Sable Island Sparrow.

IDENTIFICATION. — Length 6 to 6¾ inches; spread 9½ to 11 inches. A large robust sparrow; colors very pallid, matching very well the color of dry sand; two pale wing-bars; in spring a prominent yellow line over eye, whitish in winter.

NOTES. — Like those of Savannah Sparrow.

BREEDING. — Similar to Savannah Sparrow.

RANGE. — Breeds on Sable Island, Nova Scotia; winters from Sable Island south along the sand dunes of the Atlantic coast to Georgia.

The Ipswich Sparrow lives within sound of the breaking sea. Wherever I have seen it, my ears have been filled with the roar of pounding surf, and the bird has always been within a fourth of a mile of the outer beach. It is really at home only in treeless coastal lands, along the beaches and among the dunes. Sandy beaches backed by dunes are its favorite resorts, but it may be found also on narrow sandy beach ridges or barren beaches by the sea, where there are no real dunes. I have seen it near the edge of the woods, but never in a tree, and though it has been known to alight in one, it is usually seen, if seen at all, either in flight or on the ground. It feeds chiefly among the grasses and weeds of the dunes. When followed, its colors so blend with the sand that it easily keeps out of sight, except when startled. Then it starts up quickly and flies swiftly and rather erratically for a short distance and alights on the ground again in the concealing grasses. An observer, working cautiously and slowly, however, may now and then obtain a fair view of the bird.

Dr. Jonathan Dwight, Jr., in his interesting monograph on 'The Ipswich Sparrow and Its Summer Home,' writes as follows of the habits of this bird:

'On Sable Island, as might be expected, they were comparatively tame, although even there not permitting a very close inspection. They watch you, especially when singing from the tops of the sand-hills or the bushes, with evident suspicion, and as there is no cover they are not easily stalked. When you approach, they become restless, repeatedly crouching down as if about to fly, bobbing up again, and, finally, either slipping quietly down the opposite side of the sand-hill, or more frequently standing their ground until you are within a few yards. Meanwhile their uncertainty of mind is voiced by occasional sharp chirps, and presently they suddenly depart with brisk, undulating flight, following the inequalities of the ground until hidden by a distant hill. If pursued from place to place, they soon become very wary and will fly until they are nearly out of sight before alighting....

'They most frequented the vicinity of the ponds, and abounded towards the eastern end of the island where the hills and valleys are most extensively clothed with the Crowberry and the Juniper, in the many snug nooks and pockets of which they hide away their cosy nests or find refuge at night from the penetrating, fog-laden air....

'I well remember the first morning on the island. The sun was feebly struggling with the drifting fog that dimly revealed the treeless, ragged sand-hillocks stretching away into the distance; the air was chill, and all about me were strange sights and sounds. Amid the chorus of unfamiliar notes I soon detected those for which I had traveled far, and spied an Ipswich Sparrow singing away on an adjacent sand-peak, quite unconscious of the sensation he was creating.... It was gratifying to know that the bird really could sing, for it is one of the most silent of our winter visitors, its sole note being a sharp, dry *tsip* uttered on rare occasions.... This sad little chant is repeated several times in the minute, but rarely for more than a few minutes at a time, when the singer either seeks a new perch or devotes himself for an indefinite period to the quest for food. They sing at irregular intervals, the favorite hour being at dusk, when you may often hear round about you as many as five or six, each pouring forth his mournful trill which seems in perfect keeping with the somber surroundings. They are also more musically inclined in the early morning hours. They sang regardless of the fog, to which they are so well accustomed, nor did they, as is the wont of many birds, greet the sun as it now and again pushed aside the fog curtains with its long yellow rays. Bright days did not inspirit them, nor did dull ones depress them.... Wrapped in my coat, I have plodded along, so shut in by the cold sheets of streaming fog that I could only liken my surroundings to the sand-hills of our own coast during a winter's snowstorm, and have listened in vain for some sign of the presence of the Sparrows which I felt sure were in my vicinity. Presently one is discovered walking about on the ground in search of food, and a few minutes later he mounts a brown hummock, throws back his head, and breaks into song. Others, far and near, promptly join in chorus, and for several minutes the air fairly rings with answering songs. Then ensues a period of such perfect silence, ten, fifteen, twenty minutes, that it is hard to believe there is a single bird within earshot. If, however, you will have patience, the chorus will very possibly begin again.'

In his 'Birds of Essex County, Massachusetts,' Dr. Charles W. Townsend, who knows this species intimately through much experience with it at Ipswich, writes as follows regarding its habits while with us:

'The best place to watch them is on the beach, where the view is unobscured by grass. The beach is one of their favorite feeding-places, particularly in the seaweed or "thatch" thrown up there. Except in the coldest weather, this attracts many insects and not only are the insects found in the stomachs, but the birds may actually be seen to catch them. I have even seen them jump into the air for an insect. Beetles and small flies are the chief kinds found. The bird is a walker and runner, rarely hopping, thus differing from the Savannah Sparrow which, although a runner, prefers to hop rather than to walk.... In walking, it moves its head and shoulders in a dove-like manner. In running, the head is held low, so that the top of the head, back, and tail are parallel with the ground. Ipswich Sparrows may occasionally be seen to scratch, and they scratch vigorously, making the litter fly.... Flirting the tail nervously is frequently indulged in.

'Among the dunes, Ipswich Sparrows often alight on the seed-stalks of the beach-grass to obtain the seeds. They also, at times, alight in the bushes and even on the roofs of the few houses in the dunes. Their flight is a flickering, undulating one like that of the Savannah Sparrow, and like that bird they drop abruptly into the grass with the tail down. Like that bird, also, they frequently chase each other either in sport or anger. They often associate with the other beach- and dune-loving birds, the Horned Larks, Snow Buntings, and Lapland Longspurs. In fact, I have several times seen all four species together and that, too, at close range.'

EASTERN SAVANNAH SPARROW

Passerculus sandwichensis savanna (WILSON).   PLATE 68.

Other names: Savannah Sparrow; Ground-bird.

IDENTIFICATION. — Length 5¼ to 6¼ inches; spread 8 to 9½ inches. Slightly smaller than Song Sparrow with shorter, forked tail, a yellowish stripe over eye, pink legs; whiter below than most sparrows; darker and smaller than Ipswich Sparrow.

SONG. — *Tsip, tsip, tsip, tseeeeeee tsee-ee-ee-ee,* or *get get get bizzeeee.*

BREEDING. — In grass-lands, meadows, among sand-dunes, about edges of salt marshes or in marsh near sea beaches. Nest on ground, chiefly of fine grasses. *Eggs:* 4 to 6, greenish- or bluish-white heavily spotted and blotched with brownish and purplish-brown.

RANGE. — Breeds from northern Manitoba and northern Quebec south to northern Iowa, northern Indiana, the mountains of Pennsylvania, Connecticut, and Long Island; winters from southern Indiana and southern New Jersey south to northeastern Mexico, the Gulf coast, Bahamas, and Cuba.

The Eastern Savannah Sparrow is seen commonly in low, moist, grassy lands or drier lands near water, such as beaches or sand-dunes along the seacoast. It is common about salt marshes and river meadows, and follows river valleys into the interior, and even into the mountains, and breeds not only in the valleys but in the hills. It is most abundant, however, along the coast and in wide river valleys.

It is essentially a ground bird. It feeds, nests and sings on the ground, but it is by no means entirely terrestrial. As a boy I had read that this bird never alighted in trees. Therefore I was surprised to see a small flock of migrants fly into a tree and alight as skillfully as any other sparrow. Since then I have seen them alight on telegraph and telephone wires, trees and bushes, and they commonly alight on rocks and stumps near their nesting-places, and from such lowly watch-towers they now and then send forth their rather insect-like songs; occasionally one sings in flight. Most of those that breed in New England arrive from the south in April and are not often noticed by human eyes, as they search among grasses and weeds for their insect food. When flushed they fly swiftly away in undulating, zigzag flight and drop quickly into the grass. Both bird and song are so inconspicuous that most people seldom notice either.

When this sparrow first arrives from the South it is songless or sings very feebly, but as the May days come it bursts into full song, though even then its musical efforts do not greatly exceed those of a grasshopper. As the courtship season arrives two males may be seen occasionally engaged in a running fight, in which there is usually much more running than fighting. Dr. Charles W. Townsend says: 'In courtship the male stands on the ground and vibrates his wings rapidly above his back. He also flies slowly a short distance above the ground with head and tail up and rapidly vibrating wings.'

Both sexes engage in building the nest, incubating the eggs and caring for the young, but the female takes upon herself the greater part of the family cares. She sits closely, but when almost trodden upon by some clumsy intruder, she seeks to lead him away from her treasures by the common artifice of fluttering along the ground, dragging a leg and wing in imitation of a disabled bird.

When the young become strong on the wing, the birds gather in family groups and roam the fields and meadows. They know the art of concealment and can run rapidly close to the ground, with heads carried low, and thus they speed along for rods, keeping well under cover. When the August molt has passed, they become rather less shy and retiring, and as migration begins they may be found in upland pastures, weedy fields, orchards and gardens, where they gather the ripening seeds of weeds, as well as in meadows and marshes. In October most of them leave New England for the South, but some remain until November, and a few pass the winter along our southern coasts.

LABRADOR SAVANNAH SPARROW

Passerculus sandwichensis labradorius HOWE.

IDENTIFICATION. — 'Similar to *P. s. savanna* but wings and tarsi longer; bill shorter and thicker.'
RANGE. — Breeds in Labrador; winters southward along the Atlantic coast.

EASTERN GRASSHOPPER SPARROW

Ammodramus savannarum australis MAYNARD.   PLATE 68.

Other name: Yellow-winged Sparrow.

IDENTIFICATION. — Length 4¾ to 5½ inches; spread 8 to 8½ inches. Adults distinguished by buffy unstreaked breast and throat; a little yellow above and before eye; young similar but breasts spotted or streaked with dusky, resembling Henslow's Sparrow but not so reddish on wings.

SONG. — A grasshopper-like *tsick, tsick, tsurrrrrr.*

BREEDING. — In fields and pastures, not in marshes. *Nest:* On ground, usually sunken and well hidden, of fine grasses, etc. *Eggs:* 3 to 6, usually glossy white with sparse spots and blotches of purples, lilac and browns.

RANGE. — Breeds east of the Great Plains from southern Wisconsin, southern Ontario, and southern New Hampshire south to southern Louisiana, central Alabama, northern Georgia, and northern South Carolina; winters from southern Illinois and North Carolina south to the Bahamas, Cuba, Yucatan, and Guatemala.

The Eastern Grasshopper Sparrow is a queer, somber-colored, big-headed, short-tailed, unobtrusive little bird. It did not come by its name because of its fondness for grasshoppers, though it is never averse to making a meal of them, but because of its grasshopper-like attempt at song — if song it can be called. It is so persistent and persevering in giving forth its attempts at melody that it not only sings and sings unnoticed during daylight hours, but even awakens in the night to sing. When the novice first hears this stridulation coming out of the grass he naturally ignores it or does not connect it with a bird.

This little sparrow is not so uncommon as most people believe it to be, but its insect-like song is barely audible at one hundred yards, and if the hearer is at all tone-deaf, he will not hear it at all, even though he passes by the singing bird at a distance of twenty feet. Then again the bird keeps out of sight for the most part and runs through the grass like a little mouse. Also it is very local in its habitat. It may disappear from one town and suddenly appear in another where it was previously unknown. It may be common in one locality and unknown in a similar region near-by.

It is a bird of the coastal plain, river valleys and the lower uplands. It is rarely found at levels much above one thousand feet. Although it often nests on rather low ground, even at the edge of salt marshes, the nest is always on dry land. If in or near a meadow, it is on a rise of ground. It prefers dry, sandy fields and pastures, where the white daisy and the red sorrel grow, and I have never seen one in the woods. It is a ground bird; it eats, nests, sings and sleeps on the ground, but also sings from weed-tops, tussocks, driftwood, stones and fences. Rarely it alights in trees, and sometimes sings from a low tree-top, and in migration it may be seen at times in gardens or orchards.

Its habits are much like those of the Savannah Sparrow, but it may be readily distinguished from that species by its unstreaked breast, the yellow at the bend of its wings, and the rapid, fluttering, wren-like flight close to the ground. It usually flies up from the grass, flutters rather low and erratically for a short distance and drops, apparently exhausted, into the grass again.

It builds its nests in late May and June, and I have found two with eggs in July. They are extremely hard to find, as the female almost never flies up directly from the nest and seldom flies back to it, but scurries some distance in the concealment of the tall grass. In running in and out she wears a little path, almost imperceptible, but which may be found by a close observer. If surprised upon the nest she flutters through the grass, feigning lameness. There may be a second brood occasionally but the bird comes so late and usually goes so early that such cases, if they occur, probably are rare. The nests are frequently broken up by the mowing machine, and usually a bird leaves a locality after the grass has been cut — sometimes never to return. Its white eggs with their rings of spots around the larger end are colored so like warblers', and so unlike those of other ground sparrows, that one has no difficulty in identifying them.

When the young leave the nest, they follow the parents about for a while and in July or early August the southward movement begins. As the seeds of weeds ripen this bird feeds greedily upon them. Now and then it may be seen hovering over a tall weed regarding its seed crop, then alighting sidewise on the upright stem and reaching out, feasting 'to its heart's content.' It also feeds much on the ground. The food of the Grasshopper Sparrow, unlike that of some other sparrows, contains a very large percentage of insects.

FLORIDA GRASSHOPPER SPARROW

Ammodramus savannarum floridanus (MEARNS).

IDENTIFICATION. — 'Similar to *A. s. australis* but smaller, with larger bill, longer tarsus, and much darker coloration above, paler below.'

RANGE. — Resident in the Kissimmee Prairie region of central Florida.

LECONTE'S SPARROW

Passerherbulus caudacutus (LATHAM).

IDENTIFICATION. — Length 4½ to 5¼ inches; spread 6½ to 7¼ inches. A sharp-tailed marsh-haunting sparrow; stripe over eye, throat and breast bright buffy-ochre; wide pinkish-brown collar on nape of adult; whitish stripe through center of crown.

BREEDING. — In willow sloughs and grassy lowlands. *Nest:* On ground, of grasses. *Eggs:* 3 to 5, delicately pink, lightly spotted with brownish and black.

RANGE. — Breeds from Great Slave Lake, Mackenzie, and Manitoba south to North Dakota and southern Minnesota; winters from southern Kansas, southern Missouri, and western Tennessee to Texas, Florida, and the coast of South Carolina.

Leconte's Sparrow is an elusive inhabitant of wet marshes, willow sloughs, and grassy flats. It is like a tiny rail in its fondness for concealment, and in its weak fluttering and very brief flight when flushed. Dr. T. S. Roberts in his 'Birds of Minnesota' writes of this species: 'It is one of the prettiest of the smaller Sparrows, being arrayed in a garb of subdued but beautifully disposed chestnut, gray, black, and tawny color, having the effect of a warm, old-gold suffusion.... While, like Henslow's Sparrow and the Marsh Wrens, it occasionally sings from concealment in the dense vegetation, it is more inclined to mount to the top of a little willow or tall weed, and there, over and over again, deliver its amusingly squeaky little ditty. This makes it rather more easily found.'

Ernest E. (Seton) Thompson in his 'Birds of Manitoba' describes the singing of Leconte's Sparrow: 'Presently he throws back his head, gapes his widest, and thus with bill pointed at the zenith, arduously laboring, he is delivered of a tiny, husky, double note *"reese, reese,"* so thin a sound and so creaky that I believe it is usually attributed to a grasshopper.' — (J.B.M.)

EASTERN HENSLOW'S SPARROW

Passerherbulus henslowi susurrans BREWSTER.   PLATE 68.

IDENTIFICATION. — Length 4¾ to 5¼ inches; spread 7 to 7½ inches. A short-tailed, large-headed sparrow; finely streaked below with black; striped olive-colored head; no yellow above eye; reddish wings.

SONG. — A hiccoughing *tsi-lick'*, or *flee-sic'*.

BREEDING. — Similar to that of Grasshopper Sparrow.

RANGE. — Breeds from southern New Hampshire and New York south to northern Virginia; winters in the southeastern states to Florida.

There is a great green hill east of the city of Worcester, where farmers used to pasture cattle half a century ago, and there at the hill foot, where a never-failing spring sent forth a rivulet that watered a green field, I first made the acquaintance of this little fowl. Where the rill spread out over the meadow, keeping the roots well watered so that the grass grew rank and tall, the little male, clinging to the upper grass stems, sent forth his weak but emphatic '*flee-síc*' hour after hour. His mate kept mostly under cover of the grass, stealing along like a tiny mouse, and so well was the nest concealed that I never found it.

Rank grass in moist lowlands seems to be chosen usually by these birds as a nesting-place. Usually, I have found the bird on moist land near water, but in migration or in the South in winter it often frequents dry fields or open piney woods near some sheltering thicket.

Most of the Henslow's Sparrows arrive in southern New England in May and depart in August and September. Earlier and later birds are stragglers. There are few northern land birds whose habits are so little known. One who knows its note may find it without difficulty, but its activities on the ground, where it spends most of its time, are well hidden by the waving grass. If pursued it runs swiftly or squats and hides its head under leaves or other vegetation, or it may flutter along close to the ground until it reaches the shelter of some thicket of bushes where it sits motionless and concealed until it believes that all danger has passed. The male is ambitious enough at times to leave his grasses and weed-tops and mount the top of a fence post, from which he delivers that which with him passes for a song; but I have never seen one far from the ground, though they must leave it in migration. Some of the males have the habit of singing, if singing it can be called, after dark; sometimes they sing until midnight, and in some cases nearly all night.

WESTERN HENSLOW'S SPARROW

Passerherbulus henslowi henslowi (AUDUBON).

IDENTIFICATION. — Similar to *P. h. susurrans*, but 'in breeding plumage general color of the upper parts duller, black areas larger, chestnut areas smaller.'

RANGE. — Breeds from South Dakota and Ontario to northern Texas and Ohio; winters from southeastern Texas to northwestern Florida.

ACADIAN SPARROW

Ammospiza caudacuta subvirgata (DWIGHT).   PLATE 69.

IDENTIFICATION. — Length 6 to 6½ inches; spread 7½ to 8¼ inches. Similar to *A. c. caudacuta*, but slightly larger, paler and more uniform above, giving grayer effect; buff on sides of head and on breast and flanks paler and more washed out.

BREEDING. — About brackish or fresh marshes or on islands. *Nest:* On ground in grass, built of grass. *Eggs:* 4 or 5, pale greenish-blue marked with browns and gray.

The Acadian Sparrow is almost identical in haunts and habits with the Sharp-tailed Sparrow, and feeds on similar food (largely aquatic insects and grass seeds). So far as I know the only real difference in respect to their haunts is that the former seems rather to prefer the brackish and fresh marshes and low islands in rivers and is somewhat more northern in its breeding range, while the latter clings more closely to the salt marsh. Both races have a flight-song in spring, both frequent the salt marshes in migration, and one seems to be about as common as the other. The Acadian may seem less common usually in spring, but its greatest flight comes so late (near June 1) that it may be missed entirely by those who believe that the spring flight of land birds has passed or by those whose attention is directed toward the late shore birds.

SHARP–TAILED SPARROW

Ammospiza caudacuta caudacuta (GMELIN).   PLATE 69.

IDENTIFICATION. — Length 4¾ to 5¾ inches; spread 7 to 8¼ inches. A large-headed, short-tailed sparrow, olive-brown above, buffy below with sharply defined dark breast-streakings; blackish cap; ochre-yellow or 'burnt-orange' side of face surrounding a gray ear-patch; tail rounded, of pointed feathers.

SONG. — Short and gasping, followed or preceded by two *ticks* audible only at close range; *tick tick zeeeeeee* or *zeeeeeee tick tick*.

BREEDING. — About salt or fresh marshes. *Nest:* In tussock or on drift, or in grass, of dried grass. *Eggs:* Similar to those of Acadian Sharp-tail.

RANGE. — Breeds in salt marshes of the Atlantic coast from New Hampshire to Virginia; winters on salt marshes from New Jersey to Florida.

The Sharp-tailed Sparrow is a species of the littoral. It is rarely found far from tidal waters. To see it one must go where the flowing tide comes in. It frequents salt marshes and little bogs near the sea, and is only local in distribution where such retreats are scarce. It breeds on coastal islands as well as on the mainland. During June and July while nesting and rearing young, the bird is rather shy and hard to flush, as it prefers running on the ground mouse-like and under cover, and if flushed flies low over the reeds for a short distance to the top of a plant or bush, from which it quickly descends again to its favorite cover. I have never heard of one flying high on its breeding-grounds or alighting high up in a tree. Its highest flight, except in migration, seems to be a song-flight, which sometimes carries it up a rod or two into the air, when it flies along a bit, delivers its wheezy song, and then drops down again, as if it were trying to trace an inverted U or half-circle in the sunny atmosphere.

Breeding birds begin to appear on the coast of Massachusetts during the latter half of May, and most of them have moved south before late October. They are so secretive and keep so much under cover that little is known about their breeding habits. Dr. C. W. Townsend, who has spent much time in following the species at Ipswich, writes as follows:

'The Sharp-tailed Sparrow is one of the most interesting inhabitants of the salt marshes, on the edges of which it builds its nest in tussocks of grass, raised a few inches to escape the unusual tides, or concealed in the dead "thatch." The birds appear to be distinctly social.

In some localities several pairs are often found breeding together, while other localities, apparently equally favorable, are deserted. They may be found in all parts of the marshes, but they are particularly fond of the upper or black-grass region.

'Sharp-tailed Sparrows are rather difficult birds to observe, especially if they are vigorously followed, as they then lie close, and when flushed, soon drop into the grass and instantly conceal themselves. If, however, the observer keeps still, the birds often become quite tame and display their interesting habits. They run through the grass like mice, with heads low, occasionally pausing to look around, and stretching up to almost double their running height. They occasionally alight in bushes or small trees, and I have seen them running about a stonewall near the marsh like mice. They fly low and alight by dropping suddenly into the grass with tails pointed down.'

When the breeding season is over the Sharp-tailed Sparrow loses much of its caution and is not so given to skulking out of sight in its marshy cover.

NELSON'S SPARROW

Ammospiza caudacuta nelsoni (ALLEN).   PLATE 69.

Other name: Nelson's Sharp-tailed Sparrow.

IDENTIFICATION. — Length 5¼ to 5½ inches; spread 7¼ to 7½ inches. Breast bright ochre-buff, almost without streakings.

BREEDING. — In fresh-water marshes of the interior. *Nest and Eggs:* Similar to Acadian Sharp-tail.

RANGE. — Breeds in marshes from Great Slave Lake and west-central Alberta to southwestern Manitoba, Minnesota, and northeastern South Dakota; winters on the Atlantic and Gulf coasts from North Carolina to Florida and Texas; occurs during migration on the Atlantic coast from Maine southward.

Nelson's Sparrow, unlike the Sharp-tailed Sparrow, is a bird of the lower prairie region of the West, frequenting the neighborhood of fresh water, but during the fall migrations it flies southeastward to the Atlantic coast, where it seems to frequent mainly the neighborhood of beaches and salt marshes. Its habits are much like those of the Sharp-tailed Sparrow. It is perhaps even more shy and secretive, rarely rising in flight more than a few feet above the grass, or flying more than a few yards when startled by the approach of an intruder. If the observer can keep quiet long enough, the bird's curiosity may overcome its timidity for the time being, and it may rise to some convenient perch where it may be observed at leisure.

NORTHERN SEASIDE SPARROW

Ammospiza maritima maritima (WILSON).   PLATE 69.

IDENTIFICATION. — Length 5¼ to 6½ inches; spread 8 to 8½ inches. A dark, olive-gray, sharp-tailed, salt-marsh-haunting sparrow; lacks conspicuous head-markings of the Sharp-tailed Sparrow group, and under parts are obscurely streaked; a yellow patch before and above eye and a white streak on lower jaw.

SONG. — Short and 'buzzy,' or insect-like.

BREEDING. — In salt marshes. *Nest:* Of grasses, often under patches of drift. *Eggs:* 4 to 6, grayish-white, coarsely spotted.

RANGE. — Breeds in salt marshes of Atlantic coast from southern Massachusetts to Virginia; winters from Virginia to northern Florida.

The Northern Seaside Sparrow is well named. No land bird lives closer to the sea. It nests mostly on the ground and, like a sea bird, just above the reach of ordinary tides. So close is its little domicile to the summer tide marks that, like those of terns and gulls, it is flooded sometimes by storm tides. The salt marsh is its principal habitat and it frequents the inner shores of sea-islands lying near the coast. Its habits are similar to those of the Sharp-tailed Sparrow, but it is most common near the water's edge, where when undisturbed it often wades like a rail or a sandpiper, and where it gets much of its food.

It stays for the most part on the ground or near it, and like the other marsh sparrows runs through the concealing grass like a mouse. Often, however, the song is given from the top of some low bush, and the male indulges in a song flight, in which it emulates the Skylark, rising into the air, fluttering upward, singing the while, and finally sailing down to its perch again. Its upper plumage is so dark as to render it inconspicuous when seen against a background of dark mud. It does not seem quite so shy, however, as other marsh sparrows, and its curiosity will usually bring it to view when an observer imitates the cries of a bird in distress. Nests have been found in the grass, in or under seaweed thrown up by the tide, or even somewhat raised from the ground in bushes.

In the breeding season this bird has been rather common locally for years on the coast at Westport, Massachusetts, which is, perhaps, its most northerly nesting locality. It visits Martha's Vineyard and possibly breeds there and locally along the south shore of Cape Cod, but I have no authentic breeding records, and have only one record of its presence on Nantucket. Its principal breeding-grounds are the wide salt marshes of the New Jersey coast, and southward to Virginia. In autumn birds of this species sometimes join loose flocks of the Sharp-tailed Sparrow, and as the two species frequent a similar habitat and as one occasionally has been mistaken for the other, reports are not always reliable.

NOTE. — The 'Check-List' of the American Ornithologists' Union now recognizes six races of *Ammospiza maritima* from the region covered by this volume, and Dr. H. C. Oberholser has recently described two others, *A. m. waynei* from Georgia, and *A. m. pelonota* from the northeast coast of Florida. R. T. Peterson says in his 'Field Guide to the Birds': 'The other Seasides may be recognized by the region in which they are found breeding. In parts of Florida, where several may winter in the same locality, it is folly to attempt discrimination without collecting.' — (J.B.M.)

MACGILLIVRAY'S SEASIDE SPARROW

Ammospiza maritima macgillivraii (AUDUBON).

IDENTIFICATION. — Above darker than *A. m. maritima*, sometimes heavily streaked with blackish.

RANGE. — Salt marshes of the Atlantic coast from North Carolina to Georgia and northern Florida.

SCOTT'S SEASIDE SPARROW

Ammospiza maritima peninsulae (ALLEN)

IDENTIFICATION. — Much darker than *A. m. maritima*, upper parts darker, mainly brownish-black.
RANGE. — Salt marshes of the west coast of Florida from Tampa Bay to Lafayette County.

WAKULLA SEASIDE SPARROW

Ammospiza maritima juncicola (GRISCOM AND NICHOLS).

IDENTIFICATION. — 'The darkest and blackest race of *A. maritima*.'
RANGE. — Gulf coast of Florida from St. Andrews Bay to southern Taylor County.

HOWELL'S SEASIDE SPARROW

Ammospiza maritima howelli (GRISCOM AND NICHOLS).

IDENTIFICATION. — Upper parts slightly more olive, less grayish than *A. m. maritima*.
RANGE. — Coasts of Alabama and Mississippi, spreading to the coasts of northern Florida and Texas in winter.

LOUISIANA SEASIDE SPARROW

Ammospiza maritima fisheri (CHAPMAN)

IDENTIFICATION. — Breast and sides heavily washed with rusty buff, and streaked with gray.
RANGE. — Breeds in salt marshes on the Gulf coast from Grande Isle, Louisiana, to High Island, Texas; winters southwestward along the coast to Corpus Christi, Texas.

DUSKY SEASIDE SPARROW

Ammospiza nigrescens (RIDGWAY).

IDENTIFICATION. — Length about 5¾ to 6¼ inches; spread about 8¼ to 8½ inches. Similar to Northern Seaside Sparrow; bill smaller; *upper parts black or blackish-brown*, edged with grayish-olive and dull white; under parts white *heavily streaked with black*; lores and bend of wings yellow; wings and tail brownish edged with yellowish-olive.

BREEDING. — Similar to other Seaside Sparrows.

RANGE. — Resident in salt marshes at the northern end of Indian River, east coast of Florida.

The Dusky Seaside Sparrow occupies one of the most restricted ranges of any North American bird. It is found throughout the year in a narrow area not over twenty-five miles in length on Merritt's Island, Florida, and on the near-by mainland. A. H. Howell in his 'Florida Bird Life' says of this bird: 'The marshes inhabited by this species are rather dry and not so boggy as many of the Florida marshes. They support growths of sharp-pointed rushes (*Juncus*), interspersed with open tracts covered with a growth of salt-marsh grass (*Spartina patens*), or of glasswort (*Salicornia*). The birds live and breed in all three types of vegetation. The nests are made of fine grass stems, and are placed from four to sixteen inches above the ground, not arched, but usually concealed from view by wisps of grass carelessly arranged as if for protection from the sun.... On the Merritt Island marshes, in May, 1925, I found these Sparrows abundant, and much less shy than most Seaside Sparrows. The males were singing almost constantly from low perches on top of bunches of grass or rushes ... their song ... begins with a single (rarely double) liquid note, followed by a short, buzzing trill ... One bird was heard giving a more elaborate flight-song.' — (J.B.M.)

CAPE SABLE SEASIDE SPARROW

Ammospiza mirabilis (HOWELL).

IDENTIFICATION. — Length about 5½ inches; spread about 8 inches. *Greener above* and *whiter below* than any race of *Ammospiza maritima*, and much lighter colored than *A. nigrescens*; breast and sides streaked with brownish; yellow line from bill to eye and bend of wing yellow, sides of crown distinctly striped with black.

BREEDING. — Similar to other Seaside Sparrows.

RANGE. — Resident in coastal marshes in the vicinity of Cape Sable, Florida.

This species of Seaside Sparrow was discovered in 1918 by Arthur H. Howell and as Dr. Frank M. Chapman says, it 'is not only the latest but probably the last new species of bird to be found in eastern North America.' Its range is even more restricted than that of its congener the Dusky Seaside Sparrow, it being limited to the coastal prairie near Cape Sable in extreme southwestern Florida, 'an area about six miles in length and not more than half a mile in breadth.' It has the secretive habits of the other Seaside Sparrows. — (J.B.M.)

EASTERN VESPER SPARROW

Pooecetes gramineus gramineus (GMELIN).   PLATE 68.

Other names: Bay-winged Bunting; Grass Finch; Ground-bird.

IDENTIFICATION. — Length 5½ to 6¾ inches; spread 10 to 11¼ inches. A gray-streaked sparrow with the *outer tail feathers white;* chestnut lesser wing coverts not conspicuous.

SONG. — Two long low notes, two higher ones, then descending in chippering trills.

BREEDING. — In open upland fields and pastures. *Nest:* On ground, of grass and rootlets. *Eggs:* 4 or 5, pale greenish- or grayish-white, with dots, blotches, lines and scrawls of browns and blackish.

RANGE. — Breeds from central Ontario, southern Quebec, and Cape Breton Island south to eastern Nebraska, central Missouri, Kentucky, Virginia, and North Carolina, and west to western Minnesota; winters from the southern part of its breeding range to the Gulf coast, southern Florida, and central Texas.

Mid-March has passed and winter seems to have departed. Where but yesterday the eye swept the unbroken snowy mantle of the hills, the earth now lies bare and sodden, with here a faint vernal tinge and there a little patch of snow. Swollen streams rush murmuring to the sea. Robust Robins flutter among the crimson sumac berries, taking toll of the supply of fruit, dried on the stem. A Bluebird warbles his soft love song as he flutters from tree to tree in the old orchard, and far away, from the hill pasture, comes an 'earth-song,' a pastoral plaintive and sweet, the fine strain of the Eastern Vesper Sparrow.

In 'Our Birds in Their Haunts,' the Rev. J. H. Langille writes as follows of the song of this little poet of the fields:

'The melody of the Bay-wing, if not so sprightly and varied, still bears quite a resemblance to that of the Song Sparrow, and is expressive of a tender pathos, which may even give it the preference. It is one of the few bird-songs which might be written upon a musical staff. Beginning with a few soft syllables on the fifth note of the musical scale, it strikes several loud and prolonged notes on the eighth above, and ends in a soft warble which seems to die out for want of breath, and may run a little down the scale. Though the song is not brilliant, and rather suggestive of humble scenes and thoughts, "the grass, the stones, the stubble, the furrow, the quiet herds, and the warm twilight among the hills," it is nevertheless a fine pastoral, full of the sweet content which dwells in the bosom of nature. It is heard to the best advantage when the rosy hues of sundown are tinting the road, the rocks, and all the higher lights of the evening landscape. Then an innumerable company of these poets "of the plain, unadorned pastures" — some perched on the fences, some on weeds and thistles, but many more hid in the grass and stubble — swell into their finest chorus, while most other birds are gradually subsiding into silence. It has been well said that the farmer following his team from the field at dusk catches the Bay-wing's sweetest strain, and that a very proper name for it would be the Vesper Sparrow.'

John Burroughs describes the song as 'two or three long, silver notes of rest and peace, ending in some subdued trills and quavers.'

Although the Vesper Sparrow is a ground bird it may be seen commonly in trees, on fences, telegraph or telephone wires, and even on roofs of buildings, especially during migration, and in the love season its rapture sometimes lifts it into the air on fluttering wings, occasionally to a considerable height, where it pours forth its sweetest music ere it drops again to earth. Its lay is most frequent in early morning and near sunset, but may be heard intermittently at any hour of the day, until the night shuts down, and even in dense darkness.

Usually the bird does not become common in the latitude of southern New England until April, and it does not ordinarily build its nest until May, but nests have been found, with eggs, in April. The courtship is carried on mostly on the ground. The male walks or runs before or after the female, with wings raised, and both wings and tail widely spread, occasionally rising into the air to give his flight-song. There is much rivalry and some strife between the males.

In open pastures with short grass the nest is usually sunk in a little hollow, so that its edge is about level with the surface of the sod. When a nest is built in a tussock or a clump of weeds or bushes, sometimes it is raised somewhat above the ground. Occasionally the little domicile is built among standing grain, and now and then one is found under the shelter of a potato plant. Nest-building requires from one to two weeks, as it is frequently delayed by inclement weather. When the nest is completed an egg is laid daily. The female usually sits very closely when incubating, and often does not leave the nest until almost trodden upon, when she flutters slowly along the ground in imitation of a wounded bird. When the young are hatched, the parents eat the broken egg shells; both parents brood the young, which the female shades from the hot sun with partly spread wings, and protects from the storm with her own body. The nest is kept scrupulously clean. The young leave it in some cases in about eight days, but if not molested they are ready to fly in about twelve.

Anyone walking along a country road or through an upland pasture in spring or summer may see the bird, a plain, rather dingy, striped sparrow, running on ahead, flying only when closely approached, and now and then showing its white outer tail feathers in flight. It is a bird of the drier, upland fields, usually keeping away from houses for the most part, and rather seldom approaching swamps and watersides, but is fond of daily dust baths in country roads. When the young are on the wing, they feed about weedy fields and gardens. Although not so gregarious as blackbirds or longspurs, flocks of twenty to fifty may be seen in migration, which goes on from late September to November, after which only a few stragglers remain, some of whom winter during mild seasons along the coast from New England southward.

EASTERN LARK SPARROW

Chondestes grammacus grammacus (SAY). PLATE 69.

Other names: Quail-head; Road-bird.

IDENTIFICATION. — Length 5¾ to 6¾ inches; spread 10½ to 11 inches. Identified by chestnut ear-patch, black and white head markings, plain unstreaked breast with one central black spot, and blackish fan-shaped tail with white tip and much white on outer feathers.

BREEDING. — On prairies and other open lands. *Nest:* On or near ground, of grasses lined with rootlets, fine grass, and hair. *Eggs:* Whitish, spotted blotched, and scrawled with brown, purplish, and black.

RANGE. — Breeds from eastern Nebraska, northwestern Minnesota, central Wisconsin and southern Ontario south to southern Louisiana and central Alabama, east to western Pennsylvania, Maryland, and northwestern West Virginia; winters in southern Mississippi, southeastern Texas, and eastern Mexico.

The Eastern Lark Sparrow is a handsome, well-marked, unmistakable bird, and one of the finest singers of the sparrow tribe. It is not so terrestrial as some of the other ground-sparrows, as it alights in trees, frequenting them much after the breeding season, and in some cases nests in bushes or low trees. In spring it frequents roadsides. Hence the name 'Road-bird,' which is applied to it in the West. Another vernacular name is 'Quail-head' from the striped appearance of its head.

The song of the Lark Sparrow is somewhat like that of the Indigo Bunting, but louder, clearer, and much finer. Robert Ridgway says that it is 'composed of a series of chants, each syllable rich, loud, and clear, interspersed with emotional trills ... Though seemingly hurried, it is one continuous gush of sprightly music; now gay, now melodious, and then tender beyond description — the very expression of emotion.'

The nest-site is usually in a grassy field, a pasture, or a prairie in the neighborhood of bushes and trees. The nest is built mostly of grasses, lined with rootlets, fine grass and long hairs, and is either on the ground or in a low tree or bush.

During the mating season the males have frequent contests, often carrying their battles into the air. Mating and nesting are carried on mostly in the open, but after the young have been reared, all are likely to retire to the borders of open woodlands, or to bushy, partly wooded pastures until the molting season has passed, when in August the southward movement begins.

BACHMAN'S SPARROW

Aimophila aestivalis bachmani (AUDUBON).

IDENTIFICATION. — Length 5¾ to 6¼ inches; spread 7½ to 8¼ inches. A small sparrow with brown head, brown and gray streaked upper parts, and an unstreaked breast washed with buffy brown; line over eye buffy.

BREEDING. — *Nest:* On the ground, of grasses, domed. *Eggs:* 3 or 4, pure white.

RANGE. — Breeds from central Illinois, southern Indiana, southern Ohio, southwestern Pennsylvania, and central Virginia south to central Texas, Louisiana, Mississippi, Alabama, and northwestern Florida; winters from southern North Carolina southward into Florida.

The two races of *Aimophila aestivalis* differ but little in their habits and haunts, and the descriptive name of Pinewoods Sparrow might be applied equally well to either race. I first saw the Bachman's Sparrow at Thomasville, Georgia, in the winter of 1923, a region where in the breeding season one might expect to find intermediates between the two subspecies but where in winter only the northern race is present. At that season the birds were found in the open pine woods where there was little undergrowth of bushes but where the tall brown clumps of broom-grass furnished ideal shelter and an ample food supply for the sparrows. The birds were exceedingly difficult to identify with a glass, as they would suddenly flush from the broom-grass without warning, fly a short distance and, before any field-marks could be detected, drop quickly into the grass stems and skulk away silently, and they were seldom seen again. Several years later I met the bird on its breeding-grounds in the pineries near Charleston, South Carolina, and for the first time heard its pleasing and easily recognized song. — (J.B.M.)

PINEWOODS SPARROW

Aimophila aestivalis aestivalis (LICHTENSTEIN).   PLATE 94.

IDENTIFICATION. — Similar to *A. a. bachmani* but generally grayer; line over eye gray instead of buffy; under parts grayish-white washed with dull drab.

RANGE. — Breeds in southeastern Georgia and peninsular Florida; winters in central and southern Florida.

The song of the Pinewoods Sparrow is described by Dr. Frank M. Chapman, who says: 'In my opinion its song is more beautiful than that of any other American sparrow. It is very simple — I write it, *che-e-e-e—de, de, de; che-e—chee-o, chee-o, chee-o, chee-o* — but it possesses all the exquisite tenderness and pathos of the melody of the Hermit Thrust; indeed, in purity of tone and in execution I should consider the Sparrow the superior songster. It sings most freely very early in the morning and late in the afternoon, when the world is hushed and the pine trees breathe a soft accompaniment to its divine music.' And A. H. Howell says: 'The song, though not loud, is musically the most attractive of any of the Florida sparrows' songs. The reedlike tones are sweet and clear, suggesting the song of Bewick's Wren, but somewhat stronger and of richer quality. Successive songs, delivered by a single bird, are frequently pitched in different keys, and the phrases are varied in form as well as pitch.' — (J.B.M.)

SLATE–COLORED JUNCO

Junco hyemalis hyemalis (LINNAEUS).   PLATE 71.

Other names: Junco; Snowbird; Black Snowbird; Gray Snowbird.

IDENTIFICATION. — Length 5¾ to 6½ inches; spread 9¼ to 10 inches. Adults have slate-gray upper plumage and breast, sharply defined against white under plumage, white outer tail feathers, and pinkish bill; females duller than males in spring; young have pinkish-brown sides, and back and breast washed with brownish.

CALLS. — A characteristic *smacking* note and a metallic *clink*. SONG: A simple trill similar to that of Chipping Sparrow, but more musical.

BREEDING. — In woods, thickets, or overgrown fields. *Nest:* On (or near) ground, often behind overhanging roots, etc., of grass, roots, bark, etc., lined with finer material and hair. *Eggs:* 4 to 6, bluish, greenish, or grayish, thickly spotted with browns.

RANGE. — Breeds from northwestern Alaska, northern Manitoba, and central Quebec south to the base of the Alaska Peninsula, central Alberta, northern Minnesota, central Michigan, Ontario, Maine, Nova Scotia, and in the mountains of Massachusetts, New York, and Pennsylvania; winters from southern Ontario throughout the eastern United States to the Gulf coast.

A bleak gray day in early winter — bare trees standing stark and black against a background of white snow — a cold wind sweeping across the drifted fields — and in a sheltered, brush-filled corner, a flock of lively little gray and white birds fluttering and twittering together. The Slate-colored Junco has been aptly described as 'leaden skies above, snow below' and it is with days such as these that many people in the North associate this friendly little visitor.

This bird makes its appearance near my home in eastern Massachusetts, after a summer absence in cooler regions, as the leaves begin to fall, and it is usually an abundant autumn migrant, haunting neglected, bush-covered fields and weed-grown gardens, in company with various other seed-eating sparrows and finches. Although the majority of Slate-colored Juncos soon pass on toward the south, some remain, and with the advent of the first snowstorm or the first real cold weather abandon the windswept weed-patches and seek the bounty spread on window shelf and doorstep by their friends of the ever-growing army of bird lovers. While the cold weather continues, they usually confine themselves quite closely to a well-defined range, seldom journeying farther than from the feeding-station to a neighboring weed-patch for a change of diet or for the fine gravel which is so essential to their well-being, or to a clump of bushes or thick evergreens where they can roost and find shelter from the searching winds and driving snow.

With the return of warmer weather in spring, the winter resident Juncos leave the neighborhood of houses for fields and the edges of woodlands, where they are joined by birds which have wintered farther south, and the augmented flocks continue their journey to their breeding-grounds. While small numbers nest in the highlands of Pennsylvania, New York, and western Massachusetts, the majority seek northern New England or Canada. This Junco is a characteristic bird of the great spruce forests of Maine and of the shady ravines of the White and Green Mountain regions. Although a preference is usually shown for cool damp woods, the nest is sometimes located in an open blueberry pasture, among the piles of 'slash' in a lumber clearing, or among the buildings of a deserted logging camp.

The 'Gray Snowbird' is probably the only bird which nests above tree-limit in the White Mountains of New Hampshire, but there it may be found in summer, perfectly at home on the bare rocky cone of Lafayette or picking up crumbs dropped by tourists around the railroad station at the summit of Mt. Washington. On the fifth of August, 1926, I climbed, with a party of camp boys, up the rugged Tuckerman Ravine Trail from Pinkham Notch to the top of Mt. Washington. On the way up the trail, we heard at frequent intervals the ecstatic song of the Winter Wren, the silver notes of the Hermit Thrush, the lisping calls of Golden-crowned Kinglets, and the songs of various forest-loving warblers, among which we distinguished the Myrtle, Magnolia and Black-throated Blue Warbler. As we neared the region of stunted spruces and balsam firs about Hermit Lake, we were greeted by several small groups of Slate-colored Juncos, busily engaged in searching for food among the dense evergreens. Whole families of streaked, sparrow-like young birds, in the juvenal plumage, were calling from the thickets, and for some time we paused and watched the old birds bringing insects to their hungry offspring. As we proceeded up the ravine, we passed other groups, until, just below the rocky headwall of Tuckerman's, we came to the snowfields, at that late date still covering several acres. There, in the span of a few yards, we could pass from late winter to midsummer. Close beside the fields of snow, last year's grasses lay brown and dead; a few feet away the alder catkins and pussy willows were just coming into blossom and violets were nodding in the cold wind; beyond these, we found the yellow mountain avens and the tall white bog orchid, *Habenaria dilatata*, in bloom, and a little farther still, great showy sprays of mountain goldenrod waved in the breeze or bowed beneath the dainty weight of a silver and brown mountain fritillary butterfly. Close at hand, we heard the calls of nesting Blackpoll Warblers, while all around the snowfields sounded the smacking notes of the ever-present Juncos. One of the latter drank from 'the Stream of a Thousand Falls,' which is formed by the melting of the snow, and then bathed in the frigid waters with much fluttering and splashing of spray, reminding me of other Juncos which I have watched in midwinter, similarly engaged in bathing, but in light dry snow, just as other sparrows take dust baths in hot weather.

Reluctantly we left this region of summer snow, and clambered up over the steep headwall trail to the Alpine Gardens and across the broken rock of the windswept cone to the summit of New England's highest mountain. And there, higher even than we could climb, perched on the very ridgepole of the hotel at the tiptop of Mount Washington, was a gray and white midget of a bird, greeting us with its cheery Junco song, the only bird which is regularly found in summer in this barren place. — (J.B.M.)

CAROLINA JUNCO
Junco hyemalis carolinensis BREWSTER.

IDENTIFICATION. — Similar to *J. h. hyemalis*, but slightly larger, the upper parts, throat and breast uniform grayish slate-color *without* a brownish wash; bill horn-color.

RANGE. — Breeds in the mountains from western Maryland, Virginia, and West Virginia south to northern Georgia; winters in the adjacent lowlands.

EASTERN TREE SPARROW
Spizella arborea arborea (WILSON).   PLATE 71.

Other names: Winter Chippy; Canada Sparrow.

IDENTIFICATION. — Length 5¾ to 6½ inches; spread 8½ to 9¾ inches. A slim sparrow with brown-streaked back, reddish crown, unstreaked grayish breast with a large dusky spot in the center, and two white wing-bars; *bill dark above, yellow below.*

SONG. — A cheerful musical twittering.

BREEDING. — In thickets near water. *Nest:* On ground or in bush, of grass, roots, bark, etc., warmly lined with hair or fur. *Eggs:* 4 or 5, greenish flecked with light brown.

RANGE. — Breeds from central Mackenzie and northern Quebec to Great Slave Lake, northern Manitoba, southern Quebec, and Newfoundland; winters from southern Minnesota, Ontario, and the Maritime Provinces south to eastern Oklahoma, central Arkansas, South Carolina, and Georgia.

When the frosts of autumn chill the northland the Eastern Tree Sparrows come. We look upon their arrival as an augury of impending winter. Many of them pass on, but when the snow lies deep over hill and dale we find some still with us, sitting in flocks in sunny sheltered thickets or feeding far out in weedy fields, leaving multitudinous tracks on the snow. They linger in birches along roadsides, and feed about farmsteads, preferring open country to woodlands and seeking the companionship of man for the food material he scatters and wastes. They come with Juncos to feed in open poultry sheds or about barnyards and they come readily to farm-house doors for crumbs, seeds and chaff thrown out for the birds by kindly people. When deep snow covers most of their food, they scatter more or less, and single birds appear here and there scouting about. When they find a good food supply others soon appear. In feeding on weed seeds they take them from the ground, or pick them from the weeds, while standing on the ground or snow, but they also alight on the plants and pick off the seeds, somewhat after the manner of the smaller sparrows, Goldfinches and Pine Siskins. The winter habits of the Tree Sparrow are as an open book to all rural residents who feed birds during the inclement season. Usually by late February the northward movement toward Canada has begun.

Tree Sparrows are occasionally heard singing when deep snow covers the ground. The song is among the sweetest of sparrow notes, slightly resembling that of the Fox Sparrow. The full chorus of a flock in winter is a sound worth going far to hear.

The habits of the Tree Sparrow in its northern home are little known. Its food while with us consists largely of weed seeds and the seeds of grasses that are considered as weeds.

EASTERN CHIPPING SPARROW

Spizella passerina passerina (BECHSTEIN). PLATE 71.

Other names: Chippy; Chip-bird; Hair-bird.

IDENTIFICATION. — Length 5 to 5¾ inches; spread 8 to 9 inches. A small, slim sparrow with brown-streaked back, plain grayish under parts; crown chestnut, broad white line over eye, and black streak through eye; bill blackish.

SONG. — A simple monotonous series of dry *chips*, rapidly repeated.

BREEDING. — On farms, in orchards, gardens, in village streets, or woods. *Nest:* Of fine grass and roots, lined with hair. *Eggs:* 3 to 5, greenish-blue with wreath of blackish spots.

RANGE. — Breeds from Yukon Territory, northern British Columbia, central Manitoba, northern Ontario, southern Quebec, and Cape Breton Island south to central Texas, southern Mississippi, and central Georgia; winters chiefly in the Southern States, occasionally as far north as Oklahoma and southern New Jersey.

The Eastern Chipping Sparrow is the little brown-capped pensioner of the dooryard and lawn, that comes about farmhouse doors to glean crumbs shaken from the tablecloth by thrifty housewives. It is the most domestic of all the sparrows. It approaches the dwellings of man with quiet confidence and frequently builds its nest and rears its young in the clustering vines of porch or veranda under the very noses of the human tenants. Here and there in the wilder parts of the country Chipping Sparrows may be found in forest openings or along the shores of lakes and streams, but most of them seem to prefer the vicinity of man's dwellings.

Its reiterated chipping is one of the earliest bird-songs of the dawn, heard by the farmer as he rises for his day of toil in the fields. It is a simple, monotonous, soothing chant, sung hour after hour with the vigor, enthusiasm and abandon of the most accomplished musician; but it is rarely indeed that the bird produces any sound more musical than the simple string of *chips*. When the little birds are abundant, one singer regularly answers another on a slightly different key, so that the sound softened by distance seems gently to come and go like the breath of a sleeper in the fields.

Chippy is an early riser, often singing even before the Robin, and thus leading the morning chorus, but he does not antedate the Robin in his spring arrival. In fact he usually appears much later, in late April or May, after the early sparrows have come. We seldom see many Chipping Sparrows in New England before mid-April, and any too-previous bird of the species arriving earlier is likely to suffer with the cold. Thoreau says that he has seen one 'come too early in the spring' sitting on a limb, shivering, and drawing in its head, striving to warm it in its muffled feathers, for it is not a hardy bird, and probably only very rarely attempts to winter in southern New England in some sheltered spot near the southernmost coast.

Like the Robin it commonly nests in an apple tree in the back yard and feeds all summer about the house and barn, and some especially confiding individuals have learned to feed from the hand. Its rather fragile nest, which in good weather is built in three or four days, is composed chiefly of fine grasses and rootlets, and lined usually with horsehair, and is so lightly attached to the twigs that a sudden gust of wind may upset it or blow it away.

The egg of the Cowbird is very often deposited in the nests of Chipping Sparrows, which do not seem to resent the imposition, but, like the good foster parents that they are, tend and feed the young Cowbird until the great pot-bellied nestling is well able to care for itself. Both sexes

523

join in the care and protection of the young, which are ready to leave the nest in about nine or ten days.

Mr. Laurence B. Fletcher contributes the following: 'A nest containing young Chipping Sparrows was about five feet from the veranda in a low limb of an elm. The male bird wore a band. The female (unbanded) remained for over an hour at a time three or four inches from the nest, taking food that the male brought and feeding it to the young, which were nearly ready to leave the nest. She apparently did no hunting for food, and during an entire day (July 15th) only the male procured food. She remained quiet until she heard the call of the approaching male — then moved a little in the direction of his arrival, received the food, then turned to the nest and fed her young. The male made very frequent trips, for food was available within a short distance. The female was never seen to eat the food brought to her. It was always fed to the young, although it does not seem possible that she did not take for herself during the day some of the food furnished by her devoted mate.'

When the fledglings can fly they are seen about the door for a time, and then the little company joins with others until considerable flocks are formed, which roam over the country until late September or early October, when the southward flight usually is well under way. In August the young males begin to sing, and often their songs are unlike those of their elders; some are sweeter, others hoarse or harsh.

The Chipping Sparrow feeds mostly on insects and grass seeds. It is a redoubtable enemy of the gypsy moth, army-worm, canker-worm, beet-worm, cabbage-worm, and pea-louse. Weevils, grasshoppers, locusts and other insect pests are its common prey. It feeds to repletion in autumn on the seeds of garden weeds and grasses. It seems fond of the seeds of such weeds as ragweed, purslane and plantain. It takes some berries, usually wild fruit, and occasionally one captures a few honey-bees (probably mostly drones).

CLAY–COLORED SPARROW

Spizella pallida (SWAINSON).

IDENTIFICATION. — Length 5 to 5½ inches; spread 7½ to 8 inches. Size of Chipping Sparrow but paler and duller colored; crown striped, resembling young Chipping Sparrow, with median light streak, and not chestnut like adult Chippy; upper parts streaked black and brown, under parts unmarked white with buffy sides; dark line behind eye, not through it as in Chippy; brown ear-patch; bill light.

SONG. — A fine insect-like buzz, *ze-ze-ze-ze-ze-ze*.

BREEDING. — *Nest:* On ground or in bushes, of grasses and lined with hair. *Eggs:* Similar to those of Chipping Sparrow.

RANGE. — Breeds from southern Mackenzie, central Manitoba, and Michigan (Isle Royale) south to western Montana, southeastern Colorado, northern Nebraska, and northwestern Illinois; winters from southern New Mexico and southern Texas to central Mexico.

The Clay-colored Sparrow is a bird of the interior of North America, which shows many of the characteristics of its close relatives, the Chipping and Field Sparrows. Its chosen habitat is bush-grown hillsides, overgrown clearings, and meadows with scattered clumps of sage-brush, rose thickets, and similar areas, a type of country which in the East would be occupied by the

Field Sparrow. In appearance it is an inconspicuous, earthy-colored little bird, and is more easily recognized by its song than by any marked feather pattern.

It is a persistent singer, keeping up its thin unmusical buzzing all day long during the early nesting season. The song is usually given from a perch in a low tree or bush, and resembles that of a cicada 'but rather more rasping and unattractive than the insect's fiddling.' — (J.B.M.)

EASTERN FIELD SPARROW

Spizella pusilla pusilla (WILSON).   PLATE 71.

Other names: Bush Sparrow; Huckleberry Bird.

IDENTIFICATION. — Length 5 to 6 inches; spread 7¾ to 8½ inches. Size near Chipping Sparrow; bill pinkish, tail slightly forked; resembles Tree Sparrow but not so slim appearing and face less noticeably striped; 'this and eye-ring give bird a rather blank expression,' to quote R. T. Peterson.

SONG. — A series of ascending, descending or level-pitched notes, accelerating in speed, sometimes fading at the end, *he-ew, he-ew, he-ew, hew, hew, hew, he, heeeeu.*

BREEDING. — In open bushy places. *Nest:* In bush or briers or on the ground, of grass or weeds, often lined with hair. *Eggs:* 4 or 5, whitish, spotted with brown and lilac.

RANGE. — Breeds from southern Minnesota, southern Michigan, southern Quebec, Magdalen Islands, and southern Maine to central Texas, central Louisiana, and northern Florida; winters from Missouri, Illinois, southern Pennsylvania, and New Jersey to the Gulf coast.

On bright June days, when heat waves reflected from the warm ground shimmer over the landscape, the Eastern Field Sparrow sings. The clear, sweet, pensive chant carries far on still days, and comes down to the valley from bushy, hillside pastures and dry old fields along the edges of the woods. He sings from a huckleberry bush, from a tall weed, a fence-top, or some small birch or other pasture tree. The lay is simple but it is one of the sweetest of the sparrow songs. Rev. J. H. Langille says of it: 'The song is quite constantly repeated at short intervals, and has a rather melancholy but soothing and pleasing effect, which sensitive natures readily recognize, and do not easily forget. It is the homely, pensive poetry of the thicket, that line of land where the cultivated beauty and fertility of the fields end, and the solitude and gloom of the forest begin.'

Straggling Field Sparrows are seen sometimes in the latitude of southern New England in March, but it is not until the latter part of April that these birds usually appear in small flocks, feeding about weedy gardens and fields. During the summer, while the birds are occupied in raising their young, they are by no means such domestic birds as the Chipping Sparrows. Instead of nesting about the domiciles of man, they usually retire to old fields and bushy pastures, or low thickets along the edges of woodlands, though occasionally a pair may select some neglected garden for the home-site.

The young, like those of most ground-nesting birds, develop very rapidly. If undisturbed they may remain in the nest for nine or ten days, but if molested they may leave it by the fifth or sixth day, when they run away and hide in the grass. When the young have been reared, they repair to weedy cultivated fields, hayfields and gardens, where in the manner of Tree Sparrows they feed largely on the seeds of weeds. By September they have gathered in flocks, and soon the southward movement begins. But flocks are still passing during most of October, and a few stragglers remain later. Some of them winter occasionally along the coast of southern New England and they are common at that season from New Jersey southward.

HARRIS'S SPARROW

Zonotrichia querula (NUTTALL).

Other names: Hooded Sparrow; Mourning Sparrow; Black-crowned Sparrow; Black-headed Sparrow.

IDENTIFICATION. — Length 6¾ to 7¾ inches; spread 10¼ to 11¾ inches. A large sparrow with black face and breast or black blotch on breast; gray or buff cheeks; bill red or flesh-colored.

SONG. — Slow, drawling and monotonous.

BREEDING. — *Nest:* On ground in coniferous woods, of grass. *Eggs:* Pale bluish-green, spotted and blotched with brown.

RANGE. — Breeds in the Hudsonian Zone at Fort Churchill, Hudson Bay, Artillery Lake, Mackenzie, and probably at Great Bear Lake and just south of the Barren Lands; winters from southern Nebraska, northern Kansas, and western Missouri to southern Texas; in migration ranges east to western Ontario, southwestern Ohio, Michigan, eastern Illinois, and west to Montana, Wyoming, and eastern Colorado.

A little over a hundred years ago, on April 28, 1834, Thomas Nuttall collected the first specimen of this handsome species known to science, between Independence and Westport, Missouri, not far from the border of Kansas. Only fifteen days after Nuttall's discovery, Maximilian, Prince of Wied, also collected one of these birds on the Missouri River. It was not until 1840, however, that Nuttall published his discovery of the 'Mourning Sparrow' as he called it. On May 4, 1843, nine years after Nuttall's discovery, Audubon and his friend Edward Harris were near Fort Leavenworth, Kansas, when the latter collected a sparrow which Audubon thought a new species and which he therefore named 'Harris's Sparrow.'

For a long time nothing was known of the breeding habits of this conspicuously marked bird. In 1902 E. A. Preble collected young birds recently out of the nest, at Churchill on the west coast of Hudson Bay. In 1907 Ernest Thompson-Seton found a nest containing nearly fledged young, in the Barren Lands of Canada near Great Slave Lake. In 1930 P. A. Taverner found a nest, also containing young, at Churchill. The following year Dr. George M. Sutton went to Churchill to study the species, and the first nest with eggs was found on June 16, 1931, almost one hundred years after the taking of the first specimen of the bird.

The range of Harris's Sparrow is perhaps unique among North American birds. Swenk and Stevens in the 'Wilson Bulletin' define its breeding range as 'in the strip of dwarfed timber margining the northern edge of the forests of the Hudsonian Life Zone, from the eastern shore of Great Bear Lake to the western shore of Hudson Bay, and up to the very edge of the Arctic Barren Grounds.' Its winter range they give as 'an area of only about 200 by 900 miles extending from southeastern Nebraska to central Texas' and 'lying between the meridians of 94° and 100° north of the 28th parallel.' In migration it does not ordinarily stray very far east or west of the line between these two areas.

Alexander Wetmore, in his 'Migrations of Birds,' says of Harris's Sparrow:

'Migration is almost directly south and extends only through a comparatively narrow area along the eastern edge of the Great Plains. Stragglers come to eastern Colorado on the west and central Wisconsin and Illinois on the east, but the full migration centers through a narrow region comprising eastern Kansas and western Missouri. Here this fine bird swarms in thickets and hedgerows during October, and again in April, filling the air with its rollicking whistled calls. At the height of the migration thousands may be seen in a single day, but outside this strip, which is barely 250 miles wide, the bird is casual or rare. The cause for this limited distribution is wholly obscure, for areas at either hand seem equally suited for the needs of the bird, which has the habits of its congeners. No other bird has this distribution, which lies along the lines where forms of the eastern half of the country begin to disappear and those of the west to appear.' — (J.B.M.)

WHITE-CROWNED SPARROW

Zonotrichia leucophrys leucophrys (FORSTER). PLATE 70.

IDENTIFICATION. — Length 6½ to 7½ inches; spread 9¼ to 10¼ inches. Larger than Song Sparrow; back streaked brown, under parts pearl-gray; adult has crown conspicuously black and white (broad central stripe white, then broad black stripe, another white line, and narrow black line behind eye); lores black, distinguishing it from Gambel's Sparrow with white lores, and the rather dingy looking Nuttall's Sparrow with its narrow central crown stripes; young have head striped with brown and buffy.

SONG. — A sweet but rather short lay of five to seven notes, '*more wet wetter wet chee zee.*'

BREEDING. — Similar to White-throated Sparrow.

RANGE. — Breeds from British Columbia to California and east to Wyoming and New Mexico in the Rocky Mountains, and from limit of trees in northern Manitoba and northern Quebec to central Manitoba, southern Quebec, and in southern Greenland; winters from Lower California, southern Arizona, southern Kansas, and the Ohio Valley south to Florida, Mississippi and Louisiana, and to central Mexico.

It is a red-letter day for the novice in ornithology when he first meets this bird of distinguished appearance. Its gray vesture, black and white crown and elegant form give it an aristocratic appearance as if it were above the common herd of sparrows and in a class by itself. It arrives in the Northern States usually during the latter half of May. In some seasons few are seen, but in others it is locally common for a short time. It seems more numerous in spring than in autumn, when it usually appears in October. In spring it frequents cultivated fields, pastures, roadsides and thickets bordering fields. In autumn it may be found with other sparrows in weedy cornfields or potato fields, along the roadsides and wherever the seeds of weeds are abundant. I have seen this species in small flocks in spring, but when it comes in such numbers it usually passes north quickly. In most years one or a few are seen here and there from time to time for two or three weeks.

It prefers to feed near some thicket or brush heap, to which it can fly for safe refuge, if attacked by its enemies. In warm autumn days, like many other birds, it may vocalize softly in a 'whisper song' that can be heard only for a short distance.

WHITE–THROATED SPARROW

Zonotrichia albicollis (GMELIN).

PLATE 70.

Other name: Peabody Bird.

IDENTIFICATION. — Length 6¼ to 7½ inches; spread 8¾ to 10 inches. Larger than Song Sparrow; resembles White-crowned Sparrow but central crown stripe narrower; a broad line over eye which is yellow from bill to eye and white behind; throat white outlined with blackish from gray sides of throat and upper breast; young have black and white head markings more or less replaced by brown.

SONG. — A series of fine, clear, pensive whistles, diminishing toward the end, resembling *Old Sam Peabody, Peabody, Peabody*, in rhythm, but varying greatly in pitch; last notes sometimes ascending, sometimes descending, or all on one level.

BREEDING. — *Nest:* On or near the ground in woods or thickets, of grass, rootlets, leaves, moss, and bark-strips, lined with fine grass or hair. *Eggs:* 4 or 5, bluish, greenish-blue, or grayish-white, heavily marked with browns, gray and black.

RANGE. — Breeds from northern Mackenzie, central Quebec, and Newfoundland to central Alberta, central Minnesota, central Wisconsin, southern Ontario, northern New England, Nova Scotia, and the mountains of Pennsylvania, New York, and Massachusetts; winters from Missouri, the Ohio Valley, southern Pennsylvania, and Massachusetts south to northeastern Mexico and Florida.

It is April. At last winter has gone, after many days of snow and others of northerly and easterly gales, and the sun rises on a perfect day. The morning opens with a chorus of Robin song, mingled a little later with the trill of the Chipping Sparrow, the jingle of the Song Sparrow, the clanging of Grackles and the love notes of Flickers. Soft southeasterly breezes stir last year's leaves; flies and gnats buzz about in the sunlight; a few great bees are mumbling about in the green grass on the lawn, and frogs are croaking hoarsely at the head of the pond, as if uneasily bestirring themselves and trying their voices after the long winter sleep. Among the brush heaps, bushes, briers and sprouts of second growth clearings, along bush-bordered roads and in the edges of the pine woods where patches of snow still lie in shady places, the White-throated Sparrows range, rustling the dead leaves on the ground as they scratch with both feet. They are on their leisurely way from the sunny south to their breeding-grounds in the Northern States and in Canada.

They prefer to stay on or near the ground, and although they alight in trees they seldom perch very high. When danger threatens they are likely to fly to some thicket or heap or brush for safety. In the spring migration they seem to prefer low thickets in moist places, but in their summer home they may be found almost anywhere in bushy pastures, thickets and woods, and in fall migration numbers visit weedy gardens and cornfields.

The White-throated Sparrow is one of the sweetest singers among the sparrow tribes. The brief song that it gives occasionally during the migration is not its best music, which for its full effect should be heard on its northern breeding-grounds at evening, when, as Mr. C. J. Maynard says, 'the ledges of the mountain tops are gleaming in the brilliant moonlight and the silvery beams are finding their way through the openings in the shadowy forest, illuminating the little glades which form the home of the Sparrows. . . . Then, when all else is silent save the occasional melancholy notes of the Whip-poor-will or the distant hoot of some Owl, the effect produced by this incomparable song is surpassingly beautiful.' Like the White-crowned Sparrow this bird sings more or less at night as well as throughout the day, but most commonly at morning and evening. Its night song has caused it to be named the *Rossignol* or Nightingale

528

among the French-Canadian people of some of its northern breeding-grounds. (The same name is said to have been applied to the Song Sparrow by early settlers in the Maritime Provinces.)

Normally this sparrow breeds in the glades of coniferous forests, preferring northern firs and spruces, but on the hills from which most of the spruce has been cut it often remains to breed in waste left by the lumbermen.

Nest-building requires about a week, and apparently the female builds the nest and incubates the eggs without help from her partner. However, he assists her in feeding the young. If nothing untoward occurs the young leave the nest in about twelve to fourteen days. When the last brood has been reared, when the August molt is done, the families, which by this time have assembled in straggling flocks, begin to move southward. As they retire toward the south, a few of them (possibly young) make some rather lisping, ineffectual attempts at song, but the result will not compare with the nuptial song given on the breeding-grounds. A number of them spend the winter irregularly along the coasts of southern New England, and a few occasionally winter in the interior.

The White-throated Sparrow feeds largely on the ground, where it advances mostly by hopping, and it secures its food chiefly by scratching with its claws, digging with its bill, or by hopping up at food just out of reach. It destroys many insect pests, such as destructive beetles, grasshoppers and locusts, and eats the seeds of many troublesome weeds. It takes very little grain, mostly waste, and many wild berries.

EASTERN FOX SPARROW

Passerella iliaca iliaca (MERREM).

PLATE 72.

Other name: Fox-colored Sparrow.

IDENTIFICATION. — Length 6¾ to 7½ inches; spread 10½ to 11¾ inches. Larger than Bluebird; bright reddish color, especially bright reddish-brown tail, distinguishes it from other sparrows; heavy spotting or streaking of breast, and thick finch-like bill, distinguish it from Hermit Thrush; gray on sides of head and neck is quite variable in amount.

SONG. — Clear, full, flute-like.

BREEDING. — In coniferous forests and alder swamps. *Nest:* On ground or in bush or low tree, of grass, moss, a few leaves and rootlets, lined with feathers or hair. *Eggs:* 4 or 5, bluish-white to pale green, thickly spotted with rusty brown.

RANGE. — Breeds from tree-limit in northwestern Alaska, northern Manitoba, northern Ontario, and northern Quebec south to northern Manitoba, southern Quebec, the Magdalen Islands, and Newfoundland; winters from the lower Ohio and Potomac valleys to central Texas and central Florida; west to North Dakota in migration.

The Eastern Fox Sparrow is a bird of the lingering snow. It arrives in the Northern States commonly in March, while there is still much snow in the woods, and may be seen along the edges of woodlands, working often in thickets where the ground is bare, and scratching away as if for dear life. This is one of the few of our sparrows that scratches with both feet at once. It leaps into the air, and while off the ground scratches or kicks quickly with both its powerful feet, making them fly as well as everything they touch, before it lands on them again. Thus it is able to excavate rapidly, throwing leaves and dirt sometimes a yard or more. If after it

529

arrives, a snowstorm comes on, covering the ground with several inches of snow and cutting off most of the smaller birds from their chief source of food supply, this does not inconvenience the lusty Fox Sparrow. He excavates! Jumping and scratching he makes the snow fly, and soon is at the bottom of a hole and at his usual occupation of turning over the dead leaves and searching for seeds and insects. It is a pretty and stirring sight to see a flock of Fox Sparrows all at work in this manner, and throwing little jets of snow over the white carpet.

The Fox Sparrow is a wild bird, a bird of thicket and forest. It does not seek the habitations of man, unless driven to them by snow too hard and deep for it to penetrate. Then it will come about houses and cattle sheds to look for chaff. They are hardy birds, and if any coming to feeding-stations have succumbed to the wintry blasts, I have not heard of it. When startled from a roadside thicket or a wood road they usually either fly up into the trees or to a little distance, and when the intruder has passed they immediately go to feeding again. Along the coast they begin to sing about the first of April in damp easterly weather, which may remind them of the fog in their homes along the Labrador coast. The song, though short, is a fine clear effort, a typical song of the northern wilds. Dr. S. D. Judd says that it seems not akin to bird music, but more like the soft tinkling of tiny silver bells. Sometimes in late March a particularly vigorous bird will sing almost continuously for from five to ten minutes with hardly a pause between his individual efforts. Their musical efforts in migration, however, are not to be compared with the full song as given on their breeding-grounds.

Often the Fox Sparrows do not stay long in the Northern States, but pass on rapidly, and arrive at their northern homes while the snow is still deep in the woods. These hardy, early birds are in such haste to begin their domestic life that some of them, realizing perhaps that a nest on the snowy ground would give cold comfort, build their little domiciles in trees or bushes, but most of them wait until there is bare ground enough to receive their nests, for the ground seems to be their normal nesting-place. Having raised their young, they will be back again in October or November, passing through on their southward flight.

LINCOLN'S SPARROW

Melospiza lincolni lincolni (AUDUBON).   PLATE 72.

IDENTIFICATION. — Length 5¼ to 6 inches; spread 7¼ to 8¾ inches. Slightly smaller than Song Sparrow and with shorter tail; *more narrowly streaked below, with a buffy band across breast*; a narrow eye-ring; young grayer above than young Song or Swamp Sparrows, and striping of head more contrasting.

SONG. — Sweet, melodious, and somewhat wren-like.

BREEDING. — In or near bushy swamps. *Nest:* In a tuft of grass usually surrounded by water, of grasses. *Eggs:* 4 or 5, similar to Song Sparrow.

RANGE. — Breeds from Alaska, northern Manitoba, northern Quebec, and Newfoundland south to northern Minnesota, central Ontario, northern New York, New Brunswick, and Nova Scotia, and south in the Cascades, Sierra Nevada, and Rocky Mountains to southern California and northern New Mexico; winters from central California, southern Oklahoma, and northern Mississippi to southern Lower California, southern Mexico, and central Guatemala.

What has a bird as inconspicuous as Lincoln's Sparrow done that it must hide itself so assiduously from human eyes? It seems to dread discovery, else why should it steal so cautiously through the depths of leafy thickets, or sneak so silently along bushy stone fences? Even when singing it seems careful to keep out of sight. At least that is its usual behavior when only one or two are seen, but when half a dozen are together and singing they are not quite so cautious and may be approached with less difficulty.

This sparrow is a bird of the thicket, and in migration may be found in bushy places along low river shores or in other moist lands, along bushy fences, walls and roadsides, in rocky pastures where white pines or red cedars grow, or even on dry hillsides where its favorite thickets stand. Now and then one or two enter a village or suburban garden or back yard, and tarry for a time among the syringa or lilac bushes. The general belief that the bird is exceedingly rare along the Atlantic seaboard is not well founded. It is a regular, though not common, migrant there in spring and fall, but it is overlooked because of its retiring nature, the uncertain light in most of its shadowy retreats, and the rapidity of its passage. In spring most members of the species usually pass along within a week or ten days. In autumn their stay is longer, but then they are more silent and shy. When seen they often are mistaken for Song Sparrows, as their differently colored breasts are seldom seen, and even in autumn they resemble some young Song Sparrows.

I have found the species by itself in spring, though it may be found in company with Song Sparrows and other sparrows in autumn. If one can paddle quietly or drift with the current along a bushy river shore during a bird wave in mid-May, he may hear the song, or the bird's curiosity may cause it to expose itself. Once I saw several in this manner, two of them singing from the tops of bushes, and in plain sight. I have characterized the song as somewhat wren-like, also having a quality resembling that of the Purple Finch. Usually an approach to a singing bird must be absolutely noiseless, or he will stop singing, but by going *carefully* I have been able to hear the song many times during spring migrations. The bird creeps in and out about walls, fences and woodpiles, much like a wren, and sings usually, but not always, from the top of a bush. I have heard the song when the bird was concealed among bushes and close to the ground.

There is every reason to believe that Lincoln's Sparrow breeds in northern New England. Pairs have been seen in several localities in Maine during the breeding season. This species should be looked for in summer among the mountains of northern New Hampshire and Maine, as it breeds in mountainous regions of the West and in the Adirondacks in New York.

In the fall migration Lincoln's Sparrow appears most commonly during the latter half of September. It may be found occasionally with other sparrows in weedy gardens and potato patches or among the tall grass and bushy thickets bordering some swamp, lake or stream. It is a neat, rather slim bird of furtive mien and uneasy movement, grayer above than the Song Sparrow, but in spite of its shyness, rather inquisitive. Because of its curiosity it sometimes will come out in the open, if the observer can keep fairly well concealed. The food of this sparrow, as far as it is known, is similar to that of the Song Sparrow.

SWAMP SPARROW

Melospiza georgiana (LATHAM).

PLATE 72.

IDENTIFICATION. — Length 4¾ to 5¾ inches; spread 7½ to 8 inches. A stocky, dark sparrow with chestnut cap, grayish sides of head and breast, and a white throat similar to that of White-throat but smaller and much less conspicuous; young buffy below with fine breast streakings, and head more or less striped.

SONG. — Similar to that of Chipping Sparrow but louder and more musical.

BREEDING. — In wet meadows, bogs, swamps, and marshes. *Nest:* In tussock or low in bush, of grasses, sometimes arched over. *Eggs:* 4 or 5, similar to those of Song Sparrow.

RANGE. — Breeds from west-central Alberta, northern Manitoba, southern Quebec, and Newfoundland south to northern Nebraska, northern Missouri, northern Illinois, West Virginia (mountains), southern Pennsylvania, and New Jersey; winters from Nebraska, the Ohio Valley, and New Jersey south to the Gulf coast from southern Florida to southern Texas and central Mexico.

The Swamp Sparrow is not a public character. He will never be popular or notorious. He is too retiring to be much in the public eye, and too fond of the impassable bog and morass to have much human company; and so he comes and goes unheralded and to most people unknown. He is the dark little bird that fusses about in the mud when spring floods have overflowed the wood roads, or slips through the grasses on marsh-lined shores of slow-flowing, muddy rivers. Any watery, muddy, bushy, grassy place where rank marsh grasses, sedges and reeds grow — any such bog or slough where a man will need long rubber boots to get about — is good enough for Swamp Sparrows. In such places they build their nests. But in migration they may appear almost anywhere, though seldom distinctly seen and recognized by ordinary observers, because of their retiring habits. When they are looked for, they sneak about, mostly under cover, and hardly show themselves sufficiently for identification, but if the observer apparently takes no interest in their whereabouts and sits quietly down, curiosity may overcome their suspicions and bring them into view.

In the autumn migration many of these birds visit weedy gardens and fields with other sparrows, for they are great eaters of weed seeds. Their nesting habits are difficult to observe, but the male's song during the nesting season will give some idea of the location of the nest.

The young ordinarily remain in the nest about twelve or thirteen days, if undisturbed. Swamp Sparrows nest near water so frequently that the callow young in their first attempts at flight are likely to fall into it, and struggling as they do on the surface, they sometimes fall a prey to large frogs, fish or turtles. The following from one of my notebooks shows how one little bird bravely struggled to safety: 'Concord, August 28, 1907. This morning early as I stood on the riverbank, a bird flying toward me fell and struck the water about halfway across the stream. Immediately it fluttered swiftly along on the calm surface of the water for about a rod, and then, apparently exhausted and unable to raise itself from the water, it lay there for a few seconds, head under and tail a little raised. I looked to see some fish seize it, but no! Suddenly by a vigorous struggle it raised its body clear of the water and fluttered almost ashore, alighting on the pickerel weed at the water's edge. A few minutes later, having regained its breath and courage, it flew up into the bushes, and I saw that it was one of a brood of young Swamp Sparrows in juvenal plumage, which were flitting along the shore.'

EASTERN SONG SPARROW

Melospiza melodia melodia (WILSON).

PLATE 72.

Other names: Ground-bird; Ground-sparrow.

IDENTIFICATION. — Length 6 to 6¾ inches; spread 8¼ to 9¼ inches. A medium-sized sparrow with fairly long *rounded* tail; brown above, darkly streaked; top of head brown with inconspicuous central light stripe and broader light stripes over eye; breast grayish, heavily streaked and with a central dark spot; young resemble Lincoln's Sparrow with buffy breast finely streaked.

SONG. — Variable, rendered by Thoreau as '*Maids! maids! maids! hang up your teakettle-ettle-ettle,*' which expresses its swing and tempo; the first three notes brisk but rather long, the last few run quickly to the end.

BREEDING. — On moist land near water, in thicket. *Nest:* On or near ground, chiefly of grasses, but also other materials. *Eggs:* 3 to 7, variable, whitish with dots, spots and blotches of browns and lilac.

RANGE. — Breeds from southern Mackenzie, northern Manitoba, northern Ontario, southern Quebec, and Cape Breton Island south to southern Virginia, southern North Carolina (mountains), and northern Georgia; winters from Massachusetts and New Jersey south to southern Florida and the Gulf coast.

Song Sparrow! Well named! This is the modest, lowly avian minstrel of the brier-patch — the most persistent singer of them all. He sings day after day; awake or dreaming, he sings in the darkness of night; and, north or south, he sings every month in the year. When the mercury drops below the zero mark or when it approaches ninety degrees, still the song of 'Silver-tongue' may be heard at times, ringing, sweet and clear. He is an unquenchable optimist. Nothing seems to discourage or daunt him.

'Winter has scarcely begun to relax his icy grasp from the water and to lift his snowy mantle from off the land,' writes Mr. Charles J. Maynard in his 'Birds of Eastern North America,' 'when those harbingers of the coming spring, the Song Sparrows, begin to chant their enlivening lay about the homesteads of New England. Loud and cheerily do they sing on the brightest mornings in early March, and when they have once begun nothing seems to daunt their ardor. No matter how very stormy the weather, daylight always finds them singing. I have heard their song when the wind was blowing a gale, and the little performers were obliged to seek shelter beneath the hedges, and have seen one start to fly when the force of the blast was so great that it fairly swept him into a thicket, where he clung tenaciously to the boughs and, as if to bid defiance to the raging elements, poured forth his liveliest carol. Rightly has this species been named *melodia*, for none among our native birds sings so long or so often as the Song Sparrow.'

The Eastern Song Sparrow likes a well-watered, fertile country where thickets abound. He is normally a lowlander, but will nest in a mountain pasture if there is a 'living spring' near-by with its flowing rill. It is now generally believed that birds have descended from reptilian forms of life. If so, the Song Sparrow may well have come from amphibian ancestors, as no land bird seems more fond of water. Where no other form of bath offers he bathes in wet leaves or wet grass after a night shower, and where there is water in plenty he takes a cold bath every night after sunset, until the water freezes, and he bathes during the day whenever opportunity offers; sometimes on sunny days he lies down after a bath and spreads himself out to dry in the sun. If on the seashore, a salt-water pool does very well for his bath tub. It is interesting to see one after a hard shower striking the twigs with his wings and thus throwing the water over his plumage.

The Song Sparrow is fond of the home garden, and often nests in the berry patch or in the back yard shrubbery, and sometimes even in climbing vines on porch or veranda. A nest was found on the top of a post in a grape arbor sheltered by the vines; another in a woodshed in a sheltered nook beside the door. The nest rested on a scantling and the birds found access to it through a hole in the boarding. Another was built in a hollow fence rail.

When once this sparrow has chosen a home, nothing but death will keep it from the beloved spot. It dodges the dogs and cats, and can hardly be driven away. Once an inexperienced pair built a nest on the ground at the foot of a high tree in my garden. As is so common in such cases a cat got the young. Then the birds built again in a bush; again the stealthy cat! Twice bereaved, the mated pair grieved for a while and then fashioned a third domicile about twenty feet up in an elm tree among dense 'suckers,' where they escaped the notice of their feline enemy and reared their young in triumph.

The Song Sparrow was one of my earliest bird acquaintances, and the very first on which, at the age of thirteen, I began my self-education in the gentle art of taxidermy. Daily after school for several days I labored on that mishandled bunch of feathers in an attempt to impart to it a lifelike appearance. That first 'stuffed bird' stood for many a year in my collection, a cherished specimen. In memory I can see it now. It had much the appearance of many old museum birds of that period which, as Charles Waterton puts it, were 'stretched, stuffed, stiffened and wired by the hand of some common clown.' Since that day I have always had a peculiar affection for the Song Sparrow, and must admit that as its historian I am prejudiced in its favor.

Song Sparrows are early comers. In mild seasons a few begin to work northward in extreme southern New England about the middle of February, but it is not until some bright morning in late March that the erstwhile lifeless icebound swamp becomes resonant with their cheerful songs. In the thickets along the edges they fly back and forth singing and playing about as if spring were really here. Their early arrival, however, does not indicate very early nesting, though I remember one nest on a ditch bank, when the ground was covered with two or three inches of new-fallen snow, and when the bird left the nest at my close approach it was revealed as a little dark hole with its complement of four brown-spotted eggs framed by the white blanket of snow.

Song Sparrows spend much time in the pleasant pastime of courtship. The females seem to be modest and coy. There is considerable rivalry among the males, but their contests appear to be mainly competitions in song and flight. They chase the females and each other about through the air with fluttering wings, often sailing and singing. Their pursuit seems not to be in earnest, as, notwithstanding the rapid movement of their wings, their progress is slow. Now and then a bird pauses in his flight to sing, supported for an instant on his widespread pinions. Flight-songs also carry them up into the air. Occasionally a battle ensues between two rival males, and sometimes they even roll and tumble in the dust with locked bills and beating wings.

When the pair have mated, nest-building requires from five to ten days according to the weather and the industry of the birds. The male devotes himself more to song than to labor. Some males assist the female a little in incubation. The male stands guard much of the time until the young are hatched, when he takes over his full share of the work of defending, brooding and feeding them. The young remain in the nest from seven to fourteen days, depending on the quantity of nourishment they receive and whether they are disturbed. Like the young

534

of all ground birds they develop quickly, when well fed, and can live in the grass before they are able to fly.

Song Sparrows are brave little birds and are very devoted to their young. Should such an enemy as a snake or a turtle appear near the nest, the adults take their stand bravely before it in a position of defense, with outspread wings and depressed tails, guarding their offspring. If this bold and defiant front is not effective they may even attack the enemy, though with little hope of success. They often attack birds as large as the Hairy Woodpecker and the Catbird, when such approach the nest.

When the young of the first brood are able to fly, the female immediately begins to deposit eggs for the second brood, often in the same nest, leaving the male to care for the first, and he attends them usually until the young of the second brood have hatched, when he leaves them to help feed and care for the younger brood. In this way four broods are sometimes hatched in a season.

Song Sparrows sing more or less in autumn. Even while molting an occasional whisper song may be heard. There is more singing on warm days in October, however, than in September, and although at times the full loud spring song may be heard, most of the singing is quite different, ranging from a low connected warble to a song resembling that of the Purple Finch, and (rarely) one like that of the Vesper Sparrow. There is a particularly low, sweet, melancholy warble uttered just before the bird departs for the south. Most of the hardy Song Sparrows that winter in New England probably come to us from the northland and for the most part they pass the winter near the sea, where the ground is clear of snow in patches for a large part of the winter. A few winter in the interior, some of them well up the valleys of the Connecticut and Merrimack rivers. In severe winters, however, numbers succumb to cold and starvation.

ATLANTIC SONG SPARROW

Melospiza melodia atlantica TODD.

IDENTIFICATION. — Grayer above than *M. m. melodia*, with blackish streaking more distinct and the reddish-brown feather edging reduced to a minimum.

RANGE. — Atlantic coastal islands and edge of mainland from New York (Long Island) to North Carolina.

MISSISSIPPI SONG SPARROW

Melospiza melodia beata BANGS.

IDENTIFICATION. — General color darker and grayer than *M. m. melodia*, bill very much larger and swollen basally.

RANGE. — Mississippi Valley region; casual east to Florida in winter and in migration.

535

LAPLAND LONGSPUR

Calcarius lapponicus lapponicus (LINNAEUS). PLATE 67.

IDENTIFICATION. — Length 6 to 7 inches; spread 10½ to 11¾ inches. A little smaller than Snow Bunting; often seen with or near them, or near Horned Larks, or both, but much darker than Snow Bunting and lacking yellow and black throat markings of Horned Lark; smaller size, slender form and dark coloring should distinguish them from either of the foregoing. In flight, when seen with Snow Buntings, their *dark* sharp-pointed wings contrast with the white areas and black tips of wings of the Snow Buntings.

BREEDING. — On barren grounds and tundra. *Nest:* On ground, of grasses, moss, feathers, and hair. *Eggs:* 5 to 7, greenish, spotted thickly.

RANGE. — Breeds on Arctic islands and coasts of Greenland south to the limit of trees in Mackenzie, northern Manitoba, and northern Quebec, also in northern Europe and Asia; winters from southern Quebec and the north-central United States irregularly south to the Middle States and Texas, and in Europe and Asia to about Lat. 30° north.

The Lapland Longspur is a hardy northern species which nests in the circumpolar Arctic wastes, and which is only present in the United States and in southern Canada as a winter visitor. In migration in the United States it keeps in the interior chiefly, between the Alleghenies and the Rocky Mountains, and is rarely seen on the Atlantic seaboard. In New England it is most frequent in November and December, when it is found singly or in small flocks, usually with the Northern Horned Larks and the Snow Buntings, and it often feeds with them on the seeds of the beach grass which it picks up from the ground or the snow, though it also, unlike its companions, often alights on the grass stalks and clinging to them, feeds in that position. It is a difficult bird to find, as when approached, it is likely to squat on the ground, where, in the protective colors of its winter plumage, it seems to disappear and a number thus concealed may be easily overlooked. In the Mississippi Valley and the Prairie States, where it is sometimes very abundant and appears in immense flocks, it seeks stubble fields and plowed lands, and it is there a useful destroyer of noxious weed seeds. — (J.B.M.)

SMITH'S LONGSPUR

Calcarius pictus (SWAINSON).

Other names: Painted Longspur; Painted Bunting.

IDENTIFICATION. — Length 5¾ to 6½ inches; spread 10 to 11 inches. More buffy than other longspurs; outer tail feathers white, similar to Vesper Sparrow; male in spring has head largely black with three sharply defined white lines on the sides (black ear-patch bordered with white and with white in center).

BREEDING. — Similar to Lapland Longspur.

RANGE. — Breeds on the Barren Grounds from Mackenzie east to Hudson Bay; winters from Kansas to central Texas; east in migration to the prairies of Illinois and southwestern Indiana.

Smith's Longspur is very much like the Lapland Longspur in its general habits, but it is not as widely distributed either in the breeding season or in winter, and is merely a straggler east of the Mississippi except on the prairies of southern Wisconsin, Illinois, and southwestern Indiana, where it is a regular winter visitor. In this area it is often found in company with Lapland

Longspurs, Horned Larks, and Snow Buntings, feeding on weed seeds and small grains. — (J.B.M.)

CHESTNUT–COLLARED LONGSPUR

Calcarius ornatus (TOWNSEND).

Other name: Black-bellied Longspur.

IDENTIFICATION. — Length 5¾ to 6½ inches; spread 10 to 10¾ inches. Male in spring has pale or whitish face and throat and black breast; crown and stripe back of eye black; hind neck deep chestnut; female and winter male, sparrow-like birds with much white on tail.

BREEDING. — In open treeless prairies. *Nest:* On ground, of grass, etc., and hair. *Eggs:* 3 to 6, similar to those of Lapland Longspur.

RANGE. — Breeds from Montana, southeastern Alberta, southern Saskatchewan, and Manitoba south to east-central Wyoming, central Kansas, eastern Nebraska, and western Minnesota; winters from Colorado, Nebraska and Iowa to Arizona, Sonora, and the southern end of the Mexican tableland.

The Chestnut-collared Longspur is a bird of the prairie regions and is a mere straggler east of the Mississippi River. Dr. T. S. Roberts says of it in his 'Birds of Minnesota':

'The Chestnut-collared Longspur prefers dry upland prairies and seems to shun the neighborhood of sloughs and lakes. The male is conspicuous from its habit of perching on the tops of slender flowering plants, in which position it appears, when viewed from the front, like a coal-black little ball attached to the tops of the weeds, with which it sways back and forth in the breezes. In many of its actions and in its manner of singing it is not very unlike the Bobolink of the near-by meadows. Rising from its perching place, or it may be from the ground, it flies about in large circles in a wayward, up and down fashion, pausing ever and anon at the crest of the flight to utter, with expanded tail and fluttering wings, a short, rather feeble, but melodious song. While thus engaged in singing it presents a rather curious appearance, for, with outspread quivering wings, tail wide-spread and inclined slightly upward, and head thrown back, it resembles some oddly shaped leaf or huge butterfly fluttering in mid-air, rather than a joyous bird. As the song proceeds it sinks earthward, with the wings now extended above the back, and it appears as if about to alight but more frequently ascends again to continue on its circular course and deliver the little ditty with its accompanying physical ecstasy again and again, until, wearied at last, it comes to rest close by its listening mate, patiently guarding the nest.' — (J.B.M.)

EASTERN SNOW BUNTING

Plectrophenax nivalis nivalis (LINNAEUS).   PLATE 67.

Other names: Snow-bird; White Snow-bird; Snow-flake; Snow Lark.

IDENTIFICATION. — Length 6 to 7¼ inches; spread 12 to 13 inches. About size of Bluebird, mainly white below, brown and white above, wings white with dark tips; a plump short-legged light-colored finch that walks on the ground, and flies and wheels in compact flocks like shore-birds.

CALL NOTES. — High, sweet, tinkling, whistling notes.

BREEDING. — On Arctic shores and mountain-sides. *Nest:* On ground, of grasses, plant stalks, and moss, lined with hair, fur, wool, and many feathers. *Eggs:* 4 to 8, whitish with spots and scratches of browns.

RANGE. — Breeds in the Arctic Zone from at least Lat. 83° north to the northern parts of the mainland from Alaska to northern Quebec, also in Eastern Hemisphere; winters from Unalaska, central Manitoba, and central Quebec south to the northern United States and sporadically farther south, also in Europe to the Mediterranean, North Africa, and the Canary and Azores islands.

The Eastern Snow Bunting is a typical boreal bird. It hazards its fortune to the north wind. Its home is in Arctic wastes. It is one of the few small land birds that goes as far north as land extends, and it nests in numbers in northern Greenland. Captain Donald MacMillan says the Eskimos assert that some 'stay at Etah all winter,' but we are at liberty to doubt the evidence.

When winter really comes, when icy blasts sweep down from the north and snow fills the air and whitens field and pasture, these little birds ride down on wintry winds and whirl about the fields amid the driving snow. As they wheel and turn in concert, their brown backs and black-tipped wings veer and career about amid the snowflakes until, with a sudden swing, they turn their white under sides toward us and disappear in the snow-filled air, only to reappear as the next turn brings their backs to our view. Having swung back and forth and from side to side, and viewed their landfall from every vantage point, they glide toward the earth, alight in a patch of weeds or tall grass that projects above the snow, and running along from plant to plant, help themselves to the well-ripened seeds. While thus occupied they are always moving along over the surface of the snow, running rapidly, walking and even hopping or jumping oc-casionally, eagerly snatching, hulling and swallowing the winter offering of the weeds and grasses. They are not particularly shy, but any unusual sound or motion will send them all into the air at once. They feed mostly in the fields, but also in farmyards, about manure heaps and in the roads. Formerly before the English Sparrow came they even invaded the cities, where they picked up grain about the freight yards and found some food in suburban streets; but the belligerent sparrows soon drove them out.

John Burroughs says that this is the only one of our winter birds that really seems a part of winter — that seems born of the whirling snow, and happiest when storms drive thickest. Its calls, coming out of the white obscurity, are the sweetest and happiest of all winter bird notes. 'It is,' he says, 'like the laughter of children. The fox hunter hears it on the snowy hills; the schoolboy hears it as he breaks through the drifts on his way to school; it is a voice of good cheer and contentment.'

It nests on the hills and mountains of Arctic islands and gets much of its food along the shore, where also it finds sand for its little digestive mill. So when winter comes, many Snow Buntings naturally gravitate toward the seashore and gradually move southward along the coast. After early October they may be confidently looked for on the New England coast, while they are rarely seen in October in the interior, and often do not become at all common there until snow flies. The Snow Bunting is a harbinger of winter. It is forced southward in severe winters, for the deep snows cover much of its favorite food in the interior, and the north-ern beaches are buried in ice. The appearance of Snow Buntings in large numbers is consid-ered generally to signify the approach of a hard winter, and it certainly indicates heavy snow to the northward. The Scandinavians call them 'hard-weather birds.'

The Snow Bunting is a hardy bird — well clothed against the wintry blast. When the snow is soft, these birds are said to dive into it (as they do sometimes when pursued by hawks), and there pass the night. When the snow is frozen hard, the flocks sleep in the open, protected from the north wind only by some slight rise in the ground, by sand dunes, or by a stone wall. Once, after the flocks had gone northward, I found a lone bird in Westborough, Massachusetts, after most of the snow had disappeared. It wandered about the fields calling plaintively for its comrades, and at night it slept on a snowdrift. I found it there night after night close to a bank wall. It may have sought shelter in a crevice in the wall, for each night it sprang up from the same spot when I began to move toward it, crunching the frozen snow. The wild birds leave their resting place at the first hint of light in the east, and begin feeding while it is still quite dark. They have never been known to roost in trees at night, but some flocks frequently alight in them or on the roofs of buildings. I have seen an apple tree almost covered by a great flock of these birds, and they may be seen now and then on fences or stone walls, but I have never seen a Snow Bunting in the woods.

Sometimes in March a soft song may be heard from some male bird, but not the loud, clear song of the nesting time, which probably is never heard in our region. As spring approaches the wear of the plumage begins to show, and sometimes birds that stay late appear in the black and white dress of summer. Most of them leave for the north in February, while still in winter dress. The Eskimos kill large numbers of these birds for food, and, formerly, thousands were killed by gunners in this country. Even as late as the early part of this century great numbers were shot here illegally and sold to epicures.

APPENDIX

BIRDS OCCURRING AS 'STRAGGLERS' OR 'ACCIDENTALS' WITHIN THE RANGE OF THIS VOLUME, AND WESTERN SPECIES WHOSE NORMAL DISTRIBUTION BARELY REACHES THE NINETY-FIFTH MERIDIAN OF WEST LONGITUDE

EARED GREBE, *Colymbus nigricollis californicus* (Heermann).
  Breeds in northern Iowa; casual in Missouri and Indiana.

WESTERN GREBE, *Aechmophorus occidentalis* (Lawrence).
  Casual in Minnesota, Wisconsin, Iowa, Illinois, Michigan, Ohio and Ontario.

YELLOW-NOSED ALBATROSS, *Thalassogeron chlororhynchos* (Gmelin).
  Accidental in Quebec and Maine.

MANX SHEARWATER, *Puffinus puffinus puffinus* (Brünnich).
  Accidental in New York and Maine (or New Brunswick).

ALLIED SHEARWATER, *Puffinus assimilis barolii* Bonaparte.
  Accidental in Nova Scotia and South Carolina.

MEDITERRANEAN SHEARWATER, *Puffinus diomedea diomedea* (Scopoli).
  Casual in New York.

BLACK-CAPPED PETREL, *Pterodroma hasitata* (Kuhl).
  Accidental in Florida, Virginia, Kentucky, Ohio, Ontario, and New Hampshire.

SCALED PETREL, *Peterodroma inexpectata* (Forster).
  Accidental in New York.

PINTADO PETREL, *Daption capense* (Linnaeus).
  Accidental in Maine.

MADEIRA PETREL, *Oceanodroma castro castro* (Harcourt).
  Accidental in Pennsylvania, Indiana, and District of Columbia.

WHITE-BELLIED PETREL, *Fregetta tropica tropica* (Gould).
  Accidental in Florida.

RED-BILLED TROPIC-BIRD, *Phaëthon aethureus* Linnaeus.
  Accidental in Bermuda, and on Newfoundland Banks.

ATLANTIC BLUE-FACED BOOBY, *Sula dactylatra dactylatra* Lesson.
  Accidental in Louisiana and Florida.

WHITE-BELLIED BOOBY, *Sula leucogaster leucogaster* (Boddaert).
  Casual in Florida and Louisiana and accidental in South Carolina, New York, Massachusetts, and Bermuda.

RED-FOOTED BOOBY, *Sula piscator* (Linnaeus).
  Accidental in Florida.

SCARLET IBIS, *Guara rubra* (Linnaeus).
  Accidental in Florida and Louisiana.

BARNACLE GOOSE, *Branta leucopsis* (Bechstein).
  Casual in Labrador, Quebec, Vermont, Massachusetts, New York, and North Carolina.

PINK-FOOTED GOOSE, *Anser brachyrhynchus* Baillon.
  Accidental in Massachusetts.

ROSS'S GOOSE, *Chen rossi* (Cassin).
  Casual in Louisiana.

WHITE-FACED TREE-DUCK, *Dendrocygna viduata* (Linnaeus).
  Accidental in New Jersey.

541

SHELD-DUCK, *Tadorna tadorna* (Linnaeus).
Accidental in Massachusetts.

RUDDY SHELDRAKE, *Casarca ferruginea* (Pallas).
Accidental in North Carolina and New Jersey.

BAHAMA PINTAIL, *Dafila bahamensis bahamensis* (Linnaeus).
Casual in Florida, accidental in Wisconsin.

CINNAMON TEAL, *Querquedula cyanoptera* (Vieillot).
Casual in Louisiana, Florida, South Carolina, New York, Ohio, and Wisconsin.

WESTERN HARLEQUIN DUCK, *Histrionicus histrionicus pacificus* Brooks.
Casual south to Missouri.

STELLER'S EIDER, *Polysticta stelleri* (Pallas).
Accidental in Quebec.

MASKED DUCK, *Nomonyx dominicus* (Linnaeus).
Accidental in Vermont, Massachusetts, Maryland, and Wisconsin.

WESTERN RED-TAILED HAWK, *Buteo borealis calurus* Cassin.
Casual east of the Great Plains.

FERRUGINOUS ROUGH-LEG, *Buteo regalis* (Gray).
Casual east to Illinois and Wisconsin.

HARRIS'S HAWK, *Parabuteo unicinctus harrisi* (Audubon).
Casual in Mississippi and Louisiana, accidental in Iowa.

MEXICAN GOSHAWK, *Asturina plagiata plagiata* Schlegel.
Accidental in Illinois.

GRAY SEA EAGLE, *Haliaeetus albicilla* (Linnaeus).
Accidental off the coast of Massachusetts.

PRAIRIE FALCON, *Falco mexicanus* Schlegel.
Casual in Illinois and Minnesota.

KESTREL, *Falco tinnunculus tinnunculus* Linnaeus.
Accidental in Massachusetts.

CORN CRAKE, *Crex crex* (Linnaeus).
Casual or accidental in Newfoundland, Nova Scotia, Maine, Rhode Island, Connecticut, New York, New Jersey, Maryland, and Bermuda.

EUROPEAN COOT, *Fulica atra atra* Linnaeus.
Accidental in Newfoundland and Labrador.

LAPWING, *Vanellus vanellus* (Linnaeus).
Accidental in North Carolina, New York, Maine, Nova Scotia, New Brunswick, Newfoundland. and Labrador.

MOUNTAIN PLOVER, *Eupoda montana* (Townsend).
Accidental in Massachusetts and Florida.

EUROPEAN TURNSTONE, *Arenaria interpres interpres* (Linnaeus).
Accidental in Massachusetts.

EUROPEAN WOODCOCK, *Scolopax rusticola rusticola* Linnaeus.
Occasional from southern Quebec and Newfoundland to Virginia.

EUROPEAN SNIPE, *Capella gallinago gallinago* (Linnaeus).
Accidental in Bermuda and Labrador.

EUROPEAN JACK SNIPE, *Lymnocryptes minimus* (Brünnich).
Accidental in Labrador.

EUROPEAN CURLEW, *Numenius arquatus arquatus* (Linnaeus).
Accidental in New York.

WHIMBREL, *Phaeopus phaeopus phaeopus* (Linnaeus).
Accidental in New York and Nova Scotia.

GREEN SANDPIPER, *Tringa ocrophus* Linnaeus.
Accidental in Nova Scotia.

CURLEW SANDPIPER, *Erolia testacea* (Pallas).
Occasional in Nova Scotia, Ontario, Maine, Massachusetts, New York and New Jersey.

DUNLIN, *Pelidna alpina alpina* (Linnaeus).
Accidental in New York, Connecticut and Massachusetts.

BAR-TAILED GODWIT, *Limosa lapponica lapponica* (Linnaeus).
Accidental in Massachusetts.

RUFF, *Philomachus pugnax* (Linnaeus).
Casual in Ontario, Nova Scotia, Maine, New Hampshire, Massachusetts, Rhode Island, Indiana, and North Carolina.

WYMAN'S GULL, *Larus occidentalis wymani* Dickey and Van Rossem.
Accidental in Illinois.

THAYER'S GULL, *Larus argentatus thayeri* Brooks.
Casual in New Jersey, Illinois, and Quebec.

BLACK-HEADED GULL, *Larus ridibundus ridibundus* Linnaeus.
Casual in Massachusetts.

LITTLE GULL, *Larus minutus* Pallas.
Accidental in New Jersey, New York, Massachusetts, and Maine.

IVORY GULL, *Pagophila alba* (Gunnerus).
Casual in New York and on Lake Ontario.

TRUDEAU'S TERN, *Sterna trudeaui* Audubon.
Accidental in New Jersey.

BRIDLED TERN, *Sterna anaethetus melanoptera* Swainson.
Accidental in South Carolina, Georgia, and Florida.

WHITE-WINGED TERN, *Chlidonias leucoptera* (Temminck).
Accidental in Wisconsin.

MANDT'S GUILLEMOT, *Cepphus grylle mandti* (Mandt).
Casual to southern Quebec and Lake Ontario, accidental in New Brunswick.

ANCIENT MURRELET, *Synthliboramphus antiquus* (Gmelin).
Accidental in Wisconsin, Quebec, Ontario, and on Lake Erie.

SCALED PIGEON, *Columba squamosa* Bonnaterre.
Accidental in Florida.

ZENAIDA DOVE, *Zenaida zenaida zenaida* (Bonaparte).
Florida Keys (formerly).

WESTERN MOURNING DOVE, *Zenaidura macroura marginella* (Woodhouse).
Occasionally breeds in western Arkansas and Minnesota.

EASTERN WHITE-WINGED DOVE, *Melopelia asiatica asiatica* (Linnaeus).
Casual in Louisiana and Florida, accidental in New York.

KEY WEST QUAIL-DOVE, *Oreopeleia chrysia* (Bonaparte).
Key West (formerly).

RUDDY QUAIL-DOVE, *Oreopeleia montana* (Linnaeus).
Accidental in Florida.

SMOOTH-BILLED ANI, *Crotophaga ani* Linnaeus.
Casual in Florida and Louisiana, accidental in Pennsylvania and North Carolina.

GROOVE-BILLED ANI, *Crotophaga sulcirostris sulcirostris* Swainson.
Casual in Florida and Louisiana.

AIKEN'S SCREECH OWL, *Otus asio aikeni* (Brewster).
Northwestern Minnesota.

NUTTALL'S POOR-WILL, *Phalaenoptilus nuttalli nuttalli* (Audubon).
Western Iowa.

SENNETT'S NIGHTHAWK, *Chordeiles minor sennetti* Coues.
Northwestern Iowa.

WHITE-THROATED SWIFT, *Aëronautes saxatilis saxatilis* (Woodhouse).
Accidental in Michigan.

RUFOUS HUMMINGBIRD, *Selasphorus rufus* (Gmelin).
Accidental in Florida and South Carolina.

RED-SHAFTED FLICKER, *Colaptes cafer collaris* Vigors.
Casually east on the Great Plains in winter.

LEWIS'S WOODPECKER, *Asyndesmus lewis* Gray.
    Accidental in Rhode Island.

NELSON'S DOWNY WOODPECKER, *Dryobates pubescens nelsoni* Oberholser.
    'Casually farther east, probably to northern New England.'

LICHTENSTEIN'S KINGBIRD, *Tyrannus melancholicus chloronotus* Berlepsch.
    Accidental in Maine.

FORK-TAILED FLYCATCHER, *Muscivora tyrannus* (Linnaeus).
    Accidental in Maine, Massachusetts, New Jersey, Kentucky, and Mississippi.

SAY'S PHOEBE, *Sayornis saya saya* (Bonaparte).
    Breeds casually to western Iowa; accidental in Massachusetts, New York, Illinois, Missouri, and
        Wisconsin.

VERMILION FLYCATCHER, *Pyrocephalus rubinus mexicanus* Sclater.
    Accidental in Florida.

SKYLARK, *Alauda arvensis arvensis* Linnaeus.
    Accidental in Bermuda; introduced but not permanently established in New York and elsewhere.

BAHAMA SWALLOW, *Callichelidon cyaneoviridis* (Bryant).
    Accidental in Florida.

VIOLET-GREEN SWALLOW, *Tachycineta thalassina lepida* Mearns.
    Accidental in Illinois.

CUBAN CLIFF SWALLOW, *Petrochelidon fulva cavicola* Barbour and Brooks.
    Accidental in Florida.

CUBAN MARTIN, *Progne cryptoleuca* Baird.
    Accidental in Florida.

LONG-CRESTED JAY, *Cyanocitta stelleri diademata* (Bonaparte).
    Accidental in Quebec.

AMERICAN RAVEN, *Corvus corax sinuatus* Wagler.
    'East probably to Missouri, Illinois, and Indiana.'

CLARK'S NUTCRACKER, *Nucifraga columbiana* (Wilson).
    Casual in Missouri and Arkansas, accidental in Iowa and Wisconsin.

LONG-TAILED CHICKADEE, *Penthestes atricapillus septentrionalis* (Harris).
    East to western Minnesota and western Iowa.

COMMON ROCK WREN, *Salpinctes obsoletus obsoletus* (Say).
    Casual in western Iowa and Minnesota.

NORTHERN VARIED THRUSH, *Ixoreus naevius meruloides* (Swainson).
    Accidental in Quebec, Massachusetts, New York, and New Jersey.

RUSSET-BACKED THRUSH, *Hylocichla ustulata ustulata* (Nuttall).
    Accidental in South Carolina, Missouri, and Iowa.

CHESTNUT-BACKED BLUEBIRD, *Sialia mexicana bairdi* Ridgway.
    Accidental in Iowa.

TOWNSEND'S SOLITAIRE, *Myadestes townsendi* (Audubon).
    Accidental in New York and Illinois.

WHITE WAGTAIL, *Motacilla alba alba* Linnaeus.
    Accidental in northern Ungava.

NORTHWESTERN SHRIKE, *Lanius borealis invictus* Grinnell.
    Winters irregularly east to Minnesota.

YELLOW-GREEN VIREO, *Vireo flavoviridis flavoviridis* (Cassin).
    Accidental in Quebec.

BAHAMA HONEY CREEPER, *Coereba bahamensis* (Reichenbach).
    Accidental in Florida.

TOWNSEND'S WARBLER, *Dendroica townsendi* (Townsend).
    Accidental in Pennsylvania.

MACGILLIVRAY'S WARBLER, *Oporornis tolmiei* (Townsend).
    Casual in Illinois and Indiana.

NORTHERN PILEOLATED WARBLER, *Wilsonia pusilla pileolata* (Pallas).
    Casual in Missouri and Minnesota.

THICK-BILLED RED-WING, *Agelaius phoeniceus fortis* Ridgway.
Wanders in winter to Arkansas and Louisiana.

BULLOCK'S ORIOLE, *Icterus bullocki* (Swainson).
Accidental in New York and Maine.

NEVADA COWBIRD, *Molothrus ater artemisiae* Grinnell.
Breeds east to central Minnesota.

LAZULI BUNTING, *Passerina amoena* (Say).
Accidental in Minnesota.

BAHAMA GRASSQUIT, *Tiaris bicolor bicolor* (Linnaeus).
Accidental in Florida.

MELODIOUS GRASSQUIT, *Tiaris canora* (Gmelin).
Accidental in Florida.

ALASKA PINE GROSBEAK, *Pinicola enucleator alascensis* Ridgway.
Winters south to northwestern Minnesota.

HEPBURN'S ROSY FINCH, *Leucosticte tephrocotis littoralis* Baird.
Accidental in Minnesota and Maine.

GREEN-TAILED TOWHEE, *Oberholseria chlorura* (Audubon).
Accidental in South Carolina and Virginia.

ARCTIC TOWHEE, *Pipilo maculatus arcticus* (Swainson).
Accidental in Wisconsin and Illinois.

WESTERN GRASSHOPPER SPARROW, *Ammodramus savannarum bimaculatus* Swainson.
Breeds east to southern Minnesota.

BAIRD'S SPARROW, *Ammodramus bairdi* (Audubon).
Breeds east to northwestern Minnesota; accidental in New York.

WESTERN VESPER SPARROW, *Pooecetes gramineus confinis* Baird.
Occasional in Louisiana.

SHUFELDT'S JUNCO, *Junco oreganus shufeldti* Coale.
Casual in Illinois.

MONTANA JUNCO, *Junco oreganus montanus* Ridgway.
Casual in Maryland, Massachusetts, Indiana, and Illinois.

GAMBEL'S SPARROW, *Zonotrichia leucophrys gambeli* (Nuttall).
Casual in Massachusetts, South Carolina, Michigan, Illinois, Wisconsin, Minnesota, and Iowa.

GOLDEN-CROWNED SPARROW, *Zonotrichia coronata* (Pallas).
Accidental in Massachusetts and Wisconsin.

McCOWN'S LONGSPUR, *Rhynchophanes mccowni* (Lawrence).
Breeds east to southwestern Minnesota; casual in Illinois.

553